41: *Afro-American Poets Since 1955*, edited by Trudier Harris and Thadious M. Davis (1985)

42: *American Writers for Children Before 1900*, edited by Glenn E. Estes (1985)

43: *American Newspaper Journalists, 1690-1872*, edited by Perry J. Ashley (1986)

44: *American Screenwriters*, Second Series, edited by Randall Clark, Robert E. Morsberger, and Stephen O. Lesser (1986)

45: *American Poets, 1880-1945*, First Series, edited by Peter Quartermain (1986)

46: *American Literary Publishing Houses, 1900-1980: Trade and Paperback*, edited by Peter Dzwonkoski (1986)

47: *American Historians, 1866-1912*, edited by Clyde N. Wilson (1986)

48: *American Poets, 1880-1945*, Second Series, edited by Peter Quartermain (1986)

49: *American Literary Publishing Houses, 1638-1899*, 2 parts, edited by Peter Dzwonkoski (1986)

50: *Afro-American Writers Before the Harlem Renaissance*, edited by Trudier Harris (1986)

51: *Afro-American Writers from the Harlem Renaissance to 1940*, edited by Trudier Harris (1987)

52: *American Writers for Children Since 1960: Fiction*, edited by Glenn E. Estes (1986)

53: *Canadian Writers Since 1960*, First Series, edited by W. H. New (1986)

54: *American Poets, 1880-1945*, Third Series, 2 parts, edited by Peter Quartermain (1987)

55: *Victorian Prose Writers Before 1867*, edited by William B. Thesing (1987)

56: *German Fiction Writers, 1914-1945*, edited by James Hardin (1987)

57: *Victorian Prose Writers After 1867*, edited by William B. Thesing (1987)

58: *Jacobean and Caroline Dramatists*, edited by Fredson Bowers (1987)

59: *American Literary Critics and Scholars, 1800-1850*, edited by John W. Rathbun and Monica M. Grecu (1987)

60: *Canadian Writers Since 1960*, Second Series, edited by W. H. New (1987)

61: *American Writers for Children Since 1960: Poets, Illustrators, and Nonfiction Authors*, edited by Glenn E. Estes (1987)

62: *Elizabethan Dramatists*, edited by Fredson Bowers (1987)

63: *Modern American Critics, 1920-1955*, edited by Gregory S. Jay (1988)

64: *American Literary Critics and Scholars, 1850-1880*, edited by John W. Rathbun and Monica M. Grecu (1988)

65: *French Novelists, 1900-1930*, edited by Catharine Savage Brosman (1988)

66: *German Fiction Writers, 1885-1913*, 2 parts, edited by James Hardin (1988)

67: *Modern American Critics Since 1955*, edited by Gregory S. Jay (1988)

68: *Canadian Writers, 1920-1959*, First Series, edited by W. H. New (1988)

69: *Contemporary German Fiction Writers*, First Series, edited by Wolfgang D. Elfe and James Hardin (1988)

70: *British Mystery Writers, 1860-1919*, edited by Bernard Benstock and Thomas F. Staley (1988)

71: *American Literary Critics and Scholars, 1880-1900*, edited by John W. Rathbun and Monica M. Grecu (1988)

72: *French Novelists, 1930-1960*, edited by Catharine Savage Brosman (1988)

73: *American Magazine Journalists, 1741-1850*, edited by Sam G. Riley (1988)

74: *American Short-Story Writers Before 1880*, edited by Bobby Ellen Kimbel, with the assistance of William E. Grant (1988)

75: *Contemporary German Fiction Writers*, Second Series, edited by Wolfgang D. Elfe and James Hardin (1988)

76: *Afro-American Writers, 1940-1955*, edited by Trudier Harris (1988)

77: *British Mystery Writers, 1920-1939*, edited by Bernard Benstock and Thomas F. Staley (1988)

78: *American Short-Story Writers, 1880-1910*, edited by Bobby Ellen Kimbel, with the assistance of William E. Grant (1988)

79: *American Magazine Journalists, 1850-1900*, edited by Sam G. Riley (1988)

(Continued on back endsheets)

Twentieth-Century Spanish Poets
First Series

Dictionary of Literary Biography • Volume One Hundred Eight

Twentieth-Century Spanish Poets
First Series

Edited by
Michael L. Perna 8575
Hunter College, City University of New York

A Bruccoli Clark Layman Book
Gale Research Inc.
Detroit, London

Printed in the United States of America

Published simultaneously in the United Kingdom
by Gale Research International Limited
(An affiliated company of Gale Research Inc.)

The paper used in this publication meets the minimum requirements
of American National Standard for Information Sciences—Permanence
Paper for Printed Library Materials, ANSI Z39.48-1984. ∞™

Copyright © 1991
Gale Research Inc.
835 Penobscot Bldg.
Detroit, MI 48226-4094

ISBN 0-8103-4588-9
91-15266 CIP

Contents

Plan of the Series

The advisory board, the editors, and the publisher of the *Dictionary of Literary Biography* are joined in endorsing Mark Twain's declaration. The literature of a nation provides an inexhaustible resource of permanent worth. We intend to make literature and its creators better understood and more accessible to students and the reading public, while satisfying the standards of teachers and scholars.

To meet these requirements, *literary biography* has been construed in terms of the author's achievement. The most important thing about a writer is his writing. Accordingly, the entries in *DLB* are career biographies, tracing the development of the author's canon and the evolution of his reputation.

The purpose of *DLB* is not only to provide reliable information in a convenient format but also to place the figures in the larger perspective of literary history and to offer appraisals of their accomplishments by qualified scholars.

The publication plan for *DLB* resulted from two years of preparation. The project was proposed to Bruccoli Clark by Frederick G. Ruffner, president of the Gale Research Company, in November 1975. After specimen entries were prepared and typeset, an advisory board was formed to refine the entry format and develop the series rationale. In meetings held during 1976, the publisher, series editors, and advisory board approved the scheme for a comprehensive biographical dictionary of persons who contributed to North American literature. Editorial work on the first volume began in January 1977, and it was published in 1978. In order to make *DLB* more than a reference tool and to compile volumes that individually have claim to status as lit-

erary history, it was decided to organize volumes by topic, period, or genre. Each of these freestanding volumes provides a biographical-bibliographical guide and overview for a particular area of literature. We are convinced that this organization—as opposed to a single alphabet method—constitutes a valuable innovation in the presentation of reference material. The volume plan necessarily requires many decisions for the placement and treatment of authors who might properly be included in two or three volumes. In some instances a major figure will be included in separate volumes, but with different entries emphasizing the aspect of his career appropriate to each volume. Ernest Hemingway, for example, is represented in *American Writers in Paris, 1920-1939* by an entry focusing on his expatriate apprenticeship; he is also in *American Novelists, 1910-1945* with an entry surveying his entire career. Each volume includes a cumulative index of subject authors and articles. Comprehensive indexes to the entire series are planned.

With volume ten in 1982 it was decided to enlarge the scope of *DLB*. By the end of 1986 twenty-one volumes treating British literature had been published, and volumes for Commonwealth and Modern European literature were in progress. The series has been further augmented by the *DLB Yearbooks* (since 1981) which update published entries and add new entries to keep the *DLB* current with contemporary activity. There have also been *DLB Documentary Series* volumes which provide biographical and critical source materials for figures whose work is judged to have particular interest for students. One of these companion volumes is entirely devoted to Tennessee Williams.

We define literature as the *intellectual commerce of a nation:* not merely as belles lettres but as that ample and complex process by which ideas are generated, shaped, and transmitted. *DLB* entries are not limited to "creative writers" but extend to other figures who in their time and in their way influenced the mind of a people. Thus the series encompasses historians, journalists, publishers, and screenwriters. By this means readers of *DLB* may be aided to perceive literature not as cult scripture in the keeping of intellectual high priests but firmly positioned at the center of a nation's life.

DLB includes the major writers appropriate to each volume and those standing in the ranks immediately behind them. Scholarly and critical counsel has been sought in deciding which minor figures to include and how full their entries should be. Wherever possible, useful references are made to figures who do not warrant separate entries.

Each DLB volume has a volume editor responsible for planning the volume, selecting the figures for inclusion, and assigning the entries. Volume editors are also responsible for preparing, where appropriate, appendices surveying the major periodicals and literary and intellectual movements for their volumes, as well as lists of further readings. Work on the series as a whole is coordinated at the Bruccoli Clark Layman editorial center in Columbia, South Carolina, where the editorial staff is responsible for accuracy of the published volumes.

One feature that distinguishes DLB is the illustration policy—its concern with the iconography of literature. Just as an author is influenced by his surroundings, so is the reader's understanding of the author enhanced by a knowledge of his environment. Therefore DLB volumes include not only drawings, paintings, and photographs of authors, often depicting them at various stages in their careers, but also illustrations of their families and places where they lived. Title pages are regularly reproduced in facsimile along with dust jackets for modern authors. The dust jackets are a special feature of DLB because they often document better than anything else the way in which an author's work was perceived in its own time. Specimens of the writers' manuscripts are included when feasible.

Samuel Johnson rightly decreed that "The chief glory of every people arises from its authors." The purpose of the *Dictionary of Literary Biography* is to compile literary history in the surest way available to us—by accurate and comprehensive treatment of the lives and work of those who contributed to it.

The *DLB* Advisory Board

Foreword

This volume of the *Dictionary of Literary Biography* is the first of two devoted to Spanish poets of the twentieth century. The century began with a great revitalization of verse forms and of the Spanish language itself, when the work of the French Parnassian and symbolist poets was adapted into Spanish by the Latin American *modernistas*, especially Rubén Darío (1867-1916). His stunning verses and his electrifying personal influence—during visits to Spain (first as Nicaraguan representative to the fourth centennial of Christopher Columbus's voyage to America) and in Paris, where Spanish poets visited him— started a chain of consequences through a century, for symbolist poetics have influenced even the *anti-modernistas* who rejected Darío's neo-Hellenistic imagery and the more recent social realists who reject his legacy of devotion to art as an exclusive personal commitment.

The earliest reaction against Darío brought a rediscovery of Spain's own medieval and Golden Age poets, at a time when the quick victory of the United States in the Spanish-American War (1898) sent young Spanish writers back to their traditions to try to explain the disaster and find a way to regenerate the country. The synthesis of rediscovered writing, such as that of Luis de Góngora (1561-1627), with influences from France, such as surrealism and the "pure poetry" and criticism of Paul Valéry (1871-1945), contributed to a rebirth of Spanish poetry in the 1920s and 1930s—a great outpouring of lyric poetry comparable to the sixteenth and seventeenth centuries, when Spain adapted, reacted against, and assimilated waves of influence from the Italian Renaissance to produce its own Golden Age. For English-speaking readers Federico García Lorca is the best-known lyric poet of modern Spain; like the star one can pick out most easily in a constellation, he is surrounded by a brilliant group just beginning to be seen more clearly.

For Spanish poets the twentieth century has been similar to the sixteenth and nineteenth centuries. The Spanish Civil War (1936-1939) drove some of them abroad, brutally silenced others, and forced most to struggle to attain their full poetic stature in harsh circumstances on their native ground. Just as lives were changed by thirty or forty years of social dislocation during the rise of the Royal Inquisition in the sixteenth century or the Napoleonic invasion and wars and the absolutist reaction under Ferdinand VII in the nineteenth century, so the Spanish Civil War and the authoritarian traditionalism of the Francisco Franco dictatorship (1939-1975) have saturated these poets' biographies with history. Only now can one begin to see that exiles, victims, and survivors all belong to the same identifiable age of Spanish literature, in the way that the refugees from the Inquisition still belonged to the Spanish Golden Age or that the exiles of nineteenth-century *España peregrina* (wandering Spain) took Spain with them where they went and brought European Romanticism home with them when they returned. "Resistir es vencer" (To resist is to win) is a proverb that has proven true over and over again in Spanish history.

Except for Dámaso Alonso's *Hijos de la ira* (Children of Wrath, 1944), no book of poetry published in Spain during the ten years after the civil war was comparable in excellence to the work of Jorge Guillén, Rafael Alberti, Pedro Salinas, or León Felipe—all in exile—or of the émigré Juan Ramón Jiménez. Yet the beginnings of recovery are detectable in the literary reviews *Escorial* (1940-1950), *Garcilaso* (1943-1946), and *Espadaña* (1944-1951), and in the Adonáis Collection, a series of small volumes founded by Juan Guerrero in 1943 to choose, through the critical acumen of José Luis Cano, the best new poets. From 1956, when Jiménez was the Nobel laureate for literature, to 1977 when it was Vicente Aleixandre, Spanish poets' reputations in the English-speaking world grew steadily thanks to the work of translators, many of them academics, the best of them poets such as James Wright and Robert Bly, who shared their Spanish discoveries with their readers.

The most recent signal of the reopening of Spanish poetry to the outside world came with the establishment of the Cervantes Prize in 1976.

Alongside the system of prizes offered by Spanish publishers, the Cervantes is open to nominations from the entire Spanish-speaking world, from the twenty-one sister academies of the language of the independent Spanish-American nations, from Puerto Rico, and from the Philippines. Spain's poets among the first fifteen laureates have been Guillén (1976); Alonso (1978); Gerardo Diego, who shared the honor with Argentina's Jorge Luis Borges (1979); Luis Rosales (1982); and Alberti (1983). Most of them were in their eighties when the prize came, members of a generation for whom recognition has been too long delayed. Some of them and their successors form the subject matter of this volume.

—Michael L. Perna

Acknowledgments

This book was produced by Bruccoli Clark Layman, Inc. Karen L. Rood is senior editor for the *Dictionary of Literary Biography* series. Jack Turner was the in-house editor.

Production coordinator is James W. Hipp. Projects manager is Charles D. Brower. Photography editors are Edward Scott and Timothy Lundy. Permissions editor is Jean W. Ross. Layout and graphics supervisor is Penney L. Haughton. Copyediting supervisor is Bill Adams. Typesetting supervisor is Kathleen M. Flanagan. Systems manager is George F. Dodge. Charles Lee Egleston is editorial associate. The production staff includes Rowena Betts, Teresa Chaney, Patricia Coate, Gail Crouch, Margaret McGinty Cureton, Sarah A. Estes, Robert Fowler, Mary L. Goodwin, Cynthia Hallman, Ellen McCracken, Kathy Lawler Merlette, Laura Garren Moore, Catherine A. Murray, John Myrick, Pamela D. Norton, Cathy J. Reese, Laurrè Sinckler-Reeder, Maxine K. Smalls, and Betsy L. Weinberg.

Walter W. Ross and Timothy D. Tebalt did library research. They were assisted by the following librarians at the Thomas Cooper Library of the University of South Carolina: Jens Holley and the interlibrary-loan staff; reference librarians Gwen Baxter, Daniel Boice, Faye Chadwell, Jo Cottingham, Cathy Eckman, Rhonda Felder, Gary Geer, Jackie Kinder, Laurie Preston, Jean Rhyne, Carol Tobin, Virginia Weathers, and Connie Widney; circulation-department head Thomas Marcil; and acquisitions-searching supervisor David Haggard.

Dictionary of Literary Biography • Volume One Hundred Eight

Twentieth-Century Spanish Poets
First Series

Dictionary of Literary Biography

Rafael Alberti
(16 December 1902 -   )

Luis Lorenzo-Rivero
University of Utah

BOOKS: *Marinero en tierra* (Madrid: Biblioteca Nueva, 1925);

La amante, canciones (Málaga, Spain: Imprenta Litoral, 1926);

El alba del alhelí (Santander, Spain: Cossío, 1927);

Cal y canto (Madrid: Revista de Occidente, 1929);

Sobre los ángeles (Madrid: Iberoamericana, 1929); translated by Geoffrey Connell as *Concerning the Angels* (London: Rapp & Carroll, 1967);

El hombre deshabitado (Madrid: Plutarco, 1930 [i.e., 1931]);

Fermín Galán (Madrid: Plutarco, 1931);

Oración a la Virgen de buena leche (Paris: Pintos, 1931);

Consignas (Madrid: Ediciones Octubre, 1933);

Un fantasma recorre Europa (Madrid: Tentativa Poética, 1933); translated as *A Specter Is Haunting Europe* (New York: Critics Group, 1936);

Bazar de la providencia (negocio), dos farsas revolucionarias (Madrid: Octubre, 1934);

De un momento al otro (Mexico City: Fábula, 1935; enlarged edition, Madrid: Europe-America, 1937; enlarged again, Buenos Aires: Bajel, 1942);

Versos de agitación (Mexico City: Defensa Roja, 1935);

Poesía, 1924-1930 (Madrid: Cruz & Raya/Arbol, 1935);

Verte y no verte. A Ignacio Sánchez Mejías (Mexico City: Lira, 1935);

13 bandas y 48 estrellas, poema del mar Caribe (Madrid: Altolaguirre, 1936);

Nuestra diaria palabra (Madrid: Héroe, 1936);

Poesía, 1924-1937 (Madrid: Signo, 1938);

Radio Sevilla (Madrid: Signo, 1938);

De los sauces (Buenos Aires: Colombo, 1940);

De los álamos y los sauces (Buenos Aires: Colombo, 1940);

Entre el clavel y la espada (Buenos Aires: Losada, 1941);

La arboleda perdida, volume 1 (Mexico City: Séneca/Arbol, 1942); volume 2 (Buenos Aires: General Fabril, 1959); both volumes translated by Gabriel Berns as *The Lost Grove* (Berkeley: University of California Press, 1976);

El poeta en la España de 1931 (Buenos Aires: Patronado Hispano-Argentino de Cultura, 1942);

¡Eh, los toros! (Buenos Aires: Emecé, 1942);

Vida bilingüe de un refugiado español en Francia (Buenos Aires: Bajel, 1942);

Numancia (Buenos Aires: Losada, 1943);

Tres recuerdos del cielo (Buenos Aires: Urania, 1943);

El adefesio (Buenos Aires: Losada, 1944);

Pleamar (Buenos Aires: Losada, 1944);

A la pintura, cantata de la línea y del color (Buenos Aires: López, 1945); revised as *A la pintura. Poema del color y la línea* (Buenos Aires: Losada, 1948);

Imagen primera de ... (Buenos Aires: Losada, 1945);

¡Pueblos Libres! ¿Y España? (Buenos Aires: Comisión de Ayuda al Español Demócrata, 1946);

El ceñidor de Venus desceñido (Buenos Aires: Botella al Mar, 1947);

Coplas de Juan Panadero (Montevideo: Pueblos Unidos, 1949);

Teatro (Buenos Aires: Losada, 1950);

Buenos Aires en tinta china (Buenos Aires: Losada, 1951);

Retornos de lo vivo lejano (Buenos Aires: Losada, 1952);

Ora marítima, seguida de Baladas y canciones del Paraná (Buenos Aires: Losada, 1953);

Noche de guerra en el Museo del Prado (Buenos Aires: Losada, 1956);

Sonríe China, by Alberti and María Teresa León (Buenos Aires: Muchnik, 1958);

Los viejos olivos (Caracas: Ministerio de Educación, 1960);

Poesías completas (Buenos Aires: Losada, 1961);

Suma taurina: verso, prosa, teatro (Barcelona: RM, 1963);

Abierto a todas horas (Madrid: Aguado, 1964);

Lope de Vega y la poesía contemporánea seguido de la pájara pinta (Paris: Centre de Recherches de l'Institut d'Etudes Hispaniques, 1964);

El poeta en la calle (Paris: Librairie du Globe, 1966);

Poemas de amor (Barcelona: Alfaguara, 1967);

Libro del mar (Barcelona: Lumen, 1968);

Poemas anteriores a "Marinero en tierra" (Barcelona: V.A., 1969);

Los 8 nombres de Picasso (Barcelona: Kairós, 1970);

Prosas encontradas, edited by Robert Marrast (Madrid: Ayuso, 1970);

Picasso en Avignon (Paris: Cercle D'Art, 1971);

Canciones del Alto Valle del Aniene (Buenos Aires: Losada, 1972);

Coplas para Manuel Gerena (Seville: Gráficas del Sur, 1972);

Desprecio y Maravilla / Disprezzo e meraviglia (Rome: Riuniti, 1972);

Obras completas, 2 volumes (Madrid: Aguilar, 1972);

Poemas del destierro y la espera (Madrid: Espasa-Calpe, 1976);

Signos del día (Barcelona: Seix Barral, 1978);

Los 5 destacagados: Reparto (Seville: Calle del Aire, 1978);

Aire, que me lleva el aire: Antología juvenil (Barcelona: Labor, 1979);

Fustigada luz (1972-1978) (Barcelona: Seix Barral, 1980);

Relatos y prosa (Barcelona: Bruguera, 1980);

Lo que canté y dije de Picasso (Barcelona: Bruguera, 1981);

Obra Completa, 3 volumes (Madrid: Aguilar, 1988).

Editions in English: *Selected Poems*, translated by Lloyd Mallan (New York: New Directions, 1944);

Selected Poems, translated by Ben Belitt (Berkeley & Los Angeles: University of California Press, 1966);

The Owl's Insomnia, translated by Mark Strand (New York: Atheneum, 1973);

The Other Shore: 100 Poems, edited by Kosrof Chantikian, translated by José A. Elgorriaga and Martin Paul (San Francisco: Kosmos, 1981).

PLAY PRODUCTIONS: *El hombre deshabitado*, Madrid, Teatro de la Zarzuela, 1931;

Fermín Galán, Madrid, Teatro Español, 1931;

Los salvadores de España, Madrid, Teatro Español, 20 October 1936;

Numancia, Madrid, Teatro de la Zarzuela, 26 De-

Alberti (right) with his wife, María Teresa León, and Federico García Lorca at a Madrid café, 1934

cember 1937; revised version, Montevideo, Estudio Auditorio, 1944;

Cantata de los héroes y la fraternidad de los pueblos, Madrid, Teatro Auditorium, 20 November 1938;

El adefesio, Buenos Aires, Teatro Avenida, 8 June 1944; revised version, Madrid, Teatro Reina Victoria, 24 September 1976;

Noche de guerra en el Museo del Prado, Madrid, Teatro María Guerrero, 29 November 1978.

OTHER: Charles Pierre Baudelaire, *Diarios íntimos*, translated, with a prologue, by Alberti (Buenos Aires: Bajel, 1943);

Eglogas y fábulas castellanas, edited, with a prologue, by Alberti (Buenos Aires: Pleamar, 1944);

Gloria Alcorta, *Visages (Rostros)*, translated by Alberti (Buenos Aires: Botella al Mar, 1951).

SELECTED PERIODICAL PUBLICATION—
UNCOLLECTED: "Rafael Alberti (artículo auto-

biográfico)," *Gaceta Literaria*, 3 (1 January 1929).

Rafael Alberti first gained prominence when he received the National Prize of Literature for *Marinero en tierra* (The Land-Locked Sailor) in 1925. He was at his sister María's home in Rute, in the province of Córdoba, when the telegram arrived announcing the award for poetry, which he shared with Gerardo Diego, who won for *Versos humanos* (Human Verses). A few days later Alberti left for Madrid to collect the badly needed prize money (five thousand pesetas), and to thank the members of the committee for their vote in his favor. The members were the distinguished poets Antonio Machado and José Moreno Villa, the established critics Ramón Menéndez Pidal and Gabriel Maura, the popular playwright Carlos Arniches, and the outstanding novelist Gabriel Miró. (The committee had voted unanimously in Alberti's favor. Then Maura had proposed Diego's *Versos humanos* for a second prize for poetry, in lieu of the award for theater.

The other committee members had agreed.) From this start, Alberti's fame increased continuously. His poetry has been translated into many languages, including Czech, English, French, German, Italian, and Rumanian.

As Ricardo Gullón has pointed out, Alberti's works parallel the evolution of contemporary poetry. Due to his beginnings as a painter, he is one of Spain's most visually oriented poets. Alberti considers painting one of the greatest possible manifestations of humanity (*Cambio 16*, 5 May 1977). The visual nature of his poetic images earned him the reputation of a rebel in the realm of contemporary poetry. One of the primary themes in Alberti's works is his identification with natural elements, which frequently assume human characteristics. Roberto C. Manteiga has concluded that Alberti concentrates "on the four principal elements": earth, water, fire, and air. These fulfill a distinct symbolic function in his poetry.

In 1977 Alberti became the center of attention in Spain, due to his political writings and activities as well as to the country's sociopolitical circumstances after Francisco Franco's death. At this time Alberti became a figure of monumental importance to millions of Spaniards, the majority of whom had been previously unfamiliar with his works. The press, television, and the Spanish Communist party were instrumental in publicizing his status as the only internationally acclaimed Spanish writer still in exile since 1939. He had been residing in Rome, anxiously awaiting the day he could return to Spain. In May 1977 he stepped on Spanish soil again for the first time in almost forty years.

Alberti's life has been as stormy as the night of 16 December 1902 on which he was born in Puerto de Santa María, near Cádiz. His early instruction at home and school was marked by fanatical religious fervor. His parents, María Merello Gómez and Vicente Alberti Sánchez, operators of a winery, were devout Catholics, and Rafael attended the local Carmelite convent school until age ten. From 1912 to 1917 he studied at Saint Louis Gonzaga school, which was operated by the Jesuits. Though an average pupil in some subjects, such as mathematics and Latin, in most others he scored poorly.

His happiest childhood moments took place when he slipped away from classes to play with other truants. Around 1914 he wanted to become a bullfighter. With this ambition, he and a friend nicknamed "La Negrita" jumped pasture fences to fight grazing steers and cows. Very early in his life Alberti took pleasure in drawing and painting landscapes and seascapes. He even copied from a magazine Diego Velázquez's painting *El príncipe Baltasar Carlos*. This colorful seventeenth-century portrait depicts the young prince galloping on horseback. Velázquez later became one of Alberti's favorite painters. Alberti also cherished home theatrical productions, for which he painted backdrops. At this time he had no interest in poetry and did not anticipate his future career.

In 1917 Alberti and his family were forced to move from Puerto de Santa María to Madrid after their winery had been sold to pay bills. There he spent countless morning hours studying the paintings of Rubens, Tintoretto, Titian, Zurbarán, El Greco, Velázquez, Goya, and others in the Prado Museum. In the afternoons he studied painting in the San Fernando Academy and also with a private instructor, Emilio Coli. However, Alberti's family faced severe economic hardships, and at one point he had to help support them. His older brother, Vicente, sent him as a wine promoter to various towns in Castile for the Osborne and Terry cellars.

At the Madrid premier of Manuel de Falla's ballet *El Tricornio* (The Three-Cornered Hat) in 1919, Alberti was impressed not only by the score but also by the backdrop created by Pablo Picasso for the ballet. During that period, which gave rise to ultraism, futurism, cubism, and other artistic movements, Alberti met Jhal and Marian Paskiewicz, Robert Delaunay, and other artists by whom he was influenced. He experimented with a painting style that combines word and design in what could be described as a pictograph, which anticipates his works of forty years later. Sometime in 1922 Alberti suddenly abandoned painting, not to return to it until late in his life. He had discovered a more satisfactory medium of aesthetic expression: poetry. This reorientation resulted in a serious crisis in his personality. At one point he did not know whether he was a painter or a poet.

Alberti's poetic activity began in March 1920, when he wrote his first poem on the day of his father's death. Two other deaths that same year inspired other early poems: the tragic death of the famous bullfighter Joselito and the passing away of the great novelist Benito Pérez Galdós. Soon afterward Alberti accelerated the pace of his literary productivity. The opportunity presented itself when the trace of tuberculosis previ-

Alberti on the ranch of family friend Rodolfo Araoz near Córdoba, Argentina, circa 1940

ously discovered in his lungs recurred, but more acutely. The illness forced him to spend the summer of 1921 in the pine forest of San Rafael in the Guadarrama Mountains. He wrote with vehemence, motivated by his circumstances, the surroundings, and his reading of *Libro de poemas* (1921) by Federico García Lorca. Alberti developed a form of poetic expression different from the ultraist school and other rapidly emerging movements. He adapted some ultraist-style images but excluded from his poems the ultraist irrationalism and mechanistic themes. Again in Guadarrama during the summer of 1923 he read extensively in collections of medieval poetry and songs. These, and in particular the poetry of the Lusitanian (Portuguese) writer Gil Vicente, inspired Alberti's particular style, which was to be called "neopopularism." This term has been used by most Spanish literary critics since 1937, when Guillermo Díaz-Plaja used it for the first time in his book *La poesía lírica española* (The Spanish

Lyric Poetry). They have applied "neo-popularism" to Alberti's style to indicate that he wrote poems with folkloric themes and appearances but, contrary to anonymity poetry, he was very interested in being recognized as the author of his erudite creations. Thus he conceived his first book, *Marinero en tierra*, which he finished later at his sister's home in Rute. One of the songs in this book was influenced by Maksim Gorky's story "Malva" (1897). Alberti's two subsequent books were also written in the neo-popularist form. Despite this classification, his poetry is much more erudite than popular. The neo-popularist poems use both traditional images and avant-garde images rooted in a traditional context, as the following ballad demonstrates:

Mi vaca, la labradora,
la vaca que más quería,
por ser pirata pastora
voló sobre una almadía.

(My cow, the one used to plow,
the cow that I loved the most,
for being a pirate grazer
flew on a canoe.)

The predominant theme of Alberti's first three books is the sea. *Marinero en tierra* is written with simplicity and candor, and it played a decisive role in his resolution to become a poet. Between 1923 and 1924 he established friendships with Lorca, Salvador Dalí, Luis Buñuel, and others. One by one he met all the important poets of his age group: Pedro Salinas, Jorge Guillén, Vicente Aleixandre, Gerardo Diego, Dámaso Alonso, and more.

In addition to his poetry, Alberti wrote for the stage, but despite his literary successes, his economic situation remained constrained, and his family relations were tense. In 1926 he decided to organize an homage to Luis de Góngora for the coming year, the third centenary of his death. During the winter in Rute, Alberti began working on a book of songs, *El alba del alhelí* (The Dawn of the Lily), which he finished later in Almería at the home of his other sister, Pepita, and published in 1927. On a trip to Seville he met Ignacio Sánchez Mejías, the great bullfighter, poetry enthusiast, and playwright, and they became close friends. Passing through Málaga, Alberti visited the poets Emilio Prados and Manuel Altolaguirre, who were soon to publish Alberti's second book, *La amante, canciones* (Songs to the Beloved, 1926). This collection depicts the poet's journey across Castile to the northern coast of Spain and seems a continuation of *Marinero en tierra*, since the essential element is, once again, nostalgia for the sea. In the latter part of this second book the emphasis shifts to the Cantabrian sea, and Alberti intensifies his use of popular verse forms.

In *El alba del alhelí* he draws his themes from the traditional poetry of Andalusia. The mood of this third book is more serious than that of its two precursors, and it encompasses a wide range of themes. In the words of Manteiga: "all aspects of the Andalusian culture are explored in the work, not just the rustic aspect." The collection also contains some poems with dramatic overtones. Although Alberti's poetic creation is as vast as it is versatile, thematic unity intrinsically connects the first three books, and many themes established here—such as those concerning dreams, love, the sea, and others—are to be repeated throughout his entire work. The most important images in the early poems are of land and sea, closely followed by a significant autobiographical element.

Alberti's frequent travels throughout the country were, at times, for health reasons to rest and recuperate from tuberculosis at his sisters' homes. Other times, they were done to help the precarious economic situation of his family, who had been supporting him until he was well. He had to bring in money by going to different towns and cities promoting and selling wine from the Osborne and Terry cellars, the means of support for his entire family residing in Madrid, which was his permanent residence from 1917 to the end of the Spanish Civil War in 1939. Then he had to flee with his wife, María Teresa León, from Franco's troops and ultimately leave the country.

An extremely exciting and productive year for Alberti was 1927. One of the remarkable experiences that he had that year was meeting the composer Manuel de Falla. Since the composer had also been born in the Cádiz area, they spent an entire afternoon talking about their native region. Alberti also was on the verge of realizing his boyhood dream of becoming a bullfighter. Mejías had asked him to assist in the city of Badajoz's bullring, but Alberti failed to appear, and his debut was postponed a few weeks. It took place a month later in Pontevedra, a city on Spain's northwest coast. Rafael wore the orange-and-black toreador suit in which Mejías had mourned his brother-in-law, Joselito. At last confronted with the bull, Alberti was terrified and abandoned his bullfighting career on the spot. Later that year he participated in the grandiose homage to Góngora, but his carefree and happy years were at an end. His health deteriorated, forcing him to rest often and seek medical treatment. His financial difficulties became more acute, and, in the opinion of Joaquín González Muela, his problems were compounded by an unhappy love affair.

In 1929 Alberti published *Cal y canto* (Stone and Mortar), which marks an entirely new direction in his poetry. *Cal y canto* is an experimental work containing a few poems in free verse, and the majority in more stringent forms such as sonnets or tercets of hendecasyllabic meter. Alberti's future political commitment is already obvious in this collection, as is his emulation, however short-lived, of Góngora. *Cal y canto*, which was originally to be entitled "Pasión y forma" (Passion and Form), reflects two diametrically opposed poetic realms: on the one hand the realm of architectural elegance and frozen emotions, and on the other hand an abyss of violence and destruction. Examining Alberti's early poetry from *Marinero en tierra* through *Cal y canto*, the reader recognizes noticeable changes in his outlook on life. The poet's physical and emotional crisis is clearly reflected in the next book, *Sobre los ángeles* (1929; translated as *Concerning the Angels*, 1967), which he began before concluding *Cal y canto*. In *Sobre los ángeles* Alberti expresses his sense of failure, disillusionment, and despair. Within this deep pessimism, however, a ray of optimism sparkles in a few poems. *Sobre los ángeles* is an eminently autobiographical text, and it should not be considered entirely surrealistic.

In 1929 Alberti also entered the political scene. He hardly knew anything about politics, but he plunged into the student protests against the dictatorship of Gen. Miguel Primo de Rivera. Henceforth, political commitment played a major role both in his writings and social activities. Alberti spoke out for the rights of the working class. Many of his more tendential writings were dictated by his political convictions rather than by an abstract inspiration. Consequently the majority of his political verses seem to be lacking in artistic vision. Instead, they were intended to influence the reader. He tried to be politically effective and at the same time remain an artist, a task difficult to achieve. He sought to join the oppressed in their protest against injustice and in their struggle for freedom.

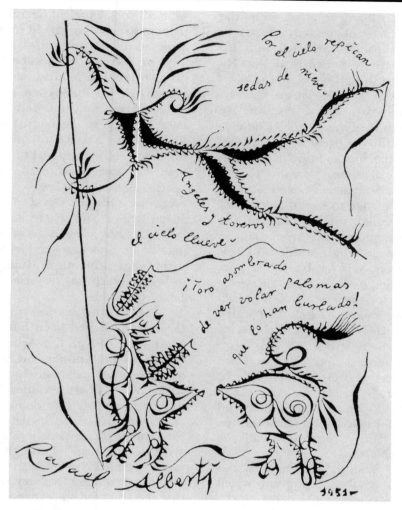

One of Alberti's "lyricographs," which combine poetry and drawing (from Marinero en tierra, La amante, El alba de alhelí, *edited by Robert Marrast, 1972)*

Early in 1930 Alberti received a desperate letter from Pablo Neruda, consul of Chile in Java. The Chilean poet announced he was sending Alberti the manuscript of *Residencia en la tierra* (Residence on Earth, 1933), enjoining him to find a suitable publisher for it, which proved to be impossible at the time. Soon afterward, Alberti met the young writer María Teresa León, and fell in love with her. Together they journeyed to Majorca. The newspapers called this scandalous and drew a parallel to the romance of Frédéric Chopin and George Sand. Upon their return to Madrid, Alberti and León were married by a justice of the peace in the suburb of Argüelles. The only guest at the wedding was León's mother.

In the spring of 1931 the newlyweds spent some time in Rota. While there, on 14 April,

they received the happy news that Spain had been proclaimed a democratic republic. That same year, Alberti became a friend of writer and philosopher Miguel de Unamuno, who had just returned from exile. The Albertis later left for France to spend the summer on the island of Port-Cross as guests of the writer Jules Supervielle, who later translated several of Alberti's works into French. They spent the winter in Paris with the group of Spanish painters residing there. At this time Alberti and Pablo Picasso entered a lasting and fruitful friendship. Alberti also met and befriended several Latin American writers, among them the Peruvian César Vallejo; the Guatemalan Miguel Angel Asturias, who later received the Nobel Prize; and the Cuban Alejo Carpentier, as well as artists of other nationalities such as Henri Michaud and Arturo Uslar Pietri.

While in Paris, Alberti received from the Spanish government a grant to study theater in Europe. To this purpose, he traveled with his wife to Germany, where he settled in Berlin. He came into contact with the group of young playwrights associated with the *Volksbühne* theater, which was then directed by Erwin Piscator. He also took part in meetings of the German Communist party. From Berlin he went to the Soviet Union, where he met the outstanding Russian writers of the day: Nicolai Aseev, Maksim Gorky, Semyon Kirsanov, Boris Pasternak, and Mikhail Sholokhov. Alberti returned to Berlin and, on 27 February 1933, witnessed the burning of the *Reichstag*. From there he went to Amsterdam in order to participate in the World Congress against the War, presided over by Henri Barbusse. He then returned to Spain via France.

Alberti was one of the more politically active writers of his generation. In 1933 he became a poet of the masses. He wrote numerous revolutionary verses, which he recited in political meetings, in workers' libraries, and even in town squares. In the summer of 1934 he met Neruda, who arrived unexpectedly in Madrid. Alberti also traveled for the second time to Moscow to attend the First Congress of Russian Writers, where he met, among others, Sergey Prokofiev and the French writer André Malraux.

Meanwhile, the Spanish coal miners and peasants in Asturias revolted, an event which caused a feeling of horror and panic among the Spanish middle class. Once the rebellion was squelched, the difficult question of the rebels' punishment had to be addressed. Disagreement ensued between Prime Minister Alejandro Lerroux and the three cabinet ministers of the Spanish Confederation of the Autonomic Right (CEDA), who were carrying out the mandates of their party leader José María Gil Robles Quiñones. After a prolonged crisis, in February 1935 Lerroux formed a new cabinet, which included five members from the CEDA, including the power-hungry Gil Robles as minister of war. Although never a prime minister, Gil Robles was able, under the tumultuous circumstances, to exercise immense power. Among CEDA's constituents were the wealthy of Spain. Gil Robles himself was an attorney for the Jesuits and possessed great eloquence. He even permitted his followers to greet him as if he were the führer. Since having visited Germany in 1933 to study Nazi propaganda, he used some of that party's tactics. He appointed Francisco Franco as chief of staff, promoted right-wing officers, expelled liberals and socialists from their posts, and embarked on negotiations to buy arms from Germany.

In Paris in 1935, Alberti was notified that his apartment in Madrid had been searched; this meant that Gil Robles was after him. Therefore he could not return safely to Spain. With the help of Palmiro Togliatti, the organizer of the Red Aid, he traveled to America. There he lectured and sought support for the Asturian revolution. He spent two weeks in New York and nearly a year in Mexico, where he met José Clemente Orozco, David Alfaro Siqueiros, and Diego Rivera, and where he published *Verte y no verte. A Ignacio Sánchez Mejías* (Seeing and Not Seeing. To Ignacio Sánchez Mejías, 1935). He spent, in addition, a month in Cuba and then returned to Spain, which was in turmoil, in 1936 after the fall of Gil Robles.

Alberti and his wife directed the magazine *Octubre*, which had been founded to express the heart and soul of the Asturian revolutionaries. He placed his writings and his life at the service of the revolutionary cause and the Spanish proletariat. When Alberti became a Communist, he radically changed his attitude toward poetry. He was caught in what Kurt Spang calls "the eternal dichotomy of the poet, who is at the same time an artist and a man." Through his social commitment, Alberti became an eminently political writer, a propagandist, and an agitator. It is true that the communism expressed in his verses may be considered social romanticism, for it propounds a total transformation of the social system. Nevertheless, several of his works after 1930 are basically Marxist. These include *Un fantasma recorre Europa* (1933; translated as *A Specter Is Haunting Europe*, 1936), *De un momento al otro* (From One Moment to the Next, 1935), *El poeta en la calle* (The Poet on the Street, 1966), and others. His zealous political commitment often weakened the poems' aesthetic quality.

At this time Alberti seemed unaware that Vladimir Ilyich Ulyanov (Lenin) was betraying Marxism. The doctrine served Lenin as a shield behind which he was promoting his own brand of revolution. Marx might have been astonished to learn what was being done in his name by Lenin and others. Marx had held that economic developments determine social evolution, shaping people's morals, politics, and culture. He never envisioned an oppressive dictatorship, and he believed that his type of proletarian revolution would succeed first in an advanced nation. But he never thought it could happen in backward Russia. Lenin had vowed to end the reign of the czars. He had been infuriated by Alexander III's hanging his beloved older brother in 1887 for having attempted to assassinate the czar. Lenin's revenge came on 7 November 1917 in Smolny. Assisted by Leon Trotsky, he imposed Bolshevism, his "new order." After Lenin's death in 1924, the logical successor would have been Trotsky. Joseph Stalin, however, seized power and exiled Trotsky. Stalin forced the collectivization of farms, which resulted in the extinction of private farms and created famine. In the 1930s he presided over the purges that exterminated additional lives, perhaps millions. This is the form of Communism with which Alberti was in direct contact during the 1930s, even though he denounced it openly in 1977. During the Spanish Republic (1931-1939), he was ignorant of the fact that Lenin's ideology and Stalin's actions were diametrically opposed to his beliefs and objectives. He did not understand Communism.

During the Spanish Civil War, Alberti edited in Madrid the magazine *El Mono Azul* (The Blue Overalls). He was secretary of the Alliance of Antifascist Intellectuals to Defend Culture. In 1937 he organized the Second International Congress of Antifascist Intellectuals and Writers, and thus came into close contact with many writers from abroad. Noteworthy are his relations with the Americans Ernest Hemingway and Langston Hughes. Alberti also participated in other cultural activities, such as the direction of the Romantic Museum. He evacuated the Prado Museum's paintings, and thus saved these treasures of art from Franco's bombs. When he left the museum by taxi, he even carried on his knees some small paintings by Goya. Alberti also served in the Republican Air Force, which kept him stationed in Madrid until the final weeks of the war. On 6 March 1939 he and his wife, with Dolores Ibarruri (La Pasionaria) and Dr. Juan Negrín, prime minister of the republic, flew from Elda (Alicante) to Oran. From there they sailed to Marseilles and finally reached Paris. The film historian Georges Sadoul took the Albertis into his home, and later they lived with Neruda. Picasso found employment for them with the radio station Paris-Mundial. At this time Alberti wrote *Vida bilingüe de un refugiado español en Francia* (The Bilingual Life of a Spanish Refugee in France, 1942), which is to a certain extent a political text.

Alberti in 1956

Shortly after Alberti's arrival in Paris, World War II began, and, with his wife, he decided to move to Argentina. Aboard the *Mendoza* they left Marseilles on 10 February 1940. On the voyage he continued working on *Entre el clavel y la espada* (Between the Flower and the Sword, 1941). The Albertis arrived in Buenos Aires on 3 March, but they did not have passports. Their friend Rodolfo Araoz hid the couple on his farm El Totoral, near Córdoba, until they obtained proper documents. Here Alberti concluded *Entre el clavel y la espada*, a clear expression of his desire to write apolitical poetry again. It contains two prologues, one in verse and the other in prose. Both hint of a future poetry devoted to beauty and devoid of violence. During the years of the Spanish Civil War and immediately thereafter, Alberti was not a productive writer. Exiled in Buenos Aires and pressed by financial need, he at first undertook such diverse tasks as drafting advertising posters, but later he wrote most of his lyric poems and stage plays there. His books published in Argentina outnumber those composed in Spain, where his works of exile were little known until the mid 1970s and were often misinterpreted. His daughter, Aitana, was born in Buenos Aires in 1941. The year 1944 marked the beginning of a new and very productive period, as Alberti published his first book written entirely in Argentina, *Pleamar* (High Tide). This loosely constructed collection of songs and poems again stresses the two complementary aspects of his work: subjective lyricism and political activism. At first glance the text appears to be similar to *Marinero en tierra*. There is, however, a sharp contrast between the clarity of the earlier poems and the sense of distance and vagueness in the poetry of *Pleamar*.

Alberti's adaptation of Miguel de Cervantes' *Numancia* was first performed in 1937 in Madrid, then, in a revised version, in 1944 in Montevideo with the well-known actress Margarita Xirgu in the lead; she had also starred in the premier in Madrid of his *Fermín Galaín* (1931). She later led the cast in Buenos Aires in his *El adefesio* (Absurdity, 1944). To date, this has been his most successful and best-known play—in terms of literary quality. His dramatic pieces never were very significant, although in Spain their value may have been enhanced by Franco's prohibition of their performance. They were read mostly by professional critics. As literary pieces their merit is considerably greater than as plays on the stage. The reader perceives those poetic qualities that largely escape an audience. When *El adefesio* was performed for the first time in Madrid in 1976 in a revised version, its weaknesses were obvious, and Alberti's reputation as a playwright declined sharply. After he attained financial security in Argentina, he had a house built in Punta del Este, Uruguay, which he named La Gallarda (The Gallant). It was an excellent place for him to relax, paint, write poetry, and host friends such as the Brazilian painter Cándido Portinari, who was living in Montevideo and painted a magnificent mural for the poet in the living room of La Gallarda.

Toward the end of World War II, Alberti traveled to Chile, where he lectured and held poetry readings. He also visited Neruda, whom he had not seen for five years. Finally, he returned to his original vocation: painting. Seen as a whole, the poetry created during Alberti's exile shows an uneven quality. It includes masterpieces, such as *A la pintura* (To Painting, 1945), side by side with texts of a more occasional character. The first version of *A la pintura* remained in-

Cover for Alberti's 1968 poetry collection, one of many to feature extensive illustrations

complete. It was published in an elaborate, limited edition. In addition to painting, it also refers to related art forms, among them line drawing and even sculpture. Alberti demonstrates his intrinsic understanding of the visual arts. The composition of the book coincided with his initial attempt to merge poetry and the visual arts in the form of "liricografías" (lyricographs). After 1947 and especially during the 1950s, he produced single copies of his calligraphic, illustrated poetry books for various exhibitions in Uruguay and Argentina. His final version of *A la pintura* (1948) is perhaps his most perfect achievement in terms of its order and structural plan.

Alberti's political convictions, first expressed in *El poeta en la calle*, proved formative for later texts. Throughout his political verses, he attacks imperialist ideologies and politics. Illustrative are *13 bandas y 48 estrellas* (13 Stripes and 48 Stars, 1936), which condemns United States interference in the Caribbean countries, and *Signos del día* (Today's Signs, 1978). During his exile in Argentina, his political fervor took on a calmer note; there is even a certain degree of resignation seen in *Coplas de Juan Panadero* (Ballads of Juan Panadero, 1949) and some of his succeeding texts. The impact of *Coplas* is considerably weakened by its excessive attention to trivialities.

During 1950 he traveled to Europe for the first time since 1940; in Warsaw he participated in the World Congress for Peace. On this occasion Picasso was awarded the Lenin Peace Prize, which Alberti accepted on his behalf.

Once he returned to Argentina, Alberti's nostalgia for Spain became more acute, and he expressed these feelings in his writings. The theme of nostalgia for past happiness is presented most lucidly in *Retornos de lo vivo lejano* (Cherished Memories of My Past, 1952). In some poems, he recalls a familiar sadness or the present loneliness of exile. Here the slightest recollection of the past is the mainstay of Alberti's inspiration.

Alberti spent two summers on the Del Mayor Loco (ranch of the Mad Major), on the banks of the Paraná river near Buenos Aires. There he composed *Baladas y canciones del Paraná* (Ballads and Songs of the Paraná, published with *Ora marítima* in 1953), which reflects his return to the simple forms of neopopularism and to the theme of the sea as the primary source of his inspiration. These poems express a strong nostalgia for the scenery he knew as a child. There is a constant dialogue between the lyrical speaker and the elements of nature, which remind him of Spain.

In 1955 Alberti traveled to Warsaw with his wife and daughter in order to attend a festival honoring the Polish poet Adam Mickiewicz. Alberti also visited Romania, Czechoslovakia, the Soviet Union, and other countries, where he was received with great acclaim. He spent a month in Paris, and in Berlin he met Bertolt Brecht, who wanted to include in the repertoire of the Berliner Ensemble Alberti's latest play, *Noche de guerra en el Museo del Prado* (A Night of War in the Prado Museum, 1956). The planned collaboration was foiled by the sudden death of Brecht on 14 August 1956. Alberti visited China in 1957 and traveled for four months across the entire country. He was honored by the aging painter Chi Pai-Shih, who dedicated his last work to Alberti. Oriental art had a considerable impact on Alberti's future graphic productivity. He considered himself a Chinese-Arabian-Andalusian painter. Returning from China, he stayed in Romania, where he agreed to translate poems by Mihail Eminescu. He also visited Italy and Paris, where he attended in 1957 the first performance of *Le Repoussoir*, the French translation of his *El adefesio*. Once again in Argentina, he bought a piece of land in the woods close to Buenos Aires. He named it "La Arboleda Perdida" in memory of a favorite spot of his youth near Puerto de Santa María. In the Argentinian woods he finished his second volume of memoirs and published it together with a republication of the first as *La arboleda perdida* (1959; translated as *The Lost Grove*, 1976). He went to the place frequently, in search of solitude and meditation, with only stray dogs for company.

Alberti always loved animals. Ever since his childhood, dogs were his inseparable companions. One dog, Centella, was his playmate on the beaches, in pine forests, and in the castles of Puerto de Santa María. He was similarly attached to Niebla, the dog of his youth in Madrid, and to Tusca, his dog in Buenos Aires. Later, when living in Rome in the 1960s, he wrote a poem entitled "A Marco" (in *Obra Completa* [Complete Work], volume 3, 1988), which is dedicated to the dog of Valerio Zurlini, a popular man known to everyone in the community. In Rome, Alberti's companion for six years was Chico, a dog he found wandering the streets of Trastevere. They became inseparable, and in 1977, when Alberti returned to reside permanently in Spain, he brought Chico with him in the airplane. He was determined that Chico would not meet the same sad fate as had befallen Centella, when old and nearly blind: "we had barbarously abandoned it to its destiny when we moved to Madrid" (*La arboleda perdida*).

In 1960 Alberti returned to his frequent travels and delivered speeches and read his poetry in Colombia, Venezuela, Peru, and Cuba. In March he exhibited for the first time his *Tauromaquia* in the National Museum of Bogotá. It is a collection of twenty-one prints on the theme of bullfighting, influenced by Goya's work of the same title. Later he displayed it in other South American cities. In 1961 he traveled to France for the celebration of the eightieth birthday of his friend Picasso. Then the Association of Argentine Plastic Artists paid special homage to Alberti on his sixtieth birthday. Various painters interpreted his poems on canvas, and he in turn displayed lyricographs and autographs in Buenos Aires.

Alberti arrived with his wife and daughter in Europe on 28 May 1963, intending to settle permanently. They spent the summer in Romania and later established residence in Rome. He decided to broaden his skills as a visual artist and studied engraving with Renzo Romero, who taught him the rare technique of lead engraving and other innovations. His first exhibition in Rome was in 1965 and included etchings of handwritten poems and ten engravings. Later in 1965 he went to Moscow to receive the Lenin Peace Prize. When he returned to Rome, he found he had been awarded the Arti Figurative di Roma first prize for his engravings. Gian Carlo Menotti invited him to the Spoleto Festival for a poetry reading, together with Salvatore Quasimodo and Neruda. For Alberti's exhibition "El lirismo del alfabeto" (The Lyricism of the Alphabet), staged in Milan in 1969, he combined painting and poetry, calligraphy and music. In 1970 the Association of Architects from Catalonia and Baleares organized a successful exhibition of Alberti's poetic and graphic works in Barcelona.

Alberti was a celebrated personality of Trastevere, the district of Rome where he lived. This popularity resulted in part from his congenial manner, in part from frequent appearances on Italian television, and most certainly from his stature as an artist. He received visitors from all over the globe, both strangers and friends. One of his regular guests was the Croatian poet Slavko Mihalic, whom Alberti in turn visited frequently. Alberti also regularly visited Picasso in Mougins, France. Among the literary by-products of these visits are *Los 8 nombres de Picasso* (The Eight Names of Picasso, 1970) and *Picasso en Avignon* (Picasso in Avignon, 1971). The last two titles are dedicated to Picasso's exhibitions in the Papal Castle of Avignon. Both these books are catalogues with prodigious interpretations of the works exhibited. For Alberti's birthday on 16 December 1972, *Canciones del Alto Valle del Aniene* (Songs from the High Valley of the Aniene) was published in Buenos Aires. Simultaneously, *Desprecio y Maravilla* (Disregard and Wonder) appeared in Rome in a bilingual (Italian/Spanish) edition.

Alberti also wrote satires not destined for publication, but known by word of mouth. His finest poetry has been popularized in song, causing him to rank among the three Spanish poets whose poems are most frequently sung by popular singers. The others are Antonio Machado and Miguel Hernández. The former is the Andalusian who in 1925 convinced the prize committee to vote for *Marinero en tierra*; the latter is the shepherd/poet from Orihuela (Alicante) who was Alberti's political comrade and friend. Composers and singers use Alberti's texts due to their rhythm and musical possibilities. In Paris, Paco Ibáñez made songs from his poem "A galopar" (Galloping) and "Nocturno y balada del que nunca fue a Granada" (Nocturne and Ballad of the Man Who Never Went to Granada). Juan Manuel Serrat sang "La Paloma" (The Dove) by Alberti with music by the Italian S. Endrigo. Luis Pastor sang Alberti's "Ser flor de mi pueblo" (To Be a Flower of My Town), and the list could continue.

Alberti was anxiously awaiting the day of his return to Spain. Upon Franco's death in 1975, Juan Carlos de Borbón was crowned king of Spain. The end of Alberti's exile seemed close. He often became euphoric and frequently talked about Spain, about Puerto de Santa María and its vicinity, especially Alcalá de los Gazules. When Alberti received the news that a partial pardon had been granted to political outcasts by King Juan Carlos, he at first thought the moment of his homecoming had arrived. This was, however, premature. Alberti remarked in Venice to José María Moreno Galván: "I cannot return under the present circumstances" (*Triunfo*, February 1976). The royal pardon kept a considerable number of political prisoners in Spanish prisons, and Alberti was waiting for total amnesty and official recognition of the Spanish Communist party. Meanwhile, Juan Carlos paid a visit to the Vatican in 1977. On 9 February Alberti went to see him and presented him with a letter from a group of Spanish refugees in Rome requesting total amnesty and an end to violence on the streets of major Spanish cities.

With the legalization of the Spanish Communist party, parliamentary elections were announced and party leaders called Alberti to serve as a congressional candidate representing Cádiz. As he told the *Diario de Cádiz*, "I accepted immediately, full of dreams and enthusiasm. I was convinced that, after almost forty years in exile, this was the only and best way for me to help the Andalusian people on their new road to democracy" (9 September 1977). He sent a poem to the populace of Cádiz announcing the end of his many years of exile. This is a gesture typical of a political candidate in order to gain the hearts of his intended constituency. These verses (printed in the same issue of *Diario de Cádiz*) are, poetically speaking, inconsequential.

When Alberti left Italy for Spain as a Communist candidate, his first step was to repudiate Stalinism to gain the trust of the Spaniards, many of whom felt uncomfortable about having reinstated the Communist party in their country. Alberti proceeded to remind them that Stalin's form of Communism already had been eradicated from the Soviet Union by the Nikita Khru-

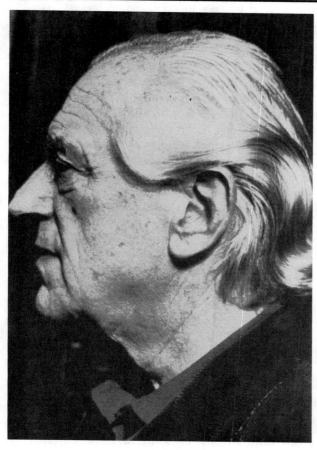

Alberti circa 1976

shchev regime. Furthermore, the Spanish Communist party, as well as the other European Communist parties, was independent from Moscow. For Alberti the Communist party of his country was only part of a strategy to achieve justice and freedom for the Spanish people. He brushed aside as stupidity the accusations that his political activism was diminishing his artistic importance. He returned with a longing for peace and prosperity, and the intense desire to serve his country. As he landed in Spain, he said, "I do not come with clenched fists, I come with open hands" (*Cambio 16*, 15 May 1977).

In the airport of Barajas he was officially received by leaders of the Spanish Communist party and by approximately five hundred Spanish Communist youths waving their flags. For example, Fina Calderón brought him a clay jar filled with soil from Cádiz and deposited it in his hands with tears in her eyes. To become the best senator to represent his province since the "Cortes de Cádiz" of 1810 (as Alberti said to Jesús Muñoz, correspondent of *Cambio 16*, referring to

the first time the Spanish parliament met to draft a constitution), he would have to win his campaign. Alberti knew he was not a professional politician; he was at times a politicized poet, an artist ready to serve his country in an hour of need. But he never considered the enormous contradictions between Communism and democracy. Unaware of political realities, he was used by professional politicians of the Spanish Communist party. At the age of seventy-four, he embarked on a new adventure as parliamentary orator. Since he did not have an explicit political platform, he reduced his campaign to a series of verse recitals.

One of his campaign highlights occurred in that spring of 1977 at Alcalá de los Gazules. Alberti expected an astounding reception in this small town surrounded by cork-tree forests and cattle ranches, situated halfway between Jerez de la Frontera and Algeciras. His expectations had a basis. When he had been contemplating his return to Spain, a newspaper reporter had asked him where he would like to reside in Spain. The poet had spontaneously answered, "in Alcalá de los Gazules." When the town's mayor learned of these intentions, he sent Alberti an official invitation to live there. For a while the prospect of a poet as a neighbor caused great excitement among the citizens of Alcalá. Alberti wanted to take political advantage of that euphoria. He wrote some campaign verses especially for Alcalá and announced well in advance the date of his arrival, in order to give the authorities and the people time for their arrangements. When the day came, Alberti appeared with his group of advisers and campaigners. He was expecting to find the streets decorated for the occasion and the authorities with the entire population gathered in the square to hear him. When he arrived, he was crushed. His expected triumphant "Palm Sunday" did not materialize. The town's authorities were in their best attire waiting for him with the municipal band in front of city hall. The band consisted of no more than fifteen players wearing soiled and faded uniforms and performing on unpolished and untuned instruments. The rest of the audience was composed of two policemen and a few dogs and chickens. As Alberti stepped out of his car, the band played the national anthem, which sounded to him like fifteen different compositions played simultaneously. He read his verses, had a glass of wine with those good Andalusians, and left.

Once elected, Alberti, working on the assumption that attire makes the politician, came to congress on his inauguration day wearing an outfit topped off by a two-tone blue coat tailored in Rome especially for the occasion. Since he had no practical solutions or specific political ideologies to offer, he probably thought that this was as good a way as any to contribute to a solution of the political dilemma of the hour. Although his was a poetic and emotional approach, it was not a realistic one. Ironically, other parliament members believed in the magic of Alberti's coat. Two Communist deputies representing Catalonia, determined to create a suit faction in the Spanish parliament, asked him to order identical coats from Rome for them.

Alberti was not equipped to confront the enormous Spanish political dilemma. He was not capable of understanding it sufficiently to suggest practical and reasonable solutions. Furthermore, he was not interested in the required political procedures to accomplish his objectives. This attitude was illustrated by a simple event in the last week of August 1977. The first session of parliament was only two weeks away. The poet had been working frantically in his hotel room on his introduction to a new edition of Lorca's *Romancero Gitano* (Gypsy Ballads, 1928), an edition which was also to include twenty etchings and a prologue by Alberti. It was approximately eight o'clock in the evening when the two intellectuals he was expecting arrived: Luis Lorenzo-Rivero and a friend. Alberti interrupted his work, greeted them, and indicated anxiety to leave his room. He felt exhausted and had no desire to speak about poetry or anything related to literature. For this reason he said he would prefer not to go out for dinner as planned. At this point the three started to the door determined simply to go downstairs and have a friendly conversation and dinner in the hotel's restaurant. The telephone rang and Alberti answered. It was a political associate who wished to discuss tactics for the coming session of parliament. In the elevator his guests began talking about Spain's present political situation. For a short while Alberti did not mind speaking in generalities and in poetic terms about the subject. But by the time the soup was served, Alberti put an end to political discussion by saying that politics did not interest him in the least.

Alberti needed desperately to be rescued from active politics and to be restored to his function as a poet. This came about on 9 September 1977, when he resigned his seat just four days before parliament was to meet: "I do not run away from the problems of my constituency and of my people. I have simply traded my congressional seat for the debates on the streets, which in my opinion are more important" (*Diario de Cádiz*, 10 September 1977). After his short-lived political adventure, Alberti became vigorously active in literary and intellectual endeavors. He began in 1978 to travel through Spain giving poetry recitations with Nuria Espert, and in 1980 he and Espert went to the United States. In 1981 he received Spain's Premio Nacional de Teatro (National Theatre Prize) and from the University Menéndez Pelayo of Santander (Spain) the Premio Pedro Salinas (Pedro Salinas Prize) for poetry. The same year he also traveled to San Juan, Puerto Rico. The following year the University of Toulouse-LeMirail (France) gave him an honorary Ph.D., and he went there to accept it. He and Espert continued their poetry recitations in 1984 in Italy, England, Venezuela, Nicaragua, France, and Switzerland. The following year the University of Cádiz made him Honorary Doctor. His wife, María Teresa, on the other hand, after their return to Spain on 27 April 1977, started to have poor health, and her situation deteriorated progressively until she passed away in 1989. On 13 July 1990 Alberti married his second wife, M. A. Mateo.

It is difficult for a poet to be both a statesman and an artist. His perception of the world will probably always be poetic. In 1981 the Spanish Royal Academy proposed Rafael Alberti for the prestigious literature prize named for Cervantes. Alberti finally received the Cervantes prize in 1983, and there is still hope that he may receive the Nobel.

Biography:
Manuel Bayo, *Sobre Alberti* (Madrid: CVS, 1974).

References:
Dámaso Alonso, "Rafael entre su arboleda," *Insula*, 198 (May 1963): 1-16;

Carlos Areán, "La imagen pictórica en la poesía de Alberti," *Cuadernos Hispanoamericanos*, 289-290 (July-August 1974): 198-209;

José Manuel Blecua, *El mar en la poesía española* (Madrid: Gredos, 1945);

Vittorio Bodini, *I poeti surrealisti spagnoli* (Torino: Einaudi, 1963);

José Luis Cano, *Poesía española del siglo XX* (Madrid: Guadarrama, 1960);

Carl W. Cobb, *Contemporary Spanish Poetry (1898-1963)* (Boston: Twayne, 1976), pp. 65-138;

Andrew Debicki, "El 'correlativo objetivo' en la poesía de Alberti," in his *Estudios sobre poesía española contemporánea* (Madrid: Gredos, 1968);

Elsa Dehennin, *La resurgence de Góngora et la génération poétique de 1927* (Paris: Didier, 1962);

Ignazio Delogu, *Rafael Alberti* (Florence: Nuova Italia, 1972);

Francisco Javier Díez de Revenga, *La métrica de los poetas del 27* (Murcia: Departamento de Literatura Española, 1973);

Antonio Gallego Morell, *La generación poética de 1927* (Madrid: Alcalá, 1966);

Jerónimo Pablo González Martín, "Alberti y la pintura," *Insula*, 305 (April 1972): 12-13;

González Martín, "La prehistoria poética de Rafael Alberti," *Insula*, 3 (December 1972): 1-7;

Joaquín González Muela, *El lenguaje poético de la generación Guillén-Lorca* (Madrid: Insula, 1955);

Ricardo Gullón, "Alegrías y sombras de Rafael Alberti," *Insula*, 198 (May 1963): 5-15;

Paul Ilie, *Los surrealistas españoles* (Madrid: Taurus, 1972);

Luis Lorenzo-Rivero, *Estudios de literatura española moderna* (Porto Alegre: PUC-EMMA, 1976), pp. 145-185;

Lorenz-Rivero, "Rafael Alberti: pintura, poesía y política, *Letras de Deusto* (January-April 1985): 5-25;

Roberto C. Manteiga, *The Poetry of Rafael Alberti: A Visual Approach* (London: Tamesis, 1978);

Barbara Dale May, *El dilema de la nostalgia en la poesía de Alberti* (Berne, Frankfurt am Main & Las Vegas: Lang, 1978);

Luis Monguió, "Rafael Alberti: Poetry and Painting," *Crítica Hispánica*, 1 (1979): 75-85;

C. B. Morris, *A Generation of Spanish Poets* (Cambridge: Cambridge University Press, 1969);

Morris, *Rafael Alberti's Sobre los ángeles: Four Major Themes* (Hull, U.K.: University of Hull Publications, 1966);

Pedro Salinas, *Literatura española del siglo XX* (Madrid: Alianza, 1972);

Solita Salinas de Marichal, *El mundo poético de Rafael Alberti* (Madrid: Gredos, 1968);

Kurt Spang, *Inquietud y nostalgia: La poesía de Rafael Alberti* (Pamplona: Ediciones Universitarias de Navarra, 1973);

José Luis Tejada, *Rafael Alberti, entre la tradición y la vanguardia* (Madrid: Gredos, 1977);

Guillermo de Torre, *Historia de las literaturas de vanguardia* (Madrid: Guadarrama, 1965);

Luis Felipe Vivanco, *Introducción a la poesía española contemporánea* (Madrid: Guadarrama, 1957), pp. 223-260;

Ana María Winkelman, "Pintura y poesía en Rafael Alberti," *Papeles de Son Armadans*, 30 (1963): 147-162;

Concha Zardoya, *Poesía española contemporánea* (Madrid: Guadarrama, 1961);

Zardoya, "La técnica metafórica albertiana (en *Marinero en tierra*)," in her *Poesía española del 98 y del 27* (Madrid: Gredos, 1968), pp. 294-336;

Emilia de Zulueta, "La poesía de Rafael Alberti," in her *Cinco poetas españoles* (Madrid: Editorial Gredos, 1971), pp. 273-343.

Vicente Aleixandre
(26 April 1898 - 14 December 1984)

Santiago Daydí-Tolson
University of Wisconsin-Milwaukee

BOOKS: *Ambito* (Málaga: Litoral, 1928);
Espadas como labios (Madrid: Espasa-Calpe, 1932);
Pasión de la tierra (Mexico City: Fábula, 1935);
La destrucción o el amor (Madrid: Signo, 1935; revised, 1944); translated by Stephen Kessler as *Destruction or Love* (Santa Cruz, Cal.: Green Horse Three, 1977);
Sombra del paraíso (Madrid: Adán, 1944);
En la vida del poeta (Madrid: Real Academia Española, 1950);
Mundo a solas (Madrid: Clan, 1950);
Nacimiento último (Madrid: Insula, 1953);
Historia del corazón (Madrid: Espasa-Calpe, 1954);
Algunos caracteres de la nueva poesía española (Madrid: Instituto de España/Góngora, 1955);
Mis poemas mejores (Madrid: Gredos, 1956);
Los encuentros (Madrid: Guadarrama, 1958);
Poesías completas (Madrid: Aguilar, 1960);
Poemas amorosos (Buenos Aires: Losada, 1960; enlarged, 1970);
Picasso (Málaga: Cuadernos de María Cristina/Guadalhorce, 1961);
En un vasto dominio (Madrid: Revista de Occidente, 1962);
Retratos con nombre (Barcelona: Bardo, 1965);
Dos vidas (Málaga: Guadalhorce, 1967);
Poemas de la consumación (Barcelona: Plaza & Janés, 1968);
Obras completas (Madrid: Aguilar, 1968; revised and enlarged, 2 volumes, 1978);
Sonido de la guerra (Valencia: Cultura, 1972);
Diálogos del conocimiento (Barcelona: Plaza & Janés, 1974);
Poemas paradisiacos, edited by José Luis Cano (Madrid: Cátedra, 1977);
Nuevos poemas varios (Barcelona: Plaza & Janés, 1987).
Editions in English: *Twenty Poems*, translated by Lewis Hyde and Robert Bly (Madison, Minn.: Seventies Press, 1977);
A Longing for the Light: Selected Poems, translated by Hyde (New York: Harper & Row, 1979);
The Crackling Sun, translated by Louis Bourne (Madrid: Española de Librería, 1981);

A Bird of Paper, translated by Willis Barnstone and David Garrison (Athens: Ohio University Press, 1982).

OTHER: Introduction to *Poesía española*, edited by Gerardo Diego (Madrid: Signos, 1932; revised, 1934);
"Nobel Lecture," in *Vicente Aleixandre. A Critical Appraisal*, edited by Santiago Daydí-Tolson (Yp-

silanti, Mich.: Bilingual Press/Editorial Bilingüe, 1981), pp. 35-40.

In 1977 the Nobel Prize for Literature was
awarded to Vicente Aleixandre, a Spanish poet
whose name and works were little known outside
Hispanic literary circles. For the rest of the
world, contemporary Spanish poetry was represented by other members of Aleixandre's generation, such as Federico García Lorca and Jorge
Guillén. After the Spanish Civil War (1936-1939)
a majority of the best Spanish poets left the country to live in exile, and Spain became for many a
land of intellectual backwardness and of no creative artistic powers. But as the Spanish political
situation began to change and interest in the country increased, the poetry of Aleixandre became
the most representative of the contemporary period in Spain. His voice bridged the gap left by the
war; the younger generations saw in his work a
connecting link with the older poets who had
died or left the country.

Since the 1920s, when he began to attend
the literary *tertulias* in Madrid, Aleixandre was always an important part of Spain's literary scene.
Because of his poor health, he maintained permanent residence in Madrid, with a few short trips
mostly within Spain. His home was a meeting
place for Spanish and Spanish-American poets
and writers for many years. There Federico
García Lorca and Pablo Neruda used to meet;
there the new poets of postwar Spain started
their careers. A member of the prestigious Generation of 1927, Aleixandre lived through the
years of the Republic, the civil war, the Franco
era, and the new democratic monarchy. He was
one of the few antifascist intellectuals of his generation who did not leave the country after the
war; consequently he was seen as a model by the
younger poets who began to write in the first
years of dictatorship. He represented the continuity of literary excellence in postwar Spain. Because he always considered himself part of a
larger scheme, the Nobel Prize awarded to him
may be seen to represent the world's recognition
not only of his personal work but of the best literature written in Spain since the great period before the war.

In his Nobel Prize acceptance speech, a text
that summarizes aptly Aleixandre's main ideas
about his art, he states that poetry is, above all,
tradition: the poet is a link between past and
future—a truism made evident in his own case.
His life covers a period of Spanish literary his-

tory that extends from the masterful Generation
of 1898 to more recent literary developments. As
a young man he was involved in a group of poets
including, besides Lorca and Neruda, Luis
Cernuda, Pedro Salinas, Rafael Alberti, and
Miguel Hernández. As a mature writer Aleixandre was given the opportunity and the responsibility of helping the younger generations searching
for a poetic inheritance half lost after the civil
war (1936-1939). In his old age he acquired the inspiring presence of a master, the consecrated
poet in whom tradition finds its continuity.

Aleixandre's works are the poetic reflection
of the circumstances in which he lived. From his
first published poems, written during a period of
highly technical and aesthetically demanding literature, to his last collection of dramatic monologues (1974), his poetry evolved in harmonious
correspondence with the main transformations in
Spanish lyric poetry. He had a clear understanding of the historical character of all artistic creation, and his own writing reflects his recognition
of what was essential in the main currents of Spanish poetic art at different historical moments.
This ability to transform his poetic diction in accordance with the times was not the result of an in-
ordinate interest in aesthetic fashion, but it was
the natural consequence of his conception of poetry and the poet.

From a theoretical position well within a tradition of contemporary poetry, Aleixandre defined the poet as a prophet or a seer. Reminiscent of the Platonic idea of poetic inspiration,
this conception and the practice it condones have
their most immediate antecedent in surrealism, although they can be traced back to early Romanticism. This visionary interpretation of the poet as
a means for other voices to express themselves,
as a spiritually superior being who can be in
touch with the cosmos and with humankind's essence, is directly related to the total immersion of
the individual writer in a tradition. Thus, in theoretical terms, Aleixandre saw himself as *the poet*,
the nameless speaker through whom all humanity talks; in his writings he even refers directly to
himself as "the poet," instead of using the first-
person pronoun. Many of his works convey a degree of anonymity, a feeling that the lyrical voice
in his poems does not belong to any definite persona, much less to the author. This absence of an
identifiable speaker is a central characteristic of
his poetic discourse and defines much of its originality within the development of contemporary
Spanish poetry.

Born in Seville on 26 April 1898, Aleixandre grew up in a period of extremely active political and intellectual life in his country. He spent his boyhood in Málaga, a fact that explains his later images of the sea and the paradisiacal world of infancy in an old provincial town in the Mediterranean. In 1909, when he was eleven years old, his parents, Cirilo and Elvira Merlo Aleixandre, moved the family to Madrid, where Vicente did his high-school and university studies. In 1919, after graduating from the University of Madrid, he began to teach at the school of business there. For a while he devoted himself to his profession and wrote on economic subjects. His trip in 1923 to Paris and London was of little consequence to his literary career.

When he began to write his first book in the 1920s, the masters of the Generation of 1898 were at the peak of their careers, and among the younger writers one could already find salient names. His own generation, which would be known as the Generation of 1927, was bewildered by the new aesthetic, philosophical, and scientific ideas of postwar Europe. The climate in the literary circles frequented by Aleixandre in those days was one of curiosity, renovation, and activity. In Madrid the literary cafés, theaters, art galleries, the Ateneo, and the very important Residencia de Estudiantes were the meeting places for poets and writers, artists, and philosophers from Spain and abroad. In the friendly atmosphere of common intellectual and aesthetic interest, Aleixandre found his first admiring readers and the motivation to become a writer.

Although during his school years he had been an avid reader, he avoided reading poetry; he was then under the impression that such a form of literature neither provided much enjoyment nor had much intellectual value. But by the age of eighteen he had changed his attitude radically and had become a fervent enthusiast of poetry, to the extent of writing it himself. His acquaintance with another young poet, Dámaso Alonso, whom he met the summer of 1917 while vacationing in Avila, was to change his attitude toward poetry. Alonso, who would not accept his friend's refusal to read poetry, introduced him to the poetry of Rubén Darío, the Latin American master of modernism, and so started him in a new adventure. Many years later Aleixandre would recall that the reading of Darío's poems produced a revolution in his spirit. He had discovered true poetry and felt infused with his great passion, one that was never to abandon him throughout the remainder of his life. During that same summer vacation he began to write, but his first publications did not appear until ten years later. While studying for his professional degrees in business and law he cultivated in silence his personal vocation, probably unaware of his talents.

It is particularly revealing that after reading Darío's poems Aleixandre was awakened to his own poetic gifts, because a spiritual correspondence existed between the two writers. For the young poet-to-be, Darío's works represented not only the manifold possibilities of language but most of all the poetic view that defines man as a passionate creature consumed by love. In Darío's writings poetic language reaches a level of communicativeness directly related to the poet's ability to create a purely fictional reality representing, in metaphorical terms, an otherwise inexpressible understanding of man and existence. No less important for such poetic effectiveness of language in Darío's works is the general tone of passionate materialism, an essential sensuality not at all alien to an unquenchable desire for spiritual transcendence. These were the aspects of Darío's literary accomplishments that inspired Aleixandre because they found an echo in his own spirit.

But the influence of the Latin American modernist is not seen in Aleixandre's first published poems. These were the result of a more immediate influence: Aleixandre wrote them when he had an intense literary relationship with other young poets who declared their interest in Juan Ramón Jiménez and the theories of "pure" poetry. Aleixandre's participation in the group's literary experimentation and theoretical discussions explains the influence of their taste on *Ambito* (Ambit), his first collection of poems, published in 1928. Aleixandre's career as a poet began in 1926 when a few of his friends sent to *Revista de Occidente* (Western Review), the new periodical founded by José Ortega y Gasset, the poems Aleixandre himself did not care to publish. They appeared that same year; the book, consisting of a tightly knit collection of interrelated poems, was soon to follow.

Ambito constitutes a basis for later developments in his art. A careful critical reading demonstrates that, although *Ambito* has many debts to other poets respected highly at the time, this first collection contains some of the peculiar characteristics of Aleixandre's work. In comparison with his later books, *Ambito* seems at first particularly different—its external characteristics are a good imitation of Jiménez's techniques. Like many

Aleixandre, Luis Cernuda, and Federico García Lorca in 1931

other young poets of his generation, Aleixandre wrote under the dictates of a rigorous concept of style and composition. Most of the thirty-five poems in *Ambito* are written in traditional verse; but the combination of different meters in some poems is the first indication of the poet's inclination toward free verse, a form that would characterize his personal style.

The other important aspect of the book is its irrational imagery, suggestive of surrealism and directly communicative of a cosmic vision of man and nature as identical in essence. Love in its widest sense is central to these compositions; it constitutes, in the poet's view, the only possible way for man to achieve the desired fusion with all matter. *Ambito* represents Aleixandre's first attempt to conform to the requisites of being a poet of his time; it is the product of several years of apprenticeship in the active workshop of his generation—the cultural life of Madrid. But it is also the result of the poet's seclusion and avocation to poetry after contracting tubercular nephritis, a chronic illness that curtailed his activities starting in 1925.

Pasión de la tierra (Earth Passion, 1935), the first good example of Aleixandre's characteristic

poetic language, is even more the result of the serious illness. It represents a new awareness gained through personal experience and study. By 1928 Aleixandre was reading the works of Sigmund Freud and James Joyce, two authors very influential in his own decision to look for a new form of literary experimentation. Although *Pasión de la tierra* was finished in 1929, it remained practically unknown until 1946. Only a few copies of the 1935 Mexican first edition reached Spain before the civil war, and consequently, in spite of its revolutionary nature, the book did not have any noticeable influence on the literary developments of the period it represents so well. Had it been published immediately after Aleixandre finished writing it, *Pasión de la tierra* would likely have become one of the major surrealist books in Spanish literature.

In *Ambito* Aleixandre was able to resolve every stylistic problem by using the well-known and already established solutions—he was working within the predetermined patterns of a tradition. In *Pasión de la tierra* the fixed channels of poetic expression were totally disrupted: language itself lacks the normal semantic values that render it meaningful. These seemingly incoherent

Vicente Aleixandre
POEMAS
PARADISIACOS

Edición de
José Luis Cano

CÁTEDRA

Cover for a collection published soon after Aleixandre was awarded the 1977 Nobel Prize. The book is a compilation of his poems on earthly paradises, written from the 1920s to the 1970s.

prose poems express within the limitations imposed by language the new reality revealed by psychoanalysis and by writers such as Arthur Rimbaud and Joyce. *Ambito* and *Pasión de la tierra* appear to be the works of two completely different poets, one a "purist" poet of aesthetic restraint and technical control, the other a vanguardist writer who follows the surrealist practice of "automatic writing." The decision to adopt a surrealistic form of expression came as a result of Aleixandre's well-informed confidence in the value of psychoanalytical theories and in the effectiveness of automatic writing. By accepting the theoretical principles behind the surrealistic method, he was stating his revolt against established poetic

objectives and methods. His interest in aesthetic experimentation common to the period was in response to the need for new techniques to express his new awareness of himself.

Between the carefully measured and well-combined verses of *Ambito* and the entirely loose prose of *Pasión de la tierra*, there is a difference not only in external form and poetic techniques but more significantly in the perspective of the speaker, his attitude, and tone of voice. Once traditional diction is attacked, the attitude of the speaker changes from dutiful acceptance of the norm to rebellious freedom. In *Pasión de la tierra* this freeing force appears in the external form of prose, releasing the new verbal flux. The model for this form had already been set forth convincingly by Joyce; Aleixandre adapted it to a still deeper search in the human psyche and its world of fascinating dreams, fears, and desires. The reasons for writing poetry in such a manner are to be found in his emotional experiences at the time. His life was centered around his innermost experiences, as illness had made him more aware of mortality. Compelled by this realization, he began a desperate and obsessive search within himself for life and its meaning.

Surrealism offered a theoretical basis and more effective ways to express his new awareness. The idealized experience of cosmic union presented in *Ambito* lacks the powerful conviction found in *Pasión de la tierra*. In the first book the perspective and the attitude of the poet are constrained by traditional principles, whereas they are free from any delimitations in the latter.

Prose is the form that best reproduces the free flow of speech, the uncontrolled stream of oneiric visions created by a web of apparently unrelated images. A return to versification in his next book, *Espadas como labios* (Swords like Lips, 1932), is a significant change. The transcription of the surrealistic, associative images into verse suggests that he was still hesitant about which form best suited his expressive needs. He never again used prose for poetic purposes, but the experiment with it in *Pasión de la tierra* left him with a keener sense of prosody. The shorter compositions in *Espadas como labios* are in traditional metrics. The main rhythmic patterns and the general tone are not new; they lack the strangeness and novelty of *Pasión de la tierra*. These poems are the products of controlled writing and reproduce a measured attitude even when the images allude to strong emotions; from this duality emerges a feeling of tension. The longer poems instead use a freer form of versification in accordance with a freer attitude of the speaker, who allows his emotional state to appear in the poem. This second type of composition, akin to both verse and prose, was improved in Aleixandre's next book, *La destrucción o el amor* (1935; translated as *Destruction or Love*, 1977) and became characteristic of most of Aleixandre's subsequent works.

Aleixandre's free verse, or versicle, is constituted by several types of repetitions, with the exception of regular rhyme and isosyllabism. Repetition is found in the phonic, the syntactical, and the semantic levels of the poems, and observable correspondences with the traditionally established meters are only circumstantial. Essential, then, to Aleixandre's verse are several stylistic devices, which, by stressing repetition, underline the value of resonance and rhythm. *Espadas como labios* contains some of them, and in *La destrucción o el amor* they become one of its defining characteristics. These reiterative techniques include anaphora, alliteration, and assonance; another technique used for the same effect is apposition. These richly rhythmic dualistic patterns convey the indecisiveness of the speaker in naming things. In some cases the poet seems to stutter in confusion, or tries unsuccessfully to put his vision into words in different ways. Behind this attitude of bewilderment there is a clear sense of the mysterious interrelation of all aspects of reality. Thus, the most characteristically Aleixandrian of all these devices is the use of the conjunction *or* not as a disjunctive but as a means of connecting two terms. The constant use of this conjunction—present even in the title of the book—provides many pairings. Duality becomes identity, and variety is a sign of unity.

Only a very detailed analysis of the poems would give an adequate idea of all the possibilities of free verse in expressing the various attitudes and emotional states of the speaker. This type of versification has its first antecedent in the combination of traditional verses used in *Ambito*; the experience with prose in *Pasión de la tierra* taught the poet how to extend the common Spanish metric patterns into a much more flexible rhythmic use of the language. Free verse became for Aleixandre the best medium to communicate his particular conception of humankind and destiny. In *La destrucción o el amor* one finds the application of Aleixandre's ideas about poetry as he stated them in his commentary for the 1934 edition of Gerardo Diego's *Poesía española*. In the first edition, published in 1932, Aleixandre had

expressed his doubts about the function and value of poetry in modern society; two years later he had a more positive outlook. Without intending an explanation of poetry, Aleixandre offers a few principles of a coherent poetic theory closely related to a general cosmic vision of humankind and nature. For him all elements of creation are only different manifestations of the one and only universal entity. In *La destrucción o el amor* he underlines this meaning through chaotic enumerations including terms referring to human aspects as well as to animate and inanimate nature: "Flor, risco o duda, o sed o sol o látigo: / el mundo todo es uno, la ribera y el párpado" (Flower, rock or doubt, or thirst or whip: / all in the world is one, the riverbank and the eyelid). Aleixandre's conception of the unity of all existing matter and of the power of love to effect this unification finds its contemporary equivalents in philosophy, theology, psychology, and natural sciences.

As in *Pasión de la tierra*, Aleixandre is driven in *La destrucción o el amor* by the desire for authenticity; he looks for poetic revelation in the subconscious, where words change their everyday meaning. It is the poet's duty to listen to the messages of the cosmos and to make of them a sensible and communicating expression.

In *La destrucción o el amor* Aleixandre is still using a form of automatic writing, except that in this case he no longer writes the utterances of an unconscious self, but rather has become the mouthpiece for all life and matter communicating itself through the deep consciousness of a man who acts under inspiration as a sibyl, a bridge between human understanding and the cosmos. In *La destrucción o el amor* Aleixandre's poetry reaches a vaguely ancient tone of pagan pantheism with mythical overtones. The poet's journey toward the attainment of the ideal takes him to the depths of existence as lived and experienced by the inner man. At this point the emotionally cautious and aesthetically restrained songs of *Ambito* have changed drastically to primal screams.

The poet's conception of reality is clearly stated and wonderfully expressed in *La destrucción o el amor*. The personal view of Aleixandre in this epoch of his life is the poetically coherent exposition of his surrealistic approach to knowledge. In this book Aleixandre has conceived a metaphorical world, a purely literary construction, through which his own interpretative view becomes evident. This world of primitive na-

Aleixandre in the 1970s

human life and death. Aleixandre's first books, the ones written before the war, are imbued with that anguished search for a meaningful explanation for existence. Irrationalism in this case is more a method than an objective in itself. Confusion and chaos are the conditions of a mind in a state of total uncertainty, but in the mass of images that fill these surrealistic books it is possible to discern the elements that in further developments will constitute a more logical understanding. With a more mature sense of his accomplishments, and aware of the circumstances surrounding him, Aleixandre had begun, in 1934, a new book, *Mundo a solas* (World Alone, published in 1950). It is a sad and pessimistic book in which he depicts humankind's loss of the primeval elemental state.

During the three years of the civil war, Aleixandre wrote sparingly, although he contributed war poems to Republican publications. It was a time of sorrow and devastation. His own house, half-destroyed in the battle of Madrid, could very well symbolize the writer and his predicament at that time. At the end of the conflict, peace brought life back to the shattered garden and rooms of the house, but many of those who frequented it in the prewar years were gone: Lorca was dead; Cernuda, Guillén, Neruda, and many others had left Spain; and Hernández was in prison, where he died a few years later. Still faithful to his old friends and ideals, Aleixandre wrote a poem to Hernández's memory, a tacit criticism of the new political regime. But while the memories of those who had gone lingered in the renovated house where Aleixandre was to continue living his reclusive life, a new group of writers started to replace them and came to visit the poet. They did not form a generational group, nor a school following the dictates of a leader; these new visitors were the first among the many postwar Spanish poets who saw in Aleixandre the inspiration of the master. The author of revolutionary surrealist books had reached maturity. Coincidentally, in 1944, an important year for the history of postwar Spanish poetry because of the publication of *Hijos de la ira* (Children of Wrath) by Dámaso Alonso, Aleixandre published his first book in almost ten years, *Sombra del paraíso* (Shadow of Paradise).

Sonnets and other neoclassical pastiches, inspired by the stale desire to believe in the reborn greatness of the empire, were the main expressions of poetry in the early days of the Francisco Franco regime. The long free verses, the sensu-

ture and oneiric images is reminiscent of *Pasión de la tierra*, but *La destrucción o el amor* has a more logical structure and a clearer language. By this time Aleixandre was moving toward a more easily understandable lyric language: this new diction reflects not only the deeper levels of subconscious knowledge but also the conscious need for order and intelligible communication.

By 1936, at the beginning of the Spanish Civil War, Aleixandre was thirty-eight years old and had survived a dangerous illness. For ten years he had suffered physical shortcomings; life and death, pleasure and pain, and desire and fear had been for him omnipresent opposites that had to affect his outlook. As a chronically ill man he was more aware than others of biological determinants; he could see in his own body the slow and unremitting process of decay and dissolution. His mind wandered with increasing anguish through the different available explanations for

ous images, and the musically ample rhythms of Aleixandre's new book were the much-needed exception. His worldview was made concrete in the imagery of the poems. With *Mundo a solas*, which only appeared in 1950 as a document of past experiences, Aleixandre wanted to express his sad realization that humans lived in a fallen state; this same idea, reminiscent of religious explanations for human inadequacy in nature, is fully developed in *Sombra del paraíso*, but with important differences. The first volume conveys in violent overtones a negative view; the dominant chord in the new one represents a more complex and richly evocative feeling of human totality. This difference between the two books, one written immediately before the war, the other during the first years of peace, is indicative of two stages in Aleixandre's understanding of reality. The first stage includes the five books written in the prewar years; they are the work of youth and convey an impression of disorder and confusion. The second stage, which begins with *Sombra del paraíso*, introduces a more harmonious, if nostalgic, view of the universe and corresponds to the mature years of the poet.

This change in Aleixandre's outlook did not happen suddenly because of the war, nor did it come as a total surprise—it is a sign of the writer's maturity reached after years of poetic meditation on life and death. Essential to this new understanding of the relationship between humankind and the universe are Aleixandre's conceptions of poetry and the poet. Although in essence they are the same ones he professed in 1934, the intensity of the conviction and its purposefulness make them appear new. What years before had been a supposition and a wish was now an accepted fact, a definite ordering of the multiple components. The poet, for Aleixandre, continues to be a seer, a person who can reveal to others that ultimate knowledge of the otherwise inexpressible truth. Aleixandre represents the poet as a gigantic being whose feet are deep inside the earth and whose head is up above, touching the sky.

Sombra del paraíso can be compared with romantic works. Everything in it is designed to underline the emotion of remembrance and the hope of recovering a lost paradisiacal state. From the conception of poetry and the poet to the images and versification, *Sombra del paraíso* stands out in contemporary Spanish letters as a document of people's eager acceptance of a degraded existence that is only a pale shadow of the original one. The speaker addresses nature, the cosmos, and other men as if he were indeed the gigantic poet of magnificent voice depicted in his own surrealistic image.

At this point in Aleixandre's literary career his work had reached its originality by an unfailing and constant effort to relate poetry and the personal search for meaning. He had applied with conviction the theory of poetic knowledge as learned from surrealism and its predecessors. *La destrucción o el amor* and *Sombra del paraíso* are two examples of poetry understood as a spiritual vocation, as a method to reach a higher form of consciousness. Partly because of his delicate health and his inability to lead a normal, active life, Aleixandre had not had other interests or devotions outside poetry; everything in his reclusive life depended on it and found in it its meaning. As in the case of a religious believer, his particular belief provided an order and interpretation to all creation. This virtually religious conviction does not correspond in Aleixandre's case to an already provided answer that the individual readily accepts and embraces as his. He went step-by-step in a personal search for an explanation of existence; this spiritual journey he described metaphorically in his commentary for *Mis poemas mejores* (1956) as an aspiration toward light.

Up to the publication of *Sombra del paraíso* the image of light pervades all Aleixandre's work and carries with it a meaning of knowledge representative of the writer's own definition of his poetic aim. This predominance of light finds its correspondence in his prose texts about poetry in which the poet is described as "illuminator, provider of light." Aleixandre's books are closely related to each other; together they form an extended structure in which there is a continuity of purpose, a slow development in his view of reality and its poetic manifestation, both represented by a growing luminosity. This light is particularly bright in *Sombra del paraíso*, the collection standing at the center of Aleixandre's whole production: it is the culmination of a process but also provides the basis for the developments that follow in the subsequent collections.

The novelty of the next book Aleixandre wrote, *Historia del corazón* (The Heart's History, 1954), which took almost ten years to finish, lies in its central subject—concrete, everyday reality. His ideas about the cosmic indistinctness of all things and of the equalizing powers of love are applied in this book in a much more restricted way—they refer only to people in society. Aleixandre ex-

Manuscript for one of Aleixandre's last poems (from Insula, *January-February 1985; by permission of the Estate of Vicente Aleixandre)*

plains this transformation by saying that *Historia del corazón* presupposes a new view and a new conception. But, more than a new conception, the book illustrates the last stage in the developmental process that Aleixandre's poetry had been following from the first compositions he wrote under the influence of Jiménez to the poems of *Sombra del paraíso*. That process was one of clarification, the journey to light that takes the poet from the universality of a cosmic view to the realization of the most immediate destiny of humankind.

In the 1950s he achieved harmony with his world and with himself. Love, on the other hand, the all-encompassing force of identification, took on the form of social love. And his voice became the voice of collective humankind, as is clearly stated in the title of his poem "El poeta canta por todos" (The Poet Sings for Everyone). An obvious consequence of this attitude is the need to stress the importance of communication, a conviction sustained also by the social poets of the same period.

With the abandonment of the visionary images found in his prewar books, the vague feeling of awe before life's mystery and the almost-sacred tone of the oracle also vanished. His interest in humankind, common people, brought other aspects of everyday reality into Aleixandre's perspective and affected greatly his inspi-

ration and discourse. The imagined reader or listener, the poetic personae, and the settings of the poems all point to a different attitude. They also bring to the forefront a factor Aleixandre started to consider only in relation to human life—the day-to-day passage of time. The attention focused on purely realistic aspects had to be complemented by an interest in realistic language—a language much nearer to everyday discourse while still maintaining a poetic force. Visionary imagery comes to be replaced in *Historia del corazón* by common visions imbued with a profoundly emotional understanding, acceptance, and exaltation of human life in a communal world:

Aquí también entré, es esta casa.
Aquí vi a la madre cómo cosía.
Una niña, casi una mujer (alguien diría: qué alta, qué guapa se está poniendo),
alzó sus grandes ojos oscuros, que no me miraban.
Otro chiquillo, una menuda sombra, apenas un grito, un ruidillo por el suelo,
tocó mis piernas suavemente, sin verme.
Fuera, a la entrada, un hombre golpeaba, confiado, en un hierro.

(Here I also went into this house.
Here I saw how the mother was sewing.
A girl, almost a woman [someone would say: how tall she is, how beautiful she is becoming]
raised her large dark eyes that did not look at me.

Another child, a little shadow, only a cry, a subtle
    noise around the floor,
touched my legs, softly, not seeing me.
Outside, at the entrance, a man was beating, confi-
    dently, a piece of metal.)

The basic principles of free verse again constitute
the stylistic basis for these new compositions.
Every form of repetition is tried in order to create the appropriate tone of chants, hymns, elegies, and songs. The poems cover the complete
range of subjects listed by Aleixandre in the prologue to the 1944 edition of *La destrucción o el
amor* as those that every poet writing for the majority of people should embrace as central: the essentially unifying aspects of love, sadness, hate, and
death. He did not include in his list, as he certainly does in his poetry, the joy of living and the
sensuous awareness of the real.

At the time of writing *Historia del corazón*
Aleixandre had reached his full emotional and intellectual maturity. Public recognition, underlined by his election to the Spanish Royal Academy in 1949, is also an indication of his complete
adjustment to circumstances and of his involvement in literary activities. He had become more
of a public man as he was invited to give lectures
and read his poems. He published some of his
nearly forgotten works, prepared anthologies
and new editions of his works, contributed to
countless poetical publications, and was extensively interviewed and honored. His poetry and
his views about it bespeak this interpenetration
of the individual with his world. Some of
Aleixandre's most important theoretical texts are
from this period and include *Algunos caracteres de
la nueva poesía española* (Some Characteristics of
the New Spanish Poetry, 1955) and the notes to
the anthology *Mis poemas mejores* (My Best Poems,
1956).

His point of view on poetics became a guiding principle among Spanish poets. Aleixandre
knew how to interpret the times, and his principles appeared as appropriate to the circumstances and the needs of that particular historical
time. In his prologue to *Mis poemas mejores*,
Aleixandre explains that, starting with *Historia del
corazón*, he believed the poet was the expression
of difficult human life and that the poet's voice either comes from his extended communitarian
heart, comforted by love, or is gathered from the
mass of the people. Aleixandre had followed a
similar path—only at a slower pace—to the one
taken by other writers of his generation who,

having practiced surrealism in the years before
World War II, had later written a poetry committed to their immediate social situation. Another
Nobel Prize winner comes to mind—the Chilean
Pablo Neruda, who was one of Aleixandre's close
friends while living in Madrid as a diplomat, and
who, like the Spaniard, had also written books of
surrealistic inspiration before the Spanish Civil
War. For him the evolution from visionary to realistic poetry was sudden and ideologically inspired. A comparison of these poets shows many
differences, but they have in common their awareness of nature and cosmos, people and society,
love and death, and the never-forgotten visionary
origin of their understanding of reality. Only
poets such as they, modern-day seers and inheri-
tors of a lyric tradition, could have authored
fully poetic realist works. In post-civil-war Spain,
Aleixandre's *Historia del corazón, En un vasto
dominio* (In a Vast Domain, 1962), and *Retratos
con nombre* (Portraits with Names, 1965) are good
examples of this new social sensibility caused by
political circumstances.

En un vasto dominio has an introductory
poem that, mirroring a growing concern among
the poets of the day, offers another declaration
of poetic principles. The attraction poets have toward *ars poetica* seems unusually conspicuous in
postwar Spanish poetry, particularly during the
period when the realistic, social style was predominant. Aleixandre himself paid less attention to
the subject in his books prior to *Sombra del
paraíso*. The preoccupation with poetics can be ac-
counted for, at least in this brief period, by the nature of literary creativity under a dictatorship. Realistic poets, whose manifest social awareness was
limited at the most to a personal testimony of
their attitude toward the troubled world, felt the
psychological need to explain their social value as
poets to themselves and to others. Aleixandre
was sensitive to the fact that there are unavoidable limitations in communication through poetry
with all people, but he did not seem to see these
facts changing the essentially communal character of the authentic poet, who continues to be
the same as the one he had described years before. His keeping intact the previous conception
of the poet as a bard of cosmic dimensions had
an influence on his understanding of realism and
its social function. Unlike the poets who confused
the levels of poetic understanding with the most
obvious everyday social and individual experiences, he saw reality in a wider perspective.

Entitled "Para quien escribo" (To Whom I Write), the introductory poem in *En un vasto dominio* uses simple, direct language, as befits the style of realistic writing; most of the emotional impact comes from the rhythmic organization of the plain discourse. The long lines are separated from one another in stanzalike units, characterized by enumeration and repetitions: "Escribo para el enamorado para el que pasó con su angustia en los ojos; para el que le oyó; para el que al pasar no miró; para el que finalmente cayó cuando preguntó y no le oyeron" (I write for the one in love for the one who walked by with anguish in his eyes; for the one who heard him; for the one who passed by and did not look; for the one who fell at last when he asked and no one listened). The similarities of the compositions in the book to some of Walt Whitman's can be attributed not solely to the metrical form but also the inspired conception of poetry and worldview that in both writers leads to a comparable expression. By listing the different types of people to whom he writes or does not intend to write, Aleixandre conveys in his first poem his basic tenets. Two of those for whom he does not write are "the gentleman with the stiff jacket" who has "furious moustaches" and raises his disapproving finger "among the sad waves of music," and the lady hidden inside a car, her lorgnettes shining "like cold lightning." These are unequivocal references to a false world of social disguise and cruel lack of sensibility—a constant motif in Aleixandre's view of creation: some forms of life are false, and, therefore, to him nonexistent. On the other hand, he writes for people who perhaps will never have the opportunity, nor the interest, to read his work: "I write for everybody. I write particularly for those who do not read my poetry." This comment coincides with a common concern among social poets who knew that they were writing for those who by education and social standing would never read their poetry. This is not the full idea behind Aleixandre's verse; he was stating once more his long-sustained belief in the universal character of the poet who is fused into the totality of humankind. Thus, to tie this interpretation in with the cosmic vision of his earlier books, natural elements are also included in the list of those for whom he writes.

Toward the end of the 1960s Aleixandre abandoned most of the elements that characterize his realistic work. Social and political circumstances had changed in Spain, making it unnecessary to sing any longer the hymns of human

Vicente Aleixandre

solidarity. Furthermore, old age had finally come to him, and with it came also more of the luminosity so cherished from the beginning. A more meditative attitude set the tone of his poems. They are grouped in two major books: *Poemas de la consumación* (Poems of Consummation, 1968) and *Diálogos del conocimiento* (Dialogues of Knowledge, 1974). These collections constitute a final development in the long process of the poet's growing understanding of the world. They are at the same time undeniably his and so novel that they fall well within the parameters of the new Spanish poetry. In his old age the master was able to renew himself because his experience had taught him the need to be open to inspiration. This came in different forms as he was able to grasp new meanings and interpret anew the presence of the world.

Poemas and *Diálogos* reintroduce as a poetic method the almost hermetic image of his surrealist period that had been abandoned by the mature poet in order to attain the much-desired ideal of communication. Aleixandre brought together in his last books all his capacities as a writer. He found himself in possession of revealed truth and could not pass the opportunity to try for the last time to put his inner visions into words. From the time of his initial experiments in *Ambito*, he had been dealing with poetry as a form of knowledge, as a method of apprehending the essences lost to science. He tried from the beginning to construct a worldview, a system of poetic ideas to account for reality. Consequently most of the critical approaches to his work had tried to explain, discuss, compare, or interpret its philosophical aspects. *Poemas* and *Diálogos* add a new, still more complex chapter to the already comprehensive system.

Poemas de la consumación includes several brief poems in short, almost traditional hendecasyllabic meter. This style of concision reproduces the succinct discourse of a wise man who does not need many words to state his ideas. Light and darkness—day and night—are once more central to Aleixandre's conception and find their correlatives in the polarities of youth and old age, the point of realization from which the book develops as a meditation on man's temporal condition. The poems are for the most part a series of short, aphoristic sentences as expressed by a detached speaker. The poet, who to a certain extent is an objective voice, transmits the emotional feeling of ultimate, wistful wisdom. It could be said again that a sybil speaks of those mysterious essences hidden to the common man.

This objective voice of knowledge changes to specific voices in *Diálogos del conocimiento*, as the poems are made up of the contrasting speeches of different characters. The structural polarity seen in *Poemas* assumes in this volume the form of long compositions that reproduce the words of two, in some cases three, speakers who sustain opposing views but do not seem to pay attention to each other's monologues. As if they were entranced by their own intellectual and emotive convictions, they talk in the same epigrammatic manner the unspecified speaker uses in *Poemas de la consumación*. In both cases the attitudes of the speakers and their tones of voice give the impression of ancient oracles. Several other factors help to produce in *Diálogos del conocimiento* the effect of entrancement. First in importance is the philosophical character of the book, which explains the abundance of apothegmatic statements. Images are also used in a similar axiomatic way. Many statements are contradictory or hermetic, and images are irrational, adding still more to the mysterious and gnomic tone. Reiterations give density and rhythm to the book; of particular interest are the several references to earlier texts by Aleixandre, whose work

acquires in such a way the fullness of a complete and self-contained system. All of these elements, supported by a brief, almost regular versification, represent his efforts to put into words the always imperfect knowledge of that which has no name and demands to be named.

After a flurry of journalistic interest caused by his 1977 Nobel Prize, the name of Aleixandre returned to a less visible position. The analysis of his contribution to Spanish letters will require still much dedication from critics, as time enhances the quality of his art. Critics have most often admired in him his ability to put into highly emotional poetic language a few basically profound ideas about being. A poet with an almost religious penchant for meditation and hymnal singing, Aleixandre has been praised for his understanding of the mysterious, for the poetic knowledge underlining his poetry, and for his capacity to communicate his luminous visions through verbal images.

Letters:

Epistolario, edited by José Luis Cano (Madrid: Alianza, 1986).

Biographies:

Antonio Colinas, *Conocer. Vicente Aleixandre y su obra* (Barcelona: Dopesa, 1977);

Leopoldo de Luis, *Vida y obra de Vicente Aleixandre* (Madrid: Espasa-Calpe, 1978).

References:

Carlos Bousoño, *La poesía de Vicente Aleixandre*, third edition, revised (Madrid: Gredos, 1977);

Vicente Cabrera and Harriet Boyer, eds. *Critical Views on Vicente Aleixandre's Poetry* (Lincoln, Nebr.: Society of Spanish and Spanish-American Studies, 1979);

José Luis Cano, ed. *Vicente Aleixandre* (Madrid: Taurus, 1977);

Santiago Daydí-Tolson, ed. *Vicente Aleixandre. A Critical Appraisal* (Ypsilanti, Mich.: Bilingual Press/Editorial Bilingüe, 1981);

Giancarlo Depretis, *Lo zoo di spechi (Il perceptive ambivalente nella poesia de V. Aleixandre* (Turin: Facoltà di Magisterio, 1976);

Hernán Galilea, *La poesía superrealista de Vicente Aleixandre* (Santiago, Chile: Editorial Universitaria, 1971);

Vicente Granados, *La poesía de Vicente Aleixandre (Formación y evolución)* (Madrid: Cupsa, 1977);

José Olivio Jiménez, *Vicente Aleixandre. Una aventura hacia el conocimiento* (Madrid: Júcar, 1982);

Gabrielli Morelli, *Linguaggio poetico del primo Aleixandre* (Milan: Gilardino-Giolardica, 1972);

Darío Puccini, *La palabra poética de Vicente Aleixandre* (Barcelona: Ariel, 1979);

Kessel Schwartz, *Vicente Aleixandre* (New York: Twayne, 1970).

Dámaso Alonso
(22 October 1898 - 25 January 1990)

Jerry Phillips Winfield
Mercer University

BOOKS: *Poemas puros, poemillas de la ciudad* (Madrid: Galatea, 1921);

La lengua poética de Góngora (Madrid: Aguirre, 1935);

Oscura noticia (Madrid: Hispánica, 1944);

Hijos de la ira. Diario íntimo (Madrid: Revista de Occidente, 1944); translated by Elias L. Rivers as *Children of Wrath* (Baltimore: Johns Hopkins University Press, 1970);

Ensayos sobre poesía española (Madrid: Revista de Occidente, 1944);

Poesía española. Ensayo de métodos y límites estilísticos (Madrid: Gredos, 1950);

Seis calas en la expresión literaria española (*Prosa, poesía, teatro*), by Alonso and Carlos Bousoño (Madrid: Gredos, 1951);

Poetas españoles contemporáneos (Madrid: Gredos, 1952);

Hombre y Dios (Málaga: Arroyo de los Angeles, 1955);

Estudios y ensayos gongorinos (Madrid: Gredos, 1955);

Antología: Creación, edited by Vicente Gaos (Madrid: Escelicer, 1956);

Antología: Crítica, edited by Gaos (Madrid: Escelicer, 1956);

Menéndez Pelayo, crítico literario (*Las palinodias de Don Marcelino*) (Madrid: Gredos, 1956);

De los siglos oscuros al de Oro (Madrid: Gredos, 1958);

Dos españoles del Siglo de Oro. Un poeta madrileñista, latinista, y francesista en la mitad del siglo XVI. El Fabio de la "Epístola moral": Su cara y cruz

en Méjico y en España (Madrid: Gredos, 1960);

Góngora y el "Polifemo" (Madrid: Gredos, 1960); enlarged, 2 volumes, 1961; 3 volumes, 1966;

*Primavera temprana de la literatura europea. Lírica, é-
pica, novela* (Madrid: Guadarrama, 1961);

*Cuatro poetas españoles: Garcilaso, Góngora, Mara-
gall, Antonio Machado* (Madrid: Gredos,
1962);

Del Siglo de Oro a este siglo de siglas (Madrid: Gredos, 1962);

*Para la biografía de Góngora. Documentos desconoci-
dos*, by Alonso and Eulalia Galvarriato de
Alonso (Madrid: Gredos, 1962);

Poemas escogidos (Madrid: Gredos, 1969);

Obras Completas: volume 1, *Estudios lingüísticos pe-
ninsulares*; volume 2, *Estudios y ensayos sobre literatura* (Madrid: Gredos, 1972, 1973);

Gozos de la vista (Madrid: Espasa-Calpe 1981);

*Antología de nuestro monstruoso mundo. Duda y amor
sobre el Ser Supremo* (Madrid: Cátedra, 1985).

OTHER: Luis de Góngora, *Soledades*, edited, with
prose version, by Alonso (Madrid: Revista
de Occidente, 1927);

*Poesía española. Antología. Poesía de la Edad Media y
poesía de tipo tradicional*, selected, with prologue, notes, and vocabulary, by Alonso (Madrid: Signo, 1935);

Gil Vicente, *Tragicomedia de Don Duardos*, edited
by Alonso (Madrid: C.S.I.C., 1942);

La poesía de San Juan de la Cruz (Desde esta ladera),
edited, with an introduction, by Alonso (Madrid: C.S.I.C., 1942);

Góngora, *Romance de Angélica y Medoro*, prose version and notes by Alonso (Madrid: Acies,
1962).

TRANSLATIONS: James Joyce, *El artista adolescente*, translated by Alonso as Alfonso Do-
nado (Madrid: Biblioteca Nueva, 1926);

Hilaire Belloc, *María Antonieta*, translated by
Alonso (Madrid: Espasa-Calpe, 1933);

T. S. Eliot, *Poemas*, translated by Alonso (Madrid:
Hispánica, 1946).

Dámaso Alonso was one of the strongest
forces in the intellectual and cultural history of
twentieth-century Spain. His contributions to literary and stylistic analysis inspired a new approach
to literary criticism, particularly in poetry. As
a member of the Generation of 1927, which
included such poets as Pedro Salinas, Jorge
Guillén, Gerardo Diego, Federico García Lorca,
Rafael Alberti, and Vicente Aleixandre, Alonso in-

itially embraced the prevailing aesthetics of "pure
poetry"—the poetry of abstraction. Yet, following
the Spanish Civil War, he began to forge an anguished and existential vision that restored the
human condition as a vital theme in Spanish poetry and offered a new freedom of technique
and style. As teacher and mentor he exerted a singular influence on an entire generation of young
poets—an influence continuing to the present
day.

Alonso was born in Madrid on 22 October
1898 into an upper-middle-class family. His famil-
ial roots were in that area where the province of
Galicia borders on Asturias, and he spent much
of his childhood in the environs around the town
of Ribadeo. His father died when he was three.
One sees in his poetry only physical reflections of
his early youth amidst images of nature and landscape. Alonso spent most of his life in the Madrid suburb of Chamartín, and his poetry is centered in the cosmopolitan capital of Spain—its
language, culture, and people. From his education in the Colegio de Jesuitas of Carabanchel, he
developed a firm intellectual foundation and perhaps a propensity in his poetry for painful and rigorous religious questioning. Reading as an adolescent the classical works of the sixteenth through
nineteenth centuries, he especially felt drawn to
the romantic verses of Gustavo Adolfo Bécquer.
Alonso recalls having written at the age of sixteen a sonnet about Medinaceli, a village where
he spent his summers. In *Los encuentros* (Encounters, 1958), the Nobel prize laureate Aleixandre
warmly recalls the eighteen-year-old Alonso as a
sensitive and ironic young man with a rare loyalty to his friends.

Alonso had intended to pursue a career in
highway engineering, but in 1916 he was forced
to abandon his studies of mathematics due to an
ulcer in his right eye. Yet he was able to read and
obtained a volume of the poetry of the Nicaraguan modernist Rubén Darío. In the summer of
1918 Alonso read for the first time the poetry of
Nobel laureate Juán Ramón Jiménez and was
profoundly moved by the verse of Antonio
Machado, whose themes of time, death, and God
were to be echoed in Alonso's own verses. In this
same year Alonso earned his *licenciatura* in law at
the University of Madrid; yet he was already committed to literature and soon changed to the
study of philosophy and letters. As a disciple of
the renowned philologist and literary scholar
Ramón Menéndez Pidal, he completed his doctorate in 1928. Having contributed to the prestig-

ious journal *Revista de Filología Española* (Review of Spanish Philology) since 1923, Alonso in these years gained the background in linguistics, literary history, and stylistics that would support his extensive literary scholarship and the development of his original concepts of criticism.

Alonso published his first book of poetry, *Poemas puros, poemillas de la ciudad* (Pure Poems, Small Poems of the City), in 1921. Considering his age, his interest in creating a "pure" poetry, and the scarcity of his poetry until the Spanish Civil War, *Poemas puros* would seem to be isolated from Alonso's later poetry. Yet in theme and technique the work is distinctly related to the anguished existential poetry written after 1936, such as *Hijos de la ira* (1944; translated as *Children of Wrath*, 1970). In *Poemas puros* Alonso creates a vital clash between poetic idealism and the tedious reality of everyday life. The imagery is bound to a simple and natural vocabulary. Although the desire to "purify" language is clear, Alonso evokes tenderness and human elegance rather than poetic beauty in language itself. This antithesis of ideal beauty and ugly reality foreshadows the tortured search for God and meaning in the later poetry of *Hijos de la ira* and *Hombre y Dios* (Man and God, 1955). The fictional speaker feels his soul caught in the trivial and commonplace of the herd in the poem "Racimos de burgeses" (Bunches of Bourgeois):

> Ando
> caído y cojo
> y triste
> y calvo.
> ¿Cuándo
> romperemos, extáticos, la luna
> amigo mío, hermano?
>
> (I walk
> dejected and crippled
> and sad
> and bald.
> When
> will we, enraptured, shatter the moon,
> my friend and brother?)

The themes of *Poemas puros*—death, night, life, eternity, love, and loneliness—would remain constant in the poetry of Alonso; yet the uneasiness of youth later became a horrible anxiety. Death is presented conceptually in this first collection and almost serenely, in contrast to its terrible semblance in the mature poetry. Loneliness and need of identity have not yet become aliena-

tion. Love is something mysterious and delicate— "the secrets of a mysterious garden"—but without the promised pain of reality. Already in *Poemas puros* the ability of Alonso to achieve symbolic unity is apparent, as is the creation of metaphors with different levels of meaning.

In 1922 Alonso lectured at the University of Berlin and in the autumn of 1923 at Cambridge University. He had already become a recognized member of the *tertulias* (literary circles) in Spain. During the school year 1923-1924 he wrote the poems of "El viento y el verso" (Wind and Poetry), which would appear in the 1925 issue of the literary review *Sí*, published by the eminent poet Juan Ramón Jiménez. "El viento y el verso" would later be published as part of *Oscura Noticia* (Dark Message) in 1944. "El viento y el verso" comprises twelve poems in which the wind becomes a symbol of the poetic search for truth in the world of prosaic reality. Just as the wind is filled with variations and nuances, the imagery of Alonso's verse creates a multiplicity of shade and meaning. The wind, as Andrew Debicki has noted in *Dámaso Alonso* (1970), serves both as a symbol of the poet's search and a metaphor defining its manifestations. In the poems "Puerto ciego de la mar" (Blind Port of the Sea) and "Ejemplos" (Examples) the wind is the watchman of the night, a primary element of the earth, a form of God, and the siesta. In "Ejemplos" the wind functions poetically as the agent of God as well as a metaphor of the conflict between the spiritual and the real. Alonso alludes to the biblical story of Martha (reality) and Mary (the poetic):

> Lo que Marta laboraba
> se lo soñaba María.
> Dios, no es verdad, Dios no supo
> cuál de las dos prefería.
> Porque El era sólo el viento
> que mueve y pasa y no mira.
>
> (For what Martha toiled
> Mary dreamt.
> God found no truth,
> God did not know
> which of the two he preferred.
> Because He was only the wind
> which moves and passes and does not look.)

From 1923 to 1927 Alonso developed strong and lasting friendships with the other members of the Generation of 1927. In 1923 he began a long friendship with the poet Pedro Salinas, and he met Gerardo Diego in 1925. Soon af-

Alonso and his wife, writer Eulalia Galvarriato, in their study, Madrid, 1962

terward his encounter with Federico García Lorca initiated an influential and enduring companionship. Meetings of this circle of poets were constant in the parks, cafés, and homes of Madrid. They spoke incessantly of poetry, both foreign and Spanish, from classical to contemporary. In 1926 Alonso published his translation of the complex *Portrait of the Artist as a Young Man (El artista adolescente)* by James Joyce. The following year, Alonso chose to commemorate the three hundredth anniversary of the death of Spanish poet Luis de Góngora with a funeral service attended by Alonso's group of poets and scholars. No one else appeared—except Alonso's mother, out of affection and a deep religious conviction. Also in 1927 Alonso completed *La lengua poética de Góngora* (The Poetic Language of Góngora, published in 1935), winning the National Prize for Literature. His prose edition of Góngora's *Soledades* (Solitudes) was published in 1927, making Góngora accessible to a new generation of readers.

During the term of 1928-1929 Alonso again lectured at Cambridge, and in March 1929 he married the gifted writer Eulalia Galvarriato, who was to be his lifelong companion. In summer 1929 he taught at Stanford University. Alonso served as a visiting professor at Hunter College in New York during the term of 1929-1930. García Lorca was in the city at the time, and he and Alonso spent considerable time discussing García Lorca's then-unpublished *Poeta en Nueva York* (1940; translated as *The Poet in New York*, 1940). Having later taught at Oxford as well as Columbia University in New York, Alonso competed for and won the chair of Spanish Language and Literature at the University of Valencia in 1933. After teaching at the University of Leipzig in

1935 and 1936, Alonso succeeded his mentor Ramón Menéndez Pidal at the University of Madrid. In this period, Alonso published significant studies on Spanish literature, including his incisive *La poesía de San Juan de la Cruz* (The Poetry of St. John of the Cross), in 1942. The scholarship of Alonso, while showing rigor and critical depth, continued to find genesis in a deep human sensitivity, and increasingly it reflected his affective concerns.

Following the publication of *Poemas puros* in 1921, and "Viento y el verso" in 1925, Alonso wrote little poetry until 1940. The ascetic and dehumanized doctrines prevailing in poetry paralyzed, in Alonso's view, his creative impulse. Throughout the life and work of Alonso there was a productive rhythm in which he accumulated experience and feeling while withdrawing into teaching, scholarship, and criticism, then released this energy in reams of poetry. It was the cataclysm of the Spanish Civil War that was to free his creative energy.

In 1944 Alonso published *Oscura noticia*, which includes sixteen original poems augmented by poems written from 1919 to 1943, as well as "Estampas de primavera" (Images of Spring)—a group of poems from 1919 to 1924. The later poetry of *Oscura noticia* reveals a mature poet who has discovered a unified core in man's existential struggle. Alonso continues the theme of conflict between spiritual values and ordinary reality; yet this duality is now more focused on the need to discover meaning in primary and concrete existence. The title of the work is from a statement of the sixteenth-century mystic poet San Juan de la Cruz: "Esta noticia que te infunde Dios es oscura" (This message with which God fills you is dark). Humankind is desperate and in need of a God who may not exist or who may be deaf to any pleas. The positive values of love, beauty, and the instinct to survive are naked and threatened in the dark and lonely night. Love would seem to relieve the pain of existence, yet in this limited world it appears ambiguous and conflicting. One is torn between the desire to touch others and the egoistic love of self.

In *Oscura noticia* Alonso portrays an almost chaotic confusion of the carnal and the spiritual. The protagonist of the poem "Destrucción inminente" (Imminent Destruction), who clearly speaks for all people, moves from interrogation to pure terror before death and God. The poem "A un poeta muerto" (To a Dead Poet) communi-

cates Alonso's personal grief concerning the senseless assassination of García Lorca during the Spanish Civil War. Alonso uses the technique of *claroscuro* to evoke light and shadow as moving images of a flight into nothingness in such poems as "Dura luz de la muerte" (Hard Light of Death). The work is filled with metaphors of multiple meanings that elicit a variance of emotions in the reader. At times, Alonso seems to describe the type of absurd hero created by the existentialist Albert Camus; yet Alonso doubts the existence of absurdity as well. The artist is gripped in the human dilemma of a limited and confused existence. The artist in the poem "Manos" (Hands) finds his hands almost atrophied in their physical incapacity to portray the artistic dream. In the well-known poem "Oración por la belleza de una muchacha" (Prayer for the Beauty of a Young Girl), Alonso celebrates the perfection of form and harmony in the title character and prays for the just, yet impossible, conservation of such beauty:

¿A qué tu poderoso mano espera?
Mortal belleza eternidad reclama.
¡Dale la eternidad que le has negado!

(For what does your powerful hand await?
Mortal beauty claims eternity.
Give her the eternity that you have denied her!)

Oscura noticia received considerable critical attention and was praised for the strength of its existential vision and the vitality of its paradox of faith and doubt. Despite—or because of—his questioning, it was certain that Alonso was deeply religious, and many critics felt that the work was influential in reinvigorating the theme of religion in postwar Spanish poetry.

Also in 1944 Alonso published his most significant and original book of poetry, *Hijos de la ira*. It is both an anguished, bitter outcry against the particular circumstances of his life and a universal protest against the injustice inherent in life. Alonso said the poems of the book were reflective of his feelings of separation and anger. He had experienced what he saw as two massive acts of outrage and insanity, the Spanish Civil War and World War II. European civilization seems to have betrayed Alonso's trust in its values. The barbarity and atrocities to be committed by the "master race" were seen earlier in a different version in the carnage and suffering of Spain's civil war. Madrid, a city of corpses, becomes a metaphor on a different level for life itself as a cemetery of anxiety in "Insomnio" (Insomnia), which begins *Hijos de la ira*, and is one of its most acclaimed poems:

> Madrid es una ciudad de más de un millón
>   de cadáveres (según las últimas estadísticas).
> A veces en la noche yo me revuelvo
>   y me incorporo en este nicho en el que
>   hace 45 años que me pudro. . . .

> (Madrid is a city of more than one million
>   corpses [according to the latest statistics].
> At times in the night I toss and turn
>   and sit up in this niche where
>   I have been rotting for 45 years. . . .)

Filled with loathing at the "sterile injustice of the world," Alonso is torn between monstrous absurdity and the need to embrace life and to comprehend it. Symbolic of the struggle with self, Alonso struggles with Goyaesque monsters of doubt and confusion in the poem "Monstruos" (Monsters) and begs God to save him amidst the terrible darkness:

> Oh Dios,
> no me atormentes más,
> Dime qué significan
> estos espantos que me rodean.
> Cercado estoy de monstruos
> que mudamente me preguntan,
> igual, igual que les interrogo a ellos.

> (Oh God,
> don't torture me any more.
> Tell me the meaning
> of these fears which surround me.
> I am encircled by monsters
> who mutely question me,
> just as I interrogate them.)

With its imagery of horror, anguish, and decay, *Hijos de la ira* is essentially poetry of protest; yet this protest is universal rather than political. The existential confrontation between the poet, God, and the universe is more direct than in Alonso's previous poetry and here underlies some of the most somber and painful verses of contemporary Spanish poetry. The intensity of interrogation recalls the poetry of Miguel de Unamuno, and, as with Unamuno, the poetry of Alonso is anthropocentric—man is its center and ultimate end. One's dark voyage balances upon the abyss, and Alonso wishes to evoke fears as immediate and tactile. Humans question, plead, and even threaten from their solitude yet, in the end, can be no more than humbled. There is a

marked biblical presence in *Hijos de la ira*, in the poet's thirst for God amidst human misery, as Alonso seems drawn to the Psalms and the Book of Job. Yet God falls silent and the poetic dialogue becomes a senseless and bitter monologue: in "Insomnio" man is portrayed, in his desperate search for God, as howling like a dog who has lost his master. Alonso is intrigued and even obsessed in his desire to somehow know his surroundings and self, such a quest being reminiscent of the poetry of his friend Vicente Aleixandre. For the most part, Alonso's tone is intense and vehement, although it varies from an elevated asceticism to the deeply human and religious, to a level of physical pain as the poet seeks to alleviate his own personal agony. The language of *Hijos de la ira* is everyday, honest speech—language one might hear in the streets of Madrid. The tension between ordinary reality and the desire for the lofty ideal, seen in *Oscura noticia*, has become less abstract and more fused to the immediate personal experience of Alonso.

However, the bleak and negative view in *Hijos de la ira* is counterpoised by the hope for God, love, beauty, and redeeming human values. The poem "Mujer con alcuza" (Woman with an Oil Jar) has received extensive critical inquiry. The protagonist, who serves as a persona of the poet, is a wandering old woman seen on the sidewalks, in a cemetery, and then on a train that runs day and night leaving off dead passengers. The train, symbolic of human lives, has neither a conductor nor a destination. The woman becomes a complex symbol of the human capacity for self-sacrifice and charity. Occasionally there appears a deep tenderness, as in such poems as "A la Virgen María" and "De Profundis" (Out of the Depths), where the speakers see and merge with God's light. *Hijos de la ira* closes with "Dedicatoria final—Las alas" (Final Dedication—The Wings), which offers a reconciliation of God and the poet, and a key to decipher the work. Engaging God in conversation, the speaker learns that his "wings" are God's gift because a poet is a glorious creature. As the last human being he will defend himself only with his gift of song—his poems—and his love of God. The love of two women, wife and mother, the poet learns, is the true wings God has given him:

> para que cuando mi Dios quiera gane
> la inmortalidad a través de la muerte,
> para que Dios me ame,
> para que mi gran Dios me reciba en sus brazos,

Frontispiece and title page for volume 1 of Alonso's two-volume collection published in 1972 and 1973

para que duerma en su recuerdo.

(so that when my God wishes, I may win
immortality through death,
so that God will love me,
so that my great God will receive me in his arms,
so that I may sleep in his memory.)

With *Hijos de la ira* Alonso also challenged the prevailing stylistics and aesthetics of poetry and was influential in motivating a new and authentic voice in postwar Spain. He stretched the limits of theme and technique. The book is a rebellion against the existing apathetic schools of surrealism and "pure" poetry. It restored the "impurities" with its *versículo*, an irregular verse with internal rhythm, as well as its multilayered metaphors and images. The technique of the work merges with its message; Alonso had found a new coherence and unity. The emotions of *Hijos de la ira* shout amidst the landscape of a chaotic and devastated universe in a perspective that changes from metaphysical to aesthetic to confessional.

In 1948 Alonso was formally installed as a member of the Royal Spanish Academy, having been elected in 1945, and served as a visiting pro-

fessor at Yale University. He also lectured in Argentina, Chile, Peru, and Mexico. In 1949 he became editor of the prestigious journal *Revista de Filología Española* (Review of Spanish Philology). His most definitive and influential critical work, *Poesía española. Ensayo de métodos y límites estilísticos* (Spanish Poetry: Essay of Stylistic Methods and Limits) was published in 1950. Studying six poets of Spain's Golden Age, Alonso interpreted the theories of the Swiss structural linguists Charles Bally and Ferdinand de Saussure regarding language and meaning. Combining their theories with his own approaches to stylistics, he emphasized the individual text itself, in contrast to the prevailing methods of literary history. He thus initiated a new school of analytical literary criticism in Spain with concern for the significance of language and the interrelationship of stylistic and affective elements in poetry.

Alonso's critical works encourage the application of varied approaches including both intuitive and analytical. In 1951 Alonso, with his friend the eminent critic and poet Carlos Bousoño, published the penetrating study *Seis calas en la expresión literaria española* (Six Samples of Spanish Literary Expression), and in 1953 Alonso taught at Johns Hopkins University. The next year proved to be crucial for him. He returned to the United States to teach at Harvard, planning to consult the libraries of Harvard and Yale to resolve some problems in literature and linguistics. For some time he had not written poetry. Departing from Barcelona on a small ship, he found himself trapped in a violent storm. As he began to read and take notes to calm himself, Alonso realized that he had begun to write poetry: "Ese muerto" (That Dead Man), in which the dead are heard crying to return to life in any form, and "Gozo del tacto" (Joy of Touch), which celebrates the most elementary of senses in the face of death. Both poems would appear in the epilogue of his *Hombre y Dios* (Man and God, 1955). The scholarly research was delayed; the immediate task was to continue what was vital—his poetry.

At Harvard and in Spain, Alonso completed the poems of *Hombre y Dios*, a powerful attempt to comprehend the complex relationship of man and God. Alonso saw this work as a continuance of the final verses of *Hijos de la ira*, where his song had been one of wrath. Alonso continued to be aware that blood was being spilled throughout the world and demanded to know the savage architects of this injustice. In the second palinode of *Hombre y Dios* he grieves for a modern society that destroys individual expression, a society whose cruel political games of "communism" and "democracy" are played with "apagados ojos y un alma de ceniza" (lifeless eyes and a soul of ashes). Yet, realizing that he must live among humans, he then turns to the conception of God. He is also deeply aware that humankind has, with courage, spiritually survived the carnage of war and oppression.

In *Hombre y Dios* Alonso envisions man and God as a symbiotic system; rather than the search for God, he seeks the presence of God as creator in man, his creation. For God and man cannot exist without each other. In the sonnet that bears the title of the book, God's love is centered in the heart of man: "Yo soy tu centro para ti, tu tema / de hondo rumiar, tu estancia y tus pensiles. / Si me desahago, tu desapareces" (I am your center for you, your theme / of deep reflection, your garden. / If I am broken apart, you disappear). While unified, *Hombre y Dios* continues Alonso's use of dramatic conflict seen in the earlier works. Existential dialogue and shifting planes of meaning create a powerful emotive content. In the poem "Mi tierna miopía" (My Tender Myopia) Alonso describes his affliction as a disguised gift al-

lowing him to focus with pleasure on the minute and simple, as well as being an opaque barrier to the world's realities. It is the way one sees God, tentatively, in vague diffusion, as in the poetry of Antonio Machado. There is considerable ambiguity in the voices of Alonso's protagonists, and the individual poems are often contradictory. Yet the multiplicity of Alonso's visions is unified by the complexity of the theme itself. The diversity of emotions, values, and impressions is formed into a matrix of human experience.

Humans are seen in *Hombre y Dios* as created in God's image because of their distinct intelligence. God grants the freedom of will to live and create even if people abuse it, because creation is freedom. In "Los cuatro sonetos sobre la libertad" (The Four Sonnets on Freedom) Alonso's religious foundation is clearly visible in the change of tone from rebellion to humility in the poem "Vida—libertad" (Life—Freedom): "Sólo sé, libertad, que allá en lo umbrío / siento el pulso de Dios; y por mí fluyes, / libre anhelar que en tiempo te propagas." (I only know freedom, that there in the shadows / I feel the pulse of God; and through me flows / the free desire that in time you reproduce yourself.)

Light continues in *Hombre y Dios* as a symbol of the creation and re-creation of the world. Yet, in God's eyes, human eyes may be almost blind, offering only the faint images of an old motion picture. The final poem of *Hombre y Dios*, "A un río le llamaban Carlos" (A River Was Called Charles), is a meditation on life, death, time, and man's essence. God does not intervene, yet is implicit in this poem, one of the most discussed of Alonso's poetry. As the speaker sits on the bank of the Charles River in Cambridge, Massachusetts, he senses time symbolically flowing in the current. The river becomes a persona from whom the speaker seeks an answer to his fate that will unify a personal and universal search. Alonso presents an allegory of the journey toward death:

Y ahora me fluye dentro una tristeza,
un río de tristeza gris,
con lentos puentes grises, como estructuras funerales grises.
Tengo frío en el alma y en los pies.
Y el sol se pone.

(And now flows within me a sadness,
a river of gray sadness,

37

with heavy gray bridges, like gray funeral struc-
tures.
My soul and feet are cold.
And the sun sets.)

Life, the celebration of the senses, free will, and
the struggle to survive are all themes of Alonso's
previous poetry. In *Hombre y Dios* they gain clarity and synthesis.

Gozos de la vista (Joys of Sight) was written
on Alonso's return from Harvard to Spain in
1954, although it was not published until 1981,
when it would also contain poems from other periods. In this work, Alonso portrays the incredible
gift God offers of human sight. Humankind
reaches a privileged level in the universe; human
eyes create and participate in the divine. This ele-
vation is balanced, however, by the imperfections
and deceptions inherent in human sight. As in
Hombre y Dios, Alonso structures an essential conflict in human nature between the nobility of people and their tragic limitations and weaknesses.
Alonso increasingly stresses human fragility and
temporality in the themes of time and death.
Gozos de la vista does not reflect the precise planning of the intentional philosophical structure of
Hombre y Dios; rather, it employs a dramatic technique that orchestrates the changing viewpoints
of its speakers. In the first poems of the collection, Alonso evokes the marvelous chromatism of
light and color. The poem "Descubrimiento de la
maravilla" (Discovery of the Marvel) reflects the
degree to which Alonso cherished his own sight:

¡Dulce espejo, retina mi aventura!
Algo exterior te azuza: saetas, hilos, tallos.
Atraes, de amor antena, centro de amor fluido.
Y al Dámaso más pozo, más larva en hondo luto
problemático cambias en Dámaso-vidriera,
torre de luz, fanal, creándose, creándote,
luz, ¿en qué nervio nítimo?, inventor de los
    Dámasos,
inventor de universos, que grita: "Luz, yo vivo. . . ."

(Sweet mirror, retina, my adventure!
Something external excites you: darts, threads,
    stalks.
You attract, from an antenna of love, the center of
    fluid love.
And you re-create the Dámaso who is more a well
    or a larva
of deep problematic mourning into a Dámaso-
    window,
a tower of light, a lighthouse, creating itself, creat-
    ing you,

light, in what innermost nerve?, inventor of Dáma-
sos,
inventor of universes, who shouts: "Light, I
    live. . . .")

In this wondrous discovery, humankind tentatively escapes physical limitations and momentarily participates in a reality that seems immortal.
Yet the protagonist Dámaso is dynamic and later
in the work is brought down again to the anguish
of his existence. As in the relationship of man
and God in *Hombre y Dios*, God seeks to view his
own creation through the eyes of the poet in the
poem "Vista humana, intuición divina" (Human
Sight, Divine Intuition). There follow prayers for
the eyes, color, and light, and Alonso describes
the varieties of blindness, which serve to distinguish the value of human perspective from that
of lower forms of life. Sight is a fragile gift, threatened by the tragedy of blindness, both literal and
symbolic; the blind cannot enter the poet's dialogue of light. Alonso begs God to let him keep
his sight or to take him completely. The section
"Visión de los monstruos" (Vision of Monsters) is
written with ironic humor as Alonso describes
the sight of animals and the mythical monster of
a faraway planet.

The theme of human frailty, even in an elevated and creative place in the universe, is emphasized by Alonso in the last sections of *Gozos de la
vista*. In the poem "Una excursión" (A Trip)
three companions on a pleasure ride enjoy a glorious landscape; they seem to escape the human
bonds of reality in their joy. Suddenly in an accident, time is stopped, and the youngest is
blinded. Humans all ultimately are seen as blind
in the face of God, who is existence, as in the
poem "Búsqueda de la luz. Oración" (Search for
the Light. A Prayer): "Carecemos de los ojos pro-
fundos / que pueden verte, oh Dios. Como el
ciego en su poza / para la luz. ¡Oh ciegos todos!
¡Todos, sumidos, / en tinieblas! . . ." (We lack the
deep eyes / that can see you, oh God. As the
blind man in his pool / lacks light. Oh blind, all
of us! All submerged / in the darkness! . . .) .
Gozos de la vista is more grounded in the personal
and immediate than *Hombre y Dios*, yet even more
philosophical in its ontological nature. Alonso
has narrowed his poetic vision to a particular
concern: that of the joy of sight and the terror
of threatened blindness, which Alonso himself
feared. Human dignity in the ability to survive or-
deals by means of love and creativity is the final
message of *Gozos de la vista*.

¿Por qué gimes, qué husmeas, que avizoras?
¿Husmeas, di, la muerte?
¿Aúllas a la muerte,
proyectada cual otro can famélico,
detrás de mí, de tu amo?
Ay, Pizca,
tu terror es quizá solo el del hombre
que el bieldo enarbolaba,
o el horror a la fiera
más potente que tú.
Tú, sí, Pizca; tal vez lloras por eso.
Yo, no.

Lo que yo siento es
un horror inicial de nebulosa;
o ese espanto al vacío,
cuando el ser se disuelve, esa amargura
del astro que se enfría entre lumbreras
más jóvenes, con frío sideral,
con ese frío que termina
en la primera noche, aún no creada;
o esa verdosa angustia del cometa
que antorcha aún, como oprimida antorcha,
invariablemente, indefinidamente,
cae,
pidiendo destrucción, ansiando choque.
Ah, sí, que es más horrible
infinito caer sin dar en nada,
sin nada en que chocar. Oh viaje negro,
oh poza del espanto:
y cayendo, caer y caer siempre.

Page from the manuscript for Alonso's 1983 poem to his dog, "A Pizca" (from the 1986 edition of Hijos de la ira *[Children of Wrath], edited by Miguel J. Flys; by permission of the Estate of Dámaso Alonso)*

Alonso continued writing major works of critical analysis, such as *Cuatro poetas españoles* (Four Spanish Poets) and *Del Siglo de Oro a este siglo de siglas* (From the Golden Age to This Age of Abbreviations), both published in 1962. He had gained international recognition with honorary degrees from the universities of Hamburg, Freiburg, Bordeaux, Rome, Oxford, Massachusetts, and San Marcos (Lima, Peru). He had served as a member of the most prestigious academic and literary associations in Spain and abroad. He continued teaching, imparting in his students his own discipline and love of language, and he exerted a singular influence on his students, who were to include Spain's finest poets and literary scholars: Carlos Bousoño, José Luis Cano, Emilio Alarcos Llorach, Fernando Lázaro Carreter, Alonso Zamora Vicente, Rafael Lapesa, Claudio Rodríquez, and Francisco López Estrada, among others. Alonso's friend the noted scholar Pedro Laín Entralgo tells of the poet's openness and cordiality in long evenings in which Alonso would recite poetry from five or six languages to aspiring young poets. Miguel Jaroslaw Flys, a former student, notes in his *La poesía existencial de Dámaso Alonso* (1969) that he called on Alonso one day and found him in the garden patiently teaching mathematics to the son of his gardener. Alonso once said to Flys that in his later years he wished to retire to some forgotten corner of the world to teach very simple things. As the Royal Academy's director for fourteen years, Alonso forged it into an instrument of professionalism and freedom of thought—a sharp contrast to General Francisco Franco's veto of Alonso's election to the academy in the past. In 1985 Alonso published his final book of poetry, *Duda y amor sobre el Ser Supremo* (Doubt and Love about the Supreme Being), in the same volume with an anthology of previous verse, *Antología de nuestro monstruoso mundo* (Anthology of our Monstrous World).

The horrors of World War II and the Spanish Civil War had drawn Alonso back to poetry and the creation of *Hijos de la ira*. In 1984 two of his closest friends, who were two of Spain's best poets, died. The deaths of Jorge Guillén and Vicente Aleixandre in great part motivated the poetry of *Duda y amor sobre el Ser Supremo*, which appeared after thirty years of poetic silence from Alonso. In contrast to the vital anguish of *Hijos de la ira*, the rigorous philosophical structure of *Hombre y Dios*, and the display of imagery and senses in *Gozos de la vista*, Alonso's final message is one of resigned introspection and sadness. Im-

mortality is the central theme, as Alonso senses the presence of death growing closer. He celebrates the liberation of the soul in the poem "Pensamientos, miradas, y sonidos en el alma eterna" (Thoughts, Glances, and Sounds in the Eternal Soul). The poet continues to search for God; however, there is a new solidity in his view of immortality. Alonso seeks to delimit the universe and to penetrate the essence of creation and death. He seeks those now embraced by death: his friends, his parents, and the great poets of his time, Unamuno, Guillén, García Lorca, and Aleixandre, as well as the great writers of Spain's past. In the poem "¿Existes? ¿No Existes?" (Do You Exist? Do You Not Exist?) Alonso returns to a constant theme of his poetry, the existence of God, asking to whom can he pray: "¿A tí? ¿Pues cómo, si no sé si existes? / Te estoy amando, sin poder saberlo. / Simple, te estoy rezando; y sólo flota / en mi mente un enorme 'Nada' absurdo" (To you? Well how, if I don't know if you exist? / I am loving you without being able to know it. / Simple, I am praying to you; and only floats / in my mind an enormous absurd "Nothing"). He loves God despite his inability to know God's existence. It is the same synthesis of doubt and love seen in *Gozos de la vista*, and in Alonso's work it represents paradox rather than contradiction.

As Flys observed on the death of Alonso in 1990, the unknowable and mysterious give great power to *Duda y amor sobre el Ser Supremo*. There is meaning in the incessant desire to know and love. In the tension of the constant struggle among doubt, love, and desire, Alonso elicits the participation of the reader in order to solve a mystery of intuition, not logic. Above all, the book is a tribute to human nobility in the desperate attempt to endure.

Dámaso Alonso became the dominant figure in literary scholarship in postwar Spain, initiating entirely new schools of criticism. He was one of the greatest intellectual influences on Spanish culture in this century. The profound themes of his poetry—existence, God, and humankind's role in the universe—achieved an intensity, precision, and emotive force that was equaled by few Spanish poets of his time. His poems reflect the natural languages of the people in a desolate atmosphere of loneliness and chaos. Yet, amid guilt and injustice, and facing a silent God, Alonso found humans to be wondrous creations who were fragile yet strong in their courage to survive. Alonso died on the morning of 25 January

1990, the day that was to mark the forty-second anniversary of his entrance into the Real Academia Española. Among thousands of messages of condolence from all over the world was one from King Juan Carlos, who referred to Alonso as simply "El Maestro."

Bibliography:
Fernando Huarte Morton, "Bibliografía de Dámaso Alonso," *Papeles de Son Armadans*, 11 (1958): 467-518.

References:
Vicente Aleixandre, "Dámaso Alonso, sobre un paisaje de juventud," in *Los Encuentros* (Madrid: Guadarrama, 1958), pp. 91-98;

Elsie Alvarado de Ricord, *La obra de Dámaso Alonso* (Madrid: Gredos, 1968);

Carlos Bousoño, "Estilística y teoría del lenguaje," *Cuadernos Hispanoamericanos*, 19 (November-December 1951): 113-126;

Bousoño, "La poesía de Dámaso Alonso," *Papeles de Son Armadans*, 11 (November-December 1958): 256-300;

José Luis Cano, *Poesía española del siglo XX* (Madrid: Guadarrama, 1960), pp. 240-260;

Andrew Debicki, *Dámaso Alonso* (New York: Twayne, 1970); translated into Spanish (Madrid: Cátedra, 1974);

Miguel Jaroslaw Flys, *La poesía existencial de Dámaso Alonso* (Madrid: Gredos, 1969);

Flys, *Tres poemas de Dámaso Alonso* (Madrid: Gredos, 1974);

Ricardo Gullón, "El otro Dámaso Alonso," *Papeles de Son Armadans*, 36 (1965): 167-196;

José Olivio Jiménez, "Diez Años en la poesía de Dámaso Alonso. De *Hijos de la ira* a *Hombre y Dios*," *Boletín de la Academia Cubana de la Lengua*, 7, nos. 1-2 (1958): 78-100;

Jorge Mañach, *Visitas españolas* (Madrid: Revista de Occidente, 1960), pp. 238-254;

José Luis Varela, "Ante la poesía de Dámaso Alonso," *Arbor*, 45, no. 172 (1960): 38-50;

Luis Felipe Vivanco, *Introducción a la poesía española contemporánea* (Madrid: Guadarrama, 1957), pp. 259-291;

Concha Zardoya, *Poesía española contemporánea* (Madrid: Guadarrama, 1961), pp. 411-428.

Manuel Altolaguirre

(29 June 1905 - 26 July 1959)

Barbro Diehl
Concordia University, Montreal

BOOKS: *Las islas invitadas y otros poemas* (Málaga: Imprenta Sur, 1926);

Ejemplo (Málaga: Imprenta Sur, 1927);

Soledades juntas (Madrid: Plutarco, 1931);

Garcilaso de la Vega (Madrid: Espasa-Calpe, 1933);

La lenta libertad (Madrid: Héroe, 1936);

Las islas invitadas (Madrid: Viriato/Altolaguirre, 1936; revised edition, Madrid: Castalia, 1973);

Nube temporal (Havana: Verónica/Altolaguirre, 1939);

Poemas de las islas invitadas (Mexico City: Litoral, 1944);

Nuevos poemas de las islas invitadas (Mexico City: Isla, 1946);

Fin de un amor (Mexico City: Isla, 1949);

Poemas en América (Málaga: Dardo, 1955);

Poesías completas (Mexico City: Tezontle, 1960); enlarged and edited by Margarita Smerdou Altolaguirre and Milagros Arizmendi (Madrid: Cátedra, 1982);

Vida poética, edited by Angel Caffarena Such (Málaga: Guadalhorce, 1962);

Poema del agua (Málaga: Curso Superior de Filología de Málaga, 1973);

Romancero de la guerra civil (Madrid: Visor, 1984);

Las islas invitadas y cien poemas más (Seville: Andaluzas Unidas, 1985);

Obras completas, edited by James Valender (Madrid: Istmo, 1986).

PLAY PRODUCTION: *El triunfo de las germanías*, by Altolaguirre and José Bergamín, Valencia, January 1937.

MOTION PICTURES: *El puerto de los siete vicios*, screenplay by Altolaguirre and Egon Eis, Posa Films, 1951;

Subida al cielo, screenplay by Altolaguirre, 1952;

Golpe de suerte, screenplay by Altolaguirre, Posa Films, 1952;

Los emigrantes, screenplay adapted by Altolaguirre from the story by Guy de Maupassant, Posa Films, 1952?;

Manuel Altolaguirre

Vuelta al paraíso, screenplay by Altolaguirre and Gilberto Martínez Solares, Posa Films, 1958;

El cantar de los cantares, screenplay by Altolaguirre, Posa Films, 1959.

OTHER: *Antología de la poesía romántica española*, edited by Altolaguirre (Madrid: Espasa-Calpe, 1933);

Federico García Lorca, *Poemas escogidos de Federico García Lorca*, edited by Altolaguirre (Havana: Verónica/Altolaguirre, 1939);

Jorge Manrique, *Coplas a la muerte de su padre*, foreword by Altolaguirre (Havana: Verónica/Altolaguirre, 1939);

Presente de la lírica mexicana, edited by Altolaguirre (Mexico City: Ciervo Herido, 1946);

Gerardo Diego, *Poemas*, selection and foreword by Altolaguirre (Mexico City: Secretaria de Educación Pública, 1948).

TRANSLATIONS: Auguste-René de Chateaubriand, *Atalá, René y El último Abencerraje*, translated by Altolaguirre (Madrid: Espasa-Calpe, 1932);

Victor Hugo, *Los trabajadores del mar*, translated by Altolaguirre (Madrid: Espasa-Calpe, 1932);

Jules Supervielle, *Bosque sin horas*, translated by Altolaguirre and others (Madrid: Plutarco, 1932);

A. S. Pushkin, *Festín durante la peste. El convidado de piedra*, translated by Altolaguirre and O. Savich (Havana: Verónica/Altolaguirre, 1939);

Luigi Sturzo, *El ciclo de la creación*, translated by Altolaguirre and Bertha Pritchard (Buenos Aires: Tiempos Nuevos, 1940);

Iwan Goll, *La canción de Juan sin Tierra*, translated by Altolaguirre and Bernardo Clariana (Havana: Verónica/Altolaguirre, 1941);

Percy B. Shelley, *Adonáis*, translated by Altolaguirre and Antonio Castro Leal (Havana: Verónica/Altolaguirre, 1941).

The youngest member of the so-called Generation of 1927, Manuel Altolaguirre, was a man whose life was entirely inspired by and devoted to poetry. He was not only a poet but also an editor, publisher, and printer of poetry. In addition, he wrote drama and, in his later years, film scripts that were largely colored by poetry; his last film, *El cantar de los cantares* (The Song of Songs, 1959), was even subtitled "cinepoema" (film-poem).

The "Brilliant Pleiad"—another name for the 1927 generation—included Federico García Lorca, Vicente Aleixandre, Pedro Salinas, Emilio Prados, Jorge Guillén, Rafael Alberti, and Luis Cernuda. These poets were more friends than anything else, since they lacked a common cause or rallying point: they did not rebel against anything in particular, be it literary taste, or social order; nor did they create any new revolutionary movement in literature.

It is true that these talented poets had certain common ideals and specific literary role models when they began to write poetry. However, they later developed different styles that were often diametrically opposed to one another. In spite of these differences, they were drawn together by Altolaguirre, who served as a sort of catalyst, publishing most of his friends' early verse; his printing shop in Málaga became a meeting place where friendships were forged or strengthened, and where ideas were exchanged. "And his poems! How much we owe to Manolo, how many he left off writing in order to print ours!" exclaimed Salinas, hinting at Altolaguirre's well-known, almost legendary generosity (in the introduction to Eleanor Turnbull's, *Contemporary Spanish Poetry*, 1968).

Despite Altolaguirre's importance to his generation both as friend and catalyst, his own literary achievements have until recently been largely overlooked, and he has sometimes (undeservedly) been labeled a minor poet. Except for his first collection of poems, *Las islas invitadas y otros poemas* (The Invited Isles and other Poems, 1926), which is highly descriptive and rich in imagery, Altolaguirre's work is almost entirely subjective and soul-searching. He communicates his main themes (love, solitude, death, and nature) to the reader via a very personal world of symbols. Pervading his poetry is a search for a spiritual existence, perceived by him as a far better one, often set against a struggle to overcome more earthly desires. Occasionally heaven and earth fuse together in harmony, especially in his last poems.

Altolaguirre is the most communicative poet of his generation. He once wrote in a "confesión estética" (aesthetic confession), published in *Poesías completas* (Complete Poetry, 1960), that poetry was his principal source of knowledge, that it taught him about the world and himself, and that there is more in store for a good reader of poetry than a good writer. He goes on to confess that he has not yet succeeded in being a good reader of his own poetry, nor is he sure that he has been able to communicate exactly what he wanted to say in his poems.

Perhaps that is why Altolaguirre kept reissuing already published poems together with new ones, introducing variants of both titles and texts of the poems themselves (not always for the better) as well as typographical changes, changes in dedications, chronology, and so on. Or maybe this phenomenon should be seen in the light of the fact that Altolaguirre was both printer and art-

Altolaguirre in 1930 (Collection of Paloma Altolaguirre)

ist as well as poet; undeniably, he loved beautiful books, and what could be more natural than for him to use his literary creations while striving to fulfill his other artistic and professional ambitions.

Manuel Altolaguirre was born in Málaga on 29 June 1905, one of seven children born to Manuel Altolaguirre Alvarez, of Madrid, and Concepción Bolín Gómez de Cádiz, who was a Malaguenian. Manuel Altolaguirre Alvarez was not only a lawyer and a judge but also a writer who had authored several plays, and who contributed regularly to a column in a local newspaper. When he died prematurely in 1910, his son Manuel was only five; consequently, the poet had very vague memories of his father and was forced to rely on others to provide information about him; they called him handsome and brave. This last epithet he had received for being outspoken in his columns, a fact that earned him another label from his son's Jesuit teachers: "impious."

At the age of five Altolaguirre wrote his first poem and dedicated it to his mother. The family cook was extremely enthusiastic at seeing his verse. During the night she took it to her own son, who was a printer, and the following morn-

ing there was a surprise waiting for Altolaguirre. He found a scroll, tied together with colorful ribbons, at the foot of his bed. Inside was his poem, beautifully printed on cardboard and decorated with flowers and butterflies. Possibly this incident laid the emotional groundwork for his vocation as a poet-printer.

Several future poets figured among his childhood friends: Prados and Aleixandre were schoolmates of his in Miraflores del Palo, a school run by the Jesuits; Alberti played regularly with Altolaguirre's older brother; and Lorca spent his summers in a house opposite Altolaguirre's grandmother's home.

Altolaguirre went to Granada in 1922 to study law, and completed his studies two years later. In the meantime he founded a literary magazine entitled *Ambos*, in collaboration with two friends, Jose María Souvirón and Jose María Hinojosa. Although only four issues were published, all in 1923, this brief venture acted as an artistic springboard for several young poets, including Lorca.

For a few months Altolaguirre went to Madrid to work for Francisco Bergamín, a lawyer, and father of another of Altolaguirre's friends, José Bergamín. However, it soon became obvious that Altolaguirre had no interest whatsoever in pursuing a legal career. Upon his return to Málaga in 1925, he founded a printing shop, Imprenta Sur (Southern Press), together with his old friend Prados, thanks in great part to the generosity of the latter's father. The shop was decorated like a boat and was a lively center for literary activity.

It was here in 1926 that Altolaguirre printed *Las islas invitadas y otros poemas*, a collection of twenty-four poems about nature, solitude, and death. It is the landscape of his native Andalusia readers meet here, colorful, luminous, and often described in pictorial images, as in "Playa" (Beach): "Las barcas de dos en dos / como sandalias del viento / puestas a secar al sol" (Little ships two abreast / like sandals of the wind / set to dry in the sun). The poems are mostly descriptive, with relatively little symbolism. Biographer John Crispin writes that although these poems present the daily battles of light and darkness, sun and moon, and masculine and feminine, "we do not have the impression that the elements are at odds with each other." Altolaguirre merely observes the "cyclical rule of opposite elements" in the Mediterranean landscape, his vision of paradise.

Litoral, Altolaguirre's second literary magazine, and one that he edited together with Prados, was published in six issues during 1926 and 1927. A typical product of the Generation of 1927, it was illustrated by young Spanish artists and has been called the best poetry magazine of that period in Europe. October 1927 saw the publication of a triple issue commemorating the three hundredth anniversary of the death of Luis de Góngora, a poet who was greatly admired by this generation. Altolaguirre contributed to the issue with his *Poema del agua* (Poem of the Water, separately published in 1973), in which he imitates Góngora's style, rich in metaphors and imagery.

Litoral also published literary supplements, such as Altolaguirre's second book of poetry, *Ejemplo* (Example, 1927). His mother had died on 8 September 1926, a date he later referred to as the most important day of his life. He had been very close to her, living with her until her death. In *Ejemplo* are several poems such as "Mi soledad llevo dentro," about loneliness caused by separation from a loved one: "Mi soledad llevo dentro, / torre de ciegas ventanas. . . . / ¡Qué juntos los dos estabamos! / ¿Quién el cuerpo? ¿Quién el alma?" (I bear my solitude within, / tower with bricked-in windows. . . . / How close we were, the two of us! / Which the soul, and which the body?). The tone in *Ejemplo* is more intimate than in his first book; the influence of Juan Ramón Jiménez, whom Altolaguirre admired very much, can be seen clearly. No longer is the poet an observer describing the landscape from a spectator's position; he wants to "amoldarse al universo, en búsqueda insoslayable de armonía" (mould himself into the universe in search of harmony), according to Milagros Arizmendi. The clouds and the sea become animated, and a dialogue takes place between the poet's soul and that of nature.

Crispin finds that several poems in *Ejemplo* are influenced by surrealism: they make sense only if explained from the perspective of a dream or dream state. Although Altolaguirre was only moderately influenced by surrealism, *Litoral* lapsed into a period during which surrealistic ideas became prevalent, especially under the editorship of Hinojosa, who took over the job in 1929 when the journal was in dire financial straits. Both Prados and Altolaguirre were still nominally members of the editorial board, however. Hinojosa remained at the helm until the journal folded later that same year, only to be resurrected briefly some fifteen years later.

Beginning in 1930, Altolaguirre's new project was a magazine, *Poesía*, that he printed and bound in his own shop; he used his favorite type, Bodoni, which had never yet been used in Spain. The first three issues of *Poesía* each consisted of three parts: poems by a classical author (San Juan de la Cruz, Fray Luis de León, and Lope de Vega); poems by a member of the Generation of 1927 (Salinas, Guillén, and José Moreno Villa); and poems by Altolaguirre himself (subtitled successively "Escarmiento" [Lesson], "Vida poética [Poetic Life]," and "Lo invisible" [The Invisible]).

Later that same year, the poet went to Paris with his portable printing press; it and his bed were the only pieces of furniture to be found in his rented room. He mixed with other Spaniards who were living there, among them Salinas and the painter Gregorio Prieto. The printing press helped Altolaguirre support himself during his two-year stay in France, a period during which two more issues of *Poesía* were published, with contributions exclusively by contemporary poets, including himself. He also published a few booklets of his own poetry, the smallest one consisting of a single six-word poem, one word printed on each page: "Escucha mi silencio con tu boca" (Listen to my silence with your mouth). It met with quite some success, was translated into French, and entered in the Paris International Book Fair that same year. According to Altolaguirre himself, this was his best commercial publishing venture.

In his poems in *Poesía* (collected in *Poesías Completas*) love and solitude are again the main themes. The influence of Jiménez can still be seen, but unlike his master, Altolaguirre never shuts himself off from the surrounding world; rather, he interprets it through his feelings. Emotions acquire an absolute value and become more real than reality itself, says Carmen D. Hernández de Trelles. María Luisa Alvarez Harvey sees the tone of intimacy as a permanent aspect of Altolaguirre's poetry from this point on. She also points out the emergence of a conflict engendered by the duality of human experience as felt by Altolaguirre—his awareness of the existence of two worlds, one quiet and intimate, the other a world "de los trenes, de los grandes vapores" (of trains and steam). At times, as in "Alta playa," he longs to escape from the earthly world to a higher existence: "Quiero subir a la playa blanca . . . a ese paisaje infinito" (I want to rise to the white beach . . . to that boundless landscape). At other times, as seen in "Dos mares,"the attractions of both worlds can be felt: "Dos mares frente a frente. / El uno un mar sin cuerpo, . . . / el otro un mar humano, / encerrado en su carne" (Two seas, face to face. / One an incorporeal sea, . . . / the other, a human sea, / imprisoned within its flesh).

Back in Spain, this time in Madrid, Altolaguirre published his next collection of poetry, *Soledades juntas* (Joint Solitudes), in November 1931, a work that has been noted for its multiple dedications, not at all unusual for this poet. Individual poems or groups of poems are dedicated to friends and fellow poets, such as Aleixandre, Salinas, Diego, Guillén, and others, while the entire book carried final dedications to Jiménez, Manuel de Falla, and Pablo Picasso. Of the more than twenty new poems in this book, the love poems have a new erotic aspect, perhaps due to the fact that the poet earlier that year had met Concha Méndez, herself a poet, whom he was later to marry.

Lips, kisses, and caresses in the poems express physical as well as spiritual love. Altolaguirre achieves harmony between the two, and according to Álvarez Harvey, the conflict between the carnal and the spiritual is less pronounced than elsewhere in his works. Crispin notes "the experience of a spiritualized sensuality in which the lovers come to transcend their individuality and fuse into a new world . . . ," and he sees the influence of Salinas, especially in the new love poetry. Altolaguirre had once confessed that his poetry was a "younger sister" to that of Salinas. In comparison to his earlier collections, *Soledades juntas* was better received by contemporary critics, who used adjectives like "intuitive" and "sensitive" to describe it.

While in Madrid, Altolaguirre lived at the Hotel Dardé, where Méndez happened to live as well. She soon joined forces with him in his printing ventures, and the two of them edited a new magazine, *Héroe*, of which six issues were eventually published. For each issue, Jiménez wrote a lyrical character portrait of a Spanish hero, including among them Altolaguirre himself. The latter was often seen with Lorca, Alberti, Aleixandre, and others at Jiménez's home, which had become a meeting place for Madrid artists and poets.

Another place where they congregated was the home of Carlos Morla Lynch, the Chilean ambassador to Spain, who kept a diary at this time and described Méndez as an intelligent and emancipated woman, energetic without being too practical, but above all good and sincere. Among the

events he recorded in his diary was the wedding of the Altolaguirres, Manuel and Concha, in the church of Chamberí on 5 June 1932. Most of Madrid's literary world was present, including Lorca, Jiménez, Guillén, and Cernuda. Morla Lynch tells how the couple were married by mistake at another altar than the one that had painstakingly been decorated for the occasion by the local sacristan, and how Altolaguirre in his good-humored way offered to go through the whole ceremony again at the appropriate altar.

The newly wed couple moved to Calle Viriato, where the printing press was installed in their basement. Altolaguirre entered upon one of the most hectic periods of his life, filled with myriad different projects. He edited an anthology of Spanish romantic poetry, *Antología de la poesía romántica española* (1933), and a new series of books, "La tentativa poética," which included works by Cernuda, Alberti, Salinas, and Méndez (using her maiden name as a writer). He translated works by Victor Hugo and Jules Supervielle, among others, and wrote a biography of the sixteenth-century Spanish poet, Garcilaso de la Vega (1933), which was more a portrait of the hero than an account of his life.

In March 1933 the Altolaguirres were stricken with sorrow by their son's death at birth. The poet expressed his feelings of loss and anguish in later poems. That same year, Altolaguirre received a scholarship from the Centro de Estudios Históricos (Center of History Studies) to investigate printing methods in England. In October the couple left for London, and not long after their arrival they began publishing a new poetry magazine entitled *1616*, founded for two purposes: to commemorate the year that Miguel de Cervantes and William Shakespeare died, and to strengthen the literary relations between Spain and England through publication of poems in the original as well as in translation.

During 1934 and 1935 ten issues were published, with poems by Lorca, Cernuda, Guillén, Neruda, and Moreno Villa, among others, as well as by the editors themselves. In addition, Altolaguirre translated several English poems into Spanish, notably *Adonáis* by Percy Bysshe Shelley, parts of which appeared in several subsequent issues, but it was not completed in translation until many years later (1941). Furthermore, supplements were published, among them a book by Ramón Pérez de Ayala, who worked at the Spanish embassy in London and helped support the magazine financially as well as artistically.

Altolaguirre, Vicente Aleixandre, José Luis Cano, and Carlos Bousoño in 1950

Altolaguirre's work as a printer was applauded in the *Times* of London, and from a typographical point of view *1616* was perhaps the most beautiful magazine he ever printed. During his stay in England, he lectured on Spanish literature at the universities of Oxford and Cambridge, and in cities such as Liverpool, Birmingham, and Manchester. In March 1935 a daughter, Paloma, was born to the Altolaguirres, who returned with their baby to Spain in June.

Altolaguirre did not let the grass grow under his feet once they were settled back home in the Madrid area. Eager to try out a new printing press he had imported from England, he set out to print *Caballo verde para la poesía* (Young Horse for Poetry), a magazine whose editor was Pablo Neruda, then an official at the Chilean embassy in Madrid. In literary circles it was quite an event, since the first issue carried the Neruda man-

ifesto in favor of "impure poetry," which caused Jiménez to distance himself from the others in the Generation of 1927. Well-known poets collaborated with newer talents, such as Leopoldo Panero and Miguel Hernández. Altolaguirre himself contributed a single romantic poem. Four issues of the magazine were published between October 1935 and January 1936; the fifth issue was never distributed due to the outbreak of the Spanish Civil War.

The fact that there were both rightists and leftists among Altolaguirre's circle of friends and acquaintances gave rise to many a stormy meeting before the war. Some, like Alberti, turned militant, proselytizing for the Republican cause. Altolaguirre, concerned about social justice, had his sympathies with the left as well, yet managed to maintain good relations with all, regardless of their political beliefs.

The Altolaguirres printed another series of poetry, this one entitled "Héroe" (like their previous magazine)—including books by Lorca, Cernuda, Neruda, and others. Altolaguirre's own *La lenta libertad* (The Slow Freedom), published in 1936 in the series, earned him the National Prize of Literature. Although there are only twelve new poems, the book has more unity than his earlier ones. He is primarily concerned with evil and social injustice, though some of the poems reflect his sorrow at the loss of his son in 1933.

The conflict of spiritual/physical duality is symbolized by a cloud in the poem "La nube" (The Cloud). As a symbol of freedom, the cloud is likened to a "blanquísima virgen" (snow-white virgin) who will lose her beauty when she (as rain) gives in to her lover (the field). Since antiquity clouds have symbolized the vague, the fugitive, and the ethereal; and the image of clouds becoming transformed into rain (tears) is an old metaphor as well. In Altolaguirre's poetry, clouds take on the added symbolism of spiritual life and freedom from material existence, and are found often enough in his poetry to earn him the name of "poeta de las nubes" (poet of the clouds)—first used by José Luis Cano.

In July 1936 Altolaguirre published his next book of poetry, *Las islas invitadas*. The civil war had just broken out, and the author dedicated his book to the Loyalists. In spite of the title, this is not a new edition of Altolaguirre's first book; rather, it is a kind of "collected works," since the poems derive from just about every book he had previously written. Only one-sixth, some twenty poems, had not been published before. A wish to reconcile heaven and earth is found in the poem "A un olmo" (To an Elm Tree); with its branches the tree can stretch into the sky (heaven, the future), at the same time as it remains well rooted in the earth (the material world, the past). This is an early manifestation of a symbol that was to become increasingly common in Altolaguirre's later works.

Shortly after the outbreak of the war, Altolaguirre joined the Alianza de Intelectuales Antifascistas (Alliance of Anti-Fascist Intellectuals), which was formed in August 1936 and included among its members such poets as Alberti, Hernández, and Bergamín. After Lorca was murdered (also in August 1936), Altolaguirre agreed to take over the former's work directing "La Barraca," a traveling theater troupe of university students who brought classical Spanish theater to the countryside. A few months later, though, Altolaguirre joined the Republican army.

He did various printing jobs for the army and printed some books as well. Paper was sometimes scarce, and conditions were usually primitive. When he printed a book by Neruda, *España en el corazón* (Spain in the Heart, 1938), the paper had been manufactured from old flags and uniforms taken from the enemy, and the wet paper had been hung out with clothespins on a line to dry.

As an intellectual, Altolaguirre felt that he was being given privileges in the army, something he bitterly resented, and he tried in vain to get posted to the front. He was in Madrid during the siege (1936-1937) and also spent time in Valencia and Barcelona during the war. In March 1937 he met and became friends with the English poet Stephen Spender, who had come to Spain to support the Republican cause. In his 1948 autobiography Spender gives yet another illustration of Altolaguirre's generosity: when the English poet told the latter that he missed having his copy of Shakespeare along with him in Spain, Altolaguirre presented him with his own copy, an eleven-volume Samuel Johnson edition, from 1786. That same year they both attended the Writers' Congress in Barcelona, which attracted many European as well as Spanish intellectuals.

Altolaguirre's literary production during the civil war is considered a parenthesis in his development as a writer, since his themes were greatly influenced by the war. Furthermore, his poems were scattered throughout various war publications and would only be assembled and published together many years later. Some of them, together with pages from his diary, appeared in *Hora de España*, a magazine that was published throughout the war and edited by several writers including Altolaguirre. Number 23 was being readied for distribution when the Nationalist army took over Barcelona.

In the summer of 1937 *El triunfo de las germanías* (The Triumph of the Brotherhood of the Guilds), a propaganda play written by Altolaguirre and Bergamín, was staged in Valencia, and in 1938 the former received the National Theatre Prize for another play, *Ni un solo muerto* (Not One Single Dead Man). Unfortunately, neither of these theater scripts seems to have survived the war.

In 1939, when the war had run its course, Altolaguirre almost had a nervous breakdown at Figueras, the last stronghold of the Republican army near the French border. His wife and daughter had already been evacuated and lived in Paris, where he later joined them when he and many other intellectuals went into exile after the war. In "El caballo griego" (The Grecian Horse—autobiographical notes published in *Obras completas*, 1986) Altolaguirre relates his experiences and feelings as he crossed the border into France. When he began acting strangely, he was first placed in an asylum and later moved to a concentration camp in France. Friends heard about his plight, and Spender invited him to come to England, but Altolaguirre chose to continue on to Paris, where he and his family lived for some time in the house of the poet Paul Eluard.

That same year (1939) the Altolaguirres decided to move to Mexico, but on the way their daughter became ill, and they had to disembark in Cuba, where they remained for almost four years. It was not long before a new literary magazine of theirs, *Atentamente*, appeared on the scene. It only lasted through two issues, but is noteworthy for carrying the first part of Altolaguirre's planned autobiography in 1940. Another magazine, *La Verónica*, was published briefly by the Altolaguirres in 1942. In the meantime they continued to work together, editing a new poetry series, "El ciervo herido" (The Wounded Hart), which included his latest book, *Nube temporal* (Temporary Cloud, 1939). According to Altolaguirre (quoted in the introduction to the 1973 edition of *Las islas invitadas*), *Nube temporal* is a book "en el aire, triste como de invierno, con algunos poemas temporales, otros menos airados, otros más permanentes . . ." (in the air, sad as winter, with some poems temporal, others less angry, others more permanent . . .). His words indicate that a double meaning was intended: the title could be interpreted as "Stormy Cloud" as well as "Temporary Cloud," the cloud in question being a symbol for war and the agony and anguish it brings.

Several of these war poems had been published earlier in *Hora de España*. Altolaguirre was deeply anguished when confronted with the terror and destruction caused by the civil war. There are elegies to Lorca and to Altolaguirre's brother Luis, who had been assasinated by the Republicans. During the four years in Cuba, Altolaguirre gave a series of lectures on Spanish authors, lectures that are now collected in *Obras completas* (1986).

Poemas de las islas invitadas was published in 1944, a year after the family had moved to Mex-

Altolaguirre circa 1959, the year of his death

ico City. By this time Altolaguirre had abandoned his wartime topics, and his poetry once again became intimate, this time with a new note of mysticism, which is mentioned by Alvarez Harvey and by Crispin. Since most of these poems were not new, there was not much reaction from contemporary critics. His next book, *Nuevos poemas de las islas invitadas*, published two years later in 1946, was a product of his seventh and last printing shop and included eleven new poems, with much the same characteristics as earlier ones.

Altolaguirre had by 1946 gone through a personal crisis; he left his wife to go and live with María Luisa Gómez Mena, whom he would marry a few years later. Although his next book of poetry, *Fin de un amor* (End of a Love, 1949), was dedicated to María Luisa, many of the poems were really written to Concha. The overall theme of this collection of mostly new poems is love, and the poet seems torn between the spiritual love inspired by Concha and the passion he felt for María Luisa.

With Prados and Moreno Villa, who also

lived in Mexico, Altolaguirre tried to revive *Litoral* in July 1944, but only three issues were ever published; his last magazine, *Antología de España en el recuerdo* (Anthology of Spain Remembered), was even more short-lived. He also published close to thirty books in the series "Aires de mi España." But his last printing shop, Isla, had been a financial disaster. His next book, *Poemas en América*, published in 1955, was the last one to appear in his lifetime. Interestingly enough, the book was printed at Imprenta Dardo in Málaga, which had formerly been his own Imprenta Sur. Although there was little new material, it nevertheless offered a representative sample of his poetry.

By this time Altolaguirre had found a new interest, working in film as a scriptwriter, then later as a producer and director. His script for the film *Subida al cielo* (whose English title is *Life and Afterlife*, 1952), directed by Luis Buñuel, won three prizes—in Mexico City, Paris, and Cannes. As a promoter and salesman for the Mexican National Film Industry, Altolaguirre traveled widely throughout the country. The unspoiled Mexican countryside spoke directly to his soul, and he saw the peasant as living simply and in close harmony with nature. His last film, *El cantar de los cantares*, is based on the translation of the biblical Song of Songs by Fray Luis de León.

In July 1959 Altolaguirre returned to Spain to present *El cantar de los cantares* at the San Sebastian Film Festival. (Except for a short visit to Spain in 1950, when he had collected material for a film and met with family and friends in Málaga and Madrid, he had not been back since the end of the civil war.) On 23 July, after the festival, he had a car accident on his way to Madrid and died three days later in a Burgos hospital.

In all the obituaries and elegies dedicated to Altolaguirre after his death, there emerges the portrait of a man who was very much loved by his friends: he was widely known for his generosity (he had literally given the shirt off his back to a refugee during the war) and could not say no to anybody; his smile was as charming and disarming in middle age as it had been in his youth; he was called Manolo or Manolito all his life (in spite of his rather tall stature), because Manuel was perceived as too formal; and he was also known among his friends as an "ángel" (to be an angel in Andalusia is to possess certain qualities such as charm, generosity, and grace).

As a poet Altolaguirre has been somewhat neglected, standing as he does in the shadow of the poets of his generation: Lorca, Aleixandre, Salinas, and others. For many years no major study of his poetry appeared, although contemporary and later critics wrote articles about it. During the 1970s and 1980s there was a new interest in his poetry, resulting in new editions of some of his books and facsimile editions of his poetry magazines, as well as several doctoral dissertations and other studies.

Alvarez Harvey sees the constant tension between body and soul, the simultaneous attraction to earth and heaven, as the main theme pervading his poetry. The desire for spirituality can be interpreted as a means of escape but also as a genuine longing for transcendence.

Crispin has studied the poet in relation to traditional archetypes. He describes Altolaguirre's personality as adolescent, both fascinated and in conflict with the mother figure. Crispin does not deny the struggle for spirituality against carnal instincts, but he interprets it as a conflict between a struggle for individual development and a desire to "regress to the bliss of an unconscious existence." Only toward the end of Altolaguirre's life did the poet reach a certain balance; through an almost religious experience inspired by Spanish mystics and the Mexican culture and landscape, he finally reached a state of mystic pantheism.

A posthumous edition of Altolaguirre's poems, *Poesías completas*, was published in 1960 with the help of Cernuda. Most but not all of the former's poetry is to be found in this book, including a section, "Últimos poemas," where some of his last poems are collected and printed for the first time. Of the reprinted poems, many are presented in later versions that Altolaguirre had himself preferred, especially the war poems, which have been considerably toned down. The enlarged *Poesías completas* (1982) is even more complete and helpful in giving information about alternate texts, changes in titles, and so on.

Although opinion is divided on Altolaguirre's place among modern Spanish poets, perhaps the last word should be given to his friend Cernuda, who writes that Altolaguirre was as great a poet as any of them, one whose production, although limited, was "nunca menor" (never that of a minor poet).

Letters:

Epistolario: De Altolaguirre a Gerardo Diego, edited by Maya S. Altolaguirre (Madrid: Caballo Griego para la Poesía, 1991).

Biographies:

M. D. Arana, "Apuntes para una biografía de Manuel Altolaguirre," *Nivel*, 43 (1962): 1-8;

John Crispin, *Quest for Wholeness: The Personality and Works of Manuel Altolaguirre* (Valencia: Albatros Hispanófila, 1983).

References:

María Luisa Alvarez Harvey, *Cielo y tierra en la poesía lírica de Manuel Altolaguirre*, (Hattiesburg, Miss.: University and College Press of Mississippi, 1972);

Alvarez Harvey, "La vida poética extraordinaria de Manuel Altolaguirre," *Cuadernos Americanos*, 170 (May/June 1970): 171-174;

Milagros Arizmendi, "El intimismo de Manuel Altolaguirre," introduction to *Poesías completas*, edited by Arizmendi and Margarita Smerdou Altolaguirre (Madrid: Cátedra, 1982), pp. 9-72;

Azorín, "Altolaguirre," in his *Crítica de años cercanos* (Madrid: Taurus, 1967), pp. 167-170;

José Luis Cano, "Manuel Altolaguirre, ángel malagueño" and "Manuel Altolaguirre, poeta de la nube" in his *La poesía de la generación del 27* (Madrid: Guadarrama, 1973), pp. 273-282;

Luis Cernuda, "Altolaguirre," in his *Poesía y literatura II* (Barcelona: Seix Barral, 1964), pp. 271-274;

Carmen D. Hernández de Trelles, *Manuel Altolaguirre: vida y literatura* (Rio Piedras, P.R.: Editorial Universitaria, Universidad de Puerto Rico, 1974);

Leopoldo de Luis, "La poesía de Manuel Altolaguirre," *Papeles de Son Armadans*, 20 (February 1961): 189-202;

Antonio Morillo, "Manuel Altolaguirre, situación y sentido de su poesía," Ph.D. dissertation, University of California, 1973;

Carlos Morla Lynch, *En España con Federico García Lorca* (Madrid: Aguilar, 1958);

C. B. Morris, "The Closed Door," in his *A Generation of Spanish Poets: 1920-1936* (Cambridge: Cambridge University Press, 1969), pp. 143-171;

Julio Neira, *Litoral: la revista de una generación* (Santander, Spain: Isla de los Ratones, 1978);

Carlos P. Otero, "La poesía de Altolaguirre y Cernuda," *Revista Nacional de Cultura*, 26 (1964): 89-96;

María de las Mercedes de los Reyes Peña, "Aproximación a la poesía de Manuel Altolaguirre: estudio del tema del agua," in *Andalucía en la Generación del '27* (Seville: Universidad de Sevilla, 1978) pp. 189-217;

Juan Manuel Rozas, *La generación de '27 desde dentro* (Madrid: Alcalá, 1974);

Rozas and Gregorio Torres Nebrera, "Manuel Altolaguirre," in their *El grupo poético del '27*, volume 2 (Madrid: Cincel, 1980), pp. 58-67;

Pedro Salinas, "Nueve o diez poetas / Nine or Ten Poets," in *Contemporary Spanish Poetry: Selections from Ten Poets*, translated by Eleanor L. Turnbull (Baltimore: Johns Hopkins, 1945), pp. 1-35;

Margarita Smerdou Altolaguirre, Introduction to *Las islas invitadas* (Madrid: Castalia, 1973), pp. 9-51;

Smerdou Altolaguirre, "El manipulador honrado de la emoción de fondo," introduction to *Las islas invitadas y cien poemas más* (Seville: Andaluzas Unidas, 1985), pp. 11-23;

Luis Felipe Vivanco, "Aprendiendo a ser buen lector de 'Las islas invitadas,'" *Caracola*, 8, nos. 90-94 (1960): 122-130.

Papers:

In the Altolaguirre Archives, Tres Cruces 11, Mexico City, articles, essays, lectures, film scripts, and plays can be found, as well as "El caballo griego" (notes for Altolaguirre's planned autobiography, published in *Obras completas*). Some letters are housed in Sala Zenobia-Juan Ramón Jiménez, Biblioteca General, Universidad de Puerto Rico.

Carlos Bousoño
(9 May 1923 -   )

C. Christopher Soufas, Jr.
Louisiana State University

BOOKS: *Subida al amor* (Madrid: Hispánica, 1945);

Primavera de la muerte (Madrid: Hispánica, 1946);

La poesía de Vicente Aleixandre: Imagen, estilo, mundo poético (Madrid: Insula, 1950; revised and enlarged edition, Madrid: Gredos, 1956; revised and enlarged again, 1968; further enlarged, 1977);

Seis calas en la expresión literaria española, by Bousoño and Dámaso Alonso (Madrid: Gredos, 1951);

Hacia otra luz (Madrid: Insula, 1952);

Teoría de la expresión poética (Madrid: Gredos, 1952; enlarged, 1956; enlarged again, 1962; further enlarged, 1966; revised and enlarged, 2 volumes, 1970; enlarged again, 1976);

Noche del sentido (Madrid: Insula, 1957);

Poesías completas (Madrid: Giner, 1960);

Invasión de la realidad (Madrid: Espasa-Calpe, 1962);

Oda en la ceniza (Madrid: Ciencia Nueva, 1967);

Al mismo tiempo que la noche (Málaga: Anticuaria El Guadalhorce, 1971);

La búsqueda (Valencia: Fomento de Cultura, 1971);

Las monedas contra la losa (Madrid: Corazón, 1973);

Antología poética (Madrid: Plaza & Janés, 1976);

El irracionalismo poético (Madrid: Gredos, 1977);

Superrealismo poético y simbolización (Madrid: Gredos, 1979);

Sentido de la evolución de la poesía contemporánea en Juan Ramón Jiménez (Madrid: Real Academia Española, 1980);

Epocas literarias y evolución (Madrid: Gredos, 1981);

Selección de mis versos (Madrid: Cátedra, 1982);

Poesía poscontemporánea (Madrid: Júcar, 1985);

Metáfora del desafuero (Madrid: Visor, 1988).

Collection: *Antología de textos críticos*, edited by Julio García Morejon (Sao Paulo: Universidade de Sao Paulo, 1969).

Since the publication of his first book, *Subida al amor* (Ascent to Love) in 1945, Carlos Bousoño has emerged from the crowd that formed Spain's first post-civil war poetic generation to become an important figure in the history of twentieth-century Spanish letters. Not only does he stand effectively alone as perhaps the best poet among this early postwar group (and one of the few Spanish poets now approaching, or in, their sixties whose poetry continues to be innovative) but he has also, and unquestionably, distinguished himself as the finest Spanish literary theorist of the last forty years. As another great poet, Francisco Brines, has maintained, it is Bousoño's steady growth as an artist over a lifetime that "le [sitúa], a mi modo de ver, como el poeta más vivo de su generación" ([ranks] him, in my opinion, as the most creative poet of his generation), a judgment also shared by José Olivio Jiménez. Although Bousoño's poetry may not yet have attracted an army of active disciples, his monumental theoretical study of contemporary poetic expression, *Teoría de la expresión poética* (Theory of Poetic Expression, 1952)—in its six editions— has greatly influenced the aesthetic formation of Spanish poets for the last quarter century. It is, therefore, not an exaggeration to call Bousoño one of the most influential figures in Spanish poetry since 1950.

As is often the case with children who grow up to greatness, the experiences of childhood are many times decisive, thus making, in retrospect, the eventual career choice seem the natural outcome of events. This is true of Bousoño in both a positive and a negative sense. Predisposed initially to an aesthetic calling by a family replete with poets and musicians, the young Bousoño was exposed at an early age to the world of art. In Asturias, the somewhat remote Spanish province where he lived, he also came to acquire the predominant vision that colors his entire oeuvre because of an unfortunate turn of events when he was ten. He was born on 9 May 1923 in Boal, a small town in northern Spain, to Luis Bousoño Canocera, a businessman, and his wife, the former Margarita Prieto Fernández de la Llana, a schoolteacher. Their only other child was Luis, presently a chemist. Two of Carlos Bousoño's uncles were poets and wrote in the Asturian dialect. One of them, Bernardo de Acevedo y Huelva, was a personal friend of the great Ramón de Campoamor and the author of a somewhat noteworthy book on the "vaqueros de Alzada" (cowboys of Alzada). Many family members were musicians, and the young Bousoño had a rich cultural life and was not discouraged from thinking that an artistic career was a worthy goal. His earliest compositions, many of them influenced by the writings of Gustavo Adolfo Bécquer, were destroyed, as is often the case, by their creator, who thought them unworthy of an audience.

Although Bousoño's first ten years were emotionally and culturally full, the unexpected death of his mother and then the almost immediate im-migration of his father and brother to Mexico, ostensibly to avoid reduced economic circumstances brought on by the Great Depression, resulted in a complete reversal of his personal well-being. Although the family was not destitute, Bousoño was forced to spend the next ten years—what remained of childhood and the greater part of his adolescence—with his great-aunt, an elderly woman who, according to Bousoño, possessed "escasa sensibilidad para los niños" (little sensitivity toward children). While undoubtedly negative, this experience proved to be the single most important factor in Bousoño's development as a poet and a decisive element in the formation of his characteristic outlook on the world: As he writes in the introduction to his *Antología poética* (1976), "El carácter de mi tía . . . y el género de vida a que, a causa de su edad, me sometió me hicieron vivir entre esas fechas, o sea, entre mis 10 y 19 años, en una angustia incesante, en una extraña sensación de agonía y no ser, que había de sellar la forma interior de mi persona, digámoslo así, definitivamente" (The personality of my aunt . . . and the type of life to which, because of her age, she subjected me made me live during those times, that is, from 10 to 19 years old, in an incessant anguish, in a strange sensation of agony and nonbeing, that sealed the inner form of my personality, in short, definitively).

Perhaps the best poem in *Subida al amor* is "Recuerdo de infancia" (Memory of Childhood), one of the few truly autobiographical glimpses anywhere in his poetry and written to his aunt to tell her, "Nunca tuviste amor" (You never had love), but "Yo sí que te adoraba. / Sí te amé, torva raíz estéril" (I adored you. / Yes, I loved you, grim and sterile root). This "sterile root" that symbolizes his adolescent experience has become not only the basis for Bousoño's particular vision of the world as expressed in poetry but also, ironically, the catalyst for a lifetime of artistic creativity. The loveless aunt, however, is merely the personal manifestation of a wider phenomenon to which Bousoño consistently responds in his poems. He constantly confronts objects and people he invests with love and in which he places his hope only to find that this love, if not misplaced, will never receive a definitive reply. The dreadful experience of adolescence gave Bousoño a firm awareness of the indifference, lovelessness, and ultimate nonexistence of the things of the world and himself, while at the same time he remains convinced that there does exist something, or some things, that will allow him, by virtue of his faith in his own love, to overcome the "extraña sensación de agonía y no ser" (strange sensation of agony and nonbeing) that always accompanies him.

With many of his intuitions about the world already formed, Bousoño received new life, so to speak, in 1943 when he left Asturias forever. Through the intervention of the poet Dámaso Alonso, whom Bousoño, then fourteen, had met at the house of a literature professor, he was able to enroll in an honors curriculum for especially promising humanities students (the "grupo especial," as it was then known) at the Universidad Central in Madrid. Although the post-civil war years were difficult ones, Bousoño claims not to have been affected by the war or its aftermath, or at least much less so than others of his generation whose poetry displays a much greater social orientation: "Creo que la guerra no influyó en mí. Tal vez porque al empezar la guerra yo tenía trece años y mi familia más cercana estaba en Méjico y por tanto fuera de las consecuencias inmediatas de ese período histórico" (I believe that the war did not affect me at all. Perhaps because at the beginning I was thirteen years old and the closest members of my family were in Mexico and thus apart from the consequences of that historical period). There are poems of his addressed to Spain, but their tone is nearly always nonsocial, in direct contradistinction to much of the poetry of the late 1940s and 1950s. Spain becomes but another object of faith in Bousoño's quest for belief in something of permanence and transcendence. Spain's greatness or misery in his poems has no connection to political events but reflects Bousoño's own general outlook, at times slightly hopeful, at others less so, though on occasion he identifies with the entire nation, as in "Dios sobre España" (God over Spain), the first and perhaps best known of his *patria* poems (in *Subida al amor*). He concludes it with a plea to God to devour both the land and the people, for they are possessed of the same hunger for transcendence that only God may rightly claim: "La misma hambre tenemos que tu garganta dura" (We have the same hunger as your harsh throat)—indicative of a more profound cause for Spain's failure to govern itself successfully.

Bousoño was involved in preparing for his *licenciatura* in literary studies in Madrid in 1946. From the start of his university career Bousoño's friendship with Alonso (one of his undergraduate professors and his eventual dissertation direc-

tor) grew steadily, as did a new friendship, thanks to an introduction by Alonso, with Vicente Aleixandre. Along with young poets such as José Luis Cano, Rafael Morales, José Luis Hidalgo, and others, Bousoño started visiting Aleixandre's house with greater and greater frequency, becoming the most faithful of the lot and learning much about poetry in the process. Although it would have been easy to have become overawed by such important figures, Bousoño's own well-formed talent allowed him to flower early on: "Yo creo que es muy positivo [tener amistades de este tipo], si uno es, asimismo, creador, y no se siente disminuido en el trato. En mi caso [con Aleixandre y Alonso], la amistad de esas dos personas formó mi personalidad y mi gusto literario en una dirección creo que correcta, y estimuló mi capacidad creadora" (I believe that it is very positive [to have friendships of this sort], if one is likewise, creative, and does not feel diminished by the interchange. In my case [with Aleixandre and Alonso], the friendship with these two people formed my personality and literary taste along a course that I believe was correct, and it stimulated my creative capacity). As for any special influence on his work by virtue of his almost daily contact with Aleixandre, Bousoño denies the possibility: "creo que no hay en mi poesía más influjo de Aleixandre que de los otros siete u ocho poetas de nuestro siglo hispánico que me han gustado más" (I do not believe there is in my poetry more influence of Aleixandre than seven or eight poets of the Hispanic contemporary era whom I have liked better). As the years passed so did the master/disciple quality that may have characterized their initial relationship. As Bousoño says, in some respects it was almost reversed: "Por ejemplo, el libro de Aleixandre *Los encuentros* [1958] fue escrito a sugerencia mía. Yo había leído algunos de los trabajos de Aleixandre sobre poetas conocidos suyos, y le hice ver lo conveniente que sería en su obra un libro de poemas de la calidad de la suya. Siempre me dio Aleixandre sus libros a leer antes de publicarlos, y a veces quitaba o ponía poemas, o corregía versos como resultado de mis sugerencias. . . . Por supuesto, esto mismo hacía Aleixandre con mis libros. . . " (For example, Aleixandre's book *Los encuentros* was written at my suggestion. I had read some of Aleixandre's pieces on poets whom he knew, and I made him see how fitting that there should be in his oeuvre a work of prose the quality of his poetry. Aleixandre always gave me his books to

A 1955 reunion of writers at the Madrid home of Vicente Aleixandre: from left to right in the front row are Bousoño, Rafael Morales, José Angel Valente, and Jesús López Pacheco; in the second row, Señora de Montale, Eugenio Montale, Aleixandre, and Señora de Gallo; in the third row, Professor Gallo, Jaime Ferrán, Leopoldo de Luis, Alfonso Costafreda, José Luis Cano, and Eduardo Cote.

read before publishing them, and sometimes he took out or added poems, or corrected verses as a result of my suggestions. . . . Of course, Aleixandre did the same thing with my books . . .).

Bousoño's university years proved to be more than simply formative; they were exceptionally creative ones as well, during which he produced two tightly woven and well-written volumes of poetry, *Subida al amor* and *Primavera de la muerte* (Springtime of Death, 1946). Both were published by Editorial Hispánica in limited editions that were distributed first to subscribers. These volumes, not reprinted for nearly a decade, had initial printings of only 425 copies each, making them nearly unobtainable in the United States. *Primavera de la muerte* has received far greater attention from scholars, possibly because the volume also contains an extensive prologue by Aleixandre, who concludes by calling Bousoño "la voz más pura que haya sonado nunca acaso, en la poesía española" (the purest voice that may have ever sounded in Spanish poetry). The greater focus on *Primavera de la muerte*

may also be due to the explicitly religious character of *Subida al amor*, which has tended to limit its appeal. Yet these two volumes should be viewed together as forming a diptych of adolescent experience—one moment ecstatic and positive, the other dejected and negative.

The explanation for the overwhelmingly ecstatic and deeply religious tone of most of *Subida al amor* surely lies with Bousoño's emotionally deprived adolescence, which gave him a deep sense that he did not exist at all—the idea of death-in-life, the dominant theme of his poetry from *Primavera de la muerte* onward. The exuberance expressed in *Subida al amor*, however, is most important, for it represents the one moment in Bousoño's life—freed from his effective imprisonment in a rural environment—when this feeling of *no ser* is banished completely, allowing him to experience reality as a pure plenitude of being of which he could not have conceived earlier. As he says in *Antología Poética*, "La muerte de mi tía y mi traslado a Madrid, me permitieron súbitamente recuperar el mundo, asumir con avidez la gracia de la luz de la realidad, recibir en mi seno más íntimo la sensación infinitiamente bienhechora de existir en el mundo. Y como yo venía de la oscuridad de la primavera, el contraste me llevó a experimentar ese existir como un existir total, pleno, glorioso" (The death of my aunt and my move to Madrid permitted me all of a sudden to recover the world, to avidly accept the grace of the light and of reality, to receive in my heart of hearts the infinitely beneficent sensation of existing in the world. And since I was coming from the darkness of privation, the contrast led me to experience that existence as a total, plentiful, and glorious existence).

It is curious that, speaking in retrospect of the period of his life that caused him to write *Subida al amor*, Bousoño does not mention the word "God," although the volume is dominated by poems dedicated to what is unmistakably the Christian God in various manifestations (as a Father-God, as Christ, and as Spirit). Yet it cannot be rightly maintained, as some of Bousoño's critics do, that this is strictly religious poetry, for Bousoño is not placing himself at the disposal of God or giving thanks for being allowed to experience the fullness of existence. Rather, he is demanding a form of love that can only be satisfied by the direct experience of the divine. Describing and addressing his own soul in the introductory poem, "Subida al amor, 1," Bousoño characterizes his human spirit in terms of the immensity of God: "Inmensa estás tocada en luz naciente. / Inmensa estás en la luz de Dios bebiendo" (Immense you are touched in the birthgiving light. / Immense you are drinking the light of God). Although this has been interpreted as a mystic longing, it could just as easily be viewed in Luciferian terms, as a quest for a special form of power—the power that, arguably, only God possesses, the power to be absolutely certain of one's existence. Bousoño's quest implied a desire for an existential space, an effectively eternal space from which all aspects of *no ser* (time, death, etc.) have been removed and in which, as this poem's final verse proclaims, there is only "claridad en el silencio . . ." (clarity in the silence).

Bousoño's initial experience of the plenitude of existence is thus expressed in religious terms that are ultimately metaphors for the real desire, for the continued certainty of his existence. Although his sentiments may be regarded as genuinely religious—that is, that the God to which he speaks is the Christian deity—there is ever present in this initial volume the idea that God and religious belief are simply the means to

the ultimate goal of becoming godlike, of becoming eternally absent from the sensation of *no ser*. His "ascent to love" is, therefore, an ascent—a quest—to find himself reflected in the cosmic mirror that is God. As he admits a dozen years later, addressing the same God in the poem "Señor"—from *Noche del sentido* (Night of the Senses, 1957)—God is, in the final analysis "semejante mío" (my look-alike). The expression and personification of all his desires is always for Bousoño the faith in existence, the will to believe in the possibility of true existence in spite of the fact that he is equally aware of the presence of death and of ultimate nonbeing.

After *Subida al amor* the Christian God ceases being the pretext for the type of plentiful existence in which nonbeing has no place. Even with the ever-growing awareness in *Primavera de la muerte* that the sensation of *no ser*, experienced so intimately during his adolescence, was not only unavoidable but in fact that ultimate truth of existence, this continuing need for a God, or a suitable godlike substitute to nurture his faith in a questioned existence, provides the dynamic for all his subsequent books. *Primavera de la muerte* represents the first painful realization, however, that it is death, not life, that is omnipresent and that what is termed human existence is in fact death, or at least one of its forms, death in its springtime.

Bousoño uses the title phrase repeatedly in this 1946 book to characterize his attitude both to life and to his poetic production, alternating at times with another somewhat less positive one, "la nada siendo" (nothingness being). He explains in *Antología Poética*: "Sin esperanza de Dios que me sustentara, el mundo se me apareció como 'la nada siendo.' . . . Pues esa fórmula no expresa todo el valor, la positividad que mis poesía atribuye a ese 'siendo' de las cosas, al ser de la realidad. He amado frenéticamente el mundo, sabiéndolo perecedero, y por eso la frase 'primavera de la muerte' . . . y no la 'nada siendo,' la que mejor puede incorporar la intuición que perdurablemente se halla al fondo de mi vida y no sólo de mi poesía. Muerte o nada sería el mundo, pero tanto que es, que está ahí para nuestros ojos enamorados, para nuestro oído, para nuestro corazón y nuestra inteligencia, tiene un gran valor, un máximo valor. . . . Una primavera, claro está, patética. Admirable y angustiosa, delicada y terrible. Entre esos dos polos . . . discurre toda mi poesía, hecha de opuestos que no se excluyen. Cada libro desarrolla esta idea, o mejor dicho, este sentimiento, de modo distinto y con tonalidades y vibraciones diferentes" (Without the hope of God to sustain me [after *Subida*], the world appeared to me as 'nothingness being.' . . . Yet this formula does not express all the value, the positivity that my poetry attributes to this 'being' of things, to the essence of reality. I have loved the world with abandon, knowing it to be perishable, and for this reason the phrase 'springtime of death' . . . and not 'nothingness being,' is the one that best incorporates the intuition that has been with me unchangingly at the heart of my being and not only my poetry. The world might be death or nothingness, but for so long as it is, as it is there for our loving eyes, for our ears, for our heart and our intellect, it has a great value, a maximum value. . . . A pathetic springtime, to be sure. Admirable and anguished, delicate and terrible. Between these two poles flows all my poetry, made of opposites that do not exclude each other. Each book develops this idea, or rather, this sentiment, each in a different mode and with different tonalities and vibrations).

The tone in *Primavera de la muerte* is one of nostalgia and general despair at the realization that not life but death is what must be faced from this point forward. Existence itself is called into question, the old beliefs quickly fading, with nothing to replace them. As the still-adolescent, yet now-disillusioned, young poet realizes in the title poem, "Pronto pasará la primavera / y veremos entonces lo que somos / la triste desesperanza, / la invernal muerte desnuda" (The spring will pass rapidly / and we will see then what we are, / sad despair, / and naked invernal death). This is quite a fall from the quasimystic ecstasy of *Subida al amor*, where the poet feels so much power at being alive that he dares to look into the eyes of God. Yet it is perhaps the final poem in *Primavera de la muerte* that reflects the predominant attitude of the volume, a nostalgia for a time before the acute awareness of time and definitive nonexistence, as its title, "Primavera sin tiempo" (Springtime Without Time), indicates. Evoking the idyllic time before life became a "primavera de la muerte," Bousoño looks back and sees other adolescents that have delighted in "su intemporal reino fugaz" (their fleeting timeless kingdom) only to discover, like himself, "el duelo que sin nombre ha existido, / ay, para volver a encarnar sin descanso" (the nameless grief that has existed, / ay, in order to incarnate itself again ceaselessly). The once-confident,

once-believing Bousoño is left with only a sense of loss.

Besides marking the appearance of *Primavera de la muerte*, the year 1946 was also important because it saw Bousoño's debut as a scholar-critic. His brilliance as a student and his growing reputation as a critic, from the reports of his professors at the University of Madrid, caused him to be invited while in Mexico (on a visit with his brother, Luis, ostensibly to see that large part of his family that had gravitated there over the years) to give a series of lectures on the resurgence of Spanish poetry after the civil war and, more important, to present a few ideas about the then-almost-unheard-of subject of literary theory, most notably at the Casino Español in Mexico City and the Instituto Tecnológico de Monterrey.

The opportunity to lecture, however, was only a small part of Bousoño's positive experience in Mexico. The trip also gave him an opportunity to reflect upon his native land. Bousoño states in *Antología Poética* that although "mi propia generación . . . ha sido con algunas excepciones, una generación que quiso tratar desde el verso los problemas políticos y sociales . . . mi poesía, cantó, en todo momento, desde supuestos distintos y se propuso otras metas" (my own poetic generation has been, with certain exceptions, a generation that tried to deal through verse with political and social problems . . . my poetry, sang, at all times, from a different source and proposed other poetic ends). His refusal to write directly about social concerns, however, does not imply an aloofness from human and societal problems. Even before the publication of *Subida al amor*, Bousoño was very much concerned with the human issues involved in living a Spanish reality. He readily admits that his having been born a Spaniard has definitively shaped his poetic consciousness. At the same time, however, the fatherland, as well as the God that hovers over it, is ultimately no more than a reflection on a grander scale of the struggle that the poet himself is experiencing. Spain, like God, mirrors an intimate reality that Bousoño attempts to bring into focus in verse. The experience of Mexico during a moment of his adolescent crisis enhanced this consciousness of the interrelationship between the poet and his cultural heritage: "De México me impresionó su españolidad, la huella enorme de España que allí hay. . . . Me pude dar cuenta de que para conocer a España y su gran esfuerzo histórico hay que pasar por Hispanoamérica" (Mexico's Spanishness impressed me, the enor-

Bousoño in the 1970s

mous imprint of Spain that exists there. . . . I realized that in order to know Spain and her great historical achievement that one must visit Spanish America).

The Mexican sojourn also presented Bousoño with the opportunity to meet, and to become friendly with, members of the Generation of 1927, most of whom were living in exile, either in Mexico or the United States. In Mexico City he spent many hours with Manuel Altolaguirre and, on subsequent visits, Luis Cernuda. He also struck up friendships with Emilio Prados, Max Aub, León Felipe, Juan José Domenchina, and Ernestina de Champourcín, as well as the critic Juan del Encina and, finally, Octavio Paz. Especially to a poet as young as Bousoño, contact with these important figures was invaluable, as attested to by the frequency with which Bousoño has evoked these experiences in interviews and in his university classes.

One of his favorite stories, however, is that of his encounter, not with a poet, but with the great composer Igor Stravinsky, who was in Mexico at the time of Bousoño's first visit in 1946. Stravinsky resided with Bousoño's uncle and also later spent some leisure time with the family at their vacation home at the shore. Stravinsky was extremely reclusive, spending most of his time in his room in the uppermost part of the uncle's house, which Bousoño describes as "una especie de torre" (a type of tower). Stravinsky would remain in his room for days at a time, even taking his meals there. On one of Stravinsky's rare outings to the family beach house, Bousoño acted as his guide on a tour of the lush terrain surrounding the estate, but the great composer turned to Bousoño and told him not to take him farther, for all nature left him indifferent. Stravinsky's statement profoundly impressed Bousoño, whose love for sensual reality put him at odds with this man of an artistic sensibility formed by another time and circumstance, which could never be Bousoño's own. This anecdote reveals that as early as 1946 a fundamental change in the objects to which he assigned value was taking place, for he had clearly moved from the quasi-mystical and otherworldly posture of *Subida al amor* to a decidedly more earthly point of view, which became dominant in the works to follow.

After his stay in Mexico, Bousoño was given the unexpected opportunity to visit the United States in the fall of 1947, substituting as a professor at Wellesley College for none other than Jorge Guillén, himself that year a visiting professor at Yale. Ironically, again, a foreign terrain—this time New England, another stronghold of Spanish Civil War exiles—afforded Bousoño other opportunities to meet some of the most gifted people of his nation as well as other well-known non-Spaniards. During his year at Wellesley, Bousoño began a friendship with the guitarist Andrés Segovia, a family friend but never before close to Bousoño.

Although Bousoño has never commented on the atmosphere he encountered in New England, he surely could have stayed longer had this been his wish. His experience at Wellesley, however, was not uneventful, for he got to meet both T. S. Eliot and Robert Frost, although the influence of neither is detectable in his poetry. One positive influence of his Wellesley year is evident in his attitude toward teaching, which changed radically during his stay: "Mi experiencia de profesor en Wellesley ... me acostumbró a la idea de que el profesor debe estar al servicio del alumno en un grado que en España no se conoce" (My experience as a professor at Wellesley ... accustomed me to the idea that a professor should be available to his student to a degree that in Spain is unheard of). Another important experience during this time was a lecture he presented at Harvard. Bousoño maintained ties at Harvard, and in fact in 1962, after the death of Amado Alonso, was offered a teaching position, which he did not accept.

Bousoño's experience of the United States, however, was not limited to New England. Along with a friend (Jorge Soriano, an engineer he met while taking intensive English classes at the University of Michigan in the summer of 1948), Bousoño literally toured the country from coast to coast, visiting New York, Philadelphia, New Orleans, San Francisco, and Los Angeles, for example. His initial impressions (he has returned at intervals over the years) are ones he carries with him to this day: "Me asombró la uniformidad de los pueblos y ciudades. . . . Esta uniformidad se compaginaba muy bien y sin duda estaba relacionada con la uniformidad de la ideología social y política del país. . . . Sentí que, paradójicamente, había en Estados Unidos una cierta tiranía de la opinión pública que en España se nota mucho menos . . . " (The uniformity of the towns and cities surprised me. . . . This uniformity went along well with and no doubt was related to the uniformity of the social and political ideology of the country. . . . I felt that, paradoxically, there was in the United States a certain tyr-

anny of public opinion that one notes in Spain much less . . .). Bousoño's opinions about the United States cannot be fully characterized as negative; it is obvious, however, that the North American reality is not his own, and he was not tempted to remain or, later, to accept the Harvard offer.

Practical matters, including the required military service for all Spanish males (Bousoño's duty was in Ceuta and Tetuán, 1949-1950), also called him back to Spain, where he became engaged in writing a doctoral thesis on Aleixandre's poetry. The dissertation, which was completed in 1949, is interesting not only because it was published the following year under the title *La poesía de Vicente Aleixandre: Imagen, estilo, mundo poético* (The Poetry of Vicente Aleixandre: Image, Style, Poetic World), but, as Dámaso Alonso maintains in his prologue, also because it was the first dissertation on contemporary poetry to be accepted by a Spanish university. The dissertation was so impressive, in fact, that Bousoño was asked to join the literature faculty at the University of Madrid in 1951, where he continues to teach—along with participation in foreign exchange programs.

At about this time two other books of criticism, or at least the ideas for them, were being formulated by Bousoño. Although he continued to write an occasional poem, criticism began to dominate his time during the early 1950s. The publication of his critical studies was equally as impressive as his poetic beginnings—three major works in three years. In addition to the Aleixandre study, he collaborated with Alonso on *Seis calas en la expresión literaria española* (Six Samples of Spanish Literary Expression, 1951), one of the first works of Spanish criticism to study poetry (as well as theater and prose) according to a standard of scientificity with regard to explanation and classification of literary phenomena. The work that Bousoño will be judged by as a critic for years to come, however, is *Teoría de la expresión poética*, one of the monumental studies in the history of Spanish criticism, which marks Bousoño (along with Alonso, Salinas, and Cernuda) as one of the greatest Spanish literary critics of the twentieth century.

In brief, *Teoría de la expresión poética* marks perhaps the first attempt by a Spanish critic to describe in scientific fashion the phenomenon of contemporary poetic expression, the dual goal being to define poetry by demonstrating how ordinary language differs from poetic language and then to proceed to examine in detail the central expressive mode of the contemporary era, irrationality. Although the work has surely been one of the most widely read and influential studies of its kind in the Hispanic world, it has been met by a certain amount of neglect in the United States (it has been translated into Rumanian but not English). The only serious review article to date by a non-Hispanic scholar (Michael P. Predmore, "*Teoría de la expresión poética* and Twentieth-Century Spanish Poetry," *Modern Language Notes*, March 1974) is decidedly critical of Bousoño's method of studying individual poems to prove his thesis rather than considering entire volumes of poetry in their chronological contexts. No doubt part of the reason for the failure of *Teoría* to captivate a non-Hispanic audience is that its principal ideas about the nature of poetry may seem to the casual observer to have been expressed elsewhere and earlier, most notably by the French structuralists of the early 1960s. Bousoño has stated, however, that precisely the opposite is the case, that he was a structuralist long before the fact: "la lectura de Saussure, padre del estructuralismo, dio origen en 1950 a una súbita iluminación que me trajo el núcleo fundamental de ese libro [i.e., *Teoría*]: la idea de que la poesía exigía la modificación del lenguaje usual. Tuve de pronto la conciencia de que había averiguado el famoso misterio de la poesía . . . (El estructuralismo francés llegó a la misma idea, por influjo del formalismo ruso, en 1964, catorce años después. He de decir que mi libro se publicó en 1952, sin influjo alguno de esa fuente)" (The study of [Ferdinand de] Saussure, the father of structuralism, gave birth in 1950 to a sudden insight that brought me to the fundamental nucleus of that book: the idea that poetry required the modification of ordinary language. All of a sudden I realized that I had discovered the famous mystery of poetry . . . [French structuralism came to the same conclusion, via the influence of Russian formalism, in 1964, fourteen years later. I must state that my book was published in 1952, without any influence from this particular source]). Perhaps some of Bousoño's insistent tone in this statement has its origin in the undeniable fact that structuralist (and poststructuralist) criticism has effectively monopolized the field of contemporary literary theory during the last fifteen years, relegating Bousoño's work in the process to a largely Spanish audience.

The year 1952, however, also marked the publication of Bousoño's first new collection of poems in over six years. Entitled *Hacia otra luz* (Toward Another Light), the volume includes both the early poetry of 1945-1946 as well as the third section, "En vez de sueño" (Instead of Dreaming), containing some twenty-two previously uncollected poems, six of which were reprinted in 1957 in *Noche del sentido*. *Hacia otra luz*, therefore, may be viewed as the transitional phase between Bousoño's adolescent crisis and the mature period that begins with *Noche del sentido*. The titles *Hacia otra luz* and "En vez de sueño" are indicative of the dilemma Bousoño faced in the years immediately following his adolescent successes. His early faith, symbolized by the Christian God, was gone. He was in need of another sustaining light that has not yet appeared. In the meantime, his poetry became a means of avoiding a life of dream, that is, the limbolike death-in-life that resulted from his adolescent crisis.

Aleixandre alludes to this prolonged period of relative poetic inactivity in the section on Bousoño in *Los encuentros*. Aleixandre actually presents two views of Bousoño—the first in a sketch of the young poet during his first days in Madrid, full of life and faith, the second depicting Bousoño on Majorca, where he habitually vacations. In the first portrait Aleixandre speaks of Bousoño's ability to assimilate time and tradition, to use them as the means to a creative end: "Sí, el impaciente, el agitado soñador de la realidad en cinco años [de aprendizaje poético] había vivido, realizándolo en sí con autenticidad absoluta y aislada, el presente sucesivo de setenta años de poesía" (Yes, the impatient, the agitated dreamer of reality in five years [of poetic apprenticeship] had lived, realizing in it himself with absolute and isolated authenticity, the successive present of seventy years of poetry). The second view, however, presents exactly the opposite, time's apparent victory over the poet who with the passing of the years has become much more passive and resigned, content to sleep rather than to imagine. In the poetry of the early 1950s, Bousoño seems directionless, as he suggests in the poem "El apóstol" (The Apostle, in *Hacia otra luz*), which is about a confused follower of Christ, whose words now have little meaning for him. Like the disillusioned apostle, Bousoño is also engaged in a type of mourning over the loss not only of faith but also of youth, as in "Tú y yo" (You and I), where he laments time's implacable movement that separates him from the time when he felt secure and loved. Yet, despite the apparent negativism of these attempts to fashion a new vision, a glimmer of hope does survive. At the conclusion of "El apóstol" the oppressive and infinite light of time ceases to be monolithic and seems to offer the possibility of another option: "La luz inmóvil, infinita, / abrió de pronto, extensa, un ala" (The immobile infinite light / suddenly opened, broadly, a wing). The reluctance of Bousoño's Christian apostle to follow a Christ no longer physically present is understandable, for to find him again means death. For Bousoño, therefore, to resurrect his lost faith requires that he confront and learn to accept the solitary beacon that directs him away from his earlier ideals toward a purely temporal reality. This search for a new faith becomes the major struggle of the mature period, which begins with *Noche del sentido* and *Invasión de la realidad* (Invasion of Reality, 1962).

The early years of the mature period were marked by an intensification of involvement with his contemporaries. A significant influence in this new phase of his poetry was undoubtedly the Alonso-Aleixandre generation—including Manuel Altolaguirre, Emilio Prados, and especially Luis Cernuda, whom Bousoño calls "uno de los poetas más grandes de su generación, y también del siglo" (one of the greatest poets of his generation, and also of this century), with whom Bousoño had frequent contact during his subsequent visits to Mexico during the 1950s. *Noche del sentido* continues to chronicle the crisis of faith introduced in *Primavera de la muerte*. Although the need for a divine or transcendent presence in his life was still present, the faith in the divine being that sustained him earlier had completely disappeared, replaced by the most painful doubting of both himself and the apparently directionless existence he found himself forced to endure. Characteristic of this frustrating predicament is "Letanía del ciego" (Litany of the Blindman), where the poet addresses the memory of his old faith, asking: "¿Dónde el camino que no veo ahora?" (Where [is] the road I no longer see?). The doubting continues throughout the first section of the volume, especially in poems such as "La duda," "Meditación desde la noche," and "La visita al cementerio" (Doubt, Meditation from the Night, and Visit to the Cemetery).

With the second section, which begins with "España en el sueño" (Spain in my Dreams), Bousoño declares his love not only for Spain but also for the sensual reality of the Spanish landscape, even though it may be ultimately no more than "vapor, fantasma, sueño" (mist, phantom, dream). Bousoño thus began to notice the physi-

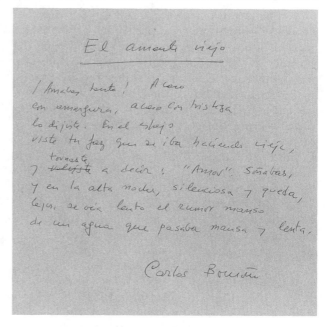

Manuscript for "El amante viejo" (The Old Lover), collected in Noche del sentido, *1957 (by permission of Carlos Bousoño)*

cal and human objects in nature that, like the God of his adolescence, seem to possess a greater permanence than the individual. Although it remained for *Invasión de la realidad* to confirm these presentiments that there do exist substitutes for God, Bousoño clearly demonstrates in the concluding poem of *Noche de sentido*, "La puerta" (The Door), that his doubting has led him to a new intuition. The poem is a meditation about an ancient door located in the Plaza Mayor of Madrid. Although men have come and gone with the passing of time, the door has survived. It thus possesses a type of permanence and eternity that Bousoño once exclusively associated with God: "Esta implacable puerta que la carcoma ha respetado. / Y aquí está segura, cerradísima, / implacable en su sin soñar / su materia sobrevivida, su materia resuelta a vivir" (This implacable door that the wood worm has respected. / And here it is safe, locked up tight, implacable in its nondreaming / its matter survived, its matter resigned and determined to live). Bousoño's final wish is for the door to open, signaling perhaps an end to the anguish and bitterness expressed throughout the volume. Implied by the image of the door, therefore, is a gateway to another existential possibility offered by a purely sensual reality whose objects provide a new orientation. This openness also signals, therefore, a new openness to himself as one of those objects.

The late 1950s also marked for Bousoño additional opportunities to solidify his relationships with his literary colleagues. One event during the summer of 1959 that greatly impressed Bousoño was a literature conference sponsored by Camilo José Cela, in Mallorca at the Hotel Formentor; it attracted writers and critics from throughout Europe. During the conference, Bousoño was able to form a discussion group with such figures as Dionisio Ridruejo, José Luis Aranguren, Carle Riba, and Gerardo Diego. In addition, he made or cemented friendships at this time with Leopoldo Panero, Juan Goytisolo, Jaime Gil de Biedma, Blas de Otero, and Gabriel Celaya. He also met Robert Graves, whose severely anti-British pronouncements surprised him.

Bousoño was quite at home in Majorca because he has spent nearly every summer since 1955 either there or in Ibiza. In 1978, with a monetary windfall for having won the Premio Nacional de Literature for criticism, he was able to buy his own summer house on Majorca in La Rápita. The summers are very important to Bousoño, who is happiest when the sun is shining brightly: "He sido feliz en medio de la luz mediteránea, que es la que más amo" (I have been happy in the midst of the Mediterranean light, which is the light I most love). Obviously, it is here where the presence of time is not as oppressive, thus affording him a peaceful counterpoint to the flux of human existence of which he is always painfully aware. This tendency to identify intensely with his surroundings, to view himself as simply a reflection of the physical reality he happens to be inhabiting at a given moment, is nowhere presented more effectively than in *Invasión de la realidad*.

If *Noche del sentido* represents the experience for the first time of himself as a minimal human creature, that is, a body without a transcendent component to assure him permanence in the cosmos, then *Invasión de la realidad* represents the opening of that body—his senses, his consciousness—to the material realm that Bousoño progressively comes to accept as the only reality. Although there is a certain consolation in this new intuition since Bousoño realizes that the exterior world is of a greater duration than human life and thus a possible means of salvation, it also lacks ultimate transcendence, leaving him in the position of being forced to embrace a new faith that leaves him unfulfilled. As he declares in "Mi verdad" (My Truth), the adolescent will that once aspired to some ultimate, cosmic truth has now,

in maturity, become confined only to the world that communicates to him through his senses:

> He aquí la fuerza que aspiró a ser cielo
> y sólo es realidad.
>
> Terrible mundo. Respirado mundo.
> Tú, mi sola verdad.
> Mi sola fe, mi solo amor profundo;
> mi sola claridad.
>
> (Here is the force that aspired to be the sky
> and now is only reality.
>
> Terrible world. Breathed out world.
> You, my solitary truth.
> My lone faith, my lone profound love;
> my sole light.)

Bousoño's progressive willingness to confront and to evaluate this material realm that paradoxically serves as both his prison and his only hope for salvation and dignity ultimately provides him the means by which to reorient his life and to come to an accommodation with the existential dilemma that has caused him much suffering. The initial sections of the volume chronicle the discovery of both the joys and the shortcomings—especially in "La gran ausencia" (The Great Absence)—of this new intuition of reality that has invaded his being; in the final section he attempts to synthesize these intuitions and experiences into a new secular profession of faith. The absence of God, and the transcendent reality that God symbolizes, leads, almost inevitably, to the divinization of the object that best exemplifies the material realm and the type of nontranscendent salvation it offers. An earthen jar thus becomes the subject of three successive poems in this final section: "El jarro," "Mirando este jarro," and "Oración ante el jarro" (The Jar, Looking at This Jar, and Prayer Before the Jar).

In "El jarro," the earthen jar is seen to embody characteristics once ascribed to God. It becomes for Bousoño "una rotunda / negación de la nada" (a rotund / negation of nonexistence), its persistence in the world generation after generation a sign to him "que no todo muere, / que algo se queda vivo entre nosotros" (that not everything dies, / that something remains alive among us). The jar thus functions as a silent intermediary between generations who discover that a communion does indeed exist among them by virtue of their experience of this artifact that outlives them. By exalting the jar, however, Bousoño indirectly affirms a place for himself and for his art which, like the jar, is destined to live on after the disappearance of the artificer. As he declares in the concluding poem of the volume, "Salvación de la vida" (Salvation of Life), his words in art will not only be the means for his individual salvation but also the hope of those who follow and to whom he addresses his poem: "Pongamos / más allá de nosotros, a salvo de la corrupción de la vida, / nuestro lenguaje . . . " (Let us place / above us, free from the corruption of life, / our language . . .). His final exhortation—"vosotros marchad" (all of you, march onward)—is precisely for his fellow human beings to search for those meager tools available to them that will make their short time in the world an occasion for affirmation and not for despair. The ultimate substitute for the absence of God thus becomes human artifice, the collectivity of human efforts. Bousoño, therefore, comes full circle, slowly acquiring in the nearly two decades since his crisis of religious faith a new, albeit reluctant, secular faith in the validity of his temporal existence and in the creative enterprise to which he has dedicated his life.

His next two volumes—*Oda en la ceniza* (Ode in the Ashes, 1967) and *Las monedas contra la losa* (Coins Against the Stone, 1973)—represent a logical continuation of the previous period, chronicling in large part the long and sometimes quite painful and confused search for the salvation heralded in the concluding poems of *Invasión de la realidad*. Citing these volumes as perhaps Bousoño's best efforts to date, both in terms of form as well as content, Francisco Brines characterizes *Oda en la ceniza* as a secular reformulation of Bousoño's earlier mystical aspiration. This volume is, however, only superficially more pessimistic than *Invasión*, for it is here where Bousoño confronts the question of the true worth of his life in relation to an ultimate destiny of nothingness. From time to time during this journey to the heart of the central mystery that confronts him, however, Bousoño is able to break free from his doubts to name the means by which he may save himself from despair. The first of these, already heralded in *Invasión*, is his art, which allows him to affirm through words, as in "El mundo: Palabras" (The World: Words), the essential worthiness of life for its own sake:

La vida.
La hermosa vida que has vivido vale.
El campo, el valle, lágrimas de lodo

Bousoño circa 1986 (photograph by EFE)

que has podido llorar, la niebla oscura.
Todo vale si es, aunque palabras
fuese. Todo vale si gime.
Todo vale si duele
junto a tu carne un mundo de palabras.

                (Life.
The beautiful life that you've lived has value.
The countryside, the valley, tears of mud
that you've cried, the dark mist.
Everything has value if it exists, even though it be
words. Everything has value if it wails.
Everything has value if there suffers
enjoined to your flesh a world of words.)

From this strophe it also becomes evident that the acceptance of human suffering itself also provides a proof that life is ultimately worth the effort to endure. Yet both the willingness to suffer and the willingness to chronicle that suffering through poetry are merely aspects of an even more noble means of salvation: love. In "Salvación del amor" (Salvation of Love) it is viewed as a principle of continuity that will assure the presence of yet another luckless generation, obsessed by the same anxieties and doubts but nevertheless the voluntary links in an existential chain that will assure eternity, if not to the individual, at least his most deeply rooted concerns. Addressing the present generation responsible for creating the world again in the next, Bousoño stresses the voluntary and ultimately selfless nature of this act of love:

> Sois vosotros los llamados, los elegidos
> para que decidáis si ha de durar el gesto
>   generoso
> de vivir como vida en más que vida,
> de aceptar con modestia ser tan sólo
> un puente en el camino,
> un puente tenebroso, esclarecido
> por el amor. . . .
>
> (You are the ones called, the elected
> so that you may decide if the generous gesture
> of living will last as life in more than life,
> of accepting with modesty to be only
> a bridge in the road,
> a dismal bridge, lightened
> only by love. . . .)

These glimpses of salvation along his odyssey of doubt lead to a final affirmation in "Precio de la verdad" (The Price of Truth), where Bousoño looks back upon his experience in order to declare that, despite the personal anguish, the searching has not been in vain:

> Es necesario haberse entendido con la malhechora
>   verdad
> que nos asalta en plena noche y nos desvela de
>   pronto y nos roba
> hasta el último céntimo. Haber mendigado después
>   largos días
> por los barrios más bajos de uno mismo, sin
>   esperanza de recuperar lo perdido,
> y al fin, desposeídos, haber continuado el camino
> sincero y entrado en la noche absoluta con valor
>   todavía.
>
> (It is necessary to have come to an understanding
>   with the wrongdoing truth
> that attacks us in the fullness of the night and sud-
>   denly awakens us and robs us
> to the last cent. To have begged afterward long
>   days
> in the lowliest neighborhoods of oneself, without
>   hope of recovering what is lost
> and at last, dispossessed, to have continued still on
>   the sincere road
> into the absolute night still with worth.)

Las monedas contra la losa continues the search for secular salvations while affirming, as in the initial poem "De curso de la vida" (In the

Course of Life), more emphatically than before, the essential impossibility of man's attainment of a definitive salvation in a "horrísona realidad verdadera" (a horrible-sounding true reality), which presents itself implacably "como un inacabable trueno de sombra" (as an interminable thunderclap of shadow). Reality being characterized sonorously rather than materially signals a shift in Bousoño's emphasis, from the concreteness of the earthen jar of a decade before to an incorporeal reality. If life-reality may be characterized as "nada siendo" (nothingness being), then it may also be characterized as insubstantial as a sound. The questioning of existence "es entonces entrar en el laberinto / toda la cuestión se reduce a pasar" (is thus an entering into the labyrinth, / the whole question becomes reduced to the passing through). More important than fruitless questioning, therefore, is the decisive act of creation. The "salvation" in which Bousoño places his faith is a personal one, inextricably tied to two antithetical forces, pain and pleasure. Pain makes the insubstantiality of reality seem more substantial, yet so does the pleasure that comes not only from the creation of art but also from its contemplation, especially in regard to music. The viselike grip of a reality no more substantial than an interminable thunderclap is released in the presence of the equally insubstantial yet harmonious melodies of classical music, as seen in his "Salvación en la música" (Salvation in Music). Along with the pain, therefore, are life's small pleasures that provide the dynamic of human existence, symbolized by music. Bousoño compares these pleasures to breezes that "Soplan físicamente . . . / más allá, en fin, del insignificante envejecer, del insignificante morir" (blow physically . . . / beyond, in sum, insignificant aging and death), breezes that momentarily liberate one from the flux and confusion that, for Bousoño, is existence.

The music about which he speaks is not a metaphor for something transcendent. In fact Bousoño has stated that listening to music is a daily and lengthy ritual for him: "Tengo mucho gusto en oír música y . . . durante años y años he escuchado todos los días cuatro o cinco horas discos de los grandes compositores" (I enjoy very much listening to music and . . . for years and years I have listened daily for four or five hours to recordings of the great composers). Like the door of *Noche del sentido*, the jar of *Invasión de la realidad*, and poetry and love in *Oda en la ceniza*, the contemplation of music becomes one more paradoxical article of faith in a world where faith is ultimately meaningless.

In the years since 1973 Bousoño has devoted himself primarily to criticism, among the most noteworthy products being *El irracionalismo poético* (Poetic Irrationalism, 1977), which won the Premio Nacional de Literatura for criticism in 1978; *Superrealismo poético y simbolización* (Surrealistic Poetry and Symbolism, 1979); and *Epocas literarias y evolución* (Literary Epochs and Evolution, 1981). This almost monumental output of writing is due, at least in some measure, to his marriage on 15 November 1975 to Ruth Crespo, "una chica mucho más joven que yo (tenía entonces ella 24 años)" (a girl much younger than I [she was at that time 24]). The marriage helped Bousoño bring a new sense of well-being and order into his life, and he gives it credit for allowing him to direct his creative and critical efforts more effectively: "Somos realmente muy felices, como nunca lo fui antes. Mi vida, antes bastante desordenada y tumultuosa, se ha ordenado . . ." (We are truly very happy, as never I was before. My life, before rather disordered and tumultuous, has become ordered . . .). This statement is a confirmation of the intimate correspondence between Bousoño's work and his personal life. His marriage and his family (his son, Carlos Alberto, was born in May 1977) seem to have begun to fill the need in his life that demanded so intensely something in which to place his faith.

Bousoño's attitudes toward sexuality are decidedly unconventional: "Nunca comulgué con los dogmas burgueses en cuanto a la moral, la sexualidad, etc." (I have never accepted the middle-class dogmas regarding morality, sexuality, etc.). But the last few years have brought him decidedly into the mainstream of both literary and intellectual life, most notably in 1979 with his induction into the Spanish Royal Academy (his acceptance address was given on 19 October 1981). Bousoño regularly participates in the academic sessions of the academy and is a member of two committees involved with incorporating new words into the official academy dictionary. His long-standing as well as newly formed friendships have been perhaps the single most important aspect of his creative life: "Concedo gran importancia a la amistad, y estas reuniones con mis amigos han constituido parte de mi vida, y sobre todo han sido incitante o excitante de una producción poética" (I concede a great importance to friendship, and these meetings with my friends have constituted a part of my life, and especially they have been an incitement or an excitement for poetic production). The friendships have come in three successive stages, the first dating from 1946 to 1956 in which Dámaso Alonso was a prominent influence; the second from about 1960 to 1973, with Felicidad Blanc (the widow of Leopoldo Panero), her son Juan Luis Panero, and the poets José Hierro and Francisco Brines being close to Bousoño; and the third still including Brines with the addition of Claudio Rodríguez and Vicente Puchol. All of the final group were also close friends of Vicente Aleixandre, the one person to whom Bousoño was closest for nearly forty years. It is from intimate and daily dialogues with his many friends that much of the inspiration of Bousoño's poetry has arisen, as attested to by the numerous dedications to these figures and others over the course of his career. Since these people are so important to Bousoño, any definitive biography must necessarily be obliged to weigh in the balance their creative impact on his work.

In the years that have passed since his first volume of poetry, Carlos Bousoño has remained an exemplary force in Spanish letters, having attained that status as both poet and critic. He has proven himself one of the most influential Spanish poets since the civil war and unquestionably the most brilliant Spanish literary critic since Dámaso Alonso and Luis Cernuda. There is every indication that his work will become a standard part of the twentieth-century canon.

References:

Francisco Brines, "Carlos Bousoño: Una poesía religiosa desde la incredulidad," *Cuadernos Hispanoamericanos*, nos. 320-321 (1976): 221-248;

José Olivio Jiménez, "*Invasión de la realidad* (1962) en la poesía de Carlos Bousoño," in his *Diez años de la poesía española: 1960-1970* (Madrid: Insula, 1972), pp. 33-60;

Jiménez, "Realidad y tiempo en la poesía de Carlos Bousoño," in his *Cinco poetas del tiempo* (Madrid: Insula, 1972), pp. 327-416;

Jiménez, "Verdad, símbolo y paradoja en *Oda en la ceniza* (1967) de Carlos Bousoño," in his *Diez años de la poesía española: 1960-1970*, pp. 243-279;

Leopoldo de Luis, "La poesía de Carlos Bousoño," *Papeles de Son Armadans*, 24 (1962): 197-209.

José Manuel Caballero Bonald
(11 November 1926 -   )

María del Carmen Caballero
S.U.N.Y. College of Technology, Farmingdale

BOOKS: *Las adivinaciones* (Madrid: Rialp/Adonais, 1952);

Memorias de poco tiempo (Madrid: Cultura Hispánica, 1954);

Anteo (Palma de Mallorca: Papeles de Son Armadans, 1956);

El baile andaluz (Barcelona: Noguer, 1957); translated by Charles David Ley as *Andalusian Dances* (Barcelona: Noguer, 1957);

Isabel Santaló, o "La moral construída (Madrid: Ateneo, 1958);

Las horas muertas (Barcelona: Instituto de Estudios Hispánicos, 1959);

El papel del coro (Bogotá: Mito, 1961);

Dos días de septiembre (Barcelona: Seix Barral, 1962);

Cádiz, Jérez y Los Puertos (Barcelona: Noguer, 1963); translated by Doireann MacDermott as *Cádiz, Jérez and Los Puertos* (Barcelona: Noguer, 1963);

Pliegos de cordel (Barcelona: Literaturasa/Colliure, 1963);

Lo que sabemos del vino (Madrid: Gregorio Del Toro, 1967);

Vivir para contarlo (Barcelona: Seix Barral, 1969);

Agata, ojo de gato (Barcelona: Barral, 1974);

Luces y sombras del flamenco (Barcelona: Lumen, 1975);

Cuixart (Madrid: Rayuela, 1977);

Descrédito del héroe (Barcelona: Lumen, 1977);

Poesía, 1951-1977 (Barcelona: Plaza & Janés, 1979);

Breviario del vino (Madrid: Esteban, 1980);

Toda la noche oyeron pasar pájaros (Barcelona: Planeta, 1981);

Selección natural (Madrid: Cátedra, 1983);

El laberinto de fortuna (Barcelona: Laia, 1984);

Los personajes de Fajardo (Santa Cruz de Tenerife: Cabildo Insular de Tenerife, 1986);

En la casa del padre (Barcelona: Plaza & Janés, 1988).

PLAY PRODUCTION: *Abre el ojo*, by Rojas Zor-

José Manuel Caballero Bonald (drawing by Zamorano; from Insula, *April 1975)*

rilla, adapted by Bonald, Madrid, Teatro María Guerrero, 1978.

OTHER: Michel Butor, *El empleo del tiempo*, translated by Bonald (Barcelona: Seix Barral, 1958);

José Ortega, *Les moissonneurs: Dessins et temperas*, introduction by Bonald (Paris: Ebro/Libraire du Globe, 1966);

Narrativa cubana de la Revolución, edited, with an introduction and notes, by Bonald (Madrid: Alianza, 1968);

Antología de la poesía rumana contemporánea, edited by Bonald and Darie Novaceanu (Barcelona: Júcar, 1972);

Luis de Góngora: Poesía, edited by Bonald (Madrid: Taurus, 1982);

Alfonso Gross, *El capirote*, introductory essay by Bonald (Madrid: Espasa-Calpe, 1984).

José Manuel Caballero Bonald wove the profile of his life in his work. In it the autobiographical and the historical, the individual and the national, complement each other. As he points out in the introduction to his poetry book *Selección natural* (Natural Selection, 1983), he himself can find many forgotten facts of his own biography by searching his work. Likewise, the reader just flipping through and reading some of Bonald's poems can experience the strength with which this man poured into his writing the amalgam of situations, knowledge, and feelings that make up a life.

Son of a Cuban father, Placido Caballero, and a French mother, Julia de Bonald, José Manuel Caballero Bonald was born on 11 November 1926 in Jérez de la Frontera, Spain. When he was nine, the Spanish Civil War broke out, and in some of his works, the ones in which he turns to his childhood, one sees the uncertainty, the anxiety to comprehend a war seen through the eyes of a child, to absorb the wartime visions of a boy who could take no other part than that of a mute, fascinated witness. That part of his work also echoes the long postwar period, which he experienced as an adolescent—a boy who examined, searched for answers, and became aware of that unsheltered historical moment, later to bear witness. Those dead fields of Spain remembered by Bonald in his poems would also be seen in the works of other poets of the Generation of 1950, as his generation is known.

In 1944 Bonald went to Cádiz to study seamanship and navigation. Here with his brother Rafael he took his first literary steps. Between 1946 and 1949 he studied philosophy and literature at Seville and wrote his first poems. Bonald remembers that these first poetic excursions were due to a crisis in his health and were tinged—perhaps because of his Cuban, French and Andalusian background—with a romanticism and a creole ornamentalism that, nonetheless, did not last long. A curiosity for examining the language, due to his readings of the modernist, symbolist, surrealist, and baroque poets, made his first book of poetry, *Las adivinaciones* (The Prophecies,

1952), somewhat a product of all those readings, especially the baroque.

This first book and his next two, *Memorias de poco tiempo* (Small-time Memories, 1954) and *Anteo* (Spectacle, 1956), tend to be autobiographical to some extent. Stories of his childhood and adolescence, wrapped in rich and colorful adjectives, form the basic "plots" of this subjective poetry. It is memory, as suggested by the title, that really shapes the thematic canvas of the second book. Thus, it is perhaps made of more impenetrable and somber poetry than is the first, although it continues along the same lines. Nevertheless, there are poems that presage a change of direction, a march toward objectivity, lexical investigation, and linguistic dominance. Hence, as Bonald says in *Selección natural*, "arises, I believe, the most frequent action of my poetry: to convert a lived experience into a linguistic experience." This is perfectly exemplified in *Anteo*, a brief book composed of four thematically related poems in which Bonald goes further into structural language, embellishing life through words. He experiments with language in his poetry. It should also be taken into account that the influences of surrealism, dadaism, expressionism, cubism, and other former literary movements are still present in *Anteo*. Nevertheless, for Bonald, this searching for the exact literary equivalency of experience enhances his capacity to investigate every aspect of the language. Poetry is for him a passionate game.

Bonald has been very prolific. In 1957 he published *El baile andaluz* (translated as *Andalusian Dances*), with simultaneous printings in French, English, and German. In 1958 his *Las horas muertas* (The Dead Hours) won the Boscan poetry prize, and it was published in early 1959. In this book Bonald does not leave behind the subjectivity of his previous work but opens himself outward to a greater extent. The poems have more social, political, and moral implications, while still being linguistically daring. His poetic expression is more a part of historical time and includes both the individual and the collective. Bonald says that *Las horas muertas* is one of the poetic texts that satisfy him most. He adds that, without a doubt, it marks a new stage in the development of his poetry.

In January 1960 he married María Josefa Ramis Cabot, moved to Bogotá as professor of Spanish literature and humanities in the Universidad Nacional, and received the Crítica prize for *Las horas muertas*. In 1961 he published *El*

Bonald (center) with Angel González and Gabriel Celaya

papel del coro (The Paper of the Heart), poems written between 1955 and 1960, and his first child, Rafael, was born. Later that year Bonald traveled to the Putumayo jungle and the Caribbean and Pacific coasts.

Bonald returned with his family to Spain in 1962 and published his first novel, *Dos días de septiembre* (Two Days in September), written in Colombia. In it he submerges himself in the customs of Andalusia, analyzing and criticizing the different social levels. Bonald wields daring descriptions and accurate literary techniques through a rich and innovative vocabulary. In *Dos días de septiembre* one finds human authenticity in an objective and smooth narration. During this same year his daughter, María Julia, was born.

His next book of poetry, *Pliegos de cordel* (Sheets of String, 1963), also written mostly in Colombia, is more realistic than his earlier ones. It is an almost didactic and documentary poetry of his inner self as well as being testimonial of his surroundings. With *Pliegos de cordel* Bonald alludes in the title to a Spanish poetic tradition, rooted in the fifteenth century and further developed

during the seventeenth. Poetry, written on *pliegos*, was sold inexpensively. Bonald revives this popular-literature tradition, creating new motifs and adapting others, deriving from it the pleasure of the past relived in the present. Those popular essences are an unmistakable part of his traditional values and his heritage.

During the same year, 1963, he published, with simultaneous editions in French and English, *Cádiz, Jérez y Los Puertos*, which is a practical and complete information guide to the region. Bonald describes it from both a historical and geographical point of view. He calls Cádiz "the oldest town in the western world" and takes the tourist through places worth seeing. He does the same with Jérez and Los Puertos, under which he includes San Fernando, Puerto Real, and Puerto de Santa María, ports lying between Cádiz and Jérez. Bonald not only pictures for the reader the area's ancient history and interesting geographical locations but its customs, peculiarities, and people, their fiestas, songs, and dances, and even their wine industry and culinary art. In 1964 Bonald's son José Manuel was born and in 1967 his son Miguel.

During 1965 Bonald lived for three months in Cuba, where he was invited by the Writers' Union; he returned in 1968 for a cultural congress. That same year he published *Narrativa cubana de la Revolución* (The Cuban Story of the Revolution), an anthology of the literature produced in that country in the first ten years since the Communists took power. The book begins with a prologue in which he tries to clarify the enmeshing of literature and revolution.

Bonald has been an avid traveler. From America to the Black Sea, he has visited every place worthy of interest. Nevertheless, his love for his native Andalusia has never ceased. For example, he crossed Andalusia often to collect an archive of recorded flamenco songs, which in 1969 Ariola-Vergara edited with the title of *Archivo del cante flamenco*, a six-record album that won the national Crítica prize. Also in 1969 Bonald's complete poems were published in *Vivir para contarlo* (To Live to Tell about It), where all his earlier poetry books are included. He added a few previously unpublished poems, written between 1964 and 1968, under the title "Nuevas situaciones" (New Situations).

In 1970 he traveled to an international poetry conference in the Netherlands and later to Rumania as a guest of the Writers' Union. During that year his fifth child, Alejandro, was born. Bonald was employed until 1975 by the Lexicography Seminar of the Royal Academy. He also worked during the 1970s as a literary editor at Ediciones Júcar, as a record producer of popular music, and a coeditor with Darie Novaceanu of the *Antología de la poesía rumana contemporánea* (Anthology of Contemporary Rumanian Poetry), published in 1972. In 1974 he published his novel *Agata, ojo de gato* (Agata, Eye of the Cat), winning the Barral prize, which he refused. In the narrative, Bonald re-creates the process of colonization of a Spanish territory. The described geographical site and its inhabitants are savage and wild. Manuela, the protagonist, a disturbing and bewildering beauty, is the symbol of the land— untamed, intense, and turbulent. This flesh-and-blood being is also a mythical one, because *Agata, ojo de gato* is a strongly mythical version of history. Bonald describes every pretemporal aspect, its origins and roots, transforming them into the site of epical adventures in a vindictive land that annihilates whatever and whoever may try to surpass its powers. Bonald's language is as elusive and irreducible as the land; readers find in *Agata* the descriptive boldness of the born writer who

surpasses the postures and limitations of school learning.

In 1975 Bonald published *Luces y sombras del flamenco* (Lights and Shadows of Flamenco) and in 1977 *Descrédito del héroe* (Discrediting of the Hero), winner of the 1978 Crítica prize. *Descrédito del héroe* was the instrument used by Bonald to make of poetry a weapon against unsatisfactory reality. This is the book for which the author feels strongest, due to his certainty of having reached with it the difficult correspondence between ideas and their expression. Using prose poems with severe, striking metaphors, Bonald searches the individual and collective humankind; he presents, through moral allegories and historical teachings, moral proposals to construct a more useful world, a reality built by better human beings.

During 1977 Bonald was named president of the Spanish Pen Club; he resigned in 1980. Also in 1977 he published *Cuixart*, and in 1979 *Poesía, 1951-1977*, as well as his version of Rojas Zorrilla's play *Abre el ojo* (Open your Eye) performed by the National Dramatic Company at the María Guerrero Theater in Madrid. Bonald received the Pablo Iglesias prize for literature.

The 1970s were very productive for him; however, so were the 1980s. His *Breviario del vino* (The Wildness of the Wine) was published in 1980, and his novel *Toda la noche oyeron pasar los pájaros* (All Night They Watch the Birds Fly, 1981) won the Ateneo de Sevilla prize. In 1982 his edition of the poetry of Luis de Góngora was published, followed by *Selección natural* in 1983, and a year later *El laberinto de fortuna* (The Labyrinth of Fortune). As with *Pliegos de cordel*, Bonald honored the literary past with *El laberinto*, since its title is the same as a famous pre-Renaissance poem by Juan de Mena. Despite the fact that Mena's *Laberinto* was framed by a stern and rigid didactic context, its rhetorical innovations reformed an otherwise precarious and lacking language in a way that was learned and practiced afterward. Mena altered almost every lexical use to open new dimensions. Bonald praised him for his audacity, because Bonald was also audacious. In his 1984 book, he follows the steps of his predecessor, likewise opening new dimensions. With every poem, Bonald entangles the expressive techniques of an articulated language with an unusual rhythmic structure, investing it with the power of a new style of poetic prose.

Bonald, throughout his career, has taught courses and participated in congresses and writers' seminars in many American and European universities, as well as publishing critical and literary works in Spanish and Latin American magazines. He has frequently contributed to other mass media and literary reviews, such as *Papeles de Son Armadans, Mito*, and *Poesía de España*. Part of his work has been published in different languages and is collected in numerous Spanish and foreign anthologies.

The life and work of José Manuel Caballero Bonald have paralleled each other. His poetry began by relating his first childhood memories. The dualism of life and art have produced poems by him that have erased the boundaries among the man, the poet, and the novelist. That interweaving has produced a spontaneous, profound style of lyric and has revealed—in narration welded by the exactness of the language, the definite word—Bonald's ability to describe, perhaps at times in enigmatic and unanalyzable ways, what he felt.

For Bonald, life, in all its aspects, is the inevitable key to the world of creation. His art is a consequence of living, an art that pleases the artist in its process, the essential equilibrium of artistic elaboration being enjoyable and being later shared by the reader. Thus, his work is doubtless the result of his joy in life. The adventure of expressing life's course and investigating the changing planes of consciousness is seen in the pages of his books. Poetry is a search, asking about one's own and others' needs in the moment in which it befalls one to live. In a way, his novels are also joined by this unity of purpose, analogous to his poetry—they emerge from a collective voice, a permanent substance in Bonald's vision of life. Recently he won yet another award, the Premio Internacional de Novela Plaza y Janés, for his novel *En la casa del padre* (In the Father's House, 1988).

References:

José Luis Acquaroni, "Caballero Bonald, un poeta al margen," *Ateneo* (May 1955);

Aurora de Albornoz, "José Manuel Caballero Bonald: La palabra como alucinógeno," in her *Hacia la realidad creada* (Barcelona: Península, 1979);

Albornoz, "La vida contada de José Manuel Caballero Bonald," *Revista de Occidente* (June 1970);

Javier Alfaya, "El misterio de la realidad," *Triunfo* (December 1977);

Harold Alvarado Tenorio, "Caballero Bonald, entre la vida y la palabra," *Espectador* (April 1980);

Alvarado Tenorio, *Cinco poetas de la generación del 50: González, Caballero Bonald, Barral, Gil de Biedma, Brines* (Bogotá: Oveja Negra, 1980);

José Batlló, ed., *Antología de la nueva poesía española* (Madrid: Bardo, 1968);

José Luis Cano, "Descrédito del heroe," *Insula* (April 1978);

José María Castellet, *Un cuarto de siglo de poesía española* (Barcelona: Seix Barral, 1969);

Camilo José Cela, "Las adivinaciones," *Clavileño* (May-June 1952);

Guillermo Díaz Plaja, "Vivir para contarlo," in his *Cien libros españoles* (Salamanca: Anaya, 1971).

Miguel Fernández-Braso, "Caballero Bonald: El realismo de la buena conciencia estética," in his *De escritor a escritor* (Barcelona: Taber, 1970);

Carmen Martín Gaite, "El fraudulento rastro de la verdad," *Diario*, 16 (9 January 1978);

Pilar Gómez Bedate, *Cinco poetas españoles* (Buenos Aires: Zona, 1964);

Félix Grande, "El lenguaje turbador de Caballero Bonald," *El País* (26 March 1978);

Homenaje a José Manuel Caballero Bonald (Sanlúcar de Barrameda, Spain: Delegación de Cultura, 1985);

José Olivio Jiménez, "Hacia la poética de J. M. Caballero Bonald," in his *Diez años de poesía española, 1960-1970* (Madrid: Insula, 1972);

Anthony Kerrigan, "Descrédito del heroe," *World Literature Today* (July 1978);

J. Lechner, *El compromiso en la poesía española del siglo XX. Parte Segunda: De 1939 a 1974* (Leiden, Netherlands: Universitaire Pers Leiden, 1975);

Charles David Ley, *Spanish Poetry Since 1939* (Washington: Catholic University of America Press, 1962);

Jorge A. Marfil, "La tradición barroca," *Informaciones* (19 January 1978);

Florencio Martínez Ruiz, *La nueva poesía española* (Madrid: Biblioteca Nueva, 1971);

Fanny Rubio and José Luis Falcó, *Poesía española contemporánea, 1939-1980* (Madrid: Alhambra, 1981);

Dámaso Santos, "La poesía que no ceja," *Pueblo* (8 June 1978);

Gustav Siebenmann, *Los estilos poéticos en España desde 1900* (Madrid: Gredos, 1973);

Rubén Vela, *Ocho poetas españoles* (Buenos Aires: Dead Weight, 1965);

Tino Villanueva, "La intención moral de J. M. Caballero Bonald en la poesía de la infancia,"

Bulletin Hispanique (January-June 1982);

Luis Antonio de Villena, "Caballero Bonald: Una vital experiencia en el lenguaje," *Insula* (June 1980).

Guillermo Carnero
(7 May 1947 -   )

Ignacio Javier López
University of Pennsylvania

BOOKS: *Libro de Horas* (Málaga: Guadalhorce, 1967);

Dibujo de la muerte (Málaga: el Guadalhorce, 1967; revised edition, Barcelona: Ocnos, 1971);

Modo y canciones del amor ficticio (Málaga: Guadalhorce, 1969);

El sueño de Escipión (Madrid: Visor, 1971);

Espronceda (Madrid: Júcar, 1974);

Variaciones y figuras sobre un tema de La Bruyére (Madrid: Visor, 1974);

El azar objetivo (Madrid: Trece de nieve, 1975);

El grupo "Cántico" de Córdoba. Un episodio clave de la historia de la poesía española de postguerra (Madrid: Nacional, 1976);

Los orígenes del Romanticismo reaccionario español: El matrimonio Böhl de Faber (Valencia: Universidad, 1978);

Ensayo de una teoría de la visión. Poesía 1966-1977 (Madrid: Peralta/Hiperión, 1979);

La cara oscura del siglo de Las Luces (Madrid: Fundación Juan March/Cátedra, 1983);

Actas del Congreso Internacional sobre el Modernismo Español e Hispanoamericano (Córdoba: Diputación Provincial, 1985);

Las armas abisinias (Barcelona: Anthropos, 1989);

Música para fuegos de artificio (Madrid: Hiperión, 1989);

Divisibilidad indefinida (Seville: Renacimiento, 1990);

La literatura al día. Vademécum metodológico y bibliográfico (Valencia: Consegería de Cultura, 1990).

OTHER: *Vicente Martínez Colomer, El Valdemaro (1792)*, edited by Carnero (Alicante, Spain: Instituto de Estudios Juan Gil-Albert, 1985);

Ignacio de Luzán, *Obras raras y desconocidas*, volume 1, edited by Carnero (Zaragoza, Spain: Instituto Fernando el Católico, 1990);

Gaspar Zavala y Zamora, *Obras narrativas: La Eumenia; Oderay*, edited by Carnero (Barcelona: Sirmio, 1990);

Pedro Montengón, *Eudoxia, El Rodrigo, Odas*, edited by Carnero (Alicante, Spain: Ediciones Quinto Centenario, 1990).

TRANSLATIONS: William Beckford, *Vathek*, translated, with a prologue, by Carnero (Barcelona: Siruela, 1969);

Vladimir Holand, *Una noche con Hamlet y otros poemas*, translated, with a prologue, by Carnero and Josef Frobelsky (Barcelona: Barral, 1970);

Theophile Gautier, *Espirita*, translated, with a prologue, by Carnero (Barcelona: Edhasa, 1971).

When Guillermo Carnero's *Dibujo de la muerte* (A Drawing of Death) was published in 1967, critics immediately pointed out the sharp difference separating this book from the mainstream of postwar Spanish poetry. From 1939, the year the civil war ended, until the second half of the 1960s, poetry in Spain dealt mostly with social topics. In his theoretical *Anatomía del realismo* (Anatomy of Realism), playwright Alfonso Sastre summarizes the aesthetic creed of this period when he states that social discourse is given preference over artistic discourse. Individual exceptions to this general orientation are rare in Spanish letters (Jaime Gil de Biedma, Claudio Rodríguez, José Angel Valente, Francisco Brines), and the practice of nonsocial poetry was generally reduced to underground groups such as "Cántico" (Canticle), an excellent and almost unknown group of Andalusian poets to whom Carnero paid tribute in a book-length study published in 1976.

Considering the social aspects of life superior to the artistic, Spanish poets during the 1950s and 1960s wrote a poetry that, at best, attempted a representation of social life and, at worst, approximated political diatribe. In fact, in its most radical form, social poetry was understood as one more activity contributing to the class struggle against social inequalities and political injustice. It was thus perceived as one of the ways to march toward final liberation from any type of social exploitation. Gabriel Celaya's poem titled "La poesía es un arma cargada de futuro" (Poetry Is a Weapon Loaded with the Future) may be considered as an extreme example of this type of literature. In this poem, form, rhetorical elaboration, and careful attention to language are considered of secondary importance and thus disregarded as purely elitist concerns.

The generation entering the literary scene in the second half of the 1960s was radically opposed to this understanding of poetry. Carnero may be considered the most outspoken member of this generation in the exposition of the new artistic creed. During the 1960s and 1970s he did not hesitate to enter into polemics with other authors, and he expressed his artistic ideas in daily newspapers (such as *Pueblo, Informaciones, Camp de l'Arpa*, and *Las Provincias*) and literary magazines (*Insula, Cuadernos Hispanoamericanos*, and *Revista de Occidente*). In these articles, he established the main differences separating early postwar Spanish poets from the members of his own generation. In one little-known but significant article of 1979, titled "Por un arte no autoritario" (Toward a Non-Authoritarian Art), he summarizes the new writers' attitudes toward former artistic forms as well as the new authors' understanding of what poetry should be in the present. The article was first published in Valencia and later in *Módulo 3*, a literary magazine published by students at the Universidad Autónoma in Madrid. Carnero writes against the narrow realism of prior generations, stating that the realists' understanding of art is an aggression against both the intelligence and the sensibility of the individual, for it forces the reader passively to accept the message given by the author. This situation creates in the reader a habit that Carnero equates to a mental deformity, for this procedure can be used to subject readers who accept literature with no critical attitude to any totalitarian ideology. In addition, Carnero rejects the basic principles set out by Sastre and other members of the immediate postwar generation, arguing that social poets, while apparently investing poetry with a transcendental message, actually dispossessed the work of art of its most basic attributes, namely the artistic. Carnero therefore senses the need to march in the opposite direction, explicitly disclaiming any kind of socially transcendental meaning for literature while claiming the importance of the work of art as art. A poem is not to be understood as a representation of life and society, as the realis-

FANTASÍA DE UN AMANECER
DE INVIERNO

"A point in space is an
argument place"
WITTGENSTEIN
Tractatus 2.0131

El tiempo anida en el color

y la memoria intuye límites
en el descubrimiento de la línea

y los tonos del aire configuran
una definición de la distancia,
miden con su cadencia y su retorno
los de las estaciones del discurso.

Así en el horizonte se refracta
un cortejo de imágenes vencidas
que desde el otro lado del cristal
encarnan en espíritu de nieve

o en la esfumada luz, gélida y limpia,
emergen de debajo de la alfombra
para con su murmullo decir
la vertical propagación del aire.

Page from the manuscript for Carnero's "Fantasía de un amanecer de invierno" (Fantasy of a Winter Dawn; from Peña Labra: Pliegos de Poesía, *Summer 1979; by permission of Guillermo Carnero)*

tic doctrines of the past maintained, but it should be thought of as a linguistic construct that has inherited a cultural tradition to which it belongs; it is not a representation of reality in the narrow sense intended by Celaya or Sastre but a part of life in the fullest sense of the expression, thereby including intellectual preoccupations, concerns about cultural inheritance, old and new mythologies, and so on. Finally, since the poem is no longer perceived as the mirror reflection of a life experience but as an experience in itself, "biographism" is carefully avoided and the poetic text stands by itself as a new reality, as Carnero told José Luis Jover in a 1979 interview.

The initial manifestations of these new attitudes toward art were not of a theoretical nature. They were books of poetry that immediately impressed critics because of the rigorous use of language and the careful attention paid to the formal qualities of the artistic work. Pere Gimferrer's *Arde el mar* (The Sea Burns), published in 1966, was the first example of the new poetry. Carnero's *Dibujo de la muerte* appeared a few months later. And more such books soon followed, testifying to the strength and general scope of this new poetic sentiment among young writers. Among the most significant are Félix de Azúa's *Cepo para nutria* (Otter Box), Marcos Ricardo Barnatán's *Los pasos perdidos* (The Lost Steps), Leopoldo María Panero's *Por el camino de Swan* (By the Road of the Swan), Antonio Carvajal's *Tigres en el jardín* (Tigers in the Garden), all of them published in 1968, and Antonio Colinas's *Preludios a una noche total* (Preludes to a Total Night) and Jaime Siles's *Génesis de la luz* (Birth of the Light), published in 1969. Finally, in 1970, the Catalan critic José María Castellet edited his important anthology *Nueve novísimos poetas españoles* (Nine Newest Spanish Poets). Although this selection has been widely criticized for its unpardonable omissions (he does not include any author that did not live in Barcelona at that time, and Carvajal, Colinas, and Siles are among the major names omitted from the selection), it meant, nonetheless, public recognition of the existence of a new generation of Spanish poets. For many years this generation has been known as the *Novísimos* in direct reference to Castellet's terminology. However, the more accurate term "Generation of 1970" and the more encompassing one of "Post-Modern Poets" are gaining acceptance among readers and critics.

The dominant and perhaps most innovative aspect of Carnero's first book is the notion that a work of art may not be taken as a supplement for the absences in life. Art and life, said José Ortega y Gasset in *La deshumanización del arte* (The Dehumanization of Art, 1925), are realities of a different nature and should be neither mixed nor confused. Carnero intensifies this dichotomy by asserting that art not only is different from life but can only capture life in linguistic terms once the living experience is over. Hence, life is lost in the distance imposed by artistic representation. The title of his book—*Dibujo de la muerte*—specifically refers to this distance metaphorically as "dibujo." This initial notion of the work of art is of fundamental importance to future developments in Carnero's poetry, namely his evolution toward metapoetry. His distance concept is perhaps best illustrated in "Capricho en Aranjuez" (Caprice in Aranjuez), one of the most representative poems of his first book:

Raso amarillo a cambio de mi vida.
Los bordados doseles, la nevada
palidez de las sedas. Amarillos
y azules y rosados terciopelos y tules
y ocultos por las telas recamadas
plata, jade y sutil marquetería.
Fuera breve vivir. Fuera una sombra
o una fugaz constelación alada.
Geométricos jardines. Aletea
el hondo trasminar de las magnolias.
Difumine el balcón, ocúlteme
la bóveda de umbría enredadera.
Fuera hermoso morir. Inflorescencias
de mármol en la reja encadenada:
perpetua floración de las columnas
Y un niño ciego juega con la muerte.
Fresquísimo silencio gorgotea
de las corolas de la balaustrada.
Cielo de plata gris. Frío granito
y un oculto arcaduz iluminado.
Deserten los bruñidos candelabros
entre calientes pétalos y plumas.
Trípodes de caoba, pebeteros
o delgado cristal. Doce relojes
tintinean las horas al unísono.
Juego de piedra y agua. Desenlacen
sus cendales los faunos. En la caja
de fragante peral están brotando
punzantes y argentinas pinceladas.
Músicas en la tarde. Crucería,
polícromo cristal. Dejad, dejadme
en la luz de esta cúpula que riegan
las transparentes brasas de la tarde.
Poblada soledad, raso amarillo
a cambio de mi vida.

(Yellow satin in exchange for my life.

Embroidered canopies, the snowy
pallor of silks. Yellow
and blue and pink velvets and tulles
and, hidden by fretted cloths,
silver, jade and subtle inlay.
How short life would be. A shadow
or a fleeting, winged constellation.
Geometrical gardens. The deep
uprooting of magnolias begins to palpitate.
Let the balcony blur, the shadowed bower hide me.
How beautiful to die. Marble
blossomings on the chained grate:
perpetual florescence on the columns
and a blind child plays with death.
Freshest silence gurgling
from corollas on the balustrade.
Silver-grey sky. Cold granite
and a hidden conduit lighted.
Let the burnished candelabra
fade among warm petals and feathers.
Mahogany trivets, censers,
or delicate crystal. Twelve clocks
chime the hours in unison.
Play of stone and water. Let the fauns
loosen their gauzy veils. Silvery, tapered brush
  strokes
sprout from the fragrant pear-wood box.
Music in the afternoon. Gothic arch,
polychrome glass. Leave me, leave me
in the light of this dome watered
by the transparent coals of the afternoon.
Peopled solitude, yellow satin
in exchange for my life [translation by Frederick
  Fornoff].)

The title of the poem evokes eighteenth- and nineteenth-century artistic representations, be it pictorial as in Goya's *caprichos* or musical as in Nikolay Rimsky-Korsakov's *Capriccio espagnol* (1887). In any case, it deals with a genre dominated by fantasy, a genre in which reason, as in Goya's paintings, has been put to sleep. Furthermore, the mention of the neoclassical village of Aranjuez insists on this eighteenth-century evocation. The speaker of the poem contemplates an artistic representation, just as the reader does.

There is contrast between the speaker's time in the poem and the time of the artistic representation. For, while the time of the representation is perennial and the poem as representation lives in an eternal present, the narrator of the poem as well as the poet are perishable. The written poem is permanent, for it has been written and published in order to endure. Its author, on the contrary, is subject to variation and time. Thus, being in different time sequences, the speaker of the poem can only relate to the artistic representa-

tion, to the permanent character of the written word, by longing to unite with it, as expressed in the imperative forms and through the substitution of life for its representation, as it is expressed in the initial and last lines of the poem.

However, the substitution does not re-create life but, rather differently, reproduces life as language. The poem, then, is not a resurrection of what died in the process, namely the living experience already lived and spent, but a renaissance of the initial experience in language. This notion of distance, and the distinction between resurrection and renaissance, may be better understood by establishing an analogy between Carnero, as well as some other poets of the 1970s, on the one hand, and, on the other, Raoul Vaneighem—author of *Traité du savoir vivre à l'usage des jeunes générations* (1967)—and Guy Debord, who wrote *La Société du Spectacle* (1974) and whose ideas were of seminal importance in the student movement of 1968. In fact, the opening remark in Debord's book—"Tout ce qui était directment vécu s'est éloigné dans une représentation"—may be used to explain the aforementioned notion of "renaissance" of the experience in the linguistic representation of the poem: what is initially lived later becomes, not a resurrection of life itself, but written language in the poem. In Debord's terminology this process (or distance) is called a "représentation"; Carnero, as mentioned, refers to it as "dibujo de la muerte."

The poet's awareness of the distance that separates art from reality determines his evolution toward a more dense and self-conscious discourse in his 1971 book, *El sueño de Escipión* (The Dream of Scipio). The term *metapoetry* is often used to refer to this and Carnero's subsequent books of poetry. A metapoem is one in which the author deliberately breaks the imaginary line separating the text as artistic construct from the text as a critical examination upon that construct, and metapoetry is the poetic discourse in which the theme—or, at least, one of the themes—is the meditation about the action of writing and the relationship between author, text, and public. Hence, a metapoem consists simultaneously of two different levels: first, a level formed by what is commonly considered a poem; and, second, one that contains a meditation on the nature, origin, and conventions of the first.

Carnero's poem "Mira el breve minuto de la rosa" (Consider the Brief Moment of the Rose), last of the "figures" in *Variaciones y figuras sobre un tema de La Bruyére* (Variations and Figures on a

Guillermo Carnero

Theme of La Bruyére, 1974), perfectly illustrates
the existence of these two levels:

Mira el breve minuto de la rosa.
Antes de haberla visto sabías ya su nombre
y ya los batintines de tu léxico
aturdían tus ojos—luego, al salir al aire, fuiste
    inmune
a lo que no animara en tu memoria
la falsa herida en que las cuatro letras
omiten esa mancha de color: la rosa tiembla, es
    tacto.
Si llegaste a advertir lo que no tiene nombre
regresas luego a dárselo, en él ver: un tallo mondo,
    nada;
cuando otra se repite y nace pura
careces de más vida, tus ojos no padecen agresión
    de la luz,
sólo una vez son nuevos.

(Consider the brief minute of the rose.
Even before you saw it, you knew its name
and the gongs of your lexicon had stunned your
    eyes;
then, when you walked out into the air,

you were immune to what could not be revived in
    your memory
by the false wound where those four letters fail
to convey that bright stain: the rose trembles, is
    touch.
If you happened to notice what has no name
you hurry back to give it one, seeking to see in it: a
    plain stem, nothing;
when another comes along and is born pure
you lack further life, your eyes suffer
no further aggression of the light,
they're only new once [translation by Fornoff].)

The poem is a meditation on a well-known poetic metaphor, the rose, taken as a substitute for
life, beauty, and poetry itself. The knowledge of
this traditional metaphor constitutes the first
level of the poem (line 2). This knowledge is
shared by author and reader, both contained in
the second-person pronoun *you*. The second level
deals with the limits of poetic experience. Specifically it suggests that it is precisely because there exists that common knowledge prior to the writing
or reading of the new poem, that both poet and
reader are unable to count this new metaphor as
an additional discovery (lines 3-7). The new
poem is a mere supplement to all that has already been said; it fills a void or it creates a new fiction (lines 8-9) that fails to modify the subject.
Carnero's metapoetry is the final outcome of his
awareness that words are veils or echoes constantly naming a void: "creemos haber vivido
porque el poema existe; / lo que parece un origen es una nada, un eco" (we think we did live because the poem does exist; but what looks like an
origin is a void, an echo).

When the young writers of the 1970s began
publishing their first books of poetry, they could
not find an awareness of poetic language among
the vast majority of postwar Spanish authors.
The mainstream of postwar poetry in Spain was directed against the political system and the inhu-
man social conditions. Authors were aware of the
system against which they rebelled, but language
was for them a tool—Celaya, for instance, talks
about the "poesía herramienta" ("poetry-tool").
Thus, in the second half of the 1960s, authors
such as Carnero expressed the conviction that
they must begin from ground zero and elaborate
an awareness of poetic language. His 1979 poetry collection, *Ensayo de una teoría de la visión*
(Essay on a Theory of Vision), may be thus considered in this respect an individual attempt to develop this awareness. The book begins with a notion of the poetic word that appears subsumed in

night and silence. It grows as a conciousness of the distance imposed by language and literature. And it concludes with the discovery that words are the final outcome of the poetic activity: "no hay más que la palabra / al final de viaje" (There is no more than the word / at the end of the journey).

Interview:

José Luis Jover, "Nueve preguntas a Guillermo Carnero," *Nueva Estafeta*, 9-10 (1979): 148-153.

References:

Carlos Bousoño, "La poesía de Guillermo Carnero," introduction to *Ensayo de una teoría de la visión. Poesía 1966-1977* (Madrid: Peralta-Hiperión, 1979), pp. 11-68; reprinted, with additions, in Bousoño's *Poesía poscontemporánea* (Madrid: Júcar, 1984);

Francisco Brines, "Integración del título en el poema," *Insula*, 310 (1972): 4;

Mirta Camandone de Cohen, "Asedio a la poesía de Guillermo Carnero," *Hispanic Journal*, 7, no. 1 (1985): 123-129.

José María Castellet, *Nueve novísimos poetas españoles* (Barcelona: Barral, 1970);

Andrew P. Debicki, "Metapoetry," *Revista Canadiense de Estudios Hispánicos*, 7, no. 2 (1983): 297-301;

Joaquín González Muela, "Dos poemas de Guillermo Carnero," in *Poemas y ensayos para un homenaje*, edited by W. F. King (Madrid: Tecnos, 1976), pp. 80-84;

José Olivio Jiménez, *Diez años de poesía española* (Madrid: Insula, 1972);

Ignacio Javier López, "Ironía, distancia y evolución en Guillermo Carnero," *Insula*, 408 (1980): 1, 10;

López, "Language and Consciousness in the Poetry of the 'Novisimos': Carnero's Latest Poetry," in *Studies in Twentieth-Century Literature*, edited by Debicki (Lawrence: University of Kansas Press, 1991);

López, "Metapoesía en Guillermo Carnero," *Zarza Rosa, revista de poesía*, 5 (1985): 37-56;

López, "Metonimia y negación: *Variaciones y figuras sobre un tema de La Bruyére* de Guillermo Carnero," *Hispanic Review*, 54 (1985): 257-277;

López, "El olvido del habla: reflexiones en torno a la metapoesía," *Insula*, 505 (1989): 17-18;

López, "El silencio y la piedra: metáforas de la tradición en la poesía española de hoy," *Bulletin of Hispanic Studies* (January 1990);

José Luis Ramos, "Meditación sobre las contrariedades del azar (Guillermo Carnero)," *Ideologies and Literature*, 1, nos. 1-2 (1985): 207-217;

César Simon, "Fracaso y triunfo del lenguaje de Guillermo Carnero," *Papeles de Son Armadans*, 83, no. 249 (1976): 249-263.

Gabriel Celaya

(18 March 1911 - 18 April 1991)

Shirley Mangini
California State University, Long Beach

BOOKS: *Marea del silencio* (Zarauz, Spain: Itxaropena, 1935);

Tentativas (Madrid: Adán, 1946);

La soledad cerrada (San Sebastián: Norte, 1947);

Movimientos elementales (San Sebastián: Norte, 1947);

Tranquilamente hablando, as Juan de Lecita (San Sebastián: Norte, 1947);

Objetos poéticos (Valladolid, Spain: Halcón, 1948);

Lázaro calla (Madrid: S. G. E. de L., 1949);

El principio sin fin (Córdoba: Cántico, 1949);

Se parece al amor (Las Palmas, Canary Isles: Arca, 1949);

Las cosas como son (Santander, Spain: Isla de los Ratones, 1949);

Deriva (Alicante, Spain: Ifach, 1950);

El arte como lenguaje (Bilbao: Ediciones de Conferencias y Ensayos, 1951);

Las cartas boca arriba (Madrid: Rialp/Adonáis, 1951);

Lo demás es silencio (Barcelona: Furest/Cucuyo, 1952);

Ciento volando, by Celaya and Amparo Gastón (Madrid: Nebli, 1953);

Paz y concierto (Madrid: Pájaro de Paja, 1953);

Vía muerta (Barcelona: Alcor, 1954);

Coser y cantar, by Celaya and Gastón (Guadalajara, Spain: Doña Endrina, 1955);

Cantos iberos (Alicante, Spain: Verbo, 1955);

De claro en claro (Madrid: Rialp/Adonáis, 1956);

Pequeña antología poética (Santander, Spain: Cigarra, 1957);

Entreacto (Madrid: Agora, 1957);

Las resistencias del diamante (Mexico City: Luciérnaga, 1957);

Música celestial, by Celaya and Gastón (Cartagena: Baladre, 1958);

Cantata en Aleixandre (Madrid: Papeles de Son Armadans, 1959);

El corazón en su sitio (Caracas: Lírica Hispana, 1959);

Poesía y verdad (Pontevedra, Spain: Litoral, 1959);

Para vosotros dos (Bilbao, Spain: Alrededor de la Mesa, 1960);

Gabriel Celaya

Penúltimas tentativas (Madrid: Arión, 1960);

Poesía urgente (Buenos Aires: Losada, 1960);

Homenatge a todó (Barcelona: Horta, 1961);

La buena vida (Santander, Spain: Isla de los Ratones, 1961);

Los poemas de Juan de Leceta (Barcelona: Literaturasa/Colliure, 1961);

L'Espagne en marche, translated into French by François Lopez (Paris: Seghers, 1961);

Rapsodia euskara (San Sebastián: Biblioteca Vascongada de los Amigos del País, 1961);

Lo uno y lo otro (Barcelona: Seix Barral, 1962);

Poesía (1934-61) (Madrid: Giner, 1962);

Episodios nacionales (Paris: Ruedo Ibérico, 1962);

Mazorcas (Palencia, Spain: Rocamador, 1962);

El relevo [play] (San Sebastián: Gora, 1963);

Versos de otoño (Jerez, Spain: Grupo Atalaya/Venencia, 1963);

Dos cantatas (Madrid: Revista de Occidente, 1964);

Exploración de la poesía (Barcelona: Seix Barral, 1964);

La linterna sorda (Barcelona: Bardo, 1964);

Baladas y decires vascos (Barcelona: Bardo, 1965);

Los buenos negocios (Barcelona: Seix Barral, 1965);

Lo que faltaba (Barcelona: Bardo, 1967);

Poemas de Rafael Múgica (Bilbao, Spain: Comunicación Literaria de Autores, 1967);

Los espejos transparentes (Madrid: Bardo, 1968);

Canto en lo mío (Madrid: Ciencia Nueva/Bardo, 1968);

Poesías completas (Madrid: Aguilar, 1969);

Lírica de cámara (Barcelona: Bardo, 1969);

Operaciones poéticas (Madrid: Corazón/Visor, 1971);

Cien poemas de amor (Barcelona: Plaza & Janés, 1971);

Campos semánticos (Zaragoza, Spain: Javalambre/Fuendetodos, 1971);

Inquisición de la poesía (Madrid: Taurus, 1972);

La voz de los niños (Barcelona: Laia, 1972);

Gustavo Adolfo Bécquer (Madrid: Júcar, 1972);

Dirección prohibida (Buenos Aires: Losada, 1973);

Función de uno, equis, ene (Zaragoza, Spain: Javalambre/Fuendetodos, 1973);

El derecho y el revés (Barcelona: Sinera/Ocnos, 1973);

Los espacios de Chillida (Barcelona: Polígrafa, 1974);

Itinerario poético (Madrid: Cátedra, 1975);

La higa de Arbigorriya (Madrid: Visor, 1975);

Buenos días, Buenas noches (Madrid: Hiperión, 1976);

Poesía abierta (Madrid: Doncel, 1976);

El hilo rojo (Madrid: Visor, 1977);

Parte de guerra (Barcelona: Laia, 1977);

Poesía, edited by Angel González (Madrid: Alianza, 1977);

Poesías completas, edited by José María Valverde, (Barcelona: Laia, 1977-1980);

Iberia sumergida (Pamplona: Peralta/Hiperión, 1978);

Memorias inmemoriales (Madrid: Cátedra, 1980);

Penúltimos poemas (Barcelona: Seix Barral, 1982);

Cantos y mitos (Madrid: Visor, 1984);

Trilogía vasca (San Sebastián: Guipúzcoa, 1984);

El mundo abierto (Madrid: Hiperión, 1986);

Ritos y farsas: La obra teatral completa (San Sebastián: Txertoa, 1989).

Edition in English: *The Poetry of Gabriel Celaya*, translated by Betty Jean Craige (Lewisburg, Pa.: Bucknell University Press / London: Associated University Presses, 1984).

OTHER: *Castilla, a Cultural Reader*, edited by Celaya and Phyllis Turnbull (New York: Appleton-Century-Crofts, 1960).

TRANSLATIONS: Rainer Maria Rilke, *Cincuenta poemas franceses* (San Sebastián: Norte, 1947);

William Blake, *El libro de Urizen* (San Sebastián: Norte, 1947);

Arthur Rimbaud, *Una temporada en el infierno* (San Sebastián: Norte, 1947);

Paul Eluard, *Quince poemas* (Guadalajara, Spain: Doña Endrina, 1954).

Gabriel Celaya arrived on the literary scene before the Spanish Civil War broke out in 1936. Yet his fame stems mainly from his so-called social poetry of the late 1940s and the 1950s, the years of rebellion by the majority of Spanish intellectuals, who felt that they could no longer turn their backs on the social and political injustice that had prevailed since the end of the civil war. Celaya can serve as a paradigm of the evolution of twentieth-century Spanish poetry, since his work displays the influences of symbolism, romanticism, existentialism, surrealism, and experimentalism, in addition to social realism. The author of more than fifty books in less than fifty years, Celaya was, most importantly, a motivating force in the development of protest poetry in Spain. His influence on younger poets and dissident intellectuals in general during the Franco regime is essential for understanding the evolution of culture and politics of the period.

Celaya was born Rafael Gabriel Juan Múgica Celaya Leceta on 18 March 1911, the son of Ignacia Celaya Cendoya and Luis Múgica Leceta. Though his legal name was Rafael Múgica, he was to use several pen names, but Gabriel Celaya is the name by which he is commonly known. He was the product of a Catholic family of the Basque bourgeoisie in Guipúzcoa. Because of his strict upbringing, Celaya became an introspective child. He discovered poetry at an early age and found it to be a perfect escape from the adult world as well as a means for self-discovery. His paternal family was of humble origins, while his mother's family was composed of doctors, musicians, and a sprinkling of adventurers. Celaya found his mother's attentions to be oppressive and seemed to prefer his father, who, though a businessman, was progressive. Nevertheless, Celaya was destined to spend most of his childhood under the protective guidance of his mother. When he became ill at the age of twelve, he was taken out of the Colegio del Pilar—part of the most liberal grade-school system in Spain even today—and was whisked off to Pau, France, by his mother. When they returned to Spain, once the young Celaya was cured, they still lived away from his father and the family home in the Basque country. Celaya's mother rented a villa for herself and her children in the region of the Escorial, the site of a majestic monastery near Madrid.

Finally, in 1925, Celaya was permitted to return to school again. Because of his age, he was not sent back to the Pilar school but spent two years hastily completing college-preparatory school, the *bachillerato*, thereby managing to reach the educational level of other boys of his age. In 1927 Celaya went off to the University of Madrid to study engineering, the logical career for a young man whose family owned a factory and expected him to carry on the business. Thanks to his father, the young Celaya moved into the famed Residencia de Estudiantes (Student Residence), where he had contact with many of Spain's most important writers and thinkers. The Residencia had housed the most illustrious of intellectuals before the civil war, including Federico García Lorca, Salvador Dalí, Luis Buñuel, Juan Ramón Jiménez, and José Ortega y Gasset. During the eight years Celaya lived in the Residencia, he had contact with many writers such as Jiménez and Pablo Neruda, the Chilean bard. Celaya's stay there was to be a turning point in his life; his engineering career quickly became a second concern to him because of his literary interests. His future poetic work was enormously influenced by the ideas and styles of poets with whom he had personal contact and even by those who had lived and worked in the Residencia before his arrival.

Also essential for his literary career were his summer vacations in 1928 and 1929 in Tours, France. Celaya's father arranged for him to spend two summers in France, which afforded him the opportunity to become familiar with foreign literature and further convinced him of his dedication to poetry. His landlady in Tours was an aristocrat, Olga Prot de Viéville, who encouraged him to read the French classics. In addition,

Drawing of Celaya by Alvarez Ortega (from Rafael Millán, Veinte Poetas Españoles, 1955)

it was in Tours that Celaya encountered the works of several writers who would most heavily influence his first poems and even many of his later ones: the German Romantics, such as Friedrich Hölderlin, and Celaya's favorite German writers, Johann Wolfgang von Göethe and Friedrich Nietzsche. About this time Celaya also discovered the French surrealists, though the surrealist style came to him even more insistently by way of the Spanish poets of the Generation of 1927, above all from Lorca, Vicente Aleixandre, Rafael Alberti, Moreno Villa, and Gerardo Diego, and their friend and companion Neruda, who lived in Madrid in the mid 1930s.

Celaya returned to San Sebastián to begin his career in the family business, Herederos de Ramón Múgica (Heirs to Ramón Múgica), in 1935; this was also the year of the publication of his first book of poetry, *Marea del silencio* (Tide of Silence). This first volume was the obvious product of the young poet who had lived those eight years in Madrid immersed in the literary life of one of Spain's most brilliant cultural periods—often called the Edad de Plata, or Age of Silver (in comparison with the seventeenth century's Siglo de Oro, or Golden Age, considered the most important cultural period in Spain's history). The administrators of the family business found the poet-engineer to be a source of public embarrassment. How could an industrial engineer and a company manager be taken seriously if he engaged in an activity as frivolous as writing poetry? Celaya was not convinced by their protests, but he did acquiesce to their demands by changing his writing name from Múgica to Celaya. So it was that the engineer Múgica and the poet Celaya managed to coexist for the next few years without ruining the family business or damaging his literary career.

Celaya continued to write under his new pen name and in 1936 won his first literary prize, the Bécquer Centennial, for his second book of poetry, *La soledad cerrada* (Enclosed Solitude, 1947). So encouraged by his literary success and the inner satisfaction it provided him, in contrast to that derived from his engineering duties, he decided to leave the family business in 1936 and set off for Madrid once again. But just as the Spanish Civil War was to change the destiny of hundreds of thousands of other Spaniards, Celaya's plans were also thwarted by it. Celaya was drafted into the Republican army, all copies of his first book were destroyed during a bombing, and his prize-winning *La soledad cerrada* was not immediately published by the Aguilar press as had been planned (finally being published by Norte over ten years later).

Before the war ended, Celaya had fought for both sides, a traumatic experience to which many soldiers were subject; taken prisoner, he was made to fight on the side of the Franco forces. When Celaya returned home in 1938, before the end of the war, he found that Spanish culture had been swallowed up by the strife. His literary friends had disappeared; they had either died in the war or, more commonly, had gone into exile. Books from foreign countries were no longer circulating in Spain; others were taken off the bookshelves by the omnipresent censors. The disappearance of surrealist literature and of many members of the Generation of 1927 especially disturbed Celaya, since in those years surrealism was the prevailing influence on his work. He married in 1938 and returned to the family firm in 1939. Though he continued to write (above all, he was working on a somewhat surrealistic and mythical book of memoirs, *Tentativas*, which

he finally published in 1946), during those immediate postwar years from 1939 to 1946 he did not publish anything.

Celaya's years of silence were like those of many intellectuals of his generation. It was a time of existential reticence, when intellectuals who did not agree with the politics of the regime remained in a state of obstinate silence. Many of them turned toward their families for consolation; poets who published in this period generally wrote of love, religious themes, and other stuff of traditional romantic poetry. It was a time of sorrow, and an extreme sense of demoralization enveloped the country. Celaya was greatly affected by this desolate atmosphere.

In 1945 he plunged into a state of depression that affected both his physical and mental well-being. He no longer found consolation in his personal life or his profession as an industrial engineer. But in 1946 his life changed entirely. He met Amparo Gastón, the woman who was to become his lifelong companion. His mental crisis ended, and he plunged back into his literary work with renewed enthusiasm. Together with Gastón, he founded in San Sebastian a small publishing house called Norte. By means of this new project, Celaya managed to publish much of his own work in the years that followed and also to recuperate lost classics, thus helping to revitalize the poverty-stricken cultural scene. Norte published the work of foreign authors such as Rainer Maria Rilke, William Blake, and Arthur Rimbaud, all of which Celaya translated. At that time, he established himself as one of the most active cultural agents among dissident intellectuals. He attributes this rebirth and renewed interest entirely to the encouragement and enthusiasm of Gastón. From 1948 to 1954 Celaya wholeheartedly contributed to the effort to reverse the death sentence the regime had pronounced on Spanish letters. Also in this period, Celaya initiated his career as one of Spain's most prolific writers, while he continued to work in the family firm. His energy and dedication were in sharp contrast to his former cultural inactivity.

Celaya's first books of poetry deal with existential themes, yet the style is reminiscent of Neruda's surrealist form of expression in *Residencia en la tierra* (Residence on Earth, 1932). *Marea del silencio* was written while Celaya lived in the Residencia de Estudiantes and clearly shows signs of his contact with Jiménez and the Generation of 1927. The book celebrates the vitality of nature in an exalted tone. Similar to the surrealist personification of nature in Lorca's *Romancero gitano* (1929; translated as *Gypsy Ballads*, 1951) are some poems in *Marea del silencio*, such as "La noche peina pausada" (The Night Slowly Combs), which includes these lines: "La noche peina pausada / sus trenzas largas y verdes; / huyen por las playas—soledad cuadrada— / mujeres de plata con ojos de nieve" (The night slowly combs / its long green braids; / through the plazas—square solitude— / flee silver women with eyes of snow).

Celaya's *La soledad cerrada* reveals a more individualistic voice and marks the colloquial fluidity that was to characterize his later social poetry. This book is also representative of another tendency in much of his work: the oscillation between joy and sorrow, desperation and hope, ironic distance and uncontrolled vehemence. Celaya's extreme moods, which he reflects in much of his poetry, were explained by him in an interview with Sharon Keefe Ugalde in her 1978 book *Gabriel Celaya*: "You see me now and I am noisy—How happy! How open! But I am a man of tremendous lows. However, I am always fighting against them. Looking at this oscillation in perspective, I see it almost as a cycle. I die and am resurrected—I mean, of course, in the sense of depression and the overcoming of it. The process is a completely conscious one. In fact, it is my obsession. I die and am resurrected just as I inhale and exhale, as if it were a type of vital rhythm."

La soledad cerrada is more densely lyrical than *Marea del silencio*. Celaya attempts to transcend the mysteries of life and death, and to break the barriers of humankind's limited understanding of existence.

Yet Celaya was to abandon this anxious search for self-knowledge in his subsequent books of 1947 and 1948, and he became simpler in his existential expression. It may be remembered that, before 1947, Celaya's mental state was very precarious, and he even considered suicide. This crisis is visible in the poems written in 1945 and 1946 when the poet expresses the emptiness of life and tragic sense of isolation he feels vis à vis the rest of the world. Yet in the books that follow—*Movimientos elementales* (Elementary Movements, 1947), for example—Celaya seems to find consolation in nature, the trivial activities of life, and the simple pleasures that communication with other human beings provides. The books immediately following *La soledad cerrada* represent an attempt to break loose from the lonely anguish of his crisis and to seek new mean-

ing through contact with others, forecasting the sense of hope for solidarity that his future social poetry was to express. There is an obvious tone of discovery in his 1947-1948 works—a tone of love, a sense of self, and a newly encountered humanism that erased the negative effects of war, his regimented life-style, and the mental crisis and alienation the poet had experienced before 1946. The effects of Celaya's new life, his encounter with Gastón, and their new literary endeavors are highly visible in his poetry after 1946.

In the most admired book of this period, *Tranquilamente hablando* (Calmly Speaking, 1947), Celaya tells of his poetic objectives. In a poem ironically titled "Mi intención es sencilla (difícil)" (My Intention Is Simple [Difficult]), he says: "No quisiera hacer versos; quisiera solamente contar lo que me pasa" (I don't want to compose verses; I just would like to talk about what is happening to me). And he does just that, expressing his feelings about the imperfection of the dehumanized world. But his own search for communion with others is a constructive and optimistic response to the effects of an indifferent world.

Tranquilamente hablando is clearly a break with the past. Its direct and colloquial style illustrates a visible desire to communicate Celaya's moods and mundane activities with sincerity and simplicity. It marks the style that was to characterize much of his social poetry: long, rambling, conversational, rhymeless verses. His intention was obviously to make a statement against the rigidly formalistic and idealistic nature of official poetry, which in those years abounded and which Celaya had begun to abhor. Above all, *Tranquilamente hablando*—published under the pseudonym Juan de Leceta—announces a "new" poet. The new pen name clearly signified a different focus on life and a change in Celaya's conception of poetry.

In the guise of Leceta he abandoned the symbolist and surrealist ties he had acquired from both Spanish and French poets. In a desire to break with the past, he cultivated a jocular and often ironic voice. The poems of this period provide an incessant dialogue between the protagonist of the poetry and the potential reader. "Leceta" tells stories or simply confesses his human flaws, his vulgarity, and his similarity to all other human beings with their weaknesses and failings. He laughs at himself outright on many occasions, writing in a conversational style, which could be viewed as understatement.

Celaya circa 1978

Celaya's first period represents little originality, and that factor has caused critics generally to ignore his initial volumes. Yet in his second period, that of Leceta and afterward, Celaya began to establish a voice that was to afford him the fame he acquired during the 1950s. Without the name of Gabriel Celaya, it would be difficult to explain the literary history of the social realist movement in Spain and the plight of dissident intellectuals in general.

His poems of this second period were seen as especially revolutionary by the young poets who were emerging on the literary scene, those of the Generation of the 1950s, also known as the Niños de la Guerra Civil, or Children of the Civil War. They had grown up on the most escapist form of poetry, that which the regime had endorsed since the end of the war. Many younger poets, until they read Celaya's work, had not envisioned poetry that was not written in tribute to romantic love or to some divine being. Suddenly they discovered that poetry could also speak of the stuff of everyday life, that it could be filled with irony and often self-deprecation. From 1947 on Celaya set the stage for literature of social protest; all other writing was considered frivolous

and immoral by opponents of the Franco regime. Inspired by the cultural ideology of postrevolutionary Russia, the body of Spanish literature written during the 1950s and the years that followed owes a large debt to Celaya's sparsely lyrical and highly colloquial poetry, entrenched in the tedium of life and its small, mundane pleasures.

Other books of this period, such as *El principio sin fin* (The Beginning Without End, 1949), reflect the same poetic tendencies as *Tranquilamente hablando*. Celaya's prolificity had begun. From 1947 to 1950, a period of three years, Celaya published eight books of poetry; in 1949 alone he published three of those books. Also at that time Celaya lectured and wrote incessantly in newspapers and journals, in addition to working on translations and a narrative called *Lázaro calla* (Lazarus Becomes Silent, 1949).

The year of Celaya's conversion into an explicitly political poet was 1951. The period that followed was to be the one that launched him into the role of intellectual hero, a dissident writer who in both his life and his work had committed himself to changing the world. It is for the work of this epoch that Celaya has been compared to his contemporaries Blas de Otero and José Hierro, who, nevertheless, today are considered by most critics to possess a finer poetic sensibility than Celaya.

The first book of the period, *Las cartas boca arriba* (The Cards Face Up, 1951), insists on Celaya's new commitment to his fellowman. The first poem, "A Blas de Otero," is dedicated to his friend and fellow poet and strongly endorses the sense of solidarity both poets were highlighting in their work. Celaya notes in this key poem his evolution into a poet of social conscience and his sense of kinship to poets of similar attitude. Another poem essential to the understanding of his social poetry is "A Pablo Neruda," dedicated to the equally politicized Chilean writer, whom Celaya had met during his days at the Residencia. In that poem Celaya expresses his ever-present fatigue in the face of daily tribulations but ends with his typical dual sentiment of despair-hope: "Poca alegría queda ya en esta España nuestra. / Mas, ya ves, esperamos" (Little hope remains in this Spain of ours. / But as you can see, we still have hope).

Las cartas boca arriba is a series of rambling monologues of an anecdotal nature, similar to the style of previous books. His next volume, *Lo demás es silencio* (The Rest Is Silence, 1952), deviates from this style, introducing Celaya's tendency toward dramatic poetry, which he was to utilize in many of his works from this time on. *Lo demás es silencio* is one eighty-page poem, a dialogue between a classically inspired Greek chorus and the so-called protagonist, who represents a member of the suffering masses. The protagonist's posture is that of the existential man, whose dramatic protest against the injustice of the world often takes on the tone of anguished lament, such as when he says: "Tal sin fondo es absurdo; tal júbilo, locura. / Debe haber otro mundo que pueda llamar mío / donde etcéteras mansos no me anulen cuando: / todo es uno y lo mismo. / Debe haber otro mundo, presiento o bien exijo. / Y por hombre doy gritos tremendos y sencillos, / gritos irremediables que levantan los muertos, / tienen casi sentido" (Such bottomlessness is absurd; such joy, insanity. / There should be another world that I could call mine / where tame etceteras cannot annul me when: / all is one and all is the same. / There should be another world, I have the feeling or I require it. / Because I am a man I shout tremendous and simple shouts, / hopeless shouts that raise the dead, / almost make sense.) The protagonist senses the absurd nature of his shouts, yet as always in Celaya and in general in the poetry of commitment of those years, he seeks a solution; he permits the voice of his poetry to salvage some glimmer of hope from his shipwrecked life. *Paz y concierto* (Peace and Agreement, 1953) reiterates his often-expressed feeling that "Nadie es nadie" (No one is anything) and that "Es triste ser un hombre" (It is sad to be a man). Yet once again the book ends with a happier note, similar to the considerably more cheerful tone of his *Entreacto* (Intermission, 1957).

Cantos iberos (Iberian Songs, 1955) contains the angry cry of political disconformity and is the book in which Celaya's most famous social poem is to be found: "La poesía es un arma cargada de futuro" (Poetry Is a Weapon Filled with Future). In this poem Celaya exposes his poetics and his politics of those years: "Poesía para el pobre, poesía necesaria / como el pan de cada día / como el aire que exigimos trece veces por minuto / para ser y en tanto somos dar un sí que glorifica" (Poetry for the poor man, necessary poetry / like our daily bread / like the air that we need thirteen times per minute / in order to be and in being we can pronounce a yes that glorifies). And he continues with his exegesis later: "Maldigo la poesía concebida como un lujo / cultural por los neutrales / que, lavándose las

manos, se desentienden y evaden. / Maldigo la poesía de quien no toma partido hasta mancharse" (I curse the poetry which is conceived as a / cultural luxury by the neutral ones, / those who by washing their hands, pretend not to understand and flee. / I curse the poetry that doesn't take a stand to the point of staining itself). Quite obvious in this poem is Celaya's criticism of contemporary official poetry, which had crowded the cultural scene until the arrival of social poetry.

Some of the poetry of Celaya's social period is overwrought with propagandistic declarations, and this factor has been one of the targets of critics. A few of the poems from *Cantos iberos*, for instance, are tediously repetitive, lengthy, and often-exaggerated chants to Spain's myth-ridden central power, Castile. Yet as Celaya himself has explained about this period, the justification for this sometimes-pedestrian style is that poetry in those years could only be used as a weapon with which to protest against social injustice. Sacrificing aesthetic considerations for ethical ones, Celaya and those who followed his lessons considered that it was more urgent to express moral issues than to worry about style or lyricism. This attitude, which could be characterized as moral realism, would be highly criticized in the 1960s by writers such as José María Castellet, who had earlier been an advocate of social poetry. But during the 1950s dissident intellectuals in general sympathized with Celaya's belief that "La Poesía no es un fin en sí. La Poesía es un instrumento, entre otros, para transformar el mundo" (Poetry is not an end in itself. Poetry is an instrument among others for transforming the world) as he stated in *Itinerario poético* (Poetic Itinerary, 1975).

By the mid 1950s Celaya had totally dedicated himself to social literature and underground politics. His poetry was beginning to circulate in the universities, which became hotbeds of rebellion. At this time Celaya decided to leave the family business, break ties with his family, and go off to Madrid with Gastón, by then his constant helpmate and his muse; not only did they work together in their publishing enterprise but also collaborated on books of poetry. Celaya was already well known in Madrid by the time he arrived there in 1956, the year of full-blown opposition by students and faculty in the universities of Madrid and Barcelona.

Shortly after his arrival in Madrid, Celaya won the Critic's Poetry Prize for his *De claro en claro* (From Time to Time, 1956). His home became one of the main meeting places for the intellectual sector of the clandestine Communist party. Celaya became a close friend and political associate of the screenplay writer and novelist, Jorge Semprún. (Semprún, then known as Federico Sánchez, was working in the underground and served as the cultural connection between the Paris party members in exile and those in Spain.) Also, Celaya's association with the young writers of the Generation of the Fifties—such as José Manuel Caballero Bonald and Angel González—began at this time. Celaya was to serve as the mentor for these younger writers, inspiring them in their literary careers and also in their commitment to dissident activity.

Celaya's description of this period in Madrid displays the enthusiasm and romantic spirit of solidarity that prevailed from 1956 to 1962: "cuando en 1956, ahorqué mis hábitos de ingeniero bungués, abandoné la fábrica de mi familia y me trasladé a Madrid, con el cielo arriba y la tierra abajo, como suele decirse. Eran, los años en que la poesía social estaba en auge. Los años en que mis libros mas considerados estuvieron. Los años de lucha y vida furiosa en que Amparitxu tanto me sostuvo. Y aunque fueron también los años de multas, cárcel, persecuciones y dificultades económicas son los que siempre añoraré. Porque entonces parecía que uno servía para algo" (when in 1956 I hung up my bourgeois engineer's frocks, I abandoned the factory and went off to Madrid, with the sky above and the earth below, as they say. They were the years that social poetry was at its zenith. The years in which my books were most admired. The years of battle and bohemian life in which Amparo supported me so greatly. And even though they were also the years of fines, jail, persecution, and economic difficulties they are the years for which I will always feel the most nostalgia. Because then it seemed that one served a purpose ([Itinerario poético]).

During that period, most dissident intellectuals felt the euphoria that Celaya reflects in his statements. Hope was high for the fall of the Franco regime. The universities all over Spain were buzzing with activism. As an integral member of the intellectual sector of the Communist party, Celaya served as a catalyst for many activities that on the surface appeared to be strictly cultural but which had expressly political undertones. Celaya was constantly involved in these activities. Of special importance to politicized poets were the acts of homage commemorating the life and work of the

poet Antonio Machado, considered to be one of the intellectual heroes of the opposition. The regime was always wary of these literary gatherings and did everything in its power to discourage such affairs. Celaya had constant problems with the censors and with government authorities who were aware of his opposition activities. He recounts how one of the acts of homage to Machado to be held at the University of Madrid had been suspended by the police. Celaya and other dissident poets defied the government and attended the function anyway. Students arrived in droves and applauded the bravery of the poets. In *Poesía y verdad* (Poetry and Truth, 1959) Celaya tells of his intervention: "Hasta que se levantó Gabriel Celaya y dijo lo que todo el mundo estaba esperando que se dijera y nadie decía por cobardía. Y entonces, el Paraninfo se vino abajo de ovaciones. Y se entendió por qué razones las autoridades habían querido suspender el acto" (Until Gabriel Celaya got up and said everything that everyone was waiting to hear and no one would say out of cowardice. That brought the house down. And the reasons why the authorities had been suspicious became clear).

During those early years in Madrid, Celaya continued to utilize the dramatic mode for his poetry. Several of those poems were "unpublishable" in Spain. For example, the collection *Las resistencias del diamante* (The Endurance of the Diamond, 1957), published in Mexico and Paris, was prohibited in Spain because it tells the story of members of anti-Franco resistance forces. The introductory poem, though, is not a dramatic one; it is rather a lament of the sad plight of the poet, wounded and broken in spirit. "Vías del agua" (Waterways—part of *Poesía urgente* [Urgent Poetry], 1960) and *Episodios nacionales* (National Episodes, 1962) are also poems in the dramatic style and retell events from the civil war.

Yet amidst this body of protest poetry, Celaya suddenly surprised his public with new work of a radically different style and thematic material. *De claro en claro* jubilantly celebrates love, its short poems vastly different from his longer, discursive social poetry. Several other books of shorter poems in this style followed, such as *Para vosotros dos* (For Both of You, 1960).

Celaya continued the use of dramatic elements, meanwhile, in poems such as *Cantata en Aleixandre* (Cantata on Aleixandre, 1959), where he utilizes fragments of Aleixandre's work and a Greek-style "coro de madres" (chorus of moth-

Celaya in 1987

ers). According to critics, this contrived attempt at juxtaposing the work of Aleixandre and his own is among the least successful of Celaya's books.

Celaya continued to write vociferous protest poetry with intermittent examples of other styles and themes until around 1962. It was then that he began to realize that the goal of reaching the masses and transforming the world through literature had been a utopian and quixotic endeavor. At this time most of the social-realist writers, especially those who had been members of the Communist party or had in some way contributed to its goal of using culture for protest purposes, became disillusioned. In 1963 a member of the party, Julián Grimau, was lured back to Spain, hastily tried, and garroted to death by the regime, to serve as a scandalously violent example to other dissidents. Many other political factors served to dissuade the activists from continuing their work in the underground. Critics began to

question the validity of social-realist literature, another factor that discouraged the intellectual sector of the Communist party from further attempts at fusing culture and politics. As Celaya himself later reflected in *Itinerario poético*, "el clima de furor y esperanza en que había nacido la primera poesía social se había ido extinguiendo con el paso de unos años en los que no se produjo más cambio que el de una derivación de nuestro país hacia una incipiente sociedad de consumo" (the climate of fury and hope into which the first social poetry had been born had begun to extinguish itself with the passage of time; they were years in which the only change that came about was that our country turned into an incipient society of consumerism).

Spain had finally emerged from its third-world status as an economically underdeveloped country, and this emergence strengthened the power of the regime. The masses had become obsessed with appliances, cars, and a flat of one's own. Yet the 1960s represented a new time of political dialogue among diverse dissident groups and a timid freedom of the press. But writers such as Celaya were tired of clandestinity and felt they had exhausted the overworked formulas of social realism. Younger social poets took to writing in a more ironic and oblique style than that of their literary forerunners.

From 1965 to 1968 Celaya groped for a way to resolve his distance from social realism and did so, above all, by returning to his experimental beginnings of the 1930s and 1940s. Most indicative of this return to his literary origins is *Poemas de Rafael Múgica* (1967), in which Celaya describes his existential thoughts by means of surrealist imagery.

Most of his work in this period of crisis—of both poetic and political identity—was not well received by Celaya's readers and is scarcely dealt with by the critics. The poet's reflections on the nature of art and its political functions, nevertheless, are important documents for understanding the disillusionment of writers who had abandoned their political activism in the 1960s. Yet perhaps Celaya's most important contributions to the understanding of the dissident intellectuals can be found in his nonpoetic work: essays and literary criticism in magazines and journals. Many of these have been collected in book form, and one of the most enlightening of these collections is *Poesía y verdad*.

Celaya's poetry became much more diversified in the late 1960s and early 1970s. In *Los espejos transparentes* (Transparent Mirrors, 1968), for example, the reader is taken into a purely imaginative world of fantasy; in *Lírica de cámara* (Chamber Lyrics, 1969) Celaya turns toward the nature of neutrons to show the irony of human existence. In many of his poems of this period the poet utilizes motifs from modern technology to illustrate his existential musings. In *Operaciones poéticas* (Poetic Operations, 1971) he uses the dramatic structure once again to convey a sense of desperation. *Campos semánticos* (Semantic Fields, 1971) and *Función de uno, equis, ene* (Function of 1, X, N, 1973) reveal a similar despair and ironic bitterness. The aggressive humor implicit in these works underlines his increasing feeling of the absurdity of life. Middle age, a sense of political and personal disillusionment, and a kind of literary bewilderment affected his works of this period. This sentiment finds its culmination in *La higa de Arbigorriya* (The Fig Tree of Arbigorriya, 1975), a dramatic poem about a clownish and ab-

surd character who reveals the inner self of the poet. It is one of Celaya's finest poems because of its reflective intensity.

Most critics believe, though, that Celaya's best work since his social poetry can be found in *Buenos días, buenas noches* (Good Morning, Good Night, 1976). Here he seems to arrive at a synthesis about life unachieved in earlier works. He no longer expresses the anger and frustration of failing to transcend the triviality of experiences but rather a resignation in the face of life's realities. In the first poem, "El neutro" (The Neutral One), he expresses indifference in the face of his formerly anguishing existential problems. In another poem, "La brisa" (The Breeze), he says: "Cuando parece que nada significa ya nada, / nos queda una alegría: / La falta de sentido: / la brisa" (When it seems that nothing means anything anymore / we are left with one happiness / senselessness: / the breeze). Celaya resolves the dialectics of his former oscillation between despair and joy through indifference. He reaches a maturity and peace in *Buenos días, buenas noches* that he had not achieved in the past, this poetry clearly lacking the tone of protest and existential anger prevalent in much of his former work.

Celaya continued to be a provocative and essential figure in the development of postwar literature and politics until his death. In 1977 he was a candidate for the Basque Communist party, though he was unsuccessful; his intention had been more that of gaining attention for the party than a serious interest in serving in parliament. But his candidacy was a sign of the interest that Celaya as a man and as a poet generated, especially in his Basque homeland, where he regularly spent several months out of the year. Alternating between San Sebastián and Madrid, he continued in later life to work on new editions of his work, which have sold with great success, given the comparatively large number of editions of many of his books.

In 1980 Celaya published *Memorias inmemoriales* (Unforgettable Memories), which is not so much a book of memoirs as it is an experimental stream-of-consciousness-type monologue in which he uses mythical figures to describe his own life. The edition marked his total release from the confines of realism.

In 1986 he received the Premio Nacional de las Letras Españolas (National Prize for Spanish Letters). Yet he died destitute and in a state of extreme depression after a long illness in 1991.

Gabriel Celaya, Rafael Múgica, and Juan de Leceta were the three faces of a poet whose work is essential for understanding the literature of the Spanish postwar period. A political and cultural spokesman for two generations whose work was thwarted by the confines of a repressive regime, Celaya wrote poetry that is a showcase for both the aesthetic and ethical concerns of modern Spanish literature. Celaya was always at the vanguard. He was capable of helping his disciples and of turning the heads of dissident writers, other intellectuals, students, and workers. Due to his inspired audacity and his direct and denunciatory poetry, he remains a figure of importance in Spanish letters. His total dedication to art and society as a joint enterprise in the lean years of Spanish culture made Celaya an intellectual hero of great stature.

References:

Angel González, Introduction to *Gabriel Celaya: Poesía*, edited by González (Madrid: Alianza, 1977);

José Olivio Jiménez, *Diez años de poesía española* (Madrid: Insula, 1972);

Sharon Keefe Ugalde, *Gabriel Celaya* (Boston: Twayne, 1978);

José María Valverde, Introduction to Celaya's *Poesía completas* (Madrid: Aguilar, 1969);

Tino Villanueva, *Tres poetas de posguerra: Celaya, González, y Caballero Bonald* (London: Tamesis, 1988).

Carmen Conde

(15 August 1901 -   )

Pilar Martin
St. John's University

BOOKS: *Brocal* (Madrid: Cuadernos Literarios, 1929);

Por la escuela renovada (Valencia: Embajador Vich, 1931);

Júbilos (Murcia, Spain: Sudeste, 1934);

Doña Centenito, gato salvaje (Madrid: Alhambra, 1943);

Don Juan de Austria, as Florentina del Mar (Madrid: Hesperia, 1943);

Los enredos de Chismecita, as del Mar (Madrid: Alhambra, 1943);

Pasión del verbo (Madrid: Marsiega, 1944);

Honda memoria de mí (Madrid: Romo, 1944);

La amistad en la literatura española, as del Mar (Madrid: Alhambra, 1944);

Dios en la poesía española (Madrid: Alhambra, 1944);

La poesía ante la eternidad (Madrid: Alhambra, 1944);

El Cristo de Medinaceli, as Magdalena Noguera (Madrid: Alhambra, 1944);

Vidas contra su espejo, as del Mar (Madrid: Alhambra, 1944);

Soplo que va y no vuelve, as del Mar (Madrid: Alhambra, 1944);

Aladino [play], as del Mar (Madrid: Hesperia, 1944 [i.e., 1945]);

Don Alvaro de Luna (Madrid: Hesperia, 1945);

Ansia de la gracia (Madrid: Adonais, 1945);

El santuario del Pilar, as Noguera (Madrid: Alhambra, 1945);

Mujer sin Edén (Madrid: Jura, 1947); translated by Alexis Levitin and José R. de Armas as *Woman Without Eden* (Miami: Universal, 1986);

Sea la luz (Madrid: Mensaje, 1947);

Mi fin en el viento (Madrid: Adonais, 1947);

Cartas a Katherine Mansfield (Zaragoza, Spain: Doncel, 1948);

Mi libro de El Escorial (Valladolid, Spain: Colegio Mayor Universitario de Santa Cruz, 1949);

Obras escogidas (Madrid: Plenitud, 1949);

En manos del silencio (Barcelona: Janés, 1950);

Iluminada tierra (Madrid: Privately printed, 1951);

Juan Ramón Jiménez, as del Mar (Bilbao, Spain: Conferencias & Ensayos, 1952);

Mientras los hombres mueren (Milan: Cisalpino, 1953);

Belén [play] (Madrid: ENAG, 1953);

Cobre (Madrid: Grifón, 1954 [i.e., 1953]);

Las oscuras raíces (Barcelona: Garbo, 1954 [i.e., 1953]);

Vivientes de los siglos (Madrid: Poetas, 1954);

Empezando la vida (Tétouan, Morocco: Al-Motamid, 1955);

Los monólogos de la hija (Madrid: Privately printed, 1959);

En un mundo de fugitivos (Buenos Aires: Losada, 1960);

Derribado Arcángel (Madrid: Revista de Occidente, 1960);

En la tierra de nadie (Murcia, Spain: Laurel del Sureste, 1960);

A la estrella por la cometa [play], by Conde and Antonio Oliver (Madrid: Doncel, 1961);

Los poemas del Mar Menor (Murcia, Spain: Cátedra Saavedra Fajardo/Universidad de Murcia, 1962);

Su voz le doy a la noche (Madrid: Privately printed, 1962);

Jaguar puro inmarchito (Madrid: Privately printed, 1963);

Viejo venís y florido . . . , as del Mar (Alicante, Spain: Caja de Ahorros del Sureste de España, 1963);

Acompañando a Francisca Sánchez (Managua: Mesa Redonda Panamericana, 1964);

Un pueblo que lucha y canta (Madrid: Nacional, 1967);

Obra poética (Madrid: Biblioteca Nueva, 1967);

Menéndez Pidal (Madrid: Unión, 1969);

A este lado de la eternidad (Madrid: Biblioteca Nueva, 1970);

Cancionero de la enamorada (Avila, Spain: Torro de Granito, 1971);

Gabriela Mistral (Madrid: Union, 1970);

El caballito y la luna (Madrid: C.V.S., 1974);

Corrosión (Madrid: Biblioteca Nueva, 1975);

Cita con la vida (Madrid: Biblioteca Nueva, 1976);

Días por la tierra (Madrid: Nacional, 1977);

La Rambla (Madrid: Magisterio Español / Novelas & Cuentos, 1977);

El tiempo es un río lentísimo de fuego (Barcelona: Ediciones 29, 1978);

Al encuentro de Santa Teresa (Murcia, Spain: Belmar, 1978);

Poesía ante el tiempo y la inmortalidad (Madrid: Real Academia, 1979);

Zoquetín y Martina (Barcelona: Ediciones 29, 1979);

Una niña oye una voz (Madrid: Escuela Española, 1979);

Un conejo soñador rompe con la tradición (Madrid: Escuela Española, 1979);

El mundo empieza fuera del mundo (Madrid: Escuela Española, 1979);

El Conde Sol (Madrid: Escuela Española, 1979);

Creció espesa la yerba (Barcelona: Planeta, 1979);

La noche oscura del cuerpo (Madrid: Biblioteca Nueva, 1980);

El monje y el pajarillo (Madrid: Escuela Española, 1980);

Soy la madre (Barcelona: Planeta, 1980 [i.e., 1982]);

Cuentos para niños de buena fe (Madrid: Escuela Española, 1982);

Desde nunca (Barcelona: Río Nuevo, 1982);

Derramen su sangre las sombras (Madrid: Torremozas, 1983);

Brocal y Poemas a María, edited by Rosario Hiriart (Madrid: Biblioteca Nueva, 1984);

Del obligado dolor (Madrid: Almarabu, 1984);

Cráter (Madrid: Biblioteca Nueva, 1985);

Hermosos días en China (Madrid: Torremozas, 1985);

Antología poética, edited by Hiriart (Madrid: Espasa Calpe, 1985);

La calle de los balcones azules (Barcelona: Plaza & Janés, 1985);

Canciones de nana y desvelo (Valladolid, Spain: Miñón, 1985);

Por el camino, viendo sus orillas (Esplugues de Llobregat, Spain: Plaza & Janés, 1986);

Centenito (Madrid: Escuela Española, 1987);

Cuentos del Romancero (Madrid: Escuela Española, 1987);

Cantando al amanecer (Madrid: Escuela Española, 1988).

OTHER: *Poesía femenina española viviente*, edited by Conde (Madrid: Anroflo, 1954 [i.e., 1955]);

Once grandes poetisas américohispanas, edited by Conde (Madrid: Cultura Hispánica, 1967);

Conde in 1920 (courtesy of Carmen Conde)

Poesía femenina española, 1939-1950, edited by Conde (Barcelona: Bruguera, 1967);

Antología de poesía amorosa contemporánea, edited by Conde (Barcelona: Bruguera, 1969);

Poesía femenina española, 1950-1960, edited by Conde (Barcelona: Bruguera, 1971);

Memoria puesta en el olvido, edited by Conde (Madrid: Torremozas, 1987).

Since the 1950s the name of Carmen Conde has been familiar in Spain to every well-educated person. Her election, however, as a member of the Spanish Royal Academy in 1978—two years before the French academy also elected its first woman, Marguerite Yourcenar—places her in the correct, solid position among Spanish writers, and, more specifically, female Spanish poets. With more than a half century of poetic production Conde is unquestionably one of the main influences, after Rosalía de Castro, on current women's poetry in Spain.

To ignore any part of Conde's life would be ignoring also the evolution of her writings. All her work is a direct reflection of her life, the poetic expression of her intense existence: the experience of the civil war in Spain, her personal encounter with Juan Ramón Jiménez, the death of her mother—all mark milestones in her literary production. Due to her sensitivity, any important or unimportant event could become the core of a composition. The fact that her poetry is based on her life does not mean it is all anecdotal. Her work is a continuous movement toward self-affirmation.

Her continuous literary output has made her accessible to all kinds of readers. She has published around eighty books in different genres: short stories, novels, plays, articles, poetry . . . but it is the last that has made her especially well known.

Her concern for women's poetry in Spanish has led her not only to make her own contribution but to research and compile what others have done. In 1954 her first publication in that field appeared, an anthology called *Poesía femenina española viviente* (Spanish Women's Living Poetry). Other such books soon followed: *Once grandes poetisas américohispanas* (Eleven Great American-Hispanic Women Poets, 1967); *Poesía femenina española*, 2 volumes (Women's Poetry from Spain, 1967, 1971); and *Antología de Poesía amorosa contemporánea* (Anthology of Contemporary Love Poetry, 1969). Her studies on Saint Theresa and Francisca Sánchez (Rubén Darío's companion) are also proof of her interest in reviving and making known women's literary and spiritual values.

One can find the most accurate details of her childhood in her own writings, for example in *Por el camino, viendo sus orillas* (For the Road, Seeing Its Edges): "Nací en Cartagena, puerto mediterráne, a las diez y cuarto de la noche de un jueves, día de la Asuncíon de la Virgen, 15 de agosto de 1901, en el piso principal de la casa número 4 de la calle de la Palma" (I was born in Cartagena [Spain], a Mediterranean port, at 10:15 P.M. on a Thursday, feast of the Assumption of our Lady, 15 August 1901, on the main floor of a house at 4 La Palma street).

The family of her father, Luis Conde Parreño, was from Galicia (in northwest Spain); her mother, the former María de la Paz Abellan, was from the South. The family lived in Morocco during Conde's early childhood. The country and its people made a deep impression on her; this is reflected, for instance, in her book *Júbilos*

(Rejoicings, 1934), which has a preface by her great master and friend Gabriela Mistral.

While still a teenager Conde published her first poems in a local newspaper in Cartagena, where she spent most of her later youth. She describes herself then as a dreamer in love with nature and life itself. Her passion for writing began with poetry and prose, including brief articles, a novel, and other narrative prose. Her first book, *Brocal* (Well-Stone, 1929), is a combination of both poetry and prose. The presence of the sea, which she contemplated every day from the windows of the office where she worked, is one of the constant elements in the book. It is full of passion and love based on her relationship with the man who, in 1931, would become her husband, the poet Antonio Oliver Belmás (known as Antonio Oliver). The book is also a result of her readings of the poetic prose of Jiménez and Gabriel Miró, two of the writers she most admired.

She wrote poems to Jiménez, sending them to him. He became enthusiastic about her work, helping to publish some of those poems in literary magazines. This contact brought her into the literary world.

Her husband proved to be her best critic. Oliver read her works and destroyed the poems he did not consider good enough. Carmen understood immediately and accepted this purification, as she intimates in *Obra poética* (Poetic Work, 1967).

Conde speaks about three stages in her poetic life. The first one centers on the publication of *Brocal* and of some of her poems and stories in newspapers (including *Liberal* and *Porvenir*) and magazines (such as *Si* and *Ley*). The influence of nineteenth-century Spanish novels is present, especially at the beginning of her poetic career.

The second period began with her marriage. She sees herself totally absorbed by the need to write poetry, to the exclusion of any other genre. *Júbilos* is the expression of this period. But the impact of the Spanish Civil War (1936-1939) caused a definite change in her literary production. The third stage followed the war.

At the start of her career, in 1929, Conde went to Madrid for the first time. There she contacted friends from the literary world such as Ernestina de Champourcin. In the capital Conde fulfilled one of her dreams, to meet personally with Jiménez and his wife, Cenobia. This friendship and contact continued till 1936, when the

Jiménezes left the country due to the civil war. Conde would not see them again.

Her interest in the diffusion of culture led Conde to create, together with her husband, the Universidad Popular de Cartagena (Public University of Cartagena) in 1931. This enterprise, too, would end with the start of the Spanish Civil War, though the university was finally reopened in 1981, with Conde as honorary president.

Personal tragedies arose for Conde and her family in 1934. Her first and only child, a daughter, was born dead, and Conde's father died a few months later.

In 1936 the Spanish "Junta de ampliación de estudios" (educational committee) gave Conde a grant to further her studies in education in France and Belgium. Then the Spanish Civil War radically changed her life and literary work, as she indicates in the preface to her *Ansia de la gracia* (Longing for Grace, 1945): "La tierra llena de muertos enseñaba a mis ojos un paisaje tremendo e inesperado" (The land covered with corpses presented to my eyes an incredible and astonishing landscape).

She did not really belong to either side in the war. She knew she had to fight for the truth and help the needy, no matter what it would take. For that reason she found herself "in no-man's-land," the title she gave to one of her poetry books (*En la tierra de nadie*, 1960). A new period was initiated in her literary life, where the presence of suffering would walk hand in hand with her longing for truth and light, as she says in *Por el camino*: "Nuestra guerra me hizo perder la fe en los hombres . . . si la verdad cambia de un lado a otro, ¿en qué hay que creer? Pues, en la honestidad, en el valor, en la responsabilidad y nada más" (Our war made me lose faith in humanity . . . if the truth changes from moment to moment, what are we to believe in? Honesty, courage, responsibility, and nothing else).

Many intellectuals left the country in those years. Conde and Oliver decided to remain. They had to use pseudonyms in order to continue publishing. Conde's production was intense: *Don Juan de Austria* (1943) and *Don Alvaro de Luna* (1945), two biographies written for children, were published under the pseudonym Florentina del Mar. The same name was used by Conde for two other children's works and two novels. Later on, in 1963, one finds *Viejo venís y florido* . . . under the same name, a series of ballads from the beginning of Spanish literature, learned by Carmen during her childhood in Me-

Conde with Vicente Aleixandre, 1941 (courtesy of Carmen Conde)

lilla, Morocco, from her Moorish friends.

During the civil war Oliver fought at the front for the Loyalists. *Mientras los hombres mueren* (While Men Die, 1953) is another book of poetry that reflects Conde's vivid impression of how useless wartime suffering can be. As she writes in *Por el camino: "Mientras los hombres mueren* fue escrito en un tiempo de intenso dolor por lo que la guerra destruía y seguirá destruyendo. . . . Todo dolor es inútil, lo supe entonces y lo sé mejor ahora. Y, sin embargo, decir en voz alta cuánto se está sufriendo por lo irremediable parece que borra todos los límites entre los demás y nosotros" (While Men Die was written in a time of intense suffering for all those things that war was destroying and would continue to destroy. . . . All suffering is useless, I found out then and I know it better now. And, nevertheless to say aloud how much one is suffering for the insoluble seems to erase all the boundaries that separate us from others).

Unable to go anywhere, she devoted herself intensively to reading and writing, surrounded by the blasts of bombs. Some of the poems written at this time, such as "El arcángel" (The Archangel), would later be included in *Obra poética*.

Conde was becoming a serious, respected poet. The book that sealed her reputation was *Ansia de la gracia*, published by the prestigious firm Adonais in Madrid. Two topics are especially prevalent in this collection of poems: love and destiny. The first part emphasizes a love for life and fellow creatures, and sorrow for the presence of mediocrity and lack of beauty in the world. A cosmic identification places her in a dialogue with nature and its creator. The mystical longing echoes in these lines: "Que si eres Tú mi forma, si vas a ser mi sino, / ¿qué tiempo éste que pierdo en no ser toda tuya?" (If You are my way, if You are going to be my destiny, / do I waste time not being yours completely?).

Most critics consider *Mujer sin Edén* (1947; translated as *Woman Without Eden*, 1986) one of Conde's major productions—the poems where she best interprets the eternal woman. Leaning on scriptural references, this book presents nevertheless a controversial interpretation; the image of oppressed women throughout history is the framework, according to some scholars. Others are more inclined toward a mystical interpretation based on Conde's admiration for Saint Theresa's writings.

Mujer sin Edén is divided into five cantos, with the woman always the center. Conde incarnates herself as this woman who represents all the women in the world. In spite of her constant lament based on physical suffering, readers are given as well an image of an eternal and transcendent body, as in "Contemplación": "Mi cuerpo se sueña / inextinguible y callado / cuerpo de la eternidad" (My body envisions itself / an inextinguishable and silent / body of eternity).

The mythical image of an angel participating in both heaven and earth is constant in these poems. The last one, "Súplica final de la mujer" (The Woman's Final Supplication), includes a startling request: the speaker asks that the flaming sword that led her out of Eden be thrust into her so that she will no longer bear babies who become men who hate.

Conde's view of women's poetry is no less universal than the rest of her conceptions. As she says in the special issue of *Cuadernos de Agora* devoted to her (August-October 1960): "Si yo soy poeta, el hecho de que soy mujer no debe permanecer ajeno a mi condición, y no se trata de hacer una obra estrictamente femenina, sino de enriquecer el común acervo con las aportaciones que sólo yo, en mi cualidad de mujer poeta, puedo ofrecer para iluminar una vasta zona que permanecía en el misterio" (If I am a poet, the fact of being a woman cannot be alien to my condition; it is not a matter of writing strictly feminine poetry, but to enrich the common cultural inheritance with the contributions that only I, being a woman and a poet, may offer to enlighten an immense field that was hidden).

In 1947, besides *Mujer sin Edén*, Conde published two more books: *Sea la luz* (Let There Be Light) and *Mi fin en el viento* (My Destiny in the Wind). *Sea la luz* includes a long title poem divided into two parts, followed by a small collection published previously: *Honda memoria de mí* (Deep Remembrance of Myself, 1944). The main topic in both is death—the need for a mystical death within oneself while one is still alive: "La muerte va dentro . . ." (Death goes inside . . .). Physical death, in the title poem, is seen on one hand as a process of material destruction, but also as a continuous ascension—life, death, eternity: "Seré llamada. . . . / Vaho de mí, / ascenderé" (I shall be called. . . . / Breath of myself, / I shall rise). And in the midst of life the poet-speaker never stops wondering about the paradox of destiny:

Siempre medida de lo inmensurable,
la paradoja. Sí, no; o sí, aún no . . .
O no, aún sí . . . Luz y sombra,
muerte o resurrección.

(Always measuring the immeasurable,
the paradox. Yes, no; or yes, not yet . . .
Or not, but still yes . . . light and shadow,
death or resurrection.)

This continuous inquiring brings echoes of the great Peruvian poet César Vallejo.

Honda memoria de mí is full of remembrances. All its poems are determined by a permanent attitude: the importance of being attentive, vigilant, as in "Velar significa querer" (To Keep Vigil Means to Want). Conde sees this vigil as a continuous state in which the human being has to live: "¡Estar despierta, velar siempre! / Quizá entonces no habría lagunas / en mi continuidad" (To be awake, ever vigilant! / Perhaps then I would not have absences / in my continuity).

Nature is the background for *Mi Fin en el viento*. The speaker sees herself in complement with the natural elements. Conde's progressive identification with nature detaches her soul more and more from her body: "¡Oh mi alma, / desligada de este pozo de mi cuerpo!" (Oh my soul, / detached from this well of my body!). This book refers also to a repeated image in Conde's poetry: the archangels, with whom she keeps up an intimate dialogue: "¡Vosotros los archangeles, oidme; / . . . descendeo para llevarme" (You the archangels, listen to me; / . . . come down to take me).

Conde's contemplation of the river Tagus in Spain inspired *Iluminada tierra* (Enlightened Land, 1951). The book is divided into four parts, and her love for nature is shown in a dialogue with God. Places she previously visited— Montserrat, Paris, London—are recalled in these poems. She denounces the suffering in the world, imploring God to alleviate it. Light appears as the liberating element in "Se hicieron país las sombras" (Shadows Became Countries):

> llegó la luz.
> Una rama crepitante,
> una selva que deslumbra.
> Toda oscuridad vencida.
>
> (the light came.
> A crackling branch,
> a dazzling forest.
> All darkness conquered.)

One of Conde's greatest loves has always been her mother. With "Doña Paz," Conde shared important and intense moments. Her *Los monólogos de la hija* (A Daughter's Monologues, 1959) is a book dedicated to María Paz Abellán on her eightieth birthday. The time they spent together is presented as a continuous present, where everything mingles with the past, and the two women blend together, as in "Riesgos de la madre" (Dangers of the Mother):

> Dejé mi infancia en un marco:
> éramos las dos iguales.
> Tomé tu mano en mi mano.
> . . . .
> ¿Eres mi hija o mi madre?
> ¡Cuántos dolores me cuestas!
>
> (I left my childhood in a frame:
> The two of us were alike.
> I took your hand in mine.
> . . . .
> Are you my daughter or my mother?
> How much pain you cause me!)

Two of the books Conde published in 1960 are *Derribado Arcángel* (Defeated Archangel) and *En un mundo de fugitivos* (In a World of Refugees). The latter includes poems written between 1939 and 1957. Some of these poems go back to the years of the civil war; in hindsight she identifies herself with the Loyalists, who lost. Nevertheless Conde realizes the importance of the present moment, beyond suffering. In "Canto al hombre" (Song to Man) she expresses a universal love, regardless of limitations: "Más allá de la vida y de la muerte, Hombre, te amo" (Beyond life and death, Humanity, I love you).

Derribado Arcángel is a book with poems of supplication about the presence of good and evil. In the twenty-first poem ("XXI") Conde prays for the victory of good: "estar soñando en paz, es mi plegaria. / ¡Oh mal presagio mío, bórrate / y déjame soñar sin pesadumbre!" (To dream peacefully is my prayer. / Oh evil token of mine, efface / and let me dream without sorrow!)

In 1963 Conde and Oliver visited Nicaragua, Panama, and Puerto Rico for the first time. In Nicaragua, Oliver received an honorary degree for the new "Cátedra Rubén Darío" (Rubén Darío Chair) he had created at the University of Madrid. *Jaguar puro inmarchito* (Pure Unfaded Jaguar, 1963) is the book Conde wrote recording her impressions of the trip. The poverty and misery of the Indians in the different cities they visited greatly impressed Conde, as shown in "Nicaragua y su garra" (Nicaragua and Its Talon):

> Pájaros sin alas, como los niños, al sol, mudos.
> El polvo, el ruido, la despiadada ciudad con
> basuras,
> . . . .
> El indio y la india están sucios, hambrientos,
> enfermos,
> sentados en cualquier pedazo de tierra, labrada o
> inmunda. . . .
>
> (Wingless birds, like children, in the sun, silent.
> Dust, noise, the pitiless filthy city,
> . . . .
> The Indian men and women are dirty, hungry, ill,
> sitting on any bit of ground, ploughed or derelict. . . .)

But Conde sees also the natural beauty and immensity of these lands. Her poems are reminiscent of those of her two masters and friends Jiménez and Pedro Salinas.

Her trips abroad did not prevent her from spending a lot of time in the Spanish country-

Conde in her study at Brocal, her house near Madrid (courtesy of Carmen Conde)

side. Brocal, the couple's house on the outskirts of Madrid (named after her first book of poems), became the place for rest and inspiration. There she finished her work on Saint Theresa and other female mystical writers, published in 1978 as *Al encuentro de Santa Teresa*.

During 1965 Carmen Conde traveled to several places; Melilla, the city where she spent her childhood, was the first one. She gave some lectures there about her poetry. Next came Greece, Turkey, and Italy. The enjoyment of these trips was always darkened by her husband's progressive heart disease. In Rome she attended a Congress of the European Community of Writers, where she met some of her colleagues from Spain.

In 1966 Carmen started teaching Hispanoamerican literature at the Institute for European Studies in Madrid. She was substituting for her husband, whose heart disease did not allow him to continue working.

The next year, Conde's *Obra poética* was published, with a prologue by Leopoldo de Luis. This publication led to her receiving the National Prize for Literature.

Her *Obra poética* includes, besides the previous publications, other books written before 1967

but never published: "Devorante arcilla" (The Devouring Clay, 1962); "Enajenado mirar" (Ravished Gaze, 1962-1964); and "Humanas criaturas" (Human Creatures, 1945-1966). The last is a long poem to her personal and literary friends: Miguel de Unamuno, Mistral, Jiménez, and others. One of the saddest years in Conde's life was 1968, when her husband died. But her literary commitments did not let her stop or retire to her suffering. She had to go to the universities of Salamanca and Melilla to give lectures previously scheduled. Part of her grief over Oliver's death is reflected in *A este lado de la eternidad* (On This Side of Eternity, 1970).

In her 1975 collection, *Corrosión*, life and death are still debating. Material substances such as marble and magma are constantly present; nature expresses human feelings, as in "Furia metódica de una lava" (Methodical Anger of Lava) and "Ruge la sombra" (The Shadow Roars). The presence of the bread and wine in "Pausa ante el origen" (Pause before the Beginning) has echoes of Vallejo's work: "Amasarte como pan, como vino incorporárteme. / Ningún alimento pudo renovarme cuerpo y alma" (To mold you like bread, to embody you in me like wine. / No food could renovate my body and soul). "A Miguel" centers on a paradox of human existence:

> No lo sé; no lo sé.
> Pero hay oscuridad.
> Una inmensa escurridiza atosigante oscuridad.
> Sí, lo sé. Hay oscuridad.
>
> (I do not know; I do not know.
> But there is darkness.
> An immense unstable oppressing darkness.
> Yes, I know. There is darkness.)

Besides writing and publishing her own poetry, Conde worked intensively in the 1970s to promote the works of her husband. She did not stop traveling. In 1974 she visited Mexico and New York. But her untiring will to write stopped at times, causing her to consider that she had already said everything she could in her poems. As she writes in *Por el camino*, "Siento la necesidad de cambiar de expresión. ¿Volver al poema en prosa; utilizar más la narrativa, o callarme de una vez?" (I feel the need of changing my expression. Maybe I should return to the poem in prose; to use the narrative style more, or perhaps silence myself altogether?). But her literary soul was strong, and she continued publishing. This active production led to her 1978 election to the Spanish Royal Academy. This well-deserved honor was accompanied, in the same year, by further publications. *El tiempo es un río lentísimo de fuego* (Time Is a Very Slow River of Fire) is one of them. This book marks her increasing preoccupation with the passing of time. Five of her stories for children were published the next year, as well as a novel, *Creció espesa la yerba* (The Grass Became Dense). In 1980 Conde received the Ateneo de Sevilla prize for her new novel *Soy la madre* (I Am the Mother, published in 1982).

A natural element, a crater, provides the title for one of her most recent books of poems, *Cráter* (1985). Conde goes back to Greek mythology, proving once more that the poet is the "collective memory," identifying herself with history. The book, written in both verse and prose, contains universal truths—for example, to reach light, one must go through shadows. Myths are updated. Humans, like gods, are seen to be made up of dreams.

In 1987 Conde was awarded the National Prize for Children's and Teenage Literature in Spain for *Canciones de nana y desvelo* (Songs for Lullaby and Vigil, 1985)—another proof of the broad scope of her literary interests and talents. Conde's voice is one of the strongest in Spanish poetry, and her work has been the basis for that of many current women poets in Spain.

References:

Esther M. Allison, "Carmen Conde, primera académica española," *Abside*, 42 (July-September 1978): 195-199;

Dámaso Alonso, *Poetas españoles contemporáneos* (Madrid: Gredos, 1952), pp. 359-365;

María Dolores de Asís, *Antología de poetas españoles contemporáneos, 1900-1936* (Madrid: Narcea, 1977);

Consuelo Bergas, "Surco de Gabriela Mistral," in *Libro homenaje a Gabriela Mistral* (Madrid: 1946);

Bonnie Maurine Brown, "Carmen Conde's *En la tierra de nadie*. A Journey through Death and Solitude," *Revista Review Interamericana*, 12 (Spring 1982): 140-145;

Pablo Cabañas, "La poesía de Carmen Conde," *Cuadernos de Literatura contemporánea*, 18 (1946): 617-624;

Susan Cabello, "The Poetic World of Carmen Conde," Ph.D. dissertation, University of Arizona, 1978;

Cuadernos de Agora, special Conde issue, 46-48 (August-October 1960);

Miguel Dolc, "Hacia el orbe poético de Carmen Conde," in Conde's *Días por la tierra* (Madrid: Nacional, 1977). pp. 9-25;

Oscar Echeverri Mejía, "Carmen Conde: A este lado de la eternidad," *Boletín de la Academia Colombiana*, 31 (October-December 1981): 291-294;

George H. Engeman, Jr., "Carmen Conde: La pasión del verbo," *Kentucky Foreign Language Quarterly*, 13 (1966): 14-19;

Engeman, Jr., "Carmen Conde: Vida y obra de la mujer poeta," Ph.D. dissertation, University of Madrid, 1962;

Homenaje a Carmen Conde (Vigo, Spain: Mensajes de poesía, 1951);

Leopoldo de Luis, *Carmen Conde* (Madrid: Ministerio de Cultura, 1982);

Luis, "El sentido religioso de la poesía de Carmen Conde," *Cuadernos de Literatura*, 6, nos. 16-18 (1949): 183-192;

Pilar Martín, "La ensoñación. Un ejemplo en la poesía de Carmen Conde," Ph.D. dissertation, City University of New York, 1991;

Emilio Miró, Introduction to *Obra poética (1929-1966)* (Madrid: Biblioteca Nueva, 1967), pp. 9-23;

Antonio Oliver Belmás, "Las conversaciones de 'Andrés Caballero,'" in his *Obras completas* (Madrid: Biblioteca Nueva, 1971);

María del Pilar Palomo, "Las escritoras: Carmen Conde," in *Historia de la literatura española*, volume 6, edited by Angel Balbuena Prat (Barcelona: Gili, 1983), pp. 256-262;

Diana Ramírez de Arellano, *Poesía contemporánea en lengua española* (Madrid: Biblioteca Aristarco de Erudición y Crítica, 1961), pp. 181-202;

Moraima de Semprún Donahue, "El paisaje ibérico en la poesía de Carmen Conde," *Cuadernos de Aldeeu*, 1 (May-October 1983): 481-491;

María Nowakowska Stycos, "Twentieth-Century Hispanic Women Poets: An Introduction," *Revista Review Interamericana*, 12 (Spring 82): 5-10;

Concha Zardoya, "Mujer sin Edén: Poema vivo de Carmen Conde," in *Poesía española del siglo XX. Estudios temáticos y estilísticos*, volume 4 (Madrid: Gredos, 1974), pp. 32-36;

Zardoya, *Poesía española contemporánea* (Madrid: Guadarrama, 1961), pp. 635-640.

Victoriano Crémer

(23 December 1909? -   )

Eric Diehl
College Montmorency, Montreal

BOOKS: *Tendiendo el vuelo* (León, Spain, 1928);

En la escalera (León, Spain, 1940);

Tacto sonoro (León, Spain: Espadaña, 1944);

Los Hombres se matan (León, Spain, 1945);

Fábula de B. D. (León, Spain: Espadaña, 1946);

Caminos de mi sangre (Madrid: Adonáis, 1947);

Las horas perdidas (Valladolid, Spain: Halcón, 1949);

La espada y la pared (San Sebastian: Norte, 1949);

Nuevos cantos de vida y esperanza I (Barcelona: Instituto de Estudios Hispánicos, 1952);

Nuevos cantos de vida y esperanza II (Barcelona: Pliegos de poesía, 1953);

El libro de Santiago (León, Spain: Espadaña, 1954);

Furia y paloma (Barcelona: Horta, 1956);

Libro de Caín (Mexico City: Compañia General de Ediciones, 1958);

Con la paz al hombro (León, Spain: Espadaña, 1959);

Tiempo de soledad (Orense, Spain: Comercial, 1962);

Diálogo para un hombre sólo (Palma de Mallorca,

Spain: Papeles de Son Armadans, 1963);

El amor y la sangre (Madrid: Punta Europa, 1966);

Poesía total (Barcelona: Plaza & Janés, 1967; enlarged edition, 1970);

Historias de Chu-Ma-Chuco (Barcelona: Plaza & Janés, 1970);

León (Madrid: Publicaciones Españolas, 1971);

Nuevas canciones para Elisa (Bilbao, Spain: Comunicación Literaria de Autores, 1972);

Lejos de esta lluvia tan amarga (Seville: Aldebarán, 1974);

El libro de Vela Zanetti (Madrid: Ibérico Europea, 1974);

Los cercos (León, Spain: Institución Fray Bernardino de Sahagún, Diputación Provincial, 1976);

El libro de San Marcos (León, Spain: Nebrija, 1980);

León insólito: Guía sentimental (León, Spain: Everest, 1981);

Tabla de varones ilustres, indinos y malbaratados de León y su circunstancia (León, Spain: Everest, 1983);

Poesía (1944-1984), 2 volumes (León, Spain: Institución Fray Bernardino de Sahagún, Diputación Provincial, 1984);

Los trenes no dejan huella (León, Spain: Garcia, 1986).

SELECTED PERIODICAL PUBLICATIONS—
UNCOLLECTED: "Esquema para un cuadro sinóptico sobre poesía y trabajo," *Poesía Española*, 8 (August 1952): 1-7;

"Un cuestionario sobre poesía social y de la otra," *Poesía Española*, 11 (November 1952);

"El trabajo y la poesía," *Revista de la Facultad de Humanidades de la Universidad de los Andes* (1960);

"Los mundos oscuros de Federico García Lorca y el *Romancero gitano* (tercera parte)," *La Estafeta Literaria*, 432 (1969): 17-19;

"Para una biografía de *Espadaña*," *Peña Labra*, 14 (Winter 1974-1975): 2-6;

"Notas para una biografía de Espadaña," *Poesía Española*, 140-141 (n.d.): 15-17.

OTHER: Francisco Ribes, ed., *Antología consultada de la joven poesía española*, includes contributions by Crémer (Santander, Spain: Bedia, 1952);

Espadaña: Revista de poesía y crítica, Volume 1-48. 1944-1951, includes introduction, articles, and poems by Crémer (León, Spain: Espadaña, 1979).

Any discussion of Victoriano Crémer's place in post-civil-war Spanish literature must take into account the two most prominent aspects of his career. First, Crémer was instrumental in founding and publishing *Espadaña* (1944-1951), which became one of the most important and influential poetry journals published in the years after the war. And second, Crémer, a product of the working class, was a poet of the people who steadfastly defended the unfortunate and downtrodden with a passion and determination that were rare among his contemporaries.

Crémer was born into a poor family in Burgos, Spain, probably on 23 December 1909, though some sources place his birth as early as 1906 or as late as 1914. His father was a railwayman who later moved his large family to the city of León, where Crémer has lived and worked ever since.

In one of his novels, *Libro de Caín* (Book of Cain, 1958), which has obvious autobiographical overtones, he describes the protagonist's arrival in the working-class barrio of Puertamoneda, where the family settled down within the depths of a large building, "Más que vivienda para seres humanos, el agujero parecía cueva de alimañas hostigadas. . . . [En el barrio] hay niños desnudos y sucios . . . mujeres terribles con tantos años que angustia asomarse a sus ojos amarillos . . . y hombres cansados, derrotados, . . . gentes duras, dramáticas y sencillas. Seres de carme y hueso, capaces de todo, por nada" (More the lair of denizens of the jungle than a dwelling for human beings. . . . The streets were full of filthy, half-naked children. . . . women whose long-suffering faces were filled with sadness and anguish . . . and tired and dissipated men . . . hard, simple people. They were flesh and blood, capable of doing anything, for nothing).

There are many references to his mother in his works. In "Ciudad amenazada" (Threatening City, in *Furia y paloma* [Fury and Dove, 1956]), he refers to the woman who "nos daba entre rezos . . . el pan nuestro de cada día . . . y con sabor a lágrimas" (between prayers . . . gave us our daily bread . . . which tasted salty from the tears). She was a coal vendor, one of the *carbonerillas* that he wrote about so poignantly in the poem of the same name (in *Nuevos cantos de vida y esperanza I* [New Songs of Life and Hope, volume 1, 1952]):

brotaban de la calle
con un corazón inmenso a las espaldas,
¿de qué nocturna mina?

Nadie las preguntaba.

Llegan a casa dobladas de negrura;

escupen tristemente negro polvo;
> descargan
su apretado botín.

> Tal vez se duerman
soñando Paraísos de escorias apagadas.

¿de qué nocturna mina?

Nadie las preguntaba.

(They erupted onto the street
with a heart-like burden on their shoulders.
Mined on which night shift?

Nobody even cared to ask them.

They arrive home bent and dirty with soot
spitting sadly, their spittle black;
> they discharge
their heavy sacks.

> Perhaps they fall asleep
dreaming of Paradises of slackened coal-fires.

Mined on which night shift?

Nobody even cared to ask them.)

Victor García de la Concha (in *La poesía española de posguerra*, 1973) has concluded that Crémer was not exaggerating the harshness of his childhood during those early years in León. The harshness and squalor were to leave a lasting impression on Crémer, producing a sensitivity to human suffering and a committed involvement that can be seen in every book and at every stage of his literary development.

At nine years of age Crémer began hawking newspapers in the streets of León to help his family make ends meet. Much like the legendary Lazarillo—of *Lazarillo de Tormes* (anonymous, 1554)—he soon left that line of work to follow other masters, serving as boy Friday to an old lawyer, and shop boy at a local pharmacy, before finally becoming interested in the printing profession at some point in his teens. He became an apprentice to a typographer, later becoming one himself.

Crémer developed an early interest in poetry and was instrumental in founding, or working on, many different journals. He was active as both a radio and newspaper journalist, all the while continuing to work as a typographer up to the end of the civil war in 1939, whereupon he was arrested and thrown in jail by the nationalist forces. De la Concha writes in *La poesía española de posguerra* that Crémer's incarceration was logical, given that, during the years of the republic, Crémer had been secretary of the Workers' Atheneum of León, a socialist-oriented literary society. And like the well-known artist, Vela Zanetti, Crémer had been an active campaigner for the Anarchical-Union Party. For these and other activities, Crémer was held in the San Marcos jail and was in great danger of being executed.

It was at this time that Don Antonio González de Lama entered Crémer's life and secured his release, literally saving him from the firing squad. Lama was a priest, himself the son of poor campesinos; he, like many others before him, had chosen the seminary and the priesthood because it offered him a chance to escape from poverty. As it turned out, Lama was also an accomplished man of letters who had been chosen to become director of the Gumersindo Azcárate Library in León, a library built from funds provided by a well-known republican family and located right across from the cathedral. It was probably in 1940 that Lama gave Crémer the job of managing the library and breathing some new life into it.

One of the innovations that Crémer and Lama organized was a *tertulia* (a literary circle) that met once a week to discuss poetry, books, and literary theory. They were soon joined by Eugenio García de Nora, with whom they were soon to collaborate in founding *Espadaña*.

There were many other such *tertulias* that sprang up in Spain during those post-civil-war years, and many poetry journals were set up to defend one or another school of poetry. These journals were a strange anomaly in Franco's Spain, for in their pages took place perhaps the most heated public ideological debates to be found anywhere in Spain. The intellectual and literary level of criticism was usually quite high, frequently going beyond the purely partisan boundaries of left and right.

One of those journals in particular, *Garcilaso*, drew the attention of the Azcárate *tertulia*. The members of the Garcilaso school, based on the ideas of sixteenth-century Spanish poet Garcilaso de la Vega, belonged to a group called "Juventud creadora" (Creative Youth), which had quite a following in and around Madrid. The "Tertulia del Gijón" was to *Garcilaso* what the Azcárate *tertulia* was to the soon-to-be-launched *Espadaña*, and the poetics espoused by the two

groups were diametrically opposed to one another.

Post-civil-war Spanish poetry had become escapist, formalist, symbolist, and generally removed from the reality of everyday life. This was perhaps the result of the hardships and broken dreams brought on by the downfall of the republic, concomitant with a loss of faith in human nature. There had been a return to classical forms, mysticism, and the long-since-vanished glories of the past. It was not the least surprising to see these poets adopt Garcilaso, a Spanish Renaissance poet, as their figurehead and standard-bearer.

The Azcárate *tertulia* took exception to this kind of poetry, which they described as cold, monotonous, and unfeeling. Following their discussions at the Azcárate, Lama published an article in *Cisneros* (1943), entitled "Si Garcilaso volviera" (If Garcilaso Were to Return), which proved to be of seminal importance, serving as a kind of manifesto that defined the standards of the emerging *Espadaña* group. Lama blasted the "garcilasistas," saying that what was needed from postwar Spanish poets was "un poco menos de forma y un poco más de vida. Menos perfección estilística y más gritos. Menos metáforas y más gritos . . . vida, vida, vida. Que sin ella todo está muerto" (less form and more life. Less stylistic perfection and more cries and shouts. Fewer metaphors and more clamour . . . life, life, life. For without it all is dead).

Crémer said that if Garcilaso were to return, he would not become Garcilaso's squire, no matter how great a knight he were—an oblique reference to the journal *Garcilaso* and an indication of just how far Crémer was from those ideas on poetry. In 1943 Crémer reacted to the start of another poetry journal, *Corcel* (published in Valencia), by complaining that too much contemporary Spanish poetry was conceived without faith or hope, was stillborn, and should thus be buried and forgotten.

In 1944 Nora successfully applied to the Delegación Nacional de Prensa y Propaganda (National Delegation of Print and Propaganda) for a permit to publish a new poetry journal, to be known as *Espadaña* (named after the great cattail, a common wetlands plant). The board of directors included Lama, Nora, and Don Luis López Santos, a university professor and important León church leader. It was felt that the censors were less likely to deny Nora a permit than Lama, who was a priest, or Crémer, who had served a prison term for his republican activities. Crémer was to take over responsibility for managing, editing, and typesetting the journal, in short, becoming a veritable factotum.

The first issue of *Espadaña* was published in May 1944; 250 copies were printed. It was "contribuir al desarrollo de la poesía española y recogar las orientaciones jóvenes de la provincia, al mismo tiempo que se da un tono de elevación cultural a la vida provinciana" (to contribute to the development of Spanish poetry, and be a focal point for the youthful poets of the province, as well as help to elevate the cultural tone of provincial life). It had been Lama's intention that the journal integrate the romantic and neoclassical tendencies into one superior kind of poetry, full of life, and free of formal constraints. The name of the journal had been put to a vote by the members of the Azcárate *tertulia*, which chose the name because of the profusion of great cattails in the Leonese countryside.

According to Fanny Rubio (in *Cuadernos Hispanoamericanos*, June 1973), the new poets led by Crémer and Nora were motivated by the desire to violate poetical taboos and rehumanize poetry, having it reflect new content, new solidarities, and new commitments. They wanted to be the leaders of the antiformalist reaction to journals such as *Garcilaso* and the ideals they stood for. Crémer himself, in the first issue of *Espadaña*, set out his philosophy clearly: "No son las reglas las que hacen el Poema; es éste él que—quebrantándolas, a veces—instaura nuevas normas" (Rules don't make poetry; rather, it is the latter which—by sometimes breaking the rules—creates new forms). Elsewhere in the first edition he writes: "Va a ser necesario gritar nuestro verso actual contra las cuatro paredes o contra los catorce barrotes soneteriles con que jóvenes tan viejos como el mundo pretenden cercarle, estrangularle. Y sin necesidad de colocarnos bajo la advocación de ningún santón literario, aunque se llame Góngora o Garcilaso" (We will have to shout our modern poetry against the four walls, or against the fourteen sonatine bars with which some world-weary young poets are trying to immobilize and strangle it. And we won't need to hide behind the advocacy of any literary saint, whether he be a Góngora or a Garcilaso).

Critics of postwar Spanish literature generally agree that 1944 was a seminal year for the revitalization of poetry in Spain; it saw the publication of Dámaso Alonso's *Hijos de la ira* (Children

of Wrath), Vicente Aleixandre's *Sombra del paraíso* (Shadow of Paradise), as well as the birth of *Espadaña*. Furthermore, it was the year Crémer published his first surviving book of poetry, *Tacto sonoro* (A Touch of Sound). Several critics mention an earlier published book of poetry, *Tendiendo el vuelo* (Taking Flight, 1928), but Crémer reportedly removed this work from his list of publications. Furthermore, the bibliographer José Simón Díaz (in *Manual de bibliographía de la literatura española*, 1966) also mentions a play, *En la escalera* (On the Stairs, 1940); however, these two works along with another play, *Los hombres se matan* (The Men Who Kill, 1945), seem to have been lost.

Ironically *Tacto sonoro* was published with financial help from an unlikely source, the poet José María Pemán, who had always maintained good relations with the nationalists. Pemán had heard Crémer reciting some of his poetry and liked it so much that he gave him the honorarium from one of his own books. Several of the poems in *Tacto sonoro* first appeared in *Cisneros*, an ideological cousin to *Espadaña*. Some critics considered the poems striking and original, while others pointed to the obvious influence of Federico García Lorca and Rafael Alberti.

As noted by Eleanor Wright, Leopoldo Panero wrote that the unity of the work lay not in the poems but in the poet's personality. José García Nieto, of *Garcilaso*, criticized Crémer's apparently poor mastery of traditional poetic forms, failing to realize that Crémer was mocking the conventions, tone, and themes of "garcilasismo."

Tacto sonoro begins with a series of poems entitled "Puertos de tierra adentro" (Interior Ports of Call), featuring Puertamoneda, the working-class barrio of León that Crémer frequently chose as the locale for his poetry and fiction. He depicts a run-down, hopelessly destitute world, one of harsh, bitter nights that yearn to become just simple, ordinary nights (in "Paisaje urbano" [Urban Landscape]). In "Viajes por el extranjero" (Travels Abroad) Crémer presents a static and emotionless world of ruin and desolation, dust and dirt, a landscape of stifling heat and bitter cold, a far cry from the Arcadian settings and sentiments so common in the poetry of the "garcilasistas."

The next section, "Cancionero del desánimo" (Songs of Discouragement), contains five songs whose message seems to be that human beings dream too much, refusing to see life as it really is: harsh, impersonal, and bitter; an asphalt

Illustration for Tacto Sonoro *(A Touch of Sound) in* Poesías, *volume 1 (1984)*

jungle of mud, misery, death, and burial; a place where moons are more symbolic of starvation and death than harvest; a place, however, of contrasts, where love can grow, reminiscent of the cactus flower that reluctantly blooms from time to time under the right conditions.

Overall, though, Crémer's view of life appears almost nihilistic. There seems little that people can do to escape life's torpor and suffering. In "Y es eso sólo la muerte" (And This Is Only Death) Crémer presents a conversation among a corpse in a casket being carried in a funeral procession, a mourner walking in the procession, and a bystander observing the funeral. The poem presents a grotesque view of death in the "tremendista" style so often used by Crémer, with its distortions of reality that remind one of Ramón María del Valle-Inclán and Lorca.

One of Crémer's "tremendista" (grotesque) techniques is to endow objects with life at the same time that living beings are robbed of vitality. In "Oda malherida al avión en picado" (Ode

Injurious to a Diving Fighter Bomber) the planes with their weapons, noise, and pollution become a kind of exterminating angel, a symbol perhaps of the planes that were even then (in 1944) laying waste to large parts of Europe and Asia (much as they had devastated parts of his native Spain some years earlier). In "Canción para submarinos" (Song for Submarines) Crémer shows the world at the mercy of these sinister mechanical denizens of the deep.

The final poems of *Tacto sonoro* touch on humankind and its relation to a possible creator. These poems are not so much concerned with the harshness of external reality as they are with the internal doubts that assail the poet, and with his anxious search to find some meaning in life. In "Hombre habitado" (Inhabited Man) the speaker reaches out to the divinity. He likens himself to a long, empty corridor whose walls are full of shadows. In the distance some footsteps are heard approaching, and he hears the deity's voice echoing through the empty shell of his humanity. Humanity and divinity meet almost face to face, and the former is given a purpose in life, namely, a commitment to his fellow humans:

¿Por qué soles y vientos y palabras?
¿Por qué espumas y pájaros y flores?

Al fin soles y vientos y palabras
se espesan en mis sombras conmovidas
por Tu presencia en mi: Hombre habitado.

(Why suns, and winds, and words?
Why foams, and birds, and flowers?

In the end, suns and winds and words
are reduced to order within my shadows
by Your presence in me: Inhabited Man.)

In general the style and themes of these poems are typical of most of Crémer's poetry, which over the years has stressed the harsh reality of life tempered by the healing possibilities of human love and dedication to the greater good of humanity. Although *Tacto sonoro* did not achieve the same success as Alonso's *Hijos de la ira* or Aleixandre's *Sombra del paraíso*, it was, nevertheless, a powerful shot in the ideological battle against the "garcilasistas." Alonso's response had been a traditional one, relying on Christian values; Crémer's was nihilist, existentialist, and ultimately humanist. In his work one catches glimpses of one of his main poetic models, Lorca, especially the Lorca of the *Romancero gitano* (Gypsy Romances, 1929) and *Poeta en Nueva York* (The Poet in New York, 1940), the latter a book with a heavy dose of social criticism.

Crémer has even suggested that his activist attitudes and worldview were inspired by previous generations, especially that of 1898. When *Tacto sonoro* was published, Fernando Gutiérrez, a literary critic, wrote an open letter to Crémer in *La Prensa* (a Barcelona newspaper) in which he blamed the war for creating such pessimistic and sad poetry. Crémer replied that the seeds had been sown much earlier by others, the Spaniard being sad and serious by nature, by education, and by environment.

The death of French poet Paul Valéry in July 1945 was the occasion for much outpouring of grief within the pages of a special issue of *Espadaña* devoted to him. Crémer, for his part, commented that few nonpoets had marked the passing of the great poet, nor had many more read his works. Crémer agreed with the general assessment of Valéry's greatness as a poet but likened the utility of his poetry to that of a solitary and inaccessible rose.

This inaccessibility of poetry to most people greatly preoccupied Crémer. In Francisco Ribes's *Antología consultada* (Reference Anthology, 1952), Crémer showed his ambivalence about his craft: on the one hand he wanted poetry to be committed to the underdog, yet on the other hand he often doubted whether poetry was at all useful in that struggle: "No vale engañarse. La Poesía es un extraño culto, sostenido por gentes de muy dudosa eficacia vital" (There is no point in deceiving oneself. Poetry is a strange craft, practiced by people whose overall effectiveness is quite doubtful).

Crémer reluctantly admitted that poetry was unfortunately not the domain of the illiterate nor the common person in society but rather of educated people and intellectuals. He wanted poetry to become accessible to those other social classes but was certain that, if it were ever to succeed in that endeavor, it would have to become clear, simple, direct, and, above all, truthful—otherwise, even silence was preferable.

In 1946 Crémer published *Fábula de B. D.* (The Fable of B. D.), a poem dedicated to Buenaventura Durruti, a militant leader of the "anarcosindicalista" (anarchist) party who had been assassinated on 19 November 1936. In writing about Durruti and how he came to be involved with the life and struggles of the Spanish worker, Crémer uses very little natural imagery, which is unusual for a Castilian poet. Nature, sad and degraded, is often transformed in Crémer's work, sometimes becoming personified, taking on the role of a protagonist, as when B. D. approaches his place of execution, where "árboles y lejanías gritan su desolación y bosques de manos rotas abren sus llagas al sol" (the trees mourn his passing and forests of broken hands open their wounds to the sun).

Crémer's main interest is humanity, and everything else is subservient to that element or seems to highlight it in some way. Crémer presents Durruti as a victim of an unjust society. Society in turn is represented by the city, the center of that injustice, an impersonal place that continues to sleep away even under the brightest sun, alluding to another motif, that of night and shadow; in Crémer's world it is night all day long.

During the years that he directed *Espadaña*, Crémer published three more books of poetry: *Caminos de mi sangre* (Streets of My Blood, 1947);

Las horas perdidas (The Lost Hours, 1949); and *La espada y la pared* (The Spade and the Wall, 1949). These books further the challenge to "garcilasismo" that had been launched by *Espadaña* and continued in *Tacto sonoro*. Crémer's poems attempt to bridge the gap between the neoclassical tradition and the modern, unfettered styles that were developing in postwar Spain. The poems are eclectic and show, above all, deep commitment; his language, if anything, has become more personal and violent, reflecting the plight of contemporary humanity and the dilemma of mortality.

He oscillates between the poles of protest and outrage, on the one hand, and despair on the other. Unlike many writers of so-called *poesía social*, who used their craft primarily to protest a particular dictatorship or rage against an unfair social order in Spain, Crémer's protests and concerns are universal and eternal. He believed that humanity's moral inertia could be surmounted only through belief in, and strict adherence to, a set of values.

Crémer seemed to have found God in *Tacto sonoro*, but God is momentarily rejected in "Mi loba blanca" (My White Wolf, in *Caminos*), reminiscent of nineteenth-century poet Francis Thompson's "The Hound of Heaven." The speaker in Crémer's poem seems afraid of God and his love; God, as the wolf, and much like Thompson's hound, seems to delight in tearing at the speaker's frozen heart. In "En tus manos" (In Your Hands) the speaker tries to avoid another encounter with God, this guardian and jailer of his flesh. "Poema" likens the poet once again to an empty hallway about to be entered by the divinity; however, they must meet as equals, face to face, indicative of the dignity and valor Crémer ascribes to humanity. "Recuerdo de la nada" (In Memory of Nothingness), in honor of Luis Cernuda, presents a landscape of iron, cement, misery, huts, palaces, factories—all unsalvageable ruins—seen through the eyes of a stranger, a man who has mysteriously returned from the threshold of death. The stranger advances slowly, painfully silent, like a sacrificial bull—dead yet alive, withdrawn inside his shell, carrying his soul in his hands—condemned to life.

In "Bienaventurados los pobres" (Blessed Are the Poor In Spirit, in *Las horas perdidas*) Crémer shows his solidarity with downtrodden workers. In a striking example of the vividness of his imagery, the speaker dreams of giving himself to these starving masses to help assuage their hunger, multiplying himself like the biblical loaves. In "Sombras" (Shadows) humankind lies trapped in "la nada" (nothingness), while God sees the situation and does nothing, abandoning people to their fate. In "Canto total a España" (A Song of Total Commitment to Spain, in *La espada y la pared*) Crémer gives full vent to his obsession with Spain and its recent history, a typical example of the inextinguishable desire of many postwar Spanish poets to discuss Spain's political and social situation, and its place in the modern world.

At the same time that Crémer was publishing these works, he continued his editorship of *Espadaña*, writing parts of each issue, contributing editorial commentary, columns such as "Tablas rasas" (Clean Slates) and "Poesía y vida" (Poetry and Life), reviews, and poetry. In number 37 Crémer included a poem, "Los hombres tienen hambre" (People Are Hungry), which he begins in typical "garcilasista" style only to explode in fury, rejecting what he had written so far as being a lot of nonsense and asking how one can talk of love, truth, and beauty when there is so much hunger and misery everywhere. He never retreats behind a search for absolute, idyllic truths; instead, Crémer and the other "espadañistas" tried to express as faithfully and beautifully as possible the life that surrounded and existed in them.

Even when his poems reflect material reality along more classical lines, Crémer always infuses them with the cries and shouts of everyday life. Although the "espadañistas" were sometimes accused of being hopeless romantics, he defended himself, saying that romanticism had really been quite superficial at times—artificial and removed from everyday reality, subjective and alienated. His poetry, on the other hand, was involved and committed both socially and historically.

During the existence of *Espadaña* two poetic tendencies developed: the earlier one, dominated by Crémer, was neoromantic, "tremendista," essentially liberal in nature, and in favor of the rehumanization of Spanish poetry; the other tendency, represented by Nora, showed a commitment to humanity by espousing Marxist ideology and adopting a socialist-realist credo. Toward the end of the journal's existence, these two tendencies gradually began to grow apart, eventually leading to a rift that culminated in its demise.

In 1949, when *Espadaña* faced grave financial difficulties, a group of poets led by Luis Rosales was instrumental in publishing a special issue of the journal dedicated to César Vallejo (number 39) and subtitled "Poesía total" (Total Poetry). Their idea was eventually to create a new journal of that same name, to be directed and edited by Crémer, but their plans fell through and the idea was stillborn. Nevertheless, the Rosales group continued to collaborate, producing issues 40 and 41 of *Espadaña*, and Crémer edited several more issues.

But the fatal blow was not long in coming; Nora, representing the politically committed Marxists, attacked Crémer and the more humanistically inclined social poets in an open letter to the editor signed by Juan Martínez, a pseudonym used by Nora. Although he later regretted his actions, Nora rebuked Crémer for including certain poets (José María Pemán, for example) in the journal and for trying to address the magazine to everyone, rather than singling out a more specifically proletarian group.

Lama answered Nora's criticism in number 47 (1950), rejecting the latter's view that poetry should try to become a vehicle of social change. But the issue was already settled. There could no longer be peaceful coexistence between these two tendencies. Too many poetical and political forces were competing for a place within the journal's pages for it to be able to continue to exist. In retrospect some have even seen the demise of *Espadaña* as the result of a carefully planned attempt by unknown forces to undermine it, but this view is not widely held.

Shortly after his comment in issue 47, Lama and his colleagues Crémer and Castro Ovejero finally decided to suspend publication indefinitely. The last issue of *Espadaña* was number 48, published in January 1951. Quite apart from everything else, the journal did win one significant battle against its chief rival: *Garcilaso* only managed to survive for three years, while its feisty competitor was able to chalk up forty-eight issues over a period of seven years.

Although details of Crémer's life after his *Espadaña* years are scarce, he continued to work in León as a literary critic and journalist until his retirement. Although his greatest literary achievement was behind him, namely his editorship of *Espadaña*, he continued to publish both poetry and prose until the 1980s. In 1951 he received the Boscán Prize for his *Nuevos cantos de vida y esperanza I*, whose title was no doubt inspired by

a work of similar name by the great poet Rubén Darío. Crémer's techniques and vocabulary had not changed, nor for the most part had his themes, although there is less of a nihilistic outlook in his later works, perhaps reflecting improvements in the social and political climate in Spain.

Underlying these poems is a feeling of the oneness of humanity, of intertwined fates, and of belief in the future and in the possibility of a better world. The focal point of that world continues to be Puertamoneda. In "Regreso" (Return) the poet slowly tours the streets of his barrio, gaining renewed vigor and inspiration from his experience. In "Friso con obreros" (Rubbing Shoulders with Workers) Crémer shows his solidarity with workers oblivious to the beauty around them as they struggle to assure their own survival, and he praises the quality and value of their work, the real heartbeat of the planet.

In "Dulce amor" (Sweet Love), a poem that underscores the difficulty of loving in a world so full of misery, a worker returns home after work only to leave again for his customary visit to the tavern for several rounds of bitter wine. "Y si ríen y gritan y golpean, es porque—¡Dios, qué vida!—da rabia beber sin alegría" (And if they laugh and shout and act a bit rowdy, it's because—God, what a life!—drinking without some fun only leads to rage). While the husband is gone, the wife remains at home to dream alone. This scene is juxtaposed to that of a bourgeois housewife in her comfortable home "escuchando, por la radio, una bella canción, mientras los niños buscan en el Atlas países coronados de yedras o corales . . ." (listening to a beautiful song on the radio while the children consult their atlases looking for countries covered in ivy or coral . . .). The drunken worker returns home to be greeted by his wife's usual disapproving stare. Who can blame them for their behavior? And "¿Quién dice amor, si la palabra estalla?" (Who can talk of love, when the very word explodes?).

In the final poem of the collection, "Nana del hijo" (Child's Lullaby), Crémer begins his poem as a typical lullaby, only to change tone abruptly as he proceeds to tell the child what life is really like: the world is a place of lies, greed, and corruption: words such as *truth* and *justice* are empty shells that mean one thing for the rich and another for the poor.

Crémer's *Nuevos cantos* belongs to a second wave of antiformalist poetry that started around the beginning of the 1950s and which can be characterized as "poesía social," a poetry showing in

Illustration for Los cercos (*from* Poesías, *volume 2, 1984*)

part an obsession with Spain and its history (particularly its recent history), a concern about commiseration with human suffering, and a dedication to exploring the real faces of existence and communicating them through poetry. The language is simple and direct, calculated to be understood by as wide a readership as possible.

In that same year (1952) Ribes came out with his celebrated *Antología consultada*, in which he published interviews with and poetry by some nine prominent modern poets. Crémer stated in his interview that he detested the poet's ivory tower. In describing his kind of poetry as collective and socially involved, he writes:

Nunca como hoy necesitó el poeta ser tan narrativo, porque los males que nos acechan . . . proceden de hechos. . . . El lector busca en el poeta al ser que le canta lo que él siente en su espíritu. Acaso le place escuchar de otros labios su propio mal. . . . El poeta, tratando de robar el fuego poético, es un loco que canta el mal de muchos. Es un loco que canta para tontos.

(Today more than ever the poet needs to be a narrator, because the evils that assail us . . . are real and factual. . . . We readers seek in the poet someone who can evoke and explain the agony that rends our spirit. Perhaps we enjoy reading about how others see and explain our human misery. . . . The poet, while trying to capture the poetic flame, is a fool who sings of others' misfortunes. He is a fool who sings for fools.)

Crémer's 1956 volume, *Furia y Paloma*, continues the style and themes of his earlier works, especially that established in *Nuevos cantos*. Many of the titles, such as "Ciudad amenazada" (A City Threatened) and "Piedra sin agua" (Rock without Water), recall earlier poems, themes, and motifs. In "Mujer redonda" (Buxom Woman) Crémer laments the fate of Woman, who is chased by Man (a "lobo furtivo"—furtive wolf) until she becomes pregnant, at which point she is left to face alone her growing child, her "amor, haciéndose" (love, creating itself), and all the pain and peril of childbearing ("¡Cómo sabe el dolor de los hijos!"—Oh, how bitter-sweet is the pain of children!).

In "Milagro en Milán" (Miracle in Milan) the narrator is approached by a beggar who says, "Buenos días, señor," as he stretches out his hand to receive a few coins, rather than what he really needs and wants—love: "Solo el hombre va con su esperanza" (Man is alone with his hope). In "Madrigal de paz" (Madrigal of Peace) the speaker offers his beloved the peace and love he has won through his daily suffering; the reply is: "¡No merezco tanto dolor!" (I don't deserve such pain!). People cry out "love," but they end up suffering and dying in silence, alone. "Invocación a Sant-Yago" invokes Spain's timeless flirtation with violence, passion, and death. The speaker pleads:

> ¡Defiéndenos, Santiago, de tu España,
> batalladora con sus propios muertos!
> De esa España de piedra . . .
> de la pasión y la muerte . . .
> ¡Defiéndenos . . .
> de la España
> que llevamos cada uno en los adentros!

> (Save us, Santiago, from your Spain,
> waging battle with its own dead!
> From that Spain of stone . . .
> of passion and death . . .
> Save us . . .
> from that Spain
> that we all carry deep within us!)

After publishing his 1958 novel, *Libro de Caín*, and more poems in *Con la paz al hombro* (With Peace on My Shoulders, 1959), Crémer published *Tiempo de soledad* (Time of Solitude, 1962), an important collection of poems that won him two more poetry prizes. Here once again Crémer writes of his existential anxieties and his concern for the material and spiritual well-being of his fellow man. The twin motifs of time and space abound throughout these poems, providing the thematic mortar that holds them together.

Often the spacial element in question is Spain, which also finds its roots within the poet's being. In "Patria de la costumbre" (A Country of Regional Customs) Crémer writes of the country that "queriéndonos, nos hace" (as it loves us, creates us), a country buried deep within all Spaniards. It is a country that provides bread, work, and little everyday miracles. "Cada hombre," he writes, "es una Patria, entera y viva, y en ella se

deshace" (Each of us is a Country, complete and alive, but one in and by which we are finally consumed). Time and space are joined together in the conjunction of person and country. At times unsure of himself in these poems, at times reverting to his search for the God within himself, Crémer ultimately reaffirms his humanistic goals as champion of the destitute and the oppressed.

Crémer's *El amor y la sangre* (Love and Blood, 1966) also won two literary awards, with the poet continuing his existential defense of the humble and downtrodden in poems such as "El tributo del miedo" (The Tribute of Fear). In "Diario de guerra" (War Diary) and "Diálogo para un hombre solo" (Dialogue for a Solitary Man), subtitled "Elegía española" (Spanish Elegy), Crémer returns to the twin themes of war and country. Out of the agony and bitterness of war, from the ashes of destruction,

> sentimos la voz de la Patria yacente,
> profunda y quieta y sola, rebozada en
> los cales de los muertos fecundos, que
> son la savia dura de su destino eterno. . . .
> Pero ¿es esto una Patria, la necesaria
> Patria que implacable reclama su tributo
> en nosotros?

> (we feel the voice of the Country as it
> lies deep in its grave, quiet and alone,
> wrapped in the lime of the abundant dead, who
> are the bitter sap of its eternal destiny. . . .
> But is this a Country, one which inexorably exacts
>   its tribute
> from us?)

In 1967 Crémer's complete works up to and including *El amor y la sangre* were published in one volume, *Poesía total*. After writing several works on different subjects—including a second novel, *Historias de Chu-Ma-Chuco* (1970); another book of poems, *Lejos de esta lluvia tan amarga* (Far from This Rain so Bitter, 1974); an essay on his native León (*León*, 1971); as well as *El libro de Vela Zanetti* (1974), a biographical sketch based on interviews with the artist Vela Zanetti—Crémer published his book of poems *Los cercos* (The Fences, 1976), in which he tries to come to terms with all the themes and ideas that preoccupied him over the years.

The speaker feels circumscribed, yet defined, by the contradictory rings (circles, fences) that surround him—rings of silence and alienation, of love, goodness, and anguish, and of inevitable death and grief over the departed. *Los cercos* begins with the title poem, which progresses through a succession of different *cercos*: "extraños, de los silencios, del amor y de la vida, de la muerte, de la tierra y de la piedra" (strange rings, rings of silence, of love and life, of death, of earth and stone), concluding with a "cerco inútil" (useless circle).

In the last poem, "Testamento inútil" (Useless Testament), Crémer tries to imagine what he can leave to his wife and children: "Repaso lo que tengo. Nada que merezca la pena ser nombrado: dos llaves, unos libros y papeles inútiles con versos que nadie entenderá" (As I look over what I have to bequeath, there is nothing worth mentioning: two keys, some books, and useless papers with poems that nobody will understand). The poet seems preoccupied with time and with the brevity of human life compared to the expanse of human and material history: "¡Cuán poca vida, Dios, para tan largo viaje!" (Such a short life, dear God, for such a long journey!). In answer to youth, who asks "¿Que mundo nos legastéis?" (What have you left us?), the poet answers that he has really nothing to bequeath to young people. His clothes are old, and his books no longer speak to youth. At the end of his life the poet is at one with his poverty, the material deprivation that fashioned and nurtured his joie de vivre. At the end of a life, all one has left in essence is a name: "Firmo y rubrico. Un nombre. Es todo lo que tengo" (Signed and sealed. A name. That is all I have).

In 1979 a complete facsimile edition of *Espadaña* was published with a dedication by Lama and an introduction by Crémer: he argues that the essential differences between *Espadaña* and *Garcilaso* were due less to the latter's form than to its ideological content "que a nosotros se nos antojaba lamentablemente alejado de la realidad de España y como decidido a disipar de la pantalla nacional los humos de la pólvora y el clamor del ser humano, tan herido" (which in our opinion seemed to be so lamentably removed from the reality of Spain and intent on removing from the national consciousness the clouds of dust and the cries of humanity, so terribly wounded). Under Franco's iron first, "Dios era Dios y el franquismo su profecía" (God was God, and Franco was his prophet). One either survived miraculously, or died miserably, "sobre todo en la España del '44, que es la España trágica y negra de las hambres . . . de los cercos, de las espadas pendientes sobre todas las cabezas" (especially in the Spain of '44, which is

the tragic and black Spain of hunger . . . of rings [boundaries], of swords hanging precariously over heads). Impelled by the spiritual climate of the time, the "espadañistas" were much more in tune with Spain's immediate past and its present, with its victims of civil war, with its sick, impoverished, ignorant masses.

It was indeed fitting as a tribute that Crémer's complete poems (including a new collection titled "Ultima instancia" [Final Requests]) were published in two well-received volumes in 1984, when Crémer was seventy-five. Although his main claim to a place of eminence among his contemporaries is as editor and guiding spirit behind *Espadaña*, Eleanor Wright suggests that Crémer, in his multiple roles as critic, theorist, and editor, as well as poet, accomplished "more than perhaps any other single writer of the 40's toward the 'rehumanización' of Spanish literature."

References:

Guzmán Alvarez, *Lírica española del siglo XX: En busca de una trayectoria* (León, Spain: Nebrija, 1980), pp. 236-240, 320-329;

Max Aub, *Una nueva poesía española, 1950-1955* (Mexico City: Imprenta Universitaria, 1957);

Rafael Bosch, "The New Nonconformist Spanish Poetry," *Odyssey Review*, 2 (February 1962): 222-234;

Enrique Casamayor, "Tremendismo poético," *Cuadernos Hispanoamericanos*, 9 (May-June 1949): 745-753;

C. Castelao, "Victor Crémer, poeta social," *Hora Leonesa* (21 February 1976);

Santiago Daydí-Tolson, *The Post-Civil War Spanish Social Poets* (Boston: Twayne, 1983), pp. 10-21, 44-48;

Miguel Fernández-Braso, *De escritor a escritor* (Barcelona, 1970);

J. L. Flecniakoska, "Victoriano Crémer, fondateur de la revue *Espadaña* et poète des pauvres et des travailleurs," in his *Etudes Ibériques et Latino-Américains* (Poitiers: Presses Universitaires de France, 1968);

Victor García de la Concha, "*Espadaña* (1944-1951)," *Cuadernos Hispanoamericanos*, 236-237 (August 1969): 380-397;

García de la Concha, *La poesía española de 1935 a 1975, Volume II: De la poesía existencial a la poesía social (1944-1950)* (Madrid: Cátedra, 1987), pp. 669-682;

García de la Concha, *La poesía española de posguerra: Teoría de sus movimientos* (Madrid: Española, 1973), pp. 37, 304-363, 392-420;

Marc Guilhamet, "Victoriano Crémer," M.A. thesis, Université de Montpellier, 1963;

Felix Grande, *Apuntes sobre poesía española de posguerra* (Madrid: Taurus, 1970);

Paul Ilie, "The Disguises of Protest: Contemporary Spanish Poetry," *Michigan Quarterly Review*, 10 (January 1971): 38-48;

Ilie, *Literature and Inner Exile: Authoritarian Spain, 1939-1975* (Baltimore: Johns Hopkins University Press, 1980), pp. 38-43, 61-63, 144;

Manuel Lamana, *Literatura de posguerra* (Buenos Aires: Nova, 1961);

J. Lechner, *El compromiso en la poesía española del siglo XX: Parte segunda, de 1934 a 1974* (Leiden, Netherlands: Universitaire Pers Leiden, 1975);

Charles David Ley, *Spanish Poetry since 1939* (Washington, D.C.: Catholic University of America Press, 1962), pp. 119-121;

Joaquín Benito de Lucas, *Literatura de la posguerra: La poesía* (Madrid: Curcel, 1981), pp. 37-38;

Leopoldo de Luis, *La poesía aprendida: Poetas españoles contemporáneos*, volume 1 (Valencia: Bello, 1975), pp. 139-140, 205-209;

Luis, "Tres afirmaciones humanistas," *Estafeta Literaria*, 259 (1963): 4-5;

J. G. Manrique de Lara, *Poetas sociales españoles* (Madrid: E.P.E.S.A., 1974);

Manuel Mantero, *Poetas españoles de posguerra* (Madrid: Espasa-Calpe, 1986), pp. 190-197;

Joaquín Marco, *Ejercicios literarios* (Barcelona, 1969);

Sergio Moratiel Villa, *La poesía en acción de Victoriano Crémer* (León, Spain: Diocesana, 1973);

Antonio Pereira, "Victoriano Crémer, el escritor al día," *Estafeta Literaria*, 467 (1971): 16-19;

Fanny Rubio, "La poesía española en el marco cultural de los primeros años de posguerra," *Cuadernos Hispanoamericanos*, 276 (June 1973): 441-467;

Rubio, *Revistas poéticas españolas: 1939-1975* (Madrid: Turner, 1976), pp. 256-272;

Rubio, "Teoría y polémica en la poesía española de posguerra," *Cuadernos Hispanoamericanos*, 361-362 (July-August 1980): 199-214;

José Angel Valente, "Poesía para el pueblo," *Cuadernos Hispanoamericanos*, 18 (November-December 1950): 471-472;

Eleanor Wright, *The Poetry of Protest Under Franco* (London: Tamesis, 1986), pp. 16-23, 29-52, 82-91.

León Felipe

(11 April 1884 - 18 September 1968)

E. T. Aylward
University of South Carolina

BOOKS: *Versos y oraciones de caminante*, volume 1 (Madrid: Torres, 1920); volume 2 (New York Instituto de las Españas, 1930);

Drop a Star: Poema (Mexico City: Ortega, 1933);

Vendrá una espada de luz, anonymous (Veracruz, Mexico, 1933);

Antología (Madrid: Espasa-Calpe, 1935);

La insignia: Alocución poemática (Valencia: Tipografía Moderna, 1937);

Poesía revolucionaria (Barcelona: Oficinas de propaganda, 1937);

El payaso de las bofetadas y el pescador de caña: Poema trágico español (Mexico City: Fondo de Cultura Económica, 1938);

El hacha: Elegía española (Mexico City: Letras de Mexico, 1939);

Español del éxodo y del llanto: Doctrina, elegías y canciones (Mexico City: Casa de España, 1939);

El gran responsable: Grito y salmo (Mexico City: Tezontle, 1940);

Los lagartos (Mérida de Yucatán, Mexico: Editorial Huh, 1941);

Ganarás la luz: Biografía, poesía y destino (Mexico City: Cuadernos Americanos, 1943);

Antología rota (Buenos Aires: Pleamar, 1947; revised edition, Buenos Aires: Losada, 1957); revised again as *Nueva antología rota* (Mexico City: Finisterre, 1974);

Llamadme publicano (Mexico City: Almendros, 1950);

La manzana (Mexico City: Tezontle, 1951);

El asesino del sueño (Mexico City: Finisterre, 1954);

No es cordero . . . que es cordera (Mexico City: Cuadernos Americanos, 1955);

El ciervo: Poema (Mexico City: Grijalbo, 1958);

Dos obras: La mordida y Tristán e Isolda (Mexico City: Colección Teatro de Bolsillo, 1958);

Cuatro poemas con epígrafe y colofón (Madrid & Palma de Mallorca, Spain: Papeles de Son Armadans, 1958);

El Juglarón (Mexico City: Ecuador, 1961);

Diré cómo murió (San Salvador: Ediciones 5° Regimiento, 1961);

¿Qué se hizo el Rey Don Juan? (Mexico City: Ecuador, 1962);

Obras completas (Buenos Aires: Losada, 1963);

¡Oh, este viejo y roto violín! (Mexico City: Tezontle, 1966);

Antología y homenaje (Mexico City: Finisterre, 1967 [i.e., 1966]);

Biblioteca León Felipe, 8 volumes (Mexico City: Málaga, 1967-1974);

Rocinante (Mexico City: Finisterre, 1969);

110

¡Oh, el barro, el barro! (Mexico City: Finisterre, 1970);

Israel (Mexico City: Finisterre, 1970);

Versos del mercolico o del sacamuelas (Mexico City: Finisterre, 1974);

Obra poética escogida, edited by Gerardo Diego (Madrid: Espasa-Calpe, 1977).

TRANSLATIONS: Marie Louise Antoinette de Régnier, *El seductor* (Madrid: Estrella, 1921);

Waldo David Frank, *América hispana* (Madrid & Barcelona: Espasa-Calpe, 1932);

Frank, *España virgen* (Madrid: Espasa-Calpe, 1937);

Walt Whitman, *Canto a mí mismo* (Buenos Aires: Losada, 1941);

Benjamin Franklin, *Autobiografía y otros escritos*, edited by Mark Van Doren (Mexico City: Nuevo Mundo, 1942);

Willa Cather, *Una dama perdida* (Mexico City: Nuevo Mundo, 1942).

León Felipe (born León Felipe Camino Galicia) is best remembered as one of the most vociferous of the poets in exile who railed against the Francisco Franco regime and the violent overthrow of the republican government in the Spanish Civil War. From his residence in Mexico City he clamored incessantly against the injustices perpetrated by the Falangist government; furthermore, through his role of *intelectual republicano*, he came to serve as the spiritual leader of many Spanish poets of the left in the postwar period.

He was born in Tabara, in the province of Zamora (region of León), in the northwest quadrant of Spain, on 11 April 1884; two years later he and his family moved to another Leonese town, Sequeros, near Salamanca. In 1893 the family took up residence in Santander on the north-central coast of Old Castile, where Felipe attended a Catholic grammar school before taking a bachelor's degree at the Instituto in Santander. His father, a notary, was old-fashioned and paid little attention to his son's sensitivity; fortunately, young Felipe was encouraged to develop his talents by his mother and an uncle.

Felipe opted for a career in pharmacy because, as Guillermo de Torre says in his prologue to Felipe's *Obras completas* (Complete Works, 1963), it entailed a very brief training period that could be completed in Madrid, a city to which Felipe was strongly attracted because of his fondness for the theater. (At the age of sixteen he had di-

rected a students' theater group in Santander.) In 1900 he moved to the Spanish capital to study for an advanced degree in pharmacy; his other intention was to gain a foothold in Madrid's theatrical circle. It was at this time that he was profoundly moved by a performance of *Hamlet*, an event which inspired a lifelong interest in William Shakespeare's works.

When Felipe's father died, Felipe hastened to finish his degree and returned to Santander (in 1908) to work as a pharmacist and assume the leadership role in the family; an older brother was unable or unwilling to discharge this duty. Felipe later accepted a similar position in Balmaceda, a town in the Basque Provinces. Once the family's financial security was guaranteed, he joined José Tallavi's theater group, in which he worked with several distinguished actresses. He later signed on with the Juan Espantaleón company and toured all the major towns and provinces of Spain and Portugal.

Some financial indiscretions caused Felipe to spend three years in a Santander jail, but he made prudent use of this time by composing verses and familiarizing himself with the Bible and *Don Quixote*. He identified strongly with Miguel de Cervantes' mock hero; Felipe came to view the balance of good and evil, of grace and sin, as the yardstick by which man's existence should be judged. By 1918 he had arranged to divide his time between idle winters in Madrid and the rest of the year, when he was employed as a pharmacy manager in sleepy Castilian towns such as Almonacid de Zorita (near Guadalajara), where he finished writing his first volume of verses (published in 1920).

In Madrid in 1919 he began to frequent the meetings of a literary circle at the Café Universal; the writer Salvador de Madariaga subsequently brought Felipe's manuscript to Enrique Díez-Canedo, editor of the magazine *España*. This publication touted Felipe's poetry and printed several of his poems a year in advance of the publication of his first volume. Given this publicity and Díez-Canedo's firm support, the young poet felt confident enough to give a public reading at Madrid's Atheneum. When *Versos y oraciones de caminante* (Poems and Prayers of a Traveler) was published, it is not surprising that it was well received.

Felipe's emergence on the literary scene coincided with the dawn of a period of renovation in the Spanish lyric that would last until 1935. Unfortunately for him, the timing was rather bad: both

Felipe (right) and an unidentified friend (left) with sculptor Victorio Macho and his bust of Felipe in Lima, Peru, 1946

the "old" school (that of Juan Ramón Jiménez and followers) and the burgeoning "ultraists" rejected Felipe's peculiar poetic style. His greatest shortcoming, from the point of view of the radicals at least, was that his verses represented a humble return to simplicity at a moment when poetry about "modern" (albeit often trivial) themes was the fashion. Felipe, the pilgrim and vagabond, would not find acceptance for his peculiar style until the mid 1930s, when the upheaval caused by the civil war would work to his advantage.

He spent the years from 1920 to 1922 as a hospital administrator on Fernando Po Island off the African coast. In 1922, en route to Africa while returning from a vacation in Madrid, Felipe abruptly decided to sail from Cádiz to Veracruz, Mexico, on the steamship *Cristóbal Colón*. Once in the New World, he used a letter of introduction by the Mexican writer Alfonso Reyes as his credential and passport to enter one of the circles of Mexican intellectuals; he came to know such notables as the reformer José Vasconcelos, painter Diego Rivera, philosopher Antonio Caso, and writers Pedro Henríquez-Ureña and Daniel Cosío Villegas.

At a Christmas celebration (*las posadas*) in 1924 Felipe met and fell in love with Berta Gamboa, who was a university professor in the United States on vacation in Mexico at the time. He followed her back to New York, and they were married shortly thereafter in Brooklyn in 1925. The early years of what would be a union full of love and mutual devotion were spent in hard economic circumstances. Felipe's career as a teacher of Spanish with the Berlitz School was abruptly terminated by his dismissal for "incompetence," although his version of the incident tells of an impatient American ballerina who demanded an intensive one-week course that would prepare her to travel in Spain but then found his pace too slow to meet her extraordinary needs.

Felipe subsequently decided to seek certification as a Spanish teacher, so he enrolled at Columbia University, where he studied under the renowned scholar Federico de Onís. By 1925 he was employed as a lecturer in Spanish language and literature at Cornell University. Berta joined him on the Cornell faculty shortly thereafter, and they remained at the Ivy League school until 1929. This period was dedicated to reading and fruitful exercise in the poetic craft, a time that he always recalled with much satisfaction. The Cornell years included the translation—with Berta's help—of Waldo David Frank's *Virgin Spain* (which he eventually published in 1937) and the preparation of the manuscript for volume 2 of his *Versos y oraciones de caminante* (1930). In this second volume one notes a more elevated tone than in the previous book; a spiritual kinship with Walt Whitman also emerges. Another influence on Felipe's verses is the Bible.

While on sabbatical leave in Mexico in 1930, he wrote *Drop a Star* (1933), a somewhat difficult and obscure work reminiscent of T. S. Eliot's *The Waste Land* (1922) and the verses of William Blake, John Donne, and the other metaphysical poets of whom Felipe was fond at the time. The attempt to give a new slant to his poetry makes *Drop a Star* a work that divides his career into two distinct periods. In this volume one notices the beginnings of a deep introspection, of a questioning about the meaning of life, and of an unfolding of profound sentiments that would be more thoroughly developed in later works. The principal image in *Drop a Star* is that of the world as a slot machine that is activated only when one drops a star into the coin deposit.

In the second year of the Spanish Republic (1932), a nostalgic Felipe returned to Spain for a visit of several months. He then came back to the United States in 1933 to accept a teaching position at New Mexico Highlands University. Shortly thereafter the Lázaro Cárdenas government in Mexico named him to direct a troupe of actors who performed on the radio for the Office of Public Education; at the same time he was hired to teach a course on *Don Quixote* for American students at the National University in Mexico City.

He returned again to his native land in 1934 to dedicate himself to some translation projects that were pending. A year later some of his close friends edited and published an anthology of his verses (*Antología*) as a homage to the poet-errant. Ever the wanderer, he journeyed across the Atlantic again early in 1936 to accept the post of cultural attaché for the Spanish Embassy in Panama, and a professorship at the university there as well. Only five months later, when the barracks revolt in Morocco in July signaled the outbreak of the Spanish Civil War, Felipe was among the first to declare his loyalty to the Republican cause. Before departing Colón for Spain on a Dutch steamer, he delivered over the radio a blistering farewell address (published in *Repertorio*

Americano, 5 October 1936) in which he excoriated certain archconservative clergy and Spanish businessmen in Panama who had openly declared their support for the rebel (Franco) cause. Returning to Madrid, he endured the October and November bombardment of that city before moving on to the safety of Valencia in January 1937 with other Spanish intellectuals. On 11 February 1937 he wrote his first major poem on the war, *La insignia*, inspired by the fall of Málaga; he later gave public readings of this work in Valencia and Barcelona, which were still in Republican hands. *La insignia* is an appeal for unity among the sundry leftist (Loyalist) factions; he calls on them to band together behind a common symbol—a single star—to defeat a foe that is detestable to them all. The poem enjoyed special popularity in anarchist strongholds and was quickly published. Instead of taking a narrow partisan stance, he seeks in the poem to rise above individual concerns by appealing to all men of a leftist persuasion to display a common spirit of heroism and willingness to sacrifice for a lofty ideal.

Ironically the same anarchists that had enthusiastically adopted *La insignia* as their own nearly took the life of its composer. Pablo Neruda, who met Felipe during the hostilities and later according to Mauricio de la Selva, called him "contradictory . . . a Nietzschean poet, a charming man," is credited with saving Felipe's life by persuading two soldiers to rescue him from an anarchist mob that was about to execute him because of some misunderstanding. It has been said that Felipe's appeal to the anarchists probably stemmed from a certain air of undisciplined, mocking rebelliousness in his wartime verses. Throughout the civil war he was attracted to the anarchist cause and was given to delivering fiery, iconoclastic—often blasphemous—anticlerical philippics in verse in areas where the anarchists were numerous.

The suffering of the Spanish nation from 1936 to 1939 provided him with a forum and theme particularly suited to his talent for epic/heroic verse. His meager aptitude for quiet, simple lyrical composition was no longer a handicap, and he took full advantage of this opportunity to raise his voice in Homeric tones to sing of the cruelty, horror, and gross injustice that he found all about him. The winds of war uprooted what had been the everyday reality of Spain and transformed certain ordinary events into heroic monuments of deep symbolic value. Felipe was now free to juxtapose the sublime with the base, to

Felipe in Mexico City during the 1960s

shuffle old and new poetic formulas in forging a new kind of epic for the times, to pour out a very personal kind of music without fear of censure from the purists.

Felipe fled Spain in early 1938 as the bombs rained down on Barcelona, but he continued to compose and read his verses even as he made his way slowly to the New World. He read prepublication selections from *El payaso de las bofetadas y el pescador de caña* (The Battered Clown and Cane-Pole Fisherman, 1938) to the public in Havana and Mexico City. He and several other exiled Spanish intellectuals found employment at the newly established Casa de España, founded by Mexican president Cárdenas in the capital city. For the next seven years, in a striking departure from his previous vagabond habits, Felipe resided in Mexico City; he fiercely embraced his role as a poet in exile and broke completely with

what he called "rotten Spain" to move toward the real essence of his homeland, which he claimed he never abandoned.

This double movement of repudiation and rediscovery was manifested in a chain of painful and often vindictive works that he produced without pause during that period: *El hacha* (The Axe, 1939); *Español del éxodo y del llanto* (The Spaniard of the Exodus and the Flood of Tears, 1939); *El gran responsable* (The Great Responsible One, 1940); *Los lagartos* (The Lizards, 1941); and finally *Ganarás la luz* (You Will Win the Light, 1943). This last work, the greatest articulation of his feelings of pain and protest, touched the hearts and souls of more readers than any of his previous efforts, and it secured for him a permanent place of honor, even among readers who did not fancy the lyric genre. His sober and precise language more than compensated for the lack of lyric quality in his verses, which were often a hybrid of prose and poetry. Rather than be narrowly political, Felipe attempts to be visionary, utopian, even quixotic in his search for justice. His subject is humankind, not just the Spaniard, and the misery people must endure. The light referred to in the title is the light of true justice, the fire that Prometheus brought down to humans in the mythical past. The poet is likewise Promethean in nature.

In the meantime Felipe had joined with fellow exiles Juan Larrea and Bernardo Ortiz de Montellano to seek the aid of Jesús Silva Herzog in April 1941 to salvage the floundering journal *España peregrina*. After several meetings the committee opted to create an entirely new publication, *Cuadernos Americanos*, for distribution in Latin America, but which would treat events and accomplishments of global significance. The first edition of the new journal appeared on 2 January 1942, and it eventually became one of the principal intellectual forums of the Hispanic world.

By 1945 Felipe was prepared to resume his previous vagabond lifestyle. *Cuadernos Americanos* was firmly established; the institution Casa de España had become the Colegio de México. He departed on an unstructured, open-ended grand tour of Central and South America, earning his way by giving public lectures, readings, and sermons at every opportunity, almost always to an enthusiastic audience. He played the role of the bearded pilgrim from Spain, his native land's authentic messenger in exile who had come to stir his listeners with religious fervor. In the hands of Felipe, the figure of Don Quixote became an epic symbol of Spain battling for justice.

At about the time of his return to Mexico, where he resided until his death in 1968, he published *Antología rota* (Fragmented Anthology, 1947), a collection of his favorite compositions from his earlier volumes, plus a few new pieces. The year 1950 marked the six hundredth anniversary of the death of Juan Ruiz, the archpriest of Hita, and, in honor of this great medieval Spanish poet, Felipe dedicated to his memory the first part of his *Llamadme publicano* (Call me a Publican, 1950). The following year Felipe turned to his original love, the theater, with the publication of *La manzana* (The Apple), a dramatic fable based on the story of Paris and Helen of Troy that Felipe called a "Dionysian film," one governed principally by fantasy and imagination. These experiments in the drama continued throughout the 1950s with skillful re-creations

and paraphrases of some of the great Shakespearean masterpieces, including *Twelfth Night* (*No es cordero . . . que es cordera* [Not a Ram . . . but a Ewe]) in 1953 (published in 1955) and *Macbeth* (*El asesino del sueño* [The Dream Murderer]) in 1954. These recastings of classics show Felipe's recommitment to a narrow, preromantic concept of originality; he emphasized the virtues of continuity within the classic tradition by a constant polishing, in successive versions and re-creations, of classic myths and traditional themes. His artistic purpose in carrying out these paraphrases was to use familiar Shakespearean works as points of departure for his own concepts and creations.

During this same period he reworked and published some brief (fifteen-minute) comic sketches he had authored in the early 1950s for Mexican television, including *Dos obras: La mordida y Tristán e Isolda* (Two Plays: A Piece of the Action and Tristan and Isolde, 1958). These and six additional sketches were eventually published in one volume in 1961: *El Juglarón* (The Teller of Tall Tales).

Felipe's poetic output waned considerably in the last decade of his life. The year 1958 saw the publication of *El ciervo* (The Stag), portions of which he had read in 1956 at the palace of Fine Arts in Mexico City. A most attractive volume, richly illustrated with sketches by promising young Spanish and Mexican artists, it was nonetheless filled with bitter verses and a spirit of self-deprecation that overtook Felipe in his final years. The poems are dominated by images of death and nothingness; the wind is his constant obsession, a haunting symbol of an implacable fate that controls all people. He himself called it a perverse book ("un libro maldito"), and it truly has all the earmarks of a poet's deathbed envoi to his reader, which may account for the false rumor of Felipe's death that circulated in Spain and Latin America in 1959. A major cause of his poetic acidity may have been the death of his beloved wife, Berta, shortly before the work was published; the sad occasion is recalled in his touching and memorable poem "Bertuca," from another 1958 work: *Cuatro poemas con epígrafe y colofón* (Four Poems with an Epigraph and a Colophon).

In his final years he often declared that he was ashamed of most of his verses, but in his eighty-second year his muse returned and he published a 216-page volume, *¡Oh, este viejo y roto violín!* (Oh, This Old and Broken Violin!, 1966). Felipe died in Mexico City 18 September 1968 at the age of eighty-four, leaving behind a rich store of verses that in recent years have been collected, edited, and published by his friends and admirers; the most notable of these anthologies is Gerardo Diego's *Obra poética escogida* (Selected Poetry, 1977).

For many young poets of the postwar generation, León Felipe has exercised a profound influence. His biblical, patriarchal countenance was often matched by the prophetic resonance of his verses, which frequently echoed like those of Isaiah, Amos, and Ezekiel. For some he was a Hispanic Walt Whitman; for others he represented the conscience of Republican Spain crying out from foreign soil in the name of justice. He relished his Promethean role as the bringer of light to the outcast and the nonconformist. From his refuge in Mexico he served as an inspiration for numerous anti-Franco poets and intellectuals in Spain and Spanish America. The most enduring monument to his memory, however, is the journal *Cuadernos Americanos*, which continues to this day to remind readers of Felipe and his quest for freedom, justice, and intellectual integrity.

References:

Manuel Andújar, "Apuntes sobre León Felipe," *Cuadernos Americanos*, 266, no. 3 (1986): 139-147;

Alfredo Cardona Peña, "León Felipe y el Viento," in his *Pablo Neruda y Otros Ensayos* (Mexico City: Andrea, 1955), pp. 117-124;

Luis Cernuda, *Estudios sobre poesía española contemporánea* (Madrid: Guadarrama, 1957), pp. 141-150;

José Francisco Cirre, *Forma y espíritu de una lírica Española* (Mexico City: Panamericana, 1950);

Gustavo Correa, ed., *Antología de la poesía española* (Madrid: Gredos, 1980), pp. 181-182, 527-528;

Germán Gullón, "La poesía de León Felipe y el contexto histórico-literario," *Cuadernos Americanos*, 266, no. 3 (1986): 170-176;

Sabas Martín, "León Felipe y el teatro," *Cuadernos Hispanoamericanos*, 411 (September 1984): 35-40;

Françoise Peyrégone, "Las metáforas del dinamismo en León Felipe," *Cuadernos Americanos*, 249, no. 4 (1983): 199-215;

Luis Rius, "La nueva poesia de León Felipe," *Cuadernos Americanos*, 164 (January-February 1966): 199-211;

Alfredo A. Roggiano, "León Felipe o el poeta del ser de España," *Cuadernos Americanos*, 266, no. 3 (1986): 184-192;

Alberto Sánchez, "Cervantismo y quijotismo de León Felipe," *Anales cervantinos*, 22 (1984): 181-198;

Mauricio de la Selva, "Otra vez León Felipe," *Cuadernos Americanos*, 198 (January 1975): 213-228;

Guillermo de Torre, Prologue to Felipe's *Obras completas* (Buenos Aires: Losada, 1963), pp. 9-26;

Laura Villavicencio, "Estructura, ritmo e imaginería en *Ganarás la luz* de León Felipe," *Cuadernos Americanos*, 183 (May-June 1972): 167-191;

Luis Felipe Vivanco, "León Felipe y su ritmo combativo," in his *Introducción a la poesía española contemporánea* (Madrid: Guadarrama, 1971), pp. 145-175;

Marielena Zelaya Kolker, "Corrientes mexicanas en la vida y obra de León Felipe," *Cuadernos Americanos*, 266, no. 3 (1986): 193-200.

Angela Figuera

(30 October 1902 - 2 April 1984)

Janet Pérez
Texas Tech University

BOOKS: *Mujer de barro* (Madrid: SAETA, 1948);
Soria pura (Madrid: Jura, 1949);
Vencida por el ángel (Alicante, Spain: Verbo, 1950);
El grito inútil (Alicante, Spain: Such & Serra, 1952);
Víspera de la vida (Madrid: Nebli, 1953);
Los días duros (Madrid: Aguado, 1953);
Belleza cruel (Mexico City: General de Ediciones, 1958);
Primera antología (Caracas: Lírica Hispana, 1961);
Toco la tierra: Letanías (Madrid: Rialp/Adonais, 1962);
Antología, edited by Alfredo Gracia Vicente (Monterrey, Mexico: Sierra Madre, 1969);
Antología total, edited by Julián Marcos (Madrid: Videosistemas, 1973);
Cuentos tontos para niños listos (Monterrey, Mexico: Sierra Madre, 1979);
Canciones para todo el año (Monterrey, Mexico: Trillas, 1984);
Obras completas, edited by Julio Figuera (Madrid: Hiperión, 1986).

Angela Figuera belongs chronologically not to the "mid-century generation," with whose writings her own are grouped, but to the "Generation of 1927," which included Federico García Lorca, Vicente Aleixandre, Rafael Alberti, Luis Cernuda, and many lesser poets. She began publishing relatively late in life, at the age of forty-six, and has been included by some commentators as the third member of the postwar "Basque triumvirate," with Gabriel Celaya and Blas de Otero (usually considered the leaders of the social poets, while Figuera is often overlooked). Chronological differences may partially explain some critical forgetfulness of Figuera, but traditional critical neglect of women writers cannot be discounted as a factor. Her wartime Republican ties may also have played a part. Whatever the reasons may be, the secondary bibliography on Figuera is sparse, and over half the titles are in the nature of *homenajes* (tributes) following her death. A large portion of the remainder comprises brief mentions in anthologies or panoramic works on postwar poetry or postwar literature generally. Discounting these and the prologues to certain editions of Figuera's works, there remain only a handful of titles, ranging from reviews and interviews to a small number of serious critical essays.

Rather than a feminist, Figuera is feminine in her poetry, with her early books celebrating motherhood, marriage, conjugal love, and domestic life. Maternity has been termed (by Roberta Quance) the axis of her poetry, with the stances adopted during the course of her career being variations on this theme. Figuera would probably have protested, at least initially, at being termed a feminist, for she proudly identified with the traditional roles of wife and mother. Her "social" poetry, part of the larger literature of engagement in postwar Europe, likewise has an unmistakably feminine and personal viewpoint, although the testimonial thematics and denunciation of injustice and oppression coincide in other ways with the social poetry authored by men. Much like Miguel de Unamuno, Figuera disliked being pigeonholed, and like this fellow Basque of an earlier generation, she, too, eschewed literary "isms" and trendy aesthetics.

Born in Bilbao, Spain, on 30 October 1902, the eldest of nine children of an industrial engineer and a teacher, Angela Figuera Aymerich enjoyed a peaceful childhood, although her mother's delicate health obliged Angela to devote much time and energy to caring for her younger siblings. Given the great importance of themes of motherhood and love for children in her poetry, this circumstance of her early years may have contributed to an especially strong development of maternal instincts. Almost from childhood Figuera wrote stories and poems but destroyed them soon afterward. One notebook with some two hundred pages of unpublished juvenilia has survived in the possession of Julio Figuera, her cousin and husband.

Angela Figuera Aymerich

After completing the *bachillerato* (high-school degree) in Bilbao in 1924, Angela Figuera had a wish to study literature, but this was stymied for two years by her father's desire that she choose a more profitable career. Eventually she began to study on her own, taking the course examinations in literature at the University of Valladolid. When her father died in 1927, Figuera's paternal uncle in Madrid sent for her so she could

attend the university there for her final year of study. As her father's death had left the family without income and dependent upon her and her grandmother, they moved in 1930 to Madrid, where Figuera taught in private schools, the Colegio Decroly, and the Montessori school, while also giving private tutorials in wealthy homes. After some three years of this difficult existence, she studied to qualify herself as a secondary-school teacher and in 1933 obtained a job in the Andalusian town of Huelva. She and her cousin Julio then married and moved there where life was relatively uneventful for some three years, save for the death of their first child due to complications during delivery.

In the summer of 1936 Figuera was taking a course in Madrid, and the outbreak of the civil war in July separated the couple when she was again expecting a child. Their only son, Juan Ramón, was born in December of that year while her husband served at the front in the Republican army. Shortly after her son's birth Figuera and her family were evacuated with other Republican refugees to Valencia, where they lived for the next two years. When her husband was transferred to a village near Murcia, she spent the final months of the war teaching there. The war's difficulties and hardships only multiplied afterward for those on the losing side; Figuera, her husband, and her other relatives lost their jobs and were obliged to begin anew. Figuera's teaching career was at an end.

During the first postwar decade Figuera devoted herself, of necessity, to her son, her home, and her writing, finishing her first book, *Mujer de barro* (Clay Woman) and publishing it in 1948. Internal evidence indicates that the poems of this first collection were written over a period of more than a decade: for example, "Muerto al nacer" (Dead at Birth) clearly refers to the death in childbirth of her first son before the beginning of the war. Figuera managed, after her book was published, to obtain work at the National Library, helping with Madrid's first bookmobile and working as a free-lance translator from 1948 to 1949. Her second collection of poetry, *Soria pura* (Pure Soria, 1949) was the result of summer vacations spent in the Sorian village of Burgo de Osma and bicycling in the surrounding countryside. The joys of the discovery of nature—earth, streams, trees, summer storms, and gentle breezes—permeate the collection, although a few somber thoughts about country folk foreshadow the poet's later social concerns.

Mid century marked the beginning of Spain's "social" literature, a neorealist movement affecting the novel, theater, and poetry alike, characterized by an attitude of covert political dissent, concentration on social and economic injustice, and a sense of solidarity with the poor, the oppressed, and the vanquished. Rigors of the Francisco Franco regime's censorship made any overt expression of opposition or criticism difficult and dangerous, and Figuera's Republican background increased the risk. Nevertheless, her growing awareness of political reprisals and persecution and of social inequities and stagnation led to a change of direction in her poetry, placing the books of her mature creative period (1950-1962) very much in the mainstream of social poetry. The decade of the 1950s is Figuera's most productive, for in it she published her most characteristic works: *Vencida por el ángel* (Overcome by the Angel, 1950); *El grito inútil* (The Futile Cry, 1952); *Víspera de la vida* (Vespers of Life, 1953); *Los días duros* (Difficult Days, 1953); and *Belleza cruel* (Cruel Beauty, 1958). She completed her last major poetry collection, *Toco la tierra* (I Touch the Earth, 1962), during the years 1959 to 1961, after which she moved from Madrid to the provincial city of Avilés to be with her husband. (He had been working there as a civil servant since 1959). Isolation from literary circles, loss of contact with other writers, and, perhaps, age combined to halt her activities in the forefront of combative poetry. Her last two books in her lifetime were for children, the first a group of narrative poems originally invented for her granddaughter, *Cuentos tontos para niños listos* (Stupid Tales for Clever Children), unpublished until several years later (1979). Figuera and her husband returned to Madrid after almost a decade in Avilés, and there she remained from 1971 until her death. During her final years, she suffered problems of the heart and lungs, dying in 1984 at the age of eighty-one. *Canciones para todo el año* (Year-Round Songs) was published posthumously (1984).

Mujer de barro contains a joyful affirmation of motherhood as the vehicle for the perpetuation of the species, a positive acceptance of womanhood as defined by patriarchal society. Reflecting the intimacy of a happy marriage and fulfilling life, the poems reveal Figuera's subjectivity as well as including some sensual erotic lyrics that blend traditional themes with then-popular forms. The brief collection has three internal divisions, the first untitled and consisting of love

poetry. The second, "Poemas de mi hijo y yo" (Poems of My Child and Me) is inspired in large measure by her son's growth (for example, there are poems marking his third and fifth birthdays, and his going to school), his games, childhood disguises, and persistent questioning. "El fruto redondo" (The Round Fruit), the third part, offers more thematic variety, from poems about the plenitude of nature in its various seasons to further erotic poetry and poems on miscellaneous topics such as insomnia, laziness, and problems of poetic expression.

Soria pura, evoking the restful months of her summers spent in rural tranquillity, expresses the relief of those who have weathered severe storms and survived, and the cautious optimism of those who have suffered, yet persevere. Figuera looks back upon wartime trials and the hardships of peace but does not dwell upon them: in the vein of Antonio Machado (whose famous lyric descriptions of the humble beauty of Soria and its surrounding countryside influenced Figuera's choice of title), she contemplates the centuries of human history imposed upon timeless nature in relation to her own present circumstances and those of her husband and son. Insofar as *Soria pura* looks backward to now mercifully distant hardships as a point of departure, the collection may be seen as transitional between the intimate, individual focus of Figuera's first poems and the more collective preoccupations of later works. Dreams, nostalgia, the simple pleasures of swimming in a mountain river or resting on the bank, memories of childhood, and a brief section of five poems written in homage to Machado round out the contents of *Soria pura*.

According to Robert Saladrigas, Figuera identified her reading of Gabriel Celaya's *Las cosas como son* (Things as They Are, 1950) as the moment of her discovery of the inadequacy of traditional lyrics as vehicles for her poetic communication. From this point onward her poetry acquires more aggressive, rebellious notes and becomes less personal and less affirmative, more critical and denunciatory. In some poetry of *Vencida por el ángel*, her next collection, she adopts an attitude of self-criticism, as the "new" Figuera denounces the egotism of the old for having sequestered herself in domestic tranquillity, ignoring the world's ugliness and problems. The title poem, which alludes indirectly to the biblical account of Jacob's wrestling with the angel, conveys a metaphorical description of the poet's attempt to close her eyes to the sufferings of humanity before being finally overcome. Some compositions of clear sociopolitical import are addressed to God (a common device among early postwar Spanish poets to avoid censorship of their works). Echoes of the civil war are both direct and indirect, as one of the longest poems re-creates an experience during the bombardment of Madrid while the poet was pregnant, and another refers obliquely to innumerable anonymous deaths. Insofar as Figuera accepted a more public and active role from this third book onward, it may be said that her attitude henceforth changed in the direction of feminism. At least, there is a heightened awareness of sisterhood in the poems, an identifying with other mothers in their problems and suffering. Figuera's compassion eventually produced a kind of promaternal politics in which she speaks out against poverty, violence, wars, and oppression.

At the same time that Figuera moved toward collective concerns and away from intimate ones, she moved further from traditional metrics in the direction of free verse and a less lyrical, more prosaic and direct expression. Even in the beginning she had seldom employed rhyme; on the few occasions that it appears, it is assonant. One of her most significant poetic devices is repetition, often acquiring ironic undertones because of some element introduced in the interim (a trait found in many poets of the "mid-century generation"). Metonymy and metaphor, the rhetorical question, litotes (understatement), prosopopoeia (personification), and dehumanization are also frequently used. Personal notes are not entirely extirpated by collective concerns, nor do political preoccupations smother all expression of such universal and eternal poetic themes as the love of parents, search for metaphysical meanings, and daily struggles with tedium and for existence.

In both *El grito inútil* and its successor, *Víspera de la vida*, the historical present with its problems and implications for women shares the stage with less temporally grounded but equally real and human concerns. *El grito inútil* recalls at times the poems of Dámaso Alonso's *Hijos de la ira* (Children of Wrath, 1944), and at other times strongly resembles the social poetry of Celaya, with the difference that Figuera focuses often upon women. Death, collective guilt, social responsibility, an idealization of labor and the working man, poverty, silence, imprisonment, exile, unemployment, and emigration are among her themes, but the main leitmotiv is a question as to

the usefulness of poetry. The first poem of *El grito inútil* implicitly queries whether the poet as woman can have any effect in her sociopolitical endeavor where so many men have failed. Looking back upon poetry-for-art's sake (seductively pleasant for readers as well as the poet), she realizes that there can be no turning back, even though she continues to doubt and wonder what she can accomplish. "Unidad" (Unity) one of her more frequently anthologized poems, appeals to the universal brotherhood of man as the only way to build a better world. "Posguerra" (Postwar) begins with a summons to war's survivors to rejoice that they are among the living, but it ends by recognizing that war has marked them indelibly and that they are only shells. "Mujeres del mercado" (Market Women), one of Figuera's most feminist pieces, presents lower-class women in the city market: prematurely aged, ragged, and dirty, choosing only the cheapest produce and worst meat, with nothing to go home to but a drunken, brutal husband in a fetid room, and perhaps another unwanted pregnancy.

The title poem of *Víspera de la vida* returns to Figuera's leitmotiv of motherhood, describing the pain and cries of childbirth, juxtaposed with the death throes of a bum, a bit of human debris that once was a man. Imagery of natural flora and fauna persists in the book, but these are no longer simple objects of delight; instead, they become signs of frustration or of ignorance. Figuera expresses solitude and alienation, previously absent from her verses, and protests against the unknown and unknowable. Childhood memories of Christmas are relived in "Entonces me nacías" (Then for Me You Were Born), while filial piety inspires a tribute to her father (and her own childish innocence) in "Cuando mi padre pintaba" (When My Father Painted). Poems devoted to Cain, Abel, her dead sister María Paz, and to her mother's death are interspersed between others concerning blood and the mother of a young poet recently drowned.

Los días duros appears somewhat out of sequence in Figuera's production, as some of the poems were written in 1950 or earlier. This group of compositions was combined in a single volume with the previously published books *Vencida por el ángel*, *Víspera de la vida*, and *El grito inútil* (all of Figuera's "social" production to that date). The previously unpublished poems are more aggressive and strident than anything by Figuera that had appeared earlier, and the posture adopted is one of solidarity with other moth-

Ha muerto un poeta. Uno de los más grandes de todos los tiempos. Que hablaba y escribía en español. Que amaba a España entrañablemente. Hablé con Pablo Neruda en París, en Setiembre de 1957. Sencillo y cordial; emotivo y apasionado en sus adentros, cuando hablaba, monocorde y pausado, era su palabra como un agua cálida y viva que se dejara caer gota a gota. Hablamos largamente. De España. Y de la poesía. Y de la poesía española. Y de los poetas españoles. Al despedirnos, lo vi pensativo. En una próxima entrevista, me dijo: "Quiero dirigirme a los poetas españoles de hoy. Cuando salí de España los dejé perdidos. Luego los ignoré. Tú me los has traído." Y, en mi presencia, escribió, para ellos, una carta emocionada y generosa que no llegó a publicarse. Han pasado dieciséis años y ahora vivimos la tristeza de su muerte. Leed su carta y sabréis como, a pesar de todo, Pablo Neruda llevó siempre a España en el corazón.

Angela Figuera Aymerich

Madrid - Setiembre - 73

Figuera's introduction to a 1957 letter she received from Pablo Neruda; this note and his letter were published in her Obras completas *(1986), edited by her husband, Julio Figuera (by permission of the Estate of Angela Figuera)*

ers the world over; at the same time, she begins to expose contradictions between, on the one hand, the cult of the Virgin and the idealization of mothers, and, on the other hand, the disempowerment of women. Figuera's most explicit rejection of her earlier, uncommitted lifestyle and limited, individual concerns appears in the title poem of *Los días duros*, as she again blames herself for having placed her roles as lover, wife, and mother foremost, writing of personal pleasures and the joys of nature instead of life's struggles and sorrows, pains and wrongs. Although she harshly judges this earlier "weakness," she nevertheless vows not to forget her love and her dreams in the newly assumed need to be strong and combative. Tears and images of violence multiply throughout the collection.

Figuera's increased combativeness produced other poems that she did not attempt for the moment to publish, perhaps realizing that they would be censored and endanger her jobs as librarian and translator. She withheld them (possibly contributing to the break in her rapid rhythm of production) until a grant to do library study in Paris in 1957 provided an opportunity to take these more overtly critical and perilous compositions out of Spain. As a former Republican, Figuera may have feared that her mail was under surveillance, at least that sent to foreign countries. In any case, the poems were in effect smuggled out of the country and sent to a friend in Mexico, who entered them in the competition for a prize instituted by Spanish exiles, the Nueva España award. The result was the publication in Mexico of *Belleza cruel* in 1958; it was not published in Spain until 1978, three years after the death of Franco. The exiled Spanish poet León Felipe wrote a polemical prologue for the collection, describing how his encounter with Figuera's work changed his mind about those who remained behind in Franco's Spain. He and many other liberal intellectuals (including the poet Pablo Neruda) had believed poetic activity in Spain to be defunct after 1939; Figuera not only brought to the outside world the revelation of her own work but that of Celaya, Otero, Victoriano Crémer, and others.

Belleza cruel reflects more clearly than any other of Figuera's books her reaction to the misery and injustice of postwar Spain. The book's title is taken from the first poem, in which she meditates on the paradox of creating art and beauty in a world of injustice and ugliness. Most particularly the reference is to "aesthetic" poetry,

art for art's sake, the "cruel beauty" that is egotistical and vain (a variation on the theme of her poems "Los días duros," "Egoísmo," and "Vencida por el ángel"). The same theme is repeated later in *Belleza cruel* in "El cielo" (The Sky) and with slight variation in "La rosa incómoda" (The Uncomfortable Rose). It is almost a commonplace of Spain's social poets, echoed in Otero's dedication of his art to "la inmensa mayoría" (the vast majority) and Celaya's definition of poetry as an instrument to change the world. In "Si no has muerto un instante" (If You Haven't Died for an Instant) Figuera proclaims that those who do not suffer and die a little with each human injustice and grief would be better buried for they are already dead, while "Libertad" (Liberty) contrasts approved behavior and conventional pastimes with the risk of thinking, dreaming, speaking of freedom. "Guerra" (War) reiterates the motif of Cain and Abel (found in at least two other Figuera collections), this time from the maternal perspective of Eve, who realizes that she has given birth to war. Society's powerful and privileged are called to account in "Balance," while the poor are exempt. The remaining poems of *Belleza cruel* reiterate many of the testimonial themes and denunciations of *Vencida por el ángel*, *El grito inútil*, *Víspera de la vida*, and *Los días duros* but do so with greater anger and directness. Figuera's style of expression in *Belleza cruel* includes notes of hostility and sarcasm and a desire to shock or to wound not present in earlier books. Figuera's target is not some vague tradition of social inequity but quite specifically the Franco regime. There are notes of demythologization (of traditional gender roles, of idealized motherhood, of the "untouchable" points of religious dogma). Figuera does not offer solutions, nor does she accept the regime's position that God or religious principles and practice provide alternatives to reform and social justice; on the contrary, at one point using the device of a poor laborer's letter to God—in "Carta abierta" (Open Letter)—she appeals to Christ as carpenter, inviting him in colloquial and cliché-filled language to join the workers' struggle. If he is not crucified again, it will only be because the current regime will not permit his speaking out. "La justicia de los ángeles" (Justice of the Angels) is a subsection of four poems, each illustrating some posthumous "poetic justice," as three mothers and one child who were overworked and underloved receive their rewards from heaven.

Angela Figuera in the 1950s

Perhaps the essentially repetitive and reiterative nature of her works published during the 1950s became apparent to Figuera, or perhaps she perceived a bit sooner than many social writers the futility of their literary struggle for reforms (as implied by the title of *El grito inútil*). Although some writers continued in the social vein through most of the 1960s, a call to change was sounded by Martín Santos in 1962 in his *Tiempo de silencio* (Time of Silence), and many writers began to expand their thematic horizons and modify their techniques during this decade. Figuera may have been among the first to recognize the need for change, or she may simply have become exhausted; she was, after all, a generation older than the other social poets. In any case, she published only one more book of poems, *Toco la tierra*, subtitled *Letanías* (Litanies), before lapsing into a prolonged silence. The prologue to this last major work insinuates her fear of repeating herself, as does the subtitle. While less forceful than the poems of *Belleza cruel*, those of *Toco la tierra* nonetheless still belong unequivocally to Figuera's most characteristic corpus and in essence constitute a coda or recapitulation. There is some sense of having completed a trajectory, having come full circle, underlined by the imagery of soil in the titles of her first and last major collections (*Mujer de barro* and *Toco la tierra*); clay and earth both allude to the feminine principle, the great mother, source of all life.

The 1986 edition of her complete works contains some thirty poems not previously published in books, several of them addressed to other social or socialist poets and others reiterating oft-repeated themes in slightly different form. For example, "Poeta puro" (Pure Poet) echoes a leitmotiv of Figuera's mature poetry, the poet's collective or social duty, but expresses it in a sonnet, perhaps the only one she wrote. "En la ardiente obscuridad" (In the Burning Darkness) conveys Figuera's reaction to Buero Vallejo's 1950 drama of that name and is dedicated to Vallejo's blind protagonist, who could not resign himself to never seeing—a dramatic symbol for the loss of liberty in Franco's Spain. "Romance de puebloespaña" (Ballad of the Spanish Proletariat) commemorates a strike by the miners of Asturias in May 1962, grimly repressed but nonetheless significant for Figuera as an indicator that the free spirit of the past lives on. Other titles are in the nature of occasional compositions, inspired by holidays (Christmas, New Year's), by world events (several refer to the Vietnam War), and by works of other poets.

Her two books for children, also written in verse, contain the only extant compositions by Figuera in perfect, complete rhyme. For the most part, the "Cuentos tontos" resemble the eighteenth-century "fábulas" (usually variants of Aesop's fables or other exemplary tales with animal protagonists) but have a more playful tone. Like some Mother Goose rhymes, however, Figuera's verses for children can occasionally pack a political wallop, as is the case with "Cuento tonto de la brujita que no pudo sacar el carnet" (Silly Tale of the Little Witch Who Couldn't Get Her Identity Card), wherein the misfortunes that befall the witch because of trying to travel without the papers the government requires are such that she totally gives up witching. The "songs" of *Canciones para todo el año* are largely of the variety that accompany children's games and dances, but occasionally Figuera's characteristic themes (such as motherhood) reappear; for example, in "La mosca" (The Fly) she imagines what might be the fate of the mother fly if the thousands of eggs she laid had to be individually nursed, bathed, put to bed, and taken to school. The humorous,

aphoristic animal characters in "Más animales" (More Animals) recall Gómez de la Serna's "greguerías" (aphorisms notably collected in *Greguerías*, 1923) with their insightful metaphors, while there are echoes of Lorca's *Libro de poemas* (Book of Poems, 1921) in "La ranita guapa y el sapo feo" (The Pretty Little Frog and the Ugly Toad) and of his frustrated attempt at lyric theater, *El maleficio de la mariposa* (The Butterfly's Evil Spell, 1919), in "Los gusarapitos, la oruga y la mariposa" (The Little Worms, the Caterpillar, and the Butterfly). One of the most interesting insights to be gained from Figuera's children's books is that she possessed a far more extensive command of poetic technique than she normally used, and that she had a rich festive and satiric vein not developed in her adult works.

Interviews:

Antonio Núñez, "Encuentro con Angela Figuera," *Insula*, 327 (1974): 4;

Robert Saladrigas, "Monólogo con Angela Figuera," *Destino* (23 November 1974): 48-49.

References:

Rafael Bosch, "La poesía de Angela Figuera y el tema de la maternidad," *Insula*, 186 (1962): 5-6;

Santiago Daydí-Tolson, *The Post-Civil War Spanish Social Poets* (Boston: Twayne, 1983), pp. 93-99;

Leopoldo de Luis, "*Toco la tierra* de Angela Figuera," *Papeles de Son Armadans*, 26, no. 78 (1962): 327-329;

Nancy Mandlove, "*Historia* and *Intra-historia*: Two Spanish Women Poets in Dialogue with History," *Third Woman*, 2, no. 2 (1984): 84-93;

Roberta Quance, Introduction to Figuera's *Obras completas* (Madrid: Hiperión, 1986), pp. 11-19;

Eleanor Wright, *The Poetry of Protest Under Franco* (London: Tamesis, 1986), pp. 154-157.

Gloria Fuertes
(28 July 1918 -   )

Martha LaFollette Miller
University of North Carolina at Charlotte

BOOKS: *Isla ignorada* (Madrid: Musa Nueva, 1950);

Canciones para niños (Madrid: Escuela Española, 1952);

Antología y poemas del suburbio (Caracas: Lírica Hispana, 1954);

Aconsejo beber hilo (Madrid: Arquero, 1954);

Villancicos (Madrid: Magisterio Español, 1954);

Pirulí (Madrid: Escuela Española, 1955);

Todo asusta (Caracas: Lírica Hispana, 1958);

Que estás en la tierra (Barcelona: Literaturasa, 1962);

Ni tiro, ni veneno, ni navaja (Barcelona: Bardo, 1966);

Cangura para todo (Barcelona: Lumen, 1967);

Poeta de guardia (Madrid: Ciencia Nueva, 1968);

Cómo atar los bigotes al tigre (Barcelona: Bardo, 1969);

Antología poética (1950-1969), edited by Francisco Ynduráin (Barcelona: Plaza & Janés, 1970);

Don Pato y Don Pito (Madrid: Escuela Española, 1970);

Aurora, Brígida y Carlos (Barcelona: Lumen, 1971);

La pájara pinta (Madrid: Alcalá, 1972);

Cuando amas aprendes geografía (Málaga: Curso Superior de Filología, 1973);

Sola en la sala (Zaragoza, Spain: Javalambre, 1973);

El camello-auto de los reyes magos (Madrid: Igreca, 1973);

El hada acaramelada (Madrid: Igreca, 1973);

La gata Chundarata y otros cuentos (Videosistemas, 1974);

Obras incompletas (Madrid: Cátedra, 1975);

Miguel: Un cuento muy moral en cinco capítulos y un prólogo (Madrid: Alfaguara, 1977);

El libro de los derechos del niño (León, Spain: Nebrija, 1978);

Las tres reinas magas: Cuento teatro (Madrid: Escuela Española, 1979);

Historia de Gloria (Amor, humor y desamor) (Madrid: Cátedra, 1980);

La ardilla y su pandilla (Madrid: Escuela Española, 1981);

Coleta, la poeta (Valladolid, Spain: Miñon, 1982);

El dragón tragón (Madrid: Escuela Española, 1982);

El abecedario de don Hilario (Valladolid, Spain: Miñón, 1982);

Así soy yo (Madrid: Emiliano Escolar, 1982);

Plumilindo: El cisne que quería ser pato (Madrid: Escuela Española, 1983);

Piopcio Lope, el pollito miope (Madrid: Escuela Española, 1983);

La momia tiene catarro (Madrid: Escuela Española, 1983);

Coleta payasa, ¿qué pasa? (Valladolid, Spain: Miñón, 1983);

La oca loca (Madrid: Escuela Española, 1983);

Yo contento, tú contenta que bien me sale la cuenta: La tabla en verso (Madrid: Escuela Española, 1984);

El domador mordió al leon (Madrid: Escuela Española, 1984);

El libro loco de todo un poco: Libro primero (cuentos, versos, aventuras, historietas, fantasías, chistes, acertijos, poesías, botijos, etc.) (Madrid: Escuela Española, 1984).

Edition in English: *Off the Map* (Middletown, Conn.: Wesleyan University Press / Scranton, Pa.: Harper & Row, 1984).

Since the publication of her first book of poems in 1950, Gloria Fuertes has gradually carved for herself a place of distinction within twentieth-century Spanish letters. Through her immensely popular poetry readings, her success as a writer for children, and her appearances on children's television, she has attained a measure of renown in Spain. Although she has never sought the acclaim of a literary elite, instead striving simply to communicate her own reality to readers from all classes of society, and to promote peace, justice, and love, she nevertheless has begun to receive serious critical attention for the poetic vitality of her forthright, energetic verse. The strength and sincerity of her personality infuse all her writings, making credible her asser-

Gabriel Celaya, Gloria Fuertes, Luis Rosales, Dámaso Alonso, Miguel Belloso, and Luis Jiménez Martos in 1971

tion that her work *Historia de Gloria* (Gloria's Story, 1980) "no es un libro, es una mujer" (isn't a book, but a woman). In person, according to José Luis Cano, Fuertes is a "madrileña castiza y sencilla, algo tímida, que gusta de los ambientes populares, del vino de las tabernas, y no se asusta por palabrota de más o de menos" (old-style Madrilenian, unaffected and somewhat timid, who likes humble settings and the wine in the taverns, and who isn't frightened by a curse word or two).

Fuertes' success with the Spanish public is no doubt due to her humor and compassion and to the candor with which she describes her life, from her childhood poverty to her struggles and successes as a gifted unmarried woman. Born in Madrid on 28 July 1918 to proletarian parents (her father was first a beadle, later a *portero* or concierge), she passed her youth in working-class neighborhoods characterized, she says, by destitution, whores, and an occasional convent. From earliest childhood she invented rhymes and, as an adolescent, loved sports; her formal higher education, however, took place in Madrid at a trade school for women, where she learned cooking, embroidery, hygiene, child care, and sewing. The death of her mother in 1934 was the first of a series of traumatic losses that included the disappearance during the civil war of a young man she deeply loved. By 1954 she was to write in "Nota biográfica," collected that year in *Antología y poemas del suburbio* (Anthology and Poems of the Urban Poor), that "Todos los míos han muerto hace años / y estoy más sola que yo misma" (All my people have been dead for years / and I'm more alone than myself).

Throughout the hardships of this early period, Fuertes wrote poems regularly, a habit she has continued throughout her adult life. Her dedication in this regard has led to the publication of numerous volumes of poetry, which are characterized by her use of colloquial language, wordplay, humor, and consistent attention to the themes of human suffering, love, injustice, and death. Her antielitist stance and de-emphasis of purely aesthetic goals (as she states in *Historia de Gloria*, she sometimes writes poorly so her readers will understand her better) have caused her to be classified as a social poet, along with many other Spanish poets who during the 1950s and 1960s cultivated socially committed expression.

The period before the 1950 publication of *Isla ignorada* (Unknown Island) found her accepting varied employment, mostly as an office worker. As Fuertes told Antonio Núñez in a 1969 interview, her experiences during the civil war, in Madrid under constant threat from bombs and shells, greatly increased the strength of her poetic vocation. In 1939 economic necessity impelled her to submit a children's story for publication; she was promptly hired as an editor by the publishing house and between 1940 and 1955 composed weekly stories for the children's magazines *Pelayo* and *Maravilla*. Throughout these years, she continued to write poetry. Although *Isla ignorada* does not chronicle these happenings, it nevertheless contains highly personal material, including what she terms her first autobiographical poem, "Isla ignorada." The book contains much nature imagery, largely missing in later works, and although social concerns emerge momentarily in the short poem "Paz que es justicia" (Peace that is Justice), they do not play the prominent role they will assume in later collections. The colloquialisms and humor so abundant later are also absent for the most part. Fuertes' tendency to eschew rhyme and regular meters, however, does begin to be apparent, as does the nascent consciousness of her identity as a poet, evident in her statement in the title poem that "Los árboles del bosque de mi isla / sois vosotros mis versos" (The trees of my island's forests / are you, my verses). In addition, she treats many of the themes that will dominate in later volumes. Although the work has been said to bear traces of earlier poetic movements in Spain, in particular of *modernismo* and the Generation of 1898, Fuertes does not acknowledge the influence of other poets on her writing, in this or any other book. She does admit to an instinctive affinity with surrealism, which may explain in part her affiliation, during this early period, with the neosurrealist "postista" movement headed by Carlos Edmundo de Ory, to whom she dedicates one of the poems in the volume. *Isla ignorada*, little no-ticed by critics at the time of its publication, is now practically unavailable.

During the early 1950s Fuertes continued to participate actively in the literary life of Madrid, working with the poetry magazine *Arquero* between 1952 and 1955 and confirming her identity as a children's poet with the appearance of three books during the same period. In 1955 she began to study library science in her spare time, which permitted her, five years later, to take a librarian's job and thus to free herself from the editorial office work that she considered the "yugo que adquirí a los 18 años" (yoke I acquired at eighteen). She later expressed (in the Núñez interview) with characteristic energy and economy the delight she felt at this change: "Eso ya era otra cosa: siempre es mejor un libro que un jefe" (That [working in a library] was something else entirely; a book is always better than a boss). Finally, it was during the 1950s that she established once and for all her original lyric voice with the publication of three new books of poetry.

The first of these, *Antología y poemas del suburbio*, was, like *Todo asusta* (Everything Is Frightening, 1958), a slender Venezuelan volume. It was poorly distributed, which perhaps explains the fact that like *Isla ignorada*, it received scant critical attention. Along with *Todo asusta*, as Francisco Ynduráin has noted, it contains the seeds of Fuertes' later work: her use of free verse, her deliberate avoidance of polish, her use of phonetically based wordplay—alliteration, puns, echoes—and her strongly autobiographical bent. At times she assumes a slightly self-deprecatory air, as in the opening poem "Nota biográfica," in which she mocks her poetic pretensions. Another technique she was to employ in later works, the simple enumeration of objects, appears in "Puesto de Rastro" (Flea-Market Stand).

The themes of *Antología y poemas del suburbio* are Fuertes' usual ones: herself, God, family, and human suffering. The most striking thematic feature of the book, however, is her advocacy for those in need; many of these poems would justify her classification as an exponent of social poetry. That poets should put their works at the service of humanity is clearly stated in the poem "No perdamos el tiempo" (Let's Not Lose Any Time), in which she exhorts her fellows to replace bourgeois literary games with the denunciation of social ills: "no decir lo íntimo, sino cantar al corro, / no cantar a la luna, no cantar a la novia, / . . . no fabricar sonetos" (not to say what's intimate, but to sing in a circle, / not to sing of

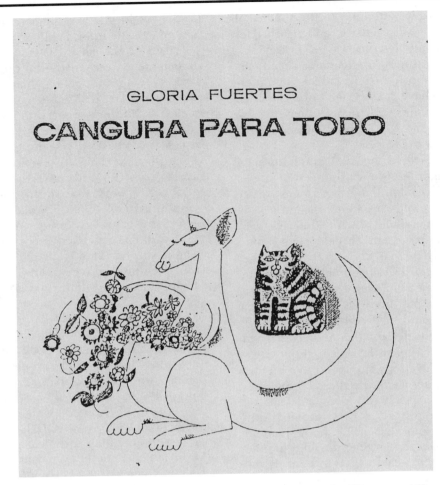

Cover for one of the first of Fuertes' many books for children, Cangura para todo *(Kangaroo at Your Service, 1967)*

the moon, nor of your sweetheart, / . . . not to construct sonnets . . .). She stresses poetry's curative, redemptive power, and its use as a practical tool.

Fuertes' commitment to denouncing social ills and her role as a critic of bourgeois values are apparent in the poem "Es inútil" (It's Useless), in which, through the use of humor, she rejects the concern expressed by the "Protectora de Animales" (Animal Protection Society) over the Spanish habit of eating fried songbirds; she suggests that a culture that gives blanket permission for the brutality of war is hypocritical to quibble over songbirds. Other poems of the collection focus on the pariahs of society, and in several cases Fuertes adopts their voice, speaking as a beggar, as a prostitute, or as a sick old man. Elsewhere in the collection, in "Un hombre pregunta" (A Man Asks), she evokes a God who "está en las manos de todo el que trabaja" (is in the hands of all who work) and who abandons those

who make war or who pray but do not love. As she says in "Poema," "canto el suburbio porque en él veo a Cristo" (I sing of the slums because there I see Christ).

With the publication of *Aconsejo beber hilo* (I Advise Drinking Thread) later in 1954 Fuertes attained, according to some, her maturity as a poet. As is usual in her works, many of the poems in the book are markedly autobiographical in ways that range from the dryly matter-of-fact to the intimate and surrealistic. Unfulfilled maternal feelings surfaces in several poems, as do her attitudes about her status as a single woman. In "Cuarto de soltera" (Unmarried Woman's Room), she complains of the early morning silence; in "No sé por qué me quejo" (I Don't Know Why I Complain) a poignant dissatisfaction underlies her insistence that she really should be happy. After all, she can live as she likes, dropping her ashes on the floor, wiping her mouth with the back of her hand, and generally doing as she pleases. Similar poems will reappear throughout her work.

In the title *Aconsejo beber hilo* Fuertes substitutes *hilo*—what crazy people drink, according to her poem "Letanía de los montes de la vida" (Litany of the Mountains of Life)—for the expected *tilo* (medicinal tea), thus playing on the notion, reiterated throughout the book, that insanity and illness are appropriate metaphors for the human condition: "tengo a mi corazón enfermo / y no tengo que darle una cucharada" (My heart's sick, / and I don't have a spoonful to give it), she states in "La pobre" (The Poor One). Throughout the book, too, she adopts a view of the poet as both seer and lunatic. Her soul, she says in "Desde siempre" (Since Forever), has always been on horseback, riding backwards; her body, she states in "Ahora . . ." (Now . . .), is "un ojo sin fin / con el que para mi desventura veo todo" (an endless eye / with which, to my misfortune, I see everything). In the poem "Escrito" (Writing) she speaks as a distracted, half-crazy young girl who acts strangely, chasing butterflies in bullfighter's garb, writing on walls, crying in closets, and praying in museums. At times, she says in "No sabemos qué hacer" (We Don't Know What To Do), a poet does not know whether to write a poem or to commit suicide.

Aconsejo beber hilo, in addition to describing the intrinsic craziness of being human, reveals Fuertes' deep existential concerns. As in practically all her works, death is a central feature of many poems. In "Dibujo" (Drawing) her portrayal of a funeral procession as a study in black and white reveals the living and the dead as two sides of the same coin:

> Envuelto en tela negra
> van cantando por la plaza,
>   por delante el muerto quieto,
> bien envuelto en tela blanca.
>
> (Wrapped in black cloth,
> They go singing through the square,
>   in front of them the quiet dead man,
> well-wrapped in white cloth.)

In other poems, her imagination transforms death into life and life into death. The dead, on the one hand, know what we do; they return to their bedrooms, they mend their stockings, as in "Los muertos" (The Dead). The dried-up, unemotional businessman, on the other hand—in "Aviso" (Warning)—is a living corpse who should be buried immediately. She continually expresses

anguish but, nevertheless, observes that when one reaches the depths of despair, someone always reaches out in rescue, as in "Siempre pasa" (It Always Happens). Social themes and love poems are less prominent in *Aconsejo beber hilo* than in some of her other works, but their presence is nonetheless felt.

In technique *Aconsejo beber hilo* resembles Fuertes' other works. Most noticeable is perhaps her frequent use of parallel constructions. In several cases she imitates nonliterary forms such as personal letters, grammar-book model sentences, and advertising slogans. Her black humor surfaces in "Guía comercial" (Commercial Guide), where she includes as one of her imaginary ads the following: "Corbatas para suicidas. Pronto" (Ties for Suicides. Prompt Service). Other instances of humor appear, as well as her typical wordplay, though these are found in lesser measure than in some of her other works. Several poems, such as "Me crucé con un entierro" (I Passed a Funeral), exhibit a marked folkloric flavor with their somewhat elliptical dialogue, brevity, and emphasis on love.

Todo asusta, in which Fuertes shifts her focus from her inner world to problems of society and of humanity in general, completes the series of books she published in the 1950s. The volume, although with limited distribution, won her the recognition of a *primera mención* (honorable mention) in an international poetry competition, the Concurso Internacional de Poesía Lírica Hispana. In the collection, she turns her attention to those who are in need either materially or spiritually, understating the personal in such love poems as "Ya ves que tontería, me gusta escribir tu nombre" (It's Silly, but I Like to Write Your Name). In many poems she indicts society for its cruelty, violence, and injustice, but she generally avoids sensationalism and melodrama by using various forms of irony and understatement. In "Tener un hijo hoy" (To Have a Child Today) she states that she prefers childlessness to raising a child to be cannon fodder. In another poem, "Lo desconocido atrae también a los cobardes" (The Unknown Also Attracts Cowards), she paints a world free of pain and injustice only to aver that such a world exists only beyond the grave. In "Hemos de procurar no mentir" (We Must Try Not to Lie) she suggests that to speak the unvarnished truth, rather than trying to make reality palatable by inventing improvements upon it, is so painful that she often chooses to remain silent. In "Es obligatorio . . ." (It's Mandatory . . .), she ridi-

Cover for Fuertes' 1970 collection of poems for children. The money from her work in children's literature supported her while she wrote and published her other poetry.

cules the hypocrisy of a society that creates rules to protect its citizens from accidents on a train but then turns around and subjects them to death in its wars: "Es obligatorio no asomarse a la ventanilla, / porque tienes que estar vivo si organizan la guerra" (It's mandatory not to lean out the windows, / because you've got to be alive if they organize a war). In "Tu parcela tendrás" (You'll Have Your Plot of Land), she "comforts" the poor, assuring them that eventually they will have a piece of land of their own—a burial plot. And the farm laborer in "Labrador" (Laborer) will some day be able to rest—in a tomb composed of the earth he plows.

The critical attitude that underlies many of the poems of *Todo asusta* extends even to Fuertes' portrayal of God in the book. In "Dios ahoga pero no aprieta" (God Chokes but He Doesn't Squeeze) apparent praise becomes an indictment; if God is patient, especially with the perverse, then he must be responsible for the evil in the world. Even her affirmation of his existence, in this poem, is more of a negative commentary on

what she observes around her than an expression of faith: "aunque parezca mentira Dios existe!" (incredible though it may seem, God does exist!). Her statement in "Oración" (Prayer) that God is "El que cuando todo se apaga, se enciende" (He who lights up when everything darkens) perhaps suggests that faith is born of despair. Even her thanksgiving reveals ambivalence; in "Acción de gracias" (Giving Thanks) her somewhat forced gratitude at not having been created a frog or a glass is considerably overshadowed by the negative implications of fear and weakness in her parting comment, "Y además gracias por no soltarme de tu mano" (And what's more, thanks for not letting me let go of your hand). These references to God, though bittersweet and ambivalent, are nevertheless evidence that, despite the muted despair of *Todo asusta*, Fuertes has not lost faith altogether, and notes of genuine optimism do appear. In "Parece que se ha dicho todo" (It Seems that Everything's Been Said) she celebrates the wonder and newness of a baby's birth, which God himself stands up to see.

In *Todo asusta* Fuertes continues to experiment with poems cast in the mold of other forms of discourse: prayers, newspaper articles, imaginary letters, and communiqués. One of the most striking of these, "Ficha ingreso Hospital General" (General Hospital Admission Card), is a stark record of a man brought in who is dying of hunger.

Although an anthology of her previously published poetry, *Que estás en la tierra* (Who Art on Earth), in 1962 brought Fuertes' works to the attention of a wider audience than before, seven years elapsed between *Todo asusta* and her next book of new poems. This hiatus may have been due in part to her acceptance, in 1961, of a Fulbright Fellowship to teach Spanish at Bucknell University in Pennsylvania, where she remained for almost three years. Despite her delight at the invitation, the new and demanding role of university professor required considerable adjustment and for a time interrupted her writing, though she eventually succeeded in composing in the United States the book *Ni tiro, ni veneno, ni navaja* (Not by Gunshot, Nor by Poison, Nor by Razor). Published in 1966, the work was awarded the Guipúzcoa poetry prize in Spain and was followed by two new poetry volumes within four years: *Poeta de guardia* (Poet on Call, 1968), generally regarded as one of her most successful works, and *Cómo atar los bigotes al tigre* (How to Tie the Tiger's Whiskers, 1969), also winner of an award in a poetry competition (the Premio Vizcaya). The 1960s thus brought Fuertes important opportunities and significant recognition. An example of critical response during this period comes from Max Aub, who called her a "poetisa de rompe y rasga" (dauntless poet) and praised her unrestrained, witty expressions.

Ni tiro, ni veneno, ni navaja reveals Fuertes' struggle with intensely negative feelings about human existence. Its poems, more philosophical than those of some of her other works, in most cases do not address specific social problems. Rather, they frequently allegorize the human condition in negative ways—as a desolate landscape in "La vida a veces es un río frío y seco y por lo tanto triste" (Life Is at Times a Cold, Dry River and Therefore Sad); as an arid garden of tears where only nettles grow in "Explicación de lo que pasa" (Explanation of What Happens); and as a long march in single file, with danger on both hands and no one at our sides, in "Voces me llaman" (Voices Call Me). In other poems she decries the hatred and selfishness that transform human beings into monsters, as in "Están vivos" (They Are Alive).

Fuertes' desperation, in *Ni tiro*, sometimes takes the form of allusions to suicide, beginning with the title itself. One can know and care too much, she implies in "No mata la calidad sino la cantidad" (It's Not the Quality but the Quantity that Kills): "sabes de todo un poco y vas al cine, / sabes de todo mucho y te suicidas" (if you know a little about a lot, you go to the movies, / if you know a lot about a lot, you commit suicide). Too much love, she affirms in the same poem, is a burial. In "La fábrica y su puerta" (The Factory and its Door) she portrays sadness as congenital; some people, she states, come out of their manufacturer's hands defective, with the umbilical cord of sadness still attached. Sorrow is part of her, a beard that grows back inexorably and must be shaved off daily in private, she writes in "Me crece la barba" (My Beard Grows). Happiness, she suggests, is elusive, so much so that "el hombre feliz" (the happy man) is a real oddity, a rare specimen on exhibit in the "Zoo de verbena" (Street Fair Zoo), in the poem of the same name. Despite the many negative feelings she expresses, however, Fuertes manages, as in *Todo asusta*, to maintain a certain faith. Just when she reaches the point of despair, she runs into God on the street, she explains in "¡Vaya encuentro!" (What an Encounter!). Calling her "Leocadia," his special name for her, he calms her down, gives her

wisdom and peace, and takes away her urge to kill herself. In "Los ciegos ven" (The Blind See) she counterbalances her awareness, expressed elsewhere in the book, of the power of hate by depicting love's transforming powers, which make the blind see, criminals cry, the mute speak, and the loquacious fall silent. In "Año nuevo" (New Year) she looks to the future determined not to suffer so much: "PROMETO no volver / a ahogaros en mi llanto, / no volver a sufrir, / sin un motivo / muy justificado" (I PROMISE not to drown you / in my tears again, / not to suffer again, / without a reason / [that is] very justified).

In *Poeta de guardia* Fuertes to some degree lives up to the promise she made in "Año nuevo." Though the book deals with her fundamentally serious themes—including death, God, and love—and though it is still an intensely personal endeavor (Fuertes described the work to Núñez as "Yo misma" [I myself]), it is written with a decidedly lighter touch than *Ni tiro*. In many poems her attitude is playful, and she includes more humor for its own sake. Her longest work up to this point, the book contains a few of the extremely brief poetic texts that in later volumes will become characteristic of her work. Many poems are more topical and more colloquial than those of earlier books, with references to Vietnam and to other current events, as well as an abundance of slang.

Poeta de guardia is divided into eight parts, with poems grouped thematically for the first time in her work. The book opens with four poems in which Fuertes defines her poetic vocation. Rather than the seer or lunatic of earlier works, she is now the "poet on call," waiting for the emergency needs of troubled humanity. She has learned to view herself and her task with considerable humor; in "Maletilla" (Amateur Bullfighter) she characterizes herself, with mock-epic seriousness, as a veteran of seven bullfights—her seven books. In "Sale caro ser poeta" (It Costs a Lot To Be a Poet) she becomes an insomniac, the hero of ghosts, and a warrior against anguish, who writes until dawn, then goes off to read at the recitals her friends organize. In "Aquí estoy expuesta como todos" (Here I Am Exposed Like Everyone Else) she portrays herself as a kind of uncanonized saint.

Following these introductory poems are the book's seven main sections. The first, "Vivir: compás de espera" (Living: Measure of Waiting), might be termed a meditation on death and on living in the face of death. While continuing to raise questions about the pursuit of happiness, Fuertes moves toward a stance more accepting of life even with all its limitations. In the second section, "¡Qué barullo en la herida! . . . (Poemas de amor)" (What a Tumult in the Wound! . . . [Love Poems]), she chronicles a profoundly felt love experience from its birth—"Una tarde al llegar a casa, / me encontré la sorpresa de quererte, / fue una bomba en mis manos" (One afternoon when I got home, / I found the surprise of loving you, / it was a bomb in my hands)—to the disappointment of its failure: "Qué poco de fiar resulta el fuego" (How untrustworthy the fire turns out to be). In the next section, "Minipoemas" (Minipoems), she tries her hand at short, mostly two-, three-, and four-line aphoristic poems full of humor and pithy wisdom, one of which begins as follows: "La muerte es una costumbre de la vida. / En las guerras la costumbre pasa a vicio" (Death is one of life's customs. / In war the custom becomes a vice). In the fourth section, "Poemas variados" (Varied Poems), death is repeatedly embodied in personified objects: a tree in Pennsylvania commits suicide, a raccoon on his way to the city lies dead on the pavement, an old doll mysteriously turns up on a child's grave, an obsolete ship is torn apart alive, and a river is threatened with death by damming.

The handful of poems that make up the fifth section, "La pica (Poemas del más allá)" (The Goad [Poems of the Beyond]), portray God's relationship with human beings in various ways: he is the dramatist who stages existence, a bullfighter (humans are the bulls), the keeper of vital statistics in his heavenly archives, and one who puzzlingly draws away whenever people feel happy. The final section of *Poeta de guardia*, which follows a group of seventeen miscellaneous poems previously published in magazines, is titled "La buena uva (poemas de buena uva)" (Good Intentions [Poems of Good Intentions]); it contains, among others, poems that fall squarely within the Spanish tradition of depicting sacred figures in a very down-to-earth light. "Zambra celestial" (Gypsy Celebration in Heaven) portrays a flamenco *jolgorio*, a tavern festivity, held at the feet of God; "Cielo de tercera" (Third-Class Heaven) describes the place where plastic flowers, cheap whores, and stray dogs go when they die; and in "Dios llama al fontanero" (God Calls the Plumber) God must cope with leaky faucets and a leaking roof in his old, dilapidated Heaven.

Poeta de guardia reflects many of Fuertes' convictions regarding poetry. Its title embodies her belief that poetry is a curative art, and its lighter tone attests to her decision, which she discussed in a 1976 interview with Tomás Fernández, to avoid writing when unhappy so as not to affect others adversely. Like all her works *Poeta de guardia* was written rapidly, spontaneously, and intuitively with little polishing or correcting, a fact that has inevitably resulted in the occasional accusation of unevenness.

Fuertes' final book of the 1960s, *Cómo atar los bigotes al tigre*, continues the trend toward a greater acceptance of human limitations, or at least toward the defusing of the tragic through humor; if one cannot tame the tiger that is life, at least one can tie up its whiskers. It has rightly been suggested that in this book Fuertes shifts her perspective from the purely personal to that of common humanity. Along with her usual techniques, she makes extensive use of personification: anguish, in "La Huéspeda" (The Guest), is portrayed as a kind of unwelcome squatter in her home; death, in "La excursión" (The Excursion), becomes a picnic outing, for which people must set their alarm clocks, without knowing for what hour; and pain, in "¿Por qué no detienen al dolor?" (Why Don't They Arrest Pain?), is a criminal on the loose, with which the United Nations should certainly deal. She treats death humorously, claiming, in "No tengo vocación de Camposanto" (I Have No Talent for Cemeteries), that she really is not cut out for cemeteries, since black does not look good on her. Jokes and riddles appear alongside fantasy that at times borders on nonsense: she describes a centipede go-go dancer, as well as octopuses whose eight arms make them formidable lovers. Her affectionate tribute to the lollipop of her childhood and her portrait of a clown suggest that in this book there is less distance between her poetry for adults and that for children.

As she moved into the 1970s, Fuertes stepped up her production of children's literature, which in the 1960s had been represented by only one book, the prize-winning *Cangura para todo* (Kangaroo at Your Service, 1967). Between 1970 and 1973 she published five children's books, and beginning in 1975 she was able to abandon completely her practice of accepting jobs teaching literature to American students in Madrid and to start living on her royalties, together with a fellowship for writers of literature for children. In addition to extending her audience to the very young, Fuertes has reached out to those who do not read or cannot buy books, traveling to Spain's provinces to read in person. She has also come out in favor of setting poetry to music as a way of broadening its appeal and has recorded some albums of her poetry.

As to her production of poetry for adults Fuertes published two books of new poetry in the 1970s, followed by a third in 1980 (*Historia de Gloria*). *Cuando amas aprendes geografía* (When You Love You Learn Geography), which received little critical attention, and *Sola en la sala* (Alone in the Living Room) both appeared in 1973. The latter book, an intimate diary not originally intended for publication, was apparently written during an intense personal crisis involving both illness and a disappointment in love. The majority of its poems are quite brief, reflecting Fuertes' intention of expressing the maximum content with a minimum number of words. Though many of its poems communicate pain and desolation, others are aphoristic commentaries on such broad issues as the pursuit of happiness.

Fuertes' extensive volume *Historia de Gloria* does not depart essentially from the themes and techniques of her earlier works, although in it she adopts a more mature perspective than before. Like *Sola en la sala*, *Historia de Gloria* consists of poems taken from her personal diary. The work is of course, markedly autobiographical; of its 760 poems, those in first person predominate, and titles such as "Autobio," "Autorretrato" (Self-Portrait), "Autobiografía," and "Autoepitafio" (Self-Epitaph) abound. Many of these refer to Fuertes' early childhood, which she characterizes in "Autobio" as "injusta y dura" (unjust and hard). Other poems describe her life as an adult— her loves, her disappointments, and her philosophy. She expresses her determination to love herself, to celebrate life, and to serve others through her poetry. *Historia de Gloria* faithfully reflects her view, expressed in 1968, that poetry has the power to combat injustice, hate, and even war. Although Fuertes has consistently valued communication over artistic refinements, she has nevertheless managed to make a solid contribution to twentieth-century Spanish poetry.

Interviews:

Antonio Núñez, "Encuentro con Gloria Fuertes," *Insula*, 270 (May 1969): 3;

Tomás Fernández, "Gloria Fuertes: poeta de todas las horas," *Libro Español* (March 1976): 92-93.

References:

Max Aub, *Poesía española contemporánea* (Mexico City: Era, 1969);

José Battló, *Antología de la nueva poesía española* (Madrid: Bardo, 1968), pp. 337-338;

Catherine G. Bellver, "Gloria Fuertes, Poet of Social Consciousness," *Letras Femeninas*, 4, no. 1 (1978): 27-38;

Rubén Benítez, "El maravilloso retablo popular de Gloria Fuertes," *Mester*, 9, no. 1 (January 1980): 21-33;

José Luis Cano, *Poesía española contemporánea: las generaciones de posguerra* (Madrid: Guadarrama, 1974), pp. 174-180;

Andrew P. Debicki, "Gloria Fuertes: Intertextuality and Reversal of Expectations," in his *Poetry of Discovery: The Spanish Generation of 1956-1971* (Lexington: University Press of Kentucky, 1982), pp. 81-101;

Joaquín González Muela, "Gloria Fuertes, 'Poeta de guardia,' " in his *La nueva poesía española* (Madrid: Alcalá, 1973), pp. 13-29;

Pablo González Rodas, Introduction to Fuertes' *Historia de Gloria (amor, humor y desamor)* (Madrid: Cátedra, 1980), pp. 25-50;

Nancy Mandlove, "Oral Texts: The Play of Orality and Literacy in the Poetry of Gloria Fuertes," *Siglo XX/20th Century*, 5, nos. 1-2 (1987-1988): 11-16;

Candelas Newton, "La palabra 'convertida' de Gloria Fuertes," *Letras Femeninas*, 13 (Spring-Fall, 1987): 1-11;

Margaret H. Persin, "Gloria Fuertes and (Her) Feminist Reader," *Revista/Review Interamericana*, 12 (Spring 1982): 125-132;

Persin, "Humor as Semiosis in the Poetry of Gloria Fuertes," *Revista Hispánica Moderna*, 41 (December 1988): 143-157;

Timothy J. Rogers, "The Comic Spirit in the Poetry of Gloria Fuertes," *Perspectives on Contemporary Literature*, 8 (1982): 88-97;

Sylvia R. Sherno, "Gloria Fuertes and the Poetics of Solitude," *Anales de la Literatura Española Contemporánea*, 12, no. 3 (1987): 311-325;

Sherno, "Weaving the World: The Poetry of Gloria Fuertes," *Hispania*, 72 (May 1989): 247-255;

Francisco Ynduráin, Prologue to Fuertes' *Antología poética (1950-1969)* (Barcelona: Plaza & Janés, 1970), pp. 7-45.

Federico García Lorca

(5 June 1898 - ?18 August 1936)

Andrew A. Anderson
University of Michigan

BOOKS: *Impresiones y paisajes* (Granada, Spain: Traveset, 1918); translated by Lawrence H. Klibbe as *Impressions and Landscapes* (Lanham, Md.: University Press of America, 1987);

Libro de poemas (Madrid: Maroto, 1921);

Canciones (Málaga, Spain: Litoral/Imprenta Sur, 1927); translated by Lorca and Philip Cummings as *Songs*, edited by Daniel Eisenberg (Pittsburgh: Duquesne University Press, 1976);

Mariana Pineda (Madrid: Farsa, 1928); translated by Robert G. Havard (Warminster, U.K.: Aris & Phillips, 1987);

Primer romancero gitano (Madrid: Revista de Occidente, 1928); republished as *Romancero gitano* (Madrid: Revista de Occidente, 1929); translated by Langston Hughes as *Gypsy Ballads* (Beloit, Wis.: Beloit College, 1951);

Poema del cante jondo (Madrid: Ulises/Iberoamericana, 1931); translated (in part) by Keith Waldrop as *Poem of the Gypsy Seguidilla* (Providence, R.I.: Burning Deck, 1967); translated (in full) by Carlos Bauer as *Poem of the Deep Song* (San Francisco: City Lights, 1987);

Oda a Walt Whitman (Mexico City: Alcancía, 1933); translated by Bauer in his *Ode to Walt Whitman and Other Poems* (San Francisco: City Lights, 1988);

Llanto por Ignacio Sánchez Mejías (Madrid: Cruz & Raya/Arbol, 1935); translated by A. L. Lloyd as *Lament for the Death of a Bullfighter* (London: Heinemann, 1937; New York: Oxford University Press, 1937);

Seis poemas galegos (Santiago de Compostela, Spain: Nós, 1935); translated by Bauer as *Six Galician Poems*, in his *Ode to Walt Whitman and Other Poems*;

Primeras canciones (Madrid: Héroe, 1936): translated by Bauer as *First Songs*, in his *Ode to Walt Whitman and Other Poems*;

Bodas de sangre (Madrid: Cruz & Raya/Arbol, 1936); translated by Gilbert Neiman as

Federico García Lorca in Buenos Aires, 1933

Blood Wedding (Norfolk, Conn.: New Directions, 1939); translated by Richard L. O'Connell and James Graham-Luján as *Blood Wedding*, in their *Three Tragedies of Federico García Lorca* (New York: New Directions, 1947; London: Falcon, 1948);

Yerma (Buenos Aires: Anaconda, 1937); translated by O'Connell and Graham-Luján as *Yerma*, in their *From Lorca's Theater: Five Plays of Federico García Lorca* (New York: Scribners, 1941);

Retablillo de don Cristóbal (Valencia, Spain: Subcomisariado de Propaganda del Comisariado General de Guerra, 1938); translated by Edwin Honig as *In the Frame of Don Cristóbal*, in his "Some Little-Known Writings of Federico

García Lorca," *New Directions*, 8 (1944): 396-402;

Obras completas, 8 volumes, edited by Guillermo de Torre (Buenos Aires: Losada, 1938-1946);

Poeta en Nueva York (Mexico City: Séneca, 1940); translated by Rolfe Humphries in his *The Poet in New York and Other Poems of Federico García Lorca* (New York: Norton, 1940);

La zapatera prodigiosa (Buenos Aires: Losada, 1944); translated by O'Connell and Graham-Luján as *The Shoemaker's Prodigious Wife* in their *From Lorca's Theater;*

La casa de Bernarda Alba (Buenos Aires: Losada, 1944); translated by O'Connell and Graham-Luján as *The House of Bernarda Alba* in their *Three Tragedies of Federico García Lorca;*

Poemas póstumos (Mexico City: Mexicanas, 1945);

Diván del Tamarit (Barcelona: A.D.L., 1948); translated by Honig in his *Diván and Other Writings* (Providence, R.I.: Bonewhistle, 1974);

Siete poemas y dos dibujos inéditos, edited by Luis Rosales (Madrid: Cultura Hispánica, 1949);

Cinco forsas breves; seguidas de Así que pasen cinco años (Buenos Aires: Losange, 1953);

Títeres de Cachiporra (Buenos Aires: Losange, 1953);

Obras completas, edited by Arturo del Hoyo (Madrid: Aguilar, one volume: 1954; two volumes: 1973; three volumes: 1986);

Conferencias y charlas (Havana: Consejo Nacional de Cultura, 1961);

Casidas (Madrid: Arte ye Bibliofilia, 1969);

Prosa (Madrid: Alianza, 1969);

Granada, paraíso cerrado y otras páginas granadinas (Granada, Spain: Sanchez, 1971);

Autógrafos, 3 volumes, edited by Rafael Martínez Nadal (Oxford: Dolphin, 1975, 1976, 1979);

El público y Comedia sin título, edited by Rafael Martínez Nadal and Marie Laffranque (Barcelona: Seix Barral, 1978); translated by Bauer as *The Public and Play Without a Title* (New York: New Directions, 1983);

Viaje a la luna, edited by Laffranque (Loubressac, France: Braad, 1980 [i.e., 1981]); translated by Richard Diers as *Trip to the Moon*, in his "A Filmscript by Lorca," *Windmill Magazine* (Spring 1963): 27-39;

Lola, la comedianta, edited by Piero Menarini (Madrid: Alianza, 1981);

Suites, edited by André Belamich (Barcelona: Ariel, 1983);

Conferencias, 2 volumes, edited by Christopher Maurer (Madrid: Alianza, 1984); translated

(in part) by Maurer as *Deep Song and Other Prose* (London: Boyars, 1980);

Ineditos de Federico García Lorca (Buenos Aires: Instituto de Estudios de Literatura Latinoamericana, 1984);

Tres diálogos (Granada, Spain: Universidad de Granada/Junta de Andalucía, 1985);

Alocuciones argentinas, edited by Mario Hernández (Madrid: Fundación Federico García Lorca/ Crotalón, 1985);

Alocución al pueblo de Fuentevaqueros (Granada, Spain: Comisión del Cincuentenario, 1986);

Teatro inconcluso, edited by Laffranque (Granada, Spain: Universidad de Granada, 1986).

Editions in English: *Poems*, translated by Stephen Spender and J. L. Gili (London: Dolphin / New York: Oxford, 1939);

The Tragicomedy of Don Cristóbal and Rosita, translated by William I. Oliver, in *New World Writing* (New York: New American Library of World Literature, 1955), pp. 187-219;

The Selected Poems of Federico García Lorca, edited by Francisco García Lorca and Donald M. Allen, translated by Roy Campbell and others (New York: New Directions, 1955);

The Cricket Sings: Poems and Songs for Children, translated by Will Kirkland (New York: New Directions, 1980);

Sonnets of Love Forbidden, translated by David K. Loughran (Missoula, Mont.: Windsong, 1989).

PLAY PRODUCTIONS: *El maleficio de la mariposa*, Madrid, Teatro Eslava, 22 March 1920;

Mariana Pineda, Barcelona, Teatro Goya, 24 June 1927;

La zapatera prodigiosa, Madrid, Teatro Español, 24 December 1930;

Tragicomedia de don Cristóbal y la señá Rosita, Madrid, Sociedad de Cursos y Conferencias, June 1931?;

Bodas de sangre, Madrid, Teatro Beatriz, 8 March 1933;

Amor de don Perlimplín con Belisa en su jardín, Madrid, Teatro Español, 5 April 1933;

Retablillo de don Cristóbal, Buenos Aires, Teatro Avenida, 27 March 1934;

Yerma, Madrid, Teatro Español, 29 December 1934;

Doña Rosita la soltera, o El lenguaje de las flores, Barcelona, Teatro Principal Palace, 12 December 1935;

La casa de Bernarda Alba, Buenos Aires, Teatro Avenida, 8 March 1945;

Lorca's parents, Federico García Rodríguez and Vicenta Lorca de Rodríguez

El público, San Juan, Puerto Rico, Theater of the University of Puerto Rico, 15 February 1978;

Así que pasen cinco años, Madrid, Teatro Eslava, September 1978;

El sueño de la vida, Madrid, Teatro María Guerrero, 23 June 1989.

Federico García Lorca's reputation rests equally on his poetry and his plays. He is widely regarded as Spain's most distinguished twentieth-century writer, his work has been translated into at least twenty-five languages, and his name is as familiar to the general reader as those of the novelists Miguel de Cervantes and Benito Pérez Galdós or the dramatists Lope de Vega and Pedro Calderón. Lorca was a major participant in the flowering of Spanish literature that occurred over the years between World War I and the Spanish Civil War—an era whose wealth and diversity have been compared to those of the sixteenth- and seventeenth-century Spanish Golden Age. He is normally categorized, therefore, as a leading member of the "Generation of 1927," a term as misleading as it is useful, but, nonetheless, Lorca's career coincided with those of certain other writers, mainly poets, who were friends and significant figures in their own right: Pedro Salinas, Jorge Guillén, Rafael Alberti, Vicente Aleixandre, and Luis Cernuda among them. It has been argued that Lorca's untimely death at the hands of a Nationalist death squad some five weeks after the outbreak of the civil war gave his reputation a special boost, in that he was rapidly transformed into a martyr figure for Spanish Republicans and for anti-Fascists from all around Europe. Be this as it may, his enduring and increasing popularity and the richness and profundity of his works show that his status as a modern classic has a sound foundation.

The major points in Lorca's life and career often seem to have coincided with significant events in the historical and political arena. For instance, the year of his birth coincided with the so-called Disaster of 1898, when Spain received a stunning double shock in losing the war against the United States and hence losing also its last remaining colonies: Cuba, Puerto Rico, and the Philippines. Lorca spent his first eleven years on the *vega* (fertile plain) of Granada, to the west of the city, his family dividing its time between two villages, Fuente Vaqueros and Asquerosa. His father, Federico García Rodríguez, was a well-off farmer and landowner; Lorca's mother, the former Vicenta Lorca Romero—his father's second wife—was a local primary-school teacher. Both parents, but particularly his mother, are thought to have exerted in their different ways a strong influence on Lorca's character and sensibility. The War of Independence in Cuba, and its subsequent loss, meant that Spain's "natural" supply of sugar was cut off; a boom in sugar beets, which thrived in the *vega*'s soil, and his father's canny business sense enabled the family to consolidate its financial position, and hence, incidentally, to support Lorca economically throughout almost the entirety of his life.

His childhood, then, was a rural and agricultural one, spent closely in contact with nature: he observed firsthand the different tasks associated with the cycle of the seasons, the lives of the farm animals, the rivers and irrigation channels that made intensive cultivation possible, the dense stands of poplars, and the insects in the grass of the meadows. He was the eldest of four children, with a brother (Francisco) and two sisters (Concha and Isabel), and this family nucleus was surrounded by domestic servants and an extended family of uncles, aunts, and cousins who lived in and around Granada. In this warm, comfortable, but relatively modest environment, Lorca would have acquired the feeling for the dynamics of nature that comes through in so many of his works, and likewise he assimilated the rural speech, customs, beliefs, superstitions, and most of all the traditional lyrics, songs, and music, which figure so frequently and prominently as part of his literary palette. At the same time, Lorca's nascent theatrical imagination received a stimulus from an itinerant puppet show he once witnessed in the village square, and soon he not only had his own cardboard theater but was also improvising texts for performances therein.

Concerned for their children's secondary education, Lorca's family moved into the city of Granada in 1909. Although his career at school was undistinguished, marked by daydreaming, a lack of application, and a greater taste for fun and jokes than hard work, Lorca's artistic sensibility was nevertheless developing throughout his teens. While his family had essentially rustic origins, it was nevertheless cultured, and its members professed a particular enthusiasm for literature. The Spanish classics and a complete set of Victor Hugo's translated works were in the

Lorca, age one, at home in Fuente Vaqueros, west of Granada

family's library. However, Lorca's first great love was music: lessons with a venerated piano teacher—Antonio Segura Mesa—led to visions of studies at the Paris Conservatory. But family opposition and the death of the aged teacher (in May 1916) meant that a career in music was stalled; Lorca remained an accomplished pianist, both in the classical repertoire and in popular Spanish songs, but his major energies would be redirected elsewhere.

Two years previously, in 1914, with some of the necessary qualifications still pending, he had commenced a preparatory year at the University of Granada. He initially embarked on a joint major in philosophy, letters, and law, but one may assume that, like many middle-class sons in Spain and like the majority of nineteenth- and twentieth-century Spanish writers, Lorca was expected by his father to become a respectable lawyer. Lorca himself had other ideas. Much of his literary juvenilia is preserved but still largely un-

Lorca and his sister Concha at the family's home in Granada

published. In his late teens he tried his hand first at prose and dramas, and then a little later at poetry. These writings are marked by a strong, sometimes overwrought romanticism, influenced stylistically by late-romantic, fin-de-siècle, Spanish-American *modernismo*, and by the work of Rubén Darío in particular. Lorca was already preoccupied by and tackling the big topics: the existence, nature, and disposition of God; the significance of Christ's life and death; the meaning of life itself; social injustice; the conflicts between the spiritual and the carnal; and the quest for a perfect, ideal, transcendent love. Brought up in a strongly and conventionally Catholic atmosphere, Lorca found himself questioning some of its most fundamental dogmas, and, at the same time, he was becoming aware that he was somehow different to most of those around him. His ill-defined longings, his highly developed sensibility, his consuming interest in philosophy, literature, music, and

the other arts, and his precocious awareness of the human condition all combined to lead him to seek the company of fellow spirits. With them he founded the Rinconcillo, a *tertulia* (loosely organized literary circle) that met in a corner of the Café Alameda, just a stone's throw from his family's house in Granada.

While the courses Lorca took at the university were mainly a tedious chore for him, nevertheless there were a few outstanding and inspiring teachers. One of these was a professor of the theory of literature and the arts, Martín Domínguez Berrueta, whose pedagogical ideas were informed by the liberal Institución Libre de Enseñanza (an independent, reformist secondary school in Madrid) and who consequently believed firmly in the educational value of travel; he organized artistic tours for selected students from the university. The first stirrings of Lorca's literary vocation can be dated to the period immediately before the first trip he took with Berrueta, and the stimulus and encouragement he received from this professor were crucial in converting him from a pianist into a writer. Lorca participated in a total of four excursions, to several different areas of Spain, in the summer and fall of 1916 and spring and summer of 1917. He returned with long, impressionistic prose accounts of his travels, and these formed the basis for his first book, *Impresiones y paisajes* (1918; translated as *Impressions and Landscapes*, 1987). This loosely structured travelogue threatens on occasions to turn into an exercise in pure style: aestheticism, synaesthesia, and endless sunsets are among the hallmarks of derivative *modernismo*, but other pieces testify to his abiding social and theological concerns, focused in meditations on such topics as the rural poverty he had observed on his travels and on the essential unhealthiness, as Lorca saw it, of the monk's way of life.

With a view to furthering and widening Lorca's education, and no doubt also with the expectation of participation in a less provincial literary life, another influential university professor and family friend, Fernando de los Ríos, supplied Lorca in 1919 with introductions to such prominent literary figures as Juan Ramón Jiménez and to the administrators of Madrid's recently moved and expanded Residencia de Estudiantes, a progressive establishment modeled after the Oxford and Cambridge colleges; it was another offshoot of the Institución Libre de Enseñanza. For the next ten years Lorca would divide his time between Madrid and Granada, staying at the "Resi," as he referred to the students' establishment, and struggling periodically to complete his law degree at the provincial university. The summers, invariably spent back home, were productive times for writing: a very high percentage of Lorca's manuscripts, when they are dated at all, are ascribed to those months in Granada, at the seashore in Málaga, or more likely in one or another of the family's houses out on the *vega*.

His life in Granada, then, rarely implied even the pretense of the exclusive and narrow pursuit of academic study, and this was especially true after composer Manuel de Falla's move to that city temporarily in 1919 and permanently from 1920 on. Lorca's piano teacher Segura and the professors de los Ríos and Berrueta had been important formative influences, and Falla was another equally significant one. Common interests in music, folklore, and Andalusia naturally drew

the composer and the poet together and led in time to a variety of collaborations.

Granada also was the scene of a visit, in the summer of 1919, by Gregorio Martínez Sierra, one of the few theatrical impresarios of the time interested in innovation and willing to take chances; impressed by Lorca's youthful compositions that he heard him read during a recital, Sierra asked him to recast and expand one of his poems as a play to be staged at Sierra's Teatro Eslava in Madrid. Such was the genesis of *El maleficio de la mariposa* (1920; translated as *The Butterfly's Evil Spell*, 1954), which is peopled exclusively with insects and whose symbolist derivation, particularly from Maurice Maeterlinck, is clear to see. The poem on which it was based is now lost, but "Los encuentros de un caracol aventurero" (The Encounters of an Adventurous Snail) from *Libro de poemas* (Book of Poems, 1921) falls into much the same genre. The play, completed under pressure and while rehearsals of act 1 were already under way, premiered in the spring of 1920 and was a dismal failure; Lorca reacted bravely, but it was seven years before he ventured again before a paying theater public.

Meanwhile, the compositions that make up Lorca's first collection of verse, the simply and generically entitled *Libro de poemas*, were beginning to fall into place. In late 1920 and early 1921 Lorca's brother, Francisco, assisted him in making a selection out of all his verse written to date. In the end no pieces dated before April 1918 were included, and the chronologically latest is ascribed to December 1920. Lorca hesitated—as he would do repeatedly in later life—over the quality of his compositions and the desirability of fixing them in print, and he delivered the completed manuscript very reluctantly to the person who was to print it, Gabriel García Maroto. As had been the case with *Impresiones y paisajes*, publication was funded entirely by Lorca's father. The poetry collection was published in July 1921, received a few kind notices, mainly from friends, and then slipped into (unjustified) obscurity.

In fact, although *Libro de poemas* suffers from many of the flaws of a poet's first collection, it also contains much that is original and worthwhile. Lorca can be seen assimilating influences of his preferred poets: Darío, Jiménez, Antonio Machado, Francisco Villaespesa, Salvador Rueda, and others, but elsewhere Lorca strikes out on new paths, nearly achieving a voice of his own. Likewise, given the essentially miscellaneous

Lorca circa 1919, at the time he went to live in Madrid's Residencia de Estudiantes (photograph by Francisco García Lorca)

nature of the collection, the style is mixed: there are formal, complex, rhetorically structured poems, usually written in correspondingly "high-art" (and therefore long-line) meters, and there are freer, lighter poems, incorporating and emulating traditional folk motifs, written—logically—in more "popular" (and hence short-line) meters. In general the book is very much in the romantic-symbolist tradition. In 1921 Spain already possessed a nascent avant-garde in the form of the *ultraísmo* movement, but save for a few outlandish metaphors—which probably owe more to Ramón Gómez de la Serna and his *greguerías* (one-line witticisms)—there is little or no avant-garde writing in *Libro de poemas*. What there is, though, is a striking inventiveness, coherence, density, and richness often to be found within the relatively conventional image making.

The same romantic-symbolist tradition can be invoked with respect to the themes. *Libro de poemas* presents a solitary, lovelorn, poetic persona, full of nostalgic yearnings, frustrated or rejected in love, pondering his mortality and the passing of time, often against a backdrop of the countryside or sunset. The religious preoccupations from Lorca's juvenilia are taken up again, if in slightly more muted terms: a cruel or indifferent God is variously represented as deaf, blind, and asleep.

By the time *Libro de poemas* was in the bookshops, however, Lorca had already turned his back on the kind of writing it exemplified, and he was elaborating a new manner that would absorb him for the next four or five years. In one bound, Lorca seems to have thrown off all traces of the high-art, long-line style of composition and all the poetic rhetoric it entailed; he opted for short, often minimal lines, arranged in loosely structured stanzaic patterns, often employing parallelism, repetition (sometimes with internal variation), exclamations, unanswered questions, and ellipses; the resulting short poems were arranged in thematically grouped sequences he called "suites." The traditional Spanish folk lyric seems to have met the haiku, at that time enjoying a vogue in Spain, and the result, in Lorca's capable hands, was a flexible mode of poetic expression, as seen in "Hacia" (Toward) from *Suites* (1983):

> Vuelve
> ¡corazón!
> vuelve.
>
> Por las selvas del amor
> no verás gentes.
> Tendrás claros manantiales.
> En lo verde
> hallarás la rosa inmensa
> del siempre.
>
> Y dirás: ¡Amor! ¡amor!
> Sin que tu herida
> se cierre.
>
> Vuelve
> ¡corazón mío!
> vuelve.
>
> (Come back
> heart!
> come back.
>
> Through the thickets of love
> you will see no people.
> You will have clear-running springs.
> In the green
> you will find the immense rose
> of always.
>
> And you will say: Love! love!
> without your wound
> closing.
>
> Come back
> my heart
> come back.)

The change in form was inextricably tied to a shift in themes, or, at the very least, the explicitness of presentation of those themes. The metrical delicacy of the compositions is matched by their understated, elliptical, suggestive, and some-times elusive content, and by a further sophistication in the forging of telling metaphors.

Lorca rarely had a firm idea for a collection of poetry before he had written the majority of the compositions that would eventually go to make it up. In this sense, most of the poems he wrote from 1921 to 1924 were not, on their inception, destined for any particular collection. Later, though, it became increasingly clear that some verses from this period fitted into the category of *Suites* (as the reconstructed book was called in 1983), and others, a little more songlike, more popular, more independent (and hence less suitelike), corresponded better to the label of *Canciones* (1927; translated as *Songs*, 1976). Still others, suites again but with a very specific content, would go to make up *Poema del cante jondo* (1931; translated as *Poem of the Deep Song*, 1987).

Suites was, of course, never published as a collection during Lorca's lifetime, and the completed manuscript has been lost. He had planned to publish it, alongside *Canciones* and *Poema del cante jondo*, in 1927, but when funds proved insufficient, *Canciones* was the sole beneficiary. *Suites* was, in the early 1980s, put together from original drafts among Lorca's papers (held by the Fundación García Lorca), with sequences that bear a strong stylistic resemblance and that are dated to the years in question. Other "suites" are probably lost, and there is no certainty that Lorca would have included all that have survived or presented them in the chronological order in which they appear, but they are more than substantial and representative enough to give a hypothetical idea of what the book would have been like.

Suites represents a major formal break with *Libro de poemas*, but there are some thematic carryovers; however, on the whole, *Suites* is a less self-indulgently melancholic book and both a more playful and a darker one than its predecessor. Nature still looms large, and in it the poet, again adopting a lyric "I," laments his broken love—as in "El jardín de las morenas" (The Garden of the Dark Women)—or again confronts the loneliness, stillness, and ultimate emptiness of a night sky. The child and childhood assume a larger role, and the poet mourns not only his lost childhood but also the children he believes he will never have (and, indeed, never had).

Poema del cante jondo, conceived and written almost completely in November 1921, represents a specific subset of these "suites," bringing together sequences dedicated to different forms of *cante jondo*, that is the pure, traditional, and un-

Lorca and Luis Buñuel at a Madrid fair, circa 1920

adulterated form of flamenco song. The principal sections in the book—each an extended suite—in no way purport to reproduce or imitate the actual lyrics of *cante jondo* but rather they seek to re-create, poetically, the impression on a hearer of a performance of these songs. The different verse types—*siguiriya, soleá, saeta, petenera* (all feminine nouns)—are each personified by Lorca with the mysterious figure of a woman who moves through the Andalusian landscape. Meter and most of the other technical features are essentially identical to those of *Suites*, with perhaps one notable exception: the poetic "I" is suppressed and all the writing is strictly third person. Thematically, the songs are presented as pure and profound expressions of the gypsy—and more generally the Andalusian—ethos. As such, their dwelling on raw emotion, the tension of the moment, enigma, death, and above all *pena* (pain, grief, sorrow)—the last of which Lorca associated intimately with the experience of Andalusian women—mark them as a channel through which the Andalusian essence finds release and form.

The later sections in the collection are more of a miscellany, and the interpenetration with not only *Suites* but also *Canciones* becomes clear. The book ends with two *diálogos*, "Escena del teniente coronel de la guardia civil" (Episode of the Lieutenant Colonel of the Civil Guard) and "Diálogo del Amargo" (Dialogue of the Bitter One). Composed in 1925, they then belonged to a quite different work, "Diálogos," which did not come to fruition and was never published in full (eight are extant). The two *diálogos* in *Poema del cante jondo* were added late in the day as a makeweight when the book was finally prepared for publication in early 1931.

The immediate stimulus for writing *Poema del cante jondo* was a project conceived by Lorca and others—including Falla—to mount a Cante Jondo Competition in Granada, an event that did indeed take place in June 1922 and is generally deemed to have been a great success. The original plan had been to publish Lorca's poetic collection to coincide with the festival, but he did at least write and deliver a lecture (largely relying on Falla's musicological researches) titled "El cante jondo. Primitivo canto andaluz" (Primitive Andalusian Song) given in February 1922 as part of the buildup to the competition and collected in *Prosa* (1969).

Lorca did not get back to Madrid at all during 1922, most likely at his parents' insistence, and this stay in Granada no doubt favored his exposure to the popular and the folkloric. If the debacle of *El maleficio de la mariposa* was still firmly in his mind, this did not dampen his enthusiasm for exploring the traditional genre of the *cristobicas*—a kind of Andalusian Punch-and-Judy show, which, like *cante jondo*, was in danger of disappearing in its original, purer forms, and which he re-created in his own puppet farce, *Tragicomedia de don Cristóbal y la señá Rosita* (*Tragicomedy of Don Cristóbal and Rosita*, written in 1921 and 1922, probably first performed in 1931, and translated in 1955). Lorca's plans and projects outstripped their realization, and during this period there was talk of Sierra putting on the play at the Eslava and also of Lorca founding with Falla a touring Andalusian puppet theater. Although neither came about, there were nonetheless further collaborations with the celebrated composer, notably a puppet-based entertainment on the eve of Epiphany 1923 for some children gathered in the living room of the Lorca family home. Lorca's main contribution was his puppet-play adaptation of a folktale, "La niña que riega la albahaca y el príncipe preguntón" (The Girl Who Waters the Basil, and the Inquisitive Prince), whose text was long thought lost but has recently been recovered (though, it is suspected, in a corrupted version). With this success behind them, Lorca and Falla now proposed a more substantial collaboration, on a comic opera to be entitled *Lola, la comedianta* (Lola, the Comedienne), of which Lorca was to compose the libretto and Falla the music. The work seems to have occupied Lorca, on and off, during 1923 and 1924; unfortunately, the project petered out, but some scenes of Lorca's text have survived and were published in 1981.

The years 1921 to 1924 are also, as has been noted, the essential period of Lorca's composition of *Canciones*, though the collection probably includes a few pieces from 1925. *Canciones* differs from *Suites* in that the poems, with one or two exceptions, stand alone as single compositions, the tone is a good deal more festive and playful, and the indebtedness to—and reinvention of—traditional verse forms is more apparent. The poems are grouped into larger sections, with such characteristic titles as "Amor," "Juegos," or "Canciones de luna" (Love, Games, or Moon-Songs). In some ways, out of Lorca's various collections of poetry, *Canciones* approaches most closely

that aesthetic propounded—or better, analyzed—in José Ortega y Gasset's influential essay *La deshumanización del arte* (The Dehumanization of Art, 1925). That is to say, in *Canciones* the poetic "I" is not prominent and there are certainly no overtly lyrical outpourings: emotions, if sensed or detected at all, are well below the surface of the text; the poetry is playful, enigmatic, and elusive; it incorporates ingenious metaphors; and it seems to serve no transcendent purpose or function. Like *Libro de poemas*, *Canciones* also participates in the trend of *neopopularismo*, shared by Alberti in his first three books. Most of the poems in *Canciones* use short-line, traditional meters, and many of them incorporate and assimilate a variety of other features and motifs from *poesía popular*. But the collection also has its darker, almost tragic side, more veiled than in *Suites:* time passes inexorably; indeterminate hopes and longings seem never to be fulfilled—or fulfillable—between the inevitable alternation of night and day, sun and moon; and in the well-known "Canción de jinete" (Rider's Song) the horseman will, of course, never reach his destination, Córdoba. *Canciones*, then, published after considerable delay in the late spring of 1927 as the first supplement of the Málaga "little magazine" *Litoral*, might well be thought of as the high-watermark of the first phase in Lorca's poetic output, in which he had indisputably achieved his own voice.

After the anomalous 1922, spent entirely in Granada, Lorca's years fell into a fairly regular kind of rhythm: most of winter, spring, and early summer in Madrid, July to September in Granada and on the *vega*, then a couple of months back in Madrid before Christmas with his family. While Lorca was most productive from a literary point of view during the summer months in Granada, these were also the years of important friendships being forged in Madrid—in particular at the Residencia de Estudiantes. In 1923 he met Salvador Dalí, in 1924 Guillén and Alberti, and in 1927 Aleixandre and Cernuda. Lorca rapidly became recognized as one of the leading lights in the new poetic generation, in what critics of the day called *la joven literatura* (the young literature). On visits to Dalí during Holy Week in 1925 and the early summer of 1927, Lorca stayed in Barcelona, Cadaqués, and Figueras, and during the second of these trips he collaborated in the premiere of his play *Mariana Pineda* on 24 June 1927 in Barcelona.

A scene from the premiere production of Lorca's first play, El maleficio de la mariposa *(The Butterfly's Evil Spell, 1920), based on one of his early poems*

The years 1924 to 1927 were also a time, after the closure of the *Suites/Poema del cante jondo/ Canciones* phase, when Lorca became engaged in a wide-ranging exploration of very different modes of poetic writing. One vein or direction is represented by what turned out to be Lorca's most successful, most popular, and best-known collection of poetry, *Romancero gitano* (first published as *Primer romancero gitano*, 1928; translated as *Gypsy Ballads*, 1951). Once more the process of gestation was a fairly lengthy and leisurely one. While a primitive version of "Romance de Don Pedro a caballo" (Ballad of Don Pedro on Horseback) dates back to late 1921, the concept of a series of Gypsy ballads and the composition of several of the poems can be ascribed to the summer of 1924. Others followed in subsequent years, and several appeared in little magazines (1926-1928) before the collection was completed in 1927 and published in mid 1928.

The eighteen poems—fifteen *romances gitanos* plus the grouping titled "Tres romances históricos" (Three Historical Ballads)—are all written in the traditional octosyllabic ballad meter, whose origins go back at least as far as the four-

teenth century and which had been perpetuated in a continuous oral tradition down to Lorca's times. His earlier collections of poetry, in differing ways, show his interest in and assimilation of that sector of *poesía de tipo de tradicional* (traditional-type poetry) that is represented by a variety of brief lyrics—*canciones, coplas, seguidillas* and the like—while *Romancero gitano* provides ample evidence of Lorca's equal enthusiasm for and absorption of the other major sector, which is constituted by the *romance* tradition. But *Romancero gitano* is not a book of imitations or pastiches. Lorca blends a skillful re-creation of traditional ballad meter and stylistic devices with a dazzling poetic language, marked above all by the abundant use of ultramodern images. "Preciosa y el aire" (Preciosa and the Wind) is representative:

Preciosa tira el pandero
y corre sin detenerse.
El viento-hombrón la persigue
con una espada caliente.

Frunce su rumor el mar.
Los olivos palidecen.
Cantan las flantas de umbría
y el liso gong de la nieve.

(Preciosa throws down the tamborine
and runs without stopping.
The wind-man chases her
with a hot sword.

The sea wrinkles its murmur.
The olive trees turn pale.
The flutes of shade
and the smooth gong of the snow sing out.)

There are rather simple, transparent images that employ a manifest Freudian symbolism; refurbished conceits, jarring and provocative, wherein one threadlike connection links two otherwise disparate realities; complex images based on trompe l'oeil effects; and "mood" images, whose internal operations are more difficult to decipher and whose principal purpose may be to create and develop atmosphere rather than a clear and specific "meaning."

Actions in the poems—their plots, so to speak, are basically intended to function as "modern myths." Their protagonists, ostensibly Gypsies, are not presented in a picturesque or anthropological vein, but rather are themselves symbols of that which is quintessentially Andalusian. Whereas Antonio Machado in his *Campos de Castilla* (1912; translated as *The Castilian Camp*, 1982) hoped to make the leap from the particular of the Castilian to the universal of humankind, Lorca intended a parallel movement from the Andalusian to the depths of the human soul.

There Lorca found *pena*, which is more than anything else what his characters and stories demonstrate; this central preoccupation is treated explicitly in "Romance de la pena negra" (Ballad of the Black Pain), whose protagonist, Soledad Montoya, is its very incarnation. Another crucial poem is "Romance del emplazado" (Ballad of the Summoned): if a few exceptional men are called to their death at a preannounced and appointed hour, then there is, Lorca implies, an unknown appointed hour waiting for each individual. The world of *Romancero gitano*, therefore, links with that of *Poema del cante jondo*, and can likewise be illuminated by his play *Bodas de sangre* (1933; translated as *Blood Wedding*, 1939), by the later version of Lorca's lecture "Arquitectura del cante jondo" (1930), and by his prose text *"Romancero gitano. Conferencia-recital"* (1935), the last two being included in his *Obras completas* (Complete Works, volume 3, 1986).

At the same time as he was working on *Romancero gitano*, Lorca was also trying his hand at a very different kind of poetry, in which he took up and refurbished several high-art, long-line meters—associated above all with poets from Spain's Golden Age—usually combining these elaborate verse forms with the modern language and image making of the 1920s. This trend in Lorca's work coincided with a broader movement in poetry, which has been termed *neoclasicismo* or *neogongorismo* and which in turn has been compared to T. S. Eliot and his contemporaries' interest in the English metaphysical poets. Lorca conceived of his major compositions in this vein as "Odas" (the title of another uncompleted book). A fragment of an ode can be dated to summer 1924, but Lorca started in earnest after his Catalonian visit in 1925 on the "Oda a Salvador Dalí," a eulogy to the young painter, a manifest token of their close friendship, and a poetic exposition of Dalí's (then) essentially cubist aesthetic. Slightly later came the "Oda al Santísimo Sacramento del Altar" (written mainly in 1928 but not finished till fall 1929) and the unfinished "Oda a Sesostris" (1928). The former is a highly heterodox and modernistic meditation on the mystery of the crucified Christ present in the Sacrament—reflecting a brief turning back to Catholicism on Lorca's part; the latter, more difficult to judge because of its fragmentary nature, takes on, in a more hermetic and rather enigmatic style, the topic of homosexuality in ancient times. (These three odes are in *Obras completas*, volume 1, 1986.)

This survey of the middle years of the 1920s would not be complete without mention of the "Poemas festivos." This title—not Lorca's own—was adopted by Francisco García Lorca (the poet's brother) and subsequently by Marie Laffranque to refer to a body of largely unpublished compositions (in the Fundación García Lorca) that fall into two categories—apocryphal poems and pastiches. Lorca and his friends in Granada invented a fictitious poet, Isidoro Capdepón Fernández, and wrote poems for him in a very out-of-date, late-romantic/*modernista* style. Sometime in the mid to late 1920s Lorca also wrote a sequence of poems imitating, and to an extent parodying, the styles of his friends and contemporaries Jiménez, Machado, Salinas, Guillén, Alberti, and others, demonstrating a keen sense of his and their established styles.

The years 1927 and 1928 also saw Lorca venturing, with serious intent, into other new fields: drawing and little magazines. For many years he had illustrated letters and odd sheets of paper with his quirky drawings—reminiscent of the

La Virgen de los Siete Dolores, *drawn by Lorca in 1924 (by permission of the Estate of Gregorio Prieto)*

work of Pablo Picasso, Jean Cocteau, and Yves Tanguy—done with pencil, India ink, or wax crayons. In 1927, encouraged by his Catalonian friends (especially the art critic Sebastián Gasch), Lorca began to take this pursuit more seriously, and an exhibition of twenty-four drawings was held in Barcelona at the Dalmau gallery. With a briefly strong zeal, Lorca planned a book of drawings; nothing came of this, but he continued drawing occasional pieces until the end of his life. Likewise, since the beginning of the 1920s Lorca had been a regular and subsequently a much-sought-after contributor to the many ephemeral literary magazines that sprang up around Spain, often directed and produced by his friends. But in 1927 Lorca started planning, with a group of younger writers, a Granadine magazine of his own, and his plans bore fruit in the two issues of *gallo* published in the spring of 1928. However, with Lorca's visits to Madrid and his shoestring budget, a third issue did not appear in the

fall, and the magazine folded.

This year 1928 was a turning point and a time of crisis, when many things came to a head. *Romancero gitano* was a big, popular success, but Lorca suspected—correctly—that most of his readers did not really understand the poems, and he chafed at what he called "mi mito de gitanería" (my Gypsy myth). The magazine *gallo* had an all-too-ephemeral effect on the public. He worked sporadically on other "Odas" and at the same time embarked on the radically different "Poemas en prosa" (never published in book form).

These were also difficult times in his personal life. As a sensitive, rather delicate, awkward youth, Lorca had had two or three crushes on young Granadine women; these were secret, adolescent passions that were confided to male friends in letters but probably never declared to the objects of his love. If Lorca felt a little different in the provincial city of his youth, the move to Madrid—and specifically the Residencia de

A photograph Lorca inscribed to the Catalonian critic Gasch

Estudiantes—made for an immediate change to a new environment where he was surrounded by many like-minded artists. There a passionate friendship seems to have grown between him and Emilio Prados, though the latter apparently invested the relationship with more importance than Lorca did. Later it was Lorca and Dalí who became an inseparable pair, and during the mid 1920s Lorca was clearly coming to terms with his own unambiguous homosexuality. The precise nature of his relationship with Dalí, at the Resi and on Lorca's two visits to Catalonia, will never be fully illuminated, but there can be no doubt that it was intense. At the same time, in Madrid, Lorca had become friends with a young sculptor at an art school, Emilio Aladrén, and it is conceivable that Dalí's apparent refusal to consummate physically his relationship with Lorca may have precipitated a stormy, physical, and relatively short-lived affair between Lorca and Aladrén, one that caused Lorca to go through the worst "crisis sentimental" of his life, in Granada during the

summer of 1928. This difficult situation and the warring emotions it engendered may in turn account for a brief turn back toward religion (even if somewhat heterodox in nature), as evidenced by his "Oda al Santísimo Sacramento" and by the unusual fact that Lorca impulsively walked as a penitent, as a member of a brotherhood, in the 1929 Easter procession in Granada.

Lorca's aesthetics were also changing at this time. Dalí, as he moved closer to the surrealism he was soon to espouse, reacted badly to *Romancero gitano*, and Lorca himself started to preach a more irrationalist position, even if he still took care to distance himself from the French way of writing. The extent of this change can be gauged by comparing two of his lectures from the second half of the 1920s. "La imagen poética de don Luis de Góngora" (The Poetic Image of Don Luis de Góngora, collected in *Prosa*) was given in Granada in February 1926 as a kind of warm-up to the 1927 tricentenary commemorations of Góngora's death, events that culminated in a trip to Seville in December 1927 in which Lorca participated. In his talk the major points are the current cult of the image, the role of imagination and objectivity (antilyricism), and the creation of modern conceits following a practice similar to that of the early-seventeenth-century works of Góngora. "Imaginación, inspiración, evasión," delivered in Granada in October 1928 and also collected in *Prosa*, totally rejects the cold, measured, rational objectivity so praised in the previous lecture; imagination is thrown out, and inspiration and evasion are the keys to a new poetics. Where the image-conceit once took pride of place, Lorca proposes the *hecho poético* (poetic event), a new kind of image that is less susceptible to rational response or interpretation and relies for its effect much less on the principle of analogy and much more on that of juxtaposition and collage.

The earliest of the "Poemas en prosa" is "Santa Lucía y San Lázaro." Written in the summer of 1927, it contains many ciphered references to Barcelona (where Lorca had just been for an extended stay), and it marks a kind of turning point, looking backward as it does to the aesthetics of *Canciones* and *Romancero gitano* (which are in turn broadly analogous in style with the Dalí of his cubist phase), and looking forward to more illogical poetic procedures developed and amplified in the subsequent prose poems. These are "Nadadora sumergida" (Submerged Female Swimmer), "Suicidio en Alejandría" (Suicide in Alexandria), "Degollación de los Inocentes" (Beheading of the Innocents), "Degollación del Bautista" (Beheading of John the Baptist), and "Amantes asesinados por una perdiz" (Lovers Murdered by a Partridge), all of which were almost certainly composed in 1928. They correspond to the new aesthetic of inspiration and evasion: they incorporate references to the modern world; they are written in a disjointed, fragmented manner; principles of logic and progression are abandoned or deliberately subverted; and the images embedded in the prose are indeed difficult, if not impossible, to respond to rationally. In many ways, then, the "Poemas en prosa" mark the closest point in his literary output that Lorca came to surrealism.

The first half of 1929 represented a personal lull for Lorca and an almost complete absence of new work. He had not thrown off the depression of the previous summer, the off-and-on relationship with Aladrén was deteriorating fast, Dalí had transferred his primary friendship to Luis Buñuel—they were working on the film *Un Chien andalou* (An Andalusian Dog, 1929)—increasing public scrutiny continued to vex Lorca, and he may, in addition, have reached a kind of artistic impasse. Early in that year he received tentative inquiries as to whether he would be interested in giving lectures in America. By the summer his family seems to have concluded that a change of scene was the only thing to pull him out of his slump, and, accompanied by Fernando de los Ríos, who was himself en route to the United States, Lorca embarked on his first trip outside Spain, leading him, via France and England, to New York's Columbia University, where he took a summer course in English language for foreigners.

The new and totally different surroundings seem essentially to have been beneficial, for Lorca, staying in a university dormitory, was soon at work again, setting down the first poems of those he would eventually gather together as *Poeta en Nueva York* (1940). The Spanish professors at Columbia had been alerted to his 25 June arrival, and he immediately got together with them and a small colony of Spaniards living in New York, some of whom he had known in Madrid. He took his English course through July and the first half of August, though without making any significant headway with the language, and when classes ended he headed north, out of the city, to stay first in Eden Mills, Vermont (with Philip Cummings, a young American he had previously met in Spain), then in the Catskills (with Angel del Río and his family), and finally in Newburgh, New York (with Federico de Onís).

Back in New York City and in a new dormitory for the fall and winter of 1929, Lorca, never an assiduous student, slacked off further. He spent a good deal of time with the Spanish professors at Columbia; Spaniards and Latin Americans residing in New York; a small circle of Americans who spoke some Spanish; a variety of American and foreign students, some of whom were living on his dorm corridor; and several Spanish friends whose visits to New York coincided with his stay. Late at night, back in the dorm room, he worked on his poetry; letters home suggest he took a lively interest in both the cinema and theater (particularly the off-Broadway "art" companies, the black reviews, and even the Chinese theater); he explored Harlem (guided by Nella Larsen) and frequented at least one of its nightspots (Small's Paradise); he was introduced to Hart Crane; Lorca directed the choir at the Instituto Hispánico; and he delivered single lec-

Lorca with Salvador Dalí at the painter's home in Cadaqués, Catalonia, 1927

tures at Columbia and Vassar College, Poughkeepsie. In October 1929 Lorca was at hand to observe in person the Wall Street crash, the panic that followed, and the immediate aftershocks; he mingled with the crowds, scanned the newspapers, and claimed to have seen a suicide's body on the sidewalk.

Poeta en Nueva York was not published in Lorca's lifetime, though it is certain that plans to do so had reached an advanced stage by the summer of 1936. Between his return to Spain (in the summer of 1930) and the outbreak of civil war, the collection underwent a process of evolution in which different phases can be identified, and Lorca used both public and private partial readings of the book as a way of testing out responses to individual compositions and to different distributions of the poems. *Poeta en Nueva York*, it seems, was originally to be an urban-centered book, and "Tierra y luna" (Earth and Moon—the

usual title for the "second" collection within it) was to be a rural one; later *Poeta* was to contain the poems that reflected the American experience more directly and contained greater social commentary, while "Tierra y luna" was to be a more abstract and metaphysical collection. At other times the two collections, in Lorca's plan, were fused into one—usually as *Poeta en Nueva York*, though for one period as "Introducción a la muerte" (Introduction to Death)—and it is clear that, as he approached a definitive formulation in the fall of 1935 and spring of 1936, the book was one, articulated into different sections that reflected its diverse orientations: urban, rural, social, philosophical, and so on. Two "first" editions were eventually published posthumously in 1940, a bilingual one in New York and a Spanish one in Mexico. The textual discrepancies between them, not as great as sometimes claimed, can be largely explained by tracing the vicissitudes of the copy text, passed on to the W. W. Norton Company in 1939 and firmly fixed thereafter, but treated in a less reverential fashion by the owner of the original heterogeneous manuscript, José Bergamín, who introduced revisions (some of dubious justification) into the text for the Mexico City edition.

Much has also been made, over the years, of the poet's unhappiness in New York and his rejection of this quintessential metropolis and prototype of the "asphalt jungle," and such a gloss is given further substance by the coincidence of his stay with the Wall Street crash. The letters home, obviously designed for family consumption, depict a very different picture, of Lorca impressed, fascinated, and often stimulated by his new environment, admiring the skyscrapers rather than denigrating them. Other accounts suggest that, while Lorca could always be counted on to serve as the life of the party, he also experienced darker moments. *Poeta en Nueva York* is divided into ten sections, each with its own title, which chart the poet-persona's passage through the arrival in the big city, getting to know New York, a trip to the countryside, the return, and a final departure for Cuba. As such, the overall shape is transparently autobiographical, but it should be noted that the poems were not written in anything like the order in which they appear in the volume, and many liberties of detail are taken that undermine any presumption of biographical fidelity or historicity.

The poems cover several themes: sharp contrasts are drawn between the innocence of childhood and the "knowledge" of adulthood; New York is depicted as a compendium of materialism, superficiality, rootlessness, soullessness, and hypocritical organized religion; humankind struggles to achieve some kind of authenticity and has great or invincible difficulty in establishing or maintaining any kind of satisfying human relationship; furthermore, humankind is subject to the twin constants of the inexorable passing of time and the inevitability of mortality. The vision could be broadly categorized as pessimistically existentialist: Lorca implies that most humans are alienated or fail to get beneath the surface of things. Partial exceptions to this rule are the blacks of Harlem—who, although oppressed and denatured, retain an atavistic spirituality—and the exemplary figure of Walt Whitman, who was properly in touch with himself and nature.

On the social level, Lorca decries the poverty and exploitation he sees around him, criti-

Lorca at Columbia University in New York, 1929

cizes Wall Street and its materialism and capitalism, rails at the pope and much of organized religion, and even looks forward to the day when, in rather vague terms, a cataclysmic upheaval is envisioned as overtaking the city, followed by the rule of nature returning. In more personal terms, this collection marks the first appearance of poems that seriously address the topic of homosexuality, notably in "Tu infancia en Menton" (Your Childhood in Menton) and "Oda a Walt Whitman" (Ode to Walt Whitman).

Poeta en Nueva York has often been classified as a prime example of Spanish surrealism, but the use of the national epithet immediately suggests that a tacit distinction is being made with regard to the original French surrealism. In fact, this form scarcely took hold in Spain, though stylistic effects commonly associated with surrealism are to be found in the poetry of some Spanish writers of this time (Alberti, Aleixandre, Cernuda). Just as in the *Romancero*, Lorca's imagistic practice in *Poeta* is quite varied. Some images work as conventional metaphors, some create a sense of mystery—"las heladas montañas del oso" (the icy mountains of the bear) means Bear Mountain in New York State; "perros marinos" (sea dogs) refers to veteran sailors—but above all *hechos poéticos* predominate, difficult images that resist easy interpretation. At the same time, the poetic discourse becomes fragmented: free verse is the form most commonly adopted, and where this extends to long, declamatory lines, the influence of Whitman is easy to detect.

Poeta en Nueva York was not the only literary work to which Lorca devoted attention during his U.S. stay. Revisions were made to both *La zapatera prodigiosa* (1930; translated as *The Shoemaker's Prodigious Wife*, in *From Lorca's Theater*, 1941) and *Amor de don Perlimplín con Belisa en su jardín* (1933; translated as *The Love of Don Perlimplín and Belisa in the Garden*, also in *From Lorca's Theater*). Lorca also penned a silent-film scenario entitled *Viaje a la luna* (published as a book in 1981; translated as *Trip to the Moon*, 1963), but it was never produced.

It was with some relief that Lorca left New York in early March 1930, traveling down the coast by train and embarking from Florida for Cuba. There he had been invited by the Institucíon Hispano Cubana to give a lecture series, and again he was received by enthusiasts of his work—Cubans, some of whom he had met in Spain in the 1920s, and Spaniards now living in or visiting Cuba. Lorca immediately fell in love with the island, with its Andalusian flavor mixed with an exotic African element. With increasing celebrity, he presented his lectures, was lionized by the artistic elite, made expeditions into the interior of the island and to Santiago de Cuba, and wrote the poem that closes *Poeta en Nueva York*, "Son de negros en Cuba" (Song of Blacks in Cuba).

In Cuba, Lorca started work on a truly revolutionary new play, entitled *El público* (1978; translated as *The Public*, 1983), the first draft of which he completed back home in Granada in August 1930. Later versions have been lost or destroyed, but the (incomplete?) first draft, published in facsimile in 1976 (in *Autógrafos*, volume 2), still affords a powerful impression of the play and is a performable script (on which the 1978 production was based). Metatheatrical in conception, its use of allegory and total abandon of verisimilitude suggest fairly close connections with expressionism. The central theatrical metaphor is used to explore Sartrean notions of acting (for others)

and being (in and of oneself); the proposition is put forward that the only ultimate truth is death itself; and the action centers on a variety of relationships, mainly between homosexuals, and embodies a plea, reminiscent of the "Oda a Walt Whitman," for a kind of pansexual liberation that would allow everyone to love as their desires dictate.

El público therefore represents Lorca's most explicit and extensive treatment of this theme, and as such it invites connection with his own personal life. Although he may have been tolerably comfortable with his homosexuality among a relatively narrow circle of friends in Madrid during the later 1920s, it was not really until his stay in New York and then in Cuba that he began to feel that he could—or should—try to write directly about the topic. If New York provided the example of laxer and more progressive morals, then Cuba, by all reports, seems to have provided the opportunity for Lorca to put a newfound openness into practice.

Reluctantly, he finally returned to Spain in June 1930. After his usual summer in Granada and Málaga, he forsook the Residencia and moved instead into a small attic apartment in Madrid. He was later joined by his brother, Francisco, and he lived there (during his times in the capital) until his family decided to move to Madrid, taking a large apartment in the spring of 1933; Christmases and summers, of course, continued to be spent in Granada at the family's Huerta de San Vicente.

According to his statements in interviews of the time, *El público* represented the direction that Lorca wanted his theater to take. Shortly after finishing this play, he commenced work on another, obviously related to it stylistically, *Así que pasen cinco años* (1978; translated as *When Five Years Pass*, in *From Lorca's Theater*), finished a year later in August of 1931. This piece, a meditation on the passing of time and the existential need to jump into the river of life, is avant-garde and experimental in manner, but it takes a step back from the extremes of *El público*.

While these radical new works represented one possible way of revitalizing the Spanish stage, which for Lorca and most of his contemporaries languished in bourgeois and commercial doldrums of self-satisfaction, the puppet theater, with its strong links to the common people, represented another. Through the 1920s Lorca revised his *Tragicomedia de don Cristóbal*, and it seems that in 1931 he wrote, using the same

First two pages from the manuscript for Lorca's ode to Walt Whitman. The poem was separately published in 1933, then included in Poeta en Nueva York *in 1940 (by permission of the Estate of Federico García Lorca).*

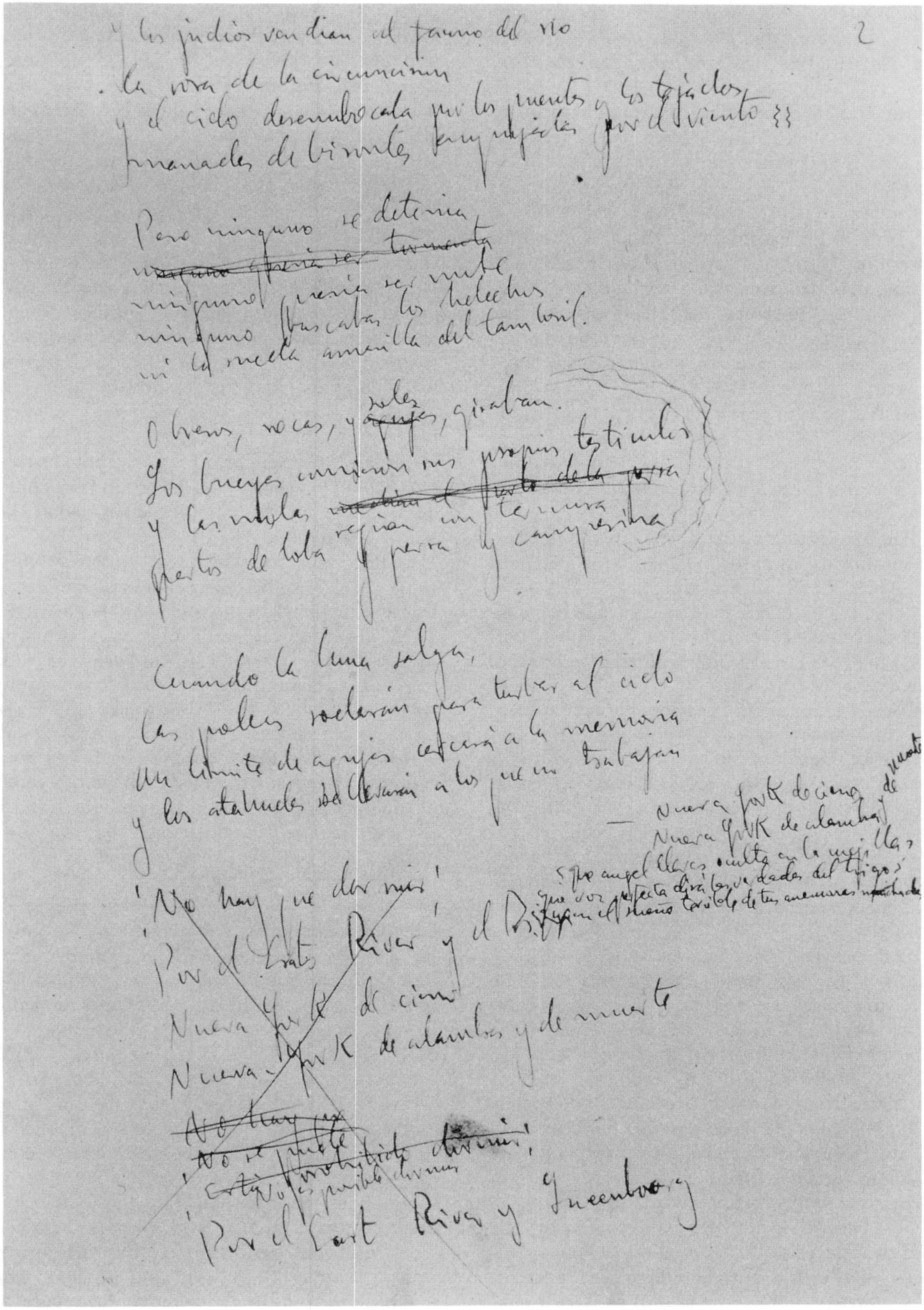

basic characters, what amounts to a second play in the same vein, the *Retablillo de don Cristóbal* (1934; translated as *In the Frame of Don Cristóbal*, 1944).

One final avenue open to theatrical reformers was to go back to the glories of the Spanish Golden Age, and this essentially was the mission of La Barraca, an experimental student-theater group set up in 1932, under the auspices of the Unión Federal de Estudiantes Hispanos and with a subvention from the newly elected Republican government, with Lorca as its artistic director. Recalling in some measure the failed plan in the 1920s for a traveling puppet theater, Lorca devoted a great deal of energy to this project for four years. Touring the country in specially adapted trucks, the troupe played a wide range of the "classics" on improvised open-air stages to audiences in villages, towns, and cities around Spain, and during school time performed in theaters in Madrid.

The major historical event of this period had been the advent of the Second Spanish Republic in April 1931. Lorca and his family were closely linked with major politicians in the Republican camp (notably Fernando de los Ríos), and their sympathies lay squarely with the Republican liberals and socialists. One of the articles of faith of the newly inaugurated regime, evolving out of nineteenth-century *krausista* thinking (based on the ideas of German philosopher Karl Krause) and the Institución Libre de Enseñanza, was the broad and enlightening value of culture and the necessity of the interaction between high art and the people. La Barraca, along with the Misiones Pedagógicas (in which Lorca was not directly involved), represented a desire to put these beliefs into practice.

In the early 1930s there was a clear shift of emphasis in Lorca's career. During the 1920s he became primarily known as a poet—above all with the success of *Romancero gitano*—though he had never neglected dramatic composition. In the 1930s, quantitatively at least, the theater seems increasingly to have predominated, partly out of his desire to reach a much wider and more diverse audience, but Lorca was far from abandoning the lyric form.

For instance, during trips to Galicia in 1932—two to give lectures sponsored by the Comité de Cooperación Intelectual (government-financed intellectual outreach program) and another as part of a La Barraca tour—Lorca conceived of the idea of writing some poems in *gallego* (Galician), the literary language par excellence of Spain at the height of the Middle Ages, and also the language of Rosalía de Castro, a nineteenth-century poetess he much admired. Thus were born at least some of the poems eventually published as *Seis poemas galegos* in 1935 (translated as *Six Galician Poems* in *Ode to Walt Whitman and Other Poems*, 1988). There is still some confusion as to the precise process of composition of these six pieces, but it is certain that a young Galician friend, and possibly lover, Ernesto Guerra Da Cal, collaborated at an early stage, providing encouragement and helping with the language, in which Lorca was not actively adept. The poems are fairly slight pieces, a kind of homage to the language and the region; they avoid the regional picturesqueness (*costumbrismo*) into which others have fallen; instead they evoke the mythic, legendary, syncretic, and superstitious aspects of Galicia, while elsewhere are certain particular preoccupations of Lorca (the drowned child or youth, the malefic moon).

Lorca's next play, and probably the one most crucial to his career, was *Bodas de sangre*. Loosely inspired by a brief newspaper article of 1928, it was substantially written in the summer of 1932 and premiered in the spring of 1933. In spirit and flavor there are close connections between it and both *Romancero gitano* and *Poema del cante jondo*, as the lectures (in *Prosa*) associated with these collections make clear. Lorca espouses a modern notion of tragedy, the most venerable of the theatrical genres and one to which the Spanish stage had to return, he believed, if a new seriousness and quality was to be injected into Spanish dramatic life. Clearly symbolist in its conception, *Bodas de sangre* is nevertheless decidedly mainstream in comparison to *El público* or *Así que pasen cinco años*. Lorca almost certainly had decided that he needed to establish himself firmly as a successful dramatist and then dictate, from a position of strength, the staging of his other, much more challenging works. The first two acts of *Bodas de sangre*, although displaying a strong symbolic charge, are relatively verisimilitudinous, but there is a change of gear in act 3, when allegorical figures and fantasy come to play important roles. The denouement, in which the young men die and the women are condemned to a life of widowhood, reflects the bleak vision of the destiny of those who give free rein to their erotic passion and of those who try to suppress it. Fully Andalusian, but again avoiding *costumbrismo*, the dark passions and evocative atmosphere, reminiscent of John Millington Synge's *Riders to the Sea* (1904), made the play Lorca's first true theatrical success, which enabled him, finally, to be financially independent of his parents. Thanks to the warm reception afforded *Bodas de sangre*, the Argentinian actress Lola Membrives and her impresario husband, Juan Reforzo, determined to give the play its Argentinian debut, and when it turned out to be a great hit, they issued an invitation to Lorca to be present when it was restaged later in 1933.

Lorca's six-month stay in Argentina—October 1933 to March 1934 (with two weeks in Montevideo in February 1934)—constitutes his second, and last, trip abroad, once again to the New World. As in the case of Cuba, Lorca's stay in Buenos Aires provided the opportunity for him to give a series of lectures to packed houses, and again he was taken to the bosom of the literary elite and lionized at the many functions he attended. Membrives took advantage of his stay to schedule runs of some of his other plays, which, with the exception of *Mariana Pineda*, all proved runaway successes. An Argentinian edition of *Romancero gitano* sold out in a few days. In Buenos Aires, Lorca made or reinforced certain significant literary friendships, perhaps most notably with Pablo Neruda, and Lorca adapted Lope de Vega's *La dama boba* (The Foolish Lady, 1613) for another Argentinian actress, Eva Franco. These months, then, saw his consecration abroad as a major, first-rank author, almost a modern classic, at a time when in Spain he was perhaps considered more as an important, up-and-coming, though still young writer.

Membrives had hoped to stage *Yerma* (1934; translated in *From Lorca's Theater*) during Lorca's stay, and when she was forced by exhaustion to end her season early, it was with that in mind that she and her husband invited Lorca to vacation with them in Montevideo. He may have started work on *Yerma* as early as 1929, but most progress was made on it in 1933, when two acts were ready. However, Membrives's plan failed. Lorca was drawn into the ever-enthusiastic literary circles of Montevideo, he repeated his Argentinian lectures, and the play was not completed until the summer of 1934. *Yerma* is the second part of a projected trilogy of rural tragedies and is a little more austere than *Bodas de sangre*. Lorca still makes use of a chorus of washerwomen, of song, and of a ritualistic and pagan final scene around a saint's shrine that is reputed to cure infertility. *Yerma* is a classic study of frustra-

tion and unfulfillment: the title character's life is focused on motherhood, but this is denied her, goading her at the end of the play to strangle her husband in a frenzy of resentment and frustration. *Yerma* was produced in Madrid at the very end of 1934, under charged political circumstances (two and a half months after the violent suppression of the Asturias uprising); its apparent paganism and impiety were denounced by the Right, but it was rapturously received in literary circles and by the great majority of the public.

The year 1934 had also seen a return by Lorca to lyric composition, an activity seemingly put on hold, with the exception of *Seis poemas galegos*, since the summer of 1931. Back then, just after the completion of *Así que pasen cinco años*, Lorca had written some pieces to which he provisionally applied the title of "Poemas para los muertos" (Poems for the Dead). These compositions probably built onto others dating from the New York period, and in particular those assigned to "Tierra y luna," whose slant was more metaphysical. But the collection was likely broken up shortly afterward, with most poems swelling the ranks of the continuing project of "Tierra y luna."

On the ocean liner returning from Buenos Aires to Spain in March 1934, Lorca wrote several new compositions, and it seems that during the later spring and early summer of that year he continued—sporadically—to pen more lyric verse. Meanwhile, in late 1933, Lorca had decided to fuse *Poeta en Nueva York* and "Tierra y luna" into one collection (for the time being to be called "Introducción a la muerte"), and, in so doing, some of the "Tierra y luna" pieces had been left out. Three of these, all dating back to August 1931, were later added to the poems of 1934, and sometime over the summer of that year Lorca hit on the idea of assembling a new collection, to be entitled *Diván del Tamarit* (published as a book in 1948; translated in 1974), split into a section each of "Gacelas" and "Casidas," that would pay homage to the Arabic poets of Muslim Spain, particularly those of Granada (*diván* is an Arabic term for an anthology or collection, and Tamarit is the Arabic-derived name of a district of the *vega* near the Lorca family's summer home; *gacela* and *casida* are two well-established Arab-Andalusian verse forms). The proof that the *Diván* is a collection conceived largely a posteriori is to be found in the fact that, on the first-draft manuscripts (in the

Fundación García Lorca), only a few of the titles originally begin with "Gacela de . . ." or "Casida de . . ." (also "Kasida de . . ."), while elsewhere these denominations are clearly written in later or only appear on later fair copies. The final manuscript was ready in the fall of 1934, and the University of Granada was slated to publish the book. However, several delays, some no doubt for practical reasons (funding?), some perhaps due to nothing more than procrastination, some possibly for political motives, meant that the volume never got beyond the stage of final page proofs before the outbreak of the civil war, and consequently it was not published until 1940, in the New York journal *Revista Hispánica Moderna*.

Diván del Tamarit is a diverse collection in that some poems recall something of the flavor of *Canciones* and others the more meditative style of *Poeta en Nueva York*, but it is nonetheless homogeneous in that all the pieces are situated between the two axes of love and death. Anecdotally, a brief, passionate, and seemingly destructive love affair is fleetingly and rather hazily evoked, almost always in the past. The poems are therefore not concerned with any one particular or lived experience but more with the repercussions of failed or lost love, with meditations on death and death in life, and on the way in which love almost inevitably leads to thoughts of death. The compositions are frequently set in, or suggest the atmosphere of, Granada; its two rivers and the fountains of the Alhambra flow through the collection in a variety of figurative transformations, as in the opening of "Casida primera del herido por el agua" (First *Casida* of the One Wounded by the Water):

> Quiero bajar al pozo,
> quiero subir los muros de Granada,
> para mirar el corazón pasado
> por el punzón oscuro de las aguas.
>
> El niño herido gemía
> con una corona de escarcha.
> Estanques, aljibes y fuentes
> levantaban al aire sus espadas.
>
> (I want to go down the well,
> I want to climb the walls of Granada,
> to see the heart pierced
> by the dark spike of the waters.
>
> The wounded child was moaning
> with a crown of frost.
> Pools, cisterns and fountains
> were raising their swords in the air.)

As for the images themselves, some recall the limpidity of *Canciones*, but many are quite dense, not quite as irreducible as those commonly occurring in *Poeta en Nueva York* but certainly more complex and difficult than those in the *Romancero*, for instance. These *Diván* compositions are in no sense pastiches, and the Arabic flavor does not really go beyond the titles; in terms of meter and content, there is no evidence of any influence or borrowing, but the overall Arab-Andalusian frame does suggest a lost world—a world of high culture and sexual tolerance—that flourished in Granada before the final reconquest of 1492.

During the summer of 1934, just when the *Diván* must have been crystalizing (the first clear mention and reading dates from September), Ignacio Sánchez Mejías was fatally gored in the ring at Manzanares. Mejías was a highly cultured man, with strong interests in literature and flamenco folklore, and an old friend of Lorca and many of his contemporaries in the Generation of 1927. Mejías had retired twice from bullfighting but still felt the lure of the ring, and at the age of forty-three he had returned, against all advice, for one last short season of engagements. It was actually during a last-minute substitution appearance that the wounding occurred; gangrene set in, and he was dead within thirty-six hours. A few weeks later Lorca started work on his *Llanto por Ignacio Sánchez Mejías* (1935; translated as *Lament for the Death of a Bullfighter*, 1937), a long poem articulated in four parts intended first and foremost as an elegy for his bullfighter friend. The work was rapidly prepared and was published the following spring.

Each part is stylistically and metrically differentiated, but they coalesce in their insistent focus on the dead man and in the narrative progression from "La cogida y la muerte" (The Goring and the Death), to "La sangre derramada" (The Spilt Blood—left on the sand of the ring after the removal of Mejías's body), to "Cuerpo presente" (Body Laid Out—lying in state in the funeral chapel before being transported for final burial), to "Alma ausente" (Absent Soul—Mejías dead, buried, and largely forgotten).

In part 1 Lorca narrates the events in discrete images, each followed by the well-known refrain, "a las cinco de la tarde" (at five o'clock in the afternoon). A sense of cosmic conspiracy is evoked, along with the idea that this is the death of no ordinary man. In part 2 the poet-persona cannot bear to contemplate the spilt blood, emblem of Mejías's life force that has flowed from

Lorca in April 1936 (photograph by Alfonso)

his body. The bullfighter is imagined disoriented in death, and also before, at the moment of facing the bull; this leads to a eulogy in ballad meter that recalls the famous fifteenth-century *Coplas en la muerte de su padre* (Verses on the Death of His Father) by Jorge Manrique. In part 3 the body has already begun to decompose, and the poet urges the mourners to face up to the inescapable fact of physical death. Finally, in part 4, in a bleak vision it is suggested that Mejías is being rapidly forgotten—save by the poet, who has sung, that is, written, of him for posterity. Lorca's *Llanto* connects more with the tradition of the *planctus* (the classical lament) than with the Christian elegy, in which a greater degree of consolation is to be found, naturally based on beliefs in the afterlife. Ultimately Lorca's poem also works on a much higher level of generality: Mejías is presented as a kind of existential hero, a notable, distinguished victim of death, one in a long and never-ending line, and thus the composition becomes a meditation on death, on how to face up to others' deaths and to the consciousness of one's own mortality. In a framework elaborated with mythic and legendary reminiscences

(particularly of the bull cults of ancient Iberia), Lorca likens but then opposes Mejías to both Christ and the pagan vegetation gods (Attis, Adonis); in this non-Christian vision Mejías will not resuscitate, and the best that can be hoped for is that his memory will live on through Lorca's poem.

With the triumph of *Bodas de sangre* at home and abroad, of *Yerma*, and of the *Llanto*, Lorca became an increasingly well-known and successful figure on the Spanish literary scene. His favorite actress, Margarita Xirgu, invited him to stay in Barcelona through the fall and early winter of 1935 and to participate in her production of various of his plays, including the premiere of his next dramatic work, *Doña Rosita la soltera* (1935; translated as *Doña Rosita, the Spinster*, in *From Lorca's Theater*). Commenced in late 1934 and finished in spring 1935, the play evokes turn-of-the-century Granada, drawing on Lorca's own childhood experiences, and has a deliciously pretentious middle-class ambiance. The action is predicated on the symbol of a rose whose bloom lasts but one day: Rosita is its female incarnation, who constantly has to wait and whose whole life, really, is indefinitely postponed. The denouement leaves her a pale, fading, middle-aged spinster, falling into a faint as the family is forced to move out of their house. The minor-key, nostalgic tone is distinctly Chekhovian, the location recalls *Mariana Pineda*, and the basic theme resembles that of *Así que pasen cinco años. Doña Rosita* did not premiere until December, but for nearly four months—September to December—Lorca participated actively in the cultural life of the Catalonian capital and was celebrated wherever he went.

After the completion of *Doña Rosita* in May 1935, two final plays occupied Lorca's last months: a third experimental and revolutionary piece, of which only act 1 is extant, now known as *El sueño de la vida* (The Dream of Life, 1989; originally published with *El Público* as *Comedia sin título*, 1978; translated as *Play Without a Title*, 1983), and *La casa de Bernarda Alba* (1945; translated as *The House of Bernarda Alba*, in *Three Tragedies*, 1947). *El sueño de la vida* returns again to metatheater, almost as an offshoot to *El público:* the set is a theater, and a rehearsal of *A Midsummer Night's Dream* is going on offstage. A character known as the Author harangues the audience and gets into an argument; shots ring out; and the theater collapses into turmoil, while a workers' uprising rages outside. Clearly the increasing politicization of the 1930s had had their effect on Lorca, most of all since the brutal repression of the Asturias uprising, and in this unfinished play he sought to combine previous concerns—authenticity, truth, love, and death—with a more explicitly sociopolitical message.

Although *La casa de Bernarda Alba* was not originally slated to complete the rural trilogy commenced by *Bodas de sangre* and *Yerma*, at some point Lorca's plans must have changed, and his intuition was surely right, as *La casa* bears many links with the two previous plays. Probably started in the summer or fall of 1935, a first draft was finished in June 1936, and he was still working on the text up to a few weeks before his death. A version of the text was rescued, and the play's first performance was given by Xirgu in Buenos Aires in 1945.

More or less simultaneous in composition with *El sueño de la vida* and *La casa de Bernarda Alba* were Lorca's last lyric verses, on the face of them very different in style and content from his earlier poems. They are the eleven "Sonetos del amor oscuro" (in volume 1 of the 1986 *Obras completas*; translated as *Sonnets of Love Forbidden,*

1989), most of which were written in November 1935, the remaining one or two in the months following. The "Sonetos" are mainly first drafts and were never organized by Lorca for publication in book form. The title of the unfinished cycle comes from secondhand sources (though it is taken from a line in one of the poems). The sonnets are all strictly traditional Petrarchan hendecasyllabics, and they all concern a lover and his beloved, their relationship, and particularly the lover's sorrows at the beloved's coldness, fickleness, incommunicativeness, or physical absence. Familiar themes reappear: the inability to attain true communion or achieve lasting solace from the consciousness of time passing and of mortality, and the paradoxical sentiment that feeling hurt, unhappy, or anguished is better than feeling nothing at all—that it protects one from an emotional "living death."

On an autobiographical level the sonnets were inspired by Lorca's relationship with Rafael Rodríguez Rapún, a young engineering student who was secretary of La Barraca from 1933 to 1935. Rapún had traveled all over Spain with Lorca and was a constant companion in Madrid; Lorca went so far as to engage him as his personal secretary. However, in the late fall of 1935 the relationship was going through a difficult period: Lorca had been away from Madrid in Barcelona, and a planned visit by Rapún had been delayed. Nevertheless, despite one possible reading of "amor oscuro" as homosexual love and despite the appearance in one poem of a masculine ending to an adjective describing the beloved, the sonnets are intended much more broadly, as an exploration of love and its sorrows on general terms. It is here that one may find an unsuspected link with *La casa de Bernarda Alba* and *El sueño de la vida:* in all three works, in different ways, Lorca depicts the difficulty of love and the problematics of human relationships, most of which seem to be, for much of the time, occasions for dissatisfaction and asperity.

The composition of the "Sonetos" can be related to a renewal of interest in that form, and in love poetry in general, which occurred on the Spanish literary scene in the mid 1930s. The style and imagery of Lorca's poems are not dissimilar to those found in the *Diván*. However, in one direction, Lorca does follow the lead offered by the sonnet's form by incorporating and elaborating oxymorons and other figurative language derived from the courtly love/Petrarchan tradition, while in another he seems to be striving, on occa-

The Lorca stamp issued in the Republican zone of Spain two years after his death

sion, toward a more transparent, more intense, apparently simpler style already foreshadowed in some of the lines of the "Poema doble del lago Edén" (Double Poem of Lake Eden, in *Poeta en Nueva York*). The Petrarchan flavor of some of the sonnets is further complicated by the sixteenth-century Spanish mystics' appropriation of courtly love language (itself an appropriation of the terminology of religious worship), language Lorca applies to a profane subject but with a series of sometimes arch literary cross-references to Saint Teresa and, particularly, Saint John of the Cross.

In February 1936 new elections brought to power the Popular Front, a loose alliance of liberal-leftist parties. The months that followed saw an increasing polarization in Spanish politics: it became increasingly difficult to be a moderate, and people aligned themselves either with the socialist-minded Republicans or with the protofascist right-ists. Sporadic acts of provocation and violence occurred, and secret military planning went ahead for a coup d'état that, when resistance proved much stronger than expected, would turn into the start of the civil war.

Nobody could be unaware of these events, and since the fall of 1934 Lorca's political sympathies had become increasingly manifest. Xirgu had left Spain to tour in Cuba and then Mexico, from whence she sent telegrams to Lorca urging him to join her there. Lorca was of two minds. He had plenty of literary work on his hands in Madrid, and it seems he was reluctant to leave Rapún behind. Events turned particularly nasty in July 1936, with killings on both sides, and Lorca eventually decided to go down to Granada, as was his wont, to celebrate his and his father's saint's day (18 July) with his family, already installed in the Huerta de San Vicente. He arrived on 14 July, and the Spanish military uprising started in North Africa on the evening of the 17th. On the 20th the Granada garrison rose in support of Franco and the other rebel generals, and that same day they took control of most of the city. A severe political purge followed on the heels of the shift of power: moving to consolidate their position, the military and the rightist politicians oversaw "official" executions, which took place in the city cemetery, while gangs of Falangists and other thugs roamed the city in cars and took "suspects"—or anyone against whom they had a grudge—on one-way rides.

Lorca had the misfortune of being in the wrong place at the wrong time. He was well known as a man of the arts, liberal minded, rumored to be a homosexual, a member of a family on intimate terms with Fernando de los Ríos, and, therefore, as far as the opposing side was concerned, a "red" beyond a shadow of a doubt. Lorca decided to stay put at the Huerta, but after several threats and searches, he moved on 9 August to a supposedly safe haven, the family house of his young poet friend Luis Rosales, two of whose brothers were prominent Falangists. Lorca's brother-in-law, Manuel Fernández-Montesinos, who had become the socialist mayor of Granada shortly before the uprising, was executed on 16 August. That same day a rightist former member of parliament, Ramón Ruiz Alonso, arrested the poet. Lorca was taken to the civil-government headquarters, under the command of Col. José Valdés Guzmán; probably spent some thirty-six hours there (contradictory evidence exists); and thence, in the early hours of

18 (or possibly 19) August, was transferred to a staging post near Víznar, a village outside Granada, where prisoners were grouped before mass executions in the surrounding valleys and ravines. The best current evidence suggests that Lorca was killed, alongside a teacher and two bullfighters, just before dawn on the morning of 18 August, and buried in an unmarked mass grave whose general location has today been determined. He was a little over thirty-eight years old.

Letters:

Cartas a sus amigos, edited by Sebastián Gasch (Barcelona: Cobalto, 1950);

Cartas, postales, poemas y dibujos, edited by Antonio Gallego Morell (Madrid: Moneda & Crédito, 1968);

Epistolario, edited by Christopher Maurer, 2 volumes (Madrid: Alianza, 1983); translated (in part) by David Gershator as *Selected Letters* (New York: New Directions, 1983);

"Federico García Lorca escribe a su familia desde Nueva York y La Habana (1929-1930)," edited by Maurer, special double issue of *Poesía*, 23-24 (1985).

Interviews:

Treinta entrevistas a Federico García Lorca, edited by Andrés Soria Olmedo (Madrid: Aguilar, 1989).

Bibliographies:

Joseph L. Laurenti & Joseph Siracusa, eds., *Federico García Lorca y su mundo: Ensayo de una bibliografía general* (Metuchen, N.J.: Scarecrow, 1974);

Francesca Colecchia, ed., *García Lorca: A Selectively Annotated Bibliography of Criticism* (New York: Garland, 1979);

Colecchia, ed., *García Lorca: An Annotated Primary Bibliography* (New York: Garland, 1982);

Andrew A. Anderson, "Bibliografía lorquiana reciente," regular listing in *Boletín de la Fundación Federico García Lorca*, 1-8, continuing (1987-).

Biography:

Ian Gibson, *Federico García Lorca*, volume 1: *De Fuente Vaqueros a Nueva York (1898-1929)* (Barcelona: Grijalbo, 1985); volume 2: *De Nueva York a Fuente Grande (1929-1936)* (Barcelona: Grijalbo, 1987); English version published in one volume as *Federico García Lorca: A Life* (New York: Pantheon, 1989).

References:

Andrew A. Anderson, "The Evolution of García Lorca's Poetic Projects 1929-1936 and the Textual Status of *Poeta en Nueva York*," *Bulletin of Hispanic Studies*, 60 (July 1983): 221-246;

Anderson, "García Lorca como poeta petrarquista," *Cuadernos Hispanoamericanos*, 435-436 (September-October 1986): 495-518;

Anderson, *Lorca's Late Poetry: A Critical Study* (Liverpool: Francis Cairns, 1990);

Luis Beltrán Fernández de los Ríos, *La arquitectura del humo: Una reconstrucción del "Romancero gitano" de Federico García Lorca* (London: Tamesis, 1986);

Carlos Feal Deibe, "Los *Seis poemas galegos* de Lorca y sus fuentes rosalinianas," *Romanische Forschungen*, 83, no. 4 (1971): 555-587;

Francisco García Lorca, *Federico y su mundo*, edited by Mario Hernández, second edition (Madrid: Alianza, 1981);

Miguel García-Posada, *Lorca: Interpretación de "Poeta en Nueva York"* (Madrid: Akal, 1981);

Ian K. Gibson, "Lorca's 'Balada Triste': Children's Songs and the Theme of Sexual Disharmony in *Libro de poemas*," *Bulletin of Hispanic Studies*, 46 (January 1969): 21-38;

Derek R. Harris, *García Lorca: "Poeta en Nueva York"* (London: Grant & Cutler, 1978);

Mario Hernández, "Jardín deshecho: Los 'Sonetos' de García Lorca," *Crotalón: Anuario de Filología Española*, 1 (1984): 193-228;

José Hierro, "El primer Lorca," *Cuadernos Hispanoamericanos*, 224-225 (August-September 1968): 437-462;

Roy O. Jones & Geraldine M. Scanlon, "Ignacio Sánchez Mejías: The 'Mythic' Hero," in *Studies in Modern Spanish Literature and Art Presented to Helen F. Grant*, edited by Nigel Glendinning (London: Tamesis, 1972), pp. 97-108;

David K. Loughran, *Federico García Lorca: The Poetry of Limits* (London: Tamesis, 1978);

Enrique Martínez López, Introduction and notes, in Lorca's *Granada, paraíso cerrado y otras páginas granadinas* (Granada, Spain: Sánchez, 1971), pp. 15-69, 319-327;

Christopher Maurer, Introduction and notes, in Lorca's *Poet in New York*, translated by Greg Simon and Steven F. White (New York: Farrar, Straus, Giroux, 1988), pp. xi-xxx, 257-276;

Maurer, "Sobre la prosa temprana de García Lorca: 1916-1918," *Cuadernos Hispanoamericanos*, 433-434 (July-August 1986): 13-30;

Norman C. Miller, *García Lorca's "Poema del cante jondo"* (London: Tamesis, 1978).

Papers:
Manuscripts by Lorca are held chiefly at the Fundación García Lorca, Consejo Superior de Investigaciones Científicas, Madrid.

Jaime Gil de Biedma

(13 November 1929 - 8 January 1990)

Shirley Mangini
California State University, Long Beach

BOOKS: *Según sentencia del tiempo* (Barcelona: Laye, 1953);

Compañeros de viaje (Barcelona: Horta, 1959);

Cántico: El mundo y la poesía de Jorge Guillén (Barcelona: Seix Barral, 1960);

En favor de Venús (Barcelona: Literaturasa/Colliure, 1965);

Moralidades, 1959-1964 (Mexico: Mortiz, 1966);

Poemas póstumos (1965-1967) (Madrid: Poesía para Todos, 1968);

Colección particular (1955-1967) (Barcelona: Seix Barral, 1969);

Diario del artista seriamente enfermo (Barcelona: Lumen, 1974);

Las personas del verbo (Barcelona: Barral, 1975);

El pie de la letra. Ensayos 1955-1979 (Barcelona: Crítica, 1980);

Gil de Biedma, edited by Shirley Mangini González (Madrid: Júcar, 1980);

Antología poética, edited by González and Javier Alfaya (Madrid: Alianza, 1981);

Volver, edited by Dionisio Cañas (Madrid: Cátedra, 1989);

Retrato del artista en 1956 (Barcelona: Lumen, 1991).

TRANSLATIONS: T. S. Eliot, *Función de la poesía y función de la crítica* (Barcelona: Seix Barral, 1955);

Christopher Isherwood, *Adiós a Berlín* (Barcelona: Seix Barral, 1967).

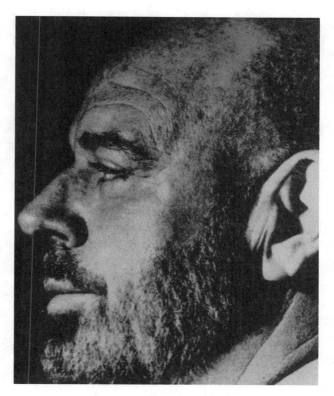

Jaime Gil de Biedma

Jaime Gil de Biedma was one of Spain's most highly respected poets, though his work is not very well known outside his own country. A member of the Generation of the 1950s, he began writing vehement poetry of social criticism in the late 1950s in the style of the first so-called social poets, such as Blas de Otero, Gabriel Celaya, and José Hierro. He later became disillusioned with the possibilities of poetry as a tool for social change and began to take an ironic stance in his work to express the disillusionment that most of the writers of his generation shared. Like his contemporaries, Gil de Biedma became more conscious of style and started experimenting with less prosaic poetic forms. Nevertheless, he differs from his group because of his educational background and experience. His knowledge of French and English and his analysis of diverse critical theories have influenced his work greatly. Because of his poetic sophistication, many of Spain's younger poets regard Gil de Biedma as the best of his generation. His insistence on erotic themes—he is the most audacious of social poets in terms of eroticism—has also distinguished him from his contemporaries. In addition, his capacity for chronicling events and often journalistically describing the repressive atmosphere of the postwar period makes him stand out among his colleagues as one of the most exceptional "poets of experience," as they are known.

Gil de Biedma was born on 13 November 1929 in Barcelona, into a family of wealthy entrepreneurs, during the year the World's Fair was held there. The fifth of eight children, he learned to read at the age of five and began grade school the following year. The Spanish Civil War broke out when he was seven, and the entire family fled Barcelona to their estate in Nava de la Asunción in the province of Segovia. They remained in Nava during the entire war, and it was there that the poet had his early education.

When the war ended, the Gil de Biedmas returned to Barcelona, though during the years that followed, the poet continued to spend a great deal of time at the Segovia estate. In 1946 he finished his baccalaureate and commenced studies in law at the University of Barcelona. It was not until 1949 that he became an avid reader of poetry and began to write. There were other changes in his life: at that time he lost his Catholic faith, and he began military service. In those college years he met those who were to contribute to his literary and political ideas, such as Carlos Barral, the poet-editor; the poet Alfonso Costafreda; Alberto Oliart, an important Spanish politician; and the novelist Juan Goytisolo. In

1951, together with most of his literary friends, Gil de Biedma became a frequent contributor to the university-sponsored journal *Laye*, which during the early 1950s served as a haven for young Barcelonian writers with progressive ideas. That same year, Gil de Biedma became a lawyer, though like many of his colleagues, he was never to practice law.

He was immersed, in the early 1950s, in Spanish Golden Age poetry; the works of French symbolists, especially Charles-Pierre Baudelaire and Stéphane Mallarmé; and the poetry of the Generation of 1927, above all that of Luis Cernuda and Jorge Guillén. In his early poems one can observe Gil de Biedma's obsession with the passage of time and his desire to recapture and preserve past moments. This poetry, influenced by his readings, is obviously more abstract than his later work, which is more concrete, heavily anecdotal, and historically descriptive. Though the poet already was conscious of what he has called his two main themes—"el paso del tiempo y yo" (the passage of time and me)—his first poetry lacks the vitality and sincerity that characterize his later work.

In 1953 Gil de Biedma went to study at Oxford, where he discovered the works of T. S. Eliot and W. H. Auden. These writer-critics were to influence definitively both the way he thought about poetry and the way he wrote it. That year the *Laye* organization published a small volume of his poetry entitled *Según sentencia del tiempo* (According to the Sentence of Time), which was his first published poetry (written in 1950 and 1951) and reveals a young poet still in search of a voice. He returned to Spain later in 1953 to study for a diplomatic career. Ironically enough he failed the exams in Spanish culture and composition and promptly abandoned his plans for a career in diplomacy. He spent that summer in Paris, translating Eliot's *The Use of Poetry and the Use of Criticism* (1933). Upon returning to Barcelona, he continued to work on the "Las afueras" poems.

In 1955 Gil de Biedma began work for the Compañía General de Tabacos de Filipinas (Philippines General Tobacco Company). His Eliot translation was published that same year. The next year marked the beginning of a change in Gil de Biedma's poetic and, above all, political attitude. Opposition activities in Spanish universities had commenced and had awakened many intellectuals to activism. It was also the year that Gil de Biedma was diagnosed as having tuberculosis—

an extremely common disease in the postwar period—and was confined to the family estate in Segovia. During this time he read assiduously and started work on his critical study of Guillén, which was published in 1960. This period is recounted in detail in Gil de Biedma's *Diario del artista seriamente enfermo* (Diary of a Seriously Ill Artist, 1974).

During 1957 and 1958, mostly spent in Segovia, he wrote many of the poems of "Por vivir aquí" (In Order to Live Here), later published as the first section of *Compañeros de viaje* (Fellow Travelers, 1959). He also established a friendship with writers such as Angel González and Gabriel Ferrater, with whom he discussed literature and politics. The poems of "Por vivir aquí" illustrate the qualities that were to distinguish Gil de Biedma from his contemporaries.

The first poem of the grouping, "Arte poética" (Poetic Art), is extremely important for understanding his work. He discusses the passage of time, the desire for communication with others, and the fear of noncommunication, as in the following stanza: "Y sobre todo el vértigo del tiempo, / el gran boquete abriéndose hacia dentro del alma / mientras arriba sobrenadan promesas / que desmayan, lo mismo que si espumas" (And above all, the vertigo of time, / the great gap opening itself toward the inside of the soul / while above swim promises / that are fainting as if they were foam). The idea becomes more concrete in the stanza that indicates the need to justify one's life: "Es sin duda el momento de pensar / que el hecho de estar vivo exige algo, / acaso heroicidades—o basta, simplemente, / alguna humilde cosa común" (It is without a doubt time to think / that the fact of being alive requires something, / perhaps heroic acts—or, simply, / some humble common act is enough).

In other poems of "Por vivir aquí" Gil de Biedma reiterates his anxiety about time; it is disconcerting, immeasurable, and irrevocable. He says in "Idilio en el café" (An Idyllic Scene in the Cafe): "Ahora me pregunto si es que toda la vida hemos estado aquí" (Now I wonder if we have been here all our lives). In another poem, "Aunque sea un instante" (Even If It's Only for a Moment), he writes: "gritamos invocando el pasado—invocando un pasado que jamás existió" (we shout, invoking the past—invoking a past that never existed). Once again he refers to the ineffable nature of time: "para creer al menos que de verdad vivimos / y que la vida es más que esta pausa inmensa, / vertiginosa" (to believe at least

that we are really alive / and that life is more than this immense, / vertiginous pause).

Practically all of the poems of "Por vivir aquí" mark some moment of the past that Gil de Biedma seeks to preserve by means of the written word, and he weaves a dreamlike atmosphere when referring to his memories of the past. His original hope of detaining the passage of time would later produce an obsessive anxiety in him, since, according to his later work, time could only result in old age, disillusionment, and death.

Gil de Biedma's desire to freeze time during the early stage of his work brings to the surface one of the most salient traits of his poetry—that of chronicling events in his life, alongside his desires and defeats, within a sociohistorical setting. By recording literary and political moments of the Franco years in his poetry, he proved to be a valuable source of information about the period, since at that time in Spain little journalistic material on these affairs was published because of the strict censorship laws. In "Noches del mes de junio" (Nights in the Month of June), he gives the year of his reminiscence, 1949, such information being frequent in his chronicle-type poetry. In other poems he gives historical or personal information with almost journalistic accuracy. In "Infancia y confesiones" (Infancy and Confessions) he says: "Mi familia / era bastante rica y yo estudiante" (My family / was quite rich and I was a student); and later, "Yo nací (perdonadme) / en la edad de la pérgola y el tenis" (I was born [I beg your pardon] / in the age of roof gardens and tennis). He thus establishes his social background so he may display a sense of guilt in the face of "historias penosas" (pitiful stories) and "caras tristes" (sad faces) that "perduraba a lo lejos" (loomed in the distance). There is always a phantasmal tone in the verses where he refers to the hungry and silenced masses of the victimized sector of Spanish society, those who had lost the civil war.

Gil de Biedma is very explicit in this period about his sense of solidarity with his literary and political companions, whom he calls fellow travelers. (This term did not have the negative, communist connotation that it did in the United States; in Spain it simply referred to those who collaborated with the underground against the Franco regime without becoming members of any clandestine political party. This was Gil de Biedma's situation in these postwar years.) "De ahora en adelante" (From Now On) is perhaps the poem that most clearly emphasizes his political solidar-

Gil de Biedma (left) with José Agustín Goytisolo, Carlos Barral, and José M. Castellet

ity with other members of his generation. He speaks of awakening suddenly from a lethargic, apolitical state to find himself surrounded by others who were seeking the same thing, that is to say, social change.

The other section of *Compañeros de viaje*, "La historia para todos" (History for Everyone), is more vehement in its protest against the mute suffering of the vanquished ones. In "Los aparecidos" (The Ghosts) their origin is explained: "Vienen / de allá, del otro lado del fondo sulfuroso, / de las sordas / minas del hambre y de la multitud / Y ni siquiera saben quiénes son: / desenterrados vivos." (They come / from over there, from the other side of the sulphuric depths, / from the deaf / mines of hunger and multitudes / And they don't even know who they are: / uninterred living beings.)

In spite of Gil de Biedma's dramatically demoralized tone when he refers to the victims of re-

pression and poverty, he ends the book with a note of hope. There is a logical reason for his optimism: *Compañeros de viaje* was completed and published in 1959, the year that hope for social change was at its zenith among dissident intellectuals. In "Por lo visto" (So It Seems) he speaks of the idea that protest and life itself are still possible in a repressive country. "Canción para ese día" (Song for that Day) also celebrates the sense of political optimism that these writers were experiencing at the time. One of his best-known verses in that poem indicates the general euphoria among dissidents: "He aquí que viene el tiempo de soltar palomas" (The time to let the doves fly is coming). Gil de Biedma promises his reader that there will be freedom; he does this, of course, in an oblique manner, since any obvious reference to revolution would have quickly been suppressed: "Palabras / van a decirse ya. Oíd. Se escucha / rumor de pasos y batir de alas"

(Words / will soon be said. Listen. One can hear / footsteps and the flapping of wings). However, the period of hope for social change soon waned.

The year of the most cohesion of the Generation of the 1950s was 1959. Many of the group attended an act of homage to the poet Antonio Machado in Colliure, France, and that same year they formed part of the "Conversaciones Poéticas" in Formentor, Majorca. There were other literary activities with political undertones in 1959, and many of these were preserved by Gil de Biedma in his book of verse entitled *Moralidades* (Moralities, 1966), inspired by the critic Yvor Winter's idea that "The artistic process is one of moral evaluation of human experience" (*In Defense of Reason*, 1947).

The first poem of *Moralidades* celebrates the poet's solidarity with his generation once again. "En el nombre de hoy" (In the Name of Today) is a chronicle-type poem reminiscent of a radio broadcast. In a more vehement tone than his previous poetry—such exacerbated irony was to characterize the rest of his poetic work—Gil de Biedma addresses his fellow travelers on 26 April 1959. Speaking directly to his companions and listing all their names, he associates them with the guilt he himself feels: "a vosotros pecadores / como yo, que me avergüenzo de los palos que no me han dado, / señoritos de nacimiento / por mala conciencia escritores / de poesía social, / dedico también un recuerdo" (To you sinners / like me, who is ashamed of the beatings which I never got, / gentlemen from birth / and because of your bad conscience writers / of social poetry, / I also dedicate a thought).

In another poem, "Conversaciones Poéticas," which describes the 1959 poetry symposium in Formentor, Gil de Biedma expresses the joy he feels during a rare moment of intense communication with his friends, and at one point he cries out in the poem: "que por favor que no volviéramos / nunca, nunca jamás a casa" (please let us / never, ever go home again). He powerfully describes the euphoria that resulted from the combined effects of literary and political dialogue and the customary consumption of large quantities of alcohol in the late night hours: "No sé si la bebida / sola nos exaltó, puede que el aire. . . . / Fue entonces ese instante de la noche / que se confunde casi con la vida" (I don't know if it was just the liquor / that excited us, maybe it was the air. . . . / But it was that instant of the night / that almost confuses itself with life).

Another poem from this book, "Un día de difuntos" (A Day of the Dead), describes an event of political importance to Gil de Biedma and his companions, that of a visit to the grave of the founder of Spanish socialism, Pablo Iglesias. Yet, many of the poems of *Moralidades* suggest the disillusionment that the social realists began to feel in the early 1960s. Already in 1959, in "Noche triste de Octubre, 1959" (Sad Night in October 1959), in his typically journalistic manner, Gil de Biedma predicts the social repression that would result from the protest movement evolving at that time.

Moralidades is undoubtedly Gil de Biedma's most important book. Its collage of styles and themes show his best work. He continues to recall lost moments in *Moralidades*, especially those of his childhood during the civil war. In "Intento formular mi experiencia de guerra" (I Try to Formulate My War Experiences), he confesses that the war had been a diversion for him, and he guiltily hastens to explain that he has changed. In a laconic final comment, typical of Gil de Biedma's style in this book, he says: "Quien me conoce ahora / dirá que mi experiencia / nada tiene que ver con mis ideas, / y es verdad. Mis ideas de la guerra cambiaron / después, mucho después / de que hubiera empezado la postguerra" (Those who know me now / will say that my experience / doesn't have anything to do with my ideas, / and it's true. My ideas of the war changed / later, a long time / after the postwar period had begun). Poems such as these, discursive and confessional, in free verse, continue to characterize the poet as a chronicler of his times.

But it is also in *Moralidades* that Gil de Biedma establishes himself as the most erotic of postwar poets. This is especially true of the poems from *En favor de Venús* (In Favor of Venus), which he had published in 1965 and later incorporated into *Moralidades*. His finest and best-known erotic poem is "Pandémica y Celeste," where he explains his most intimate desires. As in many of Gil de Biedma's love poems, the theme of homosexuality is suggested. Presenting a dialogue between his consciousness and his experience of love, "Pandémica y Celeste" serves to point up the propensity for using literary references in his work. In just this one poem, whose title is inspired by Plato's *Symposium*, he includes an epigraph from Catullus, a verse of Baudelaire's, another of Mallarmé's, and a verse translated from John Donne. Gil de Biedma's frequently flashy erudition is a quality the next gener-

Gil de Biedma

treme disillusionment for Spanish *engagé* writers, it emphasizes Gil de Biedma's sense of the uselessness of the written word: "El juego de hacer versos / —que no es un juego—es algo / parecido en principio / al placer solitario" (The game of composing verses / —which is not a game—is somewhat / similar in principle / to the solitary vices). Yet he reiterates his belief in the ideas of Winters in this poem: "Y los poemas son / un modo que adoptamos / para que nos entiendan / y que nos entendamos" (Poetry is / a method we adopt / to make others understand us / and to understand ourselves). His objective is clearly a moral one; in *Moralidades* Gil de Biedma reveals a coherence of purpose his former work did not have.

He is a prime example of the "poet of experience," being introspective but making readers aware of the image he has of himself in relation to the rest of the world. Ironically he often detaches himself from his poetry by the use of a dramatic character, "Jaime Gil de Biedma," who is, obviously, a literary projection of himself. This dramatic character—which he created after being influenced by the poetic theory of Robert Langbaum in his 1963 book *Poetry of Experience*—is nowhere more visible than in Gil de Biedma's *Poemas póstumos* (Posthumous Poems, 1968). Written between 1966 and 1968, this volume elucidates the trauma of a mental crisis he experienced in 1965 that he attributed to the loss of his youth. *Poemas póstumos* contains the culminating poems of experience in which he, toward the end of the book, includes a eulogy commemorating the death of the "young" Jaime Gil de Biedma. It is the most self-indulgent of his poetry: the author Gil de Biedma commiserates with the character Gil de Biedma. The poet is very self-derisive in this book and reproaches himself for his frivolous past, especially in "Contra Jaime Gil de Biedma" (Against Jaime Gil de Biedma). It is a book of disillusionment in the face of lost youth and lost loves, a desperate declaration concerning the search for happiness and its difficulties, and a shameless cry of jealousy in the face of those still young.

Poemas póstumos is a farewell to the young Gil de Biedma and the ushering in of the "old" man. At one point he perceptively classifies the young poet as the finer of the two. The final poem of the book announces that the older man is, albeit unwillingly, philosophical about his fate. He tells us that growing old has its charms. So in spite of the frequently caustic voice in this book, he never falls into total despair. The dramatic

ation of poets, often called the "Novísimos"—a group attracted to the classics and pop culture—admires most in the poet. This quality also distinguishes him from his contemporaries who, in general, did not have the same opportunities to travel and study abroad.

Moralidades demonstrates his consciousness of style. He occasionally uses a series of short quatrains, often in a style reminiscent of popular songs. This is true in "La novela de un joven pobre" and "A una dama muy joven separada" (The Novel of a Poor Youth, and To a Very Young Separated Lady). Both titles are somewhat ironic in their melodramatic undertones, not unlike those of popular lyrics. Other poems of this book are imitative of poets admired by Gil de Biedma: "Años triunfales" (Triumphant Years) was inspired by the poem of Rubén Darío entitled "Marcha triunfal" (Triumphant March), and "Auden's At Last the Secret Is Out" is a loose translation of a poem by Auden. Interestingly, the book ends with another metapoem called "El juego de hacer versos" (The Game of Composing Verses). Inspired by the poetic theories of Auden, this ironic poem jests about the task of the poet. Written in 1962, the year of the most excharacter Gil de Biedma is always saved by an underlying sentiment of self-love, the need for others, and a sensual zest for life. The poet Gil de Biedma has an unmitigated capacity for generating a tone of intense irony in the face of life's inherently peripatetic quality and thus rescues himself from the clutches of desperation.

Most of Gil de Biedma's poetry was brought together under the title *Colección particular* (Private Collection) in 1969. Unfortunately the book remained virtually a private collection, since nearly all of the thirty-five hundred copies were destroyed by the censors before they reached the bookstores. This factor is one which prevented Gil de Biedma from becoming more well known in Spain and abroad. Even so, in 1975 a somewhat altered edition of the book, entitled *Las personas del verbo* (The Persons of the Verb), did see print and was successfully distributed.

Gil de Biedma is the least prolific of the poets of his generation, perhaps because of the acute aesthetic demands he placed on himself. Yet *Las personas del verbo* is a brilliant testimony to his psychological evolution. It is, in addition, illustrative of the poetic and political evolution of many of the members of the Generation of the 1950s, providing some of the best examples of social poetry and then of the poetry of experience, which by the early 1960s was beginning to replace social-realist verse.

After writing *Poemas póstumos* Gil de Biedma wrote only a few poems, which he chose not to publish. He did rework and publish his diary in 1974, and he subsequently wrote numerous essays, many of which were collected in *El pie de la letra* (Literally Speaking), published in 1980, a book that generated a great deal of interest on the part of critics. This fact demonstrates the enthusiasm with which the work of Gil de Biedma was always received in Spain; he is held in such esteem that critics continue to write about his poetry and essays. Upon his death in January 1990, the poet and essayist Manuel Vázquez Montalbán (in *El País*, 15 January 1990) reasserted Gil de Biedma's popularity: "Considero su poesía la más fundamental de la posguerra, porque enseñó al poeta posterior a situarse ante la materia poética y a narrar según el ritmo poético . . ." (I consider his poetry the most fundamental of the postwar period, because he taught later poets how to position themselves before the poetic material and to narrate nostalgia according to a poetic rhythm . . .).

Until his lingering illness and subsequent death from AIDS, Gil de Biedma continued to live and work in Barcelona, frequently traveling to the Philippines. He spent much of his free time in his country home in Ultramort, a village outside Barcelona, often visiting the family estate in Nava de la Asunción. The work of Gil de Biedma, in spite of his scant literary production, is admired by writers who were contemporaries and especially by those who followed him. His ability to absorb Anglo-American poetic theory and his erotic themes made him one of the most provocative and admired twentieth-century Spanish writers. His capacity for capturing the past and preserving it in his poetry and his mastery at creating a dialogue between the poet and the dramatic personae of the poem are factors that made Jaime Gil de Biedma one of the most outstanding poets of the Spanish postwar period.

References:

Luis García Montero, Antonio Jiménez Millán, and Alvaro Salvador, eds., *El juego de hacer versos* (Torremolinos, Spain: Litoral, 1986);

Shirley Mangini González, *Gil de Biedma* (Madrid: Júcar, 1980);

Pere Rovira, *La poesía de Jaime Gil de Biedma* (Barcelona: Mall, 1986).

Angel González

(6 September 1925 -   )

Allan Englekirk
University of South Carolina

BOOKS: *Aspero mundo* (Madrid: Rialp, 1956); translated by Donald D. Walsh as *Harsh World and Other Poems* (Princeton: Princeton University Press, 1977);

Sin esperanza, con convencimiento (Barcelona: Literaturasa, 1961);

Grado elemental (Paris: Ruedo Ibérico, 1962);

Palabra sobre palabra (Madrid: Poesía para Todos, 1965; revised and enlarged edition, Barcelona: Seix Barral, 1968; revised and enlarged again, 1972; enlarged again, 1977);

Tratado de urbanismo (Barcelona: Bardo, 1967);

Breves acotaciones para una biografía (Las Palmas, Grand Canary Island: Inventarios Provisionales, 1971);

Procedimientos narrativos (Santander, Spain: Isla de los Ratones, 1972);

Juan Ramón Jiménez (Madrid: Júcar, 1973 [i.e., 1974]);

Muestra de algunos procedimientos narrativos y de las actitudes sentimentales que habitualmente comportan (Madrid: Turner, 1976; revised and enlarged, 1977);

Poemas (Madrid: Cátedra, 1980);

Aproximaciones a Antonio Machado (Mexico City: Universidad Nacional Autónoma de México, 1982);

Antología poética (Madrid: Alianza, 1982);

Estudios sobre el Siglo de Oro (Albuquerque: University of New Mexico / Madrid: Cátedra, 1983);

Prosemas o menos (Madrid: Hiperión, 1985).

OTHER: "Poesía y compromiso," in *Poesía último*, edited by Francisco Ribes (Madrid: Taurus, 1963), pp. 57-59;

El grupo poético de 1927, edited, with an introduction, by González (Madrid: Taurus, 1976);

Gabriel Celaya: Poesía, edited, with an introduction, by González (Madrid: Alianza, 1977);

Antonio Machado, edited, with an introduction, by González (Madrid: Júcar, 1979).

Angel González has most frequently been identified with a group of poets whose literary careers began with publications in the decade of the 1950s. The poetry of this so-called Generation of 1950, in basic terms, represented a response or reaction to the works of literary artists who immediately preceded them in Spain. The "poesía social" (social poetry) of these earlier writers was primarily a literature of protest and denunciation, caused by, and directed against, the prevailing sociopolitical situation of Spain in the years following the devastation related to the civil war. The poets of the Generation of 1950 continued to produce works directed to social themes, though not as consistently as their predecessors. Their focus was decidedly more universal, however, and more emphasis was placed on the art of communication than on the act of communication. As the oldest member of the poets of this second post-civil-war generation, and more than most others of the group, González oriented his work to social themes. With equal conviction as those writing immediately before him, he believed it necessary for poetry to reflect, and reflect on, the pressing problems of the surrounding world. As with his contemporaries, however, the aesthetic function of poetry was a concern of equal validity.

Born on 6 September 1925 to Pedro and María Muñiz González-Cano in Oviedo, Spain, González spent much of his early youth in this city and in the provinces of northern Spain. The youngest of four children, he was reared from eighteen months of age mostly by his mother, because his father—a professor of pedagogy in the Escuela Normal de Maestros in Oviedo—passed away in 1927 from an infection related to a leg operation. The early adolescence of González was significantly affected by events related to the Spanish Civil War. One brother was killed—possibly murdered—during the conflict, while another left home to fight on the side of the Republicans, first in Asturias, then later on the Levantine front. González's mother and sister lost their jobs

at the beginning of the war, leaving the family without a consistent and predictable source of livelihood. With no adult men in the house, financial survival was tenuous at best.

From his early years, González demonstrated a profound interest in art and music, and were it not for the economic complications caused by the death of his father and by the civil war, his study of music might have led to a career in this field. Instead, González studied law at the University of Oviedo, receiving his licentiate in 1948. Music continued to exert a powerful influence on his life, however, and by accepting an assignment as music critic for the periodical *La voz de Asturias* in Oviedo, he was able to maintain contact with this specific line of interest. In ad-

dition to his columns on music, González wrote for *La voz* on general topics of municipal concern.

The experience as a journalist eventually motivated him to travel to Madrid, where in 1951 he took a three-month course from the Escuela Oficial de Periodismo (Offical School of Journalism) in order to become accredited. Government control of the media caused González to become disenchanted with newspaper work, however. He quickly realized that the press was not serving as a source of information, but rather as a source of propaganda in support of a regime decidedly not to his liking. After passing the exams required for entry into government service he gained a position in the Ministerio de Obras Públicas (Ministry of Public Works)—first in Seville in 1954 and later in Madrid in 1956, where he remained with the ministry until 1972.

In a 1980 interview with Haroldo Alvarado Tenorio, González said that the move from Oviedo to the more vital city of Madrid changed his life: "A Madrid lo encuentro lleno de atractivos, y de muchas más posibilidades de las que me ofrecía Oviedo, que entonces me ofrecía muy pocas: . . . para mí lo mas importante fue conocer gente, frecuentar ambientes literarias, conocer una vida muy distinta de lo que había sido entonces para mí la vida . . . " (I found Madrid to be full of attractions, with many more opportunities than those offered by Oviedo, which at that time offered very few: . . . most important for me was the chance to meet people, to frequent literary ambients, to know a life quite distinct from what had been before . . .). González became a steady participant in *tertulias* (informal meetings of writers and other intellectuals) in Madrid (at the Café Pelayo) and in Barcelona; it was in these two cities in the early and mid 1950s that he became acquainted with Jaime Gil de Biedma, Juan García Hortelano, Gabriel Celaya, Vicente Aleixandre, Carlos Bousoño, Carlos Barral, and other literary critics and artists. With many of these people he established lasting friendships.

González had begun to read and compose poetry in 1944 at age nineteen, while bedridden for three years with tuberculosis in a small town in the mountains of León—twelve years before the publication of his first volume of verse. Prior to that period in León, as he told Alvarado, his exposure to poetry was minimal: "yo había leído alguna poesía que entonces todos los jóvenes que tenían libros en casa por herencía habían conocido un poquito, pues Rubén Darío, Espronceda, algunos poetas del Siglo de Oro, muestras muy insignificantes de lo que era la poesía de entonces" (I had read the poetry that most youths who had books at home, passed on through inheritance, had read, such as Rubén Darío, Espronceda, some poets of the Spanish Golden Age, insufficient samples of what poetry was at that time). The original impulse to write was provided largely by the poetry of Juan Ramón Jiménez and other poets of the Generation of 1927. The initial verses of González were written "más como pasatiempo, para llenar mis horas de ocio, de reposo, durante aquella enfermedad . . ." (more as a pastime, to fill my hours of idleness, of rest, during the illness . . .).

After recovering from his poor health, he devoted increasingly more time to poetry, but the decision to publish was difficult. The realization that the thoughts he expressed in his writings were no longer to be read only by an audience of his choosing forced him to examine his perspective on the relationship between life and art. As González confided to Emilio Alarcos Llorach: "por primera vez me preocuparon las cuestiones del valor y de la valía del arte, de su función y de su justificación" (for the first time, I became preoccupied with questions related to the worth or value of art, its function and justification). It was only upon the insistence of Bousoño and Aleixandre that González, at age thirty-one, decided to expose his writing to the general public.

Aspero mundo (1956; translated as *Harsh World and Other Poems*, 1977) is dedicated to a specific female companion, whose name is never mentioned; the volume is divided into four sections— "Aspero mundo," "Canciones" (Songs), "Sonetos" (Sonnets), and "Acariciado mundo" (Cherished World). The major part of the volume is poetry written before González moved to Madrid in 1951, but several poems in "Aspero mundo" were composed after this date. "Danae," "Alga quisiera ser" (Would that I Were Algae), and "Capital de provincia" (Provincial Capital) represent the earliest poetry of González, from his years in León.

The short prefatory title poem in *Aspero mundo* establishes the distinction that González perceives between the world as it once was and the world surrounding him at the moment. Any ideal precepts formerly held regarding life seem lost in confrontation with actuality:

Te tuve
cuando eras
dulce,
acariciado mundo.
Realidad casi nube,
¡cómo te me volaste de los brazos!
Ahora te siento nuevamente.
No por tu luz, sino por tu corteza,
percibo tu inequívoca
presencia.
. . . agrios perfiles, duros meridianos,
áspero mundo para mis dos manos!

(I held you
when you were
soft,
cherished world.
Reality almost cloud,
how you flew from my arms!

Page from a draft for "Divagación onírica" (Dreaming Digression), a poem collected in Muestra de algunes procedimientos narrativos *(A Sample of Some Narrative Procedures, 1976; by permission of Angel González)*

Now I sense you again.
Not by your light, but by your skin,
I perceive your unequivocal
presence.
. . . sharp profiles, hard meridians,
harsh world for my two hands!)

Composed after the other poems of the volume, this poem lends unity to the work by counterpointing the harsh world/cherished world dichotomy in a perspective adopted by González throughout this volume and in his entire poetic production.

In general the poems contained in the first section voice a preoccupation with the passage of time, contemplation of the distressing nature of existence on both an individual and universal level, and a conceptualization of reality as something so painful that it is best disregarded whenever possible. A denunciation of life is expressed in "Cumpleaños" (Birthday)—"Para vivir un año es necesario / morirse muchas veces mucho" (To live a year one must / die many times and many deaths)—and it is complemented by a depressing vision of self in "Para que yo me llame Angel González" (So that I May Call Myself Angel González), the first poem of the section: "yo no soy más que . . . un escombro tenaz, que se resiste / a su ruina, que lucha contra el viento, / que avanza por caminos que no llevan / a ningún sitio" (I am no more than . . . a stubborn remnant, which resists / its ruin, which fights against the wind, / which advances along roads which lead / nowhere). The despair evident in these lines is magnified by González's realization that his work will always fall short of expressing what he really feels, a sentiment powerfully conveyed by a poem titled "Me falta una palabra . . . " (I'm Lacking One Word . . .).

In contrast to the poems in the "Aspero mundo" section, much of the verse in "Canciones," "Sonetos," and "Acariciado mundo" is less negative in spirit. Frequently conveyed in these sections is the concept that physical or spiritual union with others represents one of the few human options capable of providing comfort and consolation—however fleeting. Erotic/amorous verse appears throughout the poetry of González, but, in reference to *Aspero mundo*, critics are divided as to whether the "tú" (you) to whom many poems are directed is a physical being, or rather, as Gary Auburn Singleterry has suggested, a mythical mother-goddess of the earth, representing love, fertility, and beauty. This unnamed being is most often portrayed in poems that evoke a natural world in which harmony among all elements produces a sense of lasting peace. However, the ideal world of nature vanishes in "Ciudad" (City), the final poem of the volume, which envisions a false, cold city and revives the sense of solitude defined in the initial poems of the work.

Aspero mundo was nominated for the Adonáis Prize in 1956. Though such an honor clearly acknowledges the literary merit of the volume, González, in looking back on the work, divides it into two parts—the poems of "Aspero mundo" and those of the remaining three sections. Referring to his earliest poems, early in terms of chronology but appearing in the last three sections, González classifies them (in his introduction to *Poemas*, 1980) as opaque works of an extremely literary nature "que expresaban poco o nada de mí: vagas disposiciones sentimentales, emociones más inventadas o deseadas que vividas" (which expressed little or nothing of me: vaguely sentimental lines containing emotions that were more imagined or contrived than experienced). In contrast, the poetry of the "Aspero mundo" section was composed mostly after additional readings oriented his thoughts and writings toward more defined and specific objectives. Exposure to the works of Gabriel Celaya, José Hierro, Blas de Otero, and Eugenio de Nora made González realize that life and art are not totally separate, or separable, elements. Celaya's belief that poetry should serve as a tool to transform the world was not lost on González, who recalls in his *Poemas* introduction his feelings after first reading Celaya: "Yo no estaba muy seguro de que el mundo fuese susceptible de ser transformado con palabras, pero sí creía que merecía la pena intentar algo parecido: tratar de clarificar el caos, de desvelar o denunciar las imperfecciones de la Historia, de testimoniar el horror en que me sentía inmerso . . ." (I was not sure that the world was capable of being transformed by words, but I did believe that it was worth the effort to strive for something similar: to try to clarify the chaos, to uncover or denounce the imperfections of History, to testify to the horror in which I felt myself immersed . . .). Such conclusions significantly influenced the poems of "Aspero mundo" and likewise served to guide the composition of much of González's later work.

In 1957, not long after assuming his position at the Ministry of Public Works, González was awarded a scholarship to study poetry in England—a grant provided by the government to writers with previously published material. This three-month stay abroad was followed by trips to France, Italy, Scandinavia, West Germany, and Czechoslovakia. These travels allowed him to attend various conferences on literature and meet many of his contemporaries in European and Hispanic-American letters.

Published five years after the appearance of his first book, *Sin esperanza, con convencimiento* (Without Hope, but with Conviction, 1961) is divided into five sections and was written while he was residing in Madrid. Like *Aspero mundo*, it begins with a poem built on the contrast between two worlds: "Otro tiempo vendrá" (Another Time Will Come). The speaker is immersed in the world of the present—where "es la luz del alba / como la espuma sucia de un día anticipadamente inútil ... " (the dawn's early light is like the dirty foam of a day that promises to be useless ...)—while lamenting what he has lost to the past. In contrast to much of González's previous verse, however, he expresses here the belief that "otro tiempo vendrá distinto a este" (another time will come distinct from this one). Evidently there is reason for hope. This optimistic message is repeated in "Invierno" (Winter)—this time with specific reference to the future of Spain. After relating the present condition of his country to that of a land frozen and made dormant by the cold of winter, he uses the phrases in the title of the volume when he refers to the days ahead for his homeland. As in the initial poem of the volume, the concept of the passage of time resolving the ills of the moment is evident:

> Es increíble: pero todo esto
> que hoy es tierra dormida bajo el frío
> será mañana, bajo el viento,
> trigo.
>   Y rojas
> amapolas. Y sarmiento ...
> Sin esperanza:
> la tierra de Castilla está esperando
> —crecen los ríos—
> con convencimiento.

> (It's unbelievable: but all this
> which today lies dormant beneath the cold
> will tomorrow, under the wind,
> be wheat.
>   And red
> poppies. And vine shoots ...
> Without hope:
> the land of Castile is waiting
> —the rivers are rising—
> with conviction.)

Though these two poems and the title of the volume seem to suggest a degree of optimism, this positive attitude is difficult to find with any consistency in most other poems in the book. The verse of *Sin esperanza, con convencimiento*, in general, discloses an overwhelming sense of despair with respect to the poet, Spain, and, often, all humankind. In the poem "Esperanza" (Hope) a sense of total frustration is expressed. Hope is viewed as a spider weaving expectations that consistently fail to materialize:

> Te paras
> no lejos de mi cuerpo
> abandonado, andas
> entorno a mí
> tejiendo, rápida,
> inconsistentes hilos invisibles ...
> Agazapada
> bajo las piedras y las horas,
> esperaste, paciente, la llegada
> de esta tarde
> en la que nada
> es ya posible. ...

> (You pause
> not far from my abandoned
> body and move
> in circles about me,
> spinning, rapidly,
> inconsistent invisible threads ...
> Hidden
> beneath the rocks and the hours,
> you patiently awaited the arrival
> of this afternoon
> in which nothing
> is now possible. ...)

The initial poem of the third section, "Sé lo que es esperar" (I Know What It's Like to Wait), is similar in message and tone. Like many poems of the volume, it takes advantage of the double meaning of *esperar*, which signifies "to hope" and "to wait." The first lines—"sé lo que es esperar: / esperé tantos / días y tantas cosas en mi vida"—translate as either "I know what it's like to wait: / I've waited so many / days and for so many things in my life," or "I know what it is to hope: / I've hoped so many / days and for so many things in my life." The message is basic to the entire volume: the poet has spent his life waiting in the hope that something will occur to provide meaning to life, yet time passes and he still waits and hopes. The final poem in the book manifests

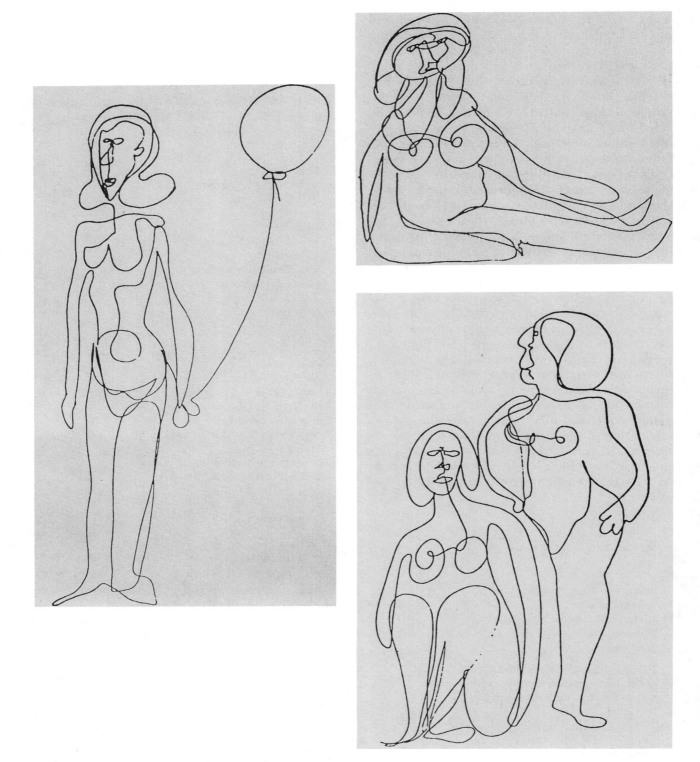

Drawings by González (from Miguel González-Gerth, "Angel González: Thirteen Poems and Some Drawings," Texas Quarterly, Spring 1977)

total despondency. The possibility of a more meaningful future is suggested, but faith in it is practically nonexistent:

> Amargo como el mar,
> y desatado
> igual que un huracán, e irremediable
> lo mismo que una piedra en su caída:
> así es mi corazón.
> > Luego
> dejadme.
> Un día como hoy nada es posible,
> y si es mi suerte lo que os preocupa
> guardad silencio y esperad
> que llegue
> un nuevo día, con el alma en vilo.

> (Bitter as the sea,
> and as untamed
> as a hurricane, and as irrepressible
> as a falling stone:
> such is my heart.
> > So let
> me be.
> On a day like today nothing is possible,
> and if it is my fate that worries you,
> maintain your silence and wait
> for a new day,
> with your soul in suspense.)

Referring to *Sin esperanza, con convencimiento*, in an unpublished interview, González stated that a central theme of the book is time. In "Otro tiempo vendrá" and "El Invierno" only time will bring a better world, yet its passage has as yet effected few changes and has merely served to heighten the sense of despair. In "El recuerdo" (Memory) thoughts of the past provide an escape from immediate reality, and the temptation to retreat into this more harmonious world is great. Several poems of *Sin esperanza, con convencimiento* reveal a concern for the transitory nature of existence. In "Mensaje a las estatuas" (Message to the Statues) González recognizes the durability of stone and its capacity to withstand the passage of years with little apparent change, but he observes that the destiny of a statue is truly like that of a man. Turning to dust, its final resting place will also be the earth.

As with many poets of his generation, memories of the civil war and a concern for its deleterious effects on Spain appear in much of González's work, beginning most noticeably in this second volume of verse. As he states in the introduction to *Poemas*, preoccupation with the war and with issues of a sociopolitical nature were un-

avoidable, given the conditions in Spain during his childhood and adolescence: "Las tensiones sociales que la República puso en evidencia, la revolución asturiana de octubre de 1934, y la guerra civil, fueron los acontecimientos más sobresalientes que jalonaron mi infancia. La posguerra fue el escenario de mi adolescencia y de mi juventud. Vivir todos esos hechos en el seno de una familia politizada, y desde el lado de los que perdieron todas las batallas, determina ciertas actitudes ante la vida (y, por tanto, frente al arte). Por ejemplo: aunque lo hubiese intentado, yo nunca hubiese podido recluirme en una torre de marfil, entre otras razones porque no hay torre capaz de resistir la presión de semejantes circunstancias" (The social tensions made evident by the Republic, the Asturian revolt of October 1934, and the civil war, were the most disturbing events of my childhood. The postwar period was the scene of my youth and adolescence. To experience all these events from within the bosom of a politicized family, and from the side which lost all the wars, determined certain of my attitudes about life [and, likewise, about art]. For example: though I might have tried, I could never have hidden myself in an ivory tower, among other reasons because no tower exists that is capable of resisting the pressure of such circumstances).

The second poem of *Sin esperanza, con convencimiento*, "El derrotado" (The Defeated One), was inspired by the predicament of González's brother, who, like many others, was forced to flee the country—remaining without a homeland and separated from loved ones. Strongest in the condemnation of the civil war and its lasting effect on Spain are the poems "Campo de Batalla" (Field of Battle) and "Entreacto" (Intermission). "Campo de Batalla" envisions the war as a tragic and devastating occurrence—as a struggle that left those who survived with little will or conviction to oppose the victors. "Entreacto" suggests that "no acaba aquí la historia" (the story doesn't end here). The civil war has come to a close, but the present moment in Spain's history is much like the break between acts of a play—the tension is high, for the villains are known, but the end is still a mystery.

Freedom of expression was severely curtailed during the years of the Franco dictatorship. Direct treatment of the theme of the civil war in particular was prohibited when González composed the works in *Sin esperanza, con convencimiento*. For this reason, these poems do

González in Madrid with Carlos and Ruth Bousoño

not condemn specific individuals or mention concrete, historical data. To avoid censorship, González was forced to evolve a poetry that might be interpreted from more than one perspective. As he affirms in the introductory pages of *Poemas*, treatment of such themes as the civil war "obligaba al uso de símbolos, alegorías y otros procedimientos alusivos ... que en cierto modo contradecían la tendencia realista entonces dominante ..." (demanded the use of symbols, allegories and other allusive procedures ... which to a certain extent contradicted the realist tendency then dominant). Referring to "Entreacto," González asserts that it was designed to suggest the provisionality of the results of the civil war, but he states that ambiguities in the poem allow for other interpretations. According to González, in "Campo de Batalla" "el tema de la guerra está planteado con una deliberada imprecisión que deriva en una imagen ... ambigua, casi intemporal y desarraigada" (the theme of the war is treated with a deliberate vagueness that results in an ambivalent, almost atemporal image).

González made use of irony in his poetry for the first time in *Sin esperanza, con convencimiento*; it was a technique of great significance to his subsequent work. He contends that his use of irony was at first motivated by a concern about censorship. The technique allowed him to criticize the sociopolitical situation yet avoid condemnation, since the message behind the double-edged words was frequently missed by the censors. Irony likewise served, according to González, to lessen the emotional burden of his poetry by creating a distancing effect. He classifies "Discurso a los jóvenes" (Discourse to the Young) as the poem with the most effective irony in his second volume. Composed in the form of an oration delivered to the next generation, yet avoiding any specific mention of Spain or concretely identifiable Spanish people or events, the poem contends that a great heritage is being passed on to the young of the nation. They must maintain the glory of the present by asphyxiating all that represents vitality. Expelled from the country should be those who dream—those who seek light and truth:

Si alguno de vosotros
pensase
yo le diría: no pienses.
Pero no es necesario.
Seguid así, hijos míos,

y yo os prometo
paz y patria feliz,
orden,
silencio.

(Should any of you
think,
I would say to you: don't think.
But it is not necessary.
Remain this way, my children,
and I promise you
peace and a felicitous homeland,
order,
silence.)

The final act yet to be performed, as suggested in "Entreacto," will be tragic if the youth follow such advice.

The themes of most importance to González's poetry are all developed in *Sin esperanza, con convencimiento*. More cohesive than *Aspero mundo*, it is a masterful collection. The opinion expressed by Florentino Martino reflects the reaction of most critics who have written about the work: "La pincelada esencial, la emoción resumida con extraña preción . . . transmiten al lector una belleza raramente alcanzada en nuestro medio" (The succinct brushwork, the emotion synthesized with strange precision . . . transmit to the reader a beauty rarely achieved in our midst [*Papeles Son Armadens*, June 1970]).

In an unpublished interview, González described the early and mid 1960s as repetitive and monotonous years in his life. Promoted to the position of assistant director of the Servicio de Publicaciones for the Ministry of Public Works, he was responsible for a monthly newsletter and also edited various technical publications from the ministry. His free time in this period, besides being dedicated to his own poetry, was directed to a perusal of the works of other contemporary Hispanic writers and poets. In the mid 1950s González had begun reading the poetry of César Vallejo, and his interest in this Peruvian increased in the 1960s. In several poems of *Sin esperanza, con convencimiento* and later volumes, themes and sentiments reminiscent of Vallejo's work are strikingly evident.

Of all his poetry, González considers his third volume, *Grado elemental* (Elementary Grade, 1962), to be closest in tone and message to the social poetry of the previous generation. Published while he was still living in Madrid, *Grado elemental* reveals a change of perspective. Though the preceding volume focuses on Spain, the Spaniard,

and humankind, likewise prevalent are poems of an extremely personal nature. In *Grado elemental* the "I" so prominent in previous volumes almost disappears. González is far less preoccupied with examining the self and more dedicated to considering others—to observing people in society, and society in general. More didactic in intent, as suggested by the title, and more political in focus, this poetry criticizes the traditional postulates upon which the values of society are based.

The reaction of many critics of this period was to reprehend those who placed life above art in their poetry. González, and others of the generation of 1950, rejected the excesses of social poetry, but in defense of committed verse in general—in 1963 in an essay titled "Poesía y compromiso" (Poetry and Commitment)—he stated that poetry evolves "de todos los estímulos que vienen dados al poeta desde fuera, incluida, por supuesto, la tradición literaria, pero teniendo presentes siempre las ideas y las realidades de cualquier tipo que caracterizan al momento histórico en el que el poema se produce" (from all the stimuli that come to the poet from without, including, certainly, literary tradition, but considering always the ideas and realities of any sort that characterize the historical moment in which the poem is produced). To those critics who believed that poetry should be directed solely by considerations of an aesthetic nature, González responded: "La poesía, como obra del hombre y para el hombre, está sujeta a tantos cambios y mudanzas como el hombre mismo. La Historia de la poesía, la Historia de la literatura, no es más que un fragmento de la Historia, que siempre es del hombre" (Poetry, as a product of and for man, is subject to as many changes as man himself. The History of poetry, the History of literature, is no more than a fragment of History, which is made by man). Life and art for González are inextricably bound together. The separation of one from the other produces poetry of shallow and superficial dimensions.

In *Grado elemental* González again employs irony, but it is irony marked by sarcasm, verging on cynicism. This negative approach is caused by what González sees as he observes society. In "Lecciones de cosas" (Lessons of Things) he portrays humankind as a destructive force—as latecomers to the planet whose presence has made the world a more hostile and violent place. The acquisition of knowledge of the intricacies of the universe, filling volumes of encyclopedias, has been used by humans to their own detriment and to the detriment of the world. The oppressive reality is a testimony to their failure to use superior wisdom in a positive, productive fashion. The fifth poem of the volume, "Prueba" (Proof), voices similar sentiments. The speaker marvels at his ability to control his own movements while commanding his hands to perform various functions. The "talent" of being able to direct actions rationally should allow humankind to become part of an ordered, perfect world. The nature of the acts performed by the hands in "Prueba," however, make the concluding lines of the poem a poignantly contradictory statement:

¡Mano, frótame la cabeza!
Mano, acércame
la silla. Desabróchale
el corsé a esa muchacha
—y tú, la otra, no te quedes quieta.
Coge
todo el dinero, mano:
incendia,
mata.
Por lo tanto
se prueba una vez más,
como decía,
el orden natural y preexistente,
la armónica hermosura de las cosas.

(Hand, rub my head!
Hand, bring
my chair closer. Loosen
that girl's bra
—and you, the other one, don't be so still.
Grab
all the money, hand:
burn,
kill.
Therefore,
one proves again,
as I was saying,
the natural and preexistent order,
the harmonious beauty of things.)

The implication is that a better world could exist, but that the human capacity for evil is a major impediment.

Constant in *Grado elemental* is a condemnation of the present—a time in which nothing is good in Spain, yet little can be done. As portrayed in "Estío en Bidonville" (Summer in Bidonville [the Slums]), Spain resembles the site of a shipwreck in which thousands of people survive, yet remain "floating," waiting to be saved from the dangers to which they are still exposed. In contrast to other volumes, in *Grado elemental* González attempts to motivate his readers to seek

to change the prevailing situation. In "Estio en Bidonville" those cast adrift by the shipwreck are told they must save themselves. Escape from the present predicament will only be realized by supreme individual effort: "Mañana es un mar hondo que hay que cruzar a nado" (Tomorrow is a deep sea across which we must swim). In "Lecciones de cosas," after observing how ants provide for their future well-being by directing themselves systematically to the tasks at hand, González suggests: "Imitémoslas" (Let us imitate them). In "Nada es lo mismo" (Nothing is the Same) the reader is warned to forget the past and focus on what is yet to come: "Habrá palabras nuevas para la nueva historia / y es preciso encontrarlas antes de que sea tarde" (There will be new words for the new history / and it is necessary to find them before it is too late). Similar to many social poets writing before him, González not only criticizes the status quo but wishes to transform it as well.

Having eliminated the theme of love almost entirely from the poetry of *Grado elemental*, González dedicated his fourth volume exclusively to a consideration of this concern. *Palabra sobre palabra* (Word upon Word, 1965) is verse of a profoundly lyrical nature that stands in stark contrast to his immediately previous or subsequent volumes. Several of the poems of *Aspero mundo* had portrayed love as the only means to find happiness and tranquility in a disquieting world, and such is the significance likewise attributed to it in *Palabra sobre palabra*. As in previous poems, however, the pleasures of love are counterbalanced by a sense of frustration. Accompanying the joy of the moment, filled with ecstasy and satisfaction, is the realization that:

Tras de tí misma,
tu ausencia se dibuja
como una nada pavorosa:
el tiempo
que debo estar sin tí
es la aguda herramienta que el destino utiliza
para cerrarme el paso a la esperanza.

(Behind you
your absence is drawn
like a forbidding nothingness:
the time
that I must be without you
is the painful device which destiny uses
to deny me reason for hope.)

Self-portrait, circa 1984 (by permission of Angel Gonzalez)

González's next work, *Tratado de urbanismo* (Treatise on Urbanism, 1967), opens with "Inventario de lugares propicios al amor" (Inventory of Places Propitious for Love), a poem that at first seems to continue the consideration of love, so preponderant a theme in *Palabra sobre palabra*. After debating over the acceptability of various locations in which to enjoy another's company, the speaker concludes that no place is totally satisfactory. The world is too full of hatred:

Por todas partes ojos bizcos,
córneas torturadas,
implacables pupilas,
retinas reticentes,
vigilan, desconfían, amenazan.
Queda quizá el recurso de andar solo,
de vaciar el alma de ternura
y llenarla de hastío e indiferencia,
en este tiempo hostil, propicio al odio.

(Squinting eyes everywhere,
tortured corneas,
implacable pupils,
reticent retinas,
are vigilant, suspicious, threatening.
Left, perhaps, is the alternative of proceeding
   alone,
of emptying the soul of tenderness
and filling it with hatred and indifference,
in this hostile time, propitious for hatred.)

This negative statement is not an isolated manifestation of bitterness. The brief interlude of love poems found in *Palabra sobre palabra* is much like the eye of a hurricane, for González, in his next works, returns to themes of social criticism evident in earlier volumes.

Tratado de urbanismo is divided into three sections of relative thematic unity. The poetry of the initial group is most closely associated with the title of the collection, for these verses are almost all directed to an analysis of urban existence. Throughout this section, the city is perceived as a hostile environment—as a cold and impersonal setting in which everything is false and where the only option is to divorce oneself from others and fill one's heart with the same antagonistic feelings that confront one on all sides. Public gardens, the zoo, and other places not overlaid by concrete are the only havens of tranquility from the pressures of existence. Even in such oases, however, as González implies in "Parque zoológico" (Zoological Park), the human is unable to forget his status as "cosa entre cosas" (thing among things). He eventually must return to the reality that "progress" has created.

The middle years of the 1960s were extremely disappointing for González. The exasperation he felt with regard to the sociopolitical situation in Spain had frequently made him, in the past, question the value of his poetry—a theme introduced in "Trabajé el aire" (I Worked the Air) in *Sin esperanza, con convencimiento*. In *Tratado de urbanismo*, "Preámbulo a un silencio" (Preamble to Silence) asserts the "inutilidad de todas las palabras" (the uselessness of all words). Looking back on this poem from the perspective of the 1980s (in the introduction to *Poemas*), González sees it as a direct response to the historical moment at that time in Spain: "Mediada la década de los 60, la inmutabilidad (más aparente que real, contempladas las cosas desde hoy) de una situación a la que yo no veía salida, me hacía desconfiar de cualquier intento, por modestos que fuesen sus alcances, de incidir verbalmente en la realidad" (Halfway through the decade of the 1960s, the immutability [more apparent than real, when contemplated from the present moment] of a situation from which I saw no escape, made me doubt the effectiveness of any intent, however modest its objectives, to alter reality by means of words). In *Diez años de poesía española* (Ten Years of Spanish Poetry, 1972), José Olivio Jiménez characterizes "Chatarra" (Scrap Metal) as one of the few expressions of hope for the future in the first section of *Tratado de urbanismo*. This poem depicts a rusted and useless piece of machinery that once functioned with rhythmic precision. A furnace will melt it and return it to its original state. From this material, "nuevas formas" (new forms) will emerge. The metaphor is quite obvious: the scrap metal is identified with humanity or society. Taking the symbolic implications of this poem literally, however, it suggests that only through the destruction of society in its present state will a better "form" come forth. Such is the nature of one of the only attempts at optimism in *Tratado de urbanismo*.

Various poems of the second section of the book are more imaginative and experimental, eschewing a political stance. "Vals de atardecer" (Evening Waltz), "Tango de madrugada" (Tango of the Dawn), and "La trompeta" (The Trumpet) exhibit a pronounced fascination with the evocative power of words to suggest other than visual images. In "La trompeta," for example, a succession of *d*'s and *r*'s within certain words generates trumpetlike staccato impulses that enhance the measured cadence of the line.

The poetic production of González declined considerably after the publication of *Tratado de urbanismo*. The turn of the decade was marked by the appearance of a short collection of verse—*Breves acotaciones para una biografía* (Brief Marginal Notes for a Biography, 1971)—dedicated by González to fellow Asturian Emilio Alarcos Llorach, who had recently completed his full-length study of González's poetry up through *Tratado de urbanismo*. Though González continued to write, various factors prohibited him from dedicating more time to his poetry. In 1970 he traveled to Mexico, accepting an invitation from the Universidad Nacional Autónoma de México to read poetry and papers at conferences. Upon concluding his stay in Mexico, he proceeded to the United States, reading poetry at the University of New Mexico. He was then invited in 1971 to serve as a visiting professor at this same institution.

The decision to accept the New Mexico offer resulted in his resignation from his post in the Ministry of Public Works. In a 1984 interview with Gracia Rodríguez, González stated that dissatisfaction with his job in Spain was in part responsible for the change: "Yo estaba muy desmoralizado por razones personales y profesionales. Trabajaba . . . en un puesto magnífico que no me obligaba prácticamente más que ir a cobrar. Situación en teoría parece ideal antes de tenerla, pero al cabo de los años te va comiendo la moral. Probablemente en ese momento pude haberme convertido en un alcohólico irremediable si no me hubiera ido a Estados Unidos ..." (I was very demoralized for personal and professional reasons. I was working ... in a magnificent post that obliged little more from me than making an appearance in order to collect my salary. This situation seems ideal beforehand, but after a few years it begins to bother your conscience. Probably at that moment I could have become an irremediable alcoholic if I hadn't gone to the United States ...).

Another factor influencing his determination to leave was his weariness with the Franco regime, coupled with his belief that, in the person of Franco and then a successor, the political/intellectual oppression exerted by the Spanish government would continue for several more years. The prospect of teaching at the college level in the United States seemed an attractive option.

While teaching in New Mexico in 1972, González met Shirley Mangini, a graduate student in Spanish, whom he married the following year. After the visiting professorship in New Mexico, González accepted similar assignments at the University of Utah, the University of Maryland, and the University of Texas. In 1975 he returned to the University of New Mexico, assuming a permanent position as a professor of contemporary Spanish literature.

Due to conflicts of interest, his first marriage ended in divorce in 1979. In 1980 he served as visiting professor at the University of California at Irvine, after which he returned to New Mexico to continue teaching courses in literature. Frequent trips to Spain since his move to the United States have allowed him to maintain long-standing friendships and establish new contacts with younger poets and writers of his country.

Such a transitory existence and the many responsibilities demanded by his new profession detracted from the free time González might otherwise have spent composing poetry. The publication of *Breves acotaciones para una biografía* was followed by two subsequent volumes of entirely new verse, the second of which appeared in 1976, one year after the poet's move to New Mexico. Recurrent themes of previous volumes persist in these publications. Various poems communication a sense of anguish at the passage of time or in the recollection of fond memories—themes especially evident in the "Poemas elegíacos" (Elegiac Poems) of *Muestra de algunos procedimientos*

narrativos y de las actitudes sentimentales que habitualmente comportan (A Sample of Some Narrative Procedures and of Some Sentimental Attitudes that Habitually Accompany Them, 1976). Love continues as a source of pleasure, pain, and frustration. "Otra vez" (Again)—in the 1977 edition of *Muestra de algunos*—and several other poems of his volumes of the 1970s show a concern for the nature of contemporary existence, with "Otra vez" condemning the bloodshed in Chile related to the overthrow of Salvador Allende. In "A veces" (At Times), in *Breves acotaciones para una biografía*, and the short poems of the *Muestra de algunos* section titled "Metapoesía" (Metapoetry), González reconsiders the potential rewards or disappointments associated with the act of creating poetry.

Breves acotaciones para una biografía marked the start of a new stage in his poetic production, one marked by a persistent desire on his part to escape from the poetic persona his previous books had defined. In terms of both form and content, many of González's later poems suggest an apparent change in attitude with regard to his conception of the purpose of art. He classifies much of this verse as a type of "antipoesía" (antipoetry). Characterized by playful parody and an ironic humor that trivializes certain themes, many of the "poems" of these volumes are apothegms, glosses, or epilogues whose abbreviated lengths allow the elaboration of only a single concept—often of an inconsequential nature. Beginning in *Breves acotaciones para una biografía*, there is a more consistent attempt to exploit the expressive potential of language. Wordplay and unconventional imagery abound, as does experimentation with structural patterns within individual poems.

This divergence toward "antipoetic" verse represents an inclination to reject traditional molds or parameters for poetic discourse, and manifests—as he states in his preliminary comments in *Poemas*—"cierto rencor frente a las 'palabras inútiles' " (a certain animosity for "useless words"). In total, however, his 1970s poetry should not be interpreted as an abandonment by González of previously held tenets regarding poetry. Negating his earlier statement in "Preámbulo a un silencio," seemingly so important to his subsequent perspective, González asserts in *Poemas*: "mi creencia en la ineficacia de la palabra poética respondía más a una decepción transitoria que a una convicción profunda. En efecto, sigo creyendo que la palabra poética, si logra alzarse hasta el nivel de la verdadera poesía, no es nunca inútil. Porque las palabras del poema configuran con especial intensidad ideas y emociones, o a veces incluso llegan a crearlas" (my belief in the inefficacy of the poetic word responded more to a temporary deception than to profound conviction. In effect, I continue to believe that the poetic word, if it manages to raise itself to the level of true poetry, is not useless. Because the words of a poem shape with special intensity ideas and emotions, and often even create them).

Poemas contains several new works composed since the publication of *Muestra de algunos*, but consists mostly of poems included under previously printed titles. The concerns that once preoccupied González have not been forgotten, but in recent times, as he expressed in an unpublished interview, he has felt "menos necesidad, menos urgencia por escribir mis intuiciones" (less need, less urgency to write my intuitions). He continues to write poetry on occasion, however, and revealed to Rodríguez the process by which most of his poetry is now composed: "Generalmente escribo en una mesa de trabajo que me he instalado en un rincón de la habitación . . . en la que vivo. Es un piso muy pequeño. Ahí escribo mis notas para clase, y a veces, entre nota y nota se me ocurre apuntar alguna idea para un poema. Si la puedo seguir, continúo, y si no, la dejo hasta reencontrarla de nuevo, con placer si aún me parece bien. . . . El reencuentro me suele situar en el mismo estado anímico en que estaba cuando la escribí, y entonces, por lo general, se vuelve a producir un nuevo alargamiento del poema, otro golpe de palabras. Y así lo voy haciendo hasta que el poema está acabado. Sólo al final puede decirse que trabajo en terminarlo . . ." (Generally I write at a work table that I have installed in a corner of the place . . . in which I live. There is very little room. There I write my notes for class, and at times, between notes an idea for a poem will occur to me. If I can follow it, I continue, and if not I leave it until finding it again, with pleasure if it seems good. . . . The reencounter usually finds me in the same spirit that I was in when I wrote it, and then, generally, this produces a lengthening of the poem, another surge of words. And this is how I do it until the poem is finished. Only at the end can it be said that I work to finish it . . .).

As a professor of literature González has edited and written critical introductions to volumes of verse by two poets—Gabriel Celaya (1977) and Antonio Machado (1979)—who significantly influenced his own work; González has also published two full-length studies on specific aspects of the poetry of Machado and Juan Ramón Jiménez. The preliminary pages of *Poemas* contain González's analysis of his own poetry.

He has generally employed free verse, avoided complex imagery, and relied most frequently on traditional symbols and a simple, direct language. There is little doubt that because of the considerable volume of his poetry directed to sociopolitical themes, and because of his explicit and forceful defense of "critical poetry" in general, he will be most often remembered for his verse related to these themes. In the opinion of José Olivio Jiménez and other literary critics, it is this fervent commitment to humankind and to life that is the force behind González's poetic efforts.

Perhaps attempting to negate the excessive importance given by some scholars to this aspect of his verse, González contends, in the introduction to *Poemas*, that a concern for the passage of time and the expression of erotic/amorous sentiments occupies more space in his work than do poems of the other vein. The most recent studies on González reflect an increasing awareness by critics of the importance of this nonpolitical verse to his total poetic statement. Disclosing emotions of an intensely personal nature, a sizable portion of his poetry is about Angel González as he attempts to define himself by confronting his own fears while recognizing his own limitations. It is in this lyrical poetry that his most memorable and compelling sentiments emerge.

Interviews:

Haroldo Alvarado Tenorio, *La poesía española contemporánea* (Bogotá: Oveja Negra, 1980), pp. 81-89;

Gracia Rodríguez, "Angel, fieramente humano," *Quimera*, 35 (January 1984): 23-29.

Biography:

Emilio Alarcos Llorach, *Angel González, poeta* (Oviedo, Spain: Archivum, 1969).

References:

Douglas K. Benson, "La ironía, la función del hablante y la experiencia del lector en la poesía de Angel González," *Hispania*, 64 (December 1981): 570-581;

Benson, "Linguistic Parody and Reader Response in the Worlds of Angel González," *Anales de la Literatura Española Contemporanea*, 7, no. 1 (1982): 11-30;

Santiago Daydí Tolson, "Oralidad y escritura en la poesía de Angel González," *Siglo*, 6, nos. 1-2 (1988-1989): 1-10;

Andrew P. Debicki, *Angel González* (Madrid: Júcar, 1989);

María Luisa García Nieto Onrubia, "Notas sobre los efectos expresivos en la poesía de Angel González," *Iris*, 2 (1987): 39-85;

Joaquín González Muela, "La poesía de Angel González en su primer período," in *Homenaje a Casalduero: Crítica y poesía ofrecidas por sus amigos y discípulos*, edited by R. Pincus Sigele and Gonzalo Sobejano (Madrid: Gredos, 1972), pp. 189-201;

José Olivio Jiménez, "De la poesía social a la poesía crítica: A propósito de *Tratado de urbanismo*, de Angel González," in his *Diez años de poesía española* (Madrid: Insula, 1972), pp. 281-304;

Florentino Martino, "La poesía de Angel González," *Papeles Son Armadens*, 57 (June 1970): 229-247;

Martha LaFollette Miller, "Literary Tradition versus Speaker Experience in the Poetry of Angel González," *Anales de la Literatura Española Contemporanea*, 7, no. 1 (1982): 79-95;

Miller, "The Ludic Poetry of Angel González," in *After the War: Essays on Recent Spanish Poetry*, edited by Salvador Jiménez-Fajardo and John Wilcox (Boulder, Colo.: Society of Spanish and Spanish American Studies, 1988), pp. 75-82;

Julian Palley, "Angel González and the Anxiety of Influence," *Anales de la Literatura Española Contemporanea*, 9, nos. 1-3 (1984): 81-96;

Gary Auburn Singleterry, "The Poetic Cosmovision of Angel González," Ph.D. dissertation, University of New Mexico, 1972;

Tino Villanueva, "*Aspero Mundo* de Angel González: De la contemplación lírica a la realidad histórica," *Journal of Spanish Studies: Twentieth Century*, 8, nos. 1-2 (1980): 161-180.

Jorge Guillén

(18 January 1893 - 8 February 1984)

Julian Palley
University of California, Irvine

BOOKS: *Cántico* (Madrid: Revista de Occidente, 1928; revised and enlarged edition, Madrid: Cruz & Raya, 1936; revised and enlarged again, Mexico City: Litoral, 1945; further revised and enlarged, Buenos Aires: Sudamericana, 1950); translated (in part) by Norman Thomas de Giovanni and others, edited by de Giovanni (Boston: Little, Brown, 1965; London: Deutsch, 1965);

La Poética de Bécquer (New York: Hispanic Institute, 1943);

Ticknor, defensor de la cultura (Havana: Fernández, 1944);

Paso a la Aurora (Aurora, N.Y.: Hammer/Wells College Press, 1944);

Cicerón, su época, su vida y su obra (Madrid: Escelicer, 1950);

Variaciones sobre temas de Jean Cassou (Mexico City: Talleres de Gráfica Panamericana, 1951);

El encanto de las sirenas (Mexico City: Panamericana, 1953);

Huerto de Melibea (Madrid: Insula, 1954);

Lugar de Lázaro (Málaga, Spain: Dardo, 1957);

Clamor, tiempo de historia, 3 volumes (Buenos Aires: Sudamericana, 1957, 1960, 1963);

Viviendo, y otros poemas (Barcelona: Seix Barral, 1958);

Federico en persona: Semblanza y epistolario (Buenos Aires: Emecé, 1959);

Historia natural (Madrid: Papeles de Son Armadans, 1960);

Language and Poetry (Cambridge, Mass.: Harvard University Press, 1961); translated as *Lenguage y Poesía* (Madrid: Revista de Occidente, 1962);

El argumento de la obra (Milan: All'Insegna del Pesce d'Oro, 1961; Barcelona: Sinera, 1969); enlarged as *El argumento de la obra y otras prosas críticas* (Madrid: Taurus, 1985);

Suite italienne (Milan: All'Insegna del Pesce d'Oro, 1964);

Tréboles (Santander, Spain: Isla de los Ratones, 1964);

Relatos (Málaga, Spain: Guadalhorce, 1966);

Homenaje: Reunión de vidas (Milan: All'Insegna del Pesce d'Oro, 1967);

En torno a Gabriel Miró: Breve epistolario (Madrid: Arte & Bibliofilia, 1970);

Guirnalda civil (Cambridge, Mass.: Ferguson, 1970);

Y otros poemas (Buenos Aires: Muchnik, 1973);

Al margen (Madrid: Visor, 1974);

Convivencia (Madrid: Turner, 1975);

Estudios (Madrid: Narcea, 1977);

Plaza mayor: Antología civil (Madrid: Taurus, 1977);

Mientras el aire es nuestro, edited by Philip W. Silver (Madrid: Cátedra, 1978);

Poesía amorosa: 1919-1972, edited by Anne-Marie Couland (Madrid: Cupsa, 1978);

Serie castellana (Madrid: Caballo Griego para la Poesía, 1978);

Algunos poemas, edited by Angel Caffarena (Santander, Spain: Institución Cultural de Cantabria, 1981);

Antología del mar (Málaga, Spain: Agora, 1981);

La expresión (Ferrol, Spain: Sociedad de Cultura Valle-Inclán, 1981);

Aire Nuestro: Final (Barcelona: Barral, 1981);

Poemas malagueños (Málaga, Spain: Publicaciones de la Diputación Provincial de Málaga, 1983);

Sonreído va el sol (Milan: All'Insegna del Pesce d'Oro, 1983);

Jorge Guillén para niños (Madrid: Torre, 1984);

Sonetos completos (Granada, Spain: Ubago, 1988).

Collections: *Selección de poemas* (Madrid: Gredos, 1965; enlarged, 1970);

Aire Nuestro: Cántico, Clamor, Homenaje (Milan: All'Insegna del Pesce d'Oro, 1968);

Antología, edited by José Manuel Blecua (Salamanca, Spain: Anaya, 1970);

Obra poética (Madrid: Alianza, 1970).

Edition in English: *Affirmation: A Bilingual Anthology, 1919-1966*, edited and translated by Julian Palley (Norman: University of Oklahoma Press, 1968).

Jorge Guillén

TRANSLATIONS: Jules Supervielle, *Bosque sin horas*, translated by Guillén, Rafael Alberti, and others (Madrid: Plutarco, 1932);

Paul Valéry, *El cementerio marino*, translated by Guillén (Madrid: Alianza, 1967).

Jorge Guillén belonged to the remarkable Spanish Generation of 1927, which boasted such poets as Federico García Lorca, Pedro Salinas, Rafael Alberti, Luis Cernuda, and the Nobel Prize winner Vicente Aleixandre. The Spanish Civil War, initially a military rebellion against the Republican regime in 1936, dispersed most of the leading poets, writers, artists, and musicians into exile. Lorca was killed by the insurgents; Alberti went first to Argentina and then to Italy; and Guillén and Salinas came to teach at universities in the United States. The name "Generation of 1927" came about because some of their most important works appeared in or close to that year, which also marked the third centenary of the death of the baroque poet Luis de Góngora, whom they admired and emulated. Lorca and Alberti were from Andalusia, in the South, while Guillén and Salinas were from the central plains of Castile. The Andalusians tended in their poetry toward a greater effusiveness, color, and brilliance, while the Castilians were more sober and restrained. Until 1936 the influence of symbolism and the trend toward "pure poetry" dominated the work of most of the Generation of 1927; but with exile and the horrors of war, their poetry became increasingly committed to the themes of history and society.

Of all the twentieth-century Spanish poets, Guillén is the one who most affirmed, quietly and without sentimentality, the value of life and the dignity of existence. "Posterity," wrote the American poet Archibald MacLeish, "if it comes upon the great resounding Yes of [Guillén's] *Cántico* [Canticle, 1928] among the tumbled fragments of our time, will not believe that No was all we had to answer to the world" (*Atlantic Monthly*, January 1961). The purity, serenity, and distance in *Cántico* (as augmented in several editions) make it stand almost alone in the works of European and American poets of this century. Guillén's affirmation and serenity are qualified, but never entirely lost, in the books after *Cántico*— the works of exile and of a turning outward toward the world and its problems.

The man himself was vital, effusive, intense, and an irrepressible conversationalist with a running, ironic commentary on a broad range of contemporary matters. One sensed, in his presence, an excitement of ideas and a vast love of life. Tall, and (until his old age) thin, he often leaned close to his interlocutor, in the Spanish manner, while confiding some information destined, apparently, for only his friend's ear.

Jorge Guillén, the son of Esperanza Alvarez Guerra and Julio Guillén Sáenz, was born in Valladolid, Spain, on 18 January 1893 and lived for the most part the relatively uneventful life of a poet and university professor. His childhood and early schooling in Valladolid are recalled in a poem from volume 2 of *Clamor, tiempo de historia* (Clamor, Time of History, 1957-1963)—"Aquellas ropas chapadas" (Those Splendid Clothes)— in which he evokes affectionately "la dulce figura del maestro / Que tan humildemente comunica" (the gentle figure of the teacher / Who so humbly communicates), a reference to his teacher Don Valentín Alonso. Guillén's father was a businessman and a member of the board of *El Norte de Castilla*, a local paper. The young Guillén's middle-class childhood was peaceful and protected, as remembered in the sonnet "Del transcurso" (Of the Passing) in *Clamor*, volume 2: "Aun vuelan, sin embargo, los vencejos / En torno de unas torres, y allá arriba / Persiste mi niñez contemplativa. / Ya son buen vino mis viñedos viejos" (The gentle martins, however, still soar / Around some towers, and the outline / Of my contemplative childhood endures. / Still my old vineyards yield good wine).

Guillén also recalled how Europe, with its mystery and grandness, beckoned to him early in his life. From 1909 to 1911 he lived in the Maison Perreyve of the French Fathers of the Oratory in Fribourg, Switzerland; this was his first direct contact with French language and culture, which were to become part of his existence for many years afterward. Later (1913-1914) a year spent in Germany—in Halle and Munich—would round out his early European education, allowing him access to major currents of art and letters. Guillén's cosmopolitanism and his rejection of narrow nationalism and easy identification with Spanish folklore—which exerted an immense attraction for some of his contemporaries— can possibly be traced to this early acquaintance with two of the great European traditions, the French and German.

At age eighteen Guillén went to study philosophy and literature at the University of Madrid, where he stayed from fall 1911 to spring 1913 in the Residencia de Estudiantes, a meeting place for writers and intellectuals of the older and newer generations. As Guillén told Claude Couffon in a 1963 interview, he saw at the Residencia the efforts of those who wanted to build a new Spain with love, care, and art, and he felt sad to realize that all this had been demolished. At the Residencia he was influenced by Juan Ramón Jiménez, a great poet then at the prime of his career, and by the philosopher José Ortega y Gasset, whose perspectivist philosophy of "vital reason" was instrumental in the formation of the ideas of the younger poets, especially Guillén, Lorca, and Salinas. In 1913 Guillén completed his *Licenciatura en Letras* (M.A. in literature) at the University of Granada.

After his year in Germany there followed a long academic career in which the creativity in him flourished and grew. The six years (1917-1923) spent as lecturer in Spanish at the Sorbonne were crucial for the formation of his style, the poetic voice of *Cántico*. The ideas of L'Abbé Henri Bremond, the theoretician of *la poésie pure* (pure poetry), were being debated in Paris, which also saw the rising movements of surrealism and cubism. It was there, during the peaceful and artistically ebullient *entre-guerres* (time between wars) that Guillén conversed with the poet Paul Valéry, the inheritor of French symbolism. Valéry's style and theories were no doubt influential in the formation of the young Castilian's lyrics, and Guillén would later (in 1967) translate Valéry's *Le Cimetière marin* (Cemetery by the Sea,

Perfección

Queda curvo el firmamento,
Compacto azul, sobre el día.
Es el redondeamiento
Del esplendor: mediodía.
Todo es cúpula. Reposa,
Central sin querer, la rosa,
A un sol en cenit sujeta.
Y tanto se da el presente
Que el pie caminante siente
La integridad del planeta.

Fair copy of a poem collected in the second edition (1936) of Cántico *(Collection of Ivar and Astrud Ivask; by permission of the Estate of Jorge Guillén)*

Drawing of Guillén by Gregorio Prieto (from Prieto's Lorca y la Generation del '27, *1977)*

1920). However, this influence should not be exaggerated: Guillén was not a "Spanish Valéry" (as some critics called him), and his mature style and concept of poetry are very different from Valéry's. Guillén was undoubtedly influenced by the symbolists, including Valéry and Stéphane Mallarmé, with regard to the perfection of traditional forms, the intensity of the image, and the use of hyperbole; but if one considers the content, the poetry of Guillén is diametrically opposed to that of the symbolists. Mallarmé sought an artistic perfection that moved farther and farther from reality, and approached the states of silence and nothingness; it is the *rejection* of reality, of the here and now, that most characterizes his work. The poetry of Valéry is essentially philosophical, as in *Le cimetière marin*. Guillén hardly ever presents discursive ideas in the form of poems. Quite to the contrary, Guillén exalts real-

ity, lived experience, the sunlight, the day, and the air; the moment is a cause of wonder; and the intensity of living is what his poetry strives to express. This celebration of common things and of the moment is close, in many ways, to the spirit of William Carlos Williams, although Williams avoided the use of traditional poetic forms.

In France, Guillén began to write the poems of *Cántico*, specifically in the beach village of Tregastel, Brittany, in 1919, as he informs readers in the first pages of that book. It was there also that he met and married the Frenchwoman Germaine Cahen (in 1921); their first child, Teresa, was born in Paris (in 1922), as was their second and last, Claudio (in 1924), who became a professor of comparative literature at Harvard. By marriage and affinity Guillén became bicultural, Spanish-French, during those years and afterward. He was later to synthesize the importance

188

of France to him in this poem from *Y otros poemas* (And Other Poems, 1973):

Confusa juventud desorientada . . .
Ya es París, si no guía, gran teatro.
Allí yo me encontré ¿Con Quién? Conmigo:
Mi amor, mi profesión, mi poesía,
El hogar, la primera criatura.
Y salí de París por clara vía.

(A confused, disoriented youth . . .
But now Paris, if no guide, a great theater.
There I met up with Whom? Myself:
My love, my profession, my poetry,
A home, my first child.
And I left Paris through a bright path.)

Guillén received his doctorate in letters from the University of Madrid in 1924, and the following year he completed his examinations for a professorship in Spanish language and literature. It is worth noting that his doctoral dissertation was on Góngora, the master of a complex, metaphoric style, who became central to the Generation of 1927—a mock book-burning of works critical of Góngora was even held in Seville in 1927, an event which Guillén, characteristically, did not attend; he rejected some of the more extravagant antics of his contemporaries. Guillén became professor of Spanish Literature at the University of Murcia for four years (1926-1929) and always remembered with affection that city and the friends he made there. It was during the Murcia period that Guillén published the first edition of *Cántico* in Madrid with Revista de Occidente, whose chief editor was Ortega y Gasset. The 1928 edition has 75 poems and 171 pages; *Cántico* was to be expanded in three more editions; the 1950 complete version contains 334 poems and 540 pages. *Cántico* was his major work until the three-volume *Clamor* began to take shape in 1957.

From 1929 to 1931 Guillén occupied the position of lecturer at Oxford University, and in 1931 he went to teach at the University of Seville. The experience of Seville, the warmth and exuberance of Andalusia, of course affected the poetry of Guillén. The Andalusian landscape, with orange trees, jasmine, and lush verdure, can be noted in such 1936 *Cántico* poems as "Verde hacia un río" (Greenness Toward a River), "Jardín que fue de don Pedro" (Garden that Was Don Pedro's), and "Verdor es amor" (Verdure Is Love), all *décimas* (ten-line poems), written during Guillén's stay in Seville.

Guillén remained in Seville until 1938. With the ouster of the Bourbon king Alfonso XIII, the Second Spanish Republic had been proclaimed in 1931. Guillén, along with most other artists and intellectuals, publicly supported the nascent Republic; but the government was beset by conflicts and divisions, and the experiment in democracy ended with the Spanish Civil War (1936-1939). The Francisco Franco-led revolt against the Republic was bolstered militarily by the Nazis and the Italian fascists. Western democracies paid some lip-service to the Republican cause, but the Non-Intervention Pact of 1936 effectively ended outside aid, except for some arms from the Soviet Union. Soon after the outbreak of the civil war came the violent death of Lorca, shot in Granada by the Falangists; a close friend of Guillén, he was one of a multitude of innocent victims on both sides of the conflict. Guillén himself was temporarily imprisoned as an enemy of the insurgents in late 1936 and early 1937 in Pamplona.

The war and the Franco victory marked the end of one of the most splendid and intense periods in the history of Spanish poetry and the arts: Pablo Picasso, Pablo Casals, and Luis Buñuel became exiles, and the great majority of the poets—such as Guillén, Salinas, Alberti, Cernuda and León Felipe—also left Spain, while the few that remained (including Aleixandre, Dámaso Alonso, and Gerardo Diego) did so not out of adherence to fascism but for personal reasons, such as health in the case of Aleixandre. One of the most remarkable younger poets, Miguel Hernández (of the Generation of 1936) died of tuberculosis in a Francoist prison in 1942.

So Guillén came as an exile to the United States in 1938. He taught for a school year at Middlebury College in Vermont, followed by a year at McGill University in Montreal. From there in 1940 he went to Wellesley College in Massachusetts, where he was to remain until 1957. The many years he spent in Wellesley are treated in an essay by Justina Ruiz de Conde (in *Homenaje a Jorge Guillén*, 1978). His children grew up there; his wife suffered a long illness there until she returned to Paris and died in 1947. Guillén spent many years in difficult solitude, unaccustomed to the daily domestic tasks he had to perform for himself, but he was an exemplary and devoted teacher of Spanish and Latin American letters, according to Ruiz de Conde: "It must be said aloud that he carried out all of his duties of professor as if he were a common soldier of literature in our department." He sought no spe-

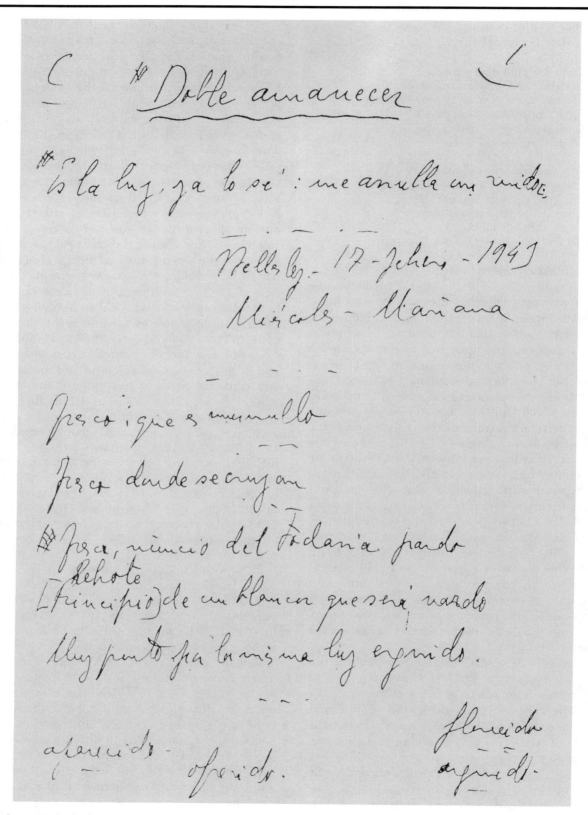

Pages from two drafts for "Amanece, amanezco" (It Dawns, I Dawn), the final version of which was published in the 1945 edition of Cántico *(by permission of the Estate of Jorge Guillén)*

C

38

Amanece, amanezca

Es la luz, aquí está: me arrulla un ruido,
Compañero del todavía pardo
Florecer de un blancor naciente, nardo
Para quien ya lo goza concebido.

Luz, luz... El resplandor es un latido.
Y se me desvanece con el tardo
Resto de oscuridad mi angustia, fardo
Nocturno entre las sombras bien hundido.

Pedro Salinas and Guillén in Middlebury, Vermont, summer 1950 (photograph by José Manuel Blecua)

cial privileges for himself, and he suffered immense indignation when the administration saw fit to terminate one of his junior colleagues. Although he was honored by the American Academy of Letters, and occupied the former chair of an American poet, Katherine Lee Bates (who had also taught at Wellesley), Guillén never became fully Americanized; he never lost his profound identity with Spain and Castile. In 1957, when he was offered the Charles Norton Eliot Poetry Chair at Harvard and was perplexed by the obligation to give a series of lectures in English, a colleague, Ella Keats Whiting, told him simply to "Be yourself," and the lectures, which were later published as *Language and Poetry* (1961), were a considerable success.

The Harvard appointment was for one year, and Guillén officially retired from Wellesley in 1958. During the following years he traveled widely in Europe and was a visiting professor at several universities, including that of Puerto Rico and the University of the Andes in Bogotá; while he was in Bogotá, in 1961, he met and married Irene Mochi Sismondi. During the 1960s he

spent extended periods in Italy and became attached to the Italian language and people; several of his books were published there. For many years he was unable to return to Spain because of his publication, in volume 1 of *Clamor*, of a long satire of Franco: "Potencia de Pérez" (Power of Pérez). When the dictator finally died in 1975, Guillén established permanent residence in Málaga, Spain, where he lived until his death. In 1977 he was awarded Spain's most important literary prize, the Premio Cervantes. Guillén died in Málaga on 8 February 1984, in the company of his family. According to an ABC News obituary on 14 February, "He died smiling and without losing his lucidity."

Cántico, as its name implies, is a hymn to being. The "I" of the poet is never exalted; his existence depends on the air, light, earth, and the presence of others. As Guillén writes in "Más allá" (Beyond): "Soy, más, estoy. Respiro. / Lo profundo es el aire. / La realidad me inventa. ¡Salve!" (I am; I am here and now. / I breathe the deepest air. / Reality invents me. / I am its legend. Hail!). The life-giving air is central to

Cántico, and Guillén's collected works would later receive the title of *Aire Nuestro* (Our Air, 1968). The poet sees himself as part of the complex harmony of nature that makes life on earth possible; the human being, the "I," while never superior to that nature, sings his love and appreciation of the world that has created him, and tries to grasp the essences of things: air, light, a walnut tabletop, a chair, a glass of water. Assuming the presence of health and peace, the air is deeply savored; the wind and the breeze fill the lungs and restore being. Together with the air is the continual presence of light. The poetry of *Cántico* is not of darkness, the unconscious, of the mysteries and ambiguities beloved by the symbolists: it is a poetry of clarity, of the conscious and palpable, of clear outlines and plenitude. There are few dreams in *Cántico*, although sleep is mentioned as a prelude to awakening and being. Light is everywhere and reveals, for example, the presence of the splendid feminine body. Light and whiteness imply ascension to higher forms of existence.

The plenitude of the universe is sensed as a sphere or circle, the most perfect of geometric forms. Most twentieth-century poets write from within the anguished self; in Guillén's work the world is seen as a perfect and harmonious sphere, and the "I" is at a center that is anywhere and everywhere. The *décima* called "Perfection" is perhaps the most complete statement of this worldview:

> Queda curvo el firmamento,
> Compacto azul, sobre el día.
> Es el redondeamiento
> del esplendor: mediodía.
> Todo es cúpula. Reposa,
> Central sin querer, la rosa,
> a un sol en cenit sujeta,
> Y tanto se da el presente
> Que el pie caminante siente
> La integridad del planeta.
>
> (The firmament is curved,
> Compact blue, over the day.
> Splendor's roundness: noon.
> All being is cupola.
> The rose, indifferent
> Center, rests, subject to the sun,
> And the present
> Gives of itself so freely
> That the treading foot senses
> The planet's integrity.)

The form of the *décima*, with its two quatrains and couplet in the center, is itself circular and per-

fect, a paradigm of the entire work. Guillén needed to use classical verse forms (the sonnet, *décima*, quatrain, and *redondilla*) to communicate his harmonious vision of the universe. His being is dependent upon all reality, and that reality is seen as symmetrical and spherical: "The *cogito* of Jorge Guillén," wrote Georges Poulet, "may be summed up thus: I am thanks to the air and the light, thanks to the revelation of a world whose admirable roundness is concentrated in me, just as my desire to embrace the sphere ascends in a circular fashion outside of myself " (in *Jorge Guillén*, edited by Birute Ciplijauskaité, 1975).

In the air and the light are the beloved objects that surround humankind and by means of which Guillén attempts to penetrate to the essences of things: the table, armchair, rose, glass of water, equestrian statue. In "Naturaleza viva" (Unstill Life) the walnut tabletop secretes within itself its past of wood and forest:

> ¡El nogal
> Confiado a sus nudos
> Y vetas, a su mucho
> Tiempo de potestad
> Reconcentrada en este
> Vigor inmóvil, hecho
> Materia de tablero
> Siempre, siempre silvestre!
>
> (The walnut confides
> In its knots and grain,
> In its long span of power,
> Concentrated in this
> Motionless vigor, become
> This tabletop, surface,
> Forever the forest!)

Sun, air, earth, sky, common objects, a summer's day with poplars, a city's streets, the love of a woman—all are joined in the harmonious, joyous, affirmative world of *Cántico*. Death is present, as it must be, but it is seen as part of a necessary symmetry, as in "Muerte a lo lejos" (Death in the Distance):

> Y un día entre los días el más triste
> Será. Tenderse deberá la mano
> Sin afán. Y acatando el inminente
> Poder diré sin lágrimas: embiste,
> Justa fatalidad. El muro cano
> Va a imponerme su ley, no su accidente.
>
> (And that will be the most sad among
> Days. Then let the hand offer and fall
> Without despair. And revering the imminent

Power I shall say without tears: come,
Just fatality. The white wall
Will impose on me its law, not its accident.)

The first (1928) edition of *Cántico* is divided
into seven sections, each of which reveals an exploration of a different classical verse form, including the quatrain, *décima*, *romance* (ballad), and stro-
phes of three and of five lines. The number *five*
seems to have a particular meaning for Guillén,
since the first part of *Cántico* is composed of
poems of five quatrains each; the complete
(1950) edition has five sections; and Guillén's entire oeuvre includes five major works: *Cántico*,
Clamor, *Homenaje* (Homage, 1967), *Y otros poemas*,
and *Aire Nuestro: Final* (1981).

Guillén slightly modified many of the
poems in *Cántico* with each successive edition,
and many of the initial poems, which appeared
at first in journals before 1928, were rewritten
for the first edition: "The changes effected on including these poems in *Cántico* emphasize the development of a personal style," according to Andrew Debicki. "We may observe how the poet
eliminates high-sounding words, suppresses the
anecdotal and circumstantial, but he points up,
on the other hand, the sensorial and dramatic impact of his poems, and also aims at more universal values."

The slight changes from edition to edition
may be illustrated by the poem "Advenimiento"
(Advent), which has a privileged position in the
first two editions, in which it is the initial poem;
in the second edition it is even set off from the
main body of the work. But in the third edition
(1945) it is the third poem, and in the 1950 edition in sixteenth place. There are few changes in
wording in the various editions, but the slight
changes in punctuation reveal a modification and
muting of the exclamatory quality of the first versions, creating a more meditative, less emotive tonality. The first two lines have a series of separated exclamations in the first three editions:
"¡Oh luna! ¡Cuánto abril! / ¡Qué vasto y dulce el
aire!" (Oh, moon! What presence of April! / How
vast and sweet the air!). But they are reduced to
a single statement in 1950: "¡Oh luna, cuánto
abril, / Qué vasto y dulce el aire!" Likewise, lines
15 and 16—"¡Arrebol, arrebol / entre el cielo y
las auras!" (Between the air and the sky / Clouds
incarnadine!)—lost their exclamation marks in
1950. A more significant change may be noted in
the sonnet "Muerte a lo lejos." The later versions
significantly change the words *con lágrimas* (with

tears) to *sin lágrimas* (without tears), in the final tercet, thus emphasizing the stoic acceptance of a future death.

The second edition of *Cántico* (1936) contains fifty additional poems; among them are two
long poems that are keystones of the completed
Cántico: "Más Allá" and the love poem "Salvación
de la primavera" (Salvation of Spring). The book
has five sections, and these two poems begin and
end the first section, called "Al aire de tu vuelo"
(In the Air of Your Flight), a quotation from
Saint John of the Cross. The second edition gives
the impression of a completed and harmonious
work, unlike the somewhat fragmented quality of
the 1928 volume. One critic, Jaime Gil de
Biedma, asserts that the great achievement of
Cántico is already present in the 1936 edition,
and he feels that the greatly augmented editions
of 1945 and 1950 do not add that much to the
splendor of *Cántico*. He may be right in the sense
that the reader tends to lose the overall vision in
the 270 poems of the 1945 version and the 334
in 1950; yet there is undoubtedly an enrichment
in the later editions.

"Más allá" sets the tone of the entire
Cántico, and, from 1936 on, it appears in the initial position, the cornerstone of the work. It contains six parts and fifty assonantal quatrains and
is a poem of awakening, of emerging from the
chaos and the half-death of sleep to morning,
light, and life. It expresses the childlike wonder
at the miracle of life that is at the heart of
Cántico. It is about the rebirth people experience
each morning. Air, light, being, joy, and the moment, the now—the major themes of *Cántico*—
are all present. The first part begins with light
and awakening:

(El alma vuelve al cuerpo,
Se dirige a los ojos
y choca.)—¡Luz! Me invade
Todo mi ser. ¡Asombro!

([Returning to the flesh, the soul
veers toward the eyes
and strikes.]—Light! It floods
all my being. Wonder!)

In the last stanza of the first part, the great
Guillénian themes of air and man's dependence
on nature emerge: "Soy, más, estoy, Respiro. / Lo
profundo es el aire" (I am; I am here and now. /
I breathe the deepest air). Guillén's poetic vision
is far removed from romantic subjectivity. He *de-*

pends on things; humankind is part of objective reality.

"Salvación de la primavera" is the major love poem of *Cántico*, and one of the great poems of love in the Spanish language. Love, then, in all of its mystery and plenitude, is added to the dominant themes of *Cántico*. Like "Más allá," "Salvación de la primavera" is a long poem; it has nine sections, all in assonantal quatrains. Physical love is celebrated, yet it is a love that, in its rapture, allows the soul to go beyond itself: "¿Irá cruzando el alma / Por limbos sin estorbo?" (Does the soul go on crossing / its limbos unhindered?). It is a love related to the mystical rapture of Saint John of the Cross, as well as the soul's journey in the romantic poetry of Gustavo Adolfo Bécquer (which Guillén wrote about in 1943). The culmination of the sexual act is clearly alluded to:

Y acuden, se abalanzan
clamando las respuestas.
¿Ya inminente el arrobo?
¡Dúrase la inminencia!

(And our answers are discovered,
Flinging themselves jubilantly.
Is an ecstasy imminent?
May that imminence last!)

At the end of the poem, the speaker's devotion to and fulfillment in the loved one is triumphantly expressed:

¡Tú, tú, tú, mi incesante
Primavera profunda,
Mi río de verdor
Agudo y aventura!

(You, you my incessant
Profound Springtime,
My river of bright verdure
And adventure!)

The third edition of *Cántico* appeared after the horrors of the Spanish Civil War and World War II. The basic form of the 1936 *Cántico*, with its five sections, is preserved; the essential character of *Cántico* as a celebration of life is also preserved. Although history and suffering begin to intrude, those poems that allude specifically to historical and social problems were to be assembled in *Clamor*. But his compilation *Aire Nuestro* has a fundamental unity, and there is no complete break between *Cántico* and *Clamor*. If it is true that *Cántico* tends toward poetic purity and an af-

firmative, joyous view of life and that *Clamor* emphasizes social criticism, it is also true that, beginning with the 1945 *Cántico*, one finds moments of anguish and disillusionment, although they remain in the background as minor, subdued themes. Such moments are in the poems "Los balcones del Oriente" (The Balconies Facing the East) and the final poem, "Cara a cara" (Face to Face).

"Los balcones del Oriente," with its title taken from Cervantes, is a description of the chaos and disquietudes of civilization:

Con una luz casi fea,
El sol—triste
De afrontar una jornada
Tan burlada—
Principia mal su tarea.
Y tanta sombra persiste
Que la luz se siente rea
De traición al nuevo día.

(With an almost ugly light,
The sun—sad
At having to confront such a
Mistaken day—
begins its task badly.
And the shadows persist so long
That the light feels guilty
Of betraying the new day.)

"Cara a cara" affirms Guillén's faith in life, but it foreshadows the social poetry of *Clamor* in its assertion of the speaker's readiness to assume responsibility for the world's ills, in his confronting "face to face" the manifestations of evil that beset modern man:

Heme ante la realidad
Cara a cara. No me escondo,
Sigo en mis trece. Ni cedo
Ni cederé, siempre atónito.

(Here I remain,
Face to face with reality. I do not hide,
I stubbornly persevere. I cede not,
Nor shall I surrender, always astonished.)

Among the noteworthy additions to the 1945 *Cántico* are the love poem "Anillo" (Ring) and "Más vida" (More Life), a celebration of birth and the continuation of life. In "Más vida" human love is transformed into the child, the son, "figura de mi amor bajo el sol" (image of my love beneath the sun). The speaker envisions a kind of immortality, the consolation of a continu-

Guillén circa 1965

ity provided by procreation and succeeding generations:

> A través de tus horas, sin descanso
> Más allá de la muerte,
> Hasta el año 2000 he de llegar
> Calladamente.

> (Across your hours, without repose
> Beyond death,
> I will touch the next century
> Quietly.)

In the first complete edition of *Cántico* (1950) the major themes of light, air, and love of course persist; one long poem, "Luz natal" (Native Light), is a description of the hills and atmosphere that surround Guillén's native Valladolid. Yet there is a subtle shift of emphasis. There are more purely domestic poems, about family, children, and grandchildren, such as "Familia" (Family), "He aquí la persona" (Behold the Person), and "Infante" (Infant). The surrounding chaos and the threat of destruction and nothingness—as in several poems of the third section, "Aquí mismo" (Right Here)—become subthemes that almost threaten, but do not overwhelm, the joyous affirmation at the core of *Cántico*. "Estación del norte" (North Station) is one of the most gloomy and pessimistic poems:

> Pero la brutal baraúnda,
> esa muchedumbre que inunda
> Nuestra común desolación. . . .
> ¿Tan turbia es nuestra incertidumbre
> Que ni un rayo habrá que la alumbre?
> El mundo se inclina a su muerte.

> (But the brutal tumult,
> That mob which innundates our common desola-
>   tion. . . .
> Is our uncertainty so sombre

That no ray of light brightens it?
The world moves toward its death.)

The final *Cántico* is dedicated to Pedro Salinas: "Amigo perfecto, que entre tantas vicisitudes, durante muchos años, ha querido y sabido iluminar con su atención la marcha de esta obra" (Perfect friend, who among so many vicissitudes, during many years, has known how to illuminate with his attention the progress of this work.)

Guillén's next major work, *Clamor*, was to appear in three parts: *Maremágnum* (Confusion, 1957), *Que van a dar en la mar* (That Will End Up in the Sea, 1960), and *A la altura de las circunstancias* (To Rise to the Occasion, 1963). *Cántico* incarnated the search for beauty, for the eternal moment, and for order and symmetry in the universe; in *Clamor* the search for order has not been abandoned, but it is often overshadowed by the poet's concern for his fellowman and a strife-tormented world. Especially in *Maremágnum* there is a poetry of commitment to the struggle for human dignity, survival, and essential worth. Each of the other two parts of the trilogy has its own character: in *Que van a dar en la mar* there predominates a prolonged meditation on death; *A la altura de las circunstancias* is a transitional work that combines the social criticism of *Maremágnum* with the affirmation of *Cántico*, and anticipates the personal reminiscences and ironic commentaries of *Homenaje*.

In *Maremágnum* the "pure poetry" of *Cántico* has been abandoned. There are politics, history, ideas, social criticism, and indignation at the world's evils. Guillén sacrificed purity to the exigencies of survival, to the "clamor" of a world that was in turmoil and accomplishing its own destruction. The title *Maremágnum* refers to a confused mass of persons and things, precisely the opposite of that harmony sought in *Cántico*. The form tends to be much freer: although the *décimas* and quatrains have not disappeared entirely, there is an abundance of free verse and poems in prose. The book's greatest single preoccupation is atomic suicide. In the long poem "Guerra en la paz" (War in Peace) the speaker contemplates the extraordinary fact that humanity is threatened with destruction yet unwilling to revolt against the almost anonymous direction of a few leaders. Poems such as ". . . Que no" (. . . Not That), "La 'U' maléfica" (The Malevolent "U"), "Nada importaría nada" (Not at All), and "Aire con época" (Air of Our Time) also explore this threat and paradox.

The long poem "Potencia de Pérez" is a clear condemnation of Franco and his regime. The dictator knew he was alluded to, and Guillén was unable to return to Spain until after Franco's death. Pérez is a common name, like Smith, that suggests the commonness, the vulgarity, of the *caudillo* (leader). The poem employs irony and sarcasm in its attacks on the several social classes that constituted the bulwark of support for Spanish fascism: the bureaucracy, the police, the party (Falange), and the clergy. Franco is presented as having built his regime on the bodies of thousands of dead:

Ahí,
céntrico ahí, perdura.
¡Cuántos le necesitan y le inventan!
Que mande
Sosteniendo aquel Orden: su desorden,
Sus bandos,
sus chanchullos patrióticos.
La tiranía avanza
con excluyente fuerza
Sobre miles y miles de caídos
Por ley de asesinato,
Entre las muchedumbres
De boca amordazada.
Dogma, sangre, dinero,
Y Pérez, Pérez, Pérez.

(There,
In the center, he persists.
How many need him and invent him!
Let him rule,
Maintaining that Order: his disorder,
His edicts,
His patriotic corruptions.
The tyranny advances
With exclusive force
Over thousands and thousands of the fallen
By law of assassination,
Among the silent
And gagged masses.
Dogma, blood, money,
And Pérez, Pérez, Pérez.)

Another social theme, racial discrimination in the United States, is the subject of the brief and powerful "El niño negro" (The Black Child):

Jugaban en la plazoleta
Con una alegría de asueto,
Violentamente menores,
Las turbas solares: chicuelos.
¡Cómo hacia la luz resaltaba,
condenado de nacimiento. . . !

(The street crowd,
Violently minor,
Played in the square,
With the joy of midday respite.
How he stood out against the light,
By birth condemned. . . !)

Another innovation of *Maremágnum* are the *tréboles* (clover leaves)—brief, ironic, gnomic poems, usually of three or four rhymed verses in the tradition of the fourteenth-century writer Rabbi Sem Tob and of Antonio Machado's "Proverbios" (in *Campos de Castilla*, 1912)—which may comment on anything from a girl's beauty, the perfidy of an acquaintance, or Franco's murdered thousands, to an admonition to his own critics: "Erudito: ¿por qué me explotas? / ¿Mis cielos se encuentran abajo, / Por entre esas nubes de notas?" (Why do you exploit me, learned dolt? / Is my heaven found down there, / Among those fuzzy clouds of notes?) Guillén was to continue to cultivate the "clover leaves" in the two other volumes of *Clamor* and was to publish a collection of this style of poetry (*Tréboles*) in 1964.

The themes of death and memory dominate *Que van a dar en la mar*, the second part of *Clamor*. The title is from a famous metaphor of the fifteenth-century poet Jorge Manrique: "Nuestros vidas son los ríos / que van a dar en la mar / que es el morir" (Our lives are rivers that will end up in the sea, which is death.) In *Jorge Guillén* (1982) Grant MacCurdy comments, regarding this second volume, that Guillén "meditates openly on the passage of time in his own life and future demise, and the personal feelings of loss resulting from the death of his first wife, Germaine." The theme of death was not absent from *Cántico* but in *Que van a dar en la mar* it is personalized, less abstract. Memories of Guillén's childhood are to be found frequently in poems such as "Aquellas ropas chapadas" (That Ancient Finery), "Patio de San Gregorio," and "Del trascurso" (Of the Passing). "Del transcurso" perhaps best sums up the meditative and gently sad mood of this collection: "Ante los ojos, mientras, el futuro / se me adelgaza delicadamente, / Más difícil, más frágil, más escaso" (Meanwhile, before my eyes, my future wanes, / Thins and dwindles delicately, / More difficult, more fragile, more spare).

A la altura de las circunstancias, the final volume of *Clamor*, returns to the joyous mood of *Cántico* without abandoning the anecdotal and meditative qualities of the first two volumes. It represents, in a sense, a synthesis of all Guillén's previ-

ous books. The overriding tone is one of faith in the future of Europe and of humanity. His poems include "Afirmación humana" (Human Affirmation)—based on the splendid spirit of Anne Frank, whose poignant diary survived the Holocaust—and "Despertar español" (Spanish Awakening), a long meditation on the meaning of Spain and Guillén's faith in its survival. In spite of the errors and afflictions of Spain's history, the speaker in "Despertar español" sees a possible future plenitude, tied to his personal realization that may only occur through language: "A través de un idioma / ¿Yo podría llegar a ser el hombre / Por fin humano a que mi esfuerzo tiende / Bajo este sol de todos?" (With the aid of my language / Could I aspire to be that man / At last human toward whom my hand reaches / Beneath this common sun?) At the end the speaker proclaims his passion for Spain: "Y no me apartarán vicisitudes / De la fortuna varia. / ¡Tierno apego sin término! / Blanco muro de España, verdadera: / Nuestro pacto es enlace de verdad" (And vicissitudes of fortune / Will not separate me. / Tender, endless passion! / White wall of Spain, exact Spain: / Our pact the truest union).

The mood changes once again in *Homenaje*, whose significant subtitle is *Reunión de vidas* (A Meeting of Lives). An epigraph states: "Fechas principales, 1949 a 1966" (Principal dates, 1949 to 1966), which clearly indicates that the collection was written not after but during the writing of *Clamor*. The title, *Homenaje*, refers in part to the scores of poems that comment on well-known writers of several nations and languages, of classical antiquity, and the Spanish Golden Age. These poems are grouped under the heading "Al margen de . . ." (On the margin of . . .), as if they were written on the margins of the original works concerned. They are poems of homage and appreciation, although an occasional satirical note is sounded. Other poems, also of homage but of a more personal nature, are dedicated to deceased friends, among them the poets José Moreno Villa, Salinas, and Lorca. There is a collection of translations, called "Variations," that Guillén made over the years, from Valéry, Rainer Rilke, Saint-John Perse, Ezra Pound, Eugenio Montale, and others. There are personal poems dedicated to his children and grandchildren, and there are even actual letters in the form of poems. This "meeting of lives" includes some of Guillén's best and most serene love poetry, such as the long "Amor a Silvia" at the work's center.

Jorge and Irene Guillén in Málaga, 1977 (photograph by Colita)

Discussing *Homenaje*, MacCurdy speaks of "the three [love poetry] modes that Guillén favors: the spiritualization of love, the inner illumination derived from the feminine image, and the manner in which the image of woman determines in part the poet's vision of external reality (*Jorge Guillén*). This poetry is more explicitly erotic than Guillén's previous love poetry, although the erotic is always transfigured into a deeper realization of the self. There are also homages to countries, especially Italy and Greece. Social criticism is mostly set aside, and the joy of *Cántico* returns in these evocations of persons and places.

Y otros poemas, his next major book, is the most difficult to characterize of Guillén's works. One finds political satire and indignation over injustice that recall *Maremágnum*; some poems touch on the horrors of slavery and of discrimination in American society; others comment satirically, or with anger, on war, consumerism, and the threat of nuclear holocaust. A group of poems—"Arte rupestre" (Rupestrine [Cave] Art) —refer, with irony, ire, or bitterness, to the outcome of the Spanish Civil War and the Franco dictatorship. The section "De Senectute" (Of Old Age) contains nostalgic and melancholic observations on old age. But perhaps the quality that most distinguishes the book from his other works may be termed "metapoetry": poems about poetic creation. Philosophical, ironic, and passionate are the brief meditations on poetry in the part called "Res poética" (Poetic Thing). At times Guillén comments on his own work, at times on the process of creation in others. He rails against the obscurity of much modern poetry and calls for the clarity he knew in Old Castile: "Dame la palabra, Castilla, / Que la luz del sol se desnuda" (Give me your word, Castile, / Which is revealed in the sun's light). His faith in poetry, as an expression of wonder at the miracle of existence, is affirmed in this brief definition:

¿Qué es poesía? No sé.
Una existe que yo nombro
Ars vivendi, Ars amandi:
Sentimiento aún de asombro
Que resplandece con fe.

(What is poetry? I do not know.

One type exists that I call
The art of living, the art of loving.
Still a feeling of wonder
That radiates with faith.)

Aire Nuestro: Final, written during Guillen's eighties, is pervaded by the serene acceptance of old age, the inevitability of death, and the continuing affirmation of life. Yet the passionate indignation at social injustice has not been silenced by age: there are poems about Franco, Auschwitz, war, man's inhumanity to man, the death of Allende, and the counterrevolution and massacre in Chile, but also there is confidence in Spain's struggling democracy. One encounters more glosses of other writers, translations (of Shlomo Ibn Gabirol, Poliziano, Cecilia Meireles, and others), and poems about the art of poetry.

The calm acceptance of death, so eloquently stated in *Cántico* ("Muerte a lo lejos"), in *Aire Nuestro: Final* includes a paradoxical mixture of an almost Olympian detachment along with a commitment to life's values and struggles. The sun, the awakening, love (of woman, family, and grandchildren) are still in the poet's thoughts. Old age is a reality: death is on the horizon; but Guillén's vitality is not extinguished by his age and is still apparent in this untitled poem:

No se ve ni se siente viejo el viejo
Cuando prorrumpe de su ser un ímpetu
Que dispara sus labios y sus brazos.
Prosigue el yo de vida ahora joven,
No el de aquel mozo desaparecido.
He ahí los deseos—bajo tiempo
Que pesa.

(The old man neither feels old nor sees himself so.
When an impulse, thrust from his lips or arms,
Breaks forth from his being.
The "I" of an always-young life,
Not that of a vanished lad, endures.
The desires are there—beneath
An oppressive time.)

Jorge Guillén left, at his death, some exemplary work and an exemplary life. Absolutely devoted to his art, he did not neglect society's ills. Today's writers and readers have much to learn from him, both with regard to the art of poetry and the art of life.

Interviews:

Claude Couffon, *Dos encuentros con Jorge Guillén* (Paris: Centre de Recherches de l'Institut d'Etudes Hispaniques, 1963);

Guillén on Guillén: The Poetry and the Poet, translated by Reginald Gibbons and Anthony L. Geist (Princeton, N.J.: Princeton University Press, 1979).

References:

Manuel Alvar, *Visión en claridad: Estudio sobre Cántico* (Madrid: Gredos, 1976);

Antonio Blanch, *La poesía pura española: Conexiones con la cultura francesa* (Madrid: Gredos, 1976);

María del Carmen Bobes Naves, *Gramática de "Cántico": Análisis semiológico* (Barcelona: Planeta, 1975);

Joaquín Casalduero, *"Cántico" de Jorge Guillén y "Aire Nuestro"* (Madrid: Gredos, 1974);

Biruté Ciplijauskaité, *Deber de plenitud: La poesía de Jorge Guillén* (Mexico City: SepSetentas, 1973);

Ciplijauskaité, ed., *Jorge Guillén* (Madrid: Taurus, 1975);

Pierre Darmangeat, *Antonio Machado, Pedro Salinas, Jorge Guillén* (Madrid: Insula, 1969);

Andrew Debicki, *La poesía de Jorge Guillén* (Madrid: Gredos, 1973);

Elsa Dehennin, *Cántico de Jorge Guillén: Une poésie de la clarté* (Brussels: University Press of Brussels, 1969);

Jaime Gil de Biedma, *Cántico: El mundo y la poesía de Jorge Guillén* (Barcelona: Seix Barral, 1960);

Joaquín González Muela, *La realidad y Jorge Guillén* (Madrid: Insula, 1962);

Ricardo Gullón and José Manuel Blecua, *La poesía de Jorge Guillén* (Zaragoza, Spain: Heraldo de Aragón, 1949);

Robert J. Havard, "The Early Décimas of Jorge Guillén," *Bulletin of Hispanic Studies*, 48 (1971): 111-127;

Ivar Ivask and Juan Marichal, eds., *Luminous Reality: The Poetry of Jorge Guillén* (Norman: University of Oklahoma Press, 1969);

Grant MacCurdy, "The Erotic Poetry of Jorge Guillén's *Homenaje*," *Hispania*, 65 (December 1982): 586-593;

MacCurdy, *Jorge Guillén* (Boston: Twayne, 1982);

Archibald MacLeish, "Jorge Guillén: A Poet of This Time," *Atlantic Monthly* (January 1961): 127-129;

Oreste Macri, *La obra poética de Jorge Guillén* (Barcelona: Ariel, 1976);

Martha LaFollette Miller, "Transcendence Through Love in Jorge Guillén's *Cántico*: The Conciliation of Inner and Outer Reality," *Modern Language Notes*, 92 (1977): 312-325;

C. B. Morris, *A Generation of Spanish Poets, 1920-36* (Cambridge: Cambridge University Press, 1969);

Julian Palley, "Jorge Guillén and the Poetry of Commitment," *Hispania*, 45 (1962): 689-691;

Palley, "The Metaphors of Jorge Guillén," *Hispania*, 36 (1953): 321-324;

Frances Avery Pleak, *The Poetry of Jorge Guillén* (Princeton, N.J.,: Princeton University Press, 1942);

José Manuel Polo de Bernabé, *Conciencia y lenguaje en la poesía de Jorge Guillén* (Madrid: Nacional, 1977);

Georges Poulet, *The Metamorphoses of the Circle* (Bal-timore: Johns Hopkins University Press, 1966);

Ignacio Prat, *"Aire Nuestro" de Jorge Guillén* (Barcelona: Planeta, 1974);

Justina Ruiz de Conde, *El cántico americano de Jorge Guillén* (Madrid: Turner, 1973);

Ruiz de Conde and others, eds., *Homenaje a Jorge Guillén* (Madrid: Insula, 1978);

Robert J. Weber, "De *Cántico* a *Clamor*," *Revista Hispánica Moderna*, 29 (1963): 109-119;

C. M. Wilson, "Modern Spanish Poems: J. Guillén and Quevedo on Death," *Atlante*, 1 (1953): 22-26;

Concha Zardoya, *Poesía española del siglo XX: Estudios temáticos y estilísticos*, volume 2 (Madrid: Gredos, 1974).

José Luis Hidalgo

(10 October 1919 - 3 February 1947)

Noël Valis
University of Michigan

BOOKS: *Raíz* (Valencia, Spain: Cosmos, 1944);
Los animales (Santander, Spain: Proel, 1945);
Los muertos (Madrid: Uguina/Adonais, 1947; revised edition, Torrelavega, Spain: Cantalapiedra, 1954); further revised and enlarged by Jorge Campos (Madrid: Taurus, 1966);
Canciones para niños (Nanas) (Torrelavega, Spain: Cantalapiedra, 1951);
Antología poética, edited by Julia Uceda (Madrid: Aguilar, 1970);
Obra poética completa, edited by María de Gracia Ifach (Santander, Spain: Institución Cultural de Cantabria, 1976).

OTHER: Arturo del Villar, "Ocho poemas inéditos de José Luis Hidalgo," includes eight poems by Hidalgo, *Papeles de Son Armadans*, 64 (December 1971): 293-327.

One can best approach José Luis Hidalgo and his poetry from the moment of his death and work one's way backward to his beginnings, for Hidalgo was the supreme poet of death. His dying at the age of twenty-seven in a Madrid sanatorium fosters a romantic vision of a young poet tragically foretelling his own death in a book of poems, *Los Muertos* (The Dead, 1947). If it were true, the task of putting Hidalgo in his proper place in modern Spanish poetry would be easier. One could imagine him the twentieth-century literary offspring of nineteenth-century poet Gustavo Adolfo Bécquer, whose influence vibrates in Hidalgo's work.

Yet the moving if sometimes angry meditation on death that constitutes Hidalgo's greatest work, *Los muertos*, was not composed in his dying hours, nor does it reflect some extrasensorial prescience on the writer's part in prophesying his own death. Indeed, Hidalgo, in the years he was creating the small but powerful corpus of the fifty-six poems in the first edition of *Los muertos*, felt infused with the light and energy of life. As his good friend and biographer, Aurelio García Cantalapiedra, says: "*Los muertos* no es el libro de

un enfermo que se siente morir; es, más bien, el libro de un hombre que se encuentra muy sano, de cuerpo y mente, y que desarrolla en sus poemas una teoría completa sobre Dios, la muerte y la externidad" (*Los muertos* is not the book of a sick man who knows he is dying; it is, rather, the book of a man who finds himself to be healthy, in body and mind, and who will develop in his poetry a complete theory about God, death, and eternity).

Unfortunately the myth of José Luis Hidalgo the man has sometimes obscured the true worth of his poetry. It is doubly ironic that this should be so, given the fact that it has been largely due to his friends' well-intentioned efforts to put Hidalgo on the poetic map by eulogizing his last moments on earth. In the process they have unwittingly contributed to the creation of that myth of the tragic, young poet dying soon after his prophecies of death.

One can better understand the special position of *Los muertos* in twentieth-century Spanish poetry by referring to the literary context in which the work was conceived. When Hidalgo started working on the poems in 1943, the dominant poetic trend was a return to more classic forms of verse, vaguely inspired by such Renaissance poets as Garcilaso de la Vega and frequently religious in tone and sentiment. While some fine poets—including José García Nieto and Vicente Gaos—were classified as *garcilasistas*, at its worst such poetry could be insipid, excessively rhetorical, and, perhaps most damaging, essentially evasive, because it did not come to grips with the harsh realities of post-civil-war Spain.

Hidalgo's work goes against this fashionable current and participates in what would be called a renewed humanization of modern Spanish poetry. Along with José Hierro, Ricardo Juan Blasco, Jorge Campos, Julio Maruri, he was a member of a group of poets Hierro designated as "La Quinta del 42" (The Draftees of 1942), and some critics have termed them the *proelistas*, referring to the fact that they were regular contributors to

José Luis Hidalgo, 1946 (painting by Ricardo Zamorano; from Rafael Millán, Veinte poetas españoles, *1955)*

Proel (1944-1950), one of the most significant poetry journals of the period. Mostly natives of Santander, in the north of Spain, they were also closely associated with another influential literary magazine of the 1940s, *Corcel* (1942-1949). In a 1939 letter to Hierro, a friend since childhood, Hidalgo anticipated the move toward a more humanizing poetry (as quoted by Hierro in *Verso y prosa en torno a José Luis Hidalgo* [Verse and Prose Concerning José Luis Hidalgo], edited by Cantalapiedra, 1971): "Valbuena [Prat] cree, con nosotros, que la poesía, después de la guerra, debe tender a una mayor humanización, pero él le da una dirección religiosa. En lo demás,

completamente de acuerdo" (Valbuena [Prat] believes, like us, that poetry after the war ought to tend toward a greater humanization, but he gives it a religious bent. In everything else, though, I am in complete agreement).

Los muertos, in particular, embodies the emphasis on poetry as, above all, a human endeavor. It was not, however, completely understood or appreciated in the 1940s and the years immediately following, when socially oriented poetry, the poetry of overt protest, became popular. Later, though, the book secured for Hidalgo a modest but firm place in the Spanish poetry of the post-civil-war period.

How did Hidalgo come to write as obsessively as he did on the theme of death? What circumstances, exterior and interior, created the kind of poetry he produced in *Raíz* (Root, 1944), *Los animales* (The Animals, 1945), and *Los muertos*?

Hidalgo was born on 10 October 1919 in Torres, Torrelavega, Spain, near Santander. He was the son of Josefa Iglesias González and César Hidalgo Ceballos, a newspaper writer. The young Hidalgo's childhood was melancholy, judging from some notes of his (quoted by Julia Uceda in her introduction to his *Antología poética*, 1970): "Yo fui un niño triste y dolorosamente sensible. Entre las nieblas de mis recuerdos de infancia, todas las sensaciones que logro vislumbrar son pequeñas heridas producidas en mi alma, las más de las veces por sucesos nimios y sin importancia aparente. Por el contrario, los grandes hechos verdaderamente dolorosos que sufrí pasaron inadvertidos para mí. Vivía un mundo concentrado, intenso: estaba siempre metido en mí mismo, sólo algunas *aristas* de la realidad lograban rozarme, *pero siempre de una manera dolorosa*" (I was an unhappy and painfully sensitive child. Hidden in the mist of my childhood memories, all the sensations that I am still able to glimpse are tiny wounds formed in my heart, brought on for the most part by trivial things, without any apparent significance. In contrast, the truly painful and important events that I suffered passed by unnoticed by me. I lived in a concentrated, intense world: I was always sunk inside myself, only a few *grains* of reality succeeded in rubbing against me, *but always in the most painful way*).

Hidalgo was an inward-looking, grave child, and the loss of his mother in 1929, when he was only nine years old, must have reinforced his sense of having been abandoned on a large and inhospitable planet. "Sí, te fuiste, te fuiste, me dejaste aquí solo / tristemente viviendo . . ." (Yes, you went away, you went away, you left me here alone / living in sadness . . .), he writes in "A mi madre muerta" (To My Dead Mother), in *Los muertos*.

From childhood on, Hidalgo concentrated on his intense inner life to such a degree that Vicente Aleixandre was to say of him in *Los encuentros* (Encounters, 1958): "Nunca la seriedad de la materia ha tenido tanta representación como en aquella figura, cuya voz se esperaba que tuviera resonancias de cueva, de cueva en piedra pura y adusta" (Never has material seriousness had such representation as in that figure, whose voice one expected to have the resonances of a cave, a cave of pure and austere stone). Yet there was tenderness and even a subtle, ironic sense of humor behind Hidalgo's gravity.

Besides poetry, he had two lifelong passions: reading and drawing. He haunted the public library of Torrelavega, which opened on 13 November 1927, and he hungrily absorbed every book he could lay his hands on: the works of philosophers such as Plato, Friedrich Nietzsche, José Ortega y Gasset, and Miguel de Unamuno; Spanish Golden Age classics by Santa Teresa de Jesús, Francisco de Quevedo, and Luis de Góngora; poetry by the Generation of 1898; intellectually significant journals such as *Revista de Occidente* and *Cruz y Raya*; and especially Gerardo Diego's 1932 *Antología* containing modern Spanish poetry. Reading Hidalgo's early work, some of which would appear in *Raíz*, one hears echoes of other poets, particularly (and not surprisingly) those in the Generation of 1927—including Aleixandre, Diego, Rafael Alberti, and Federico García Lorca.

Hidalgo's first piece of published writing, however, was not verse but prose. Appearing in Torrelavega's only weekly newspaper, *El Impulsor*, on 12 August 1934, his "Dos Ideas" (Two Ideas) is a rather abstract dialogue between matter and spirit. Its author was fourteen years old. Later, on 24 March 1935, he published in the same local paper twelve *greguerías*, (aphoristic verses) in the style of Ramón Gómez de la Serna, who had invented the terse and metaphorical minigenre before World War I. Hidalgo's predilection for the exaggerated art of the *greguería*—as in this one: "Cuando un hombre quiña un ojo, siempre hace crecer el otro" (When a man winks an eye, he always makes the other one grow larger) —parallels another interest of Hidalgo's: poster art and caricatures. Indeed, beginning in the mid 1930s, he devoted much of his energy equally to painting and drawing, and writing poetry. His first poem, "Noche" (Night), heavily influenced by Lorca, was published in *El Impulsor* on 14 July 1935, and his first show of posters and drawings was on 12 January 1936 at the Torrelavega Biblioteca Popular. Also in 1936 he collected his poetry in a manuscript entitled "Pseudopoesías" (Pseudopoetry), which, except for some poems later incorporated into *Raíz*, was never published during the poet's lifetime. These later appeared in the *Obra poética completa* (1976), edited by María de Gracia Ifach. (The same is true for other manuscripts, such as "Las luces asesinadas

Hidalgo (right) with his close friend and fellow poet José Hierro

y otros poemas" [Murdered Lights and Other Poems, 1936], "Mensaje hasta el aire" [Message as Far as the Air, 1938], and "Ciudad" [City, 1938].)

Until the Spanish Civil War, Hidalgo was only a local success. Growing up in a small town, with few cultural and intellectual resources, he had, with his indomitable will and tenacity, managed to educate and prepare himself for the arduous craft of the poet. The war deepened and universalized his experience of life, and it left him with an image of destruction so total and absolute that he could barely even talk about it. The 18 July 1936 uprising caught him in Barcelona, where he had gone to participate, as an artist, in the Olimpíada Popular. After he returned to Torrelavega, he became an instructor of drawing at the Instituto de Enseñanza Media in 1937. That same year he wrote his *Canciones para niños* (Songs for Children), a handful of lullabies his friend Cantalapiedra published in 1951. During the last months of 1937 Hidalgo was very active, writing several of the poems for *Raíz* and deepening his friendship with Hierro. But by 1938 he had been mobilized (by force) into the Falangist army and was to see action at the front in Extremadura and Córdoba. The end of the war found him in Valencia, where he formally began to study painting and drawing at the Escuela de Bellas Artes de San Carlos.

He was officially released from military service on 20 April 1942, but not before he was entrusted with one more official duty: the transfer of two political prisoners to Madrid. This episode in his life illustrates his integrity and generosity. At first he was terribly nervous, thinking the prisoners might escape, but after spending several hours in good company with them on the train, his fears subsided. By the time they arrived at the Madrid station, Hidalgo simply took out twenty-five pesetas, gave them to the men, and said: "Supongo que no tendréis dinero. Tomad esto y daros una vuelta por ahí; pero aquí a las siete, que es la hora en que tengo que entregaros" (I suppose you don't have any money. Take this and enjoy yourselves, but be back by seven, when I have to hand you over). The prisoners were dumbfounded. All along they had been planning their escape, but they were there at seven sharp, waiting for Hidalgo in the appointed place.

In the summer of 1942 in Valencia he became associated with a group of artists and writers, led by Campos, Blasco, and Pedro Caba. They met as a *tertulia* (literary circle) at the Galicia Bar. One night he read them some of his poetry, including "Hay que bajar" (You Must Go Down), one of his finest pieces from *Raíz*. It so enthused his listeners that they quickly realized it was time to declare themselves as poets of a new style of writing, infused with the human and natural in tone: no more artificiality, but always art; no mere words—or as Hidalgo himself would declare (quoted by Blasco in his *Escritos sobre José Luis Hidalgo*, 1956): "Y que por más vueltas que se le dé, la poesía se hace con pasión, más o menos contenida, pero con pasión al fin. Y que cada día me revienta más aquella frase de [Stéphane] Mallarmé cuando aseguraba que 'la poesía se hace con palabras'" (No matter what you say, poetry is written with passion, more or less restrained, but passion nevertheless. Every day that phrase of [Stéphane] Mallarmé's bothers me more and more, when he assured us that "poetry is made with words"). Elsewhere Hidalgo also says that poetry is not and cannot be logical, and that the roots of poetry are metaphor and emotion (as reported by Hierro in *Verso y prosa en torno a José Luis Hidalgo*).

Undoubtedly some of his thinking reflects the influence of the surrealists, traces of which are visible in *Raíz*. Hidalgo submitted the manuscript to the Adonais competition in Madrid and received an honorable mention for it. Consisting of a selection written between 1935 and 1943, *Raíz* was published under the Valencian imprint Cosmos at Hidalgo's own expense. With only five hundred copies circulated, today it is a rare edition. In many ways it is an apprentice product, still shining with the influences of other poets and his eclectic readings. But at the same time, as Arturo del Villar has noted, in *Poesía Española* (November 1969), it anticipates *Los muertos*, with its emphasis on death, light, and eternity, and is in its own right an interesting book.

Raíz, unfortunately, coincided with the publication in 1944 of two fundamental books of the post-civil-war period: *Hijos de la ira* (Children of Wrath) by Dámaso Alonso and *Sombra del paraíso* (Shadow of Paradise) by Aleixandre. Still, despite being rather overshadowed by these giants, *Raíz* did receive some critical attention. The anonymous *Espadaña* reviewer, for example, saw in *Raíz* "la raíz de un poeta" (the root of a poet): "Hidalgo es poeta. Tiene una sensibilidad aguda y fina, una visión lumínosa del mundo y una palpitante vibración de alma ante las cosas" (Hidalgo is a poet. He possesses an acute and very fine sensibility, a luminous vision of the world,

and the soul's trembling beat in the face of things [July 1944]).

Perhaps the most compelling element in Hidalgo's first book is the chthonic imagery employed in such poems as "Hay que bajar": "Hay que bajar sin miedo. / Hay que bajar / hasta llegar al reino de las raíces" (You must go down without fear. / You must go down / until you reach the kingdom of roots). But what at first seems like a descent into death in this "kingdom of roots," with its nauseating sense of physical decay, later becomes "el corazón de la tierra se abrirá, silencioso, para recibirnos" (the heart of the earth opening up silently to receive us) and, more important, to purify. Finally Hidalgo invites readers to go down together ("bajemos juntos") into this "vida palpitante . . . esa vida oscura de los minerales" (trembling life . . . that obscure life of minerals), for the earth not only will cleanse but will "arrojarnos de nuevo a la luz con su sudor doloroso" (throw us up into the light once more with its painful sweat). "Hay que bajar" is a reworking of the traditional inseparability of life and death. Out of renewal with the earth, with the dark, primal forces of the underworld, comes the notion that from death springs life.

Hidalgo's second book of poems, *Los animales*, is but thirty-eight pages long and consists of eleven poems. Only five hundred copies were printed and it was badly distributed, so the volume received little critical attention. Originally the poems were scheduled to appear in *Corcel*, but a censor thought he detected some irreverent ideas in one of them, "Caballo" (Horse); that issue of the journal never left the printer's. With such a diminutive book, said Antonio G. de Lama (*Espadaña*, 1946), it was rather difficult to judge the work. Still, all the poems are "lindos . . . unos en tono severo y hondo, otros que agitan rápidas metáforas" (lovely . . . some with a severe, deep tone, others fermenting with lightning quick metaphors). Diego, to whom the book is dedicated, wrote (in *Alerta*, 6 April 1947) that it was intense and original.

These precisely chiseled poems, dealing with such creatures as the horse, tiger, cat, rabbit, ant, and spider, are miniature constructions of reality beyond the human sphere. Thus in "Gallo" (Rooster) the speaker urges, "canta, canta y olvídame aunque te estoy cantando, / ronco poeta humano que no puede entenderte" (sing, sing and forget me even though I'm singing to you, / me, the hoarse, human poet who cannot understand you). In "Hormiga" (Ant) he speaks of a "medidora del tiempo, de otro tiempo / que transcurre debajo de la tierra" (measurer of time, of another time / that passes beneath the earth). The 1940s was a very active period for Hidalgo: he became friends with Aleixandre, Carlos Bousoño, Vicente Gaos, Eusebio García Luengo, Ricardo Gullón, and other writers; traveled back and forth among Santander, Valencia, and Madrid; continued to paint and hold one-man shows of his art; of course he wrote indefatigably— all this during the harsh and discouraging times of the postwar era—and he fell in love. In 1943 he met Jacinta Gil, a painter and writer who was to remain close to him until his death. (She inspired several of his love poems.) Also in that same year some of the poems of *Los muertos* were taking shape. One of the first public hints of his preoccupation with the theme of *Los muertos* came in a long poem entitled simply "Los muertos" and published in November 1944 in *Entregas de Poesía*. The journal *Escorial* printed ten other poems from the projected volume that same year.

Hidalgo had originally intended to write a book about the civil war dead, calling it "La llanura de los muertos" (The Plain of the Dead), but the scope widened and his book of "the dead" became a universal contemplation of every person's death and dying. He wrote to Blasco in April 1944 that he often felt as though he were writing the poems in a somnambulistic state, as though he were hallucinating. By 1945 he was working rapidly and with enthusiasm to complete the collection.

But in February 1946 he became ill, suffering from what was later diagnosed as a form of tuberculosis. One year later he was dead. As he lay dying in a sanatorium, his friends Hierro and Blasco helped him put the poems into some sort of order, gave titles to some that had none, divided the manuscript into parts, and lightly revised a few of the pieces. Hidalgo saw the proofs, but by then he was too weak to correct them. *Los muertos*, with five hundred copies printed, was published soon after his death on 3 February 1947. He was buried two days later, and in February 1958 his remains were transferred from Madrid to the local cemetery of Torres, his birthplace.

There was immediate critical reaction to *Los muertos*, nearly all highly favorable and much of it mixed in with lamentations over Hidalgo's early death. Melchor Fernández Almagro (*ABC*, 16 March 1947) wrote that the book is "rico en poesía de su breve experiencia humana" (rich in the poetry of his brief and human experience). The tone of many reviews is elegiac: this is not the time for a serious and calm study of the poet's work, said de Lama in *Espadaña* (1947), but a time for grief. Nevertheless, he did go on to say that *Los muertos* is mature and serene, reflecting the poet's resignation in the face of death. Similarly, José Luis Cano wrote (in *Insula*, 15 March 1947): "¿Cómo hablar hoy de este libro de José Luis Hidalgo con la objetividad crítica necesaria? ... Leerlo hoy, cuando aun brilla dolorosamente la llama del poeta, y sentimos aun el calor vivo de su muerte, resulta doblemente impresionante. Porque el libro no es sino la trémula poesía de su propia muerte, presentida, acaso deseada" (How to speak today of this book of José Luis Hidalgo's with the necessary critical objectivity? ... To read it today when the flame of the poet still shines painfully, when we still feel the intense heat of his death, becomes doubly hard to take. Because the book is but the tremulous poetry of his own death, foreshadowed, perhaps even desired). One sees already the tendency to make a myth of Hidalgo and his last book, to romanticize him.

The critics have also tried to suggest a consistency of order and attitude in the four parts of *Los muertos* that perhaps is more wished for than real. L. Fernández Quiñones, for one, sees the book's structure in these terms: first, the poet encounters death; then God; third, the poet painfully but resignedly accepts his destiny; and last, in solitude he turns toward life and carries on a melancholy self-dialogue. According to Uceda in her introduction to *Antología poética*, Hierro and Hidalgo spoke often of the order the poems would take (not the same as that in which they were written). Hidalgo envisioned "en la primera parte ... una meditación sobre el Universo como un gran cementerio ... ; en la segunda queria mostrar su rebeldía—su ira—ante el destino mortal de la creación; en la tercera, su resignación, y en la cuarta, la luz—conocimiento y aceptación—y la fe" (the first part ... in the form of a meditation on the image of the Universe as a great cemetery ... ; the second part, as an expression of his revolt—his anger—against our mortal destiny; the third, his resignation; and the fourth, the light—of knowledge and acceptance—and faith). But as this same critic notes, the four parts of the book are not distinguished that clearly from each other.

Others have tried to ascertain the dominant attitude, the emotional stance behind *Los muertos*.

José Luis Hidalgo

Many readers interpret the poems in the light of the traditional pattern of acceptance and resignation in the face of death. Emilio E. de Torre says this kind of critical pigeonholing is skewed, but he himself goes to the other extreme when he claims there is no resignation toward death in the entire book (*Hispanic Review*, Autumn 1981). In his attempt to show that Hidalgo is a *poeta vitalista*, a poet of vitality and life, he tries to ignore the elements of melancholy and pain of acquiescence to ever-present death. Hidalgo *is* a singer of life, but to live is for him "vivir doloroso" (to live sadly), as he says in the poem of the same title: "Vivir es contemplar el mundo derramado, / como una vasta muerte que nos hiela o abrasa" (To live is to contemplate the world spread out, / like a vast death that freezes or burns us).

It is impossible in Hidalgo's poetry to separate the obsession with death—with all its various and conflicting ramifications of passivity and anger, sadness and indignation—from living itself. This is the vital tension implicit in his poetry. Hidalgo's contradictory emotions and thoughts are too intertwined, too mixed together to form a consistent and systematic whole; and it would be a distortion of his work to claim for him an exclusive, hence limiting, position on a theme of such cosmic proportions. Indeed, one senses in *Los muertos* that to look upon death is so overwhelming that Hidalgo cannot commit himself to a definitive stance. To have final thoughts about death is fearsome, for the ultimate vision may be too horrifying, too hopeless, for one to bear—hence Hidalgo's inner conflict; his doubts; his dialogues with himself, with a God who may or may not exist, and with a reader who, like the poet (and even God at one point), is but one more of the dead populating Hidalgo's poetic universe.

Hidalgo says in "Espera siempre" (It Always Waits): "La muerte espera siempre entre los años / como un árbol secreto que ensombrece / de pronto la blancura de un sendero / y vamos caminando y nos sorprende" (Death always waits among the years / like a secret tree that suddenly / darkens the whiteness of a path / and we go on walking and it surprises us). Death is secret, growing obscurely like a tree, "y la muerte / va creciendo en nosotros, sin remedio / con un dulce terror de fría nieve" (and death / keeps on growing in us, irremediably, / with the sweet terror of cold snow).

Above all, death for Hidalgo is "los muertos," the dead themselves, whom the poet carries around within him like a terrible burden he cannot get rid of. In "Lo fatal" (Fate) he writes in the last stanza: "Pero ya no estoy solo, mi ser vivo / lleva siempre los muertos en su entraña. / Moriré como todos y mi vida / será oscura memoria en otras almas" (But I am no longer alone, my living being / carries the dead always deep within. / I shall die like everyone else and my life / will be a dark memory in other souls). Given the intensity of Hidalgo's goal, nothing less than the attempt to harness in the form of words that cosmic energy of life and death, light and darkness, and time and eternity, the book is relentless. *Los muertos* may even seem a bit roughhewn, its edges still raw with his insistence on his theme and the nakedness of his emotions, but Hidalgo cared less about the formal perfection of his verses than the feeling behind them. This is not to say he lacked artistry: his poems abound with the conscious use of repetitions, parallelisms, contrasts, symbolic colors and imagery, and waves of emotional intensification that build to the exploding point and are then followed by a movement of expansion and calm.

It has been argued, however, that because of his concentration on death and the highly problematic relationship between humankind, God, and eternity, his poetry suffers from a monotony of tone and, in the long run, tires the reader out. Bousoño (in Cantalapiedra's *Verso y prosa*), points to the relative lack of experience in the youthful poet as one reason for this monotony. Yet even Bousoño must admit that no one has equaled Hidalgo's emotional intensity and power, which another critic (Antonio Sánchez Romeralo) has rightfully said burns within his poetry.

Whether José Luis Hidalgo's small body of work has exerted a major influence on later poets, who largely went the route of social protest in contrast to his metaphysical bent, perhaps cannot be answered. He did, indisputably, leave traces of himself and his poetry in the circle of friends and fellow artists of the "Quinta del 42"—in particular in Hierro, who has declared that only with Hidalgo's support and friendship did he begin to take poetry seriously. It may be, too, that the song to life symbolized in Hidalgo's desire to be "el centro donde todo / ha de volver en cada cosa" (the center where everything / must return into every thing)—from "Yo soy el centro" (I Am the Center, in *Los muertos*)—has borne its fruit in the renewed awareness of being alive evident in Spanish poetry of the 1960s and 1970s. What is certain, however, is the profound universality of Hidalgo's anguished search for permanence and meaning in the midst of what seems irreversible destruction and suffering. In this, his poetry is a worthy successor to that of Quevedo, Unamuno, and Antonio Machado.

Letters:

"Epistolario," *Corcel*, 13-15 (July 1947).

Bibliography:

"Bibliografía," in *Verso y prosa en torno a José Luis Hidalgo*, edited by Aurelio García Cantalapiedra (Santander, Spain: Institución Cultural de Cantabria, 1971), pp. 365-388.

Biography:

Aurelio García Cantalapiedra, *Tiempo y vida de José Luis Hidalgo* (Madrid: Taurus, 1975).

References:

Vicente Aleixandre, *Los encuentros* (Madrid: Guadarrama, 1958), pp. 214-216;

Ricardo Juan Blasco, *Escritos sobre José Luis Hidalgo* (Santander, Spain: Isla de los Ratones, 1956);

Angel Raimundo Fernández and F. Susinos Ruiz, "José Luis Hidalgo," *Archivum*, 11 (1961): 231-322;

Lidio Jesús Fernández, "Esthétique et expression surréalistes chez José Luis Hidalgo," *Iris*, 3 (1982): 15-45;

L. Fernández Quiñones, "José Luis Hidalgo: Su poesía de la muerte," *Revista de Literatura*, 13 (January-June 1958): 79-120;

Aurelio García Cantalapiedra, ed., *Verso y prosa en torno a José Luis Hidalgo* (Santander, Spain: Institución Cultural de Cantabria, 1971);

Victor García de la Concha, *La poesía española de posguerra* (Madrid: Prensa Española, 1973), pp. 476-491;

José Manuel González Herrán, "Contenido y temas en *Los muertos*, de José Luis Hidalgo," *Boletín de la Biblioteca de Menéndez Pelayo*, 48 (1972): 407-447;

Manuel Mantero, *Poetas españoles de posguerra* (Madrid: Espasa-Calpe, 1986), pp. 53-88;

Leopoldo Rodríguez Alcalde, *José Luis Hidalgo* (Santander, Spain: Librería Moderna, 1950);

Rodríguez Alcalde, *Vida y sentido de la poesía actual* (Madrid: Nacional, 1956), pp. 219-233;

Andrés Romarís Pais, "El sistema simbólico de *Los muertos*, de José Luis Hidalgo," *Boletín de la Biblioteca de Menéndez Pelayo*, 58 (1982): 325-349;

Antonio Sánchez Romeralo, "Insistencia y contraste en la poesía de José Luis Hidalgo," *Papeles de Son Armadans*, 44 (January 1967): 51-80;

Emilio E. de Torre, "José Luis Hidalgo: Poeta vital," *Hispanic Review*, 49 (Autumn 1981): 469-482;

Arturo del Villar, "Ocho poemas inéditos de José Luis Hidalgo," *Papeles de Son Armadans*, 64 (December 1971): 293-327;

Villar, "La *Raíz* de *Los muertos*, de José Luis Hidalgo," *Poesía Española*, second series 203 (November 1969): 9-12.

José Hierro

(3 April 1922 -)

Charles Maurice Cherry
Furman University

BOOKS: *Tierra sin nosotros* (Santander, Spain: Proel, 1947); republished in *Poesía del momento* (Madrid: Aguado, 1957);
Alegría (Madrid: Adonáis, 1947); republished in *Poesía del momento*;
Con las piedras, con el viento (Santander, Spain: Proel, 1950);
Quinta del 42 (Madrid: Nacional, 1952);
Antología poética (Santander, Spain: De Heredia, 1953);
Estatuas yacentes (Santander, Spain: De Heredia, 1955);
Cuanto sé de mí (Madrid: Agora, 1957; revised and enlarged edition, Barcelona: Seix Barral, 1974);
Poesías escogidas (Buenos Aires: Losada, 1960);
Poesías completas (1944-1962) (Madrid: Giner, 1962);
Manolo Molezún (New York: Pavilion of Spain, 1964);
Libro de las alucinaciones (Madrid: Nacional, 1964);
Problemas del análisis del lenguaje moral (Madrid: Tecnos, 1970);
Farreras (Madrid: Taller, 1976);
Francisco Peinado: Aguafertes 1970-1977 (Madrid: Rayuela, 1977);
García Ochoa (Madrid: Ibérico-Europea, 1977);
Grau Santos: El crédito de la realidad (Madrid: Rayuela, 1979);
Redondela (Alicante, Spain: Rembrandt, 1979);
Antología (Madrid: Corazón, 1980);
Reflexiones sobre mi poesía (Madrid: Escuela, 1983);
7 poetas españoles de hoy (Mexico City: Oasis, 1983);
La escritura política de José Hierro (Ferrol, Spain: Sociedad de Cultura Valle-Inclán, 1987);
Agenda (Madrid: Ciudad, 1991).

OTHER: "Algo sobre poesía, poética y poetas," in *Antología consultada de la joven poesía española*, edited by Francisco Ribes, also includes poems by Hierro (Santander, Spain, 1952), pp. 99-107;

Antonio Machado, *Antología poética*, edited by Hierro (Barcelona: Marte, 1968).

SELECTED PERIODICAL PUBLICATIONS—UNCOLLECTED: "Poesía pura, poesía práctica," *Insula*, 12 (November 1957): 1, 4;
"Poésie espagnole d'aujourd'hui," *Table Ronde*, 145 (1960): 111-115.

José Hierro's prominence in contemporary Spanish letters derives from his emergence as one of the most promising younger poets during Spain's post-civil-war era, particularly through his participation with other aspiring writers in the activities of Santander's *Proel* group (who published in the journal of that name). Hierro has received several awards for his work, which is characterized by an intensely personal quality, a simple elegance of style, and a preoccupation with time and existential concerns. He makes frequent use of repetition and enjambment, and he experiments with a variety of metrical forms, including nine-syllable lines. Hierro's lifelong interest in aesthetics is reflected in the many references in his poetry to specific composers and artists and in his ability to communicate an awareness of subtle differences in color, light, and sound.

Hierro was born on 3 April 1922 in Madrid to Joaquín Hierro and his wife, Esperanza. When José was four years old, he and his family moved to Santander, his mother's native region and the one he came to identify as his own. He fondly recalls his childhood there, a period of harmony, when he and his sister Isabel found themselves surrounded by affection and protected by an introverted but loving father and a mother who was strong in character but young in spirit. José's conventional early education was followed by courses in chemistry, electronics, and other technical subjects intended to prepare him for a career in industry; however, the attraction of painting, writing, and other aesthetic concerns was so strong that he gradually abandoned his scientific pursuits.

José Hierro

In 1934 Hierro, then twelve years old, won the first of many writing honors when he received a prize (the Premio Años y Leguas) for a short story set in the Orient, a tale he later described as possessing such an affected style and well-researched, mature theme that the jury questioned its authorship and forced him to submit to an examination before bestowing the award upon him. During his early adolescence Hierro read the works of many nineteenth- and twentieth-century Hispanic writers, including Miguel de Unamuno, Juan Ramón Jiménez, Antonio Machado, and the poets of the "Generation of 1927"; however, the writer who had the strongest influence on Hierro's conception of poetry at this time was Gerardo Diego.

When the civil war broke out in 1936, Hierro's development as a budding poet came to an abrupt halt. Nationalist forces imprisoned his father in 1937, and José, forced to become the family breadwinner, accepted a low-paying job in a rubber factory. At the end of the war in 1939 he was seized, accused of subversion, and incarcerated. For the next four years he was transferred from one penal institution to another. When Hierro was finally tried, he was given a prison sentence of twelve years, but he received an early release in 1944 and returned to Santander just four days before his father's death.

Unable to locate employment in Santander, he moved to Valencia, where he spent the next three years performing mundane, nonfiction writing assignments, proving himself a dismal failure as a book salesman, and working for a road construction firm. Although Hierro found his various jobs generally unsatisfying and longed for his beloved Santander, the years from 1944 to 1947 were among his most fruitful: he composed the poetry that would constitute his first two collections and part of the third. He strengthened his friendship with fellow poet José Luis Hidalgo, who had been primarily responsible for his coming to Valencia, and became acquainted with Vicente Gaos, Jorge Campos, Carlos Bousoño, and other prominent literary figures.

In 1944, during one of Hierro's train trips from Valencia to Santander, he stopped in Madrid, where he met the distinguished poet Vicente Aleixandre, who remembered vividly his initial impressions of the young writer: "Si sin mirarle le oíais, oiríais sus risas, sus palabras joviales, sus grandes y redondas exclamaciones, como guijos lavados que reconocieseis. ¡Qué sano Pepe Hierro! . . . Pero si callaba . . . Era la hora del oscurecer. Una melancólica luz de poniente había alcanzado los ojos atardecidos. Estaban graves, serios y habría que decirlo: profundamente tristes . . ." (If you were to hear him without looking at him, you would hear his laughter, his jovial words, his large, round exclamations, like washed pebbles that you might examine. What a hearty man, this Pepe Hierro! . . . But if he became silent . . . It was as if night had fallen. A melancholy light from the setting sun had reached his darkened eyes. They became serious, grave, and one would be forced to admit it: profoundly sad . . .). Aleixandre also recorded his reactions to Hierro's poetry: "Aquellos primeros versos que yo le escuché tenían la misma recogida seriedad, la misma bruma y meditación del celaje de su país. Pero ninguna queja. Parecía que una mano inmensa y gris hubiera echado un velo gris sobre las cosas, no para ocultarlas, sino para matizarlas . . ." (Those first lines of poetry I heard him recite had the same withdrawn seriousness, the same laziness and meditative quality as the clouds above his native region. But no sign of resentment. It was as though an enormous gray hand had draped a gray covering over everything, not in order to hide it, but rather to adorn it . . .).

During the years Hierro lived in Valencia, he contributed to the journals *Corcel* and *Proel* and was destined to become the major figure in the *Proel* group, which counted among its members the three most promising young poets of the Santander region: Hierro, Hidalgo, and Julio Maruri. When Hierro returned to Santander, he became increasingly committed to the work of the *Proel* group, published *Tierra sin nosotros* (Land without Us) and *Alegría* (Joy)—both in 1947—and dedicated himself to several artistic and musical pursuits, including playing the flute and composing.

Upon its publication *Tierra sin nosotros* received little critical attention, but after Hierro became well known a short while later, the collection was read carefully and appreciated fully by the critics and educated public. More than anything else, the work is an evocation by Hierro of an often-painful past, from his early childhood and adolescence through his prison experience. The poems capture his reactions to the loss of beloved companions during and after the civil war and to the distress of being forced to grow to manhood before he was permitted to engage in the carefree pursuits of youth. Nostalgia leads him to celebrate everyday sights, sounds, and experiences too easily taken for granted: the landscape of one's native region, the changing of the seasons, the permanence of natural elements, the power of wine to warm and enliven, the joy of comradeship, and the music of life itself.

Perhaps more successfully than any other selection in his first book, "Generación" records the frustrations of an entire lost generation, the "us" referred to in the title of the volume:

No fue jamás mejor aquello.
Esto de ahora es doloroso;
pero el dolor nos hace hombres
y ya ninguno estamos sólos.
Alto fue el precio que pagamos:
miseria y llanto de los ojos,
nuestros mejores años verdes
y nuestros sueños más hermosos.
. . . .
    Así pasamos, como un soplo
de brisa azul sobre la piedra.
Sin dejar rastro, como el oro
de las hojas, cuando coronan
la frente grave del otoño . . .
    Porque no queda ni una sola
rosa plantada por nosotros.

(Nothing was ever better than that.
What we endure now is painful;
but pain makes men of us
and not one of us is alone any longer.
The price we paid was high:
misery and weeping from our eyes,
our finest green years
and our most glorious dreams.
. . . .
    Thus we go on, like a puff of air
from a blue breeze upon stone.
Without leaving a trace, like the gold
of the leaves, when they crown
the stern forehead of autumn . . .

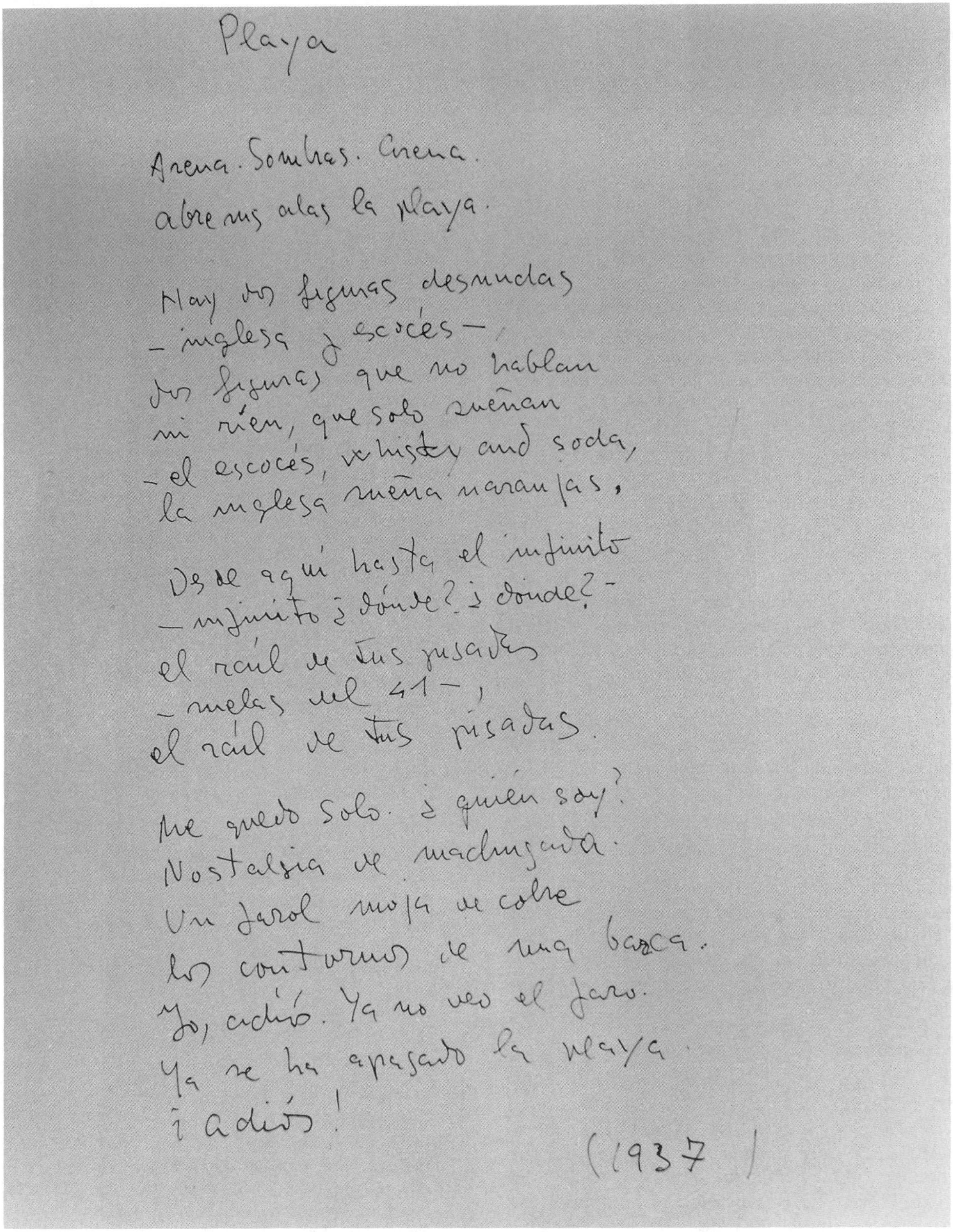

Playa

Arena. Sombras. Arena.
abre sus alas la playa.

Hay dos figuras desnudas
— inglesa y escocés —,
dos figuras que no hablan
ni ríen, que sólo sueñan
— el escocés, whisky and soda,
la inglesa sueña naranjas,

Desde aquí hasta el infinito
— infinito ¿dónde? ¿dónde? —
el raíl de tus pisadas
— suelas del 41 —,
el raíl de tus pisadas.

Me quedo solo. ¿quién soy?
Nostalgia de madrugada.
Un farol moja de cobre
los contornos de una barca.
Yo, adiós. Ya no veo el faro.
Ya se ha apagado la playa
¡adiós!

(1937)

Manuscript for an early poem first published in the Spring-Summer 1982 issue of Peña Labra: Pliegos de Poesía
(by permission of José Hierro)

214

Hierro circa 1961

Elsewhere in *Tierra sin nosotros* Hierro perceives of death as an equalizer and envisions the dead as spirits begging the survivors to allow themselves to undergo all the emotions that they could not while alive. To Hierro human experience has a decidedly universal character.

Alegría, published a few months after *Tierra sin nosotros*, drew far more critical attention. It was widely praised and earned for the poet the 1947 Adonáis Prize, awarded by a jury that included Aleixandre, Diego, and Dámaso Alonso. Because Hierro composed both volumes at approximately the same time and published them during the same year, many critics sense that they are—if not in fact, at least in spirit—two parts of a single autobiographical revelation. The experiences that motivated the writing of both works are indeed the same, yet the second book is characterized by a more deliberate existential tone. (The two collections were published together as *Poesía del momento* [Poetry of the Moment] in 1957.)

Alegría presents reflections on the transitory nature of life, meditations on death, and numerous references to time. Being alive and being happy can be synonymous, says the poet, but the path to joy is fraught with countless hardships. The introductory piece sets the tone:

> Llegué por el dolor a la alegría.
> Supe por el dolor que el alma existe.
> Por el dolor, allá en mi reino triste,
> un misterioso sol amanecía.
>
> (Through pain I reached joy.
> I discovered through pain that the soul exists.
> Through pain, out there in my sad kingdom,
> a mysterious sun was dawning.)

In "El muerto" (The Dead One) Hierro meditates on death and concludes that he is not an easy victim; because he has tasted happiness, he will never really die:

> Pero yo que he sentido una vez en mis manos
>   temblar la alegría
> no podré morir nunca.
> Pero yo que he tocado una vez las agudas agujas
>   del pino
> no podré morir nunca.
> Morirán los que nunca jamás sorprendieron
> aquel vago pasar de la loca alegría.
> Pero yo que he tenido su tibia hermosura en mis
>   manos
> no podré morir nunca.
>   Aunque muera mi cuerpo, y no quede
>   memoria de mí.

Because not even one rose
planted by us remains.)

More painful than the loss of time is the memory of dead companions who, he says in "Ellos" (Them), continue to haunt him night after night:

> Hablo
> con ellos y no entienden
> mis palabras. Los llamo
> a voces y no me oyen.
>   Ellos, lentos y vagos,
> ellos son, ellos vienen
> cada noche a mi lado.
>
>   (I speak
> to them and they do not understand
> my words. I cry out to them
> and they do not hear me.
>   Slow and vague
> they are; they come
> each night to my side.)

(But I who once felt joy tremble in my hands
shall never be able to die.
But I who once touched the sharp needles
        of the pine tree
shall never be able to die.
Those who never ever let themselves seize
that vague sensation of insane joy will die.
But I who have held its warm beauty in my hands
        shall never die.
        Although my body may die, and no memory
            of me endures.)

In several pieces Hierro laments that it is too late for him to communicate what he should have expressed to those who have died or who now live elsewhere. He observes, too, that life is at times so painful that it is like a bad dream from which there is no escape; however, through suffering, the requisite pain he refers to at the beginning of the collection, he has, by the end of the work, attained a state of imperfect, yet satisfying, joy, as seen in "Fe de vida" (Faith in Life):

        Pero estoy aquí. Me muevo,
vivo. Me llamo José
Hierro. Alegría. (Alegría
que está caída a mis pies.)
Nada en orden. Todo roto,
a punto de ya no ser.
        Pero toco la alegría,
porque aunque todo esté muerto
yo aún estoy vivo y lo sé.

        (But I am here. I go on,
alive. My name is José
Hierro. Joy. [Joy
which lies fallen at my feet.]
Nothing in order. Everything broken,
on the verge of no longer being.
        But I touch joy,
because although everything may be dead,
I am still alive and I know it.)

The selections in his next book, *Con las piedras, con el viento* (With the Stones, with the Wind), were composed in 1947 and 1948, but the volume was not published until 1950. It was received favorably, though somewhat less enthusiastically than *Alegría*. Most critics consider it to represent little departure in style and tone from his previous work. Hierro begins his third collection with a "carta" (letter) in which he acknowledges his debt to Diego and dedicates the volume to him for having served as a constant source of inspiration.

The title of *Con las piedras, con el viento* comes from one of Lope de Vega's statements to the effect that a lover customarily speaks with the stones and with the wind, and the collection is in fact Hierro's record of a love affair now ended. To overcome his grief, he seeks catharsis and must vent his feelings, even though the wind and the stones, his only audience, will not be able to hear him. By recapturing past emotions, he will be able to "desendemoniarse, / liberarse de su peso" (unleash the demon within, / free himself of his burden). In six sections, somewhat like the chapters of a novel, Hierro reflects on the love that is no more. The blissful world in which two lovers exchange romantic words and dream of their future together is shattered by circumstances he never fully understands. For a while he loses control of his senses and becomes despondent; but time provides a healing power, and he is able to admit at last, "No tienes tú la culpa. Somos / los prisioneros de ayer" (You are not to blame. We are / the prisoners of yesterday).

As in Hierro's preceding works, time is a constant element in his poetry. He realizes that there will be days and nights long after he and his beloved are dead. Love is a dynamic force without which nothing else can exist, but according to him, "sólo una vez se ama en la vida" (only once in a lifetime does one love another). To attempt to love a second time is "revivir las flores marchitas" (to revive withered flowers). He eventually becomes resigned to the fact that it is too late for reconciliation:

Ahora ya es tarde: sabemos.
(No supimos lo que hacíamos.)
Ya no hay caminos. Ya no hay
caminos. Ya no hay caminos.

(It is too late now: we know.
[We did not realize what we were doing.]
There are no longer any roads. There are no
        longer any
roads. There are no longer any roads.)

Hierro's view of the relationship becomes increasingly detached, and although he knows that from time to time memories will continue to haunt him, he accepts the reality of the present.

In 1949 Hierro had married Mari Angeles Torres, and by 1952 she had given birth to two of their four children. As he was to explain later, it is impossible for a Spanish writer to support himself solely by publishing poetry, so after he left the construction industry, he earned his living for a while in several unrelated positions, including a job in an iron foundry, an editorial post with a journal of economics, and a position teaching foreign students in Spain during the summer. Finally, in 1952, aware that his financial circumstances in Santander would continue to be limited, he accepted a post with the Editora Nacional publishing company and moved to Madrid.

That same year, the *Antología consultada de la joven poesía española* was published, containing selections by those judged by a distinguished literary panel to be the most gifted young poets. Hierro, who figured prominently among those honored in the volume, composed an introduction to his poems—"Algo sobre poesía, poética y poetas" (Something about Poetry, Poetics, and Poets)—in which he reveals his perception of the creative process: "Each poet endeavors to define poetry . . . by means of his own poems and always succeeds imperfectly in doing so. Each poem represents a failure, and, as such, is a stimulus for writing the next one." He posits the unorthodox theory that "poetry would exist even without poets," who "are mere transmitters, translators to human language." Especially to be avoided, he warns, is the tendency of some to "become enamored of the [creative] process and disdain the purpose," thereby allowing the words to "seduce" the writer, who becomes oblivious to the meaning of the composition. The poet is composed of "two distinct beings: the poet and the man. Or in other words, . . . the inspired one who receives a few words from God," and "the rational being who searches for the remainder of them."

For Hierro the evolution of a poem represents a natural sequence of events: the poet hears "a mysterious call . . . an exceedingly subtle, intense sensation that he needs to transmit." He becomes disturbed by "something made up of rhythm and color, . . . the tone, the accent, the poetic atmosphere; what is in the poem before it is written; what keeps resounding in his memory when the words have been forgotten." The writer then becomes so greatly affected by what his soul is singing to him that "he would like to sing that music to everyone else, to have them experience the same emotion that fills him." After the poet determines the dominant rhythm of the poem, he isolates the obvious metrical pattern, "verses still without words, but now with color, with greater or lesser musical tonality." This "music" enables him "to sing above it the exceedingly human lyrics of his sadness, aspirations, fantasies, memories, joy."

Hierro predicts that if one of his poems "is read by chance within the next hundred years, it will not be on account of its poetic merit, but rather because of its historical value." He proceeds with his frequently quoted assessment of the vital relationship between his own period and the poetry it has produced: "I confess that I detest the ivory tower. . . . The sign of our [times] is collective, social. Never before did the poet need to be so narrative; because the ills which lie in wait for us, which shape us, proceed from events. . . . The reader looks to the poet as the one who will sing to him what he feels in his spirit." Hierro concludes with what he terms a "provisional definition of poetry": "a gift from God by means of which the poet tells us (with words) and convinces us (with music) that he is alive. And to be alive is to carry within oneself all the weight of an epoch."

The collection *Quinta del 42* (The Draft of '42), published in 1952, differs from Hierro's previous work in its greater diversity of subject matter; and though many of the poems have an intimate quality, most can be fully appreciated without reference to other ones. Hierro describes Spain as being old, dry, and full of sadness, and he reflects on the seashore, a town plaza, and the towers of Segovia. His love for music is evident in several poems, including those in which he addresses the composer Tomás Luis de Victoria and recalls the church music of Giovanni Palestrina. Hierro's fascination with time has in no way diminished in this volume: he writes of the eternal, the ephemeral, and the passing of hours, days, seasons, years, and centuries. He dreams of childhood events and recalls painfully the misery of wasting his golden years in prison. Remembering those who have been his companions and others he may have created in his imagination, he becomes sad without really understanding why. Grieving for fellow human beings whose deaths will never be acknowledged, he recognizes his kinship with them and meditates on his own death.

In the first section of *Quinta del 42* is "Para un esteta" (For an Aesthete), perhaps his best-known poem, which reflects his poetic theory and addresses poets who become so obsessed with the sheer beauty of language that they lose sight of the true essence of their art:

> Tú que hueles la flor de la bella palabra
> acaso no comprendas las mías sin aroma.
> . . . .
> Tú que bebes el vino en la copa de plata

A Don Miguel de Unamuno
        (a través de los recuerdos de don
        Bernardo Velarde)

Era difícil encontrarte;
pensarte, como si vivieras.
Escuchábamos las palabras
que restallaron en tu lengua.
Tallado en piedra, contemplábamos
tu perpetuo gesto de piedra.
Junto a tu sueño, un perro, como
los guerreros de la leyenda.

Estrechábamos una muda mano
donde tu mano un día ardiera.
Recordábamos y volvíamos
a tí por todas las veredas.
Y era difícil encontrarte,
abarcarte, saberte; era
como erigir ciudades de oro
con sillares leves de niebla.

Page from the manuscript for Hierro's homage to Unamuno (from Peña Labra: Pliegos de Poesía, *Spring-Summer 1982;
by permission of José Hierro)*

no sabes el camino de la fuente que brota
en la piedra. No sacias tu sed en su agua pura
con tus dos manos como copa.

Lo has olvidado todo porque lo sabes todo.
Te crees dueño, no hermano menor de cuanto
  nombras.
Y olvidas las raíces ("Mi obra," dices), olvidas
que vida y muerte son tu obra.
. . . .
Y que el cantar que hoy cantas será apagado un
  día
por la música de otras olas.

(You who sniff the flower of the beautiful word
may perhaps not understand mine that have no
fragrance.
. . . .
You who sip wine from the silver goblet
do not know the path of the stream that springs
from the rocks. You do not satisfy your thirst from
its pure water
with your two hands like a goblet.
You have forgotten everything because you
  know everything.
You believe yourself to be the master, not the younger brother of all you name.
And you forget the roots ["My work," you say], you
forget
that life and death are your work.
. . . .
And that the singing that you do today will one
  day be muted
by the music of other waves.)

For his *Antología poética*, published in 1953,
Hierro received the Premio Nacional de Literatura (National Literary Prize). In 1955 he published *Estatuas yacentes* (Reclining Statues), a
255-line poem inspired by the tombs of a noble
couple in the old cathedral of Salamanca. Using
as a point of departure their memorial inscrip-
tions, he records his impressions of what life
might have been like for the knight and his lady.
Once again time becomes the unifying element,
as Hierro envisions the husband to have been a
courtier and warrior preoccupied with neither
past nor present but motivated instead by visions
of the future and of eternity. Having served his
king, honored God, and experienced the joy of
love, his life is at last complete; and he is united
in death, as he was in life, with his wife in a place
beyond the limits of time.

For his next collection, *Cuanto sé de mí* (All I
Know of Myself, 1957), Hierro received two prestigious awards, the Critics' Prize and the March Poetry Prize. In its variety the volume resembles
Quinta del 42; what unifies it is Hierro's attempt

to learn something about himself by examining
his reactions to the people and phenomena about
him. He acknowledges the power of the poet to
possess whatever he names and to immortalize
whatever he celebrates. In *Cuanto sé de mí* Hierro
writes of life, death, the evanescent, the eternal,
and of cherished experiences and painful memories. Although he appears at times to strive for objectivity, his emotions almost always surface, particularly in his poem "Requiem," a moving account
of the accidental death of a Spanish immigrant laborer in the United States. Despite an ostensible attempt to present only the facts taken from the
death notice in a newspaper, Hierro betrays his
compassion throughout, yet nowhere so strongly
as in the final lines:

Me he limitado
a reflejar aquí una esquela
de un periódico de New York.
Objetivamente. Sin vuelo
en el verso. Objetivamente.
Un español como millones
de españoles. No he dicho a nadie
que estuve a punto de llorar.

(I have restricted myself
to meditating here upon a death notice
from a New York newspaper.
Objectively. Without flight
into verse. Objectively.
One Spaniard among millions
of Spaniards. I have told no one
that I was on the verge of tears.)

Hierro's *Poesías completas* was published in
1962 and includes a prologue in which he portrays the poets of his era as "authors of complete
works," perhaps because they do not view "the
poem as a totality that begins and ends by itself,
but rather as a part, an instant of . . . life." A
poem, he says, "acquires movement only in relationship to what precedes or follows it"; and he
perceives of complete works as being "somewhat
like a film that is in the process of being shown."
Hierro then defines what is meant by the term "testimonial poet": one who, because he is inextricably bound to a "historic time," must "breathe, suffer, think, and love surrounded by others with
whom he shares much in common." Such a poet
is but "one more leaf among the millions that
make up the tree of his time," and "the only quality that distinguishes him from [those about him]
is not his greater sensibility, but rather his capacity for expression." Among the many "mute
leaves, he is a leaf that speaks out." To Hierro it

was inevitable that Spain's postwar poets were "testimonial."

Hierro judges his own poetry to be "dry and naked, spare in poetic images." He professes to favor "the everyday word, full of meaning," and poetry that is "as smooth and clear as a mirror before which the reader sits." He would like to see one of his poems "remembered by the reader not as a poem, but rather as a moment from [the reader's] own life, as is the case with certain characters in a novel who after a while" become so well developed in reader's imaginations "that we do not know whether they are real or inventions of the writer."

Hierro sees his poetry branching out into two directions: "reportajes" (reports) and "alucinaciones" (hallucinations). "Reportajes" are direct, narrative pieces possessing a theme and differing from prose only because of "the hidden, sustained rhythm that instills coldly objective words with emotion." In the "alucinaciones" "everything appears to be blanketed with fog. Emotions are vaguely discussed, and the reader sees himself hurled to an incomprehensible boundary from which it is impossible for him to distinguish the events that produce these emotions." Hierro concludes the prologue with the announcement that his next volume is to be entitled *Libro de las alucinaciones* (Book of Hallucinations).

In 1964 the eagerly awaited *Libro de las alucinaciones* was published, was enthusiastically reviewed, and earned the 1965 Critics' Prize. The nature of the volume came as no surprise to Hierro's readers, who had encountered the term *alucinación* in the titles of individual poems and division headings in *Alegría* and *Quinta del 42*. Many critics regard the *alucinación* poem as Hierro's most original contribution to date, his legacy to Spanish poetry. Several of the pieces in his 1964 collection of such poems are lengthy and have individual lines longer than those in his previous work, and the somewhat rambling style enhances the vagueness of time and space and the distance of the reader from the subject matter. Several puzzling images have led some readers to describe a few of the poems as being only slightly removed from surrealism. An air of sadness prevails as Hierro returns to subject matter with which he has dealt before: the celebration of the commonplace; painful journeys into the past; tributes to creative artists; ambivalent feelings about his homeland; the search for truth; the contemplation of death; and the fusion of past, present, and future. What is different about this collection is that Hierro utilizes the *alucinación* as the basis for his treatment of these themes.

Many of the *alucinaciones* refer to shadows and spirits of the past and leave the reader with unanswered questions. Others allow Hierro to create fresh, unexpected situations, such as the presence of St. John of the Cross, the sixteenth-century Spanish mystic, at a contemporary cocktail party in the poem "Yepes cocktail." Hierro reveals something about the new direction the collection represents and much about his art in "Teoría" (Theory), which opens the volume:

Cuando la vida se detiene,
se escribe lo pasado o lo imposible
para que los demás vivan aquello
que ya vivió (o que no vivió) el poeta.
El no puede dar vino,
nostalgia a los demás: sólo palabras.
. . . .
La poesía es como el viento,
o como el fuego, o como el mar:
da apariencia de vida
a lo inmóvil, a lo paralizado.

(When life ceases,
the past or the impossible is written down
so that everyone else may live what
the poet has already lived [or has not lived].
He cannot offer wine,
nostalgia to everyone else: only words.
. . . .
Poetry is like the wind,
or like the fire, or like the sea:
it gives the appearance of life
to the motionless, to the paralyzed.)

In 1966 Hierro reflected once more upon his poetry, which he sees as "a personal escape valve that prevents the caldron of society from cracking." Among the positive attributes of his compositions, he believes, are their innate "sincerity," a good sense of rhythm, and a certain "necessity" for their existence. He claims to be unable to write without suffering as though "one were pulling away pieces of [his] skin in order to find out what is underneath." He perceives the negative qualities of his poems to be "their monotony," "their lack of imagination," and, at times, a "prosaic quality."

During the 1970s and 1980s Hierro delivered lectures at Madrid's International Institute, at the University of Madrid, and in the United States. He has also edited an anthology of the works of Antonio Machado (1968) and has prepared several book-length works and numerous

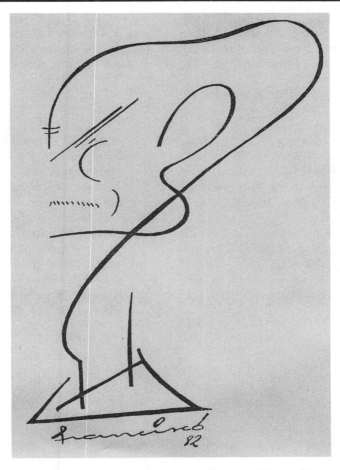

Caricature of Hierro by Francisco (from Peña Labra: Pliegos de Poesía, *Spring-Summer 1982)*

articles in the fields of art history and art criticism.

In 1974, in a volume bearing the same title as his collection *Cuanto sé de mí*, Hierro republished all his poetry. He reprinted the prologue to the 1962 edition of his complete works and added a brief preface, in which he attempted to justify his failure to compose more poetry between 1964 and 1974. Portraying himself as "an exacting man with a highly developed sense of self-criticism," he admitted that a considerable period of time had elapsed since he had written any new poetry; but he promised to resume his craft whenever poetry "makes its demands" of him. His latest collection is *Agenda* (1991).

José Hierro has established himself as an important contemporary poet. The varied themes of his work, which parallel his own joy and anguish at different stages of his life, echo the experiences and concerns of many twentieth-century people. His poetry, as he told Núñez, "does not dazzle, but in [it] one must recognize truth."

Interview:

Antonio Núñez, "Encuentro con José Hierro," *Insula*, 21 (November 1966): 4.

Biography:

Aurora de Albornoz, *José Hierro* (Madrid: Júcar, 1982).

References:

Aurora de Albornoz, "Aproximación a la obra poética de José Hierro (1947-1977)," *Cuadernos Hispanoamericanos*, 341 (1978): 273-290;

Vicente Aleixandre, "Los contrastes de José Hierro," in his *Obras completas*, second edition, revised, 2 volumes (Madrid: Aguilar, 1978), II: 358-361;

Bonnie Maurine Brown, "The Poetry of José Hierro," Ph.D. dissertation, University of Kansas, 1976;

Brown, "Point of View in José Hierro's *Libro de las alucinaciones*," *Crítica Hispánica*, 1, no. 2 (1979): 99-113;

José Luis Cano, "José Hierro," in his *Poesía española del siglo XX: De Unamuno a Blas de Otero* (Madrid: Guadarrama, 1960), pp. 483-488;

Cano, "José Hierro y sus alucinaciones," *Insula*, 20 (January 1965): 8-9;

Susan Ann Cavallo, "La poética de José Hierro," Ph.D. dissertation, University of Chicago, 1980;

Andrew P. Debicki, "José Hierro a la luz de Antonio Machado," *Sin Nombre*, 9 (October-December 1978): 41-51;

Ana María Fagundo, "La poesía de José Hierro," *Cuadernos Hispanoamericanos*, 263-264 (May-June 1972): 495-500;

Victor García de la Concha, *La poesía española de posguerra*, second edition (Madrid: Prensa Española, 1973), pp. 467-506;

María de Gracia Ifach, ed., *Cuatro poetas de hoy*, third edition (Madrid: Taurus, 1969), pp. 181-183;

Luis López Anglada, "José Hierro," in his *Panorama poético español* (Madrid: Nacional, 1965), pp. 141-145;

José Olivio Jiménez, "La poesía de José Hierro," in his *Cinco poetas del tiempo* (Madrid: Insula, 1964), pp. 155-306;

Pedro J. de la Peña, "La concepción poética de José Hierro," *Cuadernos Hispanoamericanos*, 319 (January 1977): 132-138; reprinted in *Insula*, 32 (June 1977): 3;

Rosario Rexach, "La temporalidad en tres dimensiones poéticas: Unamuno, Guillén, y José Hierro," *Cuadernos Hispanoamericanos*, 289-290 (July-September 1974): 86-119;

Douglass Marcel Rogers, "A Study of the Poetry of José Hierro as a Representative Fusion of Major Trends of Contemporary Spanish Poetry," Ph.D. dissertation, University of Wisconsin, 1964;

Julia Uceda, "Tres tiempos en la poesía de José Hierro," *Insula*, 18, no. 197 (1963): 6.

Antonio Machado

(26 July 1875 - 22 February 1939)

Carl W. Cobb
University of Tennessee

BOOKS: *Soledades* (Madrid: Alvarez, 1903 [i.e., 1902]); translated by Robert Bly as *Times Alone* (Port Townsend, Wash.: Graywolf, 1983);

Soledades, galerías y otros poemas (Madrid: Pueyo, 1907; revised edition, Madrid: Calpe, 1919); translated by Richard L. Predmore as *Solitudes, Galleries, and Other Poems* (Durham, N.C.: Duke University Press, 1987);

Campos de Castilla (Madrid: Renacimiento, 1912); translated by J. C. R. Green as *The Castilian Camp* (Portree, Isle of Skye, U.K.: Aquila/Phaethon, 1982);

Páginas escogidas (Madrid: Calleja, 1917; revised and enlarged, 1925);

Poesías completas (Madrid: Residencia de Estudiantes, 1917; revised and enlarged edition, Madrid: Espasa-Calpe, 1928; revised and enlarged again, 1933; further enlarged, 1936; enlarged again, 1965; enlarged again, 1970);

Nuevas canciones (Madrid: Mundo Latino, 1924);

De un cancionero apócrifo (Madrid: Revista de Occidente, 1926);

Desdichas de la fortuna, o Julianillo Valcárcel, by Antonio and Manuel Machado (Madrid: Fernando Fé, 1926);

Juan de Mañara, by Antonio and Manuel Machado (Madrid: Espasa-Calpe, 1927);

Las adelfas, by Antonio and Manuel Machado (Madrid: Farsa, 1928);

La Lola se va a los puertos, by Antonio and Manuel Machado (Madrid: Farsa, 1929);

La duquesa de Benamejí, by Antonio and Manuel Machado (Madrid: Farsa, 1932);

Teatro completo, by Antonio and Manuel Machado, 2 volumes (Madrid: C.I.A.P., 1932);

Juan de Mairena. Sentencias, donaires, apuntes y recuerdos de un profesor apócrifo (Madrid: Espasa-Calpe, 1936; enlarged edition, two volumes, Buenos Aires: Losada, 1943);

La guerra (Madrid: Espasa-Calpe, 1937);

La tierra de Alvar González y Canciones del Alto Duero (Barcelona: Nuestro Pueblo, 1938); *La tierra* translated by Denis Doyle as *The Legend of Alvar González* (Harrow, Middlesex, U.K.: North Light, 1982);

Obras (Mexico City: Séneca, 1940);

La duquesa de Benamejí, La prima Fernanda, y Juan de Mañara, by Antonio and Manuel Machado (Buenos Aires: Espasa-Calpe, 1942);

Abel Martín. Cancionero de Juan de Mairena. Poesías varias (Buenos Aires: Losada, 1943);

Antología de guerra (Havana, 1944);

Obra poética (Buenos Aires: Pleamar, 1944);

Las adelfas, y El hombre que murió en la guerra, by Antonio and Manuel Machado (Buenos Aires: Espasa-Calpe, 1947);

Obras completas, by Antonio and Manuel Machado (Madrid: Plenitud, 1947);

Poesías escogidas (Madrid: Aguilar, 1947; revised and enlarged, 1958);

Canciones (Madrid: Aguado, 1949); translated (West Branch, Iowa: Toothpaste, 1980);

Los complementarios, y otras prosas póstumas, edited by Guillermo de Torre (Buenos Aires: Losada, 1957);

Poesie di Antonio Machado, edited by Oreste Macri (Milan: Balcone, 1959);

Obras, poesía y prosa, edited by Torre and Auroro de Albornoz (Buenos Aires: Losada, 1964);

Antonio Machado: Antología de su prosa, 4 volumes, edited by Albornoz (Madrid: Cuadernos para el Diálogo, 1970-1972);

Yo voy soñando caminos (Barcelona: Labor, 1981);

Proyecto del discurso de ingreso en la Real Academia de la Lengua (Madrid: Observatorio, 1986).

Editions in English: *Eighty Poems of Antonio Machado*, translated by Willis Barnstone (New York: Américas, 1959);

Castilian Ilexes, translated by Charles Tomlinson and Henry Gifford (London & New York: Oxford University Press, 1963);

Selected Poems of Antonio Machado, translated by Betty Jean Craige (Baton Rouge: Louisiana State University Press, 1978);

The Dream Below the Sun: Selected Poems, translated by Barnstone (Trumansburg, N.Y.: Crossing, 1981);

Twenty Proverbs, translated by Robert Bly and Don Olsen (Marshall, Minn.: Ox Head, 1981);

Selected Poems and Prose, edited by Dennis Maloney, translated by Bly and others (Buffalo, N.Y.: White Pine, 1983);

The Landscape of Soria, translated by Maloney (Buffalo, N.Y.: White Pine, 1985).

PLAY PRODUCTIONS: Desdichas de la fortuna, by Antonio and Manuel Machado, Madrid, Teatro de la Princesa, 9 February 1926;

Juan de Mañara by Antonio and Manuel Machado, Madrid, Teatro Reina Victoria, 17 March 1927;

Las adelfas, by Antonio and Manuel Machado, Madrid, Teatro Calderón, 22 October 1928;

La Lola se va a los puertos, by Antonio and Manuel Machado, Madrid, Teatro Fontalba, 8 November 1929;

La prima Fernanda, by Antonio and Manuel Machado, Madrid, Teatro Victoria, 24 April 1931;

La duquesa de Benamejí, by Antonio and Manuel Machado, Madrid, Teatro Español, 26 March 1932;

El hombre que murió en la guerra, by Antonio and Manuel Machado, Madrid, Teatro Español, 18 April 1941.

Antonio Machado is among the five greatest Spanish poets of the twentieth century, a period blessed with fine poets, and is also respected for his book of prose articles titled *Juan de Mairena* (1936). Outside Spain, Federico García Lorca, Juan Ramón Jiménez, Jorge Guillén, and Vicente Aleixandre are better known; inside Spain, Machado is particularly revered. His first book, *Soledades* (1903; translated as *Times Alone*, 1983), emphasizes the theme of time and memory; his other major volume, *Campos de Castilla* (1912; translated as *The Castilian Camp*, 1982), imperishably captures the "Castilian" theme, exploring the essential Spanish spirit. In *Soledades* he pursues a heightened consciousness through the elaboration of memory; in *Campos de Castilla* he reveals his love of the Spanish land, a love at times bittersweet.

Antonio Machado y Ruiz was born in the Palacio de las Dueñas on the outskirts of Seville on 26 July 1875. The country estate where he was born—which was surrounded by the usual whitewashed walls—boasted fountains, lemon and orange trees, and the bright flowers typical of Andalusia. Later this childhood scenery was woven into his poetry, with the natural elements assuming symbolic values. His family belonged to the scientific, liberal tradition in Andalusia: his grandfather Antonio Machado Núñez was a doctor, professor of science, and once governor of Seville; his father, Antonio Machado Alvarez, was a lawyer especially interested in the Andalusian folk songs now called flamenco; and his mother, the former Ana Ruiz Hernández, was pliant and long-suffering, and stood by Machado in troubled times throughout his life. His paternal grandmother, also from a cultured family, often assembled the children to read to them from the ballads of Spanish history and the nineteenth-century *Leyendas* (Legends) of Gustavo Adolfo Bécquer. Antonio's older brother, Manuel, also destined to become an important poet, was born in 1874. Later two more brothers, José and Joaquín, and a sister (who died in infancy) were born.

In 1883 Machado's family moved to Madrid when Grandfather Núñez was appointed to a professorship there. For Machado the change meant that he was enrolled in the Instituto Libre, a school recently founded by Francisco Giner, which was free from the influence of church and state. During Machado's boyhood years, the fortunes of his family gradually declined; then tragedy struck when his father died in 1893, his grandfather in 1895. Both Antonio and Manuel began to pursue mildly bohemian lives during the 1890s, dabbling in various aspects of the cultural life of the capital. First Antonio wrote a series of satirical sketches for *La Caricatura*, a magazine of broad satire; then, after the brothers became friends of the actor Ricardo Calvo, Antonio played a few minor parts in the theater. With the family threatened by poverty, both brothers worked for a time for Eduardo Benot, who was developing a dictionary of synonyms.

In 1899 and again in 1902 Antonio and Manuel went to Paris to earn money as translators for the publisher Garnier. This modest job became instrumental in the Machados' participation in literary activity. Before leaving Spain, Antonio Machado had met the Nicaraguan poet Rubén Darío, captain of the new movement of *modernismo*, and Francisco de Villaespesa, Ramón del Valle-Inclán, and Jiménez, all struggling as poets. In Paris, Machado met the aging Oscar Wilde and Jean Moréas, one of the symbolist poets. During these years, he apparently wrote a collection of folk-oriented poems called "Cantares," which he later destroyed. Machado's first major effort, *Soledades*, appeared in late 1902 and was dated 1903. Although the little book achieved a measure of success, the rapidly maturing poet was soon dissatisfied with it. Certain of its poems are emphatically aesthetic, plastic, or Parnassian (characteristics of Darío's *modernista* movement); other, better ones reveal what Machado was later to call a "palpitation of the spirit." He continued to produce mainly poems of spiritual and ethical emphasis, and in 1907 an enlarged version entitled *Soledades, galerías y otros poemas* was published (translated as *Solitudes, Galleries, and Other Poems* in 1987). It was to become one of his two major books.

The publication of *Soledades, galerías y otros poemas* marks the culmination of a period in which Machado explored his inner world. With the title *Soledades*, Machado appropriated a term rich in historical and literary connotations; the word developed in the Spanish Golden Age with the poetry of Garcilaso de la Vega and reached a final baroque flowering in Luis de Góngora's *Las Soledades* (circa 1613). The specific influences on Machado's *Soledades* are poets closer to his own day: Bécquer, Darío, and the French poet Paul

José Machado's drawing of his brother's well-known character Juan de Mairena (from Insula, *February-March 1989)*

Verlaine. In the work of Bécquer, Machado discovered the short intimate lyric with simple expression; in Darío's a certain elegance of diction and verbal music; and in Verlaine's poems the suggestive use of symbol. As Machado said later, the dominant ideology of his time was subjective, and the poet pretended to sing only to himself. Soon Machado underplayed the influence of the early Darío by declaring that poetry was not sound or color values or the complex of sensations associated with the word, but the words that evoke "the deep palpitation of the spirit."

In *Soledades* Machado is essentially a poet of time and memory. Perhaps he begins as a poet *en sueños* (in dreams), relating to a complex of ideas dating to Bécquer and the romantic period. For Machado to be *en sueños* involves not an idleness in humdrum reality but the achievement of an intense state of reverie when the poet looks into his soul and attempts to expand the values of time. As a poet of memory exploring, intensifying, and creating, Machado discovered a richness in the recollections of childhood. From his living

past he settled upon a permanent image, that of the patio of his first home in Seville, with its fountains, orange and lemon trees, and flowers. In one poem, "La plaza y las naranjas" (The Plaza and the Oranges), he evokes the voices of the children chanting against the silence of the dark old plaza. His symbol for the plenitude of childhood is the rounded fruit of the orange. In another typical poem of childhood memory, "El limonero lánguido suspende" (the Languid Lemon Tree Hangs), the poet returns to the patio with the golden fruit, which he remembers he could actually reach in childhood.

Other important aspects of the theme of time and memory are his searches for love and lost youth. In "Tarde tranquila" (Tranquil Afternoon) he remembers how things might have, or should have, been: "to know some joys . . . then sweetly to remember." The reticent speaker is quietly seeking to create "fiestas of love," but love is always distant. In one of Machado's much-discussed lyrics, "Desgarrada la nube" (Torn Cloud), he recalls a scene of sun, green meadow,

Letter to Nicaraguan poet Rubén Darío, one of the first modernists, who was a friend and inspiration to Machado (from Cuadernos Hispanoamericanos, *August-September 1967; by permission of the Estate of Antonio Machado)*

lemon trees in bloom, and a sudden summer shower leaving rain drops in his beloved's hair. But a sudden disturbance shatters his reverie, and as he returns to reality, his dream vanishes "like soap bubbles in the wind."

In *Soledades* Machado establishes himself as a *poeta en el tiempo*, a poet of temporality. In a one-stanza poem, "Al borde del sendero" (At the Edge of the Path), he declares flatly, "Our life is now time," and his "sole concern" becomes the postures he will assume waiting for death. In *Soledades* Machado generally expresses the theme of time through the traditional symbols of flowing water (especially the fountain and the river) and the road. For many young poets, such as Jiménez, the streaming fountain may be erotic, but as Machado carries on a dialogue with the fountain, clearly its "eternal monotone" suggests the paralyzing flow of time. In addition to the fountain, Machado also seizes upon the ancient symbol of the river as a means of emphasizing the temporal. In his childhood studies, he must have learned some stanzas of Jorge Manrique's famous elegy, "Coplas por la muerte de su padre" (Verses on the Death of His Father), a medieval poem encapsulating the Spanish-Catholic philosophy of life, especially in the stanza declaring, "Nuestras vidas son los ríos / que van a dar en la mar / que es el morir" (Our lives are the rivers / which end up in the sea, / the sea of death). In one of Machado's major poems utilizing the river symbol, "Hacia un ocaso radiante" (Toward a Radiant West), the speaker seems to be on the Roman bridge in Soria, looking down upon the Duero River; his sense of time evokes the anguish of mortality: "Where the poor river ends, there the boundless sea awaits us." The Christian, of course, calls this the sea of life; Machado was to struggle with the problem of God and eternal life.

In Machado's searching and questioning toward the end of *Soledades*, in the poem "Leyendo un claro día" (Reading a Clear Day), he tells readers that he has been rereading his earlier poems. In these symbols of his soul he discovers the value of moral labor and the inevitability of human pain. Now he will dedicate himself to labor rather than mere song; he will work with the old griefs. First he must descend into the darkness of the soul, then he must emphasize his ethical and spiritual nature.

One of Machado's densest poems in this new category of spiritual striving is "Anoche cuando dormía" (Last Night as I Lay Sleeping),

which is clearly in the mystic tradition. He utilizes the fountain as a symbol in the first stanza, the beehive in the second, and the sun in the third. Machado seems to be following the Spanish mystic tradition of St. Teresa and St. John of the Cross, especially the former. Thus, "last night" the poet was dreaming that God's love—as a fountain flowing, a beehive working, and a sun shining—was present in his heart. In the last stanza he dreams a grander dream:

Anoche cuando dormía
soñé ¡bendita ilusión!
que era Dios lo que tenía
dentro de mi corazón.

(Last night as I lay sleeping
I dreamed—Oh illusion blest!—
That I my God was keeping
Deep down inside my breast.)

The soothing music of the poem should not muffle the sense of the stanza. In Christian mysticism, after long spiritual preparation, the mystic comes to know God directly. Here, not only is Machado's speaker dreaming, but the whole scene is an illusion. Thus Machado remains a figure hungering and thirsting after God, but finding him unreachable. As Machado puts it in another poem, "Era una tarde cenicienta" (It Was an Ashen Afternoon), he is "a poor soul in dreams / always searching for God among the mists."

Machado's poetic inspiration thus becomes threatened, for as he says in "Anoche cuando dormía," the human pains that once turned his heart into a beehive of poetic activity are threatening to tear it down like an ancient wall. Machado ends his poetic journey in *Soledades* in a confession of defeat. In the penultimate lyric, significantly called "Coplas Mundanas" (Mundane Stanzas), he declares that he has exchanged the "gold of yesterday" for the "copper pennies" of today. Generally he has traded the gold of poetry and feeling for the copper of rational ideas, philosophy, and crass reality. Specifically he has lost the gold of youth, a time of emotion and hope.

In the twentieth century the Hispanic literary world has recognized the role of Machado's *Soledades* in the renovation of Spanish poetry. Years later Jiménez made a ringing statement no one has disputed: "It fell to Machado and to me to initiate in our modern poetry the expression of the inner spirit (*lo interior*)." Machado himself

Machado and his wife, Leonor Izquierdo de Machado, circa July 1909

claimed that *Soledades* was the first book in modern Spanish poetry from which the anecdotal was proscribed. In *Soledades* Machado's themes are sharpened because of his loss of religious faith. At least a dozen of these generally simple poems have struck responsive chords in the Spanish reader, and some of the well-known lines, such as "I go along dreaming roads / of the afternoon," have become permanent additions to Spanish literary heritage.

In the early 1900s, partly as the result of Miguel de Unamuno's influence, Machado began to turn away from his semibohemian habits by preparing himself for a profession. Machado, who established contact with Unamuno after he reviewed *Soledades*, was much impressed by Unamuno, a poet driven by spiritual, intellectual, and ethical concerns at the same time. Around 1906 Machado began to prepare himself for the dreaded *oposiciones* (face-to-face encounters) between candidates for teaching positions. Machado was seeking a position as teacher of French in

the secondary schools, and he finally secured one in Soria, in northern Spain.

After a preliminary visit in the summer of 1907, Machado went up to Soria in October to assume his teaching duties. Soria is a small town in the highlands near the mountains of Aragon and thus quite cold in winter. The town was typically provincial in many ways; yet at the time it boasted four newspapers. Machado settled into a modest boardinghouse and a predictable routine of teaching. Despite his lifetime interest in learning and ideas, Machado cultivated and accepted his job as routine drudgery. He soon acquired intellectual friends, such as José María Palacio, editor of a local paper. In Machado's domestic life, he had had little contact with the opposite sex. In Soria, however, this quiet man past thirty discovered fourteen-year-old Leonor Izquierdo, daughter of his landlady. After a shy courtship they were married in July 1909—she barely sixteen, he thirty-five—in the ancient Romanesque cathedral in Soria, a concession made by Machado out of respect for her traditional feelings. The poet of *Soledades* responded happily to his new domestic life. His good fortune reached its zenith when he received a fellowship to study in Paris for a year in 1911.

In Paris, however, two years after his marriage, tragedy struck when Leonor began hemorrhaging from tuberculosis, and Machado had a desperate time reaching medical help. When she recovered sufficiently to travel, he brought her back to Soria, and it soon became obvious that she would not recover. In the following months he nursed her, but on 1 August 1912 she died and was later buried in the Espino Cemetery with the rites of the Catholic church. Unable to bear the memories of Soria, Machado asked for and received a transfer to the Instituto in Baeza, on the border of his native Andalusia.

Machado's departure from Soria in 1912 essentially terminates the second period of his poetry career, although he later added significant sections to *Campos de Castilla* when it was published in *Poesías completas* (Complete Poetry, 1917). Around 1907 he began to turn from the solipsism of *Soledades* toward the outer world. When Machado's *Campos de Castilla* was published in 1912, he earned membership in what became the famous Generation of '98, which in fact received its name at about this time. This group was responding to Spain's long decline, the culmination of which was the defeat in the Spanish-American War. Indeed, Machado became the main poet of the generation, because Unamuno was generally known as a thinker, Pío Baroja, Antonio Azorín, and Ramón de Maeztu did not write poetry, and Jiménez was considered outside the generation proper because of his lack of concern with Spanish themes. The central theme of the Generation of '98 was the problem and the destiny of Spain; therefore the major group of poems in *Campos de Castilla* deals with this theme, often called the Castilian theme, Castile being the central province in Spain. In another grouping, *elogios* (poems of praise), Machado focuses on important contemporaries who were striving to rejuvenate Spain. The third group of poems concerns Machado's love for Leonor in Soria, and many of these were written after her death. All the poems in *Campos de Castilla* look outward, toward the history and landscape of Spain, literary friends, and Machado's wife.

Under the influence of Unamuno, Machado, when he lived in the old Castilian town of Soria, began to concentrate on the regeneration of Spain. He knew that Spain was the outstanding nation in Europe around 1550, but in 1588 Spain began a decline of three hundred years, falling behind the rest of Europe, especially in progressive government and in science. The long first section of *Campos de Castilla* deals with various facets of the Castilian landscape and character, often in a hard and bitter manner, ending with a series of poems on the landscape around Soria.

After an initial "Retrato" (portrait) of himself, Machado placed "A las orillas del Duero" (On the Banks of the Duero) in a commanding position; indeed, this poem has proved to be Machado's outstanding statement on the Castilian theme in the bitter manner. Surprisingly the poem is in weighty Alexandrine couplets, the power of which can be felt in this one that expresses the theme: "Castilla miserable, ayer dominadora, / Envuelta en sus andrajos desprecia cuanto ignora" (Wretched Castile, triumphant yesterday, / Wrapped in her rags, she scorns all change today). The poem is structured in the Romantic manner of William Wordsworth. On a hot July day, the speaker sets out, crosses the Duero, goes along the road toward San Saturio, chapel of the patron saint of Soria, and finally climbs up the mountainside. Then he describes the countryside, especially the barren hills and the Duero curving around Soria. Perhaps because Castile has produced warriors, the description uses the imagery of battle; from this imagery Machado enlarges his theme and returns to the glorious Spain of El Cid and of Hernán Cortés and Francisco Pizarro. Then he contrasts the glory days with the present ones, in which the *conquistadores* have been replaced by mere traders and poor clerics. He offers no solution.

Other major poems of Machado expand on the Castilian theme. Sometimes he concentrates on Castile as a hard, rocky land, a land of denuded hills, a stern land of lofty horizons. This land has produced types of people who fit it: at one extreme the Castilian is of the race of Cain, fierce and combative; at the other he is a dull-witted soul without grace. In the poem "Por tierras de España" (Around the Lands of Spain) Machado focuses on this Cain-type, with the aim of emphasizing the divisiveness that is destroying Spain. In other poems he writes of those types in decline and decay: old poorhouse men, the criminal, and the town madman. All these Castilians have an Iberian God, an Old Testament God of vengeance.

Fair copy of a 1916 sonnet that Machado sent to Miguel de Unamuno (from Cartas de Antonio Machado a Miguel de Unamuno, *edited by José Ramón Arana, 1957; by permission of the Estate of Antonio Machado)*

In a section toward the end of *Campos de Castilla*, Machado seeks to temper his criticism of the immediate past and present by projecting hope for the next generation. The immediate past was full of lies and infamy, a time of "carnival"—that is, a time of noisy, false actions. Then Machado's own Generation of '98 appeared, eager to set things right, but Spain is still, he says, a land of brass bands and tambourines, with people who pray and yawn. But he declares that another Spain of a new generation is dawning:

Una España implacable y redentora,
España que alborea
Con un hacha en la mano vengadora,
España de la rabia y de la idea.

(A Spain redemptive and implacable,
Bursting her ancient cage,
An avenging hatchet wielded in her hand,
A Spain of idea and of righteous rage.)

But only the rage developed, in the form of the devastating civil war of 1936.

In order to concentrate on Soria alone, Machado wrote a section of lyrics entitled "Campos de Soria." In these nine short poems he creates a Soria that becomes real for his readers, most of whom have never gone to Soria personally. He emphasizes the "Silver-tinted hills, grey heights, and rocks of reddish hue"; above all, he repeats the fact that the Duero River makes a curving arc around Soria. In an elevated sense, he finds Soria mystical and warlike, this phrase referring to those fervent Catholic *conquistadores* who subjugated the New World.

During this Castilian period of looking outward, Machado, always generous, developed the idea of honoring those who were also working toward a new Spain. In his poems of praise, he attempts initially to adopt the viewpoint of the figure chosen, and then to continue in a manner acceptable to both. First is the *elogio* "A don Miguel de Unamuno," concerning, to Machado, a fiercely quixotic man with an outstanding moral stature. Perhaps the best poem of the series is the one Machado wrote for Azorín on the publication of the latter's *Castilla*. The *elogio* for Francisco Giner, founder of the Instituto Libre, ends with a ringing cry for action: "Ring out anvils; let all the bells be mute!" Machado also honors the philosopher José Ortega y Gasset and singles out for praise the medieval poet Gonzalo de Berceo and the moderns Darío and Jiménez. Although this type of poem is generally out of fashion today, Machado's elegies have been repeatedly quoted as expressing the essence of the figure being praised.

In his third important thematic group in *Campos de Castilla*, Machado expresses his love for Leonor. Of the beginning and growth of his love there is no record; his first poem concerning her is "A un olmo seco" (To a Withered Elm), about a tree he pictures growing along the Duero. The speaker, observing that the old elm has surprisingly attained some new growth, pleads for another miracle of spring, since Leonor was mortally ill at this time. But she died soon afterward, which again turned Machado inward. In Baeza the next spring, however, he recovered his equilibrium and composed one of his most remembered poems, "A José María Palacio." In Renaissance epistolary form, he writes his friend Palacio in Soria, asking if spring has reached the high country, if his favorite aspects of nature—the white-flowered brambles, the white daisies, the wildflowers, and the storks that flutter awkwardly around the bell tower—have returned. Then, almost casually, he asks his friend to take the first-blooming roses up to the Espino cemetery, "where her country is"—this is the only reference to Leonor in the poem.

Despite a certain raggedness of organization typical of Machado, *Campos de Castilla* has become a minor classic that expresses the hard and bitter aspects of the Spanish land and character and yet somehow suggests an enduring hope. Personally, it is Machado's effort, successful for a time, to look outward toward Spanish cultural and political problems, the landscape, and the domestic life. With his wife's death, the venture ended in defeat as he again retreated into the "dream" of inner consciousness and into a world he terms ironically as "metaphysical."

After leaving Soria and Castile, Machado spent seven years in Baeza, hard and lonely years. Baeza, which lies on the Guadalquiver River between Castile and Andalusia, boasts a town hall in the Renaissance style, and the Instituto where Machado taught was housed in what was once a great university. Machado had difficulty in responding to the new surroundings. In fact, although not given to histrionics, he confessed to his friend Jiménez that he thought of taking his own life after Leonor's death, but his ethical sense in using his poetic talent stopped him. His mother lived with him for a time to console him.

Antonio and Manuel Machado, who collaborated on several plays beginning in the mid 1920s

In Baeza, Machado continued his development as a man of letters. He created a modest amount of poetry, particularly poems evoking the memory of Soria, poems concerned with the Baezan landscape, and a series of "Proverbios y Cantares" (Proverbs and Songs) begun earlier, eventually included in *Campos de Castilla* as it appears in *Poesías completas*. Always a student of ideas, Machado began to organize his reading of philosophers such as René Descartes, Immanuel Kant, Georg Hegel, Gottfried Leibniz, and Henri-Louis Bergson. For some years Machado continued his college work at the University of Madrid, Ortega y Gasset being one of his professors; after struggling with requirements such as Latin he finally graduated in 1918. Moreover, Machado continued to develop his ideas as a critic of Spanish society, his mentor being Unamuno. In Baeza, Machado found complete cultural and religious stagnation.

At heart Machado never settled down in Baeza, despite his realization that the provincial town sharpened his wisdom. As early as 1914 he told Unamuno he was "resigned but not satisfied" there, and he continued half-heartedly to effect a transfer. In Baeza, Machado became for the literary world an aging poet, beset with memories. Finally in 1919 he succeeded in gaining another secondary school position in Segovia, like Soria an ancient Castilian town, but one nearer to Madrid.

Throughout the 1920s Machado's life alternated between Segovia and Madrid. His profession thus took him to towns rich in historical tradition if not in metropolitan excitement. In Segovia, for example, he found himself in one of the most striking: the famous Roman aqueduct runs into the heart of the town, and at the confluence of two small rivers, the great Alcázar castle towers above the landscape. He soon found a small concerned group for a *tertulia* (informal gathering of intellectuals), with whom he developed walking excursions through the streets of Segovia and into the countryside beyond.

Soon after his arrival in Segovia, Machado learned that a group of liberal-minded people were attempting to found a *universidad popular*, with free public lectures and a lending library. Machado, who eagerly supported the project, delivered a lecture on Russian literature, in which he claimed the Russian revolution was already a failure. He felt that the godless Communism of the Russians would return to a deeper Christian brotherhood as exemplified by Leo Tolstoy and his works. When great men of letters such as Unamuno and Ortega y Gasset visited Segovia, Machado, because of his reputation as the poet of Castile, introduced them as speakers. The Universidad Popular prospered for a decade, only to close as a result of the civil war.

For many Machado was a poet honored yet out of fashion, but in the early 1920s he began to show signs of a rejuvenation of his creative energies. In his weekend journeys to Madrid he interested his brother Manuel in collaborating as dramatists. The brothers began by adapting a Golden Age play, Tirso de Molina's *El condenado por desconfiado* (1635); then they began to write their own, usually in verse form and with historical themes. The best of their efforts is *La Lola se va a los puertos* (La Lola Goes Off to Sea), staged and published in 1929, a play in which Antonio was able symbolically to express his own life at the moment. His modestly successful efforts as a playwright came as a surprise to the Spanish literary world.

The Machados (largely Antonio) achieved an example of competent poetic theater in *La Lola*. The success of the play depends upon the depth of the two main characters, La Lola and Rafael Heredia. Antonio set out to make La Lola, a young gypsy flamenco singer, intensely human—aware of her own worth, compassionate, and of elevated spirit, characteristics she demonstrates in the dramatic action of the play. Admittedly, she becomes excessively ethereal and detached in the last act of the play. The character of Heredia, a guitarist in love with her, becomes more profound as the play progresses, for it is through Heredia's poetic dialogue that the philosopher Antonio Machado often speaks. This philosophy is bleak: people should live creatively despite the sure destruction time brings. The Machados were probably guilty of prolonging important speeches and overloading them with lyric touches, but with good actors the play carries beauty and profundity. The Machados in their plays tended to begin with real characters who drift into illusion

Drawing of Machado by Marvila (from Insula, *February-March 1989)*

in the last act. This pattern of drifting from reality into illusion is typical of Machado and all the major figures of the Generation of '98.

In the 1920s Machado also revitalized his poetic themes, especially personal ones, in a way in which poetry became embroiled with philosophy. In 1924 *Nuevas canciones* (New Songs) was published, containing mostly poems written in Baeza. First he returns to memories of Leonor, then, in a section separately published in 1926, *De un cancionero apócrifo* (From an Apocryphal Songbook), he projects a rebirth of his vital energies and a new love. Machado was approaching fifty; yet he begins here to sing of spring, of passionate rather than comfortable love, and even of jealousy. The details concerning the woman connected with this love are somewhat hazy, especially as to dates. While there is some evidence that Machado met her as early as 1926, other evidence indicates 1928. In his poetry, Machado called this autumn love Guiomar, and M. Pérez Ferrero, his first biographer, concluded she was fictitious. Then, scholars established her to be Pilar de Valderrama, a married woman who was half Machado's age. Though they met in Segovia, for some time they trysted in a café in Madrid. Given the poet's ethical sensibilities, Guiomar remained only an inspiration and not a lover.

In 1927 Machado was elected to the Spanish Royal Academy, an honor indicating the strength of his literary reputation. It is ironic that he was to occupy the chair left vacant by the death of José Echegaray, a Nobel Prize winner, since Machado and his generation rejected Echegaray's plays because of his bombast. It was 1931 before Machado got around to beginning his acceptance speech, in which he set out to define lyric poetry. Typically his ideas are clear and forceful. In his first words he surprisingly chooses to reveal his love for Guiomar—in a completely veiled fashion, of course; surely in his Andalusian sense of irony he knew he was baiting the stuffy academicians. Ultimately he stresses the important point that for the moderns poetry itself has become a problem, because for modern people lived experience itself has no meaning. In the past there was at least faith in poetry as a cultivated art. Machado's discourse trails away at the end, and he never delivered it. Thus he was never an active member of the academy.

The third and final period of Machado's poetic production was complex and shot through with paradoxes. Machado's venture into his last poetry apparently began with the philosophical idea of the absolute value of *otherness*. His attempt to blend the philosophical and the poetic commenced in a simple way in his "Proverbios y Cantares" (Proverbs and Songs), some of them dating back to 1917. In one of them he declares, "It's not the fundamental I the poet seeks, / but the essential thou." Sometime in the early 1920s he began the strange and difficult *De un cancionero apócrifo*, in which he projects himself through the persona of Abel Martín. For Martín otherness first takes the form of woman, for he declares ironically that "Without woman there is neither begetting nor knowledge." Then Martín begins to reveal his rejuvenation by exalting love. Soon, a love out of time bursts forth. These poems seem to be echoes of Pierre de Ronsard and Renaissance poets, whose courtly love was largely their own creation.

From his rich but tormented love for Guiomar the aging Machado created in *De un cancionero apócrifo* a brief collection of some of his most intense lyrics. An exceptional one is his "Recuerdos de sueño, fiebre y duermivela" (Recollections of Dream, Fever, and Nightmare), carefully structured into twelve sections, perhaps his most impressive single poem. Whereas before for Machado the dream was a controlled state of reverie, in this poem the dream sequence is presented in the Freudian manner, with time and event in confusion and with the embroilment of love, hope, guilt, and despair. In his nightmare the speaker seems to return to a love in Soria, then feel the stab of a new one; he is first tormented with jealousy and then racked by guilt. His old "road" becomes a maze of streets and alleys, all seeming to lead toward death. Many of the lines of the poem are bitterly ironic; his conclusion, that "Love always turns to ice," suggests a measure of conscious control, but the poem ends in utter frustration. His only major excursion into Freudianism is a powerful poem, though most readers have preferred his gentler ones.

With the passage of the years Machado retreated into time and memory, and hopeless yearning exudes from his "Canciones a Guiomar." At the beginning of their relationship he believed in her "dark, rose-tinted flesh" at the seashore; now in memory he retreats with her into a Renaissance garden out of time:

En un jardín te he soñado,
alto, Guiomar, sobre el río,
jardín de un tiempo cerrado
con verjas de hierro frío.

(I've dreamed you in a garden high,
Guiomar, above the river;
A garden with cold iron grilles,
Closed to time forever.)

In another lyric the speaker dreams that a goddess and her prince are escaping beyond the limits of the earth, beyond the seas, even beyond the pursuit of God himself. Finally, a much-quoted lyric is "Todo amor es fantasía" (All Love Is Fantasy), according to which the beloved does not have to exist; yet the only meaningful event in life is the brief miracle of love, and the only enduring thing is the poetry that miracle inspires.

While admitting the subjectivity of his consciousness, Machado nevertheless felt a persistent urge to overcome that subjectivity by a philosophical pursuit of otherness. In his lyric poetry of this period, his yearning becomes erotic and goes toward woman, the beloved. In the social sphere, it becomes fraternal love—brotherhood—Jesus Christ being his model. In *De un cancionero*

Page from a letter from Machado to Pilar de Valderrama, whom he called Guiomar and whose true identity was a secret until the 1950s (by permission of the Estate of Antonio Machado)

apócrifo, the ultimate yearning is toward God. For Machado God is a being that we all make, or help to make; that is, God is immanent in the human consciousness. The ironic culmination of Machado's pursuit of God is the massive and complex sonnet "Al Gran Cero" (To the Great Zero). In the sonnet, which begins as a travesty of the creation scene in Genesis, God triumphantly creates the "empty, universal egg" of nothingness. This nothingness is the complement of the poet's consciousness, just as the beloved is the "impossible" complement to the poet as lover. Finally, the sonnet suggests ironically that the "Great Zero" is God himself.

The 1936 edition of Machado's *Poesías completas* ends with four poems: two sonnets that close the Guiomar theme; "La Muerte de Abel Martín"; and "Otro clima." For the reader who has patiently absorbed Machado's poetry up to this point, the death of the alter ego Martín causes the poem concerning it to be quietly terrifying. In his "soledad" Martín is alone with the distillation of his memories: his first love has become "sacred oblivion"; the beloved herself becomes fused with death; then comes his final "great knowledge of the zero." In the last scene, as ultimate human fatigue arrives, when he raises the "limpid glass" to his lips for a final draught of salvation, the glass is filled, not with life-giving water, but with "pure shadow." Thus this penultimate poem ends in resigned courage, but Machado's tragic sense of life is evident throughout his poetry.

In 1931, with the advent of the second Spanish republic, Machado felt a surge of hope for the political future of the country. As a liberal, he always dreamed of and worked for a form of representative democracy in which the people had a voice and the military did not dominate. He was soon appointed professor in the newly created Instituto Calderón de la Barca in Madrid. For the first time, this old professor of French grammar became a professor of Spanish literature. But Machado could not change his habits: his class notebooks, later published, are dry and dull; his creative energies were going into his 1936 book *Juan de Mairena*. In Madrid he soon gravitated toward the *tertulias* in various cafés. During the next four years he sat quietly in the cafés, while his friends talked, and watched the political situation deteriorate to the point of armed conflict.

After finishing with his first persona, Abel Martín, around 1934 Machado turned his atten-

Bust of Machado sculpted by Emilio Barral in Segovia, 1926 (from Insula, *February-March 1984)*

tion to the development of a character whose name became the title of *Juan de Mairena*. Mairena first appeared in print as a flamenco guitarist in a tiny poem in the *Poesías completas* of 1917. Mairena became the major voice in the presentation of a long series of cultural articles extending into the civil war. The book's long subtitle, "Sentencias, donaires, apuntes y recuerdos de un profesor apócrifo" (Maxims, Witticisms, Notes, and Remembrances of an Apocryphal Professor), suggests that it is open-ended in structure.

Mairena is Machado's creation of the ideal professor. In his serious aspects Mairena is modeled after Socrates, and more immediately on educator Francisco Giner, Unamuno, and Ortega y Gasset. In Machado's book, Mairena is a professor of physical education who has set up a seminar on what he calls "Rhetoric," by which he means discussing philosophical ideas and cultural problems. No attendance is taken, no exams given, and Mairena, scorning the normal lectern, prefers to sit on the desk while he talks. Since Mairena is free, with no set curriculum, he can discuss anything or anyone from Heraclitus to Kant to Karl Marx, or from Unamuno to Bécquer to Lope de Vega, or even from the boxer Jack Johnson to an obscure bullfighter named Badila.

But despite the relaxed approach, Mairena's class is deeply serious. He scorns philosophical systems and prefers "apuntes" (notes); however, certain central themes are gradually developed. In the first words of the book the proposition "Verdad es verdad" (Truth is truth) is projected, and Mairena declares that even the common man is no longer convinced. Mairena retains a respect for Plato's "Ideals," or absolutes; yet he realizes that the Western world has been inundated with skepticism and relativism. Mairena is intensely interested in utilizing ideas to enhance human dignity but declares that the greatness of Platonism is not enough to cure loneliness.

For Mairena human loneliness can be alleviated only by religion, although his religious ideas are generally unorthodox if not blasphemous, especially in the Spain of the 1930s. To Mairena, Jesus is a divine figure, but he *made himself* divine. Although Mairena (and hence Machado) usually followed Unamuno in the idea that through will, desire, and suffering he could create a faith, Mairena ultimately declares that Unamuno, who dwelled upon the agonizing Christ upon the cross, did not restore Christ to his true cross. Mairena wants "to plant Christ's feet again upon the earth," to make him a human figure; Jesus becomes the ideal of immeasurable brotherly love, with God immanent in his heart. When Mairena goes on to define God, God is in the human heart. In a strict philosophical sense God becomes "The Great Zero" that Machado had earlier envisioned.

While Mairena is usually exploring the ideas of others, in some sections of the book he introduces his own projects and concerns. By his own admission, he has grown toward a youthfulness, so that not surprisingly he is interested in relations between the sexes. He reveals that among his many papers is a tragicomedy entitled "El gran climatérico" (The Grand Climax), which he declares is not influenced by Sigmund Freud. Yet Mairena defines it as a play, in twenty-one acts, with a protagonist who symbolizes the libido from adolescence until the sexual drive ceases— as Mairena observes, when man "has one foot in the grave." The protagonist is always on the stage, so frivolous dialogue that does not advance the essential theme can be avoided. Moreover, having studied William Shakespeare's works recently, Mairena uses in his play the intimacy of the soliloquy and the aside. He keeps threatening to present scenes of the play to his class, but since the students are immature he always puts it off.

Mairena's dream of being the ideal teacher, communicating with his students and having them learn to express themselves, begins seriously to fade toward the end of the book. In his own examination of conscience, Mairena finds two unpardonable faults. First, does he have the right to dish out harsh criticism of major institutions? Second, while he began in real dialogue with his students, so that one or two were given names by Machado, gradually Mairena is merely making speeches. If he cannot develop students Socratically, then his dream of a "School of the People" is doomed to failure. Of course, the pressure of the civil war ultimately forces him toward propaganda, so that he is not "free." Actually Mairena is harder on himself than the later generation has been on Machado: many have defended *Juan de Mairena* as a successful literary work and above all a vital document for understanding the Generation of '98.

In the summer of 1936 the whole country was plunged into civil war. The conflict soon became international when Germany and Italy joined the Nationalist side (led by Francisco Franco); Russia and a brigade of idealists joined the Republican side. In Spain the Nationalist cause generally included the church, the military, and the upper class; the Republican cause embraced political liberals, the working class, and most of the intellectuals. Thus Machado was a Republican on all three counts. His brother Manuel, however, partly because the war caught him in Burgos, a Nationalist stronghold, declared sympathy with the Nationalist cause. Hence brother was set against brother.

At the beginning of the war, Antonio and his family remained in Madrid. But soon the capital was under siege and the Republican government was transferred to Valencia. As a respected intellectual, Machado, along with his family, was persuaded to go there, and they settled in Rocafort, outside Valencia. Then he began his wartime task of writing articles for newspapers such as *Hora de España*—published by the Republican government—sometimes referring to Juan de Mairena. Although now in poor health, Machado stayed in contact through correspondence with various political groups, always defending the people. There is a letter to David Vigodsky in Leningrad, in which Machado stubbornly refuses to accept the economic emphases of Marxism. He

Machado speaking in Soria, Spain, in 1932. He had lived and taught there from 1907 to 1912.

prefers to dream that Russia is moving toward a spiritual ideal of Christian brotherhood. Naturally Machado's later writings are close to propaganda.

As the political situation worsened for the Republicans in 1938, Machado and his family were evacuated to Barcelona, where he continued to write for the cause. In January of 1939, with the fall of Barcelona imminent, Machado and his family joined a convoy in flight toward the French border. On this journey he encountered the horrible displacements of war if not the actual sound of bullets. The weather was cold and rainy, and the old vehicles began breaking down. He was ill with pneumonia and had to bear the horror of watching his mother, now eighty-five, suffer the same tortures of travel. Finally they arrived in Collioure, a fishing village on the Mediterranean, and Machado refused to try to go on to Paris. During the month of February both he and his mother lay ill. On 22 February he died, with his mother dying three days later; he was buried in Collioure in a civil service with political overtones, since his casket was draped with the flag of the Republic. His brother Manuel, still in Burgos, received the news from a complete stranger, who had heard it on the radio.

During the last decade of Machado's life and in the years since, he and his work have continued to be recognized by honors and tributes of respect. In 1932 Soria declared him an adopted son, and the modest poet, with some embarrassment, returned there for a celebration and for the unveiling of a plaque bearing lines of his poetry, which was placed near the road toward the Chapel of San Saturio where he used to walk. Today in Soria there is an Antonio Machado Chair at the Instituto; and crowning the hill where Soria's medieval castle used to be, is the new Antonio Machado National Inn. In 1949, the tenth anniversary of his death, the journal *Cuadernos Hispanoamericanos* of Madrid devoted a double issue to his life and work; and in 1960 *Insula* also published a Machado issue. In 1957 the Royal Academy initiated a campaign to have his remains returned to Spain; more recently there has been an attempt to set up a simple monument to him in Baeza.

Machado's permanent position in Spanish literature will depend largely upon his poetry, although his *Juan de Mairena* has remained alive. From the beginning Machado's poetry is marked by a certain intimate (though not confessional) quality he himself called a "deep palpitation of the spirit." At the start he was a *poeta en sueños*, a

Machado in the early 1930s (photograph by Alfonso)

poet of daydreams, attempting to tap the essence of memory. Little by little he became a *poeta en el tiempo*, a poet in time. By this he meant that the poet must use the specific (though limited) experiences of his life; these unique moments must be transformed into word, symbol, and music so as to become imperishable. In terms of form, Machado was always a traditionalist who avoided free verse; he pursued a form of elegant simplicity. This in no sense means his work is facile, for complexity and profundity mark many of his poems.

In his own generation, he shared poetic honors with Jiménez and Unamuno. In the next generation, that of Lorca and Guillén, for a brief time Machado was rejected because of his traditionalism. After the civil war, however, as the respected critic José Luis Cano has indicated, there was a return to Machado, one of the most impor-

tant phenomena in the evolution of postwar Spanish poetry. Little by little, Machado has become a consecrated figure while remaining a living influence. Both Camilo José Cela and Juan Goytisolo, important novelists in postwar Spain, have utilized his work. In 1959 on the twentieth anniversary of Machado's death, the writer José Marra López could say that Machado was still alive in spirit and that he awakened "a tenderness difficult to explain." For many Machado lived some words he wrote in 1904: "I see poetry as an anvil of constant spiritual activity. . . . All our efforts ought to reach out toward light, toward consciousness."

Antonio Machado, a poet of tragic vision, was sometimes given to ironic skepticism; his journeys into poetry often momentarily end in professed defeat, while the poetry itself endures. He can be compared with Robert Frost. Both Frost and Machado seem to be nature poets, the former utilizing New England, the latter Castile; in the works of both poets nature is rarely descriptive but becomes the ground for symbolic meanings. Moreover, Frost and Machado were confirmed existentialists living their moments of time bravely but tragically. And both had problems with God. When Machado, as a poet of the inner world in *Soledades*, looks into his own consciousness, he can find neither a real beloved nor a real God, and the book ends in expressed defeat. When Machado looks outward in *Campos de Castilla*, he first sees God as a God of vengeance, then as a being pursued unsuccessfully by philosophical methods. Then, in Machado's final, metaphysical period, the beloved becomes a fantasy, God becomes "The Great Zero," and only a desperate human brotherhood remains. Thus Machado's three journeys into poetry ended in implied defeats, but in the enduring poetry of those journeys is a voice speaking of the indomitable spirit of humankind.

Letters:

De Antonio Machado a su grande y secreto amor, edited by Concha Espina (Madrid: Gráficas Reunidas, 1950);

Cartas de Antonio Machado a Miguel de Unamuno, edited by José Ramón Arana (Mexico City: Monegros, 1957);

Cartas de Antonio Machado a Juan Ramón Jiménez (Rio Piedra, P.R.: Torre, 1959).

Bibliographies:

Rafael Heliodoro Valle, "Bibliografía," in *Antonio Machado (1875-1939)*, edited by Federico de Onís (New York: Hispanic Institute, 1951), pp. 91-109;

Manuel Carrión Gutiez, *Bibliografía machadiana: Bibliografía para un centenario* (Madrid: Biblioteca Nacional, 1976).

Biographies:

M. Pérez Ferrero, *Vida de Antonio Machado y Manuel* (Madrid: Artes Gráficas, 1947);

Gabriel Pradal-Rodríguez, "Vida y obra," in *Antonio Machado (1875-1939)*, edited by Federico de Onís (New York: Hispanic Institute, 1951), pp. 11-90;

José Luis Cano, *Antonio Machado, Biografía ilustrada* (Barcelona; Destino, 1975).

References:

J. M. Aguirre, *Antonio Machado, poeta simbolista* (Madrid: Taurus, 1978);

Aurora de Albornoz, *La presencia de Miguel de Unamuno en Antonio Machado* (Madrid: Gredos, 1972);

José Angeles, ed., *Estudios sobre Antonio Machado* (Barcelona: Ariel, 1977);

M. A. Baamonde, *La vocación teatral de Antonio Machado* (Madrid: Gredos, 1976);

Carl W. Cobb, *Antonio Machado* (New York: Twayne, 1971);

Cobb, *Contemporary Spanish Poetry, 1898-1963* (Boston: Twayne, 1976);

Pablo A. Cobos, *Humor y pensamiento en la metafísica poética de Antonio Machado* (Madrid: Insula, 1963);

Cuadernos Hispanoamericanos, special Machado issue (1949);

Joaquín Gómez Burón, *Exilio y muerte de Antonio Machado* (Madrid: Sedmay, 1975);

Luis Granjel, *Panorama de la generación del 98* (Madrid: Guadarrama, 1959);

Manuel H. Guerra, *El teatro de Manuel y Antonio Machado* (Madrid: Mediterráneo, 1966);

Ricardo Gullón, *Las secretas galerías de Antonio Machado* (Madrid: Taurus, 1958);

Gullón and Allen W. Phillips, eds., *Antonio Machado* (Madrid: Taurus, 1975);

Norma L. Hutman, *Machado: A Dialogue with Time* (Albuquerque: University of New Mexico Press, 1969);

Insula, special Machado issue, 158 (1960);

Pedro Laín Entralgo, *La generación del 98* (Madrid: Diana, 1945);

Leopoldo de Luis, *Antonio Machado, ejemplo y lección* (Madrid: Sociedad General Española de Librerías, 1975);

E. Allison Peers, *Antonio Machado* (Oxford: Clarendon Press, 1940);

Justina Ruiz de Conde, *Antonio Machado y Guiomar* (Madrid: Insula, 1964);

Antonio Sánchez-Barbudo, *Estudios sobre Unamuno y Machado* (Madrid: Guadarrama, 1959);

Sánchez-Barbudo, *Los poemas de Antonio Machado* (Barcelona: Lumen, 1967);

Segundo Serrano Poncela, *Antonio Machado, su mundo y su obra* (Buenos Aires: Losada, 1954);

J. B. Trend, *Antonio Machado* (Oxford: Dolphin, 1953);

Ramón de Zubiría, *La poesía de Antonio Machado* (Madrid: Gredos, 1955).

Manuel Machado

(29 August 1874 - 19 January 1947)

Michael L. Perna

Hunter College, City University of New York

BOOKS: *Tristes y alegres*, by Machado and Enrique Paradas (Madrid: Catalana, 1894);

Etcétera, by Machado and Paradas (Barcelona: López Robert, 1895);

Alma (Madrid: Marzo, 1900);

Caprichos (Madrid: Revista de Archivos, 1905);

La fiesta nacional: Rojo y negro (Madrid: Fortanet, 1906);

Poesías escogidas (Barcelona: Maucci, 1907);

Alma. Museo. Los cantares (Madrid: Pueyo, 1907);

El mal poema (Madrid: Gutenburg-Castro, 1909);

Trofeos (Barcelona: Gasso, 1910);

Alma. Opera selecta (Paris: Garnier, 1911);

Apolo. Teatro pictórico (Madrid: Prieto, 1911);

Cante hondo. Cantares, canciones y coplas, compuestas al estilo popular de Andalucía (Madrid: Helénica, 1912; revised and enlarged edition, Madrid: Renacimiento, 1916);

El amor y la muerte (Madrid: Helénica, 1913);

La guerra literaria, 1898-1914: Crítica y ensayos (Madrid: Hispano-alemana, 1913);

Canciones y dedicatorias (Madrid: Hispano-alemana, 1915);

Poesías completas (Madrid: Residencia de Estudiantes, 1917);

Un año de teatro (Madrid: Biblioteca Nueva, 1918);

Día por día de mi calendario (Madrid: Pueyo, 1918);

Sevilla, y otros poemas (Madrid: América, 1919);

Ars moriendi (Madrid: Mundo Latino, 1921);

Obras completas, 5 volumes (Madrid: Mundo Latino, 1922-1924);

Poesía: Opera omnia lírica (Madrid: Internacional, 1924; enlarged edition, Barcelona: F.E.T. & J.O.N.S., 1940);

Desdichas de la fortuna, o Julianillo Valcárcel, by Manuel and Antonio Machado (Madrid: Fernando Fé, 1926);

Juan de Mañara, by Manuel and Antonio Machado (Madrid: Espasa-Calpe, 1927);

Las adelfas, by Manuel and Antonio Machado (Madrid: Farsa, 1928);

La Lola se va a los puertos, by Manuel and Antonio Machado (Madrid: Farsa, 1929);

La prima Fernanda (Madrid: Farsa, 1931);

La duquesa de Benamejí, by Manuel and Antonio Machado (Madrid: Farsa, 1932);

Teatro completo, by Manuel and Antonio Machado, 2 volumes (Madrid: C.I.A.P., 1932);

Cante hondo, Sevilla (Madrid: Aguilar, 1934);

Phoenix: Nuevas canciones (Madrid: Altolaguirre/Héroe, 1936);

Horas de oro: Devocionario poético (Valladolid, Spain: Castellana, 1938);

Antología poética (Burgos, Spain: Zugazaga, 1938);

Antología (Buenos Aires: Espasa-Calpe, 1940);

Unos versos, un alma y una época: Discursos leídos en la Real Academia Española, con motivo de la recepción de Manuel Machado (Madrid: Españolas/Diana, 1940);

La duquesa de Benamejí, La prima Fernanda, y Juan de Mañara, by Manuel and Antonio Machado (Buenos Aires: Espasa-Calpe, 1942);

Ars longa (Madrid: Garcilaso, 1943);

Cadencias de cadencias: Nuevas dedicatorias (Madrid: Nacional, 1943);

El pilar de la victoria (Madrid: Nacional, 1945);

Las adelfas, y El hombre que murió en la guerra, by Manuel and Antonio Machado (Buenos Aires: Espasa-Calpe, 1947);

Obras completas, by Manuel and Antonio Machado (Madrid: Plenitud, 1947);

Horario: Poemas religiosos (Madrid: Nacional, 1947);

Estampas sevillanas (Madrid: Aguado, 1949);

La prehistoria de Antonio Machado, by Manuel and Antonio Machado (Río Piedras: Torre/Universidad de Puerto Rico, 1961);

Prosa, edited by José Luis Ortiz de Lanzagorta (Seville, Spain: Universidad de Sevilla, 1974);

Antología poética, edited by Margarita Smerdou Altolaguirre (Madrid: E.M.E.S.A., 1977).

PLAY PRODUCTIONS: *Desdichas de la fortuna*, by Manuel and Antonio Machado, Madrid, Teatro de la Princesa, 9 February 1926;

Juan de Mañara, by Manuel and Antonio Machado, Madrid, Teatro Reina Victoria, 17 March 1927;

Las adelfas, by Manuel and Antonio Machado, Madrid, Teatro Calderón, 22 October 1928;

La Lola se va a los puertos, by Manuel and Antonio Machado, Madrid, Teatro Fontalba, 8 November 1929;

La prima Fernanda, by Manuel and Antonio Machado, Madrid, Teatro Victoria, 24 April 1931;

La duquesa de Benamejí, by Manuel and Antonio Machado, Madrid, Teatro Español, 26 March 1932;

El hombre que murió en la guerra, by Manuel and Antonio Machado, Madrid, Teatro Español, 18 April 1941.

TRANSLATIONS: Paul Verlaine, *Fiestas galantes. Poemas saturnianos. La buena canción . . .* (Madrid: Fortanet, 1910);

Victor Hugo, *Hernani*, translated by Manuel and Antonio Machado and Francisco Villaespesa (Madrid: Farsa, 1928);

Edmond Rostand, *El aguilucho*, translated by Machado and Luis de Oteyza (Madrid: Farsa, 1932).

The older brother of Antonio Machado, Manuel was the more famous poet during the early years of the twentieth century. After a stay in Paris he brought the full force of modernism home to Spain with his adaptations in Spanish verse of symbolist techniques, especially those of Paul Verlaine. Machado did polemical and editorial work for the modernist movement and enjoyed his greatest reputation before World War I. His use of Andalusian folk poetry and flamenco lore opened the way for younger poets (such as Federico García Lorca and Rafael Alberti) to develop the themes more profoundly.

Manuel Machado y Ruiz was born on 29 August 1874 in Seville, where his parents, Antonio Machado Alvarez and the former Ana Ruiz Hernández, had met in a crowd that had rushed to the banks of the Guadalquivir River to see dolphins swimming so far upstream. His father was a Liberal whose law career was ruined by political enemies at the restoration of the Bourbon monarchy, the year Manuel was born, and who struggled to make a living as an anticlerical journalist. Living in the Triana quarter of the city, famous for its gypsy cafés and bullfighters, Manuel was practically raised on flamenco poetry, since his father collected, studied, and published many of the *seguidillas*, *soleares*, and *coplas* being sung at the time, as well as founding the first folklore society in Spain. One of the books from which Manuel was read to as a child was the *Romancero general*, a collection of more than eighteen hundred ballads that his ancestor Agustín Durán had compiled from 1828 to 1832. When Machado was nine, his family moved to Madrid and enrolled him in the Institución Libre de Enseñanza, a secular progressive school. The field trips to local workshops, nearby mountains, and forests, which were an important part of the teaching methods, and the drawing and art history classes taught by Manuel B. Cossío in the galleries and museums of Madrid stimulated Machado's powers of observation and contributed to his earliest efforts at poetry.

From 1895 to 1897 he lived with his mother's parents in Seville to complete high school and, simultaneously, to take a university degree, and there he became engaged to his cousin, Eulalia Cáceres. With a wealthy friend, Enrique Paradas, Machado published two books of youthful verse, dedicating many of his poems to local society figures. He became an enthusiast of Seville's mixture of aristocratic and gypsy café life, of bullfights and the horse fair, and participated in church festivals and Holy Week processions. When he returned to Madrid he stood out for his elegance, wit, and Andalusian manners.

In March of 1899 he went to Paris to work as a translator for Garnier Frères. There he met writers such as Pío Baroja, Oscar Wilde, and Jean Moréas and lived a bohemian life with the poets Amado Nervo and Rubén Darío. Machado's guide to literary Paris was the Guatemalan writer Enrique Gómez Carrillo, who had known Leconte de Lisle and Verlaine and kept open house for visiting Spanish and Latin American writers. For a while Machado stayed in the same cheap hotel Verlaine had lived in, since it was close to the Garnier offices, where Machado slaved away at translating short stories. After a period spent in Gómez Carrillo's rather disorderly apartment, he found a quiet place for himself near the Luxembourg Gardens where he settled down to write seriously.

In later years he remembered the storm of excitement with which the poem "Adelfos" (in *Alma* [Soul, 1900]) came to him. That seems to mark the moment when he defined his own style in relation to all the influences he was absorbing at the time: French poetry from Victor Hugo through the Parnassians and the symbolists; Darío's work in progress; avant-garde theater; and the stimulation of Paris in those years of the Alfred Dreyfus affair and the Universal Exhibition.

Back in Madrid in 1901 Machado joined Francisco Villaespesa and Ramón del Valle-Inclán on the editorial boards of *Electra* and *Juventud*—modernist reviews attacking the traditionalism of Spanish life and letters—where he published versions of poems later included in his first major book, *Alma*. Probably appearing late in 1900 or early the next year, *Alma* received a deeply sympathetic review from Miguel de Unamuno in the *Heraldo de Madrid* (19 March 1901)—collected in his *De esto y aquello* (1950). Unamuno's own moral earnestness was directly opposed to the spiritual disillusionment of Machado's poetry, but the older man praised the beginner's earnest search for inner meaning and admitted that his own conviction needed Machado's skepticism to remain in balance. The opening poems of *Alma* are reminiscent of Darío's "El reino interior" (The Inner Kingdom, in *Prosas profanas*, 1896) and Verlaine's "Colloque Sentimentale" (Sentimental Conversation, in *Fêtes Galantes*, 1869). Machado's poems on exotic themes suggested by the French Parnassians—

Cover for the 1907 collection that includes Machado's first major book, Alma, *and poems written after 1900*

"Oasis" on the Orient, "Oliveretto di Fermo" on Renaissance immorality, and even "Castilla," in which medieval Spain is treated impressionistically—are fine examples of the modernists' emphasis on the mystery of emotions that cannot be expressed in words. Traditional Spanish meters, such as the seven- and eleven-syllable *silva*, are renovated in *Alma* by the use of assonance instead of full rhyme. The artistic and spiritual refinement of "Felipe IV," a sonnet on Diego Velázquez's portrait, and the aristocratic pose of "Adelfos" both express a deeply cynical failure of willpower, which can be seen as a protest against the official optimism and vulgar practicality of the modern age. This attitude of rebellion, coupled with the innovations of their work, gradually won attention for the new poets, of whom Machado was a leader.

After another trip to Paris from 1902 to 1903, Machado settled in Madrid to lead a busy literary and café life, occasionally contributing poems and reviews to Juan Ramón Jiménez's *Helios* and acting as Darío's guide to the city when he visited Spain. In *Mercure de France* (November-December 1905) Darío reviewed Machado's next book, *Caprichos* (Caprices, 1905), which was dedicated to him. Some of the erotic verse in *Caprichos* reveals how close in attitude and theme the two poets were at the time: Machado's "Aleluyas madrigalescas" (Madrigal Hallelujahs) resemble Darío's poem "Aleluya" (in *Cantos de vida y esperanza* [Songs of Life and Hope, 1905]), which Darío dedicated to him the same year. *Aleluya* was a code word for the ecstasies of the two poets' shared recreations: drinking, chasing girls, and meeting friends nightly, all of which contributed to Darío's physical decline while it bolstered Machado's reputation of being the kind of cynical character who appeared in his poetry. A new theme appears in his poem "Domingo" (Sunday), in which the speaker feels first irritated by, then attracted to, the noise of a vulgar crowd whose simple happiness he wishes he could share. None of the poems in the book, however, is as innovative or as controlled as Machado's previous ones.

His friend Antonio Fuentes Zorita, whose bullfighting career lasted from 1893 to 1908, was the inspiration for Machado's next collection, *La fiesta nacional: Rojo y negro* (The National Sport: Red and Black, 1906). Matadors developed individual styles that attracted fanatical supporters and, at a time when Lagartijo had the most serious way of killing and Currito gave lunatic thrills, Fuentes Zorita was famous for his elegance in placing the *banderillas*. As a fan of the aesthetic and technical aspects of the *corrida*, Machado portrayed each stage of the bullfight with impressions of color, sounds, dramatic movements, and emotion:

> Y entre manchas de grana
> y reflejos metálicos,
> el toro, revolviéndose
> alza en los cuernos un pelele trágico.
>
> (And between pomegranate stains
> and metallic reflections,
> The bull, spinning
> lifts a tragic doll on his horns.)

In his poems Machado tries to capture a spectacle of many fleeting instants of beauty and daring that can hardly be grasped at the moment they occur. The finale (the bull's death) brings the tone of *La fiesta nacional* once again to the disillusionment of Machado's earlier books. Here he uses many different meters and rhymes to express in writing something that only exists in performance, while tying the emotional beauty and violence to traditional images from bullfighting lore. These poems—on a sport that represented the old Spain against which the modernists were protesting—raised objections on moral grounds from those opposed to blood sports. Jiménez disliked Machado's use of material that was not really poetic, but Darío praised the book, which was very popular.

From the poems he contributed regularly to Madrid newspapers, Machado collected new work to appear in *Alma. Museo. Los cantares* (Soul. Museum. Songs, 1907), in which he reprinted the bulk of his work to date. The poem "Cantares" from *Alma* was the stimulus for the last section of the new book, where the folklorist art of flamenco is absorbed into such fine poems as "El querer" (Desire) and "La pena" (Anguish). In "Fin de siglo" (End of an Age), concerning a delicate neoclassical poet who writes perfect verses for a polite circle of friends but who abuses his mistress, Machado is still on the attack against social conventions of poetry, but the work itself does not rise much above the level of cliché. Similarly the two sonnets entitled "Sé buena" (Be Good) have fine musical qualities, varying the accents of the alexandrine line by shifting the caesura, but the moralistic ideas expressed seem too hackneyed for most readers to give the verse much attention.

Faced with rising criticism even from his friends, Machado was perfectly willing to admit that his inspiration seemed to have failed, but far from considering himself finished, he returned to the source of much of his inspiration, translating several of Verlaine's works (1908), and preparing a new book he aggressively titled *El mal poema* (The Bad Poem, 1909). He wrote bad poems, he claimed, because his poverty forced him to write and publish quickly, without the leisure that a financially secure poet such as Jiménez enjoyed. Machado's new poems were also about "bad" people: prostitutes in "Mi Phriné" (My Phrine) and "Chouette" (Cute), and homeless crooks in "Internacional," the natural companions of the starving poet in "Invierno" (Winter). Machado's ever-increasing familiarity with prostitution and the underside of city life gave him a new subject as well as new evidence for his disillusionment. In the self-portraits he included in the book, "Prólogo-Epílogo" and "Yo, poeta decadente" (I, Decadent Poet), Machado continued to criticize the self-satisfied middle classes who pretended to appreciate art but ignored living artists and poets.

In July of 1909 a love affair with a Catalan girl led him to follow her to Barcelona, where he arrived just as the antidraft riots and the fierce repression of "The Tragic Week" broke out in the city. Abandoning his romantic adventure, he crossed the Pyrenees into France and went from there to Seville. His fiancée, Eulalia Cáceres, a cousin, had waited many years for him to be able to marry her, but when she heard of his escapades she had stopped writing to him. However, Machado renewed his courtship and they were

Canto a Andalucía
=

Cádiz, solada claridad... Granada,
agua oculta, que llora...
Romana y mora, Córdoba callada.
Málaga, "cantaora"!..
Almería dorada...
Plateado Jaén... Huelva: la orilla
de las tres carabelas...
Y Sevilla.

Manuel Machado

Fair copy of a poem collected in Phoenix, *1938 (from Gerardo Diego,* Manuel Machado, poeta, *1974; by permission of the Estate of Manuel Machado)*

married in 1910. The young couple set up housekeeping in Madrid, where Machado struggled to support his wife and his mother by contributing to reviews, translating, and turning out new books of poetry. The success of his earlier sonnet "Felipe IV" spurred him to publish a whole gallery of poems on painting, *Apolo. Teatro pictórico* (Apollo. Pictorial Theater, 1911). He covered a wide range of emotions based on his impressions of famous works, from the frenzy of Peter Paul Rubens's *La Kermesse* (Peasant Dance) to the hushed *Entierro de un monje* (Burial of a Monk) of Francisco de Zurbarán. His poems on Fra Angelico's *Annunciation* and Sandro Botticelli's *Spring* are adaptations of lines and images from Verlaine as well as careful considerations of the techniques of the paintings themselves. The book's dedication to Giner de los Ríos, director of the Institución Libre de Enseñanza, and the sonnet on El Greco, dedicated to Manuel B. Cossío, reveal the influence of Machado's studies at the Institución, where the emphasis was on personal reflections growing out of direct knowledge of works of art. Without any real system of corre-

Machado circa 1912 (from Cante Hondo)

spondences between colors and sounds, Machado still chooses his adjectives carefully to accumulate an overall impression in each sonnet. There are some musical lines, but fewer than in his early modernist books, perhaps because verbs, which have such a wide range of rhythms in Spanish, are not called for very often in describing a series of static subjects such as paintings. Some reviewers, including Eduardo Gómez de Barquero and Eduardo Ortega, regretted what they saw as a lack of polish in the sound of Machado's verses.

Then he revised and republished many of the poems from his first book, *Tristes y alegres* (Sad and Happy, 1894), as *Trofeos* (1910). The vogue for Andalusian topics stimulated him to republish other poems from his first two books, adding new flamenco lyrics, in *Cante hondo* (Deep Song, 1912), which sold a thousand copies in twenty-four hours. Deciding to pursue a regular career, Machado entered the Universidad de Madrid and studied for the competitive exam to be a civil-service librarian, which he passed in 1913. He was appointed to the government university in Santiago de Compostela but quickly arranged a transfer back to Madrid, to work in the Biblioteca Nacional. This allowed him to resume the café life of a respected writer in the capital.

A collection of his articles defending modernism, *La guerra literaria* (The Literary War, 1913), drew a favorable review from Unamuno. In 1916 he became the theater critic of the daily *Liberal*, which marked the height of his literary and social acceptance. His poorer and less well known brother Antonio lived with him in Madrid during 1917 and 1918 while attending the university. The poetry Manuel continually published in newspapers was collected in *Sevilla, y otros poemas* (1919), which seems marred today by superficial Andalusianism, but which influenced the atmosphere in which García Lorca prepared his *Poema del cante hondo* (Poem of Deep Song, 1921). The force of a deep, unspoken emotion behind the simple language of flamenco is what Machado aims at in his versions of popular songs.

Machado also contributed to other poets' magazines—for example, Julio Carol's *Alfar* in 1920 and Jiménez's *Indice* in 1921—poems that were collected in *Ars moriendi* (The Art of Dying, 1921). This book was another "farewell" to poetry, like *El mal poema* in 1909, but Machado this time explains his lack of inspiration as the effect of prosperity instead of poverty: "El poeta de Adelfos dice, al fin" (The Poet of Adelfos Says, Finally) contrasts his present happiness with the despair that fired his early work. Still, as the book's title suggests, the inescapable approach of death gives him new motives for writing in fear and resignation. Shallow poems mixed in with fine ones make this book hard to evaluate as a whole.

Machado did indeed have a stable life and a reputation that was spreading beyond Spain. In 1924 he was a cofounder of the *Revista de la Biblioteca, Archivo y Museo de Madrid* (Review of the Library, Archive and Museum of Madrid) at the Biblioteca Municipal, of which he became the director in 1925. In 1928 he also took over the Museo Municipal. He was one of the few intellectuals able to accept the dictatorship of Gen. Miguel Primo de Rivera in those years, since Machado considered politics unimportant. While collected editions of his poetry appeared regularly, he was more interested in the theater, writing on average a play a year with his brother Antonio from 1926 to 1932. The actress Lola Membrives was their most frequent leading lady, enjoying a great success with *La Lola se va a los puertos* (Lola Goes Off to Sea) in 1929. In that same year, the dictator's son, Jose Antonio Primo de Rivera, who later founded Spain's fascist party, the Falange, was one of the speakers at a banquet to honor both Machado brothers as playwrights. Friends used to guess which scenes each brother had written and always guessed wrong, to the authors' great amusement. Politics made it difficult to produce funny plays, however. *La prima Fernanda* (Cousin Fernanda) had been written before the crisis that ended the monarchy in 1931, but reached the stage afterward (in April), so that many audience members saw the satirical scenes as directed against the fallen court. Man-

Machado in the 1940s delivering a reading of his poetry

uel in particular was angered by so many student strikes and demonstrations; he was more interested in events such as the return of El Gallo to the Madrid bullring after six years' absence in South America. In 1934 his conservative reaction to the rising turmoil of the Second Republic forced Machado's resignation from the paper *Libertad*, for which he had written since 1919, and he retired to the company of his friends in his favorite cafés.

The young poet Manuel Altolaguirre convinced him to publish again and suggested the title for the collection, *Phoenix* (1936). At the age of sixty-two Machado took stock in "Nuevo autorretrato" (New Self-Portrait), based on one of his childhood photographs with a music box; his whole life seemed to be a listening for the music of things as the world passed by. Much of the book is a series of impressionistic sketches of cities of Spain, seasons, and landscapes. Some poems on modernist themes (sensuality, exotic places, lost youth) appear in the section "Confetti." Reaction to *Phoenix* was lost in the chaos of the summer of 1936 as the civil war erupted. Machado and his wife had gone to Burgos to visit Eulalia's sister in a convent, and the revolt isolated the couple in a house full of guests, including the bullfighters Marcial Lalanda and Antonio and Manuel Bienvenida. Burgos became the capital of the Nationalist zone, and once Machado realized he could not return to Madrid, he went to the Nationalist Oficina de Propaganda to ask for work. After the police approved his application, he became one of the leading writers on the Francisco Franco side during the war, even though some questioned his loyalty, since his brother was so prominent on the other side, in the Republic. Manuel Machado's propaganda poems were collected as *Horas de Oro* (Golden Hours, 1938), mostly occasional pieces in traditional meters: heroes of Spain's past such as Charles I, Velázquez, and Guzmán el Bueno are paired with Generals Franco, Moscardó, and Mola, and conservative thinkers such as Menéndez y Pelayo; cities that went Nationalist or were captured early in the war are hailed in sonnets; and religious subjects include replacing a crucifix in a school (illegal under the Republic) and prayers to Saints Augustine, Theresa, and Ignatius of Loyola. Machado had been in the process of converting to Catholicism before the war, under the influence of his wife and a Jesuit confessor, so this book amounts to a public profession of faith. The sonnet on Fra Angelico's painting from *Apolo* was reprinted in *Horas de Oro*, where it is no longer a sensual description of a work of art but a religious meditation on the Annunciation of the Virgin.

In 1938 the Real Academia Española (Spanish Royal Academy), meeting with a remnant of its members in the Franco zone, elected Machado a member in spite of the objections of some fanatics that his early bohemian and cynical verse made him unfit for the honors of the new Catholic, traditionalist Spain they were fighting to establish. Machado's inaugural address, included in *Unos versos, un alma y una época* (Some Verse, a Soul, and an Era, 1940) drew further criticism, since he recounted his biography in a way that stressed his mature rejection of the follies and vices of French culture, which in any case he had merely observed. His youthful errors were forgiven amid pride that he was a truly Spanish poet.

In early 1939, as the war ended, he received news that his brother Antonio had died in a refugee camp in Collioure, France. When Manuel arrived, he found that his mother had died there as well. There was no criticism of his trip, out of respect for his personal feelings and because of a short-lived campaign in Spain to claim that Antonio had been secretly sympathetic to the Franco cause. Manuel returned to Madrid in time for Franco's victory parade, to which he contributed a poem, and, after another police investigation, he resumed his old job at the museum. His literary activities were semiofficial, as a juror on prize committees and a cofounder of Musa Musae, a society to bring together writers even if they had been on the wrong political side. The Falangist-controlled Editora Nacional published an enlarged edition of his 1924 collected poetic works, *Poesía: Opera omnia lírica* (Poetry: Complete Lyric Works, 1940), and his verse was recited at religious and civic festivals. He was able to use his influence to save the jobs of some politically suspect writers, though he did not respond to an appeal to free Miguel Hernández from prison. As a symbol of poetry he presided at many banquets, such as the ones he and the painter Ignacio Zuloaga gave in 1941 to honor the great retired matador Juan Belmonte. He supported the new poetry reviews *Escorial* and *Garcilaso*, calling himself the oldest of the young poets and the youngest of the old. In 1943, aged sixty-nine, he released *Cadencias de cadencias: Nuevas dedicatorias* (Cadences of Cadences: New Dedications), which shows he could write in the neoclassical style of the *Garcilaso* movement, at times as well as any of its younger members. Many of his poems, similar to his earlier approaches to painting and bullfighting, focus on moments in the performing arts: in the section "Epinicios" (Triumphs) he includes tributes to actors and actresses in performances that deserve to be remembered; in "Epicidios" (Eulogies) he praises recently deceased Madrid sculptors, musicians, and operetta composers. Machado includes a neoclassical self-portrait, "El viejo jardinero" (The Old Gardener), presenting himself in the garden of poetry, as well as a personal protest against old age: "Omega." The book closes with eleven devotional sonnets under the heading "Horario" (Book of Hours, which gave a title to the collection of all his religious verse, the posthumous *Horario* (1947).

Manuel Machado (photograph by Alfonso)

In 1944 retirement from the municipal museum was mandatory for Machado, and in the same year the appearance of the review *Espadaña* made it obvious that the newer generation of poets was no longer interested in the officially approved styles. Even the Franco regime was toning down its crusading rhetoric as it became clear that Adolf Hitler was losing the war, so that Machado's praise of the crusade, published as recently as the year before, was discreetly ignored. Machado devoted himself to home life and religious devotions, though occasionally he would publish a poem in the Monarchist daily *ABC* that contained implicit criticism of Franco (Machado had become a royalist). He fell ill attending a friend's funeral in January of 1947 and died at home a few days later, while his fellow members of the Spanish academy were attending their annual New Year's banquet.

Manuel Machado's best work was done early in his life, when he contributed to the growth of modernism in Spain. His experiments with Spanish verse resulted in poems of permanent value in *Alma*, and in some of the poetry of *Alma. Museo. Los cantares*; *El mal poema*; and *Ars moriendi*. His flamenco poetry was what his contemporaries knew him for, although in later years it became superficial. This fact, coupled with his support for the Franco regime, has led to a critical blindness to his real excellence in those books that contain little or none of the Andalusian mystique he cultivated. At his best he gives a poem apparently spontaneous, sincere emotion in the midst of musical elegance and verbal finesse.

Biography:

Gerardo Diego, *Manuel Machado, poeta* (Madrid: Nacional, 1974).

References:

Giovanni Allegra, "Manuel Machado e il male di Saturno," in his *Il Regno Interiore: Premesse e sembianti del modernismo in Spagna* (Milan: Jaca, 1982), pp. 189-218; translated by Vicente Martín Pindalo as "Manuel Machado y el mal de Saturno," in his *El reino interior: Premisas y semblanzas del modernismo en España* (Madrid: Encuentro, 1990), pp. 200-232;

Dámaso Alonso, "Ligereza y gravedad en la poesía de Manuel Machado," in his *Poetas españoles contemporáneos* (Madrid: Gredos, 1952), pp. 50-102;

J. Gordon Brotherston, *Manuel Machado: A Revaluation* (Cambridge: Cambridge University Press, 1968);

Gerardo Diego, "Manuel Machado (1874-1947)," in his *Crítica y poesía* (Madrid: Júcar, 1984), pp. 253-261;

Gillian Gayton, *Manuel Machado y los poetas simbolistas franceses* (Valencia, Spain: Bello, 1975);

Ricardo Gullón, "Relaciones entre Juan Ramón y Manuel Machado," in his *Direcciones del Modernismo*, second edition, enlarged (Madrid: Gredos, 1971), pp. 210-227;

Juan Ramón Jiménez, *El modernismo: Notas hacia un curso (1923)* (Mexico City: Aguilar, 1962);

Francisco López Estrada and others, *Doce comentarios a la poesía de Manuel Machado* (Seville, Spain: Universidad de Sevilla, 1975);

Miguel de Unamuno, *De esto y aquello* (Buenos Aires: Sudamericana, 1950), I: 184-192.

Papers:

The Biblioteca Machado is at the Institución Fernán González, Burgos, Spain.

Rafael Morales

(31 July 1919 -)

Paula W. Shirley
Columbia College, Columbia, South Carolina

BOOKS: *Poemas del toro* (Madrid: Hispánica/Adonais, 1943);

El corazón y la tierra (Valladolid, Spain: Santarén/Halcón, 1946);

Los desterrados (Madrid: Hispánica/Adonais, 1947);

Poemas del toro y otros versos (Madrid: Aguado, 1949);

Canción sobre el asfalto (Madrid: Poetas/Radio, 1954);

La pintura de Juan Guillermo (Madrid: Ateneo, 1957);

Antología y pequeña historia de mis versos (Madrid: Escélicer, 1958);

Entrevistas de Clarinero (Mexico City, 1958);

La máscara y los dientes (Madrid: Española, 1958);

Dardo, el caballo del bosque (Madrid: Doncel, 1961);

Granadeño, toro bravo (Madrid: Nacional, 1964);

Poesías completas (Madrid: Giner, 1967);

La rueda y el viento (Salamanca, Spain: Alamo, 1971);

Antología poética (Barcelona: Pozanco, 1979);

Obra poética (Madrid: Espasa-Calpe, 1982);

Reflexiones sobre mi poesía (Madrid: Escuela Universitaria, 1982).

OTHER: *Literatura contemporánea española e hispanoamericana*, edited by Morales and others (Madrid: O.F.E., 1964);

Los 100 poetas mejores de la lírica castellana, edited by Morales (Madrid: Giner, 1967).

Rafael Morales is one of the most lyrical and humanistic poets of the post-civil-war era in Spain. Whether describing a solitary lover, a fighting bull, or an old jacket, he evokes the lyricism he perceives in all things. Among contemporary Spanish poets he has been admired for his innocence and the childlike love of all people that serves as a base for his poetic explorations.

Born in Talavera de la Reina, Spain, on 31 July 1919, Morales grew up during the turbulent periods of King Alfonso XIII's reign, of the short-lived Republic, and of the civil war. Morales remained in his hometown to complete his *bachillerato*, but moved to Madrid to pursue the *licenciatura* in romance philology at the University of Madrid. During World War II he received a scholarship to study in the Facultad de Letras de Coimbra in Portugal. Since that time he has written several articles on Portuguese literature. He was for many years a professor of literature at the University of Madrid and secretary of the Department of Literature and Philology of the Juan March Foundation. For several years he was director of the journal *Estafeta Literaria*. In addition to his poetry, Morales has written some children's books.

During the time Morales attended the University of Madrid, whose buildings had been severely damaged during the civil war, he and the other students of the Facultad de Filosofía y Letras had to meet in other quarters, the Caserón de San Bernardo. While efforts were underway around them to repair the physical and social devastation of the war, the students argued in *tertulias* (literary circles) and read their poetry to each other. This dynamic atmosphere shaped young Morales's literary career.

He had written his first poem at age seven and had first published some lyrics when he was fourteen. His early poetry was influenced by his idol, Vicente Aleixandre, whom he met in 1936 and whose prizewinning *La destrucción o el amor* (Destruction or Love, 1935) had impressed Morales deeply. But at twenty-one he produced his first group of poems that separated his work from such influences, and it brought him a great deal of attention from people important in the literary world. The collection was published in 1943 as *Poemas del toro* (Poems of the Bull).

In his semiautobiographical work *Antología y pequeña historia de mis versos* (Anthology and Little History of My Verses, 1958) Morales describes the inspiration for his first book of poetry. In the summer of 1940 Morales was home in Talavera de la Reina, on vacation from his university studies, when he had an experience he was soon to

translate into poetry. He attended the stockyard sales one day and stopped to observe some restless bulls. Later on in the day, remembering the most persistently troublesome bull of the lot, he felt the need to write a poem. That sonnet, "El toro," was to become the first in *Poemas del toro*. Morales wanted to write more lyrics on the subject, and as soon as he returned to Madrid, he visited his mentor Aleixandre, who responded enthusiastically to the sonnets. Morales held a reading for his fellow students, a reading also attended by Gerardo Diego and Aleixandre. José María de Cossío, the historian and critic of the bullfight, had already seen the sonnets and asked for autographed copies. Some of the poems were soon

published in the prestigious magazine *Escorial*.

Morales was asked to participate in a series of poetry readings at Madrid's Ateneo, where his work was enthusiastically received. His poems were heard by José Luis Cano, Rafael Montesinos, and José García Nieto. *Poemas del toro* became the first poetry published in the Adonais Collection, which was initiated by Juan Guerrero and Cano. Morales's book met with considerable success. The critics praised him, and the first printing quickly sold out. *Poemas del toro* is, not surprisingly, dedicated to Aleixandre.

Cossío, feeling the excitement of discovery, wanted the pleasure of writing the prologue to the first edition. Because the fighting bull had been a constant, if not overworked, theme in Spanish poetry, Cossío expressed delight in discovering a poetic voice speaking with "un matiz de emoción lírica muy personal o singular que puede llevarnos al delicioso engaño que llamamos novedad" (very personal or singular shading of lyric emotion that can lead us into the delicious illusion we call originality). In volume 2 of Cossío's *Los toros* (1947) he devotes a lengthy discussion to "Los toros y la poesía," in which he asserts that Morales's "El toro" is the last great taurine poem written in Spanish: "El vigor de la expresión, lo misterioso y tremendo del sujeto, la realización afortunadísima del poema, justifican este juicio. Y el enfoque de tema tan elaborado como ha podido verse a lo largo de estos apuntes, enaltece con su novedad, su originalidad y su hondura, la poesía de la fiesta de toros" (The vigor of expression, the mystery and power of the subject, the fortunate realization of the poem, support this judgment. And the focus given to such a complicated subject as seen in these notes ennobles with its novelty, originality, and depth, the poetry of bullfighting).

Morales's taurine poetry is informed by a single concept—that of the creature as an elemental force. Perhaps the best-known poem of his first collection, "El toro" bristles with the serenely contained fury of the beast in whose "piel poderosa se serena / su tormentosa fuerza enamorada" (powerful skin is calmed / its stormy enamored force). The tone of the series is somber, suggesting the dignity of this powerful animal that is born in order to die. Morales writes in "Plaza desierta" (Deserted Plaza): "Pasó la vida por aquí llevada / pasó un gran mar, un viento, una tormenta / pasó mugiendo un toro hacia la nada" (Life passed, swept through here / A quiet sea, a wind, a storm passed / A bull passed roaring toward nothingness), lines that suggest the bond shared by all living things whose struggle to survive inevitably ends in death.

Most taurine poetry had dealt with the bull as an element in the *fiesta brava*, or as an overworked symbol; Morales changed that. His poems present the bull as an entity apart from the bullfight, and they show a new sensitivity to the creature's experience of freedom, inevitably followed by pain.

The majority of *Poemas del toro* focuses on the *toro bravo*, but there are some poems dedicated to cows and calves, and a few poems use the bull as a metaphor for longing, disappointment, and even Spain. At first reading, anyone

knowledgeable about modern Spanish poetry might suppose the influence of the poet Miguel Hernández in Morales's taurine poems, but Miguel D'Ors in his thorough work on the *Poemas del toro* rejects this notion, declaring that the similarity between some sonnets of the two writers is based on their knowledge of the Golden Age poet Francisco de Quevedo.

Formally Morales demonstrates domination of and facility with the traditional sonnet form. Most of his *toro* poems observe the *abba abba cdc cdc* rhyme scheme. In *Antología y pequeña historia* Morales asserts that for him the sonnet is easy and that he is attracted to it for that reason, but he also expresses what is essential for every writer of lyrics: "Al poeta que le falla la forma, le falla todo. Ideas poéticas las tiene cualquiera, lo difícil es expresarlas como corresponde" (The poet who lacks form lacks all. Anybody has poetic ideas, the hard thing is to express them fittingly).

Luis López-Anglada hailed 1943 as a milestone in Spanish poetry for two reasons: Pedro de Lorenzo's manifesto in the first issue of *Garcilaso*; and the publication of *Poemas del toro*. *Garcilaso*, which published some of Morales's poetry, was intimately associated with the group of young poets called the "Juventud Creadora" (Creative Youth), but Morales has always resisted being labeled according to any poetic group or school.

Even while finishing the *toro* poems, Morales began working on his next group, the ones in *El corazón y la tierra* (The Heart and the Land, 1946). He has called this book (in *Antología y pequeña historia*) "el libro condenado, el libro maldito que ha de padecer un largo purgatorio" (the condemned, damned book that is to suffer a long purgatory). Impelled by financial needs in 1945, Morales gave the journal *Fantasía* all the poems he had. These poems lack the unifying theme and spirit of the *Poemas del toro*, and Morales claims that some were destined for the trash can. Nevertheless, when early in 1946 Halcón of Valladolid, Spain, wanted to publish his new poems from *Fantasía*, he agreed, adding some but not removing the ones he considered inferior. Even through several reprintings and its 1967 inclusion in *Poesías completas*, the 1946 version of *El corazón y la tierra* remained intact because Morales did not want to spend time editing old material.

Three themes predominate in *El corazón y la tierra*: love, landscape, and death. These poems are filled with images of mist, silence, solitude, and nothingness. The landscapes are usually empty, and lovers are separated. In "Tierra he de ser" (Land of Being) human destiny is described unflinchingly in the final couplet: "¡Que terrible es pensarse si se ama / vecino eterno de la eterna piedra!" (How terrible to wonder if one loves, / eternal neighbor of the eternal rock!).

One of Morales's poems frequently included in anthologies is from this *El corazón* series—"A un esqueleto de muchacha" (To a Skeleton of a Girl), an homage to Lope de Vega: "Aquí el cuello de garza sostenía / la alada soledad de la cabeza / y aquí el cabello undoso se vertía" (Here the crane's neck held / the winged aloneness of the head / and here the wavy hair flowed down).

Morales has always rejected attempts to categorize him or his work, but perhaps none has rankled more than the claim that *El corazón y la tierra* was the initiator of *tremendismo*. The *tremendista* (grotesque) emphasis on the most negative and monstrous elements of human existence is often associated with a novel, *La familia de Pascual Duarte* by Camilo José Cela; nevertheless, the term was used to describe *El corazón* because of poems such as "Paisaje" (Landscape):

El cielo plomo gris que se derrumba
sobre el pavor silente del paisaje,
es un inmenso buitre hambriento y sordo,
un infinito dios, amenazante.

(The lead grey sky that falls
on the silent fear of the fields
is a great hungry deaf vulture,
an infinite, threatening god.)

With regard to Morales's work, the *tremendismo* tag is probably of more historical than poetic interest. A more useful poetic category for *El corazón* is that of neoromantic. Morales himself says the book is a reaction against the neoclassicism in vogue at the time of its publication. In spirit and language much of *El corazón* is in the tradition of the great romantic Spanish poets José de Espronceda and José Zorrilla.

When *Poemas del toro* was published in 1943, it was greeted as a revival of a humanitarian strain in poetry that had been subdued by formalism. Morales's collection *Los desterrados* (The Exiles), first published in 1947, was a further development of this trend. The publication background of the book shows Morales's compassion, which is demonstrated frequently in his work. He

recounts the events leading to the publication of *Los desterrados* in *Antología y pequeña historia*: Cano wanted to publish Morales's new poems in the Colección Adonais, and it was agreed that *Los desterrados* would appear, followed by *Los muertos* (The Dead, 1947), a group of poems by Morales's and Cano's friend José Luis Hidalgo, who had been writing, gravely ill of tuberculosis, in a sanatorium. Hidalgo knew of Morales's work in progress, having heard some of it in their *tertulia* at a café, El Cocodrilo, and Morales had even given him an offprint of seven poems that had appeared in *Escorial*. When it became clear that Hidalgo would not live long enough to see his book come out if the original plan were followed, Cano asked Morales if he would consent to a change in order, so that there would be a chance for Hidalgo to see his book in print. Morales quickly agreed, but although the publication process was hastened, Hidalgo died before *Los muertos* was published. Morales links this event with the purpose of *Los desterrados*, describing it as a book that tries to exalt compassion and charity.

The five-part structure of *Los desterrados* conforms to a hierarchy of Christian concerns. In the first section, "Las enfermedades" (The Sicknesses) four poems portray isolation based on illness or disfigurement. The images repeatedly convey absence and abandonment, as in "Los enfermos" (The Sick): "en esta carne que se siente llena / de una ausencia brutal, de inmensa herida" (in this flesh which feels full / of a brutal absence, of immense wound); and in "Los ciegos" (The Blind):

Sombra son nada más, tan sólo sombra,
nube de carne que en el suelo pasa;
en su entraña el abismo, y en su frente
un celeste silencio sin estrellas.

(They are shade, no more, only shade,
cloud of flesh passing over the ground;
in their heart the abyss, in their face
a heavenly starless silence.)

The second section, "Soledad, pena y olvido" (Solitude, Pain, and Oblivion), explores the isolation of the emotions, where sadness and loneliness rule. In "Los abandonados" the poet reveals the desolation of being alone:

Cuando uno queda solo, cuando queda
el alma sola doloridamente,
cuando todos olvidan que vivimos

Fernandez Spencer, Rafael Montesinos, Morales, and Blas de Otero at a May 1953 meeting of writers

estamos muertos ya, somos ausentes.
Si en otro corazón no vive el hombre,
ha muerto ya, Dios mío, para siempre.

(When one remains alone, when the soul
remains painfully alone,
when everyone forgets that we live
we're already dead, we're absent.
If man lives in no other heart,
He is already dead, my God, forever.)

This poem, while not the best Morales offers in this volume, certainly expresses most clearly its theme: that one must be loved in order to be truly alive, that a person alone is an absence.

In the next sections, titled "Los sueños y la muerte" (Dreams and Death) and "El corazón y la nada" (The Heart and Nothingness), poems describe the desolation of death, memory, old age, and disbelief. In the poem "Los ateos" (The Atheists) solitude is created by the absence of God. "Los idiotas," the last poem in the fourth section, also reminds readers of the atheist's condition: "Los idiotas son carne de la nada, de nadie; / son soledades vivas, desiertos corazones" (The idiots are flesh of the nothingness, of no one; / they are living solitudes, deserted hearts).

The book ends with a poem under the section title "Oración." "Invocación al señor" is a sonnet/prayer that in the octave asks God to eradicate the pain and agony that fill the human heart, and in the sestet accepts suffering, if it is deserved, but asks God's divine warmth for sustenance.

In his essay on Morales, Leopoldo-Eulogio Palacios describes *Los desterrados* as "poesía en que el hombre aparece representado en los ejemplares de nuestra especie más dignos de lástima . . ." (poetry in which man is represented by the most pitiful examples of our species). Morales, from his earliest poetic efforts, has demonstrated profound compassion. In an interview with Salvador Jiménez in *Españoles de hoy* (Spaniards of Today, 1966) Morales said the human virtue that most fascinates him is charity, but what has most disappointed him is the lack of love for one's fellow people. This tension runs through every volume of poetry Morales has written, finding full expression in *Los desterrados*.

Between 1947 and 1953, because of a full schedule and fatigue, Morales was unable to write as much as he wanted. And yet, when in 1954 his new collection *Canción sobre el asfalto*

(Song on Asphalt) was finally ready for publication, it was greeted as his best effort and was awarded the prestigious Premio Nacional de Literatura for that year.

In his first three books Morales's role was that of the rehumanizer of Spanish poetry. *Canción* signaled for him the beginning of an era of social poetry, which is not to say that he championed a specific political or social cause, but rather that the poems of *Canción* call for a greater awareness of and sensitivity to other human beings and to objects as well. Julio López in *Poesía y realidad en Rafael Morales* (1979) aptly describes the humanistic concerns of Morales: "*Canción sobre el asfalto* incide de lleno en la necesidad de humanizar las ciudades monstruosas en que vivimos mediante una solución de signo espiritualista que entra en un claro humanismo cristiano, de cuño evangélico, capaz de hacer a los hombres más humanos y sensibles, dispuestos a conmoverse no sólo ante sus semejantes sino incluso ante los objetos más miserables que, a partir de ese momento se tornan en compañeros y en humanos" (*Song on Asphalt* meets completely the need to humanize the monstrous cities we live in with a spiritual kind of solution, a clear Christian humanism, of evangelical stamp, that makes men more human and sensitive, able to sympathize not only with their fellow creatures but with the meanest objects, which then become human and companions).

The themes of presence and absence dominate *Canción sobre el asfalto*, with the primary focus on the city. It is the environment that frequently robs humankind of humanity (presence) and forces people into spiritual isolation (absence). Highly diverse topics are treated in the poems: ragpickers, the silence of a suburb, the Christ child, and the poet's shoes.

Lyrics that present details of the urban landscape are invariably full of sadness, describing solitary activities. In "Los barrenderos" (The Street Sweepers) the carts of the workers carry "acongojadas flores y muertas mariposas, / billetes del tranvía, brutalmente arrugados" (choked flowers and dead butterflies, / trolley tickets, brutally wrinkled). The remnants of life are visible throughout these poems.

Within the second of four sections, "Lejos queda el asfalto" (Asphalt Remains Far Away), several religious poems express the joy of the Virgin and Christ child, the Crucifixion, and faith. Juxtaposed with these are two about Adam and the fall, suggesting the limits of human nature and alienation from God, the presence who gives meaning to life.

Some of the most felicitous lyrics of *Canción* focus on objects, again suggesting presence/absence. In "Soneto triste para mi última chaqueta" (Sad Sonnet for My Last Jacket) the speaker reflects on his jacket, which will one day be empty—"cobijará una ausencia, una lejana memoria de la vida presurosa" (will cover an absence, a far memory of hurried life). Similarly the final poem, "Cancioncilla de amor a mis zapatos" (Little Love Song for My Shoes), is a paean to the thin soles that separate people from earth:

> Bajo la suela delgada,
> siento la tierra que espera . . .
> Entre la vida y la nada,
> ¡que delgada es la frontera!
>
> (Under the thin sole
> I feel the earth waiting . . .
> Between life and nothing,
> How thin the border!)

Morales's most frequently translated poem and the one that has been most often selected for anthologies, "Cántico doloroso al cubo de la basura" (Sorrowful Canticle to the Garbage Can), presents a trash can in maternal terms: "En ti se hizo redonda la ternura, / se hizo redonda, suave y dolorosa" (Tenderness became round in you, / became round, soft and sorrowful). The can lovingly embraces the most humble of objects—an apple peel, a dusty bit of banana. Morales's artistry exalts the humble and the forgotten.

Images of the city—asphalt, bricks, neon, and cement—abound. López says, "La estructura de *Canción sobre el asfalto* viene entonces a simbolizar la estructura misma de la ciudad: un mundo de objetos, seres, personas y problemas anudado y atenazado por un cinturón de cemento, luces de neón y columnas de humo negro" (The structure of *Song on Asphalt* comes to symbolize the very structure of the city: a world of objects, beings, persons, and problems knotted and tied by a cement belt, neon lights, and columns of black smoke).

Morales worked on poems for another collection for approximately five years, finding it difficult to write because of his professorial duties. In 1957 he received a grant from the Fundación Juan March, which assisted him in the preparation of *La máscara y los dientes* (The Mask and the Teeth), published in 1958. An unusual volume,

Morales circa 1960

and to some extent a departure for Morales, *La máscara* describes one day in the life of a nameless male office worker. Morales called it "lirodrama," saying (in *Poesías completas*), "no me he propuesto desarrollar un poema novelesco, sino una acción tratada líricamente, que no es igual" (I have not proposed to develop a novelistic poem, but an action treated lyrically, which is not the same).

The action Morales refers to is organized in sections beginning with "El alba" (Dawn) and moving through aspects of the man's daily experience, such as "El tranvía" and "La oficina," to "La noche" (The Night) and "Punto final" (Final Point). The anonymous protagonist is not depicted fully as an individual but as a symbol of modern, urban humankind, living quietly, desperately alienated from other people. As his day progresses, readers realize that each day is the same, equally meaningless: "Aunque mañana empiece un nuevo día, / nunca las naves llegarán al puerto" (Though tomorrow may start a new day, / the ships will never make port).

Biblical allusions are abundant, as one expects in Morales's work. Indeed, *La máscara* is marked by biblical themes: the fall, the flood, and divine wrath, all typically expressed in an acer-

bic tone. Morales's social and Christian concerns merge in *La máscara*. López contrasts these poems with those in *Canción sobre el asfalto*, saying that *La máscara* is more violent and unbridled, showing a much crueler and less compassionate world: "La decepción ante la pérdida de la belleza y de la bondad, el eskepticismo nacido del paraíso perdido para siempre por virtud de los resabios maliciosos del Adán oficinista, del cainismo y de la concepción selvática del mundo, engendran un libro amargo, menos positivo que el anterior, con todos los destellos que pueda tener (que los tiene) de conmiseración e incitación a la fraternidad" (Disillusionment at the loss of beauty and goodness, scepticism born of paradise lost forever by the vicious habits of the office Adam, of Cainism and a jungle idea of the world, engender a bitter book, less positive than the previous one, whatever traces there may be [there are] of commiseration and appeals to brotherhood).

Sounds and images assault urbanites, who become indistinguishable from objects around them. A surrealistic description of a streetcar ("El tranvía") conveys life's meaninglessness:

> Y el tranvía prosigue,
> avanza, avanza,
> con su carga tumultuaria de tempestades,
> con su gran viento azul de telegrama,
> con sus corazones indefensos,
> con aburrimientos esteparios,
> con sueños,
> con zapatos,
> con esperanzas,
> con corbatas,
> con odios,
> con pañuelos,
> con el plural ramaje de la vida.
>
> (And the tram runs on,
> advances, advances,
> with its tumultous load of tempests,
> with its great blue telegram wind,
> with its helpless hearts,
> with boredoms boundless as the steppes,
> with dreams,
> with shoes,
> with hopes,
> with ties,
> with hates,
> with handkerchiefs,
> with the tangled branches of life.)

In *La máscara y los dientes*, by choosing an anonymous, contemporary antihero and placing him poetically within biblical tradition, Morales communicates the vulnerability and helplessness of all human beings who, since Adam and Eve, have yearned for paradise and found instead a prison.

Morales, in the prologue to his *Poesías completas*, describes his poetry as faithful to "lo esencial humano y artístico...." He goes on to set forth the three bases upon which his poems are created: "la búsqueda de la belleza expresiva, que afecta al aspecto formal; la atracción de la realidad del mundo, que afecta a los temas; el amor, que afecta al contenido esencial, al sentido más profundo y universal de toda ella" (the search for expressive beauty, which affects the formal aspect; the attraction of the reality of the world, which affects the themes; love, which affects the essential content, the most deep and universal sense of it all).

Reviewing the *Poesías completas* for *Crónica de Poesía*, Emilio Miró stated that Morales, an existential poet, is a religious one, and the absence of God in the heart of man does not mean God does not exist, but rather that man has abandoned and denied him. Miró's final remarks underscore Morales's significance: [this work] "lo coloca—lo confirma, mejor dicho—en uno de los primeros puestos de la poesía española contemporánea" (places him—better, confirms him—in one of the first places of contemporary Spanish poetry).

Morales further developed his "lirodrama" form in a 1971 publication—also funded by a grant from the Fundación Juan March—*La rueda y el viento* (The Wheel and the Wind). More loosely organized than *La máscara*, it is a rather free-flowing series of lyrics divided only into part 1 and part 2. In an afterword Morales describes *La rueda y el viento* as an "eslabón o episodio independiente ese drama, o quizá farsa, de la vida humana que inicié con mi libro *La máscara y los dientes*" (link or episode independent of that drama, or farce, of human life that I began with my book *La máscara y los dientes*).

La rueda is frequently more symbolic than *La máscara*, particularly in its presentation of characters. The office worker of *La máscara*, although a representative of modern humankind is, nonetheless, a fairly distinct entity. The characters who move through the pages of *La rueda* are types, such as the Samaritan.

The epic intentions of this volume quickly become apparent as readers are immediately immersed in the dawn of a New World, the biblical Genesis: "La luz despliega lenta / su tierno desper-

tar de madreselva / ... / la candorosa aurora edénica del mundo" (The light spreads slow / its tender honeysuckle wakening / ... / ingenuous edenic dawn of the world). Fresh and recently awakened, the heart gives itself to dreams and breaks the wall of night. But, as in the biblical paradigm, the Eden of *La rueda* is invaded by vice. Walls are erected that keep people separate from others: "Cada uno su muro contra el otro construye" (Each one his wall against the other builds). Images of walls, labyrinths, and closed doors signal isolation. God is present, but unrecognized: "pasa el amor, herido, con su cruz, sin delito, / junto al muro de helada rigidez persistente" (Love passes, wounded, with his cross, blameless, / by the wall of frozen stiffness persistent).

The poems become less biblical in imagery as a series of repetitious lyrics suggest the spatio-temporal repetition of life:

> Olas, olas, olas, olas ...
> con el hombre, con el viento;
> zapatos que van, que vienen
> con la risa, con los sueños;
> ramas, ramas, ramas, ramas
> con el hombre, con el viento;
> zapatos que van, que vienen
> con los vivos, con los muertos;
> arena, arena y arena
> siempre y siempre en movimiento ...
>
> Y la rueda gira y gira
> con el hombre, con el viento. ...
>
> (Waves, waves, waves, waves ...
> with man, with wind;
> shoes coming, going,
> with the smile, with dreams;
> Shoots, shoots, shoots, shoots,
> with man, with the wind;
> shoes coming, going
> with the living, with the dead;
> sand, sand and sand
> always and always moving ...
>
> And the wheel spins and spins
> with man, with the wind. ...)

Part 2 proclaims a world in which "La diosa Tecnos" (The Goddess Tecnos) reigns; the machine is now God. Humankind remains without peace or rest, and the world continues to repeat itself:

> Va cambiando de actores,
> pero no se advierte el cambio.

Las máscaras son las mismas,
iguales los escenarios.

(It's changing actors
But the change isn't noticed.
The masks are the same,
The scenes the same.)

A fatalistic tone persists throughout *La rueda y el viento* and makes the human tenure on earth seem uncompromisingly miserable. The narrative voice often moralizes as Morales expresses the tyranny of vice that keeps Man, the protagonist, enchained.

La rueda y el viento did not break new ground as Morales's other volumes of poetry had. As a more abstract successor of *La máscara y los dientes*, it failed to strike the same responsive chord as the original "lirodrama" had. *La rueda* is not without its fine moments, but the repetition of moral themes expressed in an unremittingly negative tone often wears down the patience of a reader who expects to find in Morales's work a balance between celebration and despair.

Obra poética, published in 1982, is a most useful collection of Morales's poetry and includes *Poemas del toro, El corazón y la tierra, Los desterrados, Canción sobre el asfalto, La máscara y los dientes,* and *La rueda y el viento*. In addition, a set of previously unpublished poems entitled "Prado de serpientes" (Meadow of Serpents) brings together twenty-one lyric pieces written between 1969 and 1981. The epigraph to the latter work is a phrase from Pleberio's lament in *La Celestina*. This litany of the grief-stricken father centers on the vile and dangerous labyrinth of life in which people are destined to confront misery, and it compares life to a meadow of serpents. "Prado de serpientes" presents themes of loneliness, solitude, and nostalgia with an occasional expression of affirmation to lighten the bleak mood. A clear evocation of these themes is found in "Ahora que el otoño me unce a su tristeza," in which the speaker is drawn by autumn into the sadness of goodbyes and memory. Some of these poems focus deeply on an emotion or an image that comes to life through Morales's lyrical expression. Morales's poetic gift is still impressive in these later poems. The revelation lying in wait in an ordinary object continues to be characteristic of his poetic impulse.

Rafael Morales has been, according to C. D. Ley, "one of the most read poets of his generation. His poems have been reprinted more frequently than those of any other poet after 1939." The poetry of Morales is a compendium of Spanish poetic traditions spanning the baroque and romantic ages as well as the Generation of '27. But Morales has not depended solely on tradition as a source of poetic forms, and certainly not as a source of themes. *Los desterrados, Canción sobre el asfalto,* and his "lirodramas" have had a profound influence on post-civil-war Spanish poetry, placing humanity—including the humble and forgotten—once again at the center of poetic concerns.

Interview:

Salvador Jiménez, *Españoles de hoy* (Madrid: Nacional, 1966).

References:

Vicente Aleixandre, *Los encuentros* (Madrid: Guadarrama, 1958);

Victor G. de la Concha, *La poesía española de posguerra: Teoría e historia de sus movimientos* (Madrid: Española Soto, 1973);

Miguel D'Ors, *Los Poemas del toro de Rafael Morales* (Pamplona, Spain: Universidad de Navarra, 1972);

C. D. Ley, *Spanish Poetry Since 1939* (Washington, D.C.: Catholic University Press, 1962);

Julio López, *Poesía y realidad en Rafael Morales* (Barcelona: Pozanco, 1979);

Luis López-Anglada, *Panorama poético español: Historia y antología, 1939-64* (Madrid: Nacional, 1965);

Leopoldo-Eulogio Palacios, *El juicio y el ingenio y otros ensayos* (Madrid: Española, 1967).

Leopoldo Panero

(17 October 1909 - 27 August 1962)

Ana María Alfaro-Alexander
Castleton State College

BOOKS: *Guía artística y sentimental de la ciudad de Astorga*, by Panero and others (León, Spain, 1929);

La estancia vacía, Fragmentos (Madrid: Escorial, 1945);

Escrito a cada instante (Madrid: Escélicer, 1949);

Canto personal. Carta perdida a Pablo Neruda (Madrid: Cultura Hispánica, 1953);

C. Martínez Novillo (Madrid: Dirección General de Bellas Artes, 1959);

Poesía 1932-1960 (Madrid: Cultura Hispánica, 1963);

Antología, edited by Juan Luis Panero (Esplugas de Llobregat, Spain: Plaza & Janés, 1973);

Obras completas: Poesías; Prosa, 2 volumes, edited by Juan Luis Panero (Madrid: Nacional, 1973).

OTHER: *Antología de la poesía hispanoamericana*, 2 volumes, edited by Panero (Madrid: Nacional, 1944, 1945).

Leopoldo Panero's reputation as a lyric poet has continued to grow since his death, as complete editions and exhaustive critiques of his work have become more generally available. Among Spanish poets who defined themselves generationally, Panero had the misfortune of belonging to the ill-fated "Generation of 1936." Its members had barely started on their work or had recently emerged from the shadow of the brilliant and coherent "Generation of 1927," when Spain suffered that almost total cultural eclipse instituted by the insurgent victors of its civil war. During the ensuing years of seemingly interminable dictatorship—when major poets were silent or absent and ideas were anathema—Panero's quiet, insistent lyrics, which celebrate the acceptable themes of family, landscape, religion, and death, came increasingly to prominence. At the time of his death he was regarded, along with Luis Rosales, Dionisio Ridruejo, and Luis Felipe Vivanco, as representative of the generation's "Garcilasismo," the adherence to Renaissance formulas as a sign of fidelity to Spain's traditionalist culture. In Panero's case this is more by default than by design; his poetry became increasingly personal, differing from his contemporaries. However, his eclecticism, intense cultivation of his vocation, and meticulous craftmanship did fulfill critic Torrente Ballester's definition of the mission of the "Generation of '36" as being the continuity of Spanish culture.

Leopoldo Panero Torbado was the youngest boy born to Moisés Panero and Máxima Torbado de Panero in Astorga, in the Spanish province of León. Astorga, in which he spent an idyllic childhood, was to remain his home both emotionally and physically throughout his life. Almost all the themes he elaborates in his mature poetry originated in the pristine experience of his childhood and youth. His love of literature was encouraged during visits to the home of his maternal grandparents in the company of his brother Juan. The grandparents lived in the adjacent mountains and possessed an unusually large library. Juan was closest to Leopoldo of all the children and it was with Juan that he later boarded at the secondary school run by the Saint Bernard Brothers of the Christian Doctrine in San Sebastián. After his first years of college in Valladolid, Panero, his brother Juan, and their friends Luis Alonso Luengo and Ricardo Gullón spent the summer of 1928 publishing a weekly literary review, *Humo*. The four young men also put together a study of their town, which they called *Guía artística y sentimental de la ciudad de Astorga* (Artistic and Sentimental Guide to the City of Astorga), published in 1929. The same year saw the death of Panero's grandfather, the first of the great personal losses that were ultimately transformed into the only major theme of his poetry not present in his serene childhood—his recurrent meditations on temporality and death.

It was also during 1929 that Panero demonstrated initially his talents as a prose writer and also began to compose poetry. At that time he was a law student at the University of Madrid.

Leopoldo Panero, circa 1960

He began frequenting the capital's cultural circles in the company of others, such as Antonio Maravall, José Ramón Santeiro, José Antonio Muñoz Rojas, and Luis Filgueira. Panero then established the periodical *Nueva Revista*, which published his "Crónica cuando amanece" (Chronicle When It Dawns, 1929), "Poema de la niebla" (Mist's Poem, 1930), and a panegyric to the new vanguard poetic movement *creacionismo*.

Panero's earliest efforts strongly reflect the influence of Jorge Guillén's cerebral approach to poetry. This master so impressed the fledgling poet Panero that he committed Guillén's *Cántico* (Canticle, 1928) to memory. Panero's first poems belong to the so-called pure poetry, which attempted to refine emotion and experience to a quintessential state of illumination by purging poetry of narrative and description. After some time, he began to experiment, making use of

free verse, Dadaism, and the shifting oneiric imagery of surrealism. He was ultimately either uneasy or unsatisfied with modernism, and it disappeared from his work after 1936. In his later critical discussions of these schools, he claimed that the moral cynicism of surrealism had dismayed him, but he credited the experimentation and ferment with bringing a freshness to language.

In the fall of 1929 Doctor César Alonso Delás diagnosed Leopoldo Panero as suffering from tuberculosis and sent him to the Royal Sanatorium of Guadarrama, where he stayed for eight months. There he became strongly attached to another youthful patient, Joaquina Márquez, who died some months later in a Swiss sanatorium. The poignant melancholy of this association echoes throughout his "Versos de Guadarrama" (in the journal *Fantasía*, 1945; collected in *Obras*

Panero with his wife, Felicidad, and son, Juan Luis, in the 1940s

completas, 1973). In the summer of 1930 Panero returned to Astorga and retired to the mountains to strengthen both body and soul. There he read as much as he could. He also became more reserved and isolated and began to develop the persona readers recognize as the mature Panero: a grave attitude preserves a lyric sensibility that blossoms in isolated communion with the timeless landscape of his native mountains. "Esa pequeña hoja" (That Little Leaf), completed in 1931 but unpublished until it appeared in *Noreste* in fall 1934 (also in *Obras completas*), although stylistically modernist, begins to signal his mature work in its use of metaphor and the treatment of landscape as the subject matter of a poetic world.

It was during this period that he completed "Versos de Guadarrama," which had been gestating during his convalescent walks at the sanatorium. It is an outburst of old-fashioned, simple lyricism that he did not dare publish in those modernist times; he kept it among his papers until the changed climate of 1945. In the early 1930s he enjoyed good health and traveled to study French and English literature in Tours, Poitiers, and Cambridge. Stimulated by these new experiences, he continued to publish modernist and surrealist poems in magazines all across Spain.

In July 1936 the Spanish Civil War began, and Panero's outlook on life drastically changed. The war did away with all freedom. His regular meetings at the Café Universal had labeled him as subversive, and on 19 October 1936 he was arrested and accused of collecting funds for the outlawed "Socorro rojo" (Red Aid) while abroad. Neither his brother Juan, who had joined the Nationalist army, nor his father was able to intervene. However, Panero's capable, strong-willed mother took the lead in his defense. She had saved all his written requests for money from abroad as well as the receipts of the money orders they had sent him, clearly demonstrating that he had been on a private trip and not a politically funded mission. She then sought the intercession of Miguel de Unamuno—Panero had traveled with him as his interpreter while they were in England. Lastly she called on a remote relative, Carmen Polo, the ultraconservative wife of Gen. Francisco Franco. Thanks to her, Panero was freed and returned to Astorga in November.

Despite the acquittal, police visits to his home continued. Finding himself unable to live under the conditions of constant threat, he joined the Nationalist forces, thereby allaying further suspicion. The peace thus attained was short-lived. On 7 August 1937 Juan died in an automobile accident. The effect on Leopoldo was devastating and lasting. From this time onward he abandoned all flirtation with modern themes, though not their meters. At this point his anguish provoked great changes.

"Adolescente en sombra" (Adolescent in Shadow, 1938)—in *Poesía 1932-1960* (1963)—the poem to the memory of his brother, brought something radically new. Elegiac poetry had provided Spanish literature with some of its finest achievements and most profoundly moving verse from Jorge Manrique's lament for his father through Antonio Machado's tribute to Giner de los Ríos. These poets had praised the worth of the departed, his character, and his contribution to society. Instead of this, Panero recreates his own intensely emotional experience of the childhood world shared with his brother and from which his brother's presence is inseparable. He recalls their childhood in Astorga and their adolescence beside the sea in San Sebastián. Panero's attempt to retain the sensitive child's subjective, even solipsistic, perception of the world by transforming it into the never-ending symbolic universe of poetry became, from this point on, the poignant hallmark of his vision.

Shortly before the war ended, Panero married the writer Felicidad Blanc y Bergnes de las Casas, and in 1939, with hostilities over, he actively resumed publishing in periodicals. It was not until April 1945 that *Escorial*, the Falangist literary review, published the first portion of his long autobiographical poem "La estancia vacía" (The Empty Stay, collected in *Obras completas*). Written in the unrhymed hendecasyllables that were to be his most commonly used meter and interspersed with sonnets, it is his attempt to sum up his inner life from infancy to the 1940s. With it he distanced himself from his childhood ties to establish an independent existence. The poem received a warm critical acceptance from the other writers of *Escorial*. Dionisio Ridruejo, the assistant editor, called Panero the best poet of the time; Pedro Laín Entralgo, the editor and mentor of the *Escorial* group, welcomed Panero's poem as among the most original and important of Spanish lyric poetry.

In 1945 "Versos de Guadarrama" appeared in *Fantasía*, the supplement of the *Estafeta Literaria*. These verses from Panero's sanatorium days had been closeted until now, when, in the al-

tered climate of the time, their sentimental and traditional bitter-sweet theme of hopeless love among forested mountains appealed to the public. Panero's feeling for nature, his almost pantheistic enthusiasm, results in poetry that overflows with nostalgia, as exemplified in "El viejo estío" (The Old Summer):

> La nieve borra el campo blanco y lento,
> y el Guadarrama duerme bajo el frío
> triste del corazón . . . (¡Igual que el mío,
> oh Guadarrama, tu latido siento!).

> (The snow erases the slow white fields
> And Guadarrama sleeps beneath the sad
> Heart's cold . . . [Like my own,
> Oh Guadarrama, I feel yours beat!].)

The same government that had incarcerated him for his English excursion nine years earlier now approved of his newly published conservatism and sent him back to London, first as librarian and then as director of the Spanish Institute, for a period of two years. There he spent much time and labor translating the English Romantics into Spanish and wrote "Canto al Teleno" (Song to [Mount] Teleno, in *Obras completas*), which won first prize at the Floral Games of the Jérez Harvest Festival in 1948. He returned that year from England for the commemoration of the tenth anniversary of the death of the Peruvian poet César Vallejo. Panero and Vallejo had been friends in Madrid and the Peruvian had visited him in Astorga. The memorial Panero had addressed to him in 1943, "César Vallejo" (in *Obras completas*), was already regarded as one of Panero's finer poems.

On his return to Spain, Panero decided to take command of his work by anthologizing both his unedited and his published poems. He had until now attempted to maintain his freedom by incorporating every poetic influence that affected him without adopting any specific one. He hoped that a rigorous selection of what was undeniably his would enable him to distinguish his own voice by the mastery or the purging of these innumerable influences. The effort succeeded beyond all expectation. *Escrito a cada instante* (Writing at Every Moment) was published in 1949 and immediately solidified its author's reputation. The work became the subject of major critical studies, and Panero himself declared it the first publication that fully satisfied him. It was awarded both the Spanish Royal Academy's Fastenrath Prize and The Premio Nacional de Literatura in 1949.

Fair copy of a poem by Panero, a song praising the meadows of Sepueda, in the province of León (from Cuadernos Hispanoamericanos, *volume 63, 1965; by permission of the Estate of Leopoldo Panero)*

Panero in the 1950s

Escrito a cada instante has a double meaning: in each flash of time the poet decodes the name of God and comes close to God, but simultaneously this truth escapes him and so must be written again. This zeal for attaining a vision even as he senses his repeated failings is precisely how Panero arrives at creation, how his poems are born. His life is a continuous creation, or, better, a never-ending reception of divine inspiration that then translates into poetry.

Feeling new confidence, he accepted a cultural mission for the Franco government. With three other poets, Antonio Zubiaurre, Luis Rosales, and Agustín de Foxa, he left in November 1949 for a tour of Latin America, expecting an overwhelming welcome. In Bogotá, Havana, and Caracas, they received mixed receptions, ranging from enthusiasm through incomprehension of the Spanish reality down to manifestos calling for their expulsion. The authors of these manifestos, of course, were easily dismissed by the visiting representatives of Franco's cultural establishment as communist intellectuals. Consequently, upon his return to Spain, Panero immediately joined the official Institute of Hispanic Culture, as editor of its new magazine, *Correo Literario*, in order to reestablish Hispanic-American literary relations with Spain on a proper basis.

In the spring of 1953 Panero came across a Spanish exile magazine from Mexico, *Nuestro tiempo*, containing a poem that attacked a Spanish writer. He immediately recognized his nemesis from the tour: Pablo Neruda, a poet and leftist ideologue, and a friend and guide to all of Madrid's Republican poets who had himself fought for the Republic. By June Panero finished work on *Canto personal. Carta perdida a Pablo Neruda* (Personal Canto. Lost Letter to Pablo Neruda, 1953), an overly long patriotic and Christian attack on Neruda's *Canto general* (1950). Panero's inspiration in this case was undoubtedly political, and even though its initial expression

Panero, Vicente Aleixandre, and Dámaso Alonso, circa 1957

may be powerful, one cannot but notice the loss of lyrical sensibility, a loss that turns many of his verses into vulgar padding. *Canto personal*, properly enough, was awarded the José Antonio Primo de Rivera prize by the Falangists. Panero's more unbiased critics suggest that this polemic be considered apart from his lyric production.

In his last years Panero returned to publishing his works in periodicals. From June 1957 to March 1960 he was the literary reviewer for the weekly *Blanco y Negro*. Since his days as a reviewer for the Madrid daily *El Sol* in the 1930s, Panero had always acknowledged Unamuno and Antonio Machado as his mentors. To commemorate the twentieth anniversary of Machado's death, in 1959 Panero published two poems with the title "Desde el umbral de un sueño" (From the Threshold of a Dream) in *Cuadernos Hispanoamericanos*. The same year, Camilo José Cela's monthly *Papeles de Son Armadans* published Panero's "Siete poemas." In 1960 *Cuadernos Hispanoamericanos* published "Romances y canciones" (Ballads and Songs) and what is considered his last if not his major masterpiece, "Cándida

puerta" (Shining Door). After these 1959-1960 poems (all in *Obras completas*) he suspended all further publication to work on a book about Christ, "La verdad en persona" (The Truth in Person), to which he had been led by his increasing religiosity, but he died in his Madrid home on 27 August 1962 before completing the project.

"Cándida puerta" therefore stands as his last and major profession of faith—a metaphor of eucharistic communion. He had been invited to submit poetry to a religious festival, the Juegos Eucarísticos in Toledo, Spain, in 1959 but declined until struck by an observation during the first communion of the poet Luis Rosales's son. The shining door in Panero's poem refers to the door of the tabernacle on a Catholic altar, where the Host is kept, and in this case also to the town bakery. There bread, the people's main staple, is baked at night. This nighttime labor conveys a humble and loving care for mankind. The bread becomes a holy gift. The smell of burning heather, according to Panero, will reach the whole world and grant it the flavor of bread. The small-town bakery becomes universal:

Más que el olor del brezo montañoso
es bueno el que ahora nace de su leña,
y empaña o mueve las estrellas altas,
alzado por el viento, que da al mundo
como un tibio sabor de pan de aldea.

(Better than the burning mountain heather
The odor born of your wood
Enwraps or moves the highest stars,
Raised by the wind that gives the world
A sort of warm flavor of village bread.)

There is a transition in the poem, almost a misplaced prayer:

No puedo definirte sino amándote.
Razón más honda el corazón no tiene
que ésta de no tener ninguna otra,
para llamar, Señor, tocar tu puerta,
y, sin razón, pedirte que le abras.

(I cannot define thee but by loving thee.
My heart has no deeper reason
Than this: having no other it calls,
Lord, it knocks on thy door
And foolishly asks that thou open for it.)

This eucharistic door is also that of the town bakery, where "el pan desnudo" (the naked bread) is found. Panero's voice ascends a mystical scale: "Cándida puerta" is a personal hymn, a spiritual song in which the symbol of the bakery becomes the poet's desire to reach that "Cándida puerta." Moreover, Panero seems to hear his name pronounced by the one (God) that inhabits this tabernacle. Ecstatic, the poet transcends his mortal being to embrace a blissful, an almost divine state of being:

Ya el templo soy yo mismo en mi palabra,
y pertenezco a su sustancia viva
de modo simple pero real: amando.

(Now the temple I am myself in my word,
And belong to its living substance
A simple, real way: loving.)

Following Panero's death, his following and critical reputation grew even more substantial. Since 1963 the Instituto de Cultura Hispánica has awarded an annual poetry prize in the name of Leopoldo Panero.

Biography:

Ricardo Gullón, *La juventud de Leopoldo Panero* (León, Spain: Diputación Provincial de León, 1985).

References:

César Aller, *La poesía personal de Leopoldo Panero* (Pamplona, Spain: Universidad de Navarra, 1976);

Dámaso Alonso, "La poesía arraigada de Leopoldo Panero," in his *Poetas españoles contemporáneos* (Madrid: Gredos, 1952), pp. 333-358;

Eileen Connolly, *Leopoldo Panero: La poesía de la esperanza* (Madrid: Gredos, 1969);

José García Nieto, *La poesía de Leopoldo Panero* (Madrid: Nacional, 1963);

María de las Mercedes Marcos Sánchez, *El lenguaje poético de Leopoldo Panero* (Salamanca: Universidad de Salamanca, 1987);

Alberto Parra Higuera, *Investigaciones sobre la obra poética de Leopoldo Panero* (Bern, Germany: Herbert Lang / Frankfurt: Peter Lang, 1971);

Juan Sardo, *El Dios de Leopoldo Panero* (León, Spain: Institución Fray Bernardino de Sahagún de la Excelentísima Diputación Provincial, 1978);

Luis Felipe Vivanco, "Leopoldo Panero, en su rezo personal cotidiano," in his *Introdución a la poesía española contemporánea*, third edition revised, 2 volumes (Madrid: Guadarrama, 1974), II: 255-310.

Dionisio Ridruejo

(12 October 1912 - 29 June 1975)

Teresa Scott Soufas
Tulane University

BOOKS: *Plural* (Segovia, Spain: Printed for the author, 1935);

Primer libro de amor (Barcelona: Yunque, 1939);

Poesía en armas: Cuadernos de la Guerra Civil (Barcelona: Jerarquía, 1940);

Fábula de la doncella y el río (Madrid: Nacional, 1943);

Sonetos a la piedra (Madrid: Nacional, 1943);

Poesía en armas: Cuadernos de Rusia (Madrid: Aguado, 1944);

En la soledad del tiempo (Barcelona: Montaner & Simón, 1944);

Don Juan (Madrid: Nacional, 1945);

Elegías (Madrid: Adonais, 1948);

En once años (Madrid: Nacional, 1950);

Dentro del tiempo (Barcelona: Arión, 1960); revised and enlarged as *Diario de una tregua* (Barcelona: Destino, 1972);

En algunas ocasiones (Madrid: Aguilar, 1960);

Hasta la fecha (Madrid: Aguilar, 1961);

Escrito en España (Buenos Aires: Losada, 1962; revised, 1964);

España 1963: Examen de una situación (Paris: Centro de Documentación y Estudios, 1963);

Cuaderno catalán (Madrid: Revista de Occidente, 1965);

122 poemas (Buenos Aires: Losada, 1967);

Casi en prosa (Madrid: Revista de Occidente, 1972);

Entre literatura y política (Madrid: Seminarios, 1973);

Castilla la vieja, 2 volumes (Barcelona: Destino, 1973, 1974);

En breve (Málaga, Spain: Litoral, 1975);

Primer libro de amor, Poesía en armas, Sonetos (Madrid: Castalia, 1976);

Casi unas memorias, edited by César Armando Gómez (Barcelona: Planeta, 1976);

Poesía, edited by Luis Felipe Vivanco (Madrid: Alianza, 1976);

Sombras y bultos (Barcelona: Destino, 1977);

Los cuadernos de Rusia, edited by Gloria de Ros and César Armando Gómez (Barcelona: Planeta, 1978);

Cuadernos de Rusia, En la soledad del tiempo, Cancionero de Ronda, Elegías (Madrid: Castalia, 1981).

OTHER: "El poeta rescatado," prologue to *Obras completas* by Antonio Machado (Madrid: Espasa-Calpe, 1941).

While writing his poetry (some eight hundred poems in all), Dionisio Ridruejo led a life of crisis, surrounded by and involved in the turmoil of war, exile, court trials, and imprisonment. His life, like his poetry, reflects the reversals and contradictions characteristic of the man who at a very early age had attained positions of importance within the Falangist party only to suffer confinement and banishment after his break with the Francisco Franco regime. The traditional spirit that politically motivated the young Ridruejo led him initially to produce verses based on popular poetry or in keeping with the poetic expression of Garcilaso de la Vega. After Ridruejo's disillusionment over the failure of ideals espoused during the Spanish Civil War, the thematic content of his poetry changed, coming finally to express a spiritual turning point in the face of solitude, time's passing, and growing maturity. His extensive poetic output and the recognition he gained as a political activist under difficult circumstances ensured that the voice of Ridruejo, poet and orator, was heard by many in Spain.

Born on 12 October 1912 in Burgo de Osma in the Spanish province of Soria, Dionisio Ridruejo Jiménez was the only son of Dionisio Ridruejo Martín, a local merchant and banker, and Segunda Jiménez Ridruejo. Due to the early death of his father in 1915, Ridruejo and his sisters were brought up by their mother in company with his great aunt and his maternal grandmother. Though his household was not a literary one, the youngster showed interest in writing poetry, his first compositions being completed before he was thirteen. This initial affinity had

Dionisio Ridruejo, 1940

been fostered in an informal way by his grandmother, who continuously shared with the family her great repertory of romances and folksongs, which Ridruejo claimed in *Primer libro de amor* (First Book of Love, 1939) "me . . . sonido siempre por dentro" (always sounded within me). His early education, begun in Segovia in a school run by the Marist Brothers and then continued in Valladolid in a Jesuit school, was finally completed in 1927 in another Jesuit institution, Charmartín de la Rosa, in Madrid. After abandoning his original plan to study engineering at the Escuela de Ingenieros Industriales, he entered the Universidad de María Cristina in El Escorial in 1928. Having spent six years of study there and additional time at the Universidad de Madrid, he obtained his law degree but never practiced as a lawyer. From 1935 to 1936, following his inclination to write and in preparation for what would be an important aspect of his career, he studied journalism in Madrid's El Debate, the only school in

Spain offering such a course of study at that time.

As a university student and young adult, Ridruejo's sympathies with Falangist ideals were strong. Indeed, in 1929 his first published poems appeared in the university newspaper, a rightist publication whose original title *El Gurriato* was changed to *El Escorial.* Entering formally into membership in the Falange Española with his three sisters in May 1935, Ridruejo took the first step toward the political activity that would lead to a most successful yet short-lived rise to positions of importance within the party. Between 1936 and 1941 he served as the local political officer of propaganda in Segovia, the regional chief of the Falange, and ultimately as national propaganda officer. His early and successful political career was not without problems, however, for Ridruejo was against the unification movement of the party. His protest led to the resignation of his regional position in April 1937 and a direct declaration to Franco of his dissent.

Ridruejo in his Madrid office, circa 1938. He was Francisco Franco's director general of propaganda from 1938 to 1941, when he resigned in disillusionment with Franco's policies.

In February 1938, however, Ridruejo was named director general of propaganda, a position which, he later affirmed in *Casi unas memorias* (Almost Memoirs, 1976) plunged him into the "jungla del poder" (jungle of power). The jurisdiction of this post had always been vague, and Ridruejo's grandiose ideas for reorganizing the instruments of communication admittedly went far beyond the limits of available funds and his own authority. In the meantime, nevertheless, his office became the meeting place for a *tertulia* (discussion group) for literary figures and artists. Among those in attendance were the essayist Pedro Laín Entralgo, poets such as Luis Felipe Vivanco and Leopoldo Panero, novelists including Juan Antonio Zunzunegui and Ignacio Agustí, the painters A. José Caballero and José R. Escassi, the sculptor Emilio Aladrén, and the dramatist/novelist Gonzalo Torrente Ballester, all of whom were part of the group who collaborated on the founding of the magazine *Escorial* in 1940.

The poetry written by the young Ridruejo during this period of intense political activity is not political, however, but amorous, sensual, and descriptive. The poems of *Fábula de la doncella y el río* (Fable of the Maiden and the River, 1943), composed between 1935 and 1940, are a reworking of an original composition entitled "Canciones de la niña del río" (Songs of the Girl of the River), which uses the rhymes and meter of popular poetry to tell the story of a girl from her birth to her wedding day. The narrative stanzas of the early poem are interrupted by short verses with various creatures of nature offering praises to her. Ridruejo read this work in October 1935 to a group of friends (Samuel Ros, Xavier de Salas, and Xavier de Echarri among them). Their dislike of it was unanimous, and the original work was not published for the first time until 1961 in the volume of Ridruejo's poetry entitled *Hasta la fecha* (Until Now).

With its baroque title and its romantic style, *Fábula de la doncella y el río* reflects a change of expression and poetic structure from its forerunner

"Canciones." The poems deal with a girl who is both real and symbolic, as is the river that represents her lover. She is the eternal adolescent awaiting the arrival of love: "Espera la doncella en la alegría, / en la angustia sin nombre, en el desvelo; / de esperanza se mueve y abandona" (The maiden waits in happiness, / in anguish without name, awake; / she moves in hope and leaves). Vivanco considers the final section—"Rapto y elegía final" (Rapture and Final Elegy)—in which death and love are combined, to be some of Ridruejo's finest poetry.

Ridruejo continued to write poetry of love, but in *Primer libro de amor* the amorous poems take on a more personal and subjective quality compared with those of *Fábula de la doncella y el río*. The first (1939) edition, whose publication was directed by Juan Ramón Masoliver, was printed on a fine grade of paper with one hundred copies decorated by hand, reproductions of sixteenth-century Italian volumes. There are eight sections to *Primer libro*, six of which are principally sonnets that abound in plastic and descriptive elements. One sonnet, for example, begins with the following strophe:

Junto al silencio verde va ligera,
hacia una sed, la acequia en flor de hielo
y en la sombra del ave el tibio suelo
da hoja y fecha feliz de primavera.

(Near the green silence goes lightly,
toward a thirst, the channel flowering with ice
and in the shadow of the bird the lukewarm soil
brings forth the leaf and happy date of spring.)

Beneath the stylized form there runs the thread of a subjective story, as indicated by several of the individual titles, such as "Despedida a la puerta del colegio" (Farewell at the Door of the School), "Al tren de las colegialas" (At the Train of the Schoolgirls), "El llanto en el jardín" (The Weeping in the Garden), and "Idilio en el río" (Idyll in the River). Evident in Ridruejo's poetry from here on is the inclination toward a thematic unity, not unlike the thematic books produced by the Generation of 1927. Ridruejo specifically acknowledged the influence exerted on his writing by Pedro Salinas's *La voz a ti debida* (The Voice Owed to You, 1933).

An amplified and corrected version of *Primer libro de amor* was published in 1950 in the anthology *En once años* (In Eleven Years). Judging the first edition to be flawed both in poetic style and content and marred by insufficient proofreading, Ridruejo undertook some corrections that were, for the most part, minor changes. Additional small alterations were made for *Primer libro*'s 1961 publication in *Hasta la fecha*. Another anthology—*Primer libro de amor, Poesía en armas, Sonetos*—published in 1976 several months after Ridruejo's death, contains further editorial changes by Ridruejo, primarily in the section entitled "Cánticos a Aurea" (Songs to Aurea), incorrectly labeled "Cánticos a la Aurea" in *Hasta la fecha*.

In the anthology *En once años* there are two books with the same title, *Poesía en armas* (Poetry in Arms, the first published in 1940, the second in 1944). As their subtitles indicate, nevertheless, they are indeed different, for the early book is "Cuadernos de la Guerra Civil" (Notebooks of the Civil War) while the later volume is "Cuadernos de Rusia" (Notebooks from Russia). The poems about the civil war, written during the years of that conflict, are not among the best of Ridruejo's works. They are ideological and propagandist in nature, and he was tempted to eliminate them completely from *En once años*. However, these poems are included in that collection as well as in *Hasta la fecha* and *Primer libro de amor, Poesía en armas, Sonetos*, for Ridruejo came to believe that they reflect his youthful idealism.

Ridruejo's poetic production of the war years was accompanied by a growing disillusionment with the nation's and the party's failure to attain the ideals that had inspired him. Though in 1940 he founded *Escorial* with Laín Entralgo, among others, the years 1940 and 1941 were politically the most difficult and contradictory for the poet. A brief anecdote related in 1978 by Carlos Rojas gives an indication of Ridruejo's deep dissatisfaction with Franco in the early 1940s. In attendance with others at the unveiling of a full-length portrait of the *Caudillo* (Franco) by Ignacio Zuloaga, Ridruejo witnessed an exchange between the artist and his subject. Upon hearing Zuloaga's statement, "Excelencia, yo no sé si esto está bien o está mal. Pero sí sé que es mi obra maestra" (Excellency, I do not know if this is good or bad. But I do know that it is my masterpiece), a claim Zuloaga was frequently heard to make upon completion of a portrait, Franco burst into tears. Ridruejo's reaction was to say within earshot of Franco, "Vaya llorón" (What a crybaby). Turning angrily, Franco exclaimed, "¡Ridruejo! ¡Yo lloro cuando quiero!" (Ridruejo! I cry when I want!), whereupon the poet

Cover for Ridruejo's 1943 collection, which includes poems written from 1934 to 1942

responded "Esto es lo malo" (This is what is wrong).

Filled with frustration and disappointment during this period, Ridruejo nevertheless clung to the hope and conviction of his dreams of bettering the country while, as he later explained, each day brought a new defeat for those ideals in the face of disappointing reality. The cycle of dissatisfaction intensified. Resigning his position as director general of propaganda in February 1941, Ridruejo abandoned his political career. He took advantage of a singular opportunity later the same year by enlisting in the Blue Division on its way to participate in the Russian campaign. His enlistment was motivated not only by his belief that fascism could both represent the model for a rational Europe and serve as the means of defeating the Soviet movement, but also by his desire to escape the contradictions he faced in

Spain and the disgust he felt with Spanish politics.

The poetry that this Russian experience prompted Ridruejo to write marks an expansion of theme, for he deals with his time as a soldier (1941-1942), recording his states of mind within the verses of *Poesía en armas: Cuadernos de Rusia* as if writing a spiritual diary. This phase in his poetry is described by Vivanco as going from the neobaroque to a style heavily influenced by Antonio Machado. The two most important factors in his trek across the Russian countryside were the solitude endured by one who faces death for the first time and, conversely, the feeling of communion with the small band of men with whom he served and shared danger.

In this poetry Ridruejo no longer speaks of imaginary, indistinct, bucolic landscapes as in *Primer libro de amor*, but instead he describes viv-

274

Ridruejo with his wife, Gloria, and their children, Gloria and Dionisio, 1953

idly the settings and sights around him, as in the following lines:

> Suelo de turba, barro que es escoria,
> negro y frío fangal que guarda el fuego,
> tierra anterior al hombre, tierra y bosque
> viudos del caos y vírgenes del tiempo.

> (Peat soil, mud that is slag,
> black and cold bog that guards fire,
> land earlier than man, land and forest
> widowers of chaos and virgins of time.)

Death is likewise faced as a reality rather than as a mere abstract concept. Ridruejo was forced by his journey through Russia and the loss of many of his companions to accept the presence of death, an awareness reflected in this poetry. Indeed, Ridruejo himself (as quoted by Gaspar Gómez de la Serna) declared his desire to write poetry that was "más esencial y simple; temáticamente más amplia y atenta a la Creación; interiormente más refrenada, más honda; expresivamente más clara y refinada" (more essen-

tial and simple; broader and more attentive thematically to Creation; inwardly more restrained, deeper; expressively clearer and more refined).

Forced to return from Russia in 1942 because of poor health, Ridruejo made a brief visit to Germany before going back to Spain and came into contact with individuals who exemplified the dangers of Adolf Hitler and his followers. Once in Spain, having come through his experience in Russia, Ridruejo felt stronger in his own convictions and free of the crisis of ideals that had so afflicted him earlier. His dissatisfaction with the Falangist party led him to write a letter directly to Franco outlining his complaints and suggestions for changes. In addition, he resigned all positions and affiliations with the party, even giving up his position at *Escorial* because of the support the magazine received from the government. There were no immediate official reactions to his decision, and during the rest of the summer Ridruejo made some attempts to practice law and continued to speak out against the governmental policies with which he disagreed.

By October 1942 the official silence was broken, and Ridruejo was placed under police surveillance and prohibited from leaving the city of Ronda. He was, moreover, held back from publishing certain books of poetry that were ready for the press (among them, *Fábula de la doncella y el río* and *Sonetos a la piedra* [Sonnets to Stone, 1943]), nor could he write for any newspaper. Though he had been chosen to receive the Premio Nacional de Literature, he could not do so. He faced financial difficulties for the first time, but the monetary aid and support of close friends, including some of his companions from the Russian campaign, saw him through.

However, Ridruejo's period of confinement (1942-1947) had some beneficial aspects. He spent time with nature, his books, and a few intimate friends, which made for a more peaceful existence than he had known for quite a while. He even came to an understanding with the police assigned to guard him, agreeing to check in with them once a day in exchange for their willingness not to follow him too closely. Ironically, in December 1942 he was awarded the Cruz Roja de Mérito Militar for his service with the Blue Division.

In February 1943 Juan Ramón Masoliver invited Ridruejo to the Barcelona region to finish out his sentence. Permission to make the move was granted in May. *Fábula de la doncella y el río* and *Sonetos a la piedra* were finally published this same year. Composed during the years 1934 to 1942, the poems of the latter reflect two facets Vivanco identifies as "biografía" and "geografía." Some of these poems deal with stone in its natural state in cliffs, volcanos, and mountain summits. The geological stone is complemented by the artistic stone in poems about statues, edifices, and ruins. Also treated are the cities important to Ridruejo; their plazas, gardens, street corners, and architecture become the focal points. Reflecting the poet's growing concern with time's passage, these sonnets express philosophic as well as sentimental concerns. In "A una ruina" (To a Ruin) Ridruejo says:

De un tiempo usó la eternidad tu musa,
mas fuiste con el tiempo amortajada
y la materia fue materia y nada
y ni aun recuerdo la razón confusa.

(For some time eternity used your muse,
but you were shrouded with time
and the material was material and nothing
and I do not even remember the vague reason.)

The poetry written just before and during Ridruejo's initial period of confinement is of a mature quality, reflecting the disillusionment and existential suffering of one who has experienced solitude and who is fully aware of the passing moments. His forced return to the countryside of Spain brought with it the inspiration evident in *En la soledad del tiempo* (In the Solitude of the Time, 1944), in which, with Machadoesque treatment, he makes poetic confessions. *Cancionero de Ronda* (Songbook of Ronda, published with *Cuadernos de Rusia* and other collections in 1981), also written during his detention, relates, in verses that again show Machado's influence, the physical and spiritual "walks" taken by Ridruejo in his solitude—at once interior and exterior journeys.

Between 1943 and 1945, still confined, Ridruejo wrote the poetry of an important book entitled *Elegías* (not published in its entirety until 1948), in which his disillusionment reaches its fullest expression. Describing the poems as Ridruejo's "desengaño del mundo en palabra" (disillusionment with the world in words), Vivanco adds that *Elegías* is "plenamente creación espiritual o imaginativa" (completely a spiritual and imaginative creation). The passage of time, Ridruejo's errors, and his internal rebellion against those errors are the root of the *desengaño* that finds expression in these long poems. Though written during a time of personal plenitude just before and during the first months of his marriage, *Elegías* nevertheless gives evidence of Ridruejo's painful dissatisfaction with life in Spain. Years later in reference to the distressing process that helped to produce *Elegías*, Ridruejo wrote in *Casi unas memorias* that the content of *Elegías* "ofrece un testimonio tan sincero como completo de aquella etapa de mi vida interior" (offers a testimony as sincere as it is complete of that period in my life).

On 26 June 1944 Ridruejo married Gloria de Ros and moved with her to Llavaneras, where they rented a house. Allowed to travel briefly, he took Gloria on a honeymoon to Majorca, and while there, at the urging of friends, he interviewed Franco's adversary Manuel Hedilla, who was under confinement on the island. This action stirred up fresh governmental distrust of Ridruejo, and he was given a choice of living under guard either in Cádiz or Castellón de la Plana. In September, however, he received permission to continue residing in Llavaneras. That year saw the publication of *Poesía en armas: Cuadernos de*

Ridruejo circa 1960

Rusia and *En la soledad del tiempo*, as well as the completion of *Elegías*.

The latter years of his confinement were primarily spent writing for such newspapers as the *Vanguardia, Solidaridad Nacional, Hoja del Lunes*, and *Arriba*. In January 1947, at the insistence of friends who were close to Franco, Ridruejo met with the dictator in Madrid. This necessitated a secret trip to the capital city, from which he was still barred, so that he could explain to Franco his suggestions for ways to avoid future violence in Spain. No reaction, either negative or positive, was ever registered, and as Ridruejo wrote later (in *Casi unas memorias*), it was "como si [el episodio] no hubiera sucedido" (as if [the episode] had never taken place). In September, nevertheless, a partial lifting of the restrictions upon him meant that he could reside in any part of the country except Madrid and its environs or Valladolid.

By the end of 1948 his period of living under guard was completely over, and with the help of a highly placed government official, Ridruejo secured a job with the Prensa del Movimiento (Press of the Movement) in Italy as a correspondent without political duties. Before Ridruejo could begin his new position in Rome, his government sponsor was replaced by a successor who changed the poet's contract to one that outlined a more substantial journalistic position that included political coverage. Ridruejo refused the offer, arranging instead to work in Rome as a "simple periodista" (simple journalist) for the Agencia Pyresa, which distributed foreign features and news stories to the Prensa del Movimiento. During his stay in Italy he published in 1950 the edition of his complete works entitled *En once años*, for which in December of that year he was awarded Spain's Premio Nacional de Literatura. His two-and-a-half years in Italy represented freedom from his recent confinement in Spain, and the return to his native country in June 1951 was a return to reality and his commitments. In December he was named director of Radio Intercontinental.

In 1952 the industrialist Alberto Puig interested his friend Ridruejo in collaborating on the journal *Revista*, published in Barcelona with a popular format that supported the liberation of the country and afforded an opportunity for expression of topics relevant to life in Catalonia and the potential for new movements among the working classes and unions. Ridruejo contributed not only his own efforts but enlisted intellectuals from Madrid to express their liberal views in *Revista*. With opposition from such groups as the Opus Dei, there were often times when the magazine and its contributors suffered censorship and restrictions.

Ridruejo's political activity, though unofficial and not in line with government policies, was once again strong. Lecturing often to groups and schools, and writing articles and treatises with more political zeal, Ridruejo felt increasingly removed from his original youthful positions. In April 1955 at the Ateneo of Barcelona he delivered a polemic that openly criticized the Franco regime. Charges were initiated against him, but the only real consequence of his address was the loss of further invitations for speaking engagements.

Since 1954 Ridruejo had been actively involved with militant students, and in February 1956 he suffered his first imprisonment for such involvement after helping a university-student group obtain signatures on a petition in behalf of the right of expression for young writers. This action led to a violent demonstration in which one Falangist was shot and killed. Though arrested and jailed again in 1957 after statements made in the magazine *Bohemia* published in Havana, Ridruejo did not modify his antigovernment activities. After his release from prison in September of that year, he founded the illegal Partido Social de Acción Democrática. In February 1959 he was tried for his activities, but his sentence of twenty months in jail was suspended due to a governmental reprieve prompted by the coronation of Pope John XXIII.

The decade of the 1950s saw very little poetic output by Ridruejo. In 1961 the new edition of his complete works, *Hasta la fecha*, was published. To this volume he added some new poems and subtracted others, so the content of the various collections differs somewhat from the material in *En once años*. In March 1962 he published *Escrito en España* (Written in Spain), a prose account of his thoughts on Spain's political situation. In *El correo catalán* (30 December 1980) Rojas called the book "la crítica más inteligente y más devastadora del franquismo publicada hasta la fecha" (the most intelligent and devastating criticism of *franquismo* to the present). Later in 1962 the authorities made Ridruejo choose between permanent exile or confinement on the island of Lanzarote. Choosing exile, Ridruejo settled in Paris to take his place among the members of what he called the "amarga paella del exilio" (the bitter stew of exile). He traveled to New York to deliver political speeches and to Puerto Rico, where he taught classes in Spanish literature and civilization at the University of Puerto Rico. In 1963 his literary efforts were turned toward collaboration on the short-lived *Boletín Informativo*, edited in Paris at the Centro de Documentación y Estudios and expressing anti-Franco sentiments. Later that year the center published Ridruejo's essays in book form as *España 1963*.

In April 1964 an initial attempt to return clandestinely to Spain failed, and Ridruejo was forced to go back to the border. A second attempt was successful, and upon his arrival in Madrid he sent a letter to the Director General de Seguridad, Carlos Arias Navarro, announcing his return. This action earned him another arrest and detention, and he spent some weeks in Carabanchel prison.

Ridruejo's politically outspoken addresses continued to provoke governmental reactions. In 1966, after delivering a speech to the Facultad de Ciencias Políticas y Económicas de Madrid on the state of Spanish universities, he was once again arrested and this time fined twenty-five thousand pesetas. The following year Ridruejo published in Buenos Aires *122 poemas*, which comprises poems selected from earlier works and slightly revised.

Suffering from longstanding heart problems, Ridruejo went to Germany for a few weeks in 1968 to seek treatment. From there he went to the United States and taught Spanish literature at the University of Wisconsin in Madison. After some additional time spent in Puerto Rico and in Austin, Texas, he returned to Spain in 1970. In December of that year he wrote to Tomás García Rebull, the capitán general of Burgos, interceding for a group of militant Basques recently tried by a military court. His political activity continued, and among his writings in the next few years were important political declarations.

Drawing by Ridruejo published in the 1976 edition of his Primer libro de amor *(by permission of the Estate of Dionisio Ridruejo)*

In 1974 Ridruejo went to Mexico to participate in a *homenaje* (testimonial) to León Felipe. On 16 April of the following year he received his own *homenaje* in Madrid, proffered by friends and admirers during a time when his health problems were worsening. To the five hundred or so persons in attendance Ridruejo spoke of the need for a collective "convencimiento de que los españoles podemos convivir y competir en libertad sin matarnos unos a otros" (conviction that Spaniards can live together and compete in liberty without killing each other); his speech was included by Jesús Aguirre in *Dionisio Ridruejo* (1976). Though gravely ill, Ridruejo was nevertheless active until shortly before his death, publishing a book of poetry entitled *En breve* (Briefly) in 1975 and delivering an address over the BBC about his political beliefs. On 26 June 1975, how-

ever, he entered the Clínica de la Concepción in Madrid, where he died of a heart attack three days later.

Ridruejo has left behind a legacy of challenges to his compatriots. Posthumously published works, along with his works already in print, keep fresh in the public's mind certain political contradictions and Ridruejo's responses to them, which characterized his life and art. In his BBC declaration, published in *Casi unas memorias*, Ridruejo said: "Me interesa poder morir con la conciencia a punto. Con la evidencia de haber obrado con sinceridad, con honradez y con solidaridad. Y si me da usted a elegir entre el destino de un poeta cuyos versos serán repetidos dentro de cinco siglos y el de un ciudadano que ha ayudado a que sus vecinos vivan un poco mejor, elijo, aunque parezca mentira, esta última

Ridruejo in the early 1970s

aspiración" (I am interested in being able to die with a clear conscience. With evidence of having acted with sincerity, with honor, and with solidarity. And if you ask me to choose between the destiny of a poet whose verses will be repeated after five centuries and that of a citizen who has helped so that his neighbors live a little better, I choose, although it might seem a lie, this last aspiration). In Ridruejo's case the second aspiration does not preclude the other.

References:

Jesús Aguirre, ed., *Dionisio Ridruejo, de la Falange a la oposición* (Madrid: Taurus, 1976);

Francisco Gómez Bellard and others, *Homenaje a Dionisio Ridruejo* (Madrid: USDE, 1975);

Gaspar Gómez de la Serna, "La poesía de Dionisio Ridruejo," *Clavileño*, 12 (1950): 41-51;

Homenje a Dionisio Ridruejo: Retratos de amigos por Alejandro Vidal (Madrid: Labor, Moneda & Crédito, 1977);

Emilio Miró, "Dionisio Ridruejo," *Insula*, 235 (1966): 5;

Manuel Penella, "El diario de Dionisio Ridruejo," *Cuadernos Hispanoamericanos*, 274 (1973): 179-182;

Jorge Rodríguez Padrón, "Para un lúcida meditación," *Cuadernos Hispanoamericanos*, 274 (1973): 173-178;

Carlos Rojas, "A Dionisio Ridruejo," *Destino*, 12 July 1978, p. 31;

Luis Felipe Vivanco, Prologue to *Hasta la fecha* (Madrid: Aguilar, 1961), pp. XI-XXXVIII;

María Zupanchich, "Two Moments in the Life and Poetry of Dionisio Ridruejo," *Romance Notes*, 10 (1969): 218-225.

Carlos Sahagún

(4 June 1938 -)

Patricia E. Mason
University of South Carolina

BOOKS: *Hombre naciente* (Onil, Spain: Silbo, 1955);

Profecías del agua (Madrid: Rialp, 1958);

Como si hubiera muerto un niño (Barcelona: Estudios Hispánicos, 1961);

Estar contigo (León, Spain: Provincia, 1973);

Memorial de la noche: 1957-1975 (Barcelona: Lumen, 1976);

En la noche (Málaga, Spain: Guadalhorce, 1976);

Primer y último oficio: 1973-1977 (León, Spain: Institución Fray Bernardino de Sahagún," 1979);

Las invisibles redes (Pamplona, Spain: Pamiela, 1989).

OTHER: *7 poetas españoles*, edited by Sahagún (Madrid: Taurus, 1959);

Francisco Ribes, ed., *Poesía última*, includes poems and notes by Sahagún (Madrid: Taurus, 1963);

E. C. Riley, *Teoría de la novela en Cervantes*, translated by Sahagún (Madrid: Taurus, 1966);

Vicente Gaos, comp., *Antología del grupo de 1927*, edited by Sahagún (Madrid: Cátedra, 1975);

Blas de Otero, *Poemas de amor*, selected, with a prologue, by Sahagún (Barcelona: Lumen, 1987).

With a writing career that began in the mid 1950s, Carlos Sahagún belongs to the second generation of post-civil-war poets, the so-called children of the war. Although his subject matter is largely drawn from his experiences, his poems evoke the collective experience of all those who lived through the Spanish Civil War and its aftermath. As his work evolved into the 1970s, his poetry increasingly came to reflect his personal commitment to social and political change.

Sahagún was born during the civil war, on 4 June 1938, in Onil, in the southeastern Spanish province of Alicante. He left in 1956 to study at the University of Madrid, where he obtained a bachelor's degree in romance philology in 1959. Although his first collection of poetry, *Hombre*

naciente (Growing Man), was published in 1955 when he was only sixteen, and he had won the 1956 José Luis Hidalgo prize for several individual poems, his full-fledged writing career is usually considered to have begun in 1958 with the publication of *Profecías del agua* (Prophecies of Water). Since then he has published six collections of his poetry, in addition to many poems that have appeared in magazines.

Written in only two months, *Profecías del agua* won the prestigious Adonáis poetry prize for 1957. In a series of poems composed around the water motif of the title (a motif that recurs throughout his poetry and symbolizes freedom, purity, and the life force), Sahagún recalls his childhood and adolescence amid the chaos of the years immediately following the war, as in "Manantial" (Source):

Parece que fue ayer, qué no era el año
mil novecientos treinta y ocho. Bosques
en llamas, altas
palmeras encendidas, hombres muertos
me rodeaban, lo recuerdo todo

(It seems that it was yesterday, not the year
nineteen thirty-eight. Forests
in flames, tall
palm trees alight, dead men
surrounded me, I remember it all).

One of the most highly praised poems in *Profecías del agua* is "El preso" (The Prisoner) written in memory of the poet Miguel Hernández, who was also from Alicante. In it Sahagún juxtaposes and equates the repression of postwar Spain with the imprisonment of Hernández:

Volar . . . Pero ¿quién vuela,
qué azules horizontes nos cerraron
con llave y para siempre, qué alegría
nos han quitado a los vencidos?
. . . .
sin esperanza como están los ciegos
de nacimiento, duerme, entrega al aire

281

Carlos Sahagún

lo que es del aire, roza la alta reja.
Porque las rejas son como las cuerdas
de una guitarra triste, y nadie rasga
esa guitarra, y nadie viene nunca
desde la vieja libertad

(To fly . . . but who flies,
what blue horizons did they lock away
from us forever, what happiness
have they taken from those of us who were
    defeated?
. . . .
without hope, like those who are blind
from birth, render to the air
what is the air's, lightly touch the high bars.
Because the bars are like the strings
of a sad guitar, and no one strums
that guitar, and no one ever comes
from the old freedom).

Yet despite the pessimism, and the fact that he views his childhood as having been destroyed by the war, there is still optimism about a better future, as seen in "Agua subterránea" (Underground Water):

En algún sitio
si cruzáis la frontera, si nos vamos
de este jardín quemado, sé que hay flores
de libertad
. . . .
decidme
que aun teneis fe, que no nos han quitado
la fe

(Somewhere
if you cross the frontier, if we leave
this charred garden, I know there are flowers

282

of freedom
. . . .
tell me
you still have faith, that they haven't taken away
our faith).

In 1960 and 1961 Sahagún taught Spanish at the University of Exeter in England. Although he had completed his next collection, *Como si hubiera muerto un niño* (As If a Child Had Died), in April 1959, it was not published until 1961, after it had won the 1960 Boscán prize. The poems again explore the world of his childhood and adolescence in the aftermath of the war. Running through the book are the motifs of growing up, the loss of childhood, and the bitter-sweet experience of first love. When love ends, the speaker looks back nostalgically on his childhood as a refuge from the pain, but the child in him is dead and there is no going back, as in "Niños en peligro" (Children in Danger):

Nunca, nunca
debí salir de allí. Ya la alegría
no volverá aunque vuelva yo, los niños
no volverán. Desmesuradamente
mis manos—aunque vuelva yo—crecieron
para el amor, para el dolor.

(I should never, never
have left there. Now happiness
will never return even if I go back, the children
won't return.
My hands—even if I go back—grew bigger
for love, for pain.)

But his concerns also reach beyond the purely personal, as seen in "Cosas inolvidables" (Unforgettable Things), with its insistence that the past not be forgotten, and that shared responsibility for Spain's future take precedence over individual happiness:

Por mí, por nuestro amor de cada día
nunca olvides, te pido que no olvides.
Los dos nacimos con la guerra. Piensa
lo mal que estuvo aquella guerra para
los pobres. Nuestro amor pudo haber sido
bombardeado, pero no lo fue.
Nuestros padres pudieron haber muerto
y no murieron. ¡Alegría! Todo
se olvida. Es el amor. Pero no. Existen
cosas inolvidables. Esos ojos
tuyos, aquella guerra triste, el tiempo
en que vendrán los pájaros, los niños.

(For me, for the love we share everyday
never forget, I beg you not to forget.

We two were born with the war. Think
how bad that war was for
the poor. Our love could have been
shelled, but it wasn't.
Our parents could have died
and they didn't. Happiness! Everything
is forgotten. It's love. But no. There are
things that cannot be forgotten. Your eyes,
that sad war, the time
when birds will come, and children.)

Sahagún has said that both *Profecías del agua* and *Como si hubiera muerto un niño* are works that came out of a period when poetry fulfilled a need for self-expression. He refers to this idea in "País natal" (Native Land), from his 1979 collection, *Primer y último oficio* (First and Last Office):

Más allá del confín donde desfallecía
la libertad de todo un pueblo
buscaba yo el fulgor de las palabras
para salir de aquel silencio.

(Beyond the horizon where
the liberty of a whole people
languished I sought the brilliance of words
to escape that silence.)

From 1965 to 1971 Sahagún lived in Segovia, where he taught Spanish literature at the Instituto Andrés Laguna. In 1971 he left to live and teach in Barcelona. His next collection of poems, *Estar contigo* (To Be With You), was finally published in 1973, twelve years after the publication of *Como si hubiera muerto un niño*. Only a few new poems had appeared in the interim, and almost all of these are in Francisco Ribes's 1963 anthology *Poesía última* (Latest Poetry). Sahagún himself has stated that the two years following the completion of *Como si hubiera un niño* were unproductive from a creative point of view but crucial years in his political development. In 1963 he wrote (in his notes in *Poesía última*) that during this period he became convinced of the need for revolution. Political commitment changed his life and also, in all likelihood, certain aspects of his poetry; he realized that he, too, bore responsibility for the millions of people throughout the world living in misery and poverty. He set forth his definition of social poetry: "[it] proposes a transformation of the world or, at the very least, of the structures of the society in which the poetry is created . . . it has obvious critical characteristics, inasmuch as it presents us with a clearly unjust situation and tries to overcome it. And above all else, it has a profoundly moral content.... Strictly speaking at this time, social poetry is to be understood as that which exposes the corruption and defects underlying the bourgeois organization."

In the notes that accompany his poems in the Ribes anthology, Sahagún analyzed the creative process. The stimulus for the poem, he wrote, comes from those moments in the poet's life that have affected him most deeply. The actual creation of a poem is something spontaneous and automatic, and it usually begins with rhythm and a series of emotionally charged images. But even though it originates involuntarily, for the poem to achieve its final form there must be a conscious choice of words, and finding the right words to fit the rhythm may prove problematic. In some cases the poet may have to leave gaps to be filled in later, and as a result the composition process may sometimes be interrupted for years. A poem can only be effective if the emotion is genuine and has been expressed in an original way. If either of these conditions is not met, then merely writing on socially relevant topics is not enough to validate the poem. Self-expression, an analysis of one's own feelings, is more important than communication with eventual readers. And given the inherent ambiguity of poetic language, the latter may in any case prove to be impossible.

Sahagún's new poems in the Ribes anthology are included in *Estar contigo*, which in certain respects marks a departure from his previous poetry. The central themes of lost childhood and love are still important, but the work as a whole is much more politically oriented, and there is the stylistic innovation of the prose poem. The titles and content of several of the poems indicate that they were composed in 1960 and 1961, when Sahagún was living outside Spain. Teaching in England and traveling through Europe in the early 1960s had allowed him to experience a world outside the oppressiveness of the Francisco Franco dictatorship, and this self-imposed exile evoked in him a nostalgia for Spain that has been compared with that expressed by the poets forced into exile after the civil war. In "Puentes del Elba" (Bridges of the Elbe) he writes:

Si ahora estuviéramos de pronto
allí, junto a aquellos olivos
. . . .
Pero España está al sur de estas palabras
como si se nos hubiera perdido.

(If now, suddenly, we were

there, beside those olive trees
. . . .
But Spain lies south of these words
as though lost to us.)

The first poems of *Estar contigo* are filled with memories of his childhood in the Andalusian city of Almería. In "Preludio" it is apparent that the horror of those years still haunts him:

De nada sirve haber corrido el mundo,
saber que no estoy sólo (mas conocí la soledad),
salir del tiempo de las privaciones,
y entrar en un tiempo favorable
. . . .
si cada día regresa la imagen de Almería
y me acompaña fiel, insoslayable,
la sordidez de aquellos años.

(It does no good to have roamed the world,
to know that I'm not alone [but I knew loneliness],
to escape from times of hardship,
and enter into a favorable time
. . . .
if every day the image of Almería returns
and faithful and undeflectable,
the squalor of those years accompanies me.)

Despite such memories, childhood is still a time to be looked back on as a world of limitless potential before reality took effect. And even though the promise of childhood was destroyed by the war, its aftermath, and the passing of time, the child in him remains as a symbol of hope: "Sé que, a pesar de las derrotas, él perdura y nos vence, superviviente de todos los naufragios" (I know that in spite of the defeats, he endures and conquers us, a survivor of all the shipwrecks).

From memories of his childhood, Sahagún turns to the positive force of love in "Junio" (June): "lo cierto es el amor, lo poderoso, / lo que ha triunfado sobre los derrumbes" (what is certain, what is powerful, / what has triumphed over disasters is love); but memories of the past still intrude, as he recalls "desde qué tristeza hemos venido, / desde qué infancia que nos han quitado" (what sadness we have come from, / what a childhood they took away from us).

In the last two sections of *Estar contigo* Sahagún moves away from recollections of his own past to an attack on the corruption and injustices of the Franco regime. In "De la vida en provincias" he castigates Spain for its passivity, its acceptance of "un gobierno de gángsteres mediocres" (a government of mediocre gangsters):

Cover for the 1973 collection that includes Sahagún's first prose poems

abdicar, doblegarse, sonreír,
darse al mejor postor con voluntad
de servicio, aceptar humildemente
las migajas del gran festín, ¿qué son
sino el más puro ejemplo de hidalguía
española?

(giving way, submitting, smiling,
willing to serve, giving oneself
to the highest bidder, humbly accepting
the crumbs from the feast, what are
these if not the clearest example of
Spanish nobility?)

His concern for freedom and justice also extends beyond Spain. In a poem on the death of Che Guevara ("Octubre, 1967") he envisions freedom, solidarity, and justice someday prevailing:

al abandono de la noche triste

sucederá la aurora compartida,
nunca la soledad.
Ser hombre significa desde ahora
ser guerrillero de la libertad.

(When we leave this sad night
a shared dawn will follow,
never loneliness.
To be a man signifies henceforward
to be a fighter for freedom.)

The final poem, "Epitafio sin amor" (Epitaph Without Love), looks forward to a future after an unnamed dictator's death. After the last vestiges of the regime have been dismantled, "en el silencio que quedaba en pie / fue posible por fin la primavera" (in the silence that remained, spring at last was possible).

In 1976 *Memorial de la noche* was published. With some revisions, additions, and deletions, it contains the poems of *Profecías del agua, Como si hubiera muerto un niño*, and *Estar contigo*. It also presents twelve new poems in a final section entitled "En la noche." Later that year, these poems were published separately in a limited edition of one hundred and fifty copies. In 1979 they were reprinted in *Primer y último oficio*.

Primer y último oficio won the 1978 province of León prize and the 1981 Premio Nacional de Poesía. The poems were written between 1973 and 1977, a period encompassing the end of the Franco regime, but the overall tone is one of pessimism, as the poet looks at an uncertain future and a past destroyed by the circumstances of history. Like all of his generation, he is caught in the struggle between remembering and forgetting the past. But his awareness of the power of the written word and the consequent responsibility of the poet to bear witness make obliterating the past from his memory a moral impossibility. He writes in "Invierno y barro" (Winter and Mud): "Pues fracasó la realidad de entonces, / no sucumba el poema, no haya olvido" (Since the reality of that time failed, / let the poem not succumb, let us not forget.

Everyone who lived through the war and the postwar years is, according to Sahagún, burdened with the responsibility for what occurred, whether one was actively involved in events or a mere bystander, an issue raised in Sahagún's "Septiembre 1975," which commemorates the execution of five Basque terrorists:

cinco vidas segadas descendieron
hacia la sombra, no hacia la derrota,
símbolos de un presente envilecido
que lentamente y sin piedad acaba . . .
Y más allá de la crueldad del tiempo
los que fuimos testigos somos cómplices
. . . .
la certidumbre de sus muertes
hoy nos atañe a todos

(five lives cut down descended
into darkness, not to defeat,
symbols of a degraded present
that slowly and pitilessly is drawing to an end . . .
And beyond the cruelty of this time
those of us who were witnesses are accomplices
. . . .
the certainty of their deaths
today concerns us all).

The opposition between light and darkness, day and night, runs through *Primer y último oficio*, particularly in the second part, which includes eight of the twelve "En la noche" poems. Spain is living through "esta noche que no va a dar jamás al alba," (this night which is never going to see the dawn), and perhaps there is to be no brighter future. Although the Franco era is finally drawing to an end, the future is uncertain. Signs of hope may be deceptive, and the long night that Spain has lived through may not disappear with the dictator's death. In "Libertad inmediata" (Immediate Liberty) Sahagún says:

se anuncia al fin la decepción del alba:
más allá de la puerta hay otra puerta,
también cerrada para nuestro daño

(At last they announce the disappointment of the
    dawn:
behind the door is another door,
also closed to our detriment).

Pessimism about the future is even more pronounced in "Para este otoño súbito" (For This Unexpected Autumn). The dictator is dead but,

Ahora en la incertidumbre de esta muerte,
contemplo a solas una luz difusa,
cada vez más lejana. Hay en las playas
pura lluvia sin fin, y en los caminos
igual desesperanza, más arboles sin vida
para este otoño súbito.

(Now in the uncertainty of this death,
I contemplate alone a diffused light,
all the time more distant. On the beaches there is
endless pure rain, and on the roads
the same despair, more lifeless trees
for this unexpected autumn.)

Despite the horrors of the past and the uncertainties of the future, not all Sahagún's memories are unhappy. There was love, and with the memory of love comes a sense of hope and a dream for a better future, as seen in "Vegetales":

Estamos en el bosque,
amor mío,
en la espesura de los años
vividos duramente
bajo la tiranía de las frondas,
en situación de seres vegetales
. . . .
pasa
por nuestro sueño un leñador amigo
desbrozando la noche,
abriendo para siempre el camino del alba.

(We are in the woods,

my love,
in the thickness of the years
lived harshly
under the tyranny of the foliage,
like vegetative beings
· · · · · · · · · · · · · · · ·
through
our dream a friendly woodsman
passes cutting through the night,
opening forever the way to the dawn.)

Sahagún has published no new volume of poetry since *Primer y último oficio*. However, *Las invisibles redes* (Invisible Nets), mostly an anthology of love poems selected from his earlier works, was published in 1989. The final section consists of five new poems from an unfinished volume to be entitled "El lugar de los pájaros" (The Place of the Birds). The melancholy that is characteristic of Sahagún's work pervades these poems, too, with the loneliness and longing where "nadie llega en lo oscuro a consolarme" (no one comes in the darkness to console me). Yet there is also a sense of readiness to experience love and passion again.

Indelibly marked by his childhood experiences in the civil war and its aftermath, Sahagún has been acclaimed as one of the most authentic of the Spanish postwar poets for the uncompromising ideology and intense emotion he expresses in his poetry, and the sparseness and lucidity of his poetic language.

References:

Andrew P. Debicki, "Carlos Sahagún: Metaphoric Transformation," in his *Poetry of Discovery: The Spanish Generation of 1956-1971* (Lexington: University Press of Kentucky, 1982), pp. 142-164;

Julio Rodríguez Puértolas, "La poesía de Carlos Sahagún: Memoria de una generación," in *Entre la cruz y la espada: En torno la España de posguerra*, edited by Jorgé Manuel López de Abiada (Madrid: Gredos, 1984), pp. 299-311.

Miguel de Unamuno

(29 September 1864 - 31 December 1936)

Michael L. Perna

Hunter College, City University of New York

BOOKS: *Paz en la guerra* (Madrid: Fernando Fe, 1897);

De la enseñanza superior en España (Madrid: Revista Nueva, 1899);

Tres ensayos (Madrid: Rodríquez Serra, 1900);

En torno al casticismo (Madrid: Fernando Fé, 1902);

Amor y pedagogía (Barcelona: Henrich, 1902);

Paisajes (Salamanca, Spain: Calón, 1902; enlarged edition, Madrid: Aguado, 1950);

De mi país: Descripciones, relatos y artículos de costumbres (Madrid: Fernando Fe, 1903);

Vida de Don Quijote y Sancho, según Miguel de Cervantes Saavedra, explicada y comentada (Madrid: Fernando Fe, 1905); translated by H. P. Earle as *The Life of Don Quixote and Sancho* (New York: Knopf, 1927);

Poesías (Bilbao, Spain: Rojas, 1907);

Recuerdos de niñez y de mocedad (Madrid: Suárez, 1908);

Mi religión y otros ensayos breves (Madrid: Renacimiento, 1910); translated by Stuart Gross as *Perplexities and Paradoxes* (New York: Philosophical Library, 1945);

Por tierras de Portugal y de España (Madrid: Renacimiento, 1911);

Soliloquios y conversaciones (Madrid: Renacimiento, 1911);

Rosario de sonetos líricos (Madrid: Española, 1911);

Contra esto y aquello (Madrid: Renacimiento, 1912);

Del sentimiento trágico de la vida en los hombres y en los pueblos (Madrid: Renacimiento, 1912); translated by J. E. Crawford Flitch as *The Tragic Sense of Life in Men and in Peoples* (London: Macmillan, 1921);

El espejo de la muerte (Madrid: Renacimiento, 1913);

La venda. La princesa doña Lambra [plays] (Madrid: Libro Popular, 1913);

Niebla (Madrid: Renacimiento, 1914); translated by Warner Fite as *Mist: A Tragicomic Novel* (New York: Knopf, 1928);

Ensayos, 7 volumes (Madrid: Fortanet/Residencia de Estudiantes, 1916-1918); translated in part by Flitch as *Essays and Soliloquies* (London: Harrap, 1924; New York: Knopf, 1925);

Abel Sánchez, una historia de pasión (Madrid: Renacimiento, 1917); translated by Anthony Kerrigan as *Abel Sánchez and Other Stories* (Chicago: Gateway/Regnery, 1956);

Tulio Montalbán y Julio Macedo (Madrid: Novela Corta, 1920);

Tres novelas ejemplares y un prólogo (Madrid: Calpe, 1920); translated by Angel Flores as *Three Exemplary Novels and a Prologue* (New York: Boni, 1930);

El Cristo de Velázquez (Madrid: Calpe, 1920); critical edition, edited by Victor García de la Concha (Madrid: Espasa-Calpe, 1987); translated by Eleanor L. Turnbull as *The Christ of Velazquez* (Baltimore: Johns Hopkins University Press, 1951);

La tía Tula (Madrid: Renacimiento, 1921);

Sensaciones de Bilbao (Bilbao, Spain, 1922);

Andanzas y visiones españolas (Madrid: Renacimiento, 1922);

Rimas de dentro (Valladolid, Spain: Cuesta, 1923);

Teresa: Rimas de un poeta desconocido presentadas y presentado por Miguel de Unamuno (Madrid: Renacimiento, 1923 [i.e., 1924]);

Fedra [play] (Madrid: Pluma, 1924);

L'Agonie du Christianisme, translated (into French) by Jean Cassou (Paris: Rieder, 1925); translated by Pierre Loving as *The Agony of Christianity* (New York: Payson & Clark, 1928); Spanish version published as *La agonía del cristianismo* (Madrid: Renacimiento, 1931);

De Fuerteventura a París: Diario íntimo de confinamiento y destierro vertido en sonetos (Paris: Excelsior, 1925);

Como se hace una novela (Buenos Aires: Alba, 1927);

Romancero del destierro (Buenos Aires: Alba, 1928);

Dos artículos y dos discursos (Madrid: Historia Nueva, 1930);

Sombras de sueño [play] (Madrid: Teatro Moderno, 1930);

El otro [play] (Madrid: Espasa-Calpe, 1932);

San Manuel Bueno, mártir y tres historias más (Madrid: Espasa-Calpe, 1933); translated by Kerrigan as "St. Emmanuel the Good, Martyr," in *Abel Sánchez and Other Stories* (Chicago: Regnery, 1956);

El hermano Juan; o, El mundo es teatro [play] (Madrid: Espasa-Calpe, 1934);

La ciudad de Henoc, comentario, 1933 (Mexico City: Séneca, 1941);

Antología poética, edited by Luis Felipe Vivanco (Madrid: Escorial, 1942);

Cuatro narraciones (Barcelona: Tartessos, 1943);

Cuenca Ibérica (lenguaje y paisaje) (Mexico City: Séneca, 1943);

Temas argentinos (Buenos Aires: Institución Cultural Española, 1943);

Almas de jóvenes (Buenos Aires: Espasa-Calpe, 1944);

Viejos y jóvenes (Buenos Aires: Espasa-Calpe, 1944);

El caballero de la triste figura (Buenos Aires & Mexico City: Espasa-Calpe, 1944);

Paisajes del alma (Madrid: Revista de Occidente, 1944);

La dignidad humana (Buenos Aires & Mexico City: Espasa-Calpe, 1944);

La enormedad de España (Mexico City: Séneca, 1945);

Soledad [play] (Buenos Aires: Espasa-Calpe, 1946);

Antología poética, edited by José María de Cossío (Madrid: Espasa-Calpe, 1946);

Algunas consideraciones sobre la literatura hispano-americana (Madrid: Espasa-Calpe, 1947);

Visiones y comentarios (Buenos Aires: Espasa-Calpe, 1949);

Mi Salamanca, edited by Mario Grande Ramos (Bilbao, Spain: Misericordia, 1950);

Madrid (Madrid: Afrodisio Aguado, 1950);

Unamuno in 1883, when he was a university student in Madrid

De esto y de aquello, 4 volumes (Buenos Aires: Sudamericana, 1950-1954);

Obras completas, 16 volumes, edited by Manuel García Blanco (Madrid: Afrodisio Aguado, 1950-1958);

Vida literaria (Buenos Aires: Sudamericana, 1951);

Cancionero: Diario poético, edited by Federico de Onís (Buenos Aires: Losada, 1953);

España y los españoles, edited by Manuel García Blanco (Madrid: Aguado, 1955);

Inquietudes y meditaciones (Madrid: Aguado, 1957);

En el destierro, edited by García Blanco (Madrid: Pegaso, 1957);

Cincuenta poesías inéditas (Madrid: Papeles de Son Armadans, 1958);

Mi vida y otros recuerdos personales, edited by García Blanco (Buenos Aires: Losada, 1959);

Teatro completo, edited by García Blanco (Madrid: Aguilar, 1959);

La esfinge (Madrid: Alfil, 1960);

El pasado que vuelve (Madrid: Alfil, 1960);

Del diario poético (Buenos Aires: Losada, 1961);

Cuentos, 2 volumes, edited by Eleanor Krane Paucker (Madrid: Minotauro, 1961);

Mi bochito, edited by García Blanco (Bilbao, Spain: Arturo, 1965);

El gaucho Martín Fierro (Buenos Aires: América-lee, 1967);

Diario íntimo (Madrid: Alianza, 1970); selections translated by Martin Nozick as *The Private World* (Princeton, N.J.: Princeton University Press, 1984);

Poesía completa, edited by Ana Suárez Miramón, 4 volumes (Madrid: Alianza, 1987-1989).

Editions in English: *Poems*, translated by Eleanor L. Turnbull (Baltimore: Johns Hopkins University Press, 1952);

Selected Works, edited by Anthony Kerrigan and others (London: Routledge & K. Paul / New

York: Bollingen Foundation, 1967);

The Last Poems of Miguel de Unamuno, translated by Edita Mas-López (Rutherford, Madison & Teaneck, N.J.: Fairleigh Dickinson University Press, 1974).

PLAY PRODUCTIONS: *La esfinge*, Las Palmas, Gran Canaria, Spain, Teatro Pérez Galdós, 24 February 1909;

La difunta, Madrid, Teatro de la Comedia, 27 February 1910;

Fedra, Madrid, Salón del Ateneo, 25 March 1918;

La venda, Madrid, Teatro Español, 10 June 1921;

El pasado que vuelve, Madrid, Teatro Español, 10 July 1923;

Raquel encadenada, Barcelona, Teatro Tivoli, 7 September 1926;

Sombras de sueño, Salamanca, Spain, Teatro Liceo, 24 February 1930;

El otro, Madrid, Teatro Español, 14 December 1932;

Medea [based on Lucius Anneas Seneca's *Medea*], Mérida, Spain, Anfiteatro Romano, 25 June 1933.

Miguel de Unamuno was such an important public figure and intellectual mentor in Spain during the first third of the twentieth century that his fame as a polemical essayist and philosopher overshadowed his poetry during his lifetime, and since his death his reputation has also depended more on his prose works than on his verse. He is known as a religious thinker, a philosopher who is only marginal to the main stream of Western thought, or, to students of Spanish, a writer of paradoxical novels and essays. Yet Unamuno thought of himself always as a poet, and because he valued feeling over reason and the individual over society, everything he wrote features an unsystematic and poetic use of language to express psychological and emotional dilemmas, self-contradictory thoughts, and sudden insights. When his poetry first appeared, it was criticized for being weighed down with intellectual arguments, but now the best of his poetry is appreciated for expressing intimate, personal concerns in lively language. As early as the 1950s Unamuno's work influenced Spanish poets such as José Hierro, Rafael Morales, and José Luis Hidalgo, who preferred simple concepts and colloquial turns of phrase to stylized refinements or exalted emotion. Unamuno was not in love with

words, he used them as means to search for truth.

Born on Saint Michael's day of 1864 in Bilbao, Miguel de Unamuno y Jugo spent most of his first thirty years in that progressive, commercial city. During those years Bilbao enjoyed a growing prosperity and had a liberal, outward-looking atmosphere, both due to the rapid expansion of Basque banking and the export of Biscayan iron ore. Unamuno's father, Félix, who died when Unamuno was six, had been overseas and returned prosperous; he spoke foreign languages and collected a small library of history, philosophy, and science. Unamuno's mother, Salomé Jugo, exemplified Basque tradition in her deep Catholic piety and the strict upbringing she gave her children. This contrast of one social ethos with another played a part in Unamuno's first adolescent crisis, when his urge to become a priest was checked by his love for his childhood sweetheart, Concepción (Concha) Lizárraga. Even his early childhood memories of the siege of Bilbao by the reactionary Catholic army in the Second Carlist War were of both kinds of Basques (intellectual and religious) locked in bitter combat. His deep desire to reconcile the opposites, or at least to accept them both, controls the structure of Unamuno's first published novel, the largely autobiographical *Paz en la guerra* (Peace in War, 1897), just as it informs the conflict of themes and moods in his later poetry. When Unamuno went to Madrid at sixteen for university studies, he disliked the big city and its frivolity, and dedicated himself to reading in the library, learning German and English to read Georg Hegel and Herbert Spencer, and straying off campus mostly to attend talks at the Ateneo, a liberal literary society with a good library. By age twenty he had written a doctoral thesis attacking as ridiculous most of the then-current theories of the origin of the Basque language and people. With his degree in hand he returned to Bilbao to work as a private tutor, while he studied for and took *oposiciones* (competitive national examinations for teaching posts), until in 1891 he placed first in Greek. This gave him a professorship at the university in Salamanca, where he moved with Concha, his new bride. Secure in his career, Unamuno began to attack the stagnation he saw at the university and in Spain as a whole. He wrote articles for *La Lucha de Clases*, the socialist paper in Bilbao; he insisted on teaching Greek as a living language to the point of reading the Argentine *gaucho* poem *Martín Fierro* to his students for comparison with

Self-caricature by Unamuno (from Insula, *June 1971; by permission of the Estate of Miguel de Unamuno)*

Homeric epics; and he published essays, later collected as a book, *En torno al casticismo* (On Authentic Tradition, 1902), advocating the reform of Spain by the adoption of European cultural and scientific values. But when his third child developed meningitis in 1897, Unamuno suffered a terrifying spiritual crisis: he could find comfort neither in his intellectual convictions nor in the childhood Catholicism to which he attempted to return. A fear of death began to change Unamuno's thinking and writing in the decade before he published his first poetry. Gradually he abandoned socialism, since not even the attainment of a just society would solve the greatest human problem, death. He changed his mind about modernizing Spain, arguing instead, in *Vida de Don Quijote y Sancho* (1905; translated as *The Life of Don Quixote and Sancho,* 1927), that Spain's true nature lay not in technological but in spiritual supremacy, in the tradition of Saint Teresa of Avila, Saint John of the Cross, and Cervantes' character Don Quixote—whose chivalric mission Unamuno interpreted as a struggle to attain immortality.

Thus the major themes in Unamuno's poetry, from the time he began to publish it at age forty-three·to his death at seventy-two, had developed in his younger years. Unable to believe the official, institutional dogmas of religion, he suffered from the need that God exist so that his death would not mean total annihilation.

Reason offered him no consolation for death, and he could not abolish reason by the will to believe. Loving Spain for its particularity, for its difference from Europe, he still could not abide its moral and mental stagnation. He attempted to combine passionate emotions with ideas in his poetry, using poetic license to harmonize all discord. At war with himself, he saw poetry as a weapon for spiritual warfare, so he would write a poem about anything that happened to him as a way of keeping a diary of spiritual self-examination. The techniques he uses in his verse follow from his goal of telling the intimate truth about himself. The honesty of the poem is more important than the beauty of the language. While he shared this conviction with a greater poet, the then-obscure Antonio Machado, it set him against the leading poets of his time, and against the dominant style of *modernismo*, led by Rubén Darío. The modernists preferred exotic and musical words for elevated thoughts and beautiful verse; Unamuno chose rough, ordinary vocabulary from common Spanish. Where the modernists crafted a thought to fit a single verse for parallel sense and sound, Unamuno's thought rushes past the end of the line so that sense is more important than sound. As a result Unamuno's poetry was an anomaly when it first appeared, his books rarely went into second editions, and he even began to take pride in his unfashionableness, once telling a friend, "I have just flung another volume of my verse at the public's indifference."

In the years before he published *Poesías* (1907), Unamuno prepared and revised his poetry in the midst of a very busy life. He was appointed rector of the Universidad de Salamanca in 1900, so every day after teaching for two hours he did administrative work. Then after lunch and a regular siesta, besides writing articles or essays, he would take a long walk, normally on the Zamora road to the north of Salamanca. In 1899 and 1900 he was working on a translation of Giacomo Leopardi's poem about nature's indifference to insignificant man, "La Ginestra" (1836), and telling friends that he planned to publish it soon with two dozen of his own poems.

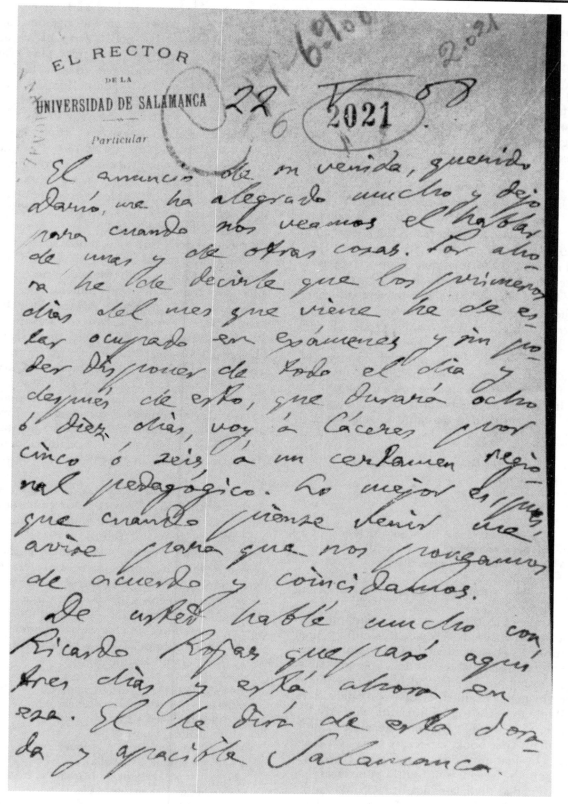

Page of a letter from Unamuno to Nicaraguan poet Rubén Darío, a leading exponent of modernism (from Cuadernos Hispanoamericanos, *August-September, 1967; by permission of the Estate of Miguel de Unamuno)*

Seven years later he had 210 poems, many of them influenced by Leopardi's free verse. Unamuno also reproduced free verse from English and Catalan, translating Samuel Taylor Coleridge and Joan Maragall, as well as from two Italian poems by Giosuè Carducci. Coleridge and Leopardi provided models for the kinds of subjects Unamuno chose: philosophic discourses or vague musings on the events of daily life, on the poet's impressions of nature, or on visits to cathedrals in the cities and small churches in the countryside.

Unamuno's love of ancient Spanish places owes less to Coleridge than it does to the idea he shared with other members of the Generation of 1898—such as Antonio Machado and José Martínez Ruiz (Azorín)—that Spain's regeneration required her intellectuals to penetrate the spirit of the neglected, rural countryside and abandon the false culture that urban and political sophisticates had imitated badly from abroad. Unamuno's variant on this theme was the need to rediscover the secret, ignored history (*intrahistoria*) of Spain as it lies hidden in the provinces. Having lived for sixteen years in the provincial calm of his university town, he wrote an ode, "Salamanca" (in *Poesías*) thanking the city for giving him this insight:

> bosque de piedras que arrancó la historia
> a las entrañas de la tierra madre,
> remanso de quietud, yo te bendigo,
> ¡mi Salamanca!

> (great forest of stone that drew out the history
> from the deep recesses of mother earth,
> backwater of quietude, I bless thee,
> my Salamanca!
> —translation by Eleanor L. Turnbull).

For this ode of thirty-one stanzas Unamuno uses the *cuarteta sáfica* of seventeenth-century poet and latinist Esteban Manuel de Villegas: three unrhymed hendecasyllables and a pentasyllable, thus opposing an ancient and learned technique to the rhymed alexandrines of his modernist rivals. While the effect is both traditional and idiosyncratic, this ode has become the most famous poem of his first book, especially since it was set to music by Joaquín Rodrigo and performed as a cantata on the seven hundredth anniversary of the Universidad de Salamanca in 1953. When the book was published, however, Unamuno's status as the rector of the university and his fame as a polemical essayist in his newspaper columns made

him a hard poet to review, and no regular reviewer for any paper printed a reaction that went beyond noting the book's overall casualness about verse form and the new poet's appeal more to the heart and head than to the ear, all of which were points Unamuno himself had proclaimed in the poems and in earlier essays.

Between 1907 and the year of his next poetry book, *Rosario de sonetos líricos* (Rosary of Lyric Sonnets, 1911), Unamuno continued to turn out essays on metaphysics, religion, and travel. He visited Portugal, wrote about it, and met a kindred spirit there: the poet Texeira de Pascoaes. Unamuno was attracted to Pascoaes's metaphysical bent; his desire to regenerate Portugal through exploring the national *saudade* (nostalgia), which he saw as a blend of pagan, Christian, Roman, and Semitic inheritances; and his preference for the "sculptural" qualities of English verse over the musicality of the French. The main difference was that Pascoaes was exclusively a poet and the leader of a poetic movement with his journal *Saudade*. Unamuno's interest in Portuguese soon led him to read Antero de Quental, a poet who had led Portugal's reformist Generation of 1870 but who had abandoned politics to write cycles of sonnets chronicling his search for a new faith to replace Catholicism; Quental combined German metaphysics, Buddhism, and other disparate elements in his new system of philosophy.

When Unamuno sat down to do a sonnet cycle he finished 128 poems for publication between his forty-sixth birthday in September 1910 and the beginning of February 1911. He admitted to a friend that, in spite of the title *Rosario de sonetos líricos*, his sonnets were more tragic than lyric, and indeed he sees himself in the sonnets as a tragic hero condemned to an unjust fate. For Unamuno death is the most unjust of fates, but resigning oneself to dying is a vile surrender; it is better to fight on hopelessly, as he urges in "Razón y fe" (Reason and Faith):

> Levanta de la fe el blanco estandarte
> sobre el polvo que cubre la batalla
> mientras la ciencia parlotea, y calla
> y oye sabiduría y obra el arte.
> Hay que vivir, y fuerza es esforzarte
> a pelear contra la vil canalla
> que se anima al restalle de la tralla,
> y hay que morir!, exclama. Pon tu parte
> y la de Dios espera, que abomina
> del que cede. Tu ensangrentada huella
> por los mortales campos encamina

hacia el fulgor de tu eterna estrella;
hay que ganar la vida, que no fina,
con razón, sin razón o contra ella.

(Raise the white standard of faith
over the dust that covers the battle
while science chatters, and wisdom
falls silent and hears, and art works.
One must live, and you are forced to force yourself
to fight the vile mob
that gets excited by tearing away your lash,
and exclaiming "One must die!" Do your part
and expect his from God, who hates
whomever surrenders. March your bloody trail
over the fatal fields
toward the gleam of your eternal star;
you must win life, which dies not,
with reason, without reason, or against it.)

The last tercet of the poem shows how far Unamuno is from ancient tragedy, where the grandeur of the hero increases because of the absolute hopelessness of the fight, since Unamuno's implication is clear that God may give the prize of eternal life to a truly great fighter even though he loses the battle. This attitude in the *Rosario de sonetos líricos* was expanded into a central theme of Unamuno's major work, *Del sentimiento trágico de la vida en los hombres y en los pueblos* (1912; translated as *The Tragic Sense of Life in Men and in Peoples*, 1921), as Unamuno argues that the prize of immortality goes only to those who struggle most fiercely against doubts to win it, not to those whose faith assures them that they will be rewarded, nor to those who abandon faith for reason—as though God is the result, not the cause, of man's longing to live beyond death. Beside developing a major idea that would later be expanded into his greatest essay, Unamuno develops a new kind of control over language in *Rosario de sonetos líricos* by forcing his thought into the compressed form of the sonnet. His Spanish becomes more concise, and the strong, even violent enjambments never break the classic rhythms allowed in Spanish sonnets, where the stresses can vary back and forth along the eleven-syllable lines. In general the best of Unamuno's sonnets can stand comparisons to Francisco de Quevedo's, though each of them is an occasional piece in the sense that it has a date attached to it or a quote from some author that the sonnet glosses.

This gain in control marks the beginning of the long process of Unamuno becoming a better poet, and he worked at it by rewriting slowly and repeatedly his longest and greatest poem *El*

Cristo de Velázquez (1920; translated as *The Christ of Velazquez*, 1951), which Pedro Salinas called the greatest religious poem since the seventeenth century. Begun in 1913 from a desire to write a truly Spanish Christology, even if not by the church's definition of Christ nor the state's of Spain, the poem reached fifteen hundred lines in its first draft, when Unamuno went to Madrid in early 1914 to read it at the Ateneo. Choosing a biblical tone for his work, he decided to create a Spanish equivalent for John Milton's blank verse. He was pleased with the effect his reading had on an audience that could follow the interior rhythm of his thought, and he was sure he had made the right choice of meter: an unrhymed variant of *estancia*, eleven-syllable verse in stanzas of flexible length, a form used since the sixteenth century for odes, songs, and eclogues. He continued expanding his poem through years when his academic career became embroiled in politics: while Spain was officially neutral in World War I, Unamuno's stand in favor of the British and French alliance got him removed from the rectorship by the conservative, pro-German faction at the university. His friends secured him a deanship there in 1915 but he refused it. On a visit to Catalonia in 1916, among the ruins of the monastery of Poblet, Unamuno read a revised version of *El Cristo de Velázquez* to his friends. When it was published in October of 1920 it ran to 2,538 lines, a long meditation on the symbolism of Christ as seen in one of the greatest Spanish paintings.

The subject of the actual body of Christ gradually replaces the painting as the poem progresses, developing the theme that the resurrection of Christ's suffering, human body is a promise to the believer that his own body will be resurrected as part of his salvation. In the first section of thirty-nine poems the visual immediacy of Velázquez's image of Christ, its serenity and beauty, calm the fears of the viewer and evoke meditation, praise, and worship through a series of allegorical names for Christ (Ecce-Homo, Lamb, Wine, Eagle, Lion, and so on) taken from scripture and devotional literature. A second section of fourteen short poems evokes the moment of Christ's death. Third, the parts of Velázquez's painting are described in twenty-seven meditations on the parts of Christ's body. The last eight poems and final prayer declare that Christ has accomplished his promise to save the soul and resurrect the body of the viewer who encounters him and believes. Convinced that the flesh-and-blood Christ of Spanish art was the

Unamuno and his wife, Concha, in 1916

key to his people's faith, Unamuno wanted to re-create in his poem the direct, undogmatic experience of belief. In fact the Christ figure by Velázquez is one of the least tortured in the tradition of Spanish Crucifixions, and the painting's sensory qualities seem to have occasioned the most sensual imagery Unamuno ever wrote. Far from being an orthodox devotional figure, Unamuno's Christ is a heroically mythical being, a quixotic spirit in the image of Unamuno's own ideal of Spanishness. Since its publication *El Cristo de Velázquez* has been less studied as a poem than mined for evidence in arguments over whether Unamuno himself was an atheist, a heretic, or a Catholic.

While *El Cristo* was in press, Unamuno spent the summer of 1920 preparing a volume of travel sketches, *Andanzas y visiones españolas* (Spanish Travels and Visions, 1922), which contains some of his most frequently anthologized poetry. Although most of *Andanzas* is prose that had been sold to weekly and daily newspapers soon after each of the excursions Unamuno made through Spain and Portugal from 1907 to 1914, each piece is a poetic description of some spot, and publishing them together, Unamuno main-

tained they were all poems whether written in prose or verse. The opening sketch of the ruined monastery at La Granja de Moreruela contains four meditative sonnets like the ones he published in *Rosario de sonetos líricos* in 1911, the year he wrote the sketch. At the end of the book there are eight "Visiones rítmicas" (Rhythmic Visions): four are printed as prose but when read aloud reveal by their rhymes that they are written in verse. Then, to confound readers who demand mechanical perfection in poetry, the third verse of the third stanza is lacking in the final "prose" poem, "Junto a la vieja Colegiata" (By the Old Collegiate Church)—a sly joke because the description is complete without the "missing" verse. On the other hand, both metrical and formal perfection help to make deeply moving expressions of "En un cementerio de lugar castellano" (In the Cemetery of a Castilian Place), with its imagery of cemetery walls to which sheep run across the plains in a summer storm, and "En Gredos" (In Gredos), a hymn to Castile's wildest mountains. These two poems present Unamuno's most frequent themes: death as an escape from the storms of history into the peace of eternity; and the land itself as the timeless renewer and lasting symbol of Spanish life. Seen in the context of the Generation of 1898 to which he belonged, Unamuno's early work is the most poetic contribution to *la cuestión de España* (the problem of Spain), which constantly preoccupied all his contemporaries, but seen within the continuing development of Spanish poetry, his subjects—family, country, and religion—had become anomalies. Poems he wrote in his mid forties and published through the next decade and a half were the basis for what reputation he had as a poet during his lifetime; another creative period would come in his mid sixties, but the later work would only become known after his death.

Written from 1907 to 1910, the twenty poems of *Rimas de dentro* (Rhymes from Within, 1923) express Unamuno's inner anguish at the passage of time and his bitter fear of death as personal annihilation, themes he was developing philosophically in *Del sentimiento trágico de la vida* during the same years. These themes provide the only unity in *Rimas de dentro*, otherwise simply a gathering of poems on disparate subjects (seeing wild reeds, riding a train, looking into his childhood nursery, and so on) that he read to a group of friends on 5 May 1923 at the Ateneo in Madrid. Present was José María de Cossío, editor of a private series called "Libros para amigos no destinados a la venta" (Books for Friends Not for Sale), who convinced Unamuno to let him publish the poems together. As part of the editor's campaign his brother, Francisco de Cossío, reported on Unamuno's performance in the Valladolid daily *El Norte de Castilla* (10 May 1923), and the book was produced in the Cuesta print shop within a month. In the book is one of Unamuno's greatest poems, "Aldebarán." The speaker asks the bright red star a series of questions, wondering if it watches him back, whether it is lonely, or perhaps it is just a drop of blood in the living body of the universe. When the sun dies and the solar system dissolves, will the star watch human deaths? And when will death take the star itself ?

¿Cuando frío y oscuro
—el espacio sudario—
ruedes sin fin y para fin ninguno?

(And when, cold and dark,
—in the shroud of space—
you roll endlessly to no end?)

Yet before the cosmos dies, the speaker will take it as a pledge of eternal mystery that Aldebaran

will shine its blood-red light on his own grave. The only acceptance of death he reaches is resignation to living and even dying in the doubts of his hope and ignorance. The first national review of *Rimas de dentro* was by the poet Gerardo Diego in an article for José Ortega y Gasset's new review *Revista del Occidente* in 1923. Diego had published his sonnets (*Soria*, 1923) in Cossío's series just before Unamuno's book, and later Diego would choose "Aldebarán" as one of the Unamuno poems for his widely read anthology *Poesía española, antología* (1932). When Jorge Guillén, under the pseudonym Pedro Villa, reviewed Unamuno's book in the Salamanca paper *La Libertad* on 16 January 1924, it was clear that, as a poet, Unamuno was about to be promoted into a precursor of the rising generation.

During the month of June 1923, on vacation in Palencia, Unamuno reread the *Rimas* (1871) of Gustavo Adolfo Bécquer, a melancholy romantic whose love poetry continued to be popular, though younger poets were adverse to his sentimentality. Attracted emotionally to Bécquer, Unamuno began to write Becquerian *rimas* as a relief from the political crisis of that summer (in the *Cortes*, the Spanish Parliament, the Liberals were demanding an investigation of the Spanish army's disastrous defeat at Anual in 1921, when it attempted to conquer Morocco). By the winter of 1923-1924 Unamuno published *Teresa: Rimas de un poeta desconocido presentadas y presentado por Miguel de Unamuno* (Teresa: Rhymes of an Unknown Poet Presented by Miguel de Unamuno), another book of mixed prose and verse. The poems are set within a story almost like the frame device of a nineteenth-century novel. Unamuno claims to be only the editor of these verses sent to him by Rafael, a young poet in a provincial city, to tell the story of his love for Teresa, her lingering death from tuberculosis, and the poet's grief-stricken eagerness to follow her to the tomb. Constructing *Teresa* from such romantic clichés allows Unamuno to develop the theme that each person lives beyond death as the person he or she has been for others: as Rafael's poetry has re-created the Teresa he loved, so Unamuno's editing has cheated death of the best Rafael. Unamuno adds a series of his own notes on Rafael's versification and choice of rhymes, plus an essay of farewell ("Despedida") to defend the idealism of Rafael's poems from the depressing reality that surrounds it. Realizing that the critics' reception would be poor—for 1924 was a year in which innovative poetry reigned: Rafael

Unamuno in exile in Hendaye, France, where he lived from 1925 to 1930 (photograph by Guereo)

Alberti's *Marinero en tierra* (Sailor on Land) had won the National Poetry Prize while still in manuscript, and Pablo Neruda's *Veinte poemas de amor y una canción desesperada* (Twenty Love Poems and a Desperate Song) was sweeping the Spanish-speaking world—Unamuno prefaced *Teresa* with the essay "Unamuno, poeta," which the great modernist poet Darío had done for *La Nación* of Buenos Aires (2 May 1909) to salute Unamuno's first poem of fifteen years earlier. *Teresa* seems of interest now as an example of Unamuno's chaste, if somewhat morbid, idea of love and as an echo of Bécquer.

Before the first copies of *Teresa* reached Unamuno, political events forced a great change in his life which would make him an international cause célèbre in political exile and give him a renewed reputation through the 1920s as a religious thinker. With the idea that "Since I am king, let me govern," Alfonso XIII connived in a military coup (13 September 1923) to make Gen. Miguel Primo de Rivera dictator. Unamuno joined the outraged Liberal politicians in pouring out a stream of polemical articles full of invective and sarcasm. On 22 February 1924 he was exiled without his family to the island of Fuerteventura in the Canaries. Once settled in tiny Puerto del Rosario he began keeping a diary of sonnets, which would become *De Fuerteventura a París: Diario íntimo de confinamiento y destierro vertido en sonetos* (From Fuerteventura to Paris: Intimate Diary of Confinement and Exile Poured Out in Sonnets, 1925). Again in an agitated time of his public life he chose to write in the most traditional verse form. For the first three months his poems were almost exclusively attacks on his political persecutors. After the end of May, when he became aware that friends were trying to arrange his escape by yacht to France, he wrote more and more about his encounter with the vastness of the ocean: he had replaced his afternoon walks out from Salamanca by roaming nightly, when the heat of the African sun lessened, along the shores of the island. Unamuno left Fuerteventura on 11 July 1924 aboard a private schooner and arrived in Paris at the end of August. By the end

Drawing of Unamuno by Bagaria (from Luis S. Granjel, Retrato de Unamuno, 1957)

of the year he had added another thirty-seven sonnets to complete his book, with reflections on what it was to be in exile after being a prisoner. Feeling himself even more Spanish in a foreign country and obsessed with loneliness and fears for his sanity, Unamuno began at the end of this book to develop themes that would fill his next work of poetry, *Romancero del destierro* (The Ballads of Exile, 1928).

In Paris Unamuno became aware that his exile had caused an increase in the sales of his books. When he got the sales figures for the second trimester of 1924 from his Madrid publisher, Renacimiento, he compared the figures for the same period of 1923 and wrote an article, "De economía literaria" (On Literary Economy), which he sold to the Madrid weekly *Nuevo Mundo* (14 November 1924). Singling out *Andanzas y* *visiones españolas* and *Rosario de sonetos líricos* as his two fastest-selling poetry books, he attacked the idea that poetry does not sell, citing the popularity of Gustavo Adolfo Bécquer and the local Salamanca poet José Gabriel y Galán, and Darío's steady sales year after year; then Unamuno praised the readers of poetry for rereading and replacing their books as novel readers seldom do. His hope of appealing to the popular market shines through the article but was far off the mark, for in Paris he was lionized for a year by the progressive intellectuals who knew him primarily as the author of *Del sentimiento trágico de la vida*. As such he was given a contract for *L'Agonie du Christianisme* (The Agony of Christianity, 1925), a book he completed and turned over to his French translator on 13 December 1924, so that the French and the English (1928) translations appeared before it came out in Spanish (1931).

Miguel de Unamuno

Unamuno the explorer of religious psychology completely obscured Unamuno the poet in his contemporary international reputation (Henry Miller, for instance, writing his surrealistic novel *Black Spring* [1936] in Paris invokes Unamuno, Fyodor Dostoevski, François Rabelais, and Walt Whitman as his inspirations), but the dramatic, personal arguments of *La agonía del cristianismo* are the bases for many of the poems of *Romancero del destierro*, the first four poems of which show that, for Unamuno, Paris had become the place where he would die without seeing Spain again. In August 1925 he moved to Hendaye, the French Basque city just across the Bidasoa River from Spain. In sight of the Pyrenees, living again in a Basque port that was a smaller version of his childhood home, he sold articles regularly to *Hojas Libres* (Free Papers)—Eduardo Ortega y Gasset's Spanish exile weekly in Bayonne—in a furious campaign against the Spanish monarchy and for a Republic. The ballads of the *Romancero* are really political journalism in verse, but from the thirty-seven poems that precede the ballads, critics have been im-

pressed with Unamuno's eerie premonition of death in "Vendrá de noche" (It Will Come By Night); his feeling that life dissolves back into the universe in "¿Qué es tu vida, alma mía?, ¿cuál tu pago?" (What is your life, my soul? What your reward?); and his temptation to find peace with the Basques on a little hillside in "Orhoit Gutaz" (Remember Us):

> calle el porqué . . . vivamos
> como habéis muerto, sin porqué, es lo cuerdo . . .
>
> (Silence the why . . . let us live
> as you have died, without why, it's the sane
>   thing . . .).

Romancero del destierro was the last book of poetry that Unamuno published in his life, but on 1 March 1928 he put the first poem into what would become a series of little notebooks, to which he kept adding entries until 28 December 1936, three days before he died. Meanwhile his public life became a storm of political involvement: on 28 January 1930 King Alfonso attempted to regain some popularity by removing the dictator, Primo de Rivera, and on 10 February Unamuno crossed the bridge to Irún; he made a triumphal procession with friends; supporters, and students for four days across Spain to Salamanca. Within the year he was restored to a professorship. After the king fled Spain and the Republic was proclaimed in April 1931, Unamuno became rector of the university again (22 May 1931), and on his retirement at age seventy (29 September 1934) he was named rector for life. By that time, amid increasing violence between left and right extremists, he was calling on students not to follow their elders into the insanity of dissolving the nation in partisan hatreds; he correctly predicted and warned against the communist-socialist-anarchist revolt, which broke out in Asturias on 4 October 1934. The next coup d'etat, by the Army (18 July 1936), he supported as a means to end the chaos. Yet when the coup turned into civil war, Unamuno saw his friends arrested and executed in the methodical repression the army carried out to consolidate its hold on the rebel zone. At the next university convocation (12 October 1936) Unamuno exploded into denunciations of the rebellion; Gen. Francisco Franco granted permission to shoot him, but, to avoid international bad publicity, the old man was removed from the rectorship and confined in strict house arrest, where he died on New Year's Eve, 1936.

While Unamuno's final speech as rector and his last days became a story in standard histories of the Spanish Civil War (one might call it the legend wherein he buried his other selves), the poet Luis Felipe Vivanco edited the first general collection of Unamuno's poetry, *Antología poética*, in 1942, printed at the press of the new literary journal *Escorial*, which had been begun by writers on the Franco side during the war. Vivanco included the whole of *Rimas de dentro* in the anthology, generous selections from each of the other books, and seventy-two poems from the notebooks of 1928-1936. In 1946 José María de Cossío edited another *Antología poética* of Unamuno (including fifty-one poems from the notebooks), which has been in print ever since. Finally, the former Republican ambassador to the United States Federico de Onís edited the entire notebooks as *Cancionero: Diario poético* (Book of Songs: Poetic Diary, 1953). Many of the 1,755 poems are banal occasional pieces; some are witty uses of sound for emotional effect. When Unamuno plays with the Spanish place names that have *esdrújulo* (penultimate) accents, he makes each half-line a classic Spanish octosyllable while building a fast rumble of music to accompany what lasts longest in Spain, the geography and the language:

> Ávila, Málaga, Cáceres,—Játiva, Mérida, Córdoba,
> Ciudad Rodrigo, Sepúlveda—Úbeda, Arévalo, Frómista.
> Zumárraga, Salamanca—Turégano, Zaragoza,
> Lérida, Zamarramala,—Arracundiaga, Zamora,
> Sois nombres de cuerpo entero,—libres, propios, los de nómina,
> el tuétano intraductible—de nuestra lengua española.

> ([cities' names]
> You are whole-bodied names,—free, personal, the ones that count,
> The untranslatable pith—of our Spanish language.)

This love for words themselves is a constant in all of Unamuno's writing: in his philosophy he often abandons logic to argue from etymology; his fictional characters muse on words that unsettle or hurt them. These habits prompt some of his finest poems in *Cancionero*. As a poet Unamuno reveals his personal traits with paradoxically less of the embarrassing self-dramatization that sometimes mars his prose. He wrote always proclaiming his honesty but in the fear that he was falsifying something intimate by his exhibitionism in bringing it to light. There was inexpressible, untranslatable mystery for him in his own personality as in the universe, but he seemed to come closest to it in the hours when he felt himself offstage and set down his poetry for himself.

Letters:

El porvenir de España, by Unamuno and Angel Ganivet (Madrid: Renacimiento, 1912);

Epistolario a Clarín, edited by Adolfo Alas (Madrid: Escorial, 1941);

Unamuno y Maragall, Epistolario y escritos complementarios (Barcelona: Edimar, 1951);

Epistolario Ibérico: Cartas de Pascoaes e Unamuno (Nova Lisboa, Portugal: Cámara Municipal de Nova Lisboa, 1957);

Trece cartas inéditas de Miguel de Unamuno a Alberto Nin Frías, edited by Pedro Banadelli (Buenos Aires: Mandrágora, 1962);

Unamuno en Canarias, edited by Sebastián de la Nuez (Santa Cruz, Tenerife: Universidad de La Laguna, 1964);

Cartas inéditas de Miguel de Unamuno, edited by Sergio Fernández Larraín (Santiago, Chile: Zig-Zag, 1965);

Unamuno y sus amigos catalanes, edited by José Tarín-Iglesias (Barcelona: Peñiscola, 1966);
Cartas, 1903-1933 (Barcelona: Aguilar, 1972);
Unamuno "agitador de espíritus" y Giner: Correspondencia inédita (Madrid: Narcea, 1977).

Bibliographies:

Manuel García Blanco, "Crónica unamuniana," in *Cuadernos de la Cátedra Miguel de Unamuno*, 1 (1948): 103-136; 2 (1951): 133-148; 3 (1952): 5-12, 81-104; 4 (1953): 85-105; 5 (1954): 185-211;

Federico de Onís, "Bibliografía de Miguel de Unamuno," *La Torre (Revista General de la Universidad de Puerto Rico)* 9, nos. 35-36 (1961): 601-636;

Pelayo H. Fernández, *Bibliografía crítica de Miguel de Unamuno (1888-1975)* (Madrid: Porrúa, 1976).

Biographies:

Arturo Barea, *Unamuno* (New Haven: Yale University Press, 1952);

Margaret Thomas Rudd, *The Lone Heretic* (Austin: University of Texas Press, 1963);

Emilio Salcedo, *Vida de Don Miguel* (Madrid: Anaya, 1964);

Frances Wyers, *Miguel de Unamuno: The Contrary Self* (London: Támesis, 1976).

References:

Manuel Alvar, "Unidad y evolución en la lírica de Unamuno," in his *Estudios y ensayos de literatura contemporánea* (Madrid: Gredos, 1954), pp. 113-138;

Carlos Blanco Aguinaga, *El Unamuno contemplativo* (Mexico City: Colegio de México, 1959);

Blanco Aguinaga, *Unamuno, teórico del lenguaje* (Mexico City: Colegio de México, 1954);

Luis Cernuda, "Miguel de Unamuno (1864-1936)," in his *Estudios sobre poesía española contemporánea* (Madrid: Guadarrama, 1957), pp. 71-82;

Birute Ciplijauskaité, "Los valores fónicos en la poesía de Unamuno," *Hispania*, 71 (March 1988): 31-37;

Rubén Darío, "Unamuno, poeta," *La Nación* (2 May 1909); reprinted in his *El modernismo y otros ensayos*, edited by Iris M. Zavala (Madrid: Alianza, 1990);

Gerardo Diego, *Poesía española contemporánea* (Madrid: Taurus, 1959), pp. 59-83;

Diego, "Poesías del norte (Miguel de Unamuno, Basterra, Rio Sáinz)," *Revista de Occidente*, 2 (1923): 128-132;

Manuel García Blanco, *Don Miguel de Unamuno y sus poesías* (Salamanca, Spain: Universidad de Salamanca, 1954);

Victor García de la Concha, Introduction to Unamuno's *El Cristo de Velázquez* (Madrid: Espasa-Calpe, 1988), pp. 5-84;

Luis S. Granjel, *Retrato de Unamuno* (Madrid: Guadarrama, 1971);

Josse de Kock, *Introducción al "Cancionero" de Miguel de Unamuno* (Madrid: Gredos, 1968);

Allen Lacy, *Miguel de Unamuno: The Rhetoric of Existence* (The Hague: Mouton, 1967);

Julián Marías, *Miguel de Unamuno* (Madrid: Espasa-Calpe, 1943); translated by Frances M. López-Morillas (Cambridge, Mass.: Harvard University Press, 1966);

Ciraco Morón Arroyo, "Unamuno: Poesía y filosofía," in *Miguel de Unamuno*, second edition, enlarged, edited by Antonio Sánchez Barbudo (Madrid: Taurus, 1990), pp. 375-390;

Martin Nozick, *Miguel de Unamuno: The Agony of Belief* (Princeton, N.J.: Princeton University Press, 1971);

Mario J. Valdés, *Death in the Literature of Unamuno* (Urbana, Ill. & London: University of Illinois Press, 1966);

Valdés and María Elena de Valdés, *An Unamuno Sourcebook: A Catalogue of Readings and Acquisitions with an Introductory Essay on Unamuno's Dialectical Enquiry* (Toronto: University of Toronto Press, 1973);

Pedro Villa [Jorge Guillén], "Correo literario: La poesía en 1923," *Libertad*, 16 January 1924;

Luis Felipe Vivanco, "Dos grandes poetas retrasados: Unamuno y Antonio Machado," in his *Introducción a la poesía española contemporánea*, third edition, 2 volumes (Madrid: Guadarrama, 1974), I: 24-40;

Howard T. Young, "Miguel de Unamuno: The Oldest Struggle," in his *The Victorious Expression: A Study of Four Contemporary Spanish Poets* (Madison: University of Wisconsin Press, 1964), pp. 3-31.

José Angel Valente

(25 April 1929 -   )

Margaret H. Persin
Rutgers University

BOOKS: *A modo de esperanza* (Madrid: Rialp/
Adonáis, 1955);

Poemas a Lázaro (Madrid: Indice, 1960);

Sobre el lugar del canto (Barcelona: Literaturasa/
Colliure, 1963);

La memoria y los signos (Madrid: Revista de Occidente, 1966);

Siete representaciones (Barcelona: Bardo, 1967);

Breve son (Madrid: Ciencia Nueva/Bardo, 1968);

Presentación y memorial para un monumento (Madrid: Poesía para Todos, 1970);

El inocente (Mexico City: Mortíz, 1970);

Las palabras de la tribu (Madrid: Siglo Veintiuno,
1971);

Punto cero (Barcelona: Barral, 1972; enlarged,
1980);

El fin de la edad de plata (Barcelona: Seix Barral,
1973);

Número trece (Las Palmas, Gran Canaria, Spain: Inventarios Provisionales, 1973);

Ensayo sobre Miguel de Molinos (Barcelona: Barral,
1974);

Interior con figuras (Barcelona: Barral, 1976);

Material memoria (Barcelona: Gaya Ciencia, 1979);

Siete cántigas de alén (Sada, La Coruña, Spain: Castro, 1981);

Tres lecciones de tinieblas (Barcelona: Gaya Ciencia,
1981);

La piedra y el centro (Madrid: Taurus, 1982);

Mandorla (Madrid: Cátedra, 1982);

Poesía y poemas (Madrid: Narcea, 1983);

El fulgor (Madrid: Cátedra, 1984);

Entrada en materia (Madrid: Cátedra, 1985);

El inocente; seguido de Treinta y siete fragmentos (Barcelona: Orbis, 1985);

Al dios del lugar (Barcelona: Tusquets, 1989);

Obra poética, 2 volumes, edited by Andrés Sánchez Roybana (Barcelona: Ambit Serveis,
1990).

OTHER: "Conocimiento y comunicación," in
Poesía última, edited by Francisco Ribes (Madrid: Taurus, 1963), pp. 157-159.

José Angel Valente is in a group of Spanish
poets who came to the fore in the late 1950s and
1960s, which also includes such writers as
Claudio Rodríguez, Carlos Sahagún, Francisco
Brines, Eladio Cabañero, and Angel González.
The work of this group cannot be classified very
easily: it reaches beyond the social orientation of
earlier post-civil-war poetry and also deepens the
philosophical queries about humanity's position
that appear in the work of earlier poets such as
José Hierro and Blas de Otero. The common de-
nominator of the poetry of this later group can
be found not in its proclamation of certain
shared themes or its utilization of a particular
style but rather in its attitude regarding the creative act. Poetry is seen as both the cognition and
the communication of modern human reality.
Thus poetry is not just a result and a reflection
but a conscious process.

Valente was born on 25 April 1929 in
Orense, Galicia, Spain, and thus belongs to the second generation of poets who came into prominence after the disastrous Spanish Civil War
(1936-1939). He began his university education
at the Universidad de Santiago de Compostela in
the faculty of law, but in 1947 he moved to Madrid, where he studied philosophy and letters at
the Universidad de Madrid. He received his licentiate diploma in romance philology in 1953. From
1955 to 1958 Valente was a lecturer in the Department of Hispanic Studies at Oxford University in
England, from which he received the Master of
Arts degree. Soon after, he moved to Geneva,
Switzerland, where he is an official with the
United Nations; his residence is nearby in
Collongues-sous-Salève, France. Aside from his
works of poetry, he also frequently contributes
critical articles to literary journals and has done
translations of poets such as Gerard Manley Hopkins, Constantino Cafavis, and Eugenio Montale.

With the other members of Valente's generation, he shares the sense of poetry as the creation
of a new reality. In his essay "Conocimiento y
comunicación" (Knowledge and Communication),

José Angel Valente, circa 1960

his ars poetica, Valente affirms that "the poet does not function basing himself on the knowledge of previous material experience, but rather this knowledge is produced in the very creative process and is, in my opinion, the central element of what we call poetic creation. The instrument through which knowledge of a certain subject of experience is produced in the process of creation *is* the poem itself. I wish to say that the poet is familiar with the zone of reality upon which the poem rises up in giving it poetic form: the act of expression in the act of coming to know. . . . Every poem, then, is an exploration of the material of previously unknown experience, which constitutes its object."

Thus, for Valente, the poem itself is the only way by which its creator can know reality in its fullest sense. The poet expresses this reality by forming another one in the creative act. Exploration and discovery are inherent in the poetic process. This view finds expression in Valente's poems; these often become real processes in and

of themselves. They embody the idea of process both as a theme and as a method of communication. Clearly the poet must come to grips with the limitations of language itself. These limitations make his task difficult, since language is both the vehicle and the barrier to experiencing reality. But, according to Valente, the poet must continue in his task, in spite of the inherent ambiguities, inconsistencies, and imperfect approximations that language entails. It is within the context of these difficulties that the reader's role becomes paramount. Both poet and reader must approach the language of poetry as a starting point: poet, word, idea, and reader all participate in the ongoing process of the creative act.

In spite of Valente's preoccupation with the creative task, his poetry is deeply rooted in the circumstantial existence of man. José Olivio Jiménez states that the group of writers to which Valente belongs has produced "poetry written face to face with man, history and life." In all of Valente's poetry, one notes his commitment to

Drawing of Valente by Zamorano (from Insula, *March 1972)*

his personal and historical circumstances. This focus on his environment, including its social and political aspects, also permits him to speculate on the final destiny of humanity. Valente combines his musings on a universal plane with observations on daily life—on the lack of communication, on politics, or on family relationships, for example.

A modo de esperanza (In the Manner of Hope, 1955) was Valente's first book of verse and won the coveted Adonáis literary prize. In this collection Valente confronts directly the problems of death and human loss. For the most part the poems are devoid of rhetorical artifice and tend to communicate their meaning on an intellectual rather than emotive level. In spite of the fact that he ponders subjectively his existential, social, and metaphysical condition, a certain realistic tone can also be noted. Valente presents for the reader particular scenes and episodes from every-

day existence, so he never completely becomes abstract.

Valente received the Crítica prize in 1960 for his second book of poetry, *Poemas a Lázaro* (Poems to Lazarus), published that year. The themes of death and loss are important, but in this collection he enriches his language and depth of expression. His symbols take on a murky and purely personal significance, but they contribute to emphasizing the fundamental theme of the collection: the anguish of human existence. Fear, nothingness, death, love, social responsibility, patriotic loyalty—all are treated from a philosophical perspective that tends toward nihilism and existentialism.

As Andrew P. Debicki noted in 1982, "One evident characteristic of [Valente's next book of poetry,] *La memoria y los signos* [Memory and Signs, 1966], written between 1960 and 1965, is the poet's concern with the historical and social

Valente circa 1990 (photograph by María Moreno)

context in which he grew up and lives. One whole section of the book focuses on reminiscences of the Spanish Civil War and its effects on a number of people; individual poems of various sections deal with human relations in the light of social circumstances, with patterns of life and death in one's family, with specific episodes of biography." In the final section of the book, Valente offers a possible interpretation of the worth of poetic creation: it can be used as an antidote to the false values of a hypocritical and bankrupt society. Valente also views the creative process as a search for self. Poems and poets decipher, define, reflect, and incarnate one another.

In his first three collections Valente deals directly with objective reality, and in his later books of verse he confronts more of its complexities, subtleties, and distorted images. He utilizes more allusions and intertextual links to inform his verse, and thus he provides for the reader a richer fabric with which to construct shadings of meaning. In *Siete representaciones* (Seven Representations, 1967), for example, Valente makes use of the whole of Judeo-Christian heritage in his meditation on the seven deadly sins. His scathingly ironic tone will likely remind the reader of similar invectives in Francisco de Quevedo's poetry.

The collection entitled *Breve son* (Brief Sound, 1968) was composed from 1953 to 1968 and includes compositions of two different types. The first style includes very short poems with lyrical, rhythmic cadences reminiscent of the popular, traditional poetry of the Middle Ages and the Renaissance. Valente includes Galician themes and ambiences as well as poems of love. The second type reflects a more bitter tone: the poems are ironic, at times sarcastic, and often demonstrate his mordant sense of humor. But Valente never loses sight of his basic preoccupation with the relationship of poetry to reality. Once again, the creative act is viewed as a method of coming to know an untrustworthy reality.

Both published in 1970, *Presentación y memorial para un monumento* (Presentation and Memorial for a Monument) and *El inocente* (The Innocent One) offer critical and accusing views of contemporary society. But Valente takes consummate care in couching his vituperation in resonant verses. In the first collection he often focuses on irreconcilable extremes, such as duty versus pleasure or Nazism versus Judaism, only to reject summarily all forms of dogmatism. The second collection brings into clearer focus the agony of the individual. Valente speaks from a perspective of doom, desperation, and vacuity.

Valente's *Interior con figuras* (Interior with Figures, 1976) and *Material memoria* (1979) are murky meditations on reality, life, and the creative act. For their meaning many of the poems depend on intertextual links with other literary works (including previous texts of Valente), well-known personages, historical events, and cultural circumstances. He retains the ironic and often biting tone of his previous works. Both collections also include various prose selections. In spite of the overall pessimistic tone, Valente concludes on an upbeat note; he is able to overcome the darkness of despair through the literary process. His salvation and that of the world around him is to be won through the creation of the word.

The two central factors that serve to identify and describe Valente's whole poetic productions are the theory/method of the poem as process and the utilization of intertextual resonances that enrich the reader's experience. Although Valente could be classified as an intellectual poet, he never loses sight of everyday reality. He creates concrete experiences and episodes, from which readers must form their own conclusions. Valente favors simple, uncluttered verse, devoid for the most part of rhetorical devices. But because of the philosophical basis from which he begins, the simplest of terms, descriptions, and evocations of common experience often take on symbolic or allegorical overtones. Thus his poetry is more conceptual than emotive, more suggestive than descriptive. He is a product of his age: his art reveals the society that produced it. He is not a political ideologue; rather, he wishes to know reality through his art and make it comprehensible to others in the same terms.

Interview:

Ana Basualdo, "Valente, poeta," *El País*, 240 (20 May 1990): 1-3.

References:

Andrew P. Debicki, *Poetry of Discovery* (Lexington: University Press of Kentucky, 1982), p. 115;

José Olivio Jiménez, "Poética y poesía de la joven generación española," *Hispania*, 49 (May 1966): 196.

José María Valverde
(26 January 1926 -   )

Michael L. Perna
Hunter College, City University of New York

BOOKS: *Hombre de Dios: Salmos, elegías y oraciones* (Madrid: Instituto Nacional de Enseñanza Ramiro de Maeztu, 1945);

La espera (Madrid: Cultura Hispánica, 1949);

Estudios sobre la palabra poética (Madrid: Rialp, 1952);

Versos del domingo (Madrid: Barná, 1954);

Guillermo de Humboldt y la filosofía del lenguaje (Madrid: Gredos, 1955);

Storia della letteratura spagnola (Turin: Radio Italiana, 1955);

Il Don Chisciotte di Cervantes (Turin: Radio Italiana, 1955);

Cartas a un cura escéptico en materia de arte moderna (Barcelona: Seix Barral, 1959);

Historia de la literatura universal, 3 volumes, by Valverde and Martín de Ricquer (Barcelona: Noguer, 1957-1959); volume 4, *La literatura de Hispanoamérica* (Barcelona: Planeta, 1977);

Poesías reunidas, hasta 1960 (Madrid: Giner, 1961);

Breve historia de la literatura española (Madrid: Guadarrama, 1969);

El profesor de español (Valparaíso, Chile: Ediciones Universitarias, 1971);

Enseñanzas de la edad (Barcelona: Barral, 1971);

Azorín (Barcelona: Planeta, 1972);

Antonio Machado (Madrid & Mexico City: Siglo XXI, 1975);

Ser de palabra y otros poemas (Barcelona: Ocnos, Barral, 1976);

Joyce (Barcelona: Dopesa, 1978);

Antología de sus versos (Madrid: Cátedra, 1978).

OTHER: *Antología de la poesía española e hispanoamericana*, 2 volumes, edited by Valverde (Mexico City: Renacimiento, 1962);

Antología de la literatura española e hispanoamericana, edited by Valverde and Martín de Ricquer (Barcelona: Vicens-Vives, 1967);

Antonio Machado, *Nuevas canciones, De un cancionero apócrifo*, edited by Valverde (Madrid: Castalia, 1971);

Antonio Machado, *Juan de Mairena (1936)*, edited by Valverde (Madrid: Castalia, 1972);

Azorín, *Artículos olvidados de J. Martínez Ruiz*, edited by Valverde (Madrid: Narcea, 1972);

Azorín, *Los pueblos, La Andalucía trágica y otros artículos (1904-1905)*, edited by Valverde (Madrid: Castalia, 1973);

"The Generation of 1936, Almost from Within," in *Spanish Writers of 1936: Crisis and Commitment in the Poetry of the Thirties and Forties*, edited by Jaime Ferrán & Daniel P. Testa (London: Tamesis, 1973), pp. 45-48;

Luis Felipe Vivanco, *Antología poética*, edited by Valverde (Madrid: Alianza, 1976);

Miguel de Unamuno, *Antología poética*, edited by Valverde (Madrid: Alianza, 1976);

Ernesto Cardenal, *Antología*, edited by Valverde (Barcelona: Laia, 1978).

TRANSLATIONS: Friedrich Holderlin, *Doce poemas* (Madrid: Adonáis, 1950);

Thomas Merton, *Veinte poemas* (Madrid: Adonais, 1954);

Rainer Maria Rilke, *Cincuenta poesías* (Madrid: Agora, 1957);

Las buenas noticias del reino de Dios [the Gospels], translated by Valverde and Father José R. Díaz (Madrid: Guadarrama, 1960);

Charles Dickens, *Pickwick y otras obras* (Barcelona: Planeta, 1963);

Johann Wolfgang von Goethe, *Fausto y otras obras* (Barcelona: Planeta, 1963);

Rilke, *Obras* (Barcelona: Plaza & Janés, 1967);

William Shakespeare, *Teatro completo*, 2 volumes (Barcelona: Planeta, 1967, 1968);

Herman Melville, *Moby Dick y otras obras* (Barcelona: Planeta, 1968);

El Nuevo Testamento (Madrid: Cristiandad, 1967);

Los Cuatros Evangelios (Madrid: Guadarrama, 1968);

Bertholdt Brecht, "Todos los años en septiembre; Cambio de las cosas; La infamia; Contento de comer carne; No necestio lápida," *Insula*, 300-301 (November-December, 1971): 3;

James Joyce, *Ulises* (Barcelona: Lumen, 1976);

José María Valverde, circa 1960

Christian Morgenstern, *Canciones de la horca* (Madrid: Visor, 1976);

T. S. Eliot, *Poesías* (Madrid: Alianza, 1978).

SELECTED PERIODICAL PUBLICATIONS—
UNCOLLECTED: "Numancia: Tragedia en un prólogo y tres actos," *Teatro: Revista Internacional de la Escena,* 8 (June-August 1953): 63-77;

"Rafael Alberti and Luis Felipe Vivanco," *Malahat Review,* 47 (1978): 62-64.

As a Catholic poet José María Valverde is broadly representative of the literary situation in post-civil-war Spain. His poetry of the 1940s and 1950s appeals, in conversational language, to the general reader's concern with daily life, religion, and family. Later, in the course of a busy career as a teacher, translator, and literary historian, he introduces moderate social criticism and an interest in the nature of language and consciousness into his verse, which is for him simply the form

in which he writes his personal thoughts, opinions, and memories. He develops a fine sense of irony concerning the uses to which God is put in the social and political life of Spain.

Valverde was born on 26 January 1926 in Valencia de Alcántara, a few miles from the Portuguese border in the southwest of Spain, and spent his childhood in Madrid. His first discovery of poetry was in his father's library, where he read Rubén Darío, Juan Ramón Jiménez, and Antonio Machado, as well as Charles Baudelaire and Paul Verlaine. Valverde began to write at age thirteen and at seventeen his work appeared in the "Antología-Manifiesto" of the "Juventud Creadora" group in the weekly *Español* (17 April 1943). That same year, while a student at the University of Madrid, he mailed a collection of his work to Jose García Nieto, the editor of *Garcilaso,* who began publishing Valverde's poems that would later appear in *Hombre de Dios* (Man of God, 1945). For this first book, Dámaso Alonso wrote a preface hailing Valverde as a sincere new poet in search of God. Many of these poems present his Christian childhood as a happy state without fears or doubts, and they invoke his past faith as they include meditations on his own death, the meaning of existence, and the value of unattractive and unhappy people around him. An insistent repetition of themes in this first book leads to a form that Valverde develops as his own: several poems become part of a larger poem that carries on a dialogue based on an idea. The poems of the section "Elegía y oración del arroyo" (Elegy and Prayer of the Stream), for instance, become the changing voice of a stream as it moves through the stages of its journey. This conversational structure of Valverde's poems separates them sharply from the intense lyricism of Federico García Lorca and Rafael Alberti, work Valverde admired but found very different from his own voice. His personal search for God in the midst of youthful doubts and elegiac meditations sets a theme that will persist in his later work even as it broadens to include humankind's relation to God generally.

In 1948 Valverde received his licenciate from the University of Madrid and, while continuing to do graduate work there, completed *La espera* (The Waiting, 1949). Life is waiting for the complex revelation of truth that may come only at death, a theme influenced by the later poems of T. S. Eliot. The book is dedicated to Leopoldo Panero, who, like Luis Felipe Vivanco and Luis Rosales, was his poetic mentor and friend. Sharing with them basic Catholic beliefs as a background for his feelings, Valverde includes a spiritual dimension in the love poems and reflections on human loneliness in *La espera*. On the threshold of life, at the end of adolescence, he realized that the depths of human feelings cannot be expressed by the verbal games of poetry, but ultimately must lead to silence. Hopes and fears for the future alternate with memories in these verses; concrete experience in the present is always presented in a philosophic or religious perspective rather than with lyric immediacy. *La espera* won the José Antonio Primo de Rivera National Prize for Literature in 1949.

From then until 1955 Valverde taught at the Spanish Institute of the University of Rome, lecturing for Radio Italiana on Spanish literature and finishing his doctorate for the University of Madrid in 1952 with a book on Wilhelm von Humboldt's philosophy of language, an interest that would appear in his own poetry some years later. By 1953 Valverde had completed a novel,

"San Fernández" (unpublished), and a short prose play, "Numancia" (unproduced but published that year in the journal *Teatro*). The mystical strength of the earth is the theme of the play, which presents the Roman siege of Numancia (133 B.C.) in a realistic modern setting as it affects a family of peasants living near the city. Though each generation's world dies with the members of that generation, the traditional values of Spain—heroism, rebellion, endurance, and the power of motherhood—are presented as continuing through the centuries.

By contrast, Valverde's next book of poetry, *Versos del domingo* (Sunday Verses, 1954), focuses on the immediate joys of his life in Italy. The book asserts his sense that poetry is a simple activity rather than a great mystery and is something that can be finished on Sundays without conflicting with the week's working routine. In 1952 Valverde had married Pilar Hedy Gefaell, their first two children being born in Rome, and the love poems "Air Mail" and "Más allá del umbral" (Beyond the Threshold) reveal his new, secure acceptance of reality and emotion. Also in those years he met the poet Dionisio Ridruejo—then a disillusioned fascist living in Rome after a term of banishment in a small Catalan village—who was the first to applaud a new photographic language in Valverde's work. The scenery around Rome, for instance, in "Montes de azul" (Mountains of Blue) stimulates a dialogue between the life of nature from its beginning and the stages of awareness of a baby from the moment of its birth; the visual impressions of both voices carry philosophic and social connotations. Valverde is here beginning to escape from his interior ghosts and to develop a new sense of himself. The thirst for eternity, dominant in his earlier books, no longer prevents his enjoyment of the ordinary pleasures so dear to the Italians among whom he lives. Valverde's usual verse forms continue to be free-rhyming *endecasílabos* (eleven syllable lines) and assonant shorter lines (*arte menor*), but with this book he begins to publish a few sonnets, still as independent poems but soon to be integrated into the larger units of his work.

The modest experiments of *Versos del domingo* and Valverde's new attention to daily life are not only the results of his encounter with Italy and his family happiness. They are also the first creative fruits of his theoretical work, including *Estudios sobre la palabra poética* (Studies on the Poetic Word, 1952). In contrast to the classic poetry of the Spanish ascetics who approached God

Drawing of Valverde by Arovedano (from Rafael Millán, Veinte poetas españoles, *1955)*

by eliminating the things of this world, the modern religious poet tends to share the twentieth century's increasing concentration on the natural and man-made objects around him. According to Valverde, when any poet writes about a phenomenon outside himself, he escapes his own existence, but at the same time the new poem he has created redefines him, giving him a better self. Thus behind the poem lies the drama of the poet's destiny, a drama revealed in his attitude to the words he writes. From his existential view of poetry Valverde concludes that his search for salvation must lead through the things of this world, as he submits to the ordinariness of life by the humility of using a clear, simple style in his verse. Just as the great mysteries are inherent in daily routine, his deepest poetic insights require

a sincere, if prosaic, language.

In 1955 Valverde returned to Spain to teach aesthetics at the University of Barcelona. Years of constant scholarly and editorial work on Spanish and European literature and art followed. Renewed close contact with his friends led to many poetry projects: in 1957 he, Rosales, Panero, and the philosopher Jose L. Luis Aranguren read Rainer Rilke together. Soon Valverde began to work on a book-length poem, "Voces y acompañamientos para San Mateo" (Voices and Accompaniments for St. Matthew; collected in *Poesías reunidas*, 1961). The immediate stimulus for the work and one of the two voices in the dialogue of its sections is a series of readings from the Gospel, presented as daily scenes in the life of Jesus. Prosaic objects and routine events are introduced with photographic realism, then are transformed by questions, parables, and miracles that the seemingly ordinary Jesus injects into normal existence. The language of these sections shows some influence of César Vallejo. In counterpoint to the miracles, a series of poems based on Valverde's family life reinterprets his childhood and his hopes for the future in the face of his new feelings for his own children, another source of the book's popular appeal to the Spanish lay reader of religious verse. This emphasis on a broad readership owes much to the work Valverde was doing at the time with Father José R. Díaz, translating all four Gospels into everyday Spanish as *Las buenas noticias del reino de Dios* (The Good News of the Kingdom of God, 1960).

Also published with "Voces y acompañamientos" in *Poesías reunidas* is another long poem in sections, "La conquista de este mundo" (The Conquest of This World). It is a series of ironic odes on civilization—from cave paintings through consumerism—alternating with sonnets on the shortness and fragility of personal lives. The changes in tone, from a survey-course prose style to intimate anecdotes and from admiration to irony, make "La conquista de este mundo" an interesting experiment that does not quite hold together its panoramic and intimate aspects, though the individual poems are finely organized meditations. Ten years later Valverde was to suppress four of the twenty sections of the poem to improve its coherence and heighten the effect by giving it a faster rhythm (in *Enseñanzas de la edad* [Teachings of the Age, 1971]). A similar editing was to retain and rearrange fifteen of the original twenty-five sections of "Voces y acompañamientos" into its definitive version, also in *Enseñanzas*.

For the 1960s, however, *Poesías reunidas*, which won the Premio de la Crítica in 1962, presented a complete if disputed image of Valverde as a poet. He seems to have had two sets of readers, each noticing one aspect of his work while ignoring or subordinating others. Inside Spain many felt that Valverde was a safe Catholic writer who agreed with their social ideas because he shared their religious interests. A conservative literary historian, J. M. Castro Calvo, claimed that, in contrast to the work of more skeptical and bitter poets influenced by Alonso's *Hijos de la ira* (Children of Wrath, 1944), such as Gabriel Celaya and Blas de Otero, Valverde's more compassionate, Christian resolution of his doubts made his poetry some of the best of its kind. On the other hand, the exiled critic Max Aub, while also linking Valverde closely to Alonso, characterized him as a believer with open eyes, praised his simplicity as being close to the people, and stressed his attitude to God as one of questioning as part of a search for truth and for an end to human pain and loneliness. In both cases critics and readers paid more attention to the content of Valverde's work for their own ideological purposes than to his experiments with structure and overall meaning.

Some of the differences in critical opinion and Valverde's own drastic but careful revision of his work correspond to a major change in his life. The university students of Spain, angry at having to belong to the Francisco Franco regime's official student union, held a long sit-in at Madrid in February 1965. Several professors joined them on the fourth day of the demonstration, which brought on a police attack as they marched to deliver a petition to the university chancellor. Among the faculty dismissed permanently from their jobs was Valverde's friend Aranguren. Resigning his post in solidarity with his colleagues, Valverde continued to meet his students and fellow poets at cafés in Barcelona in near cloak-and-dagger conditions, since meetings of more than thirteen were forbidden. This atmosphere of a "free university" with an uncontrolled curriculum led to debates on new aesthetic, linguistic, and political theories. By 1967 Valverde had to leave Spain to find a teaching position. After a semester at the University of Virginia he went to the University of Trent, Ontario, in 1968 as a professor in, and then chairman of, the Spanish department. The tumult and uprooting of these years and the intellectual freedom he found in Canada were the conditions as well as the subjects of his next poems.

In 1971 he published *Enseñanzas de la edad*, including the revised versions of "Versos y acompañamientos" and "La conquista de este mundo," as well as those parts of his earlier books he still approved. The change in his thinking is clearly expressed by his comments on his earlier, conversational elegies in "Sobre mi imposibilidad de escribir una elegía madrileña" (On My Inability to Write a Madrid Elegy). He realizes that his childhood was lived in the midst of an unhappy and non-Christian Madrid, which was divided into the winners and losers of the civil war; it was a city where hatred and fear caused general hypocrisy. His new work in *Enseñanzas* is grouped under the title "Años inciertos" (Uncertain Years), divided by themes into three sections. First, in "Preámbulos de la fe" (Preambles of Faith), he no longer sees God as the perfect, dogmatic being of the church and society but from a perspective tempered with irony and love for the downtrodden who reject formal faith. "Estampas de costumbres" (Society Prints) contains a series of sketches of the pretensions and realities of America and of political and artistic protestors. Finally, *El profesor de español* (The Spanish Professor, which was separately published, also in 1971) reflects on the myths of the profession through a survey written in the different period styles of Spanish literature. Valverde sees the glorifying of the Spanish language as an excuse for the crusading intolerance of the past or for the ignoring of the plight of the poor majority of the present Spanish-speaking world with its angry hopes for a more just future.

The internal structure of Valverde's multi-sectioned poems is more complicated in *Enseñanzas*: voices clash within sections rather than between sections. But the basic elements of a text and his commentary are the same: the classics of Spanish literature now provide the kind of starting point that the Gospels did earlier. And far from making a literary game of his reading, Valverde's Spanish professor is just as anxious as his Gospel reader was to apply the lessons of the text to the lives even of those who do not read its message. In this context the new work in *Enseñanzas* reflects a decade when North American and European academics tried to make their specialized work relevant to general social problems.

This combination of linguistic and social concerns also marks Valverde's next book, *Ser de palabra y otros poemas* (Word Being and Other Poems, 1976), in which he renounces personal subjects to discuss such themes as his change in attitude to Cuba or the Christian idea of the millennium vis-á-vis the global disaster threatening modern industrial civilization. In the title poem the reality of language, "wordbeing," opposes the physical, objective reality of nature—an opposition based on Humboldt's views that the structure of each language reveals an inner spiritual form or world, and that language itself links the spiritual and physical worlds. The poem is thus part of a century-old tradition of congenial acceptance of German philosophical idealism in Spain, which poets then adapt to their own creative uses,

much as Antonio Machado adapted Gottfried Wilhelm von Leibnitz. Indeed, Valverde's study *Antonio Machado* (1975) was published some twenty-three months earlier than *Ser de palabra* and a comparison of the two is illuminating. In the sections of the long title poem Valverde speculates on the glory and danger of language, both as the struggle of the human spirit to rise from primitive sounds to thought and as the source of dangerous illusions that can destroy mankind. Valverde's poetry also includes language as the cause of creativity and suffering: "El robo del lenguaje" (The Theft of Language)—an exposé of financial jargon used to intimidate the poor—quotes and refutes an earlier poem from "La conquista de este mundo" on finance as a human invention that improves life. The final section of the book, "Maneras de hablar" (Ways of Speaking), tries to recapture the voices of recently deceased friends and family as well as those of authors such as Jean-Jacques Rousseau and Miguel de Cervantes. Each poem contains some variation of the tension between the personal and the metaphysical, between reality and the imagination. As a poet in exile, Valverde merged his personal sense of loss into a search for general truths that included a new historical dimension.

In 1977, after the death of Franco and the reappointment of the professors fired twelve years earlier, Valverde was invited to return to the University of Barcelona. Also, the publisher Cátedra asked him to prepare a selection of his poems for a volume presenting four poets of the 1940s. That collection did not appear, but he edited his own *Antología de sus versos* (1978) and wrote a preface in which he evaluates his previous work. As a literary historian he is ironically aware that belonging to a certain generation or even returning to Catalonia in a time of renewed Catalan ideology may be used as shortcuts to interpret his poetry. In fact his academic, religious, and social concerns combine in ways that differentiate him from such movements. A workmanlike borrowing of and experimenting with diverse elements and forms is the most constant mark of his writing, which makes predicting the course of his future poetry a difficult task. Between the formal restraint and religious thought of the Generation of 1936 and the irony and prosaic language of the Generation of 1950, Valverde is developing a life's work along individual lines, just as he continues to build up the meaning of book-length poems from the relations between their parts.

References:

Vicente Aleixandre, "El equilibrio de José María Valverde," in his *Los encuentros: Semblanzas personales alusivas a poetas españoles* (Madrid: Guadarrama, 1958), pp. 289-295;

Dámaso Alonso, "En busca de Dios," in his *Poetas españoles contemporáneos* (Madrid: Gredos, 1952), pp. 373-380;

José L. Luis Aranguren, "Filosofía y crítica de poesía," in his *Crítica y meditación* (Madrid: Taurus, 1957), pp. 65-75;

Max Aub, *Poesía española contemporánea* (Mexico City: Era, 1969), pp. 202-204, 231;

José L. Cano, "Notas sobre José María Valverde," in his *Poesía española contemporánea: Generaciones de posguerra* (Madrid: Guadarrama 1974), pp. 165-173;

J. M. Castro Calvo, *Historia de la literatura española*, 2 volumes (Barcelona: Cresda, 1965) II: 316;

Victor G. de la Concha, "La poesía arraigada de José María Valverde," in his *La poesía española de posguerra: teoría e historia de sus movimientos* (Madrid: Editorial Prensa Española, 1973), pp. 458-464;

Giuseppe De Gennaro, "L'esperienza poetica di José María Valverde," *Letture*, 20 (June 1965): 427-446;

Pedro Lain Entralgo, "El espíritu de la poesía española contemporánea," *Cuadernos Hispanoamericanos*, 5-6 (September-December 1948): 51-86;

Francisco Lucio, "José María Valverde: Una palabra poética actual," *Ínsula*, 306 (May, 1972): 15;

María Isabel Paraíso de Leal, "José María Valverde: Trayectoria de una vocación asumida," *Cuadernos Hispanoamericanos*, 185 (May 1965): 383-402;

Mary Paraíso de Leal, "Valverde y su dilema: ¿Épica o Lírica?" *Papeles de Son Armadans*, 66 (May 1972): 231-239;

Luis Felipe Vivanco, *Introducción a la poesía española contemporánea*, 2 volumes (Madrid: Guadarrama, 1974) I: 81-83, 289.

Luis Felipe Vivanco

(22 August 1907 - 21 November 1975)

Clark Colahan
Whitman College

BOOKS: *Cantos de primavera* (Madrid: Héroe, 1936);

Tiempo de dolor (Madrid: Aguirre, 1940);

Continuación de la vida (Madrid: Gallades, 1949);

Alberto Sartoris (Santander, Spain: Escuela de Altamira, 1951);

Primera bienal hispanoamericana de arte (Madrid: Aguado, 1952);

El Escorial (Barcelona: Noguer, 1953); translated by John Forrester as *The Escorial* (Barcelona: Noguer, 1956);

Angel Ferrante: Estudio (Madrid: Gallades, 1954);

El descampado (Madrid: Papeles de Son Armadáns, 1957);

Introducción a la poesía española contemporánea (Madrid: Guadarrama, 1957; enlarged, 2 volumes, 1974);

Memoria de la plata (Madrid: Rialp, 1958);

Lecciones para el hijo (Madrid: Aguilar, 1961);

Los ojos de Toledo: Leyenda autobiográfica (Barcelona: Barna, 1963);

Moratín y la ilustración mágica (Madrid: Taurus, 1972);

Los caminos (1945-1965) (Madrid: Cultura Hispánica, 1974);

Prosas propicias (Esplugas de Llobregat, Spain: Plaza & Janés, 1976);

Antología poética, edited by José María Valverde (Madrid: Alianza, 1976);

Azorín (Madrid: Fundación, 1979);

Diario, 1945-1975 (Madrid: Taurus, 1983).

RECORDING: *Me llamo Luis Felipe Vivanco*, La Palabra MLL 005, 1964.

OTHER: *Poesía heroica del imperio*, edited by Vivanco and Luis Rosales (Madrid: Jerargvía, 1940);

Antología poética: Miguel de Unamuno, edited by Vivanco (Madrid: Escorial, 1942);

"Raíces temporales de la imaginación," in *Homenaje a Xavier Zubiri* (Madrid: Moneda & Crédito, 1969), pp. 731-742.

SELECTED PERIODICAL PUBLICATIONS—
UNCOLLECTED: "La desesperación en el lenguaje," *Cruz y Raya*, 8 (April 1933): 149-158;

"Amor suficiente," *Cruz y Raya*, 12 (February 1934): 129-134;

"Música celestial de Gustavo Adolfo Bécquer," *Cruz y Raya*, 19 (October 1934): 5-58;

"El arte humano," *Escorial*, 1 (October 1940): 141-150;

"Aproximándome a la poesía temporal y realista," *Proel*, second series 6 (Spring-Summer 1950): 15-27;

"La humildad de ser poeta," *Correo literario*, 1-11 (June-November 1950);

"Poesía lírica y mundo técnico," *Cuadernos Hispanoamericanos*, 186 (June 1965): 464-479.

An important lyric and philosophic poet of the Generation of 1936, Luis Felipe Vivanco saw his life and work severely disrupted by the Spanish Civil War and by the fact that he worked with the Falangist party and then broke with it and retired from public life in 1945. Although, as an architect, he always supported himself and his family, because of his consuming interest in literature, literary theory, and aesthetics, as well as his personal integrity, he came to a be a good friend of most of the major poets of the time and analyzed their work and its history in his *Introducción a la poesía española contemporánea* (1957), which was awarded the Premio de Fastenrath by the Spanish Real Academía. He also did several translations, notably of the poetry of Rainer Rilke and Paul Claudel. An advocate of avant-garde directions in art and literature, Vivanco served as chairman of the board of the National Museum of Contemporary Art and participated in the projects of the progressive Escuela de Altamira group of artists and thinkers.

With the exception of the work of his last years, the concerns and emotions expressed in Vivanco's poetry are personal rather than social, a tendency derived primarily from his imagina-

Luis Felipe Vivanco, circa 1960

tive and philosophic temperament, but it was also reinforced by the oppressive intellectual situation in Spain during much of his adult life. In his *Introducción a la poesía española contemporánea* he divides the postwar poets into "those who believe that in order to be true to others you must begin by being true to yourself, and those who believe that you must begin by being true to a cause." As this polarized formulation suggests, the repressive political circumstances created in Vivanco a certain need for justification, one growing out of self-doubts about the validity of a poetry that could be interpreted as tacit acceptance or surrender to the forces in control of the nation. Unquestionably, his association with Francisco Franco's government colored for many years afterward the public's attitudes toward his work, as well as his own view of it. In a melancholy retrospective in *Los caminos* (The Roads, 1974) he described the time after the civil war as "a clumsy and failed attempt at adaptation (mea culpa!) to the his-

toric circumstances," after which he only managed to "take negative refuge in an intimate, existential attitude and a lyric expression incapable of approaching the reality of this world."

However, when not viewed against the disturbing background of the political scene, the validity of his themes becomes a false issue, since they formed an integral part of a steadfastly pursued way of life that included literary theory, poetry, and personal conduct. His writings are one expression of a larger creative effort that centered on a search for essence and authenticity. Strongly influenced in his youth by San Juan de la Cruz (for whom he named his only son) and St. Teresa, he described as "pseudo-mysticism" his looking beneath the surface of the world for a deeper philosophic and religious meaning. Much of his poetry re-creates the emotions of exaltation or frustration experienced in his attempts to approach God through manifestations in beauty, nature, and human love.

Drawing of Vivanco by Zamorano (from Insula, *December 1975)*

While in the mystic tradition all of life must be a preparation for the higher vision, Vivanco emphasized that insight itself takes place through *ensoñación*, a dreamlike, meditative frame of mind. Although an altered state of consciousness has always been associated with poetic inspiration, in Vivanco's thinking there is a strong influence of the Generation of 1927, which at the time he entered the Spanish literary scene was establishing the surrealist doctrine of the primacy of the unconscious mind. When combined with Vivanco's view that God is the final reality to be revealed through poetry, the result was what has been called surrealism *a lo divino*, a typically Spanish philosophical and mystical quest reminiscent of those of Miguel de Unamuno and Antonio Machado, but adapted to somewhat later theories of poetry and psychology. The 1920s vanguard influence was also decisive in Vivanco's style, because, although his writing had both periods of turbulent profusion of detail and ascetic simplicity, it is overwhelmingly the images alone—by and large without the support or hindrance of characters, plot, or systematically developed concepts—that carry his poems. In a natural way his striving for metaphysical essence is reflected by a concentration on images that seek to summarize and bring together thoughts and feelings. His lifelong involvement with art was also doubtless a contributing factor to his emphasis on the pictorial in his poetry.

The eldest of five children, Vivanco was born on 22 August 1907 in El Escorial and, while growing up, lived primarily there and in Madrid. His father was a judge, and his mother, Rosario Bergamín, an exceptionally well-read woman from an upper-middle-class professional family, was always emotionally close to him and proved instrumental in helping him begin his dual career as poet and architect. As his mother held strong religious beliefs, he had a thorough Catholic up-bringing that included attending Marianist schools. When Vivanco was fourteen, his father was transferred temporarily to Toledo, Spain, and took his family there with him.

In maturity Vivanco re-created and re-shaped that time between childhood and adolescence in *Los ojos de Toledo* (The Eyes of Toledo, 1963), a collection of memories selected from the perspective of a later self-awareness. He portrays himself as having been shy and dreamy, still tied to his parents and unable to make real contact with others in the city: "I should have joined the casino, learned to play pool, and turned fifteen knowing how to make bank shots off of three or five sides of the table—as many sides as possible—and become used to using public urinals and tipping waiters. Instead of that, I used to hike with my father through the hills that face the city, inventing the men and women shut up in their houses and making up a sort of private world of my own, the only one to which I wished to belong."

Vivanco often projected this image of himself as a dreamer unable to cope with life's practicalities. In a list of his wife's good qualities in *Los ojos*, for example, he includes her patience with his inability to make enough money.

After a few years in Toledo, the young Vivanco returned to Madrid with his family and entered the preparatory program in architecture at the University of Madrid, through which he later became a close friend of the painter Rafael Zabaleta. Vivanco's interest in art also led him to frequent the Museum of Reproductions and the Prado, where he did drawings of Greek statues. He continued in the regular university architecture course, receiving the Ph.D. in 1932; he then began working for his uncle, Rafael Bergamín, with whose architectural firm he was associated for several years. Friendship with the philosopher Xavier Zubiri strengthened Vivanco's inclination toward philosophy, and he enrolled in the college of philosophy and letters at the University of Madrid. However, the war intervened before he received a degree, and afterward, feeling that the quality of the faculty was no longer on the same level, he chose not to continue.

During these student years he was active in campus politics, with a leftist stance in conflict with his family's conservative position, and in 1931, the year the Republic was established, he became president of the Professional Association of Architecture Students, part of the national organi-zation of university students. He wrote later that he was a Republican until 1936, when he underwent a serious emotional crisis that, together with a disenchantment with the Republic, led him to be reconciled with his family and feel that a more authoritarian government was necessary to restore order. Nevertheless, although a convinced Catholic throughout his life, he never sided with the reactionary branch of the church in Spain, and he felt vindicated by the changes in social policy instituted at Vatican II.

While at the university Vivanco wrote a considerable amount of poetry, in the earliest years in the style of Antonio Machado and most of which Vivanco later destroyed. He was introduced into literary circles by another uncle, José Bergamín, and formed strong friendships with the poets Luis Rosales and Leopoldo and Juan Panero. Vivanco's uncle Pepe, who shared with him a liberal Catholicism and interest in avant-garde literary movements, was then editing a review called *Cruz y Raya*, to which Vivanco contributed literary criticism and theory.

The most important poetry to come out of this period was his surrealist/creationist book *Memoria de la plata* (Silver Memory, 1958), which, although most of the poems were later reworked, was written when he was twenty to twenty-four. He told José María Valverde that the book began to take shape when Rafael Alberti spent part of a summer—probably in 1928—with him at the Vivanco family's home at El Escorial. Vivanco's mother did not approve of the friendship, and so would not let Alberti stay the night indoors. He was obliged to sleep in the fields, being allowed inside in the morning to shave, to eat, and to visit Vivanco. This contact with the author of *Sobre los ángeles* (Concerning the Angels, 1929) converted Vivanco to the vanguard style.

The title of *Memoria de la plata* is a quotation from San Juan de la Cruz referring to the images generated by imagination and memory. The book is dedicated to Gerardo Diego, who was writing and becoming known in a style derived from the poetry of Vicente Húidobro, and Vivanco subsequently emphasized that the book was begun at the time of the famous Luis de Góngora centenary in 1927. The primary theme of the collection is the tension Vivanco felt between a mystical ideal of perfection—in love, poetry, and morality—and the limitations he found in himself and others.

Of the eleven poems in the collection, "My Song from the Highest Tower" expresses this

Luis Rosales, Pablo Neruda, and Vivanco

idea most directly, while "Silhouette of Abantos" best demonstrates the kaleidoscopic profusion of images typical of his style at this point. In the latter poem the reader is shown a collage of scenes that include bucolic rural surroundings; the violence and decay of a modern city; God as an architect preparing designs and budgets for the construction of the poet; a phosphorescent grasshopper that represents the temptations of the flesh; and other equally unlikely visions. There is also at times a surprising humorous tone, which, in combination with a Catholic worldview, makes the collection a noteworthy addition to the legacy of the Generation of '27. The poetry Vivanco wrote in the following years, however—including *Cantos de primavera* (Spring Chants, 1936) and *Tiempo de dolor* (Time of Pain, 1940)—while continuing and emphasizing the intensity of religious idealism, changed markedly to a more subdued, almost neoclassic style influenced by Claudel. But while Vivanco subsequently reworked and pub-

lished the poems of *Memoria de la plata*, he later consistently rejected the work of this period, describing it as something he had surpassed.

In 1936 Vivanco's father felt that he and his family were threatened by "uncontrolled" political factions, so he and Luis took refuge in an embassy. During the war the entire family sided with Franco, and Vivanco worked as a writer for the Falangists in Granada, Pamplona, and Burgos. When literary life resumed in Madrid after the conflict, he frequented a group of writers that met in the Lyon Café, a *tertulia* (literary circle) that had been active earlier but was now expanded and included Ricardo Gullón, Gerardo Diego, Manuel Machado, and Luis Rosales. Vivanco also contributed poetry and literary and artistic criticism to the journal *El Escorial*, which had the government's seal of approval. Nevertheless, like the editor Dionisio Ridruejo, Vivanco was committed to conciliation and sought to avoid discrimination against those who had fought on the Republican side. In general he was careful not to judge people unnecessarily or hastily, and he always saw them as individuals.

In 1949 he accepted an invitation to join the Escuela de Altamira, a newly established association of painters, sculptors, architects, poets, and critics interested in contemporary aesthetic movements. Although the group was active only through 1951, its meetings at Santillana in September of 1949 and 1950 gave Vivanco the opportunity to present papers on architecture as well as art and literature. These make clear that, had he lived in a society more open to innovation, he would almost certainly have experimented in architecture as he did in poetry.

His participation in Altamira was typical of a period of emotional stability and new creative vitality that dated from two events in 1945: his withdrawal from political connections into what he characterized as a deliberately and intensely personal and artistic life, and his marriage to María Luisa Gefaell. The daughter of an Austrian Jew who had emigrated to Spain and converted to Catholicism, she was a highly talented musician who had studied at the Madrid Conservatory and in Munich. She later became a respected and successful writer of children's books. They had three children, and the marriage was happy. Summers were spent in the rural countryside of the northwest corner of the peninsula.

These changes in Vivanco's life were immediately reflected in the 1940s poems of Los caminos, poems that established a new tone in his writing and were the starting point for his best-known collections, Continuación de la vida (Life Continues, 1949), El descampado (City Lot, 1957), and "Lugares vividos" (Places I Have Lived, written in 1965 and published together for the first time in Los caminos). A search for God is still central in Los caminos, but the mood is more serene. There is an irrepressible tenderness toward family and nature, as exemplified in "Presentation to the Birds," which begins: "With my new little girl under my arm I go out into the springtime." A nostalgic yearning for the peace of the country is a recurring motif, notably in the title poem of El descampado (included in Los caminos). Such themes represent what Vivanco found most authentic and worth preserving in disillusioning postwar times. His poetic language partakes of the same need to reach an essential simplicity. In sharp contrast with his vanguard work, metaphor is practically eliminated, things are called by their names, and there is a direct, often reverent vision of the world as divine creation.

In this time of retreat into poetry, family, and self, which was never so complete as to exclude numerous friendships and even considerable responsibilities within the world of literature and art, there were moments of discouragement and a sense of isolation. For example, in the poem "For an Up-and-Coming Young Man" he writes: "No one hears the heartbeat of my abandonment. . . . / I am left with my doubts, my fragments, and my years." But recognition came sooner than it did to many writers and came well before Vivanco's death of a heart attack in 1975. The academy's award in 1957 for his history of contemporary Spanish poetry came the same year as Dámaso Alonso's enthusiastic praise in his prologue to El descampado, and later (in 1974) Vivanco received the Critics' Award for his best-known poetry, that in Los caminos.

Throughout his middle and old age his writing continued to evolve. He undertook several sorts of verse in a more conversational and expositional format, as well as the poetic prose of Lecciones para el hijo (Lessons for One's Son, 1961). But his most surprising book was the posthumous collection Prosas propicias (Propitious Prose, 1976). In spite of the title (that alludes ironically to Rubén Darío's Prosas profanas, 1915), the book consists mainly of stanzas that look like free verse but read like groupings of conventional metric lines. It marks a return to the volcanic creationism of his youth but with a new freedom of expression and, particularly in a section reserved for political expression, images formed from a powerful fusion of long-considered ideas and long-contained emotions.

Perhaps due to the security brought by age and having won respect for his work, and certainly because of the more tolerant political atmosphere in Spain, Vivanco expresses himself again in Prosas propicias with the vehemence more typical of his youth but on a much wider range of topics. Always intensely personal, he records his emotional/intellectual reactions, sometimes with humor and often with anger, to the events at the end of his life. His most private experiences generated poems such as "Jubilación (22 Agosto 1972)" (Retirement [22 August 1972]) and "Clínica," the latter subdivided into "Adios a la próstata" (Good-bye to the Prostate) and "Olvida los motores" (Forget the Motors). There is a section dedicated to friends, and these poems, like those that consist entirely of social and political criticism, often reveal a previously undocu-

Vivanco in the early 1970s

mented side of Vivanco. "Insomnia 73," for example, is dedicated to Alonso on the thirtieth anniversary of his *Hijos de la ira* (Children of Wrath, 1944) and begins: "Madrid est una ciudad de más de tres milliones de cadaveres (según a las últimas estadísticas). / Te quedaste corto, Dámaso, te quedaste mui corto en tu cálculla enfurecido de la putrefacción y el crecimiento unanimes" (Madrid is a city of more than three million corpses [according to the latest statistics]. / You came up short, Dámaso, you came up very short on your raging estimate of the unanimous rot and growth). In other poems Vivanco wrote in protest of, or in solidarity with the protest of, specific events and ideas, as in "Satire," directed to Valverde when he resigned his chair at the University of Barcelona after J. L. Aranguren had his taken from him in Madrid for political reasons. *Prosas propicias* was left unfinished at Vivanco's death, but a list of the titles of the poems he had intended to write and include in it, as well as the title of another projected book, "El rabo por desollar (poesía política)" (The Worst Is Yet to Come [Political Poetry]), confirms that this openly critical social expression was a new direction in which his work was moving.

It can perhaps be fairly said that his children's actions near the end of his life represented an extension of this commitment, as both Juan and Soledad suffered persecution by the government for their political activism. Soledad had to flee the country, and Franco's death probably saved Juan from execution; in a dramatic farewell, Juan was brought in handcuffs to Vivanco's bed shortly before the poet died.

While Vivanco's life and personality have commanded respect from contemporary Spanish critics, most of whom were friends of his, his work has been relatively little read and studied. There has been praise for and emphasis on his search for what is authentic in both life and literature, even though his concerns were not such as to make him a popular success. His life and personal qualities have become a prominent topic in the few studies done on him. This focus is illuminating, in that his poetry is always lyrical and closely tied to his circumstances, and he sought to live the ideas he developed in his poetics. Certainly his talent for friendship opened channels for influence in his poetry and provided insights for his literary criticism. But his work can also stand on its own for its intensity, its technical variety and quality, and its reflection of the spiritual trajectory over sixty years of a poet whose underlying attitudes evolved, by and large, like those of his countrymen.

References:
Dámaso Alonso, Prologue to Vivanco's *El descampado* (Madrid: Papeles de Son Armadáns, 1957);

Lucía Cerrutti, "La poesía de Luis Felipe Vivanco," Ph.D. dissertation, University of Madrid, 1972;

Ricardo Gullón, "Luis Felipe Vivanco, Joven," *Cuadernos Hispanoamericanos*, 311 (May 1976): 265-279;

Victorino C. Rodríguez, "Luis Felipe Vivanco: Poeta de la insistencia," Ph.D. dissertation, University of Southern California, 1974;

José María Valverde, Introduction to *Luis Felipe Vivanco: Antología poética* (Madrid: Alianza, 1976).

Books for Further Reading

Allegra, Giovanni. *Il Regno Interiore: Premesse e sembianti del modernismo in Spagna.* Milan: Jaca Books, 1982. Translated by Vicente Martín Pindado as *El reino interior: Premisas y semblanzas del modernismo en España.* Madrid: Encuentro, 1986.

Alonso, Amado. *Materia y forma en poesía.* Madrid: Gredos, 1955.

Alonso, Dámaso. *Ensayos sobre poesía española.* Buenos Aires: Revista de Occidente Argentina, 1946.

Alonso. *Poetas españoles contemporáneos*, third edition, revised. Madrid: Gredos, 1969.

Barella, Julia. *Después de la modernidad: Poesía española en sus distintas lenguas literarias.* Barcelona: Anthropos, 1987.

Baur, Carlos, ed. and trans. *Cries from a Wounded Madrid: Poetry of the Spanish Civil War*, bilingual edition. Athens, Ohio: Swallow Press, 1984.

Bousoño, Carlos. *Teoría de la expresión poética*, fifth edition, revised. Madrid: Gredos, 1970.

Brihuega, Jaime. *Manifiestos, proclamas, panfletos y textos doctrinales: Las vanguardias artísticas en España, 1910-1931.* Madrid: Cátedra, 1979.

Cañas, Dionisio. *Poesía y percepción: Francisco Brines, Claudio Rodríguez y José Angel Valente.* Madrid: Hiperión, 1984.

Cano, José Luis. *Poesía española contemporánea: Generaciones de posguerra.* Madrid: Guadarrama, 1974.

Carreño, Antonio. *La dialéctica de la identidad en la poesía contemporánea: La persona, la máscara.* Madrid: Gredos, 1982.

Ciplijauskaite, Biruté. *El poeta y la poesía, del romanticismo a la poesía social.* Madrid: Insula, 1966.

Cobb, Carl W. *Contemporary Spanish Poetry (1898-1963).* Boston: Twayne, 1976.

Concha, Victor G. de la. *La poesía española de 1935 a 1975*, 2 volumes. Madrid: Cátedra, 1982.

Concha. *La poesía española de posguerra: Teoría e historia de sus movimientos.* Madrid: Española, 1973.

Connell, Geoffrey N. *Spanish Poetry of the "Grupo Poético de 1927."* Oxford: Pergamon, 1977.

Daydí-Tolson, Santiago. *The Post-Civil War Spanish Social Poets.* Boston: Twayne, 1963.

Debicki, Andrew Peter. *Poetry of Discovery: The Spanish Generation of 1956-1971.* Lexington: University Press of Kentucky, 1982.

Díez de Revenga, Francisco Javier. *Panorama crítico de la generación del 27.* Madrid: Castalia, 1987.

Espadaña: Revista de poesía y crítica, Volume 1-48. 1944-1951. León, Spain: Espadaña, 1979.

Espada Sánchez, José. *Poetas del sur*. Madrid: Espasa-Calpe, 1989.

Ferrán, Jaime, and Daniel P. Testa, eds. *Spanish Writers of 1936: Crisis and Commitment in the Poetry of the Thirties and Forties: An Anthology of Literary Studies and Essays*. London: Tamesis, 1973.

Fuentes Florido, Francisco. *Poesías y poética del ultraísmo*. Barcelona: Mitre, 1989.

Geist, Anthony J. *La poética de la generación del 27 y las revistas literarias: De la vanguardia al compromiso (1918-1936)*. Barcelona: Labor-Guadarrama, 1980.

Gullón, Ricardo. *Direcciones del modernismo*, second edition, revised. Madrid: Gredos, 1971.

Hamer, Louis, and Sara Schyfter. *Recent Poetry of Spain: A Bilingual Anthology*. Old Chatham, N.Y.: Sachem, 1983.

Havard, Robert G. *From Romanticism to Surrealism: Seven Spanish Poets*. Cardiff, Wales: University of Wales Press, 1988.

Ilie, Paul. *The Surrealist Mode in Spanish Literature*. Ann Arbor: University of Michigan Press, 1968.

Jiménez, José Olivio. *Cinco poetas del tiempo (Aleixandre, Cernuda, Hierro, Bousoño, Brines)*, second edition, revised. Madrid: Insula, 1972.

Jiménez. *Diez años de poesía española: 1960-1970*. Madrid: Insula, 1972.

Jiménez and Dionisio Cañas. *Siete poetas españoles de hoy*. Mexico City: Oasis, 1983.

Jiménez Fajardo, Salvador, and John C. Wilcox, eds. *At Home and Beyond: New Essays on Spanish Poets of the Twenties*. Lincoln, Nebr.: Society for Spanish and Spanish-American Studies, 1983.

Ley, Charles David. *Spanish Poetry Since 1939*. Washington, D.C.: Catholic University, 1962.

Lucas, Joaquín Benito de. *Literatura de posguerra: La poesía*. Madrid: Cincel, 1981.

Manrique de Lara, José Gerardo. *Poetas sociales españoles*. Madrid: E.P.E.S.A., 1974.

Mantero, Manuel. *Poetas españoles de posguerra*. Madrid: Espasa-Calpe, 1986.

Morris, C. Brian. *A Generation of Spanish Poets, 1920-1936*. Cambridge: Cambridge University Press, 1969.

Pauliuno Ayuso, José. *La poesía en el siglo XX: Desde 1939*. Madrid: Playor, 1984.

Pérez Bajo, Javier. *La poesía en el siglo XX: Hasta 1939*. Madrid: Playor, 1984.

Persin, Margaret H. *Recent Spanish Poetry and the Role of the Reader*. Lewisburg, Pa.: Bucknell / Cranbury, N.J.: Associated University Presses, 1987.

Pont, Jaume. *El postismo: Un movimiento estético-literario de vanguardia*. Barcelona: Mall, 1987.

Pritchett, Kay. *Four Postmodern Poets of Spain: A Critical Introduction with Translations of the Poems*. Fayetteville & London: University of Arkansas Press, 1991.

Provencio, Pedro. *Poéticas españolas contemporáneas*, 2 volumes. Madrid: Hiperión, 1988.

Rubio, Fanny. *Revistas poéticas españolas, 1939-1975*. Madrid: Turner, 1976.

Rubio and José Luis Falco. *Poesía española contemporánea: Historia y antología (1939-1980)*. Madrid: Alhambra, 1981.

St. Martin, Hardie, ed. *Roots and Wings: Poetry from Spain, 1900-1970; A Bilingual Edition*. New York: Harper & Row, 1976.

Salinas, Pedro. *Literatura española: Siglo XX*, second edition, revised. Mexico City: Robredo, 1949.

Siebenmann, Gustav. *Die Moderne Lyrik in Spanien*. Stuttgart, Germany: Kohlhammer, 1965. Translated as *Los estilos poéticos en España desde 1900*. Madrid: Gredos, 1973.

Soufas, C. Christopher. *Conflict of Light and Wind: The Spanish Generation of 1927 and the Ideology of Poetic Form*. Middletown, Conn.: Wesleyan, 1989.

Vélez Julio. *La poesía española según "El País" (1978-1983)*. Madrid: Orígenes, 1984.

Videla, Gloria. *El ultraísmo: Estudios sobre movimientos poéticos de vanguardia en España*, second edition, revised. Madrid: Gredos, 1971.

Villanueva, Tino. *Tres poetas de posguerra: Celaya, González y Caballero Bonald (Estudio y entrevista)*. London: Tamesis / Wolfeboro, N.H.: Longwood, 1988.

Vivanco, Luis Felipe. *Introducción a la poesía española contemporánea*, third edition, revised and enlarged, 2 volumes. Madrid: Guadarrama, 1974.

Wright, Eleanor. *The Poetry of Protest Under Franco*. London: Tamesis / Dover, N.H.: Longwood, 1986.

Young, Howard, T. *The Victorious Expression*. Madison: University of Wisconsin Press, 1964.

Zardoya, Concha. *Poesía española del siglo XX: Estudios temáticos y estilísticos*, 4 volumes. Madrid: Gredos, 1974.

Zuleta, Emilia de. *Cinco poetas españoles (Salinas, Guillén, Lorca, Alberti, Cernuda)*, second edition, revised. Madrid: Gredos, 1981.

Contributors

Ana María Alfaro-Alexander...*Castleton State College*
Andrew A. Anderson...*University of Michigan*
E. T. Aylward...*University of South Carolina*
María del Carmen Caballero...............*S.U.N.Y. College of Technology, Farmingdale*
Charles Maurice Cherry..*Furman University*
Carl W. Cobb ....*University of Tennessee*
Clark Colahan...*Whitman College*
Santiago Daydí-Tolson ....*University of Wisconsin-Milwaukee*
Barbro Diehl...*Concordia University, Montreal*
Eric Diehl ....*College Montmorency, Montreal*
Allan Englekirk ....*University of South Carolina*
Ignacio Javier López ....*University of Pennsylvania*
Luis Lorenzo-Rivero...*University of Utah*
Shirley Mangini ....*California State University, Long Beach*
Pilar Martin...*St. John's University*
Patricia E. Mason...*University of South Carolina*
Martha LaFollette Miller ....*University of North Carolina at Charlotte*
Julian Palley..*University of California, Irvine*
Janet Pérez...*Texas Tech University*
Michael L. Perna ....*Hunter College, City University of New York*
Margaret H. Persin...*Rutgers University*
Paula W. Shirley ....*Columbia College, Columbia, South Carolina*
C. Christopher Soufas, Jr.......................................*Louisiana State University*
Teresa Scott Soufas ....*Tulane University*
Noël Valis...*University of Michigan*
Jerry Phillips Winfield ....*Mercer University*

Cumulative Index

Dictionary of Literary Biography, Volumes 1-108
Dictionary of Literary Biography Yearbook, 1980-1990
Dictionary of Literary Biography Documentary Series, Volumes 1-8

Cumulative Index

DLB before number: *Dictionary of Literary Biography*, Volumes 1-108
Y before number: *Dictionary of Literary Biography Yearbook*, 1980-1990
DS before number: *Dictionary of Literary Biography Documentary Series*, Volumes 1-8

A

C

G

I

J

M

N

Q

R

S

U

V

W

Y

Z

(Continued from front endsheets)

80: *Restoration and Eighteenth-Century Dramatists,* First Series, edited by Paula R. Backscheider (1989)

81: *Austrian Fiction Writers, 1875-1913,* edited by James Hardin and Donald G. Daviau (1989)

82: *Chicano Writers,* First Series, edited by Francisco A. Lomelí and Carl R. Shirley (1989)

83: *French Novelists Since 1960,* edited by Catharine Savage Brosman (1989)

84: *Restoration and Eighteenth-Century Dramatists,* Second Series, edited by Paula R. Backscheider (1989)

85: *Austrian Fiction Writers After 1914,* edited by James Hardin and Donald G. Daviau (1989)

86: *American Short-Story Writers, 1910-1945,* First Series, edited by Bobby Ellen Kimbel (1989)

87: *British Mystery and Thriller Writers Since 1940,* First Series, edited by Bernard Benstock and Thomas F. Staley (1989)

88: *Canadian Writers, 1920-1959,* Second Series, edited by W. H. New (1989)

89: *Restoration and Eighteenth-Century Dramatists,* Third Series, edited by Paula R. Backscheider (1989)

90: *German Writers in the Age of Goethe, 1789-1832,* edited by James Hardin and Christoph E. Schweitzer (1989)

91: *American Magazine Journalists, 1900-1960,* First Series, edited by Sam G. Riley (1990)

92: *Canadian Writers, 1890-1920,* edited by W. H. New (1990)

93: *British Romantic Poets, 1789-1832,* First Series, edited by John R. Greenfield (1990)

94: *German Writers in the Age of Goethe: Sturm und Drang to Classicism,* edited by James Hardin and Christoph E. Schweitzer (1990)

95: *Eighteenth-Century British Poets,* First Series, edited by John Sitter (1990)

96: *British Romantic Poets, 1789-1832,* Second Series, edited by John R. Greenfield (1990)

97: *German Writers from the Enlightenment to Sturm und Drang, 1720-1764,* edited by James Hardin and Christoph E. Schweitzer (1990)

98: *Modern British Essayists,* First Series, edited by Robert Beum (1990)

99: *Canadian Writers Before 1890,* edited by W. H. New (1990)

100: *Modern British Essayists,* Second Series, edited by Robert Beum (1990)

101: *British Prose Writers, 1660-1800,* First Series, edited by Donald T. Siebert (1991)

102: *American Short-Story Writers, 1910-1945,* Second Series, edited by Bobby Ellen Kimbel (1991)

103: *American Literary Biographers,* First Series, edited by Steven Serafin (1991)

104: *British Prose Writers, 1660-1800,* Second Series, edited by Donald T. Siebert (1991)

105: *American Poets Since World War II,* Second Series, edited by R. S. Gwynn (1991)

106: *British Literary Publishing Houses, 1820-1880,* edited by Patricia J. Anderson and Jonathan Rose (1991)

107: *British Romantic Prose Writers, 1789-1832,* First Series, edited by John R. Greenfield (1991)

108: *Twentieth-Century Spanish Poets,* First Series, edited by Michael L. Perna (1991)

Documentary Series

1: *Sherwood Anderson, Willa Cather, John Dos Passos, Theodore Dreiser, F. Scott Fitzgerald, Ernest Hemingway, Sinclair Lewis,* edited by Margaret A. Van Antwerp (1982)

2: *James Gould Cozzens, James T. Farrell, William Faulkner, John O'Hara, John Steinbeck, Thomas Wolfe, Richard Wright,* edited by Margaret A. Van Antwerp (1982)

3: *Saul Bellow, Jack Kerouac, Norman Mailer, Vladimir Nabokov, John Updike, Kurt Vonnegut,* edited by Mary Bruccoli (1983)

4: *Tennessee Williams,* edited by Margaret A. Van Antwerp and Sally Johns (1984)

5: *American Transcendentalists,* edited by Joel Myerson (1988)

6: *Hardboiled Mystery Writers,* edited by Matthew J. Bruccoli and Richard Layman (1989)

7: *Modern American Poets,* edited by Karen L. Rood (1989)

8: *The Black Aesthetic Movement,* edited by Jeffrey Louis Decker (1991)